W9-BBL-557

3 4028 06915 4749
HARRIS COUNTY PUBLIC LIBRARY

200.973 Wil
Williams, Peter W.
America's religions : from
  their origins to the
twenty-first century
                      $35.00
            ocn190760651
3rd ed.   12/22/2008

America's Religions:
From Their Origins to the Twenty-first Century

AMERICA'S RELIGIONS

FROM THEIR ORIGINS TO THE TWENTY-FIRST CENTURY

Peter W. Williams

THIRD EDITION

UNIVERSITY OF ILLINOIS PRESS

Urbana and Chicago

Publication of this book was supported by a grant
from Susanne F. Webb.
© 1990, 1998, 2002, 2008 by Peter W. Williams
All rights reserved
Manufactured in the United States of America
1 2 3 4 5 C P 5 4 3 2 1
♾ This book is printed on acid-free paper.

Some earlier versions of this book appeared under
the title *America's Religions: Traditions and Cultures.*

Library of Congress Cataloging-in-Publication Data
Williams, Peter W.
America's religions : from their origins to the
twenty-first century / Peter W. Williams. — 3rd ed.
p.   cm.
Includes bibliographical references and index.
ISBN-13 978-0-252-03305-6 (cloth : alk. paper)
ISBN-10 0-252-03305-1
ISBN-13 978-0-252-07551-3 (pbk. : alk. paper)
ISBN-10 0-252-07551-X
1. United States—Religion.
I. Title.
BL2525.W485   2008
200.973—dc22   2007052617

For Jeremy Adams

teacher extraordinary

firm friend

Contents

Illustrations follow pages 164 and 328.

Preface to the Third Edition

The passage of six years since the second edition of *America's Religions: From Their Origins to the Twenty-first Century* has brought the need for some fine-tuning to the earlier text. The impact of the events now universally known as "9/11" has permanently affected the status of Muslims in the United States as well as American policy toward Muslim countries. The subsequent invasion of Iraq in 2003 has raised once again the idea of "American exceptionalism," the notion that the United States has a particular, indeed providential, mission in world history to, in Woodrow Wilson's phrase, "make the world safe for democracy." The Iraq incursion has unfolded as part of the agenda of George W. Bush, described by some as the most intensely evangelical president in American history, whose policies have been shaped not only by traditional "born-again" personal religiosity, but also by a Religious Right that has persisted as a major force in American electoral politics since its origins in the 1970s.

The social issues focused on by the Religious Right have also affected the internal lives of many American religious communities: the status of gay marriage, in particular, has threatened to tear asunder the unity of the Episcopal, Methodist, and Presbyterian churches. The Catholic Church, in the meantime, has been plagued by the surfacing of numerous accusations of sexual abuse of young people by their clergy, with corresponding questions being raised about the culpability of Catholic bishops for not having taken more decisive action in responding to such abuse. All of these issues have helped shape the revisions that distinguish this edition from its predecessors.

In addition, scholarship in the area of American religion, past and present, has continued to flourish. The expanded bibliographical section is an attempt to keep pace with that scholarship through the addition of a substantial number of new titles.

Finally, the chapter with which the previous edition ended has been dropped in favor of a prolonged reflection on the emergence of the Religious Right. Although some have been startled by the upsurge of this combination of religious and political action as a force in American life, I attempt to demonstrate that, although it might not have been predictable, its components can be easily traced from the beginnings of Anglo-American religious history. I conclude with some personal reflections on this conservative turn in American religious life in the context of the concluding reflections of my own mentor, the late Sydney E. Ahlstrom, in his monumental *A Religious History of the American People,* now a third of a century old.

In preparing this new edition, I am indebted especially to my Miami colleagues Frederick Colby on matters Islamic; Scott Kenworthy on early Christianity and Eastern Orthodoxy; and Lisa Poirier on Native American religions. The discussion of recent controversies in the Episcopal Church has been shaped by electronic conversations with David Hein of Hood College; Eugene Y. Lowe Jr. of Northwestern University; Thomas Mason of the Indiana Historical Society; and Robert Prichard of the Virginia Theological Seminary. Paula Kane of the University of Pittsburgh has been most helpful in reviewing my treatment of American Catholicism, as has Charles Lippy of the University of Tennessee with evangelicalism and the Religious Right. Finally, my students, Whittney Barth, Katie Hladky, and Myev Rees, have helped me understand better various aspects of contemporary evangelicalism.

Preface to the Second Edition

America's Religions: From Their Origins to the Twenty-first Century is a historical introduction to the religions that are currently practiced in the United States. Although it is intended primarily as a textbook for use in colleges, universities, and theological schools, it may also interest the general reader as a survey of this country's religious traditions. Although it does not pretend to be absolutely comprehensive—there are far too many groups in the United States to make that goal realistic—I have tried to make it as inclusive as possible; therefore, it may also serve as a reference work as well, providing basic information on a wide variety of groups and movements.

The immediate occasion of this book's writing was an unannounced office visit by a publisher's representative seeking manuscripts. As a result, *America's Religions* was initially published by Macmillan in 1990 and subsequently reissued, first in a preliminary version and now in this thoroughly revised and expanded edition, by the University of Illinois Press. The book's roots can be found in my teaching, now a third of a century in duration. Starting with part-time work during my graduate career at Yale in the late sixties and continuing through three decades at Miami University, I have been attempting to convey the story of America's religious development to successive generations of undergraduates and a smattering of more advanced students as well. Most of these chapters have their origins in the detailed lecture outlines which I gradually began to prepare and distribute to my students in the frequently reinforced belief that such devices cut down on note-taking and enhance the process of active listening.

The lessons that I have tried to incorporate into these outlines and resulting text reflect what any good teacher presumably learns soon: challenge your students, but help them to meet your challenge by also understanding what they don't already know and meeting them at least halfway. Although faculty tend to romanticize a past in which all students were eager, industrious, and well prepared—they weren't—it does seem true enough that many American students today are not overly familiar either with the basics of the Jewish and Christian traditions (including the Bible) or with the history of their own nation. Whatever tooth-grinding I may have quietly exercised in contemplation of this state of affairs, I early on decided that the best response to this lack was to try to fill the manifest vacuum. Instead of attempting to cover the entirety of American religious development in one course, I split the content into two (now three) courses, taking the time in each to explain as carefully as possible the backgrounds of each of the traditions we set about studying. This approach is reflected especially in the first section of this work, which is devoted to the religious histories of those peoples—Africans, American Indians, Jews, and Christians—who provided the cultural stock out of which the nation's traditions developed. In subsequent chapters, I try in this revised edition to provide similar backgrounds for those traditions which have been introduced more recently, especially by Spanish-speaking people, Muslims, and the followers of the major Asian religions.

Another feature of this book is the introduction of religious terminology as it becomes relevant, together with definitions and pronunciations where they seem called for. I have also tried to use as rich a vocabulary as possible in preference to "dumbing down" the language—or, for that matter, the content. With regard to the latter, I am convinced that religion, like any other human phenomenon, can only be understood in its full cultural and historical contexts as well as its contemporary manifestations. While trying to avoid detail for its own sake, I have tried to present as full a portrait as possible of the traditions discussed here, in terms of their beliefs, practices, and organizational structures as well as their origins and development.

In my own courses, I have chosen not to begin with 1492 (or 1620, or whenever) and move forward with one story; in the introduction to this book, I comment on the problems of treating American religious history as a unified story. This work is in fact arranged in roughly chronological order, and may be used in that fashion. For those, however, who prefer to approach the materials selectively and/or topically, I have provided an alternative table of contents to aid in this rearrangement of chapters.

As far as possible, I have tried to portray the religious traditions discussed here as fully and sympathetically as possible. However, as many theologians have pointed out, one should not mistake human attempts to worship the divine with the divine itself. Religions are aspects of human culture, and they and their fashioners partake of the same foibles as all others who share in the finite and fallible human condition. Therefore, I have tried to avoid treating my subject matter as solemn and humorless, in recognition that *homo religiosus* occasionally takes a pratfall or even acts in dubious faith. I also recognize, as do most scholars these days, that complete neutrality and detachment from one's subject matter is impossible, although that impossibility should be taken as a limit against which objectivity necessarily collides rather than a pretext for casting off any claims to treat one's subject as fairly as possible. My own tradition, the Anglican, easily accommodates this combination of detachment, engagement, and irony, as behooves any church founded by an ax murderer.

The difficulties of putting together a work of this sort require some comment. As the bibliography—one of the most greatly enhanced parts of this revised edition—demonstrates, the literature on religion in the United States has grown to staggering proportions. When I was a graduate student during the late 1960s, it would not have been impossible to have read virtually every significant piece of writing on the subject. Today, a student of the field is hard pressed to keep up even with one's own subspecialty. It is therefore not possible to represent this work as a synthesis of all the scholarship in the field. It can't be done anymore. I have tried, however, to draw upon as much of the best scholarship, old and new, as time and strength have permitted, to weave together an account of the most important forces that have shaped the nation's religious life as well as many of its broader cultural patterns. My debts are therefore beyond enumeration, beginning with my own mentor, the late Sydney E. Ahlstrom and his *A Religious History of the American People*; my coeditor, Charles H. Lippy, and the hundred or so contributors to our *Encyclopedia of the American Religious Experience*; my numerous excellent colleagues in what are surely two of the most congenial niches in academe, the American Society of Church History and the North American Religions Section of the American Academy of Religion; and generations of Miami students who have made me continually rethink my accounts of the history of religion in the United States. I trust that the bibliography and occasional note sufficiently recognize the sources of the scholarship on which I have particularly drawn.

Besides these general acknowledgments, more particular thanks need to be rendered to a number of colleagues who have been directly involved at various stages of this book's coming into being. Liz Dulany, Pat Hollahan, and their colleagues at the University of Illinois Press have been both supportive and very, very patient. James Bratt, Thomas Tweed, and Grant Wacker all read substantial portions of the manuscript to good effect. The following clergy and scholars provided information and feedback on their individual areas of expertise: African American religions, Albert Raboteau; Anglicanism, John Nicholas Gill and David Holmes; Asian religions, Alan Miller, Brian Moynahan, and Liz Wilson; Baptists, David L. Bartlett; Campbellites, Harry Baker Adams and Abraham Malherbe; early Christianity, Roy Bowen Ward; church and state, John F. Wilson; Congregationalism, Mary Kupiec Cayton, William Duffy, and William Hobbs; Eastern Orthodoxy, John Erickson and Phillip Lucas; Islam, Newell Booth, Hugh Halman, and Aaron Hughes; Judaism, Robert Goldy and Harold Forshey; late twentieth-century religion, Charles Lippy; Latino religion, Reed Anderson and Wayne Elzey; Latter-day Saints, Philip Barlow and Anne and Robert Wicks; Lutheranism, Fred Cook and Christa and Leonard Klein; Methodism, Charles Wallace; New Age, Catherine Albanese; Presbyterianism, R. John Harris and

Prudence Zimmerman; Roman Catholicism, Michael Beatty, Patricia Hollahan, Paula Kane, and Mary Jo Weaver; the South, Curtis Ellison and Jack Temple Kirby.

Jeremy Adams of Southern Methodist University, to whom this volume is dedicated, is an enduring reminder of the value and power of undergraduate teaching. Finally, my family must receive their due share of credit on general principles. I therefore acknowledge with gratitude and an abundance of warmth: my mother, Harriet E. Williams; my wife, Ruth Ann Alban Williams; my stepchildren, Dana Alban Meyers and Jonathan Alban Schneider; their significant others, David and Laurie; their children, Alban, Macy, and Remington Schneider and Bailey and Clara Meyers; and, of course, the inimitable Fanny and Gwinnie and their predecessors, Brent, Bronwyn, and Tory.

Topical Guide to Chapters

America's Religions follows the organizational scheme outlined in the preface, which is a modified chronological approach. For those wishing to organize courses or reading in other ways, this book can be utilized more topically as well, with little violence done to the narrative flow. The following indicates which chapters deal with the principal religious traditions covered here. Chapters in parentheses are relevant as background to the tradition indicated, but can be safely omitted.

America's Religions:
From Their Origins to the Twenty-first Century

Introduction:
Telling Stories

Not all that long ago, American religious history was something of a family affair. The "master narrative," or overarching framework, for the enterprise could be described in a book title by Baptist church historian Winthrop Hudson: *The Great Tradition of the American Churches.* Hudson and others were firmly rooted in a Protestant tradition based on the premise that the churches of the Reformation, divided as they might be into distinct denominations, provided the norm for the American religious experience. Despite their differences on sometimes arcane issues of belief, practice, and governance, Baptists, Methodists, and Presbyterians were, after all, cousins, united in having shaped a great nation based on principles, such as democracy and the work ethic, that were firmly Protestant in origin. Both necessity and idealism had combined to tolerate, if not always welcome, other religious communities, but Jews, Catholics, and others were expected to conform to these broad, nondenominational Protestant norms, and in many ways actually did so. Others, such as African Americans, were overwhelmingly Protestant in adherence, but not a great deal was expected of their highly emotive interpretations of the Baptist, Methodist, and pentecostal traditions. Still others, such as Episcopalians and Lutherans, were also within the Protestant fold, but were marginalized respectively by elite social status and elaborate liturgy on the one hand or by ethnic and geographical isolation on the other. To paraphrase a famed fictional English parson, our (semifictional) religious historian might have said, "By religion I mean the Protestant religion, and by the Protestant religion I mean white, middle-class, English-speaking, evangelical Protestants, especially those of Calvinist lineage—Congregationalists, Presbyterians, American Baptists, Methodists, Disciples of Christ, and low-church Episcopalians."

During the intervening decades between the 1950s, when this mindset predominated, and the turn of the twenty-first century, many things have happened to affect dramatically the way in which the story or stories of religion in the United States are told. The election of John F. Kennedy and the ecumenical council known as Vatican II dramatically lowered the walls of mutual suspicion that had previously kept Catholics apart from the mainstream of cultural and political life. Growing revulsion against the Holocaust helped discredit genteel and not-so-genteel anti-Semitism. The Civil Rights Movement of the 1950s and 1960s not only overturned deeply entrenched patterns of legal segregation in the South but also forced white Americans to reexamine their premises about race. The feminist and gay rights movements of succeeding years both created a new discourse about sexuality and gender roles, and also helped precipitate a countermovement in the form of the (New) Religious Right, which can be interpreted as a vehicle through which previously marginalized conservative Protestants found their way into the political and social mainstream.

As more and more outsiders were thus brought into this "mainstream," the very notion of an American religious and cultural mainstream began to grown precarious. First, any number of communities founded on identity—whether based on religion, ethnicity, gender, or sexual orientation—began to stake a claim for legitimacy and empowerment, sometimes to the exclusion of other such claimants. Second, a renewed surge of immigration from widely scattered parts of the world continued to bring to the United States large numbers of adherents of religious traditions, such as Islam and Hinduism, which had previously been represented in religious narratives as footnotes or afterthoughts. Third, a growing skepticism about or indifference to institutions of all sorts—governmental, religious, educational, professional—together with the traditions to which they appealed for authority, had a profound impact on the role that institutional religion was to play in American life. Americans are still arguably the most religious people on earth, as measured both by institutional affiliation and personal self-description, but the configuration of their religious behavior has shifted considerably in the interval.

Sydney Ahlstrom, one of the greatest religious historians of the previous era, characterized history as "telling a plausible story," and set out to do so on an epic scale in his 1973 classic, *A Religious History of the American People*. Ahlstrom took as his theme what he called "the Great Puritan Epoch," which spanned over three centuries from the English settlement of the Atlantic colonies to the election of a Roman Catholic president in 1960. Although Ahlstrom emphasized the impact of Protestant culture on the development of American institutions and values, he concluded with the realization that this epoch had now reached an end, symbolized by the election of a non-Protestant to the nation's highest office but involving a great deal more as well. Even so, Ahlstrom thought that the religious development of the United States could be contained within a unified narrative framework, albeit a lengthy and complex one.

Although some students of American religion since Ahlstrom's time have continued to fill in the gaps that remained within his vast framework, others began to suggest that perhaps the telling of such a unified, centralized story was neither possible nor desirable. Catherine Albanese, for example, in her *America: Religion and Religions* of 1981, no longer "privileged" Protestantism as deserving of more space than any of a number of other traditions, from Jewish to Native American. Robert Orsi, although not rejecting historical narrative, supplemented it with oral interviews in his *Madonna of 115th Street* (1985) and *Thank You, Saint Jude* (1996), to try to delineate the thoughts and feelings of the actual participants in American Catholic devotional life, rather than relying entirely on institutional annals and "official" theological accounts. Other recent scholarship, such as that collected in Thomas Tweed's 1997 *Retelling U.S. Religious History* has focused on the religious experience of women, of religious and ethnic minorities, of geographical and cultural regions outside the East Coast, and on the everyday character of "popular," "vernacular," "lived," or "material" religion. Some of these emphases—such as, say, African American religion—are susceptible to narrative treatment, whereas others are less so.

Is it still possible to present a narrative account of the religious life of the people of the United States as a unified whole? Or shall we, in postmodern fashion, regard each locus of individual or group religious experience as an equally valid and useful entrée into understanding something about the American religious scene, while making no claims to seeing a whole which most likely does not even exist? What I am setting out to do in the following pages is something different from either, although it partakes of both approaches in passing. While recognizing that each religious community has its own unique character and story, we can also acknowledge the commonalities that they share—in part because religious communities tend to be subject to the same sociological patterns of development, and in part because of their interaction with the same dominant American social and cultural system in which they find themselves located and with whose rules and givens they somehow have to come to terms.

First, it is necessary to distinguish between what we might, in a rough and ready sort of way, call personal and public religion. *Personal religion* is the experience of the individual, which is at some level always unique, though at the same time it is always mediated through some sort of public structures. Autobiography or personal narrative, whether composed spontaneously or elicited by an interviewer, is the most direct source of this kind of religious material, and is by nature pluralistic. As such, it is hard to reduce to a broader narrative, although it might supply valuable illustrations of more general tendencies. Narratives such as *The Autobiography of Malcolm X* and Dorothy Day's *The Long Loneliness* might thus provide a useful counterpoint to this work in classroom use.

This book sets out to delineate the major features of public religion as they have unfolded in what is now the United States over the past half-millennium—the nearly five centuries since the first arrival of Europeans on the North American continent. For our purposes, *public religion* may be defined as the religious expression and organization of a group of people who have constituted themselves, formally or informally, as a religious community. The life of each religious community, whether in early, more spontaneous stages or in later, more consciously organized form, creates normative patterns and expectations to which individual members are expected to conform. Although groupings such as "civil religion" and "the New Age" strain the definitions of community, they nevertheless have communal dimensions that can be treated as public phenomena.

My premise is that each major wave of conquest, colonization, and settlement—including those of indigenous peoples prior to the time of Columbus—brought with it religious institutions, beliefs, and practices as part of the larger cultural "baggage" that every society generates and carries along as it migrates. When such a cultural configuration becomes sufficiently established, it may usefully be called a *tradition*. Religious traditions, then, provide groups of people with a complete way of encountering the ultimate questions of human existence through myths, rituals, belief systems, organizations, and special personnel without having to start again from the beginning. Those who follow them, through choice or necessity, participate in a *religious culture*, a pattern of belief, action, and even feeling that governs their existence not only on special occasions but in everyday life as well. The more exclusive and self-contained a society, the more total will be the control that this culture exercises over its members. This book therefore begins with delineations of some of the most important religious traditions that were brought to North America especially during the colonial period, including the Jewish, Eastern Orthodox, Roman Catholic, and various Reformation (Protestant) strains. In addition, those traditions—more diverse and diffuse because not recorded in writing—of Native Americans and Africans are sketched as well. Later arrivals, such as Islam and the religions of Asia and of Spanish-speaking peoples, as well as those traditions, such as Mormonism and pentecostalism, that are indigenous to the United States itself, are introduced as the book unfolds.

Another major aspect of public religion is *religious institutions*—the social structures through which religious culture is transmitted and implemented. The generic sociological term for such a structure is *church*, which may indicate a material place for worship, a local congregation, a regional or national institution, or the totality of the membership, past, present, and even future, in a religious community. Religious institutions are carried on through personnel, in this country often consisting of trained and compensated professionals, known as *clergy*, who carry out and on the work of religion: conduct of public worship, individual counseling, education, and even such seemingly "secular" activities as fund-raising and office administration. Much of the literature, whether historical or sociological, about religion is focused on these institutions, their activities, and their personnel, because they are prone to leave written records that are easily accessible to scholars. These records include their intellectual activity, *theology*, which consists of the ongoing attempt of religious leaders to relate the deposit of original revelation—for example, the Bible—on which their traditions are founded to the realities of contemporary thought and experience. These formal, public structures of religion provide the frameworks in which individuals shape their own personal religious lives.

The forms of organization that have come to characterize American religious life have differed in some important ways from their predecessors and counterparts in other societies. Central to the American religious configuration has been the phenomenon of denominationalism. In medieval and Reformation-era Europe, religious groups had either the status of an *established church*—recognized and supported by the government to the exclusion of all others—or a dissenting sect, composed of a small number of zealous believers who pursued their independent course outside the law and frequently at the risk of their lives. The pluralism of New World society, later given the force of law by the First Amendment, introduced a new kind of religious organization—the *denomination*—which was both self-supporting and free from external interference. The term originally arose as a descriptor for the many Protestant groups—Baptist, Congregational, Methodist, Presbyterian—that resembled one another in fundamental beliefs but differed on matters of worship and organization. Eventually, however, other traditions, such as Catholic, Jewish, and even Buddhists, began to take on many of the characteristics of these Protestant groups as they adapted to the ground rules of the American scene. Furthermore, many aspects of popular religious practice, such as revivalism, "civil religion," and what in recent years has been called "spirituality," have coexisted with the more formally structured denominations as crosscurrents of religious influence.

The other public aspect of religion in the United States that warrants close examination consists of the many ways in which it interacts with the broader society and culture. One important facet of this interaction is what is often referred to as the realm of "church and state," that is, the formal conditions and restrictions that the civil government imposes on religious organization and practice. During the colonial era these conditions varied widely, ranging from nearly universal tolerance in Pennsylvania and Rhode Island to the establishment of one church at the expense of all others in Massachusetts and Virginia. The adoption of the First Amendment as part of the Bill of Rights in 1791, however, permanently altered this state of affairs, first at the federal and later at the state level. It is now the universal practice in this country to prohibit government at any level from actively promoting or penalizing any kind of religious belief, as well as any practice that does not conflict with other civil goods. The implications and limits of this policy of benign neutrality are continually being tested by courts and legislatures, but the fundamental premise that religious tolerance is good and that both establishment and persecution are not is so deeply embedded in the national consciousness as to render serious challenge unthinkable.

The First Amendment and its history of interpretation lie at the core of the public life of America's religions outside the bounds of their own institutions. They are also among the most important things that are distinctly American about American religion. The United States was the first nation to make widespread religious tolerance a fundamental premise of public policy, and it remains unusual, if not unique, in this coexistence of widespread and fervent religious activity within a legal matrix of rigorous nonestablishment. However, there are a variety of ways in which the development of religion in America has been affected by other aspects of distinctively American social and cultural circumstances. These ways also constitute an important part of the public story of religion in America. Just as the laws of the nation apply uniformly to all religions, so do all necessarily partake in the broader social, cultural, and intellectual currents of American life, and become part of a larger, common story. Among these constitutively American circumstances are: mobility, immigration, British culture, slavery and race, democracy, populism, capitalism, nationalism, pluralism, and Americanization.

Mobility has been a continuing fact of life not only for the United States and its colonial antecedents but for the entire human history of the North American continent. Mobility has taken the forms of geographical mobility and of social mobility. *Immigration* and *in-migration*—movement respectively into and around the nation—are the two major forms of geographical mobility. Anthropologists are in general agreement that the ancestors of today's American Indians originally came across a land bridge that linked Alaska and Siberia. (Recent evidence also suggests possible non-Asian origins for some aboriginal peoples as well.) Although most nations have experienced both immigration and emigration to some extent, the United States is unusual in the number of immigrants that have come to its shores over the centuries; the variety of sources of that immigration, which include virtually the entire world; the ongoing process of immigration, which has taken place during most of its colonial and post-independence history, with only occasional interludes of severe legal limitation; and the mixture of voluntary and involuntary immigrants, the latter represented primarily by the African slave trade. The United States, in short, is a "nation of immigrants" (or their descendants) on a vast scale. The consequence for religion, naturally, has been the importation of the traditions of every populated continent to these shores as the stuff out of which America's religious communities have evolved. The net result has been an ever-changing, de facto pluralism of religions and cultures that make up the American mosaic.

In addition to continuing immigration, Americans have from their beginnings practiced *in-migration*—movement from one place to another within the boundaries of the nation. The European experience of a family's inhabiting the same town or farm, or even the same house, over several generations, has been rare in this nation. In-migration has frequently been linked with social mobility, a possibility much more closely linked with the United States than with the countries of origin of most immigrants. The extent of the possibilities for social mobility in America has been keenly debated, but the idea of such mobility is firmly implanted in the mythology of American life. The problem with such an ideal, however, is that the emergence of a market economy dominated by large corporations following the Civil War led to severe modifications in the sorts of opportunities for social and economic betterment available to ordinary citizens, especially those not possessed of significant social and cultural as well as financial capital. The incompatibility of the ideal of unlimited opportunity for all with the reality of these new limitations has led to severe stresses in American life, such as those manifested in the Populist movement (discussed below).

Even though the United States has taken on the characteristics of a microcosm, attracting and absorbing immigrants from all over the world, not all peoples and their cultures have found themselves on an equal footing upon arrival on these shores. From virtually their earliest contact with Europeans, the native peoples of the continent found themselves marginalized and eventually either decimated through disease and warfare or else relegated to remote reservations. The imperial powers of France and Spain, bringing with them Catholic religion and clergy, had little success in establishing permanent outposts in what is now the United States. From early in the seventeenth century, it was rather the British who established colonial outposts through which English language, laws, values, and religion would, by the time of independence, become dominant through law and/or custom. Britain, to be sure, was not at all homogeneous, and had earlier become itself a mini-empire, consisting of the dominant Anglo-Saxon English and the various native Celtic peoples—Scots, Irish, Welsh, and Cornish—whom they had at one time or another subdued and incorporated into the United Kingdom. The earliest British immigrants, therefore, already embodied some cultural and considerable religious pluralism, because the North Atlantic colonies proved a convenient refuge for religious dissenters in danger or discomfort in the old country.

Whatever their differences, however, most early British settlers shared some cultural commonalities: the English language, English legal traditions, and some variety of Protestant Christianity. Although the colonies eventually split from the "mother country," Britain and the United States continued to share this common cultural seedbed while each developed in parallel ways democratic polities, capitalist economies, imperialistic foreign policies, and both evangelical and liberal versions of religion. Pluralistic as American life has become, it is impossible to deny the deepest of lineages from the culture of Great Britain.

If the British was the most privileged of cultures, that of African Americans re-mained in many ways at the opposite end of the spectrum at least until recently. Virtually all of the immigration out of Africa to the colonies and the subsequent United States prior to the Civil War was involuntary. Africans were enslaved by one another, sold to Europeans, transported at great peril across the Atlantic, and dispersed among the British and other European colonies in the New World until (officially, at least) the American government outlawed the slave trade in 1807. Even after Emancipation, most African Americans, though no longer enslaved, were compelled to live under highly restrictive and discriminatory conditions, whether by law in the South or by custom elsewhere.

The result has been a schizoid strain in American culture, since the presence of dark-skinned people in considerable numbers has provoked reactions qualitatively incomparable with the milder ambivalence that European Americans have felt toward other "races." (Anthropologists today have largely abandoned the idea of race as a viable biocultural category, despite the fact that groups of people do share some common genetic patterns, but they do continue to regard it as a powerful social construct.) Despite the repeal of racially based laws since the 1960s, African Americans continue to live with a legacy of slavery and institutionalized discrimination. On the other hand, they have generated some of the most powerful indigenous forms of American cultural expression, especially in the realm of music, and for decades have played a dominant role in the emergence of a national popular culture. This cultural impact has been highly significant in the realm of religion as well, ranging from the prophetic rhetoric of the Civil Rights Movement to the cross-fertilization of black and white styles of evangelical worship. What was once a rigid color line continues as an ambivalent process of symbiosis, a yin-yang exchange in which each culture is simultaneously attracted and repulsed by the other in a tense but ultimately creative manner to produce a new and distinctive synthesis.

The existence of slavery as a legal institution was for decades one of the principal challenges to the ideology of *democracy,* one of the most revered terms in the American political vocabulary and a major intellectual export commodity from the United States to the rest of the world as well. The linkage between democracy and Protestant Christianity has been the subject of considerable historical speculation, and will probably never be settled entirely. However, it seems clear enough in broad outline that the two have had a close and reciprocal interconnection during the course of American history. Both the congregational governance of the Puritan churches of colonial New England and the more aristocratic vestries of Virginia's Anglican churches demonstrated the reality of the power of the laity in the conduct of religious affairs, and even the ultimately hierarchical Roman Catholic church began its career in the New Republic with a bishop elected by his priests. The balance of power between clergy, laity, and hierarchy has varied within each tradition over time, but the general direction has been that of the empowerment of those whose profession is not religion. Similarly, the ideology of popular enfranchisement in the secular political realm has generally been embraced and promoted by most of America's religious communities, albeit with considerable variation as to how much power, especially in the realm of moral conduct, should be the affair of civil government.

The way in which democratic ideology has been acted out during the past two centuries has been strongly tinged with that distinctively American social force, populism. *Populism* is the belief that the moral as well as the economic, social, and political core of American society subsists in the middle ranks — "the middling sorts," as they were known in the nineteenth century — who were active, self-sufficient producers rather than the parasitic wealthy on the one hand or dependent slaves or servants on the other. Populist notes were sounded early on by the followers of that Democratic odd couple, Thomas Jefferson and Andrew Jackson, as well as in later years by a variety of politicians ranging from Abraham Lincoln to William Jennings Bryan to George Wallace and George W. Bush. Evangelical Protestantism, which frequently fostered a kind of spiritual entrepreneurialism in the persons of revivalists and their latter-day successors, has always demonstrated a special affinity for the populist temperament, an affinity that resulted in the later twentieth century in an explicit alliance between a newly populist Republican Party and the emergent New Religious Right.

The relationship of *capitalism* and Protestantism has also been debated avidly since the time of Max Weber's classic sociohistorical treatise, *The Protestant Ethic and the Spirit of Capitalism,* of 1904–5. Whatever the cause-and-effect relationship between the two may have been during the colonial era, it is undeniable that all American institutions have had to relate to the emergence of a national (now international) capitalist economy since at least the time of the Civil War. As R. Laurence Moore has argued, many religious groups, especially the various Protestant denominations who found themselves in a highly competitive market situation in the nineteenth century after the legal abolition of any religious establishment, resorted to the promotional techniques of the emergent economic order in their quest for a maximal "market share." And, although many religious groups have benefited greatly over the years from the support of members grown prosperous in the industrial order, most major religious communities have also mounted powerful critiques of the social abuses that have issued from that order, from the Protestant "social gospel" to Catholic "liberation theology." More recently, some evangelical Protestant groups have openly embraced capitalism as God-given in their broader apotheosis of "traditional American values," as have Catholic neoconservative writers such as Michael Novak.

Those same groups that today view capitalism as a divinely mandated form of the economic order are in historical continuity with a tendency to view the broader American nation as under supernatural protection and guidance. The notion of the United States as an exceptionally favored society and people has roots in the English Reformation, and took definitive shape in the New England Puritan idea of a new Israel in covenant with God. This notion, often couched in millenarian terms, has taken many twists and turns over the nation's history, especially in times of war or other national crisis. The debacle of Vietnam, however, brought this notion, now expressed in the form of "civil religion," into considerable question. Although *religious nationalism* is still endorsed by the Religious Right, the pluralism and secularism of American society by the year 2000 had weakened its appeal, especially outside the South, which remained a stronghold of traditional religion and politics.

Another theme that pervades the American religious landscape, both past and present, is that of *pluralism* and diversity. The territory that composes the United States today has always housed a pluralistic population, even in the centuries prior to the coming of any Europeans. The arrival of the latter was from the first pluralistic as well, with Spanish and French Catholics competing with British Protestants for territorial hegemony. The British themselves were by no means religiously unified, and the thirteen colonies reflected the rival religious ideologies of Anglicans, Baptists, Catholics, Puritans, and Quakers. Independence and the First Amendment institutionalized pluralism as a fundamental principle of the Republic; although the latter did not guarantee a warm spirit of tolerance, it did at least make overt persecution of religious dissent very difficult. As William Hutchison has pointed out, there is an important difference between a legally enforced tolerance and a positive welcoming of difference as a sign of cultural health and vitality. The acceptance of a pluralistic population has generally been more pragmatic than intentional, and active opposition to "others" is still very much a theme of American life at the turn of the millennium in the realm of public policy issues such as immigration restriction and prayer in the public schools.

A final theme that must be addressed before proceeding to the broader story is that of Americanization. *Americanization* is an elusive term: it is a process that has been ongoing in the United States since the beginnings of its colonial antecedents, and its meaning has changed over the decades and centuries. In the beginning, Americanization involved a coming to terms with the physical circumstances of existence in a new, sparsely populated continent by voluntary newcomers from Europe and involuntary migrants from Africa. The interaction of these various groups eventually began to result in a new consciousness—political, social, and even religious—of what it meant to live not simply as exiles or emissaries from an old world but rather as residents of a new one. Before long, it involved the adaptation of subsequent newcomers to institutions and habits of mind that had by now become established as distinctively American patterns of living. It also began to acquire ideological dimensions, as those already established in power exerted pressure on the newly arrived to conform to their patterns, and as the government passed successive laws regulating the flow of immigration. By the later twentieth century, a reaction had occurred in which many groups based on particularistic identities argued that American society should be founded on a perpetuation of difference rather than a pressure to conform to a single norm.

The arguments continue, but it is undeniable that these issues and forces involved in the Americanization process have made a profound impact on America's religious traditions and communities. It should be noted, though, that the reaction of new religious groups to the pressures of Americanization have by no means been uniform or invariably positive. As R. Laurence Moore has pointed out, many groups have Americanized, seemingly paradoxically, by taking a self-conscious stand as outsiders within the broader American scene. In a number of cases, as with Catholics and Protestant evangelicals, they have presented themselves as upholders of true American values in a society that is in the process of abandoning such values. In other cases, such as the slave community, marginalized groups may have superficially conformed to dominant patterns while covertly creating a very different religious culture of their own. Very few groups, however, can avoid coming to terms with the pressures of the broader society; even the Old Order Amish now use telephones on occasion.

In telling the story of American religion, then, one must tell both one story and many stories. The latter are as numerous as there are religious groups, perhaps even as there are religious individuals. These stories overlap and intersect, but are never identical, and no one can be accurately singled out as the paradigmatic story. Catholics now have more impact on the public realm than do Congregationalists, and one can only speculate on what role Muslims might play a half-century from now. The story to which all must be referred, though, is a more unified if extremely complex story, that of the evolution of a distinctly American social, political, legal, and economic order, which has provided both the explicit ground rules as well as the subtler cultural cues that have been extremely difficult for any group living and growing in the United States to screen out. The story of religion in the United States is that of the interaction of individual religious groups with the broader social order. It is that story and those stories which I will now try to tell.

PART I

THE TRADITIONS

A. Oral Traditions

According to conservative estimates by archaeologists, writing on tablets dates back to roughly the middle of the fourth millennium B.C. (3500–3300), whereas the earliest alphabets used in the ancient Near East appeared less than four thousand years ago. The use of writing to record religious lore became important in the Western world quite early in the human experience, but even the Hebrew Bible (Old Testament) began as a collection of oral traditions. For centuries after scripture began to be codified in written form, the vast majority of people even in the West were unable to read, and its preservation and interpretation was entrusted to a small elite of rabbis or priests. It was not until the Reformation era that literacy, abetted by the invention of printing with movable type, began to spread widely. The radical notion that all people should be able to read and write did not gain great currency until the settlement of North America by English-speaking Protestants in the seventeenth century.

In the areas of the world that remained isolated from the forces of modernization, oral culture predominated until recent times. This was very much the case among Native American, African, and African American cultures until at least the nineteenth century. The transmission of religious traditions through memory and word of mouth—often in astounding quantity and complexity—has certain features that differentiate it from the written lore to which most Americans are accustomed. Changes and borrowings occur frequently but with little notice, so that the process is more fluid, more protean than that which takes place with a set of fixed sacred texts. The role of the few "religious specialists"—priests, shamans, medicine men—who constitute a people's collective memory also takes on a very special character. They determine what is to be remembered and what discarded.

This is not to say that oral traditions have disappeared in our own day. Folk preachers, both black and white, continue to cultivate their art, which is ostensibly based on written scripture but often takes on a life of its own. Radio and television have also opened up whole new avenues for oral religious expression. Some very ancient motifs of traditional religion, such as healing and the warding off of evil, manifest themselves throughout the spectrum of traditional, folk, and popular cultures. The texture of the religious life of a people who have lived for centuries without contact with the technology and values of modernity, though, differs substantially from the world of Jimmy Swaggart and Oral Roberts. The first two chapters of this survey of the American religious experience are an exploration of the religious cultures of the aboriginal inhabitants of North America and Africa in order to evoke this texture. This can only be done in a very general way, given both the multiplicity and complexity of these traditions. Also, as soon as these traditions began to come into the consciousness of Europeans and European Americans, they immediately began to change through the inevitable cultural contacts—many of them forced—that occurred. In later chapters, the metamorphoses of these traditions—as they encountered, embraced, adapted, or resisted the Christianity of European America—will unfold in all of their own complexity.

CHAPTER 1

The Varieties of Native American Religious Life

Beginning a survey of the religions of what is now the United States with the American Indian, or Native American, peoples has a number of advantages. In the first place, it helps to overcome a historic blindness induced by a preoccupation with America's European cultural heritage, to the detriment of religious impulses that do not fit readily into European American categories. Secondly, it raises a number of issues about the basic character of religion that are not as readily apparent in the exclusive study of the traditions of the modern West. Thirdly, it obeys strictly the logic of history—a "chrono-logic"—in beginning at the beginning, with the aboriginal inhabitants of a very old continent. Fourthly, it opens up an array of highly diverse yet in some ways curiously similar religious experience and expression that most contemporary Americans have easily written off as exotically "other" or have so romantically idealized that it bears little resemblance to reality.

The notions of "Americanness" and "Indianness" in themselves have always been problematic. The American "Indians," of course, were not what Columbus thought them to be, that is, residents of southern Asia. On the other hand, as Sam Gill has pointed out, the term *Indios* in Columbus's day referred generically to any of the inhabitants of the part of the world that lay east of the Indus River. Since many, if not all, of the ancestors of the American Indians had most probably originated in Siberia and crossed what was then a land bridge across the Bering Strait to Alaska at some remote time in prehistory, Columbus may have not been so far off in his identifying these "new" people as Asians. The notion of "America," as distinct from the sought-after Asia, came hard and slowly to the cognitively bewildered European newcomers. The subsequent development of the "United States" out of a contiguous collection of European colonies and areas inhabited by aboriginal peoples was also a process that took time and required active feats of imagination to rationalize. Two recent works of scholarship, Edmundo O'Gorman's *The Invention of America* and Garry Wills's *Inventing America,* indicate in their convergent titles the intellectual difficulties involved in making sense first out of an entire hemisphere and, much later, of the new political creation of a group of transplanted English colonists wanting to become an independent nation.

Although the idea of "America" today carries with it the features and values of a modernized, technologically sophisticated society very remote from the life of the continent's aboriginal peoples, there are some intriguing ways to argue that these people were archetypically American. In the first place, like all subsequent inhabitants of North America, the Indians were immigrants. As we have already noted, their ancestors probably arrived from Siberia in pursuit of big game. Secondly, like later immigrants and more settled Americans as well, they were a mobile people, ultimately fanning out from the Bering Strait through two continents, all the way south to Tierra del Fuego. For some, mobility was more or less continuous as they adopted nomadic patterns in pursuit of game. Others, such as the agriculturists of the south, became more settled, but never escaped from the periodic need to readjust to new circumstances often engendered by intercultural encounters or changes in the natural environment. Thirdly, as Americans of today are proud to claim for themselves, these Native Americans were an infinitely adaptable people. Even though they lacked sophisticated technology, they adjusted their life-patterns to environmental circumstances ranging from the Arctic to the tropics, and learned to extract a living from the most varied of circumstances. The ultimate encounter with Europeans was no exception: the animals and firearms of the Spanish were rapidly adopted by the Plains Indians, for example, and the latter's myths began to incorporate the previously unknown horse as an archetypal symbol.

Finally, like Americans of later times, the earliest Americans were extraordinarily varied in the cultures they developed. Just as the diet, the language, the religions, and the other components of the American culture of our own day have been enriched from the endless rubbing of shoulders of almost infinitely varied national stocks living together, so did the aboriginal peoples continually diversify, lend, and borrow in response to changing circumstances. This diversity was maintained over the years through the lack of continual interaction made possible by today's means of cultural homogenization—widespread literacy, mass media, centralized educational and political institutions. However, Native American cultures were by no means static. Ecological changes or social dynamics continually prompted these peoples to migrate and come into contact with others, whether peaceably or otherwise, and cultural borrowing and assimilation were ongoing factors in the evolution of Native American culture. The Aztec civilization that Cortés and his followers beheld on their arrival in Mexico was an imperial creation, and many peoples had been forced by the powerful Aztecs to submit to a not always very welcome yoke. Myth and ritual changed their contents to embrace new circumstances, a process that continued through the fusions of Indian and Christian themes in the Peyote religion of the late nineteenth and twentieth centuries.

Because of this remarkable cultural and religious diversity stretched over both space and time, it is difficult to be both general and meaningful in the discussion of Native American religions. One runs the risks in doing so of generating a series of abstractions in need of endless qualification and counterexamples, or else an equally endless chain of anecdotes and descriptions having little to do with one another. Still, there are some ways of approaching the topic that illuminate the general patterns of Native American religious expression and its underlying characteristics, especially insofar as it differs significantly from the characteristics of religion in the modernized society to which most of us have become accustomed.

First, there are a number of ways of perceiving the world that are characteristic of traditional cultures in general and Native American peoples in particular. Religion itself, for example, is a concept for which most such cultures lack specific words. In contemporary American society, religious activity tends to become compartmentalized and relegated to a specific time and place, for example, Sunday morning at church. In traditional cultures, the religious or symbolic life of a people is instead frequently integrated into the fabric of daily activity, so that any act connected with what the culture identifies as significant takes on a religious meaning. For premodern cultures especially, the production or acquisition of food is of central importance—in contrast with most of contemporary American society, in which only a small percentage of the population is directly engaged in agricultural work. Therefore, the killing of an animal or the harvest of the year's supply of maize (corn) is not just a routine, "secular" event but rather one surrounded with ritual or ceremonially developed as a constant reminder of the cosmic significance of the particular act. Perhaps the saying of grace before meals, now largely abandoned in homes where parents and children keep wildly different schedules and communicate through notes on the refrigerator door, is an example of the way in which such practices linger and eventually dissolve in the solvent of modernity.

Another aspect of Native American religious life that differentiates it from much of contemporary American experience is its relationship to the social order. In the pluralistic America of today, religion is seen, and regarded by law, as a matter of individual choice among any number of conceivable alternatives. In fact, our choice may be more constrained by our own situation in society than may be readily apparent, but the theoretical range of options remains open. In traditional societies, however, the religious life of a people is coextensive with the people itself, and seldom extends beyond a coherent social group. It would be as unlikely, for example, for a Navajo to adopt the religion of the Apache as it would be to begin speaking the Apache language, even though cross-fertilizations may occur among religions or languages.

A system of religious practices therefore develops within the context of the experience of a particular people, remains confined among that people, and is virtually the only option open to any of the members of the people, although change is always possible through commonly accepted visionary experience. This relationship of religion to society is reflected in tribal naming, where the word a people uses to describe themselves frequently means "the people" or "human beings." For an individual group, their own experience of the world is normative and exclusive, and is regarded as universal only in the sense that the religions of other peoples are irrelevant to their own situation. Other peoples, and their religions with them, are not "really real." Society, culture, religion, and cosmos are coincident, and together constitute the sum of reality for a particular people as long as they manage to cohere as a self-sufficient group.

Two other basic cultural categories that have direct implications for religion are the ways in which a given people perceive and experience time and space. For contemporary Americans, both time and space are usually experienced as linear and divisible, and subject to precise measurement and manipulation. The theory of relativity may have modified these notions at a high level of scientific abstraction, but the logic of modern life dictates otherwise in our everyday round. Clocks and watches are everywhere: on our walls and desks and wrists. Complex organizations such as businesses, hospitals, and universities depend on a precise synchronization of activity, and woe to those who are habitually late. Space is similarly compartmentalized: parking spaces, apartments, house lots, and offices all represent the division and privatization of the space in which we daily live and work.

Among traditional peoples, however, time and space are generally experienced in other ways. Verb tenses in Native American languages frequently lack the clear-cut distinction of past, present, and future characteristic of the linear interpretation of time implicit in English and other Indo-European tongues. In the modern West, time progresses in a straight line, from an origin through the present into a future that will be distinct, and hopefully better, than what has preceded it. Implicit in this schematization of time is the notion of progress, which reached its apogee in the optimism of the Victorian era when technology and democracy promised to bring about a secular millennium of peace and prosperity here on Earth.

This sense of time is by no means universal, and in fact is quite recent in the course of human history. Far more typical of the world's peoples is an experience of time as an endless repetition of the same events, with humans striving eternally to emulate the patterns handed down by the gods or other superhuman beings in the mythical time of beginnings. Left to themselves, humans tend to muddy the proverbial waters and are in need at regular intervals of returning to this "strong time" of origins—*illud tempus,* in Mircea Eliade's phrase—to bring the course of the world back into line with the original, divinely given paradigms for human action. Instead of inevitable progress, regress is the normal course of things, and must be regularly compensated for if life is to continue.

Similarly, space in the sense of clearly delineated land belonging to a particular person is alien to the sensibilities of most traditional peoples. For nomadic hunting peoples especially, the notion of fixed space as in any way significant is virtually non-sensical. Land is provided in the order of things for human habitation and use, but it can be said to "belong" to an individual or group only insofar as they are actually inhabiting or otherwise utilizing it. On the other hand, almost all peoples engage in making certain aspects of space symbolically significant, thus creating order, or *cosmos,* out of what is otherwise undifferentiated chaos unfit for human habitation. For the Navajo, for example, the world (in the sense of cosmos) is delineated by four sacred mountains at its corners. Whether these are actual, physical mountains is of secondary importance. What is ultimately important, rather, is the sense of orientation, of living in a space that is organized spiritually for human existence.

In some cases, actual topographic features, especially mountains, take on this orienting function. For nomadic hunters, such as the Sioux of the Great Plains in the nineteenth century, their renowned Sun Dance ceremony could be performed anywhere. The coming together of scattered people for the ceremony was a symbolic affirmation of their unity, which was not always visually apparent. In the Sun Dance, as in the rituals of many other peoples, a tree was set into the ground to constitute a pole representing the center of the cosmos—an *axis mundi,* or world axis, in the phrase of Eliade. This center was none the less real because its location was arbitrary—in the Indian worldview, it was more real than any naturally rooted tree since its ultimate reality was bestowed by the ceremonies performed around it.

Just as Native Americans experienced time and space in ways significantly different from members of modernized societies, so was their interpretation of and relationship with the complex of forces and entities we call "nature." Just as modernized peoples distinguish sharply between past, present, and future, so do we experience nature as sharply different from ourselves. Human beings hold a special place in the universe, a distinctiveness supported by the early chapters of Genesis. Domestic animals occupy an intermediate role, but the rest of nature, the realm of plant and animal life, is frequently perceived as so different from our own realm that it is subject to dominance and manipulation for our own purposes with impunity.

It is interesting that one of the ways in which the traditional cosmos of the Native American peoples has reentered our own worldviews has been through the ecological crisis that was first perceived by Rachel Carson and other environmentalists in the 1960s. Although much sentimentalization and distortion of American Indian modes of perception has occurred in the process, the essential insight that has been recently appropriated by many contemporary Americans is valid—namely, the idea that the American Indians regarded humans as one among a number of animate forces in the world that had to live in harmony with one another if life was to continue in a tolerable fashion.

A good example of this relationship is the practice of some peoples, such as the northern Saulteaux, of addressing and propitiating a bear before killing it at the end of a hunt. The Indians were not vegetarians who shuddered at the idea of taking life. Rather, they recognized the claims of all life to a place in the cosmos and the proper respect that different life-forms owed one another in the divine ecology. The logic of that ecology dictated that humans were to use bears as a source of nutrition, but that did not reduce the bear to the status of the object of sport or casual violence. Human and bear each had a proper role to play in the cosmic round, but the significance of that round had to be repeatedly and carefully reasserted each time an act of potential disruptiveness was anticipated.

The same sense of participating in a cosmos in which all beings formed an inter-related continuum also shaped Native American conceptions of the supernatural realm. In the Christian worldview, God and humanity are radically distinct from one another, even though the latter may have been made in the image of the former. Calvinistic Protestantism, which helped to shape the modern world-picture even more than other varieties of Christianity, carried this contrast to an extreme, and insisted that the Divine Word was the only possible point of contact between the two realms.

For American Indians, however, the monotheism characteristic of the principal Western religions—Judaism, Christianity, Islam—is simply absent. In some cases a particularly powerful creator god may be ultimately responsible for the world's coming into existence, but such a god usually then takes on the characteristics of what Eliade calls a *deus otiosus*—an "otiose" or inactive god who takes little interest in the subsequent fate of that creation. More usually, Native American creation stories, which vary greatly in their precise content, are narratives of the activities of different kinds of supernatural beings who help humanity emerge from nothingness or some primordial condition of existence into the mundane world. For both the Navajo and the Zuni, for example, the original inhabitants of the world emerged from underground. In other versions, the Earth Diver—a diving bird or animal—brings soil up from beneath the primordial water that had covered the world and sets the process of creation in motion. This latter motif, incidentally, was widespread among peoples of eastern Asia, the probable ancestral home of the natives of the New World.

Many other sorts of supernatural beings inhabit the Native American cosmos. In the Seneca creation account, which is shared by many other peoples as well, a good twin brother brings a perfect world into being, after which his bad twin proceeds to foul it up. Supernatural forces in animal or bird form, as in the case of Earth Diver, also can play roles in world-creation. Another sort of figure related to the Seneca creator-twins is generically known as the Culture Hero. This being plays a role in many myths, such as those of the Algonkians, as the source of human life-patterns. The Culture Hero is not really a god but nevertheless lives in a realm of mythic beginnings rather than in the here-and-now of the everyday world.

Still another widely known *theriomorph*—a humanlike character in the form of an animal—is the Trickster, who frequently appears as a raccoon, coyote, or other proverbially mischievous creature. Many stories chronicle Trickster's exploits in playing jokes on other characters and frequently in the end on himself. A number of these have to do with sexual adventures, often of the most grotesque sort, or with excrement, illustrating the fact that the Native American religious outlook can accommodate many things that the Westerner of average piety would view with scandal or at least considerable distress.

The typical Native American spiritual world, then, is highly pluralistic. Humans do not themselves possess the powers of divine beings, but can avail themselves of this power, and avoid its ill effects, through maintaining a proper relationship with all aspects of the cosmos in which this power inheres. Again, our example of the bear and bear killer is pertinent: the bear itself is not necessarily divine, but one's interaction with the bear can be the occasion in which sacred power is unleashed for better or worse. Such power may also inhere in certain natural features such as mountains, but only those that for some reason are singled out as specially significant for a particular people or individual.

The most specifically religious dimension of Native American life consists of the means employed by native people to align themselves with benevolent sacred power and to avoid or rid themselves of harmful forces. Here, again, there are not sharp dichotomies between good and evil as in most Western religious systems. As illustrated in the story of the twin brothers who bring humanity into being, power for good or evil is situational; the power itself seems to be undifferentiated in its essence and can be put by different personalities to different purposes. The general Native American attitude toward the dead similarly illustrates this theme. In the first place, there is no sharp differentiation between the existence led by the living and the dead; the two realms of existence are more in continuity than disjunction, and their relationship is not seen as particularly problematic. Few cults of the dead, such as are common among traditional African peoples, existed in North America. Secondly, Christian missionaries were often frustrated in trying to persuade their Indian listeners that they needed to be afraid of punishment in the world to come for sins committed in this life. Such ideas were simply unintelligible to them, for the notions of radical sin meriting radical punishment, and that punishment being visited on the dead, were utterly alien to their patterns of thought.

The principal means of assuring harmony between humans and the spiritual powers of the universe lay in the retelling of myths in the context of the performance of ritual. As Eliade repeatedly points out, "myth" in this sense lacks the connotation of falsity that it has taken on in ordinary discourse. A myth in the context of Native American religion should rather be understood as a story told to explain the way in which the cosmos and its various significant components came into being. The beginning of the book of Genesis is a good example of a creation myth: "In the beginning God created the heavens and the earth." Whether and how this statement may be literally, historically true is still the subject of heated controversy among American Christians today. We can define it as "myth" not on the basis of such criteria but rather because of what is does—that is, it explains how the cosmos came into being. We have already referred to several Native American creation myths, of which the variety is almost inexhaustible. What all have in common, regardless of their particulars, is the emergence of cosmos—purposeful order—out of chaos.

A myth is basically a story, an example of the fondness for narrative form typical of societies in which the transmission of culture takes place orally rather than in writing. Such a story, however, does not exist in isolation to be enjoyed simply for its literary and aesthetic qualities. Rather, it becomes operative in the context of ritual, usually with the accompaniment of music and dance. Even here, the complex of activity is not simply a "multimedia" event but is aimed at bringing the participants into effective contact with the spiritual world. What we have, in short, is worship or liturgy, the end of which is to establish—or, more properly reestablish—an efficacious relationship between two or more realms of being.

The content and function of myth and ritual can best be understood in the context of "the eternal return" we discussed earlier—the return from the limitations of earthly life and time to the "strong time," *illud tempus*. The idea of worship is not simply to recall fondly the way things were in the beginning but to restore the pattern of everyday life to harmony with the cosmic patterns revealed to humanity in the beginning, in *illo tempore*. Such an attitude is by no means confined to oral cultures. For example, the Jewish seder meal at Passover or the Christian celebration of the Eucharist are both rituals that aim at a return to a time or event that established a basic pattern for the proper relationship between the human and the divine. Before anything more specific can be accomplished, the general pattern of harmony between the two spheres, which does not last forever but must be renewed at periodic intervals, has to be reestablished.

The performance of myth and ritual is not always connected with the achievement of specific goals, but a sense that benefits of some kind will ultimately result is a safe assumption. At the deepest level of significance, they might be viewed as an integral part of a common quest for "ontological security"—a sense that life has ultimate meaning and purpose, that the transient lives of humans are anchored in a deeper, more enduring reality. Because an individual's sense of reality is profoundly rooted in participation in the collective life of a people, the reenactment of the beginnings of the world also have the function of reaffirming that sense of peoplehood, of existing not simply as isolated individuals but as a social unit. This becomes particularly important for nomadic peoples, such as the Sioux of the Plains, and their renowned Sun Dance was the occasion for their reassembling as a group and reasserting their collective sense of community.

Specific rituals might also be performed at crucial times in the life of a people, such as the onset of a war or a hunt. Among agricultural peoples such as the Creeks (Muskogee), for example, the Green Corn ceremony, a festival celebrating the first fruits of the annual maize planting, was held near midsummer, with the earliest ears of corn being offered in thanksgiving for this indication that another year's sustenance was in prospect. Presumably some of the ceremony's significance was a collective desire to ensure the continuation of the earth's bounty in years to come. Whatever role such intentions may have played, however, the broader context of the ceremony was that of an annual rite of collective and cosmic renewal. A *bosquito* or "busk" was an integral part of the ceremony, which extended for several days, in which both individuals and houses were purified of the real and symbolic dirt that had accumulated over the previous year. (Thoreau praised this practice in *Walden* as an admirable means of simplifying one's life.) Old fires were extinguished and a new one kindled, offenses were forgiven, and the new crops could be eaten after extended fasting. The levels of parallel symbolic activity should be evident: at once the individual, the society, the village, nature, and by extension the entire cosmos were joining in a round of purification and renewal.

Ritual also played an important role at crucial stages in the life of the individual as well as in society as a whole. Emergence into adulthood, often at the onset of puberty, was the most frequent occasion for the observation of these "rites of passage." Young women usually went through a ritual involving temporary isolation at the onset of menstruation. The vision quest for males in the hunting cultures of the North, such as the Massachuset of New England or the Ojibwa (Anishinaabe) of the Great Lakes, tended to be more dramatic. A boy would be conditioned over the years to expect to undertake the quest for a uniquely personal vision putting him into contact with the supernatural world and thereby authenticating his entry into the adult world. After appropriate ritual preparation, the vision might be achieved after days spent in the wilderness with no food or water; in the case of the Sun Dance, intense pain brought about through suspension on ropes fastened to needles inserted into the flesh induced a trance state conducive to visionary experience. In some societies narcotic drugs or tobacco smoking were utilized to help induce an appropriately altered state of consciousness as well.

As for other critical stages of life, births were not usually celebrated in public, although the mother and child might later be presented to the group in a ceremony. Most peoples did not seem to have elaborate ceremonies focusing on marriage, except for puberty rites that prepared young people to be eligible for matrimony. At the termination of life, funeral customs vary considerably, although many northern peoples practiced burial on elevated platforms. In the case of the Hurons, this was a temporary resting place; every fifteen years, the remains would be collected and interred in a great Feast of the Dead, after which the entire village would change its location.

Other problematic aspects of life requiring ritual mediation were illness and witchcraft, the first sometimes resulting from the practice of the second. It is interesting to note that, although native peoples lacked the sophisticated medical technology of today, many aspects of their approach to the issue of healing are finding increasing favor in an age when *holistic medicine,* dealing with all aspects of a person and not simply his or her physical condition, is becoming a watchword. Again, American Indians did not draw the sharp distinctions between body, mind, and spirit that have been characteristic of the modern Western world-picture. Rather, disease was the result of a lack of harmony between the afflicted individual and broader spiritual forces. This disharmony might be induced by natural causes, in which case treatment with herbal medicines might be efficacious. However, illness might also be the result of taboo violation, contact with ghosts, witchcraft, or "soul loss," so that a supernatural remedy must be invoked to reestablish proper harmony between the sufferer and the cosmos.

The close relationship between curing and the supernatural is indicated in the fact that what we might call religious specialists or "professionals" in Native American cultures have the remedy of disease as one of their primary functions. In settled agricultural tribes, such as the Pueblo, this function may be institutionalized in the form of voluntary societies of men concerned with the crucial affairs of the people. Even where the "medicine man" operates as an individual rather than a member of a group of religious specialists, he derives his power more from the possession of traditional ritual lore thought to be efficacious in bringing about cures than from any special personal gifts. Disease is often thought to result from the presence in the body of a foreign object that has entered through supernatural means, such as witchcraft. In such a situation the medicine man brings about a cure through sucking it out and displaying the object—often a feather—to the afflicted person. To the skeptical Westerner, this may appear as a sort of sleight of hand, which it probably is in a literal sense. From the native point of view, however, the point is that the source of affliction has been localized in something tangible, and the literal origins of the offending object are not particularly interesting or relevant.

Another sort of religious specialist found more frequently in northern, hunting cultures is the shaman, a name derived from the particularly intense version of this practitioner originally found in Siberia. The shaman is characterized not so much

by the possession of traditional knowledge but rather by his (or sometimes her) personal ability to engage in trance-voyages in the supernatural realm. Such individuals
are often psychologically marginal—perhaps even borderline psychotic in modern
parlance—but are valued by their fellows as rarely gifted individuals with direct access to other realms of being. Such abilities are valued both in the broader religious
realm as the bringers of the visions that are the ultimate source of myth and ritual,
and more specifically as possessed of healing powers. For someone who has "lost
his soul"—one possible source of disease—recovery is only possible if the shaman
undertakes a journey into the supernatural realm to recover and restore it.

The roles of shaman and medicine man were by no means mutually exclusive,
and the combination of factors giving them authority varied from people to people.
Similarly, shamans may not be at all the only people with access to visions. Among
the Massachusets, for example, the shaman or "powwow" was recognized as having
supernatural authority only as long as he could continue to "produce" accounts of
communication with the spirit world, interpret dreams, and cure illnesses. His powers
were different not so much in kind but in degree from others, and private visions could
be obtained by many people in appropriate circumstances. The status of "powwow,"
then, had to be continually reaffirmed, and such a person had continually to reassert
his claim to power if he was to retain respect in a highly individualistic society.

As we have seen, witchcraft was regarded by many peoples as an important cause
of illness, and the power of shamans or medicine men was frequently exercised to
counteract its effects. Witchcraft, or the intentional use of spiritual power by an
individual to do harm to others or to act out of pure self-interest, is by no means
confined to American Indian societies; its emergence in Salem in 1692 and as a part
of much African American lore in the antebellum South indicates European and
African antecedents as well. Among the Navajo especially, belief in witchcraft is
pervasive and has given rise to a complex lore distinguishing among different sorts
of witchcraft and prescribing means of avoiding its effects or curing them once they
have been worked. Even among contemporary Navajo who have become thoroughly
assimilated into European American culture, such beliefs still surface, at times of
stress especially, and witchcraft accusations and occasional killings have taken place
well into the twentieth century. Among some peoples, medicine men or shamans
who had a suspiciously low rate of success in saving people from various afflictions
might well be accused of witchcraft themselves, since the power manipulated by
healers and sorcerers was essentially the same. Although witchcraft beliefs are common in many cultures, a particular preoccupation with witchcraft is often indicative
that a community is undergoing severe stress and change, and that someone must
be found to blame for it and thereby reverse the ill effects.

In this survey of what we might broadly identify as "religious life" among the native peoples of North America, we have already come across instances of the effects
of cultural change, particularly that induced by contacts with European American

society. As this contact became widespread and it became apparent that the old ways could not be continued indefinitely, Native peoples reacted in a number of ways. A substantial number simply died, killed by the epidemic diseases introduced by Europeans against which they had no immunity. Others engaged with Christianity, a response that was especially common when a traditional culture was faced with nearly total collapse in the face of white incursions. Finally, a number of "pan-Indian" movements, usually incorporating distinct religious dimensions, began to emerge during the late nineteenth century. Some of these, such as the Ghost Dance, ultimately failed, whereas others, such as the Peyote religion, endure to the present. These stories will be taken up in later chapters.

CHAPTER 2

The African Background of New World Religions

In many ways, the traditional religions of Africa were similar to those of the aboriginal peoples of North America. In both cases, knowledge and lore were transmitted orally, rather than in written form, in the manner of traditional cultures. Religious and mythological systems varied considerably from region to region and people to people, although a number of themes were common to most. Supernatural beings were plural rather than singular, as in monotheistic religions, and the line between this world and the supernatural was not sharply drawn. Religion was not identifiable with an organizational structure and a statement of beliefs in propositional forms, but rather with the myths and rituals that were periodically retold and enacted in the course of a people's common life. These are all characteristics of other traditional peoples' religious experience as well, and such similarities should come as no great surprise.

Similar also are the changes that arose in both cases through the shock of cultural contacts, often unsought and unwelcome, between these traditional peoples and the aggressive newcomers from Europe who sought to extend their hegemony overseas. Both the overtures of Christian missionaries and the responses of native peoples resulted in adaptation and innovation within the old frameworks. What distinguished the African American experience from the Native American was not the shock of European American imperialism nor the emergence of new religious forms, nor even the wide-scale suffering and death that resulted from these hostile contacts. Rather, the most significant differences resulted directly from the character of the coming of the African peoples to the New World. This migration took place not through free choice, as had been the case with most other immigrant groups, but rather through a forcible, involuntary massive population movement in the context of the slave trade and the institution of slavery. This context dominated African American life until the American Civil War, and its consequences have been inescapable to the present day.

A further distinction can be made between the character of the patterns of black settlement and subsequent life in the two hemispheres of the Americas. Slavery itself was an institution that had pervaded colonial society—English, French, Portuguese, and Spanish—from Maryland through the West Indies and deep into South America, and which had reached even as far north as New England for a time. Its character varied considerably over these two continents. The tendency of the British was to plant permanent colonies of settlers in the New World, while the Iberians regarded their vast lands more as arenas from which valuable goods could be extracted to enrich those who had remained at home in Europe. All of the colonizing powers agreed that Africans were not the human equivalent of Europeans, and therefore could be enslaved with impunity. Although the work of Bartolomé de las Casas on behalf of the aboriginal peoples of the Americas may have had some marginal effect in alleviating the condition of the Africans, they consistently were regarded as the lowest estate of humanity, and thus susceptible to the grossest forms of exploitation.

In South America and the West Indies, African slaves vastly outnumbered Europeans and were also less likely to be systematically separated from their fellow tribespeople than was the case in what would become the United States. Conditions were thus far more propitious in Ibero-America and the Caribbean for the continuation of the traditional cultures of Africa, especially those of the western Guinea coast from Gambia to the Congo, the source of the largest percentage of the possibly twelve million slaves who reached New World shores alive. Although the living and working conditions of those few who had survived the arduous, forcible crossing of the Atlantic from Africa to the New World—the "Middle Passage"—were oppressive, the bitterness was partially offset by the possibility of keeping alive the old ways, including religion. The Catholic Church's missionaries attempted to spread the Christian Gospel among the slaves, but their numbers were too few, and many of the plantations too isolated, to make a great deal of difference.

As was the case with many Native Americans, who in North America were occasionally enslaved but without lasting success, the more usual response of traditional peoples to new and powerful cultural forces was not a rigid maintenance of the old but a blending of old and new. The religions of West Africa varied in detail but generally involved belief in a creator god, or *deus otiosus,* who was not actively involved in the subsequent course of earthly affairs. More relevant to everyday matters were a host of lesser divinities that were immanent within the natural realm and who served as the tutelary deities of local villages and other social units. These supernatural beings reflected the most important concerns of a particular people, and priests conducted sacrifices on altars to propitiate them and ensure that life continued smoothly. These priests could also acquire considerable political power and reputation.

Just as these divinities represented practical concerns in the midst of everyday life, so were the ancestors of a particular people regarded as continuing as a relevant presence in the here and now. They served as guardians of their descendants' laws and customs, and could play an intermediary role between humans and supernatural beings. Consequently, burial rites were of considerable importance, and it was incumbent on the living to make sure that the dead were content. Further, just as divinities could enter into the bodies of their devotees and manifest themselves in spirit-trances, so did the ancestors continue to live on in their progeny. A firm line, in short, did not exist between the natural and the supernatural or the living and the dead. These different realms of being instead coexisted in an ongoing mutual interaction, so that human well-being was intimately involved in a broader, ecological pattern of relationships.

This active, pluralistic cosmos was brought to New World shores by the African emigrants, where it came into contact with the Roman Catholicism of the French, Spanish, and Portuguese masters. For the most part, the Africans regarded this new faith not as something completely alien, to be accepted or rejected as a whole, but rather as a source for creative borrowings and adaptations. Where the radical monotheism of North American Protestantism was uncongenial, the panoply of ceremonies and saints that Catholicism offered presented numerous correspondences, at least on the surface, with the rituals and divinities of African practice. The result was the development of a variety of new, creolized religions, blending elements of African and Catholic practice into new wholes. These included Candomblé in Brazil, Shango in Trinidad, Obeah in Jamaica, and, most familiar in the United States, Haitian Vodun (or Vodou) and Cuban Santería.

Vodun is the new religious movement that emerged in French colonial Haiti and that has subsequently coexisted with Catholicism as the dominant religion of that nation to the present day. Its career in Haiti, where it had been an illicit folk religion for most of its existence, took on a sinister turn in the twentieth century when it was utilized by President "Papa Doc" Duvalier as an instrument of political terror. Vodun came to North America early with Haitian blacks who began to arrive in Louisiana, also a center of French creole (i.e., colonial) culture, after the Haitian revolution around 1800. In New Orleans, where it became known as *voodoo,* it flourished during slavery days, especially under two priestesses, mother and daughter, both named Marie Laveau, and focused on the cult of a snake god known as "Li Grand Zombi," a practice probably derived ultimately from Dahomey in Africa. During its heyday, New Orleans voodoo was an organized system, characterized by practices of African origins such as ritual dancing, trance possessions, and sacrifices. However, as its influence spread beyond into the rural South, it lost much of its coherence and disintegrated into a collection of magical practices known as "hoodoo" or "rootwork" best regarded not so much as religion but rather as folklore. (Magic is usually distinguished from religion in that the former is aimed at immediate, specific, this-worldly results attained through the manipulation of occult forces, without regard to any larger metaphysical or moral system.)

More recently, the influx of Cuban refugees in the Miami and New York metropolitan areas brought with them another African Caribbean religion known as *Santería*—the "way of the saints." Santería is derived from the traditional religion of the Yoruba, the dominant African people in Cuba, who continue to live in and around present-day Nigeria. The religion of the Yoruba and its transformation into African American Santería is exemplary both of traditional African religion and its Old and New World metamorphoses.

The first important thing to note about the Yoruba and their religion is that neither people nor religion is uniform or unchanging. The Yoruba, who today are estimated to number anywhere from five to ten million, are divided into a number of groups who maintain independent traditions of religion and culture. They are united, however, by a common language and an agreement on the centrality of the sacred city of Ife—the Yoruba's *axis mundi,* or center of the cosmos, and the continuing locus of religious power. According to Benjamin Ray, their creation myth reflects the conquest during the fifteenth century of the Ibo (or Igbo), who had been the first to live in the vicinity of Ife.

Whatever its specific political and historical purposes, this creation myth is typical of those of many African peoples. Its first character is Olorun, the "owner of the sky," who is the Yoruba's "high god." (The meaning of his older name, Olodumare, is not as clear. Newell Booth suggests that the clarity of "Olorun" may indicate the more recent influence of monotheistic Christianity and Islam in the area.) He is also associated with the cosmic serpent, manifested in the rainbow. Olorun resides in the sky (*Orun*) as a *deus otiosus,* an ultimate source of power who has little direct relation to life in the other half of the cosmos, namely, the earth (*Aiye*). Humans living in the latter realm can relate directly not to Olorun himself but rather with *oris(h)as*—which can be loosely translated as "gods" or "divinities"—and human ancestors now residing in Orun.

Because Yoruba religious practice is not highly centralized, there is no definitive creation account but rather a number of variants on a theme. In one typical version, Orishanla (also known as Obatala), the first-created and principal *orisha,* was charged by Olodumare with creating the world from some earth and a five-toed chicken, who set to work spreading the earth about. In the version of the story told at Ife, Orishanla became drunk on palm wine before finishing the job, which was completed by his brother Oduduwa. Upon awaking, Orishanla got into a fight with his brother, which may echo the long-past struggle between the Yoruba and the Ibo. The result was the victory of Oduduwa, who became the first divine king of Ife and thus legitimated the ongoing rule of the Yoruba. Orishanla, however, was not vanquished but rather given the task of creating the first humans. His presence is manifested especially in dwarfs and others of abnormal shape, who are regarded as sacred beings and reminders of Orishanla's power.

Many other gods—who are not always clearly differentiated from one another and whose identities may overlap—also make up the Yoruba pantheon and are associated with particular locales, peoples, and aspects of nature. Ogun, for instance, is associated with metals and war, and is invoked in situations where these phenomena are involved. Ogun is supposed to have been the first king of Ife. When the earliest humans, newly created by the gods, did not respect him, he went off to kill himself. A similar story is associated in some traditions with Shango, the god of thunder and lightning. Shango was a bad king who was so hated by his subjects that he hanged himself. When he heard someone say that he had done so, though, he became angry and destroyed the talebearer with lightning. As a result, he has always been known as "the king who did not hang himself."

Ogun is particularly interesting in his dual role as god and human. Now a god, he began on earth as a human, and thus is also identified as a dead ancestor residing in the world beyond. As such, he is one of many intermediaries between the realms of Orun and Aiye. Ancestors are particularly important for the Yoruba in this mediating function. Not all the dead are regarded as "ancestors" in the strong sense; those who have led an unworthy life are relegated to a hot and dry land of broken potsherds. The good, however, ascend to the "good heaven" of Olorun and the orishas, and are venerated by their descendants. Some remain important simply for their families, whereas others—the "deified ancestors"—have shrines maintained for them by whole towns. Gods and ancestors alike are regarded as important conduits of supernatural power.

A final aspect of Yoruba belief and practice that deserves mention is their attitude toward individual destiny. All people are made up of a physical and a spiritual component. Before birth, they choose a destiny, which is identified with an ancestor but which is forgotten upon birth. This destiny is somewhat malleable for better or worse, but cannot be affected without a recovered knowledge of its character. This knowledge can only be acquired through the activity of a diviner (*babalawo*). The babalawo establishes contact with the supernatural world through a process involving the transfer of palm nuts rapidly from hand to hand and the working out of a set of traditional parables that correspond to the results of this process. These parables point to specific advice about one's destiny and life-course, and are accompanied by sacrifices.

These traditional practices are still very much alive among the Yoruba, though their character is continuously subject to change along both geographical and temporal lines. The importation of Christianity and Islam to West Africa has affected the nature of the traditional religion, and has also resulted in the emergence of new, syncretistic religions. As Joseph Murphy has demonstrated, this adaptability is clearly illustrated in the religious life of the Yoruba after their forcible transplantation to the New World. In Cuba, where Roman Catholicism was officially established and traditional religions outlawed, the Yoruba adapted their ancestral practices to the symbolism of the Catholic pantheon of saints, who became identified with various orishas. Santería shrines thus ostensibly honor Catholic saints, but in their deeper meaning actually are dedicated to Yoruba orishas. Saint Barbara, for example, is depicted in Western iconography as mounted on horseback; in Santería, she becomes equated with Shango, who is similarly represented in Yoruba tradition. In contemporary America, Santería is usually practiced in the home, where shrines are assembled consisting of Catholic devotional objects such as saints' statues and pictures combined with traditional African elements such as stones consecrated by priests or priestesses in ceremonies involving blood from animal sacrifices.

The *botánicas,* or religious goods stores, that are familiar features in Caribbean neighborhoods in America's large cities are exotic reminders that the African heritage is very much alive and well in America today. Their appeal, however, is not so much to blacks with deep roots in America but rather to more recent immigrants from the West Indies whose ancestors were better able to preserve over the decades a direct line of continuity with their African origins. In addition, recent immigrants from Africa itself are adding a new element of complexity to the religious makeup of American cities from Manhattan to Lewiston, Maine, as they bring with them varieties of Christianity, Islam, and tribal religions.

B. The Mediterranean Matrix

The origins of the religions and culture we call "Western" lie in the eastern reaches of the Mediterranean basin and date back at least four millennia. The roots of the culture that has flourished in Europe and North America and by the late twentieth century had extended its reach around the entire globe are complex. Most of its languages are of the Indo-European family, which most likely originated in the Indian subcontinent. Much of the Western heritage of thought, education, law, and politics can be traced to ancient Greece and Rome, which successively dominated their environs for many centuries.

The religions of classical antiquity, however, survive mainly in the names of gods and goddesses now affixed to intercontinental missiles. The religious tradition that now dominates the West and is well represented throughout the rest of the world had its origins among a Semitic people who only briefly enjoyed a rather limited political dominance in part of the Middle East, and were soon conquered and scattered. Their sacred writings—the Hebrew Bible or Old Testament—had their origins in oral traditions and incorporated preliterate and even "Oriental" elements as they expanded and were gradually codified. Their bearers, who became known as the Jewish people, eventually dispersed throughout the world, and never greatly expanded their numbers. Their very survival as a people over the centuries has been radically problematic and constitutes one of the most gripping stories of the twentieth as well as earlier centuries.

It was only through the spread of a messianic movement that originated among the Jews of the later Roman Empire that this Hebrew tradition became the basis of a powerful and aggressive world religion. After the first Christians accepted the premise that their converts did not first have to become Jews, their way became clear for universal evangelization. In the twilight of imperial Rome, a persecuted Jewish sect with apocalyptic expectations eventually became the official religion of the entirety of Europe, and still later of Europe's overseas empires. Even as both Judaism and Christianity began to lose ground to secularism, it became obligatory in public pronouncements to invoke the (somewhat nebulous) "Judeo-Christian tradition" as the groundwork of our society and culture.

For all of these transformations, there is no doubt that the religion of the large majority of Americans has some sort of historical connection with the religious heritage of the Mediterranean basin that took shape between two and four millennia ago. To understand Judaism and Christianity, then, we have to survey those origins, and see how three distinct traditions—the Jewish and the Eastern and Western Christian—arose in a political and social context that was hardly favorable to their growth, but in which, despite all odds, they eventually flourished and dominated.

1. JUDAISM AND THE EMERGENCE OF HISTORICAL RELIGION

CHAPTER 3

The Jewish Tradition

Judaism, even more than most religions, is intended to be lived rather than simply believed or accepted. Certainly most religions teach that their precepts must be translated into everyday practice rather than remain at the level of nominal belief.

The Jewish tradition, however, has more explicitly than most maintained that to be a good Jew is not primarily to believe the correct ideas but to do the correct things. Such deeds are known as *mitzvoth* (MITZ-vahs), or, in the singular, *mitzva(h)* (MITZ-vah).* A mitzvah is literally a divine commandment or, more broadly, a good deed or work performed for God's glory. In Jewish tradition, there are 613 specific mitzvoth: 365 of these are negative, and the remaining 248 positive injunctions relate to ritual observance and also to just and proper relations among people. Even among Jews who do not regard such detailed tradition as binding, the notion of mitzvah as a general obligation to live justly in the world is still powerful.

Judaism has thus always emphasized *orthopraxis*—correct action or living—over *orthodoxy*—correct belief, and has seldom been given to drawing up creeds containing specific propositions about God that have to be accepted by believers. On the other hand, there are a cluster of symbols, rituals, texts, and roles, as in most modern religions, that form the core around which the varieties of Jewish practice have unfolded. The traditional triad of foci has been God, Torah, and Israel.

The relationship of the Jewish people with their *God* is summarized in the central prayer of their tradition, the *Shema* (sh'MAH) (Deuteronomy 6:4–7):

> Hear, O Israel: The Lord our God, the Lord is One!—And thou shalt love the Lord thy God with all thy heart, and with all thy soul, and with all thy might. And these words, which I command thee this day, shall be upon thy heart, and thou shalt teach them diligently unto thy children, and thou shalt talk of them when thou sittest in thy house, and when thou walkest by the way, and when thou liest down, and when thou risest up. And thou shalt bind them for a sign upon thy hand, and they shall be for frontlets between thine eyes. And thou shalt write them upon the door-posts of thy house and thy gates.

In addition to mandating certain practices of worship, the Shema conveys a vivid sense of the character of the God of the people of Israel—one God, who enters into a personal, covenant relationship with his chosen people and in return demands their undivided allegiance. Although the nature of God has subsequently been debated and questioned by Jewish thinkers, the centrality of the notion of a single, personal god to historic Judaism is clear.

The second term in the central triad is *Torah*—the Pentateuch, or first five books of Hebrew scripture traditionally attributed to Moses. These five books are regarded as the holiest part of scripture, and are kept in scroll form in the Ark of the Covenant at the heart of the synagogue. Torah may also refer in an extended sense to the remainder of Hebrew scripture—or, even more broadly, to the "sacred wisdom" of the tradition.

---

*Spellings and pronunciations of transliterated Hebrew words vary because of the lack of exact English equivalents for some sounds such as that variously represented as *h* or *ch*. In some cases, such as here, various transliterations will be ackowledged by using parenthesis in the first occurrence.

In addition to Torah and the rest of scripture, Jewish tradition is based on a related collection of lore known as the *Talmud* (or simply Talmud). The Talmud is the collective body of interpretations of scripture that developed as a central part of Jewish life since the fifth century B.C. It is sometimes called "oral Torah," following the tradition that it was delivered by God in oral form to Moses at the same time that he received the written Torah. The Talmud is lengthy and complex, and consists of *Mishnah*—a collection of ritual laws—and *Gemara,* or records of rabbinical discussions of Mishnah. Basically, it represents the application of deductive logic to scripture to develop an ethic, *(H)Aggadah,* and a code of law, *Halakah,* for the guidance of the Jewish people. During the ages when Jewish communities were semiautonomous, the Talmud formed the legal system and body of precedents on which their governance was based. Rabbis functioned in such contexts as governors and judges, and continued to apply Talmudic principles and precedents to everyday situations. Even though a *Beth Din,* or rabbinic court, is unusual among assimilated American Jews, such judgments are still preferred to those of the civil courts by some traditionalists. Still another body of extrabiblical lore is *Midrash,* numerous collections of rabbinical interpretations of or sermons based on scripture.

The third member of this triad is *Israel,* the name of both a holy land and its holy people. Although the physical relationship of the Jewish people to the land of Israel has been problematic over the centuries, the restoration of independence in recent years has revived Israel as a powerful emotional, religious, and political symbol for American Jews regardless of their specific theological propensities. Similarly, the Holocaust forcibly reminded Jews throughout the world of their collective identity and relationship as a people, despite periodic efforts to reinterpret that identity in more universalistic religious terms—that is, by stressing the commonality of Judaism with other religions rather than its uniqueness.

Although all Jews are traditionally expected to participate actively in religious observance, a number of specialized religious roles have emerged over the centuries. After the Temple disappeared as the focus of Jewish worship, the role of the priest, who conducted cultic sacrifices therein, became obsolete. In place of the priest emerged the *rabbi,* or "teacher," who has persisted to the present as the Jewish religious leader in diaspora. Traditionally, the rabbi—a title and function dating back to the sixth century B.C.—served as a scholar of Torah and Talmud who could apply that knowledge practically to the needs of the Jewish community. In the American context, however, where no rabbis even existed until the 1840s and where the model of the Protestant minister has been widely influential, the role of the rabbi has changed significantly. For example, many American rabbis now preach regularly—a function unknown in earlier years in Europe—counsel, administer, and perform the myriad organizational tasks familiar to most American clergy. In addition, women are now ordained by the Conservative, Reform, and Reconstructionist branches of American Judaism in what is certainly a distinctive departure from tradition.

Among many traditional Jews even today, one of the primary functions of the rabbi is the supervision of the laws of *kashrut,* or dietary code derived from the Book of Leviticus. The original motivations for this code have been the subject of considerable speculation, but over the centuries its maintenance has emerged as a primary sign of holiness of life for the observant Jew. The operative everyday word here is *kosher,* which means ritually clean and fit to eat. (In its broader contemporary sense, it also is used informally by Jews and Gentiles alike to mean "OK" or legitimate.) The following are some of its more important features:

1. Pork and shellfish, together with a long list of foods from animals seldom encountered today, are *trayf,* that is, not fit to eat. Trayf animals are those whose features do not conform to certain criteria—for example, mammals should both chew their cud and have cloven hooves and fish possess both scales and fins.
2. Meat and milk products are not to be mixed. A kosher kitchen will have two sets of dishes, one for each. Even an accidental mixing renders such dishes unclean, so that they have to be ritually purified or destroyed.
3. Even animals such as cattle that are potentially fit to eat have to be slaughtered in a kosher manner, so that the blood is drained from the brain immediately. A *shochet,* or special functionary trained in the laws of kashrut, must perform such butchering under rabbinic supervision.

Keeping kosher, then, is one of the most visible ways in which traditional Jews manifest their piety. From a secular viewpoint, kosher food has the virtue of being free of many controversial chemical additives widely used today and is also obtained through a humane method of slaughtering animals.

Another traditional Jewish role is that of *chazzen,** or cantor. Prior to the advent of the first rabbis in America in the 1840s, congregations employed *chazzonim* to lead them in prayer. Although their voices were their leading feature, many other aspects of synagogue life also devolved on them in earlier days in the absence of a rabbi.

Although worship for Jews is manifested in private prayers, in study, and in the round of daily life, it is also carried out, as in most organized religions, at specific times and places in public. The physical setting for public worship bears several names:

Shul—"school" or "house of study," a traditional Yiddish term;
Synagogue—probably most familiar, originally signifying the congregation meeting in diaspora for worship, and later coming to mean primarily the building used for worship;

**Chazzen,* like *shochet,* is one of a number of Hebrew and/or Yiddish words beginning with the "ch" sound that is articulated as a strong guttural emerging from deep in the throat. This sound is also found in German but not in English. In many cases, such as *Hasidism* and *Hanukkah,* the initial *c* is dropped in transliteration.

Temple—which no longer exists in its ancient sense as a place for conducting sacrifices, revived by Reform Jews as a synonym for synagogue, with the implication that the temple of old was permanently superseded by this new institution.

Because Jewish life in diaspora has been conducted in so many different host cultures, no authoritative styles of synagogue design have ever emerged, and American synagogues have undergone a variety of phases of architectural development. Synagogue arrangements always include an Ark of the Covenant for the Torah scrolls and one or more *bemas,* or platforms for reading tables. In traditional synagogues, women are sequestered from and invisible to men; in more contemporary arrangements, families usually sit together in pews. Although God may not be represented in pictorial form, other religious themes are frequently depicted in synagogue art.

For public prayer to be valid, Jewish tradition dictates that a *minyan,* or group of ten adult male Jews, be present. (A rabbi, however, is not essential.) Daily and Sabbath prayer are conducted according to a fixed ritual in one of several versions of the *Siddur* or prayer book—an English version for Reform, Hebrew for most others. The sequence of prayer varies at different times of the day—morning, afternoon, and evening—and may include praises of and petitions to God, readings from the Torah, and the recitation of the Shema. As an adjunct to public worship, traditionally inclined men as a measure of respect wear a *yarmulke* (YOM-muk-kah), or skullcap (also know as a *kipah* [KEE-pah]); a *tallit,* or tasselled prayer shawl; and *tefillin,* or phylacteries, which are leather containers, attached to the left arm and head by leather straps, in which scrolls with scripture verses are kept. A similar practice on the domestic side is the affixing of *mezuzahs,* or prayer scrolls, to the doorposts of Jewish homes.

The core of Jewish worship, however, is the weekly observance of the Sabbath—*Shabbes* in Yiddish, or *Shabbat* (shah-BOTT) in Hebrew. Sabbath begins at sundown on Friday and continues until the corresponding time of Saturday. (The Christian Sabbath, or Sunday observance, is derived from the Jewish custom, but uses a different reckoning of time—as Reform Jews have occasionally attempted.) On the Sabbath all work ceases. Meals and other necessities are provided for beforehand, so the entire day may be consecrated to rest and worship—"re-creation" in the root sense. Public worship is held on Friday evening and, most especially, on Saturday morning, and domestic rituals, such as the mother's lighting the candles before the Friday evening meal, extend the observance into the home as well. Contemporary Jews adhere to these rites with varying degrees of strictness, but the weekly Sabbath is without question the core of Jewish religious life.

In addition to the weekly Sabbath observance, Jewish worship focuses on a yearly cycle of holidays, the occurrence of which is governed by a traditional lunar calendar utilized today almost solely for such ceremonial purposes. Two holiday sequences are observed almost universally by American Jews: Passover, in the spring, and the High Holy Days (or "Days of Awe"), which begin early in the fall with Rosh Hashanah, the New Year, and end with Yom Kippur, the Day of Atonement. Others, such as Sukkoth and Purim, are folk festivals rather than solemn religious observances, and are not usually the occasion of remaining home from school or work. Yet another, (C)Hanukka(h), has come to occupy a distinct place in the interaction of Jewish tradition with American culture.

Passover, or *Pesach* (PAY-sock), usually occurs in the spring fairly close to the Christian Easter, and was the occasion of Jesus's "Last Supper." Passover commemorates the archetypal event in the sacred history of Israel, the deliverance by Yahweh of the Hebrew people out of Egyptian bondage. Its celebration extends over eight days (seven in Israel), which are preceded by a ritual cleansing to ensure that not even the slightest trace of leavened bread or other foods with leavening remains in the house. The highlight of Passover is the *seder* (SAY-durr), at which all of the family gather for a ritual meal.

The seder meal consists of two primary components: a specific array of foods and wine, and a special liturgy called *(H)Aggadah* (Hah-GAH-dah).

The foods include the following:

Karpas—parsley or another green vegetable symbolizing spring and rebirth;
(C)haroset(h)—a mixture that usually includes chopped apples, nuts, wine, and spices, signifying the materials from which the Hebrews made bricks while serving as Egyptian slaves;
Maror—bitter herbs (usually horseradish), reminiscent of the bitterness of Egyptian bondage;
Beitzah and *Zeroa*—a roasted egg and bone, symbols of the sacrifices once brought to the Temple;
Matzo(h)—unleavened bread, recalling that made in haste once the departure from Egypt was to begin.

Sweet kosher wine is also served to all, including children. The (H)Aggadah service is led by the father or oldest male family member present, and consists of prayers and readings from the Talmud and from the Book of Exodus. A favorite part of the family-oriented service is the posing of the traditional question "Why is this night different from all other nights?" by the youngest son, with four similar ritual questions and answers following.

Rosh Hashanah (roshe ha-SHO-nah), the Jewish new year that celebrates the creation of the world, inaugurates the ten-day cycle of High Holy Days (Days of Awe). Services are held in the synagogue and are marked by the periodic blowing of the *shofar*, or ram's horn. The cycle ends with *Yom Kippur* (yahm KIP-pur), or Day of Atonement, which is also observed at the synagogue rather than in the home. The theme of this holy day and its special chanted liturgy, the *Kol Nidre*, is repentance and forgiveness for offenses committed during the past year—a ritual of individual and collective spiritual renewal.

Other festivals that are not quite of the same stature but are still frequently observed include *Succot(h)* (or *Sukkot* [SOOK-ess or SOOK-ote]), the Feast of Booths (or Tabernacles) which begins the fifth day after Yom Kippur. This is a thanksgiving holiday in which the booths set up by observant families recall the transient character of the forty years spent in the wilderness after the Exodus. *Purim* (POOR-im), the Feast of Lots, commemorates the deliverance of the Jews of Persia from mass extermination by the wicked royal minister Haman, as narrated in the Book of Esther. Its celebration is festive, and includes the booing of the name of Haman by children during the synagogue service.

Another holiday commemorating a specific historical event is *(C)Hanukka(h)* (HAHN-ah-kah, beginning with the guttural "ch" sound), or "Feast of Lights." Although the holiday commemorates the successful rebellion of Judah "the Hammer" and his followers, the Maccabees, against Syrian oppression in the second century B.C., its celebration has taken on a very different significance in the American context. As Christmas came to assume a larger and larger role in American secular as well as religious life, Jewish children felt excluded from the gentile world that seemed to explode yearly in caroling, gift buying and giving, and the rest of the interwoven commercial, festive, and sacred observances that the holiday acquired. As a response, Hanukkah was elevated from the status of a relatively minor holiday into a seasonal alternative to Christmas. This is very much a home-centered observance, with one of eight candles on the *menorah,* or candleholder, lit daily with a ninth. This is symbolic of an oil lamp that burnt for eight days on one day's supply of fuel during the Maccabean revolt. Popular customs include the making of *latkes,* or potato pancakes; games played with a *draydl,* or spinning top traditionally made from clay; and the giving of Hanukkah *gelt,* gilt-wrapped chocolate coins resembling those of the Maccabean era. Some Jews eager to approximate gentile customs even further—and with tongues often firmly in cheek—add a "Hanukkah bush," or Christmas-tree substitute, and even have visits from "Hanukkah Harry" or "Uncle Max the Hanukkah Man," obvious counterparts to a well-known Christmas figure.

These and other holidays (described by Michael Strassfeld in *The Jewish Holidays*) correspond to the yearly round of observances that characterize many religions. Individual Jews and Jewish communities observe them with different degrees of intensity, though a great many Jews observe Passover and the High Holy Days with special reverence. In addition to the weekly Sabbath observance and the yearly round of holidays, the Jewish tradition also acknowledges in symbol and ritual special times in the individual life cycle. The first of these is the *bris,* or circumcision performed on male infants eight days after birth. The infant's foreskin is surgically removed by a *mohel* (MOY-ull), who is not a rabbi but rather a man specially trained in this craft.

The next stage of life that is ritually mediated comes at age thirteen—on or about the onset of puberty—in the ceremony of *Bar Mitzvah*. At this time, a Jewish boy becomes a "son of the commandment" (the meaning of the phrase) by reading a prayer and a passage from the Torah in Hebrew. The ceremony, in which the boy announces "Today I am a man," is preceded by instruction in Hebrew school and immediately followed by a great celebration of family and friends. Its immediate origins lie in late medieval Europe, although the symbolic recognition of coming of age has much deeper historical roots. A *Bas* or *Bat Mitzvah* ceremony for girls is of considerably more recent origin, practiced mainly in Reform and Conservative congregations. The latter traditions also may add, or substitute, a confirmation ceremony later in one's teens.

Early marriage and the bearing of children was traditionally encouraged among Jews, although contemporary Jewish demographics in America have tended in the opposite direction so greatly that some leaders fear that the community may eventually die out from attrition. The Jewish wedding, however, has taken its place in the American array of ethnic celebrations as a particularly lavish and joyful event—much like the Bar Mitzvah. A traditional wedding is performed with the couple standing under a *(c)huppa(h)*, or canopy. At the end of the ceremony, the groom breaks a glass under his foot, which is usually (but not definitively) explained as a reminder of the destruction of the Temple and the sufferings of the Jewish people. Although many Jews now simply obtain secular divorces when necessary, Jewish law allows for religious divorce, or *get,* under certain circumstances.

Although funeral practices differ among contemporary Jews, tradition calls for a simple burial in white linen garments in a plain wooden coffin (on the grounds that conspicuous consumption is inappropriate at such an occasion, and that all are equal in death). Cremation has never been permitted in traditional Judaism. The funeral service is equally simple, and features the recital of the *Kaddish* (KOD-dish). On each anniversary of a death, the family of the deceased may light a *Yahrzeit* (or *Yortzeit*) candle in their memory.

The cycle of Jewish observances, then, is a complex one that has developed over the centuries from the time of ancient Israel, with many additions and adaptations in the intervening centuries. Rituals are celebrated both in the home and in the synagogue, depending on the character of the observance. Some themes that intertwine among the many observances are the sanctity of daily life and the ongoing need to fulfill the demands of the covenant. In their combination of traditional practices and everyday concreteness, these observances demonstrate vividly much about the character of the Jewish religion.

From the Religion of the Hebrews to the Restoration of Israel

It has become a commonplace in discussing American Judaism to begin with "the problem of Jewish identity": what does it mean to be Jewish? It is also proverbial among Jews that where you have two Jews, you'll find three opinions. Jews as well as Gentiles (non-Jews) find this question both centrally important and vexingly difficult to answer. What follows will contribute, if not to an answer, at least to an exploration of the question's dimensions.

The question asserts itself from the beginning of Jewish history and is manifest in the multiplicity of names for the Jewish people, which have to be sorted at the outset. What, for instance, is the difference between *Jewish* and *Hebrew* when used as adjectives to identify a people and their religion, tradition, and scripture? And, when those who attack Jews are called *anti-Semites* or *anit-Semitic* how does this multiplication of terms further expand, or confuse, the question of who the Jewish people may be?

To begin at the end, *Semitic* is a generic term that designates a family of languages spoken primarily in the Middle East. This Semitic language family is not part of the Indo-European group that includes English, Yiddish (the vernacular language of many Jews in the past), and most other modern European languages. Other Semitic languages are Arabic, spoken by many Muslim peoples; Ethiopic, which is still in use in northeastern Africa; Aramaic, the vernacular of the Middle East at the time of Jesus; and a variety of long-extinct tongues spoken by contemporaries of the ancient Hebrew people, such as Akkadian, Moabite, and Phoenician. The use of *Semitic* to refer specifically to the Jewish people—usually in the construct *anti-Semitic* and its variants—is relatively recent, and frequently derogatory.

The related words *Jewish* and *Jew* originated in the later biblical period, and will be introduced and explained a bit later. The word *Hebrew,* the original meaning of which is not clear, can be used to designate a specific Semitic language, namely, that utilized by a particular group of ancient Near Eastern people. The linguistic name became attached also to the people among whom it was spoken. These "Hebrews" differed from their neighbors in their seminomadic character and by supporting themselves not through settled agriculture but rather as herders. Their identity as a distinct people with an even more distinct religion is attributed in the Book of Genesis to the calling of the patriarch (paternal ruler) Abraham. The god who thus called Abraham would from that time on be regarded as the god of the Hebrews and from the time of Moses would be known as *Yahweh*. Similarly, the Hebrew people would no longer be defined simply by language or kinship but by their allegiance to this, their god.*

At Yahweh's instruction, Abraham moved from Mesopotamia into the land of Canaan, later known as Palestine. The story of Abraham and his descendants—the *patriarchs* of Israel—is legendary in character, but may be rooted in historical events taking place around the first quarter of the second millennium B.C.—that is, 2000–1750 B.C.**

It is with Abraham and his covenant with Yahweh that the history of the Hebrews as a chosen people properly begins. Abraham's willingness to sacrifice his son Isaac demonstrated his devotion to Yahweh, and Isaac's son Jacob founded the twelve tribes that constituted the people of *Israel*—the name Jacob received after successfully wrestling with God himself (Genesis 32:22ff.). One of Jacob's sons, Joseph—he of the many-colored coat—was forced by his brothers into Egypt, where he prospered as Pharaoh's prime minister. Later, the rest of Jacob's family were forced by famine into Egypt as well, where they benefited from Joseph's position. This privileged status was later lost under "a new king over Egypt, who did not know Joseph," and the Hebrews were reduced to the status of slaves. It was this unpleasant situation that provided the context for the most dramatic event in the history of the Hebrew people, the memory of which is crucial for their identity to the present day.

The Book of Exodus retells the story of the emergence of Moses, rescued by Pharaoh's daughter from the bulrushes, raised in the royal court, and forced to flee into the land of Midian after killing a brutal Egyptian overseer beating Hebrew slaves. While living as a herdsman, Moses experienced a *theophany,* or appearance of the

---

*The meaning of the name Yahweh remains uncertain, although some scholars have argued that it is an invocation of God's role as creator. Although *Yahweh* is the form that is widely accepted as closest to the biblical *YHWH* (spelled in Hebrew consonants only without vowel points, and now usually pronounced YAH-way), it is not that which is commonly used by Jews. *Adonai* (ah-doh-NOI, "lord") and *Elohim* (ell-oh-EEM, meaning uncertain) are Hebrew forms used as substitutes. Many Jews even alter these slightly when uttering them.

**The question of indicating dates illustrates the profound influence that Christianity has had on the entire course of Western history, including the calendar. The calendar introduced by Julius Caesar in 46 B.C. was adopted by Christians, and the convention of fixing dates with reference to the supposed year of the birth of Jesus gradually spread throughout the West during the early Middle Ages. The calendar used almost universally today is based on a reform of this Christianized Julian calendar introduced by Pope Gregory XIII during the sixteenth century. Although most American Jews use the Gregorian calendar for everyday reckoning, some depart from it in two ways. When using, they substitute C.E. ("Common Era") and B.C.E. ("Before the Common Era") for A.D. (*Anno Domini*, "in the year of [our] Lord") and B.C. ("Before Christ") respectively. For ceremonial purposes—for example, in dating the cornerstone of a synagogue—the Jewish calendar devised by Hillel II (ca. A.D. 360) is sometimes used. This system reckons years by adding 3761, based on a traditional reckoning of the date of creation, to the Gregorian date. For convenience, however, the usual forms of B.C. and A.D. will be retained throughout this work.

divine: he encountered Yahweh, the god of the Hebrew people, in the form of a burning bush. Moses returned to Egypt at Yahweh's command, presented himself as a champion of the Hebrews against Pharaoh, brought down a series of plagues on the Egyptians when Pharaoh proved unyielding, and ultimately led his people safely through the parted waters of the Red (or, more accurately, "reed") Sea. From here Moses and his people journeyed to Mount Sinai, which Moses ascended to receive the Decalogue, or Ten Commandments, on two stone tablets. After years of wandering in the wilderness, the people finally entered into the promised land of Canaan—without Moses, who died after only glimpsing it.

It is this story of deliverance that has remained normative—the "root experience"—for the Hebrew (or Jewish) people ever since; in it are contained and developed the major themes that define the character of the Hebrew people and their covenantal relationship with their god, Yahweh. These themes are not restricted to the Hebrew religion; they are also the basis for the central theological conceptions and beliefs that would later inform the two other religions that have dominated the Western world in the course of its history—Christianity and Islam. It is worth pausing here to develop briefly some of these themes.

1. In contrast with the religious systems of the other ancient Near Eastern peoples among whom the Hebrews arose and lived, the god of the Hebrew people was the only god with which they were permitted to have a relationship. This religion eventually developed into a full-fledged *monotheism,* or belief in one god to the exclusion of all other deities. This was the first such religion of any consequence ever to arise in human history.

2. In addition to his singularity, another characteristic of this god of the Hebrews was his concern with human history itself. The deities of the neighboring peoples—not unlike those of prehistoric Africa and the Americas—were primarily representations of natural forces and had to be appeased to ensure the continuing fertility of the soil. On the contrary, the Hebrew god Yahweh took a direct interest and role in the course of specific human events. In particular, he was concerned with the fortunes and misfortunes of his chosen people, the Hebrews. On occasion he appeared to their representatives—as in the cases of Abraham, Jacob, and Moses—and actively interfered in the historical realm, as in his deliverance of the Hebrew people out of bondage in Egypt. His name *Yahweh* most likely means that he is a god who acts in human affairs.

3. As should by now be apparent, this god Yahweh is a personal god, not simply a personified force of nature. He has a name—actually, several, of which Yahweh (sometimes mistransliterated as "Jehovah") is the most central and sacred. He enters into direct relationships with individuals, at times in such dramatic forms as his wrestling with Jacob. Nor is he eternally unchanging,

at least in appearance, as shown in the different ways and circumstances in which he manifests himself to the Hebrews.

4. The basic form in which Yahweh's successive relationships with his people of Israel take place is through the form of the covenant. A *covenant* is a relationship between two parties, and in a sense is a sort of contract. Unlike a simple contract entered into for the straightforward exchange of goods, services, or money, however, a covenant is personal and open-ended, without specific stipulations as to who owes what. In the present day, when impersonal contracts predominate, marriage might be an apt illustration of a covenant relationship. The covenant Yahweh entered into with Moses at Sinai was most likely based on suzerainty or vassalage treaties employed by other ancient Near Eastern peoples, in which personal, open-ended allegiance would be pledged by the weaker party in return for protection by the stronger. This theme of a stronger and weaker party was incorporated into this biblical covenant. Yahweh, of course, was the stronger one who offers deliverance and prosperity to his people if they keep their covenant with him, and punishment should they transgress its terms.

The record of these covenants between Yahweh and his chosen people is the major theme and connecting thread through the religious annals of the Hebrews—the *Bible.* (Christians refer to these Hebrew scriptures as the *Old Testament,* while Jews generally prefer the terms *Hebrew Bible* or *Tanak,* an abbreviation of the Hebrew words for the three divisions of scripture: Torah, the Prophets, and Writings.) *Bible* is derived from the Greek *ta biblia,* or "books." Although the Bible is sometimes bound as and referred to as a single book—for example, "the Good Book"—it is in fact a collection of writings of various kinds, compiled over several hundred years, often from earlier oral traditions, and reflecting the collective religious experience of the Hebrew people in a wide variety of circumstances expressed in many different literary genres. Very briefly, the books of the Hebrew Bible can be summarized as follows:

1. The *Torah,* or *Pentateuch,* sometimes called "the five books of Moses," to whose authorship they were traditionally attributed. These are regarded by Jews as the most sacred core of scripture and, inscribed on scrolls, are central to Jewish worship. The first, Genesis, begins with an account of the creation of the cosmos and the world by Yahweh, proceeds with the story of the introduction of evil and death into the world in its account of Adam and Eve, retells other legendary stories such as those of the Tower of Babel and Noah and the Flood, and then emerges into early historical times in its accounts of the patriarchs Abraham, Isaac, Jacob, and Joseph. Exodus, as we have already seen, narrates the story of Moses and the deliverance of the Hebrew people from bondage in Egypt, a story which is continued in

Numbers and Deuteronomy. Leviticus is composed primarily of detailed cultic regulations concerning ritual purity.*

2. Books in a second group narrate the history of the Hebrew people in Canaan, the era of the Judges, the establishment of the monarchy under Saul and his successors, the division of the land into the two nations of Israel and Judah, their conquest by their enemies, and the destruction of the Temple (586 B.C.) and its rebuilding (520–515 B.C.). These books include Joshua, Judges, Ruth, 1st and 2d Samuel, 1st and 2d Kings, 1st and 2d Chronicles, Ezra, Nehemiah, and Esther.

3. A third major category of biblical literature is the *prophetic* books, of which the "major"—that is, longer—prophets, Isaiah and Jeremiah, are among the best known. The Hebrew prophets, who flourished during the eighth through the sixth centuries B.C., did not set out to foretell the future in a literal way but rather announced impending judgments by Yahweh if the Hebrew people did not observe the terms of the covenant. These "prophecies" were denunciations of ethical transgressions, such as the exploitation of the weak by the powerful. The force of their message can be summarized in the words of Micah (6:8): "What does the Lord require of you, but to do justice and to love kindness and to walk humbly with your God?" The ethical thrust of biblical prophecy and the call to social justice rather than simply cultic purity as the proper fulfillment of the covenant has been a major motif through the subsequent history not only of Judaism but of Christianity as well.

4. The final grouping of books of Hebrew scripture consists of "Wisdom literature" and other poetic works, such as Job, the Psalms, Proverbs, Ecclesiastes, and the Song of Songs. Some of these works, such as Job, are profoundly steeped in the Hebrew sense of the relationship between the divine and the human; others, such as Ecclesiastes and Proverbs, reflect a notion of "wisdom" that was international in character and somewhat at odds with traditional Hebrew sensibilities in its individualism and lack of a historical perspective.

Over many centuries and with much editing, this collection of highly diverse literature coalesced into a *canon,* or list of works commonly acknowledged as divinely inspired. A number of respected but not fully accepted books, such as Maccabees and Tobit, were relegated to the periphery and known as *apocrypha.* This canon of

*Greek names for a number of books of Hebrew scripture derive from the *Septuagint,* a Greek translation prepared during the Hellenistic period during the second and third centuries B.C. Until recently, Roman Catholics employed names of some Old Testament books derived from the Septuagint, which differed from other usage. There is now general agreement among the major religious traditions on English usage, however.

Hebrew scripture was probably closed, or regarded as complete and definitive, around the end of the first century A.D.

At the core of the collection of scripture is the history of the Hebrew people in successive covenants with Yahweh. The earlier books celebrate the deliverance of Yahweh's people out of bondage and into a spectacular hegemony in the days of the kingship of David and Solomon in their glory. The previous description of some of the later books, though, makes it clear that the subsequent epochs were less than triumphant. With the death of Solomon in 922 B.C., the kingdom split into two separate entities, Israel in the north and Judah in the south. Israel then fell to the Assyrians in 721 B.C. Later, during the days of Jeremiah the Prophet (ca. 600 B.C.), the kingdom of Judah began to succumb to internal disarray and the superiority of external forces, culminating in the Babylonian king Nebuchadnezzar's destruction of Jerusalem in 586 B.C. Although the Jerusalem temple was rebuilt in 520–515 B.C. and lasted until its final destruction by the Romans in A.D. 70, the days of the Hebrew people as independent in their own land were clearly over. From this time onward, their normative state was not one of territorial hegemony but rather of *Diaspora*—a scattering, eventually through the entire world, in which they had to make as best a peace as they could with the various "host" cultures among whom they dwelt.

One of the most significant of these host cultures for the subsequent development of Jewish religion and culture was the Hellenistic. It was so called from the dominance of Greek language and civilization spread through the eastern Mediterranean basin and beyond by Alexander the Great, who conquered Palestine in 332 B.C. It was the displacement of Hebrew by Greek as the language of learned discourse that eventually led to the production of the Septuagint, or Greek translation of Hebrew scripture, as well as to a shift in philosophical and theological attitude reflected in the "Wisdom" tradition and the later writings of the great Philo of Alexandria and alien to the mainstream of Hebrew thought. It is also during these years that a metamorphosis was taking place in the vocabulary used to characterize the Hebrew people. The word *Jew* is ultimately derived from the Hebrew name for the kingdom of Judah. After the Exile (from Judah and Jerusalem to Babylonia, ca. 600 B.C.) it began to gain currency as a designation for any of what we now refer to as the "Jewish" people (as distinct from "Gentiles" or *goyim,* that is, non-Jews. *Goy* or, in its plural form, *goyim,* is a Yiddish word derived originally from Hebrew, and often used with a disparaging undertone). The transition from "Hebrew" to "Jew," witnessed in Greek, Latin, and modern European forms of the latter word, is indicative of a major change in self-identification by a Jewish community for whom Hebrew was no longer the language of everyday discourse.

The Diaspora remained the normative condition of what were now known as the Jewish people until only recently, with the reestablishment of the state of Israel as a Jewish homeland following World War II. Jews continued to live in the eastern Mediterranean area under a variety of rulers, but an abortive revolt against the Romans in A.D. 66 resulted in the ultimate destruction of the Temple four years later and the death of perhaps a million of the rebels. After continued suppression and revolts during the ensuing decades, a measure of stability was finally attained after the death of the Emperor Hadrian in A.D. 138. The ancient Jewish land of Judaea, now renamed Palestine by the Romans, continued to serve as a center for the faith until even more drastic restrictions on Jewish life were imposed by Christian dominance in the fifth century. Babylonia became the center of Jewish life in the Middle East, while more and more Jews began to fan out along the frontiers of the empire.

Two major groups of Jews, who would ultimately have a major impact on American Jewish history, emerged in the course of this process of dispersion. One of these was the *Sephardim,* or Sephardic Jews, who fanned out through northern Africa and into the Iberian Peninsula (Spain and Portugal). Although Muhammad (570–632), the founder of the new religion of Islam, was hostile toward Jews, as well as Christians, for their refusal to accept himself as the prophet of Allah, his successors tempered their positions. The end of Christian hegemony in Iberia at the hands of the Muslims in the eighth century ultimately proved beneficial to the Sephardim, who developed a flourishing culture there and proved invaluable to their "hosts" in a variety of ways. Sephardic Jewish civilization was in turn stimulated by the growth of Muslim philosophy.

This generally happy relationship of cooperation and interaction came to an end in the late fifteenth century with the defeat of the Muslims and the "reconquest" and unification of Spain by the "Christian monarchs," Ferdinand of Aragon and Isabella of Castille. Catholicism of the most militant sort now became equated with Spanish nationalism, and Jews were given the unpleasant choices of exile, conversion to Christianity, or death. It is ironic that it was in 1492, the year of Columbus's first encounter with the New World—a voyage in which he was accompanied by Spanish Jews—that the Sephardim were forced into yet another painful exile. Many of the participants in this new diaspora found refuge eventually in the anti-Spanish Netherlands and their New World colonies, and later established the first Jewish presence in what would become the United States. Jews who converted to Christianity became known as *Marranos,* and spread through the Spanish empire in the New World as well as remaining in Iberia. Recently, a number of families in New Mexico have made public the surreptitious observance of Jewish customs, many of them only in vestigial and dimly remembered form, that has continued among them to the present day.

The other Jewish group of major significance for our story is the *Ashkenazim,* or *Ashkenazic Jews.* (The name comes from a descendant of Noah who was thought to have settled in the general area of Germany.) The Ashkenazim followed the routes of the Roman legions during the later days of the Roman Empire and the early Middle Ages to settle across northern and central Europe. The focus of Ashkenazic life was in the German-speaking area, although some were dispersed in France and England, and large and influential communities developed in Poland and Russia. The tension in which they lived with the dominant Christians set many of the themes for Gentile-Jewish relations in later times, by no means always for the better. Although not in the same category with heretics—Christians who deviated from the orthodoxy of the Roman church and who were therefore always outlawed—the Jews occupied an ambiguous position in medieval Christian thought. By law, they were barred from owning agricultural land and were generally compelled to live in special areas. In the more urbanized reaches of the West, these were called *ghettoes,* or districts of a city solely reserved for Jewish habitation. Here Jews were accorded some autonomy and their rabbis enjoyed considerable prestige and power. (The word *ghetto* [GETT-oe] is of Italian origin and uncertain meaning.) In the less rapidly modernizing east of Europe, Jews lived instead in villages called *shtetls* (SHTET-uls or SHTATE-uls; that is, "little cities").

Thus isolated geographically, Jews were unique in their status in other ways as well. The prohibition of the medieval church on usury—lending money at interest—did not apply to Jews, who at times served as moneylenders to popes and bishops. This special advantage served on the one hand to permit the accumulation of considerable fortunes, as in the case of the fabled house of Rothschild. On the other hand, it helped reinforce the negative stereotype of the Jew as Shylock, the grasping moneylender who showed no mercy toward Gentiles. Another dimension of this negative image was the Jew as Christ-killer, which was perpetuated at higher levels of discourse through a reading of the Gospels as placing the responsibility for the death of Jesus on the Jews. More popularly, the image of the Jew as murderer was reinforced by the folkloric belief that Jews kidnapped gentile children to use them as sacrifices in secret rituals. Folklore depicted the Jew alternately as in league with Satan and also as the perpetual exile—"the wandering Jew"—doomed to live forever without a fixed abode as punishment for the crime of deicide ("god-killing"). The result, not surprisingly, was periodic outbreaks of violent anti-Semitism, particularly in times of crisis or popular excitement such as the Crusades, when mobs invaded the ghettoes and slaughtered Jews. Although, needless to say, this folklore had no factual basis, it legitimated Christians' using Jews as scapegoats and objects for the fulfillment of deep and perverse fantasies.

The situation of medieval Jewry, though continually precarious, was conducive to the perpetuation of a very traditional religious culture in which rabbis enjoyed great influence and prestige as teachers, judges, and arbiters with the gentile world. By a combination of choice and necessity, most Ashkenazic Jews lived in an entirely Jewish world. Their worship, lifestyles, and worldviews were shaped by the traditional lore of the Talmud, and their religious practice was highly conservative. This is not to say that a rich religious culture did not develop and flourish; however, its direction lacked the stimulus provided the Sephardim by Islamic civilization, since positive interaction with the Christian world was unusual. Innovations that did emerge in some quarters were *Hasidism,* a mystical movement with anti-intellectual implications, and the rationalism of Baruch Spinoza, the seventeenth-century philosopher who was disowned by his fellow Amsterdam Jews and forced into exile by them for his radicalism.

It has been said with some justice that the Middle Ages in Europe lasted much longer for Jews than for Christians, since the isolation of the former outlived the era of the Renaissance by several centuries. It was the eighteenth century—"the Age of Enlightenment"—that saw the first major confrontation between the Jewish community and what we have come to regard as "the culture of modernity." On the one hand, the Enlightenment and the French Revolution, which was inspired partly by Enlightenment ideals of rationality and universalism, led to the emancipation of Jews in France and elsewhere from the legal constraints that had traditionally been imposed on them. Jews were free to leave the ghettoes and to live as Gentiles if they chose, enjoying the full privileges of citizenship.

On the other hand, an intellectual and religious response from within the Jewish community was already in the making. Moses Mendelssohn (1729–86), a learned German Jew, set about to bring what he saw as the essence of Judaism into conformity with the principles of the Enlightenment. Mendelssohn argued that Judaism as a religion could be both theoretically and practically separated from the baggage of traditional Jewish culture that had accumulated over the centuries and that stood in the way of the adaptation of the Jewish people to modern civilization. Essentially Judaism, when properly understood, was an eminently rational faith and embodied those tenets— the existence of an omnipotent god, freedom of the human will, immortality of the soul—which Enlightened thinkers generally agreed were deducible from reason and observation without the dubious benefit of revelation, tradition, and authority. Jews, then, could participate readily in the broader life of the gentile community. They would no longer be distinguishable by dress, dietary habits, or other superficial customs, but solely by their embracing a system of religious belief that was at once distinct from Christianity while conforming with the avant-garde intellectual trends of the time. Paradoxically, however, Mendelssohn himself observed fully the customs of traditional Judaism and believed that they had been revealed directly by God to Moses.

Mendelssohn's thought laid the foundations both for enthusiastic participation in emancipation in Europe and the New World and also for a new religious strain that would become known as *Reform*. Unfortunately, the problems of being a Jew in a predominantly gentile society did not disappear in the aura of the Enlightenment. In Russia, which throughout the nineteenth century remained one of the most retrograde sections of Europe, traditional anti-Semitism vented itself in the form of pogroms (poh-GROHMZ), raids by armed Cossack soldiers on Jewish settlements—the shtetls that dotted the broad agricultural belt that stretched between the Black Sea and the Baltic, in which relations between Jewish artisans and merchants and their gentile peasant neighbors were never entirely amicable. (The comments of Polish peasants in the film Shoah demonstrate the abiding suspicion and dislike of mercantile Jewish "outsiders" that has been part and parcel of peasant culture for centuries.)

Anti-Semitism was seldom as virulent in the more modernized western parts of Europe during the nineteenth century as it was further east. In the twentieth century, however, it was the very Germany that had been a seedbed of Enlightenment thought and modern scientific development that erupted in a violence against the Jewish people on a scale unprecedented in human history. In other parts of the European American world, including the United States and Italy, Jews received some blame for the devastating depression of the 1930s, but in most cases these mutterings had little important result without the further catalyst of Nazism. It was in Germany that the devastation of World War I, its subsequent settlement that resulted in ongoing political and economic chaos and bitter resentments, and the further blow of worldwide economic collapse came together to mobilize ancient folklore and modern ideology and fantasy into a massive program of genocide. Germany's very real problems were blamed by Hitler and his National Socialists on the Jewish community, who were depicted as part of an international conspiracy of financial manipulators who had brought on the depression and served Jews at the expense of any national loyalties.

Although it resurrected some of the charges against Jews that had been common in medieval Christian lore, Nazism also repudiated Christianity as a "slave morality" unworthy of a master race. It appealed to a primordial, mythic Teutonic spirit that had been emasculated by the Christian exaltation of weakness, and set out to destroy all—especially the Jews—who stood in the way of its triumphant path to world dominion. It is worth remembering that the majority of the victims of the Nazi program of death and terror were not Jews but a variety of peoples deemed inferior by the Nazis—Poles and other Slavs, German Catholics, Gypsies, homosexuals. However, the campaign against none of these was as systematic, determined, and hate-filled as that against the Jews, who were singled out for total eradication. What has since come to be called the *Holocaust*—a word of Greek origin used to indicate a burnt offering such as that (*Shoah*) of the ancient Hebrews—was intended by the Nazis to be the "final solution" to the "Jewish question." It came frighteningly close to achieving its goals, at least in Continental Europe. Between five and six million Jews died under the most hideous circumstances in the gas ovens of Auschwitz, Buchenwald, Bergen-Belsen, Treblinka, Ravensbrück, and other concentration camps. After World War II, the once multitudinous Jewish communities of Germany, Poland, and the rest of central Europe had been nearly exterminated, and many of the survivors chose to emigrate to the United States, Israel, or elsewhere rather than attempt to continue life in such a grim context.

Needless to say, the Holocaust was one of the most definitive events of Jewish history in the twentieth century, and an enormous literature has been generated attempting to understand and express its anguish, its sources, and its meaning. At almost exactly the same time that the victorious Allied armies were liberating the concentration camps, however, another movement of extraordinary consequence for all of the Jewish people was beginning to achieve fulfillment. During the nineteenth century many Jews, especially those under the influence of Mendelssohn and the Reform movement, had accepted the Diaspora as the normative condition of the Jewish people. They thought it not only necessary but desirable that Jews should continue to live scattered among various gentile societies, from which they should be distinguishable only in religion. For other Jews of a wide variety of intellectual backgrounds, however, a very different movement was beginning to coalesce under the name of *Zionism*.

Some supporters of the restoration of an independent Jewish homeland—preferably in Palestine, the historical land of Israel—were motivated by a deeply religious drive for the restoration of traditional Judaism. (Most religious Jews, however, were opposed to the movement in its early, more secular forms.) Others saw Zionism as a pragmatic campaign to free Jews from the threat of anti-Semitism which was manifest even in such "enlightened" nations as the France in which the Jewish army officer Alfred Dreyfus had been framed for treason and sent off to Devil's Island before his ultimate exoneration. The central catalytic figure in modern Zionism was Theodor(e) Herzl (1860–1904), an Austrian Jew who promoted the idea through his book *Der Judenstaat* ("The Jewish State") of 1896 and his organization the next year of the World Zionist Congress. The cause was furthered by the Balfour Declaration of 1917, in which the British pledged the restoration of Palestine as a Jewish homeland in the context of their wresting the territory from Turkey at the end of World War I. After a series of advances and retreats, the Zionist cause prevailed in 1948, when the newly founded United Nations proclaimed the independence of the State of Israel. After several decades of precarious, sometimes violent, and always controversial existence surrounded by Arab neighbors, Israel continues to provide a focus of identity for Jews throughout the world.

The story of the Jewish people is the oldest continuous such narrative in the Western world. Jewish history has oscillated among a number of poles: Diaspora and homeland; reason and tradition; prosperity and suffering. Lacking a central organization, Jews have been free to adapt their beliefs and practices within a wide variety of cultural and intellectual circumstances. Whatever the multitudinous varieties of understandings of Jewish identity that have emerged, however, there has always remained a deep sense of shared history, of constituting a people whose collective experience has been, however troubled, still infinitely rich and meaningful. However much they may differ on its meaning, Jews can hardly help but continue to regard themselves as a "chosen people."

CHAPTER 5

The Eastern Orthodox Tradition

The Jewish community in the Roman Empire at the time of Jesus of Nazareth was by no means unified. It can be described as consisting of a number of sects or factions—Pharisees, Sadducees, Essenes, and Zealots, to name some of the best known. In this context a new sect arose that believed that the Jewish god was acting through Jesus of Nazareth to transform the whole created realm. One of the first major disputes among these early "Christians" was whether they were required to continue to practice all of the dictates of the traditional Jewish law, and therefore should require that male gentile converts be circumcized. The answer provided by Peter, Paul, and other disciples assembled at the Council of Jerusalem (Acts 15) was in the negative. Christianity—as this new religion would come to be known—was to be universal, welcoming all, rather than restricted to the people of Israel. Paul especially was instrumental in spreading the Gospel—the "Good News"—of Jesus throughout the Roman Empire. According to tradition, both he and Peter were martyred and buried in Rome, the imperial capital.

Although Christianity was thus from the beginning destined to be a "universalistic" rather than a "particularistic" faith, its rapid spread was not at all to the liking of the Roman authorities. The first three centuries of its existence were spent in a twilight world of dubious legal standing in which violent persecution might break out at any time—as it did under the emperors Nero, Decius, and Diocletian. Although the Jews had negotiated with the Romans a right to continue their traditions, the Christians were unwilling to do so. The loyalty of the Christians was always to a higher power, and they were willing to suffer torture and death rather than seek earthly permission for worshiping the one true god. Their early gatherings for worship were of necessity covert, taking place in private homes or sometimes literally underground in catacombs.

Another characteristic of early Christianity was what has been called its "eschatological world picture." *Eschatology* is the branch of theology that deals with the "last things"—in Christian tradition, death, judgment, heaven, and hell. For these earliest Christians, it dominated their entire religious view. Given the precarious situation in which they found themselves, and their belief that Jesus would return again to earth soon, these Christians placed little hope or confidence in earthly life. They regarded it as a holding action against the forces of evil; it could at any moment give way to a radical transformation of the whole created realm. Revelation, or the Apocalypse—the final book of Christian scripture, or "New Testament"—is a document reflecting a specifically eschatological worldview. It relates in symbolic form this final consummation of things, for which Christians waited eagerly and in anticipation of which they were prepared to make the most drastic sacrifices.

This situation changed dramatically early in the fourth century with the triumph of Constantine in a struggle for leadership of a divided and declining empire. According to legend, Constantine, who was the son of the Christian (later saint) Helena, was preparing for the Battle of the Milvian Bridge against his rival Maxentius in 312. He beheld in the sky the sign of the cross and the words *In hoc signo vinces*—"by this sign you shall conquer." Conquer he did and, upon accession to the imperial throne, set about making Christianity not only legal but the favored religion of the empire. Although he did not himself receive baptism until the end of his life, a common practice at the time, his reign stands as the most critical turning point in the fortunes of Christianity from the time of Jesus and his followers at least until that of Charlemagne's crowning as Holy Roman Emperor nearly five centuries later.

Constantine not only favored Christianity but as emperor actively intervened in its internal affairs. Christians had established communities throughout the Mediterranean world by this time, but they had become torn by one of a series of controversies over the precise nature of the man Jesus whom they acknowledged as the Son of God. A party led by a priest named Arius in Alexandria held that, although Jesus was the *Logos*—the Word, or Son of God—incarnate, this Son of God was not equal to God the Father, but rather was created by him. Another party rejected this "subordinationist" Christology (that is, interpretation of the nature of Christ), and maintained that the Son was truly divine and the equal of God the Father.

To settle this controversy, Constantine convened the bishops, or local leaders, of the Christian world in 325 at the town of Nicea as the first ecumenical, or worldwide, council in the history of Christianity. The principal work of the Council of Nicea was the settling of the Arian controversy in a document still widely regarded as authoritative in many churches, the Nicene Creed. This creed, or brief statement of the essentials of the faith, begins "We believe in one God, the Father Almighty [or All-Governing], creator of all things visible and invisible."* It rapidly proceeds to settle the issue in dispute with the words "And in one Lord Jesus Christ, the Son of God, begotten of the Father as only begotten, that is, from the essence of the Father ... begotten not created ..." Arius and his followers were thus confounded and relegated to the status of heretics. Though they held their own in the East for several decades and gained some converts among the barbarian tribes encroaching on Ro-

---

*Source of text: John H. Leith, ed., *Creeds of the Churches* (Garden City, N.Y., 1963), p. 30. The more familiar form used in many churches today was the work of the later Council of Constantinople.

man dominion in the West, they eventually lost the contest to the "Orthodox"—that is, "correct believers"—as the victors became known.

Although the creed and its contents are themselves extremely significant turning points in Christian development, the active role of the emperor in convening and supervising the council was also of the utmost importance for the subsequent relationship between the Christian church and the civil order. Instead of living a precarious existence as at best a suspect community, Christians began to enjoy a privileged status that would last through the Middle Ages—an epoch in which the term "Christendom" would describe the dominance of Christianity throughout most of Europe. On the other hand, the price of this new status was the constant danger of civil encroachment into the church's affairs, as Constantine's own benevolent intercession into the Arian dispute demonstrated.

Still another action of Constantine with decisive consequences for the future was his abandonment of the ancient capital of Rome in favor of the city of Byzantium in Asia Minor—later renamed "Constantinople" (the *polis* or city of Constantine). An imperial representative remained behind in Italy at the city of Ravenna, but as the post-Constantinian empire in the West began to crumble, his presence was ineffective. The power vacuum that thus developed was filled instead by the head of the church in the West, namely the bishop of Rome. This latter figure, who was gradually acquiring exclusive rights in the West to the title of *pope* (that is, "papa" or "father"), had emerged as the most influential of the leaders of Christianity in the West, and by virtue of his location was heir to much of the administrative talent and the broader cultural, legal, and political tradition of the Roman Empire. In the longer run, the pope began to make claims of supremacy over all of the other leaders of the church in the East—claims which were almost universally accepted in the West, where Latin and its derivatives remained dominant, but rejected in the East, where Greek held sway. This issue of papal supremacy continues to the present day as a major source of division between the Eastern Orthodox and Roman Catholic churches.

Although no formal break was to occur for centuries, the geographic isolation and cultural and linguistic diversity that characterized Rome and Constantinople gradually gave rise to the division of Christianity into two separate spheres, western and eastern. The story of the West is continued in chapter 7, "Western Catholicism from the Time of Constantine." In the East, the firm hold of the emperor established by Constantine set a tone that would impress itself on what would become known as the Byzantine Empire and its church for centuries. The church was clearly subordinate politically to the state, and enjoyed little of the independence that characterized its counterpart in the West. Rather, a new culture emerged that focused on the imperial court (which has given rise to the use of "Byzantine" to describe extremely convoluted internal politics), the Greek language, and a version of Christianity preoccupied more with mystic symbolism than with law and logic.

During the period that has come to be known as the Middle Ages, East and West grew apart as much from inertia as active hostility. Six more ecumenical councils took place in the years between Nicea and Nicea II in 787. Probably the most significant of these was Chalcedon (451), at which the question of whether Jesus was fully human as well as fully divine was settled in the affirmative. This made heretical the teachings of the so-called *Monophysites* (from the Greek words for "one nature"), whose refusal to speak of Jesus as being "in two natures" as compromising the unity of Christ appeared to the conciliar fathers to question his full humanity or to make it different from our own.

These differences appear to today's Orthodox as more verbal and cultural, and were largely held by ethnic groups such as Copts and Armenians at the margins of the empire. (Representatives of the non-Chalcedonian tradition, now usually referred to as "Oriental Orthodox" and including the Armenian Apostolic Church and various Coptic and Syrian Jacobite groups, are in continuing dialogue with the Chalcedonian churches.) As a result of this dispute, those Eastern churches that accept the council's decree favor the term Chalcedonian as a self-designation. These seven councils were accepted as fully authoritative by both Eastern Orthodox and western Catholics, while subsequent councils through Vatican II have been acknowledged as authoritative only by the latter.

Estrangement between East and West continued to grow during these and succeeding centuries, focusing at times on what may seem minor theological controversies such as the insertion of the *filioque* clause into the Nicene Creed in the West. (*Filioque* means "and from the Son," indicating that the Holy Spirit did not proceed from God the Father alone.) Representatives of the pope and the "Ecumenical Patriarch," as the archbishop of Constantinople had come to be known, mutually excommunicated one another in 1054, again over issues that in retrospect seem too unimportant to have been the real cause of the estrangement. The most serious blow to these steadily deteriorating relations came in 1204 with the sacking of Constantinople during the Fourth Crusade. This holy war was ostensibly being waged against the Muslims, but Eastern Christians felt the wrath of the West as well. For most of the time from then until the goodwill that Vatican II generated with the invitation of Eastern observers by Pope John XXIII, the two camps stood in mutual enmity despite their profound underlying similarities. Although no longer hostile, the relationship between the Roman Catholic and Eastern Orthodox churches is characterized by division over issues of governance—especially the supremacy of the pope—rather than those having to do with the nature of God, salvation, and the like.

The Byzantine Empire eventually began to lose its hegemony to the powerful forces of Islam that during the Middle Ages had overwhelmed most of the Middle East and North Africa. The final blow came with the fall of Constantinople in 1453, after which Orthodox Christians in Muslim lands had to accept a subordinate political status. By this time, however, Eastern Christianity was no longer confined to the Mediterranean basin. Where missionaries had fanned out from Rome to spread its version of Christianity among the peoples of France, Germany, and the British Isles, envoys from the East were performing similar work in the areas of Europe to their north. Saints Cyril and Methodius are celebrated in tradition as the original apostles to the Slavic tribes in the ninth century, and the name of the former is perpetuated in the "Cyrillic" alphabet for transcribing Slavic languages, which he is credited with having devised. In the long run, these early efforts were eminently successful: in 988 the Kievan Rus, the forerunner of modern Russia and Ukraine, was converted to the Eastern version of Christianity, and in 1448 the Russian church based at Moscow declared itself to be *autocephalous*, which in modern times has meant an autonomous national or ethnic church within the Orthodox "family." In 1721, Tsar Peter the Great subordinated the Russian church to the state, thus constricting its autonomy in a way that lasted until the 1917 revolution—after which the church experienced even greater restrictions under Communist antireligious policies. The breakup of the USSR and the Warsaw Pact in the early 1990s removed Communist-era restrictions from Orthodox churches in Russia and neighboring lands, and a dramatic resurgence of vitality has since resulted.

By the time of significant migration of Orthodox Christians to the New World in the late nineteenth and early twentieth centuries, the world of Orthodoxy stood apart from both Roman Catholicism and the various Protestant traditions in the West. It zealously guarded its traditions and adherence to the teachings of the seven ecumenical councils, but remained geographically and politically limited by the circumstances of its history. Its historical core was located in the great ancient patriarchates—the seats of the oldest and most prestigious Christian communities and their bishops—of Constantinople, Alexandria, Antioch, and Jerusalem. (Rome originally had been ranked first among the patriarchal sees but, after the East-West split of 1054, the Orthodox have given Constantinople the place of honor.) Muslim conquests, a long tradition of subordination of church to state, the Russian Revolution of 1917, and the political fragmentation of southeastern Europe, where Orthodoxy was strongest—all combined to produce a problematic fragmentation as much as the healthy decentralization on which the Orthodox have always prided themselves. At the time the great emigration began, Orthodox Christians could be found in significant numbers in what are now Greece, Romania, Bulgaria, Albania, Serbia, and the eastern reaches of the old Soviet Union, as well as in the Middle East. The specific story of Orthodoxy's coming to America begins in Russia—although, as we shall see later, its ways of passage were intriguingly circuitous.

In the Eastern Orthodox tradition, which has thus taken shape over the centuries, stress has always been placed on the act of worship. This is not to say that belief is unimportant: the very term *orthodoxy* is indicative of a commitment to "correct belief." Orthodoxy shares with the other liturgical traditions a foundation in the creedal statements of the early church and the first seven ecumenical councils. These established particularly the doctrines of the Trinity and the dual nature of Jesus Christ as both divine and human as the firm dogmatic basis of Christian belief. Conformity to the teachings of these councils is the hallmark of orthodoxy, and any faith statements that are not in harmony with them are by definition *heterodox*—that is, "other" or false belief.

Given a shared commitment to these early creeds, however, there has still been room for significant divergences in interpretation and emphasis between East and West. One of the most influential of the "Church Fathers" of the West was Cyprian (d. 258), the bishop of Carthage in North Africa, whose writings dealt primarily with the nature of the church. Of even greater importance in the long run was Augustine (354–430), bishop of Hippo (also in North Africa), whose *Confessions* detailed the story of his personal conversion and whose *City of God* developed a theology of God's awful power and the corresponding finite and sinful character of humanity. Together, Cyprian and Augustine represent characteristic Western emphases respectively on the importance of the institutional church and on a pessimistic view of human nature, stressing the radical gulf between the human and the divine. Although later Western theology, such as that especially of Thomas Aquinas in the thirteenth century, was rather more hopeful in its appraisal of human possibilities, Augustine remained in the background as the most powerful and original exponent of a distinctively Western standpoint.

The theological writings of the Eastern church fathers, written in Greek rather than Latin, represent a very different point of view. Prominent among their number were Athanasius, Gregory of Nyssa, Gregory Nazianzen, Basil the Great, and John Chrysostom, all of whom flourished during the fourth century. (The study of the thought of the Eastern and Western church fathers together is known as *patristics*.) As opposed to Augustine's doctrine of predestination, which is based on God's power and goodness and on human depravity and helplessness, the theology that emerged in the East was instead grounded in a much more optimistic appraisal of the human condition. Central to Orthodox thought is the term *theosis,* or "divinization," which refers to the human capacity for being transformed into the divine likeness. The emphasis is therefore not on a divine remission of the penalties for human sin but rather a putting off of the constraints of mortality while still on earth and a participation in the divine nature instead.

This transformation has its locus in the *liturgy*—that is, the collective and public worship of God. The emphasis here is not on thought but on being—or, rather, the gradual transformation of one's being through participation in divine worship. Eastern Orthodox liturgy is in its basic outlines similar to that of the Roman Catholic Church: the structure of the eucharistic service is not radically different; the cycle of the liturgical year is followed through its various seasons; and seven *sacraments,* known as *mysteries,* are recognized, together with a number of other rites that have a sacramental or grace-mediating quality. The differences lie more in nuances, emphases, and interpretations that make the liturgy of supreme importance in the Orthodox tradition and that differentiate it in significant ways from the practices of the other liturgical traditions. Unlike the Roman Catholic Church, which has only allowed worship in the vernacular since Vatican II in the 1960s, the Orthodox churches have a long tradition of the use of national languages in liturgical practice.

When entering an Orthodox church, one is struck at first by the physical differences that set it off from those of other Christian communities. Greek churches usually are laid out in the form of a "Greek cross," that is, with all four arms of equal length, and capped with a rounded dome in the Byzantine tradition. Typical Russian Orthodox churches differ in having one or more "onion domes," in which the crest rises to a sharp point. The interiors of these churches are even more distinctive. In almost every direction, including the vertical, one beholds scores of icons, one of the most singular aspects of Orthodox belief and worship, as well as numerous frescoes and mosaics. In Orthodox usage, an icon is a stylized, two-dimensional depiction of a sacred subject, usually on a wooden background. The themes may include Jesus or the Trinity; the saints recognized by Orthodoxy, especially the Virgin Mary, known as *Theotokos* or "God-bearer"; or important events in the history of the church. The image depicted on each icon is not the product of an individual artist's imagination but rather an objective revelation of an aspect of the Incarnation. It is, in short, an *epiphany*—a manifestation of the divine in the midst of this world. As opposed to the Western artistic tradition, where originality has been prized, icons are not supposed to be original but rather to be copied, often by monks, in a manner as faithful to the divinely revealed prototype as possible.

Icons are thus an essential key to understanding the importance that Orthodoxy places on worship. They are physical vehicles through which the human and the divine come into contact—windows between the two worlds—and thus means through which the human can take on a progressively more divine character. Their arrangement in a church is prescribed by tradition. In the ceiling or dome is the icon of *Christos Pantocrator*—Christ, the Ruler of the Universe. The *Theotokos* with the Christ Child can be found above the sanctuary in the apse (the projection at the rear of the area where the altar is located). The majority of icons are arranged on the iconostasis. This is a large screen that divides the sanctuary, which is reserved for the priest and his assistants, from the nave, where the congregation sits or, more frequently, stands during the lengthy service. The *iconostasis* emphasizes the mysterious character of the eucharistic celebration; the icons on it represent Jesus and other figures important in the Christian experience. Through the mediating function of the icons and the sacramental mysteries performed before them, the believer comes into the presence of the divine, and in the Eucharist receives a foretaste of the heavenly realm.

The liturgy itself usually follows one of two traditional rites, those identified with St. John Chrysostom and with St. Basil the Great. In addition, there is a Liturgy of the Pre-Sanctified Gifts, where a previously consecrated Communion is distributed at specific times during Lent. Although the liturgy was traditionally celebrated in

Greek, Old Church Slavonic, and other languages of the Old World, it has in recent times been translated into English to accommodate the large majority of American Orthodox no longer familiar with these ancestral tongues. Practical considerations have also led most to abandon the traditional Julian calendar for everyday purposes, although it is still used for determining parts of the liturgical cycle. Other differences from Western practice include the use of the term "Epiphany" to designate the commemoration of the baptism of Jesus, rather than the appearance of Jesus to the Magi; the use of leavened bread mixed with wine in the distribution of the Eucharist; and the practice of *chrismation,* an anointing administered immediately after baptism, rather than in a separate, later rite such as the West's sacrament of confirmation.

In addition to the seven sacraments or mysteries shared with the Roman church, Orthodoxy recognizes a number of other rituals as sacramental in character. Among these is the administration of the *tonsure*—a symbolic clipping of hair—to those taking monastic vows. Monasticism has played an important role in Orthodoxy from early on, and Mount Athos on the Greek coast has been a major center of Orthodox spirituality. Monasticism also plays an important role in Orthodox polity, since bishops are usually elevated from the ranks of celibate monks. (Widowers who have taken monastic vows are also eligible.) Other clergy may marry before they receive ordination, but are thereafter barred from the episcopate. Clergy, laity, and bishops all participate in councils that set policy for the entire communion. In the United States, the scarcity of bishops and clergy in the early years led to a stronger role for the laity in governance. The exact character of polity varies according to the size, needs, and traditions of the several branches of Orthodoxy represented in North America, but continuity within the apostolic succession of bishops is a constant.

In the Christian spectrum today—especially in the United States—Eastern Christianity remains something of an anomaly. In terms of Will Herberg's classic typology of "Protestant, Catholic, Jew," Eastern Christians fall through the cracks (together with Anglicans, many of whom reject such easy classification). Although Eastern ways of belief and worship closely resemble those of the more familiar Roman Catholic tradition in many ways, the issue of papal supremacy has placed the Orthodox churches in closer alliance with the Protestant churches on such matters as participating in the National and World Councils of Churches. (Their conservatism on a number of social issues, however, has led some Orthodox churches to grow cautious about participation in these ecumenical bodies and even to the complete withdrawal of others.) Although their ethnic identities remain distinct and in many ways restrictive, their continued vitality on the American scene is a caution against too facile a reduction of America's religious communities into generic categories that are easy to think of but poor reflections of a complex reality.

The Roman Catholic Tradition

The Roman Catholic Church is the largest single religious organization in the United States today. Like those of many religious groups, its name, bestowed on it after the English Reformation by Anglicans hostile to the papacy in Rome, originally had derogatory connotations. In recent times, however, the name is widely accepted in English-speaking countries as proper and official. Until the Reformation era, the modifier "Roman" was unnecessary, because the Catholic Church, with its center in the Roman papacy, was officially the only representative of Christianity in Western Europe. Despite the challenges that began in earnest with Luther's protests in the early sixteenth century, the Roman Catholic Church represents to this day the largest single tradition within the Christian religion, as well as the most universally dispersed.

Roman Catholicism affirms the traditional teachings of the early church as expressed in the creeds of Nicea and Chalcedon, the decrees of subsequent ecumenical councils (worldwide assemblages of bishops, held periodically, such as the most recent Second Vatican Council, commonly called Vatican II), and the dogmatic pronouncements of the popes. It shares with virtually all other Christian groups a belief in the inspired and authoritative character of the Hebrew and Christian scriptures (the Old and New Testaments) together with the so-called Apocrypha.

However, it also maintains that scripture can only be interpreted properly through the *magisterium,* or teaching authority, of the institutional church. The fullness of this authority resides in the papacy, which is the custodian of the body of teaching known as tradition. *Tradition* is based on revelation as contained in scripture, but also includes doctrines, such as the bodily assumption of the Virgin Mary into heaven. These are not explicit in scripture but have developed within the Catholic community over the centuries from implicit scriptural evidence. The pope is further able to make infallible pronouncements on matters of faith and morals when he speaks *ex cathedra,* that is, officially from his "chair"—a symbol of his office.

A major key to understanding the Catholic theological perspective is through its approach to the relationship of the realms of "Nature" and "Grace." The Catholic Church has traditionally taught that the realm of nature is God's creation. Though finite and flawed, nature, including humanity, is fundamentally good. Human nature has been corrupted by original sin; still, it is capable of redemption through divine grace, which is potentially available to all of humanity.

The usual channel of such grace is the sacraments. These rituals, seven in number, are said to have been instituted by Jesus Christ. They are ordinarily administered by the clergy, who are thus empowered by ordination to the priesthood (itself a sacrament) or, in some cases, by a bishop (for example, confirmation and ordination). Sacraments employ both verbal and material elements, and are examples of the Catholic belief that grace, or divine saving power, does not repudiate but rather builds on and perfects a natural substratum.

As should be evident from the above, the Catholic Church has always placed great emphasis on the institutional church as an intermediary between the divine and the human. From the time of the Council of Trent (1545–63), the church was identified primarily with the clergy, or priests, and the hierarchy, or bishops headed by the pope. The Second Vatican Council (1962–65), however, redefined the character of the church through a much greater emphasis on the role of the laity (a category which includes nuns and sisters, who, though "religious professionals," cannot receive ordination because of their sex).

Traditional Catholic ethics, which is frequently called "moral theology," is based on the notion of *natural law,* an idea that correlates with the theology of nature and grace. This fundamental approach in both theology and ethics is derived from the thought of the thirteenth-century philosopher St. Thomas Aquinas (1225–74), who adapted the categories of the Greek philosopher Aristotle for Christian purposes. According to natural law theory, all important human activities have a proper goal that is defined by nature and knowable by reason unaided by grace. For example, sexual intercourse has as its natural goal procreation, and the use of artificial contraceptives to thwart the fulfillment of this goal is unnatural and therefore immoral.

Needless to say, this particular application of natural law theory has been extremely controversial. Since Vatican II, a diversity of teachings on a wide variety of ethical matters, including the morality of nuclear warfare and capital punishment as well as sexuality in its various forms, has arisen within the American Catholic community. (The difficulties of the American ethicist Charles Curran and the German theologian Hans Küng with the Vatican over their teachings on a variety of matters from contraception to papal infallibility are illustrative of the ferment and tensions within the international Catholic community.) Similarly, new theological approaches influenced by contemporary philosophical movements such as existentialism and phenomenology have arisen to challenge traditional scholastic philosophy and theology based on Aquinas's teachings. Central to this reconceptualization of theology has been a movement away from a focus on objective, external processes, goals, and criteria toward an emphasis on the individual self in personal relationship with God and the Christian community. Continental European theologians such as Bernard Häring, Karl Rahner, Hans Küng, Bernard Lonergan, Pierre Teilhard de Chardin, and Edward Schillebeeckx—some of them still controversial—have all exercised an important influence on contemporary American Catholic thought.

One way of understanding both the centrality of sacramental worship to Catholicism and the ways in which thought and practice have changed significantly in the wake of Vatican II is to look more carefully at each of the seven sacraments, a number fixed during the later Middle Ages after long debate as to the precise number. These seven can be separated analytically into two categories: those that are usually received once (at most) during the course of the life cycle, and those that are received on a regular basis.

To begin with the latter, the rite that has traditionally been known as *Penance* has undergone some of the most dramatic reinterpretation in recent years. For centuries Penance had been administered on a very individualistic basis in which penitents would confess their sins to the priest, usually while kneeling in a confessional (a wooden box designed for the purpose with screens between priest and penitents to provide an atmosphere of anonymity). After confessing their sins, penitents would receive absolution, or a declaration of divine forgiveness, from the priest, and be assigned a set of prayers or other pious acts to be performed as a condition of this forgiveness. Criticism of this approach arose on the grounds that the process had become too mechanical and impersonal, with excessive emphasis on a legalistic and objective recitation of particular deeds. As a result of post–Vatican II shifts in perspective, the sacrament, now known as *Reconciliation,* more frequently takes place with the priest and penitent facing one another. Emphasis is placed on a subjective transformation of one's priorities and relations with others. The practice of a more generalized absolution of whole groups has come into use in some parts of America, but does not enjoy official institutional sanction as an ordinary procedure.

The other sacrament that is intended to be received on a regular basis is the *Eucharist*—also known as "Holy Communion"—which is the core of the church's central ritual, the Mass. The Mass, which is closely paralleled by the eucharistic rites used by Anglicans and Lutherans, developed gradually over many centuries, and still uses Latin and Greek forms to indicate sections that originated in early Christian usage, though it is now rendered solely in the vernacular. The following is an outline of the Mass as now usually celebrated by American Catholics:

A. Introductory Rites
    1. Entrance hymn
    2. Greeting by celebrant and response by people
    3. Rite of blessing and sprinkling with holy water (on special occasions)
    4. Penitential rite: general confession of sin and absolution, including the *Kyrie Eleison*: a Greek form, "Lord have mercy"
    5. The *Gloria,* retaining its Latin name: "Glory to God in the highest . . ."
    6. The opening prayer

B. The Liturgy of the Word
    1. Old Testament reading
    2. A psalm, recited alternately by the reader and the congregation
    3. New Testament reading
    4. Gospel reading
    5. The homily (sermon)

6. The profession of faith (the Nicene Creed)
7. General intercessions: prayers for specific categories of intentions

C. The Liturgy of the Eucharist
1. The Offertory
2. The Preface
3. The *Sanctus*: "Holy, holy, holy . . ."
4. The prayers of the Canon and the Consecration
5. The memorial acclamation (one of several forms)
6. The final doxology
7. The Lord's Prayer
8. The Sign of Peace: the congregation greets one another
9. The breaking of bread, with recitation of the *Agnus Dei*: "Lamb of God, you take away the sins of the world, have mercy on us."
10. Administration of Communion (bread and wine)
11. Silent prayer after Communion

D. Concluding Rite: greeting, blessing, and dismissal

The Mass takes its name from its concluding words in Latin, *Ite, missa est:* "Go, you are sent forth." Its exact form has varied over the centuries; the present-day English version is based on the Latin form dating to the time of the Council of Trent, which led to the standardization of a great deal of Catholic practice. In addition to the use of the vernacular, the reforms of Vatican II have brought about several other note-worthy changes. Instead of being turned toward an altar, the celebrant (that is, the priest) now faces the congregation over an altar table that has been moved out from the wall. The congregation takes a more active role in responding to the priest, and participates in bringing forward the elements (bread and wine) and in exchanging the sign of peace (usually a handshake). Scripture is read by lay people, including women. The priest is free to improvise some of the prayers, which formerly had set forms, and is also encouraged to present a well-crafted homily or sermon, an art form frequently neglected in earlier American Catholic practice.

Music during worship is another area in which considerable change has taken place since Vatican II. During the nineteenth and earlier twentieth centuries, Catholic liturgical music was rather eclectic, and tended toward the operatic or sentimental when used at all. The liturgical movement led in the United States by the Benedictine monks at St. John's Abbey in Collegeville, Minnesota, emphasized the revival of Gregorian chant as part of a new stress on a dignified, participatory liturgy. Since Vatican II, chant has yielded to congregational singing, an experience to which many Catholics had never been accustomed. Current collections used in Catholic worship reflect the general broad range of sources found in the hymnals used by Episcopalians, Lutherans, and Presbyterians, though some with specific Catholic themes—for example, devotion to Mary—provide small notes of distinctiveness.

"Folk Masses" with guitars and folksongs became popular during the late 1960s, and are still celebrated in some parishes.

The other five sacraments can be arranged in the order of the progress of the individual human life cycle. Parallels with these rituals in many other religious cultures present no problem theologically; the Catholic idea of grace building on and completing what has already been anticipated in nature legitimates these correspondences or, in some cases, appropriations. The same argument holds for the divisions of the liturgical year, which are betokened by the changing colors of the vestments of the priest and the cloths draped over the altar. This annual cycle begins with Advent, a period of waiting and preparation, which is observed during the four Sundays preceding Christmas. Christmas Day, which is not fixed on the (unknown) actual birthdate of Jesus but rather on the Roman festival of the unconquered sun, is another good example of the appropriation of religious symbols from other cultures with a Christian reinterpretation. The year continues through other major holy days commemorating major events in the life of Jesus (his Epiphany and Circumcision); of Mary (her Immaculate Conception—that is, freedom from original sin—and bodily Assumption into heaven); and those of other saints, especially All Saints' Day on 1 November. Easter, preceded by the forty penitential days of Lent and coming usually in the early spring, is another good example of the coincidence of an event of the utmost significance for Christians—the Resurrection of Jesus—with both the Jewish Passover and the more general celebration of the annual renewal of nature.

The first of what might be called the sacraments of the life cycle is that of Baptism, or Christian Initiation. Baptism was available in the early church only to adults after a considerable period of instruction. After Christianity had become the official religion of the empire, it was routinely administered to newborn infants by sprinkling (aspersion) rather than immersion. Although infant baptism is still the norm, a new emphasis since Vatican II has also revived the importance of the symbolism of the initiation of adults in the early Christian manner. Because infant baptism is a vicarious process, with the parents and godparents providing the witness, the sacrament of *Confirmation* provides for a conscious completion of the initiatory process by the "candidate" at a later age. In traditional American Catholic practice this took place around the age of eight or nine, but more recently is carried out in adolescence. Baptism is performed by a priest, although lay people may confer it in unusual circumstances; confirmation is ordinarily administered by a bishop. In newer Catholic churches, the baptismal font, or basin, has been replaced by a larger structure in the narthex, or "gathering."

The onset of adulthood traditionally involved a choice between marriage or the religious life, each of which was acknowledged sacramentally. Holy Orders, or ordination, is the ritual of entry into the priesthood, and is also administered by a bishop. Women entering religious orders participate in elaborate ceremonies in which they take solemn vows, but these are not technically sacraments. Matrimony, or marriage, does have a sacramental character, and is technically dissoluble only through an annulment, or declaration that a proper marriage has never taken place because of nonconsummation, lack of free consent on the part of both parties, or other technical reasons. In practice, the binding character of both of these sacraments has come into question in recent years. Diocesan marriage tribunals have extended the grounds of annulment to psychological as well as physical and legal criteria, and many Catholics simply obtain civil divorces. The status of divorced Catholics, who are technically unable to receive Communion, is thus a sensitive point, and many support groups have arisen to help them deal with the situation. Similarly, the reappraisals of the priesthood brought about by Vatican II have resulted in many priests seeking and obtaining dispensation from their vows, whereas others have simply left.

The last of the "life cycle" sacraments was formerly known as "Extreme Unction"—the anointing with oil of the gravely ill and dying. Its revised name, "the Anointing of the Sick," has given it a less dire character; it is no longer administered solely to those close to death, but rather in cases of reasonably serious illness, with an emphasis on its life-affirming character, and may be administered communally. Cremation of the dead had long been banned because it had at one time been practiced as a denial of Catholic teaching on the resurrection of the body. More recently, though, it has reemerged as a permissible option under some circumstances. Burial in consecrated ground—that is, a Catholic cemetery—is still the preferred means of the disposal of the earthly remains of the dead.

A final topic of distinctively Catholic belief and practice is the complex of devotions focusing on Jesus, the Virgin Mary, and the saints. Many of these practices originated in the "Baroque" era of piety that flourished in France and Italy during the seventeenth and eighteenth centuries. Prior to Vatican II, "para-liturgical" practices such as the recitation of the Rosary and other prayers and pious acts focusing on the Virgin Mary and the saints had become central to the religious life of many Catholics, and were promoted actively by many religious orders. The liturgical movement helped undermine these practices by its focus on the Mass as an event in which the laity were to participate actively, rather than attend to their own devotions while the priest conducted the liturgy unilaterally. The emphasis on the dialogic character of worship promoted by the council has resulted in a deemphasis on devotional practices, though many older Catholics still find them rewarding and many conservatives actively advocate their revival. On the other hand, the new interest in female religious symbolism promoted by the feminist movement in theology has focussed attention on the significance of the Virgin Mary, though from a very nontraditional perspective.

As should be clear from the discussion of the development and general character of Roman Catholicism, the tradition's stress on the importance of the institutional church as a channel for divine grace, together with its Roman heritage, combine to create an elaborate and intricate structure of organization and governance. The basic structure of the Catholic Church is hierarchical, that is, resembling a pyramid in which power is concentrated at the top and is diffused downward through increasingly broader layers.

At the very top of this pyramid of authority is the bishop of Rome—the *pope*—who as supreme pontiff holds ultimate authority over the entire church. The pope is assisted in his duties by the curia, or cabinet, which consists primarily of cardinals (see following paragraphs) and other bishops residing in Rome who preside over the various divisions of papal government, with corresponding titles such as "secretary of state." The pope and his advisors reside in the Vatican City, a small area of only a few acres within the city of Rome but entirely independent politically and possessing all of the agencies of government. These include a diplomatic corps with representatives throughout the world's capitals, and even a small army of sorts, the colorful Swiss Guards. The Vatican is all that remains of the Papal States, a belt of territory that bisected the Italian peninsula and over which the pope presided as political ruler until the achievement of Italian unification in 1870.

The *College of Cardinals,* which supplies the highest level of staffing for much of the Vatican's activities, is a group of men, of late about 130 in number, whose sole official duty is the election of a new pope when the office falls vacant by death or, rarely, by abdication. (The pope traditionally serves for the remainder of his lifetime after election.) Almost all of the cardinals are bishops, usually archbishops of major cities, appointed by the pope. Until recently, the college (and the papacy) were dominated by Italians, but since the reign of John XXIII it has become more cosmopolitan in membership, with a number of third-world cardinals appointed in the last few decades. (The election of John Paul II, formerly archbishop of Kraków, Poland, as pope in 1978 also put an end to the longtime hold on the papacy by Italians.) Although any Roman Catholic male can theoretically be named a cardinal, in practice the college's ranks have been filled by prominent archbishops.

The rank of cardinal is largely honorific, with the election of the pope as the only distinctive function. More central to the church's structure is the office of *bishop.* Bishops are said to be direct successors of the apostles, and the doctrine of the apostolic succession is crucial to the church's notion of authority. (This idea is also accepted by a number of other religious groups, such as the Eastern Orthodox and Anglican churches, but the Roman Catholic Church does not recognize all of these claims as valid.) Administratively, bishops preside over territories called *dioceses,* geographical units into which virtually the entire earth is divided. Each bishop has full power over the ecclesiastical life of his diocese, including finances, property, personnel matters (especially the assignment of priests), and teaching and worship. A bishop answers directly only to the pope, although the notion of collegial sharing of authority with clergy and laity has become more important since the Vatican II. In terms of worship, two of the seven sacraments of the church, ordination to the priesthood and confirmation, can ordinarily be administered only by bishops.

Although all bishops are considered to be successors to the apostles, not all bishops have equal prestige and authority. Bishops of large and important cities in the Catholic world are often given the title of *archbishop*, a designation that goes with responsibility for a particular territory known as an *archdiocese*. Bishops of other cities are officially known as *suffragan* bishops; however, they enjoy the same fullness of power as an archbishop, whose only real additional function is the right to convene the bishops of his *province*, that is, the territory composed of the dioceses of which his, the archdiocese, is first among equals. Archbishops or bishops of large dioceses may also be assisted by *auxiliary* bishops. Finally, a bishop *coadjutor* is sometimes appointed when a bishop is old or infirm. Such a bishop functions as an assistant until the senior bishop's death or retirement, at which time the coadjutor automatically becomes bishop in his own right.

Bishops, cardinals, and popes are all chosen ultimately from the ranks of the *priesthood*, the basic group of "professional religious" men in the church whose professions are given spiritual legitimation through the sacrament of ordination. Priests are distinguished from the laity primarily through their power to administer the sacraments. However, priests have many other duties and functions, including the administration of a parish, or basic geographical division of the church (usually a town or urban neighborhood, all of the Catholic inhabitants of which are in theory expected to attend the church designated for that parish), pastoral counseling, preaching, and the various other activities usually associated with the Christian ministry. A priest who is in charge of a parish is known as a *pastor* or *rector*; any assistants he might have are called *assistant pastors* or *curates*. *Monsignor* is an honorary title sometimes bestowed by the pope on senior priests as a special recognition of their services.

Not all priests, however, are assigned to parishes, especially those belonging to religious orders. The major division of the priesthood is usually given as that between the *secular* clergy, who are part of the diocesan hierarchy and who answer directly to a bishop, and the *regular* clergy, who belong to religious orders such as the Jesuits or Dominicans and who answer to their order's superior. The term *secular* does not indicate a lack of religious zeal, but rather refers to this sort of priests' residence in the world (Latin *saeculum*), usually in a parish. Regular clergy, on the other hand, are those who live according to a rule (Latin *regula*), frequently in communities by themselves apart from the secular world. Regular clergy were originally monks, such as the Trappists, who continue to live in monasteries and have little contact with the outside world. Others, such as Jesuits, Dominicans, and Franciscans—orders of priests, brothers, or *friars* originating in the later Middle Ages or Catholic Reformation eras—are active in the world, and may function as missionaries, teachers, or at times as parish priests. Members of religious orders usually take vows of poverty, chastity, and obedience as part of their commitment, whereas secular clergy may own private property. The latter, however, are supposed to be obedient to their bishops, and cannot marry under the prevailing code of church discipline.

In addition to the clergy, other members of the church dedicate their lives totally to religion without being ordained. Men in this category are usually known as brothers, who perform menial tasks in some religious orders, or who sometimes, as in the case of the Christian Brothers, belong to orders composed primarily of unordained men who engage in teaching and other distinctive tasks (including wine making). Women, on the other hand, are not able to receive the sacrament of ordination under any circumstances, but are able to enter into religious orders and take vows similar to their male counterparts and likewise live in community. Although women religious are usually referred to generically as *nuns,* this term is more properly reserved for those who live in communities secluded from the secular world and dedicated to a purely contemplative life. Religious women who engage in such tasks as teaching and nursing, such as the Sisters of Mercy and the Sisters of Charity, are technically referred to as *sisters.* (In the United States, though, this distinction has never been much observed.) Since religious women cannot be ordained, their status is technically that of *laity* (as opposed to clergy).

Finally, the large majority of the world's Roman Catholics are not ordained and do not belong to any religious order, but live their lives in the secular world in the pursuit of any number of occupations while presumably attending church and receiving the sacraments with some regularity. These are the laity, or laymen and laywomen. In the years before Vatican II, these laity were generally regarded as rather passive in their role in the church in comparison with the clergy and other religious, and did not ordinarily play a major role in the decision-making and teaching roles of the church. In more recent times, however, the role of the laity has been redefined in more positive and active terms. This activity has taken such forms as participation in parish councils, which help in the planning and execution of parish activities, and in teaching at a variety of levels, from parochial elementary schools, which can no longer rely on large numbers of teaching sisters, to seminary theological faculties.

This lengthy account of the belief, worship, and organizational structure of Roman Catholicism indicates the importance placed by this tradition on the objective, formal aspects of the religious life. This has been in large part an outgrowth of its distinctively Roman cultural heritage, with an analysis of which the following chapter begins. The development of the Western, Roman tradition of Christianity over nearly two millennia can be read as an ongoing interplay or dialectic between these powerful forces of order and other impulses in revolt against a centralization, uniformity, and traditionalism perceived as overly rigid and spiritually deadening. In some cases—most dramatically the era of the Reformation—that tension has resulted in a revolutionary sundering of the unity that Roman Christianity has so prized. In others, it has led to the flourishing of internal diversity. That dialectic received new impetus in the later twentieth century as a result of Vatican II, and any ultimate resolution of those tensions remains doubtful. This is perhaps for the best: were it to be achieved, it might be a sign that the tradition's centuries-old vitality was finally nearing a close.

Western Catholicism from the Time of Constantine

Each of the three words that make up its modern name reveals some important aspects of the character of the Roman Catholic Church. Its association with the city of Rome dates to the earliest days of the Christian religion and the residence there of the apostles Peter and Paul. Peter, the chief of the apostles, gradually came to be regarded as the first of an unbroken line of bishops of the city. The text of Matthew 16:18ff. ("And I say unto thee, thou art Peter, and on this rock I shall build my church") is regarded by Catholics as evidence that Jesus himself was the source of the original authority of the Roman bishop's office.

In a monumental shift in the history of Christianity, the Roman emperor Constantine (d. 337) elevated Christianity from the status of a suspect and potentially treasonable "underground" religion to the official creed of the empire. In another epoch-making act, he removed the imperial capital to Byzantium (which was subsequently renamed "Constantinople") early in the fourth century A.D. The Roman bishop, who had acquired the title of "pope" ("father"), thus found himself the leader not only of the official religion of the West but in many regards the civil ruler as well. He was faced with the problem of serving not just as spiritual but as temporal administrator for Italy, the western reaches of northern Africa, and other territories not directly under the aegis of Constantinople. The pope and his staff therefore found themselves becoming diplomats, distributors of relief, and even occasional military figures in dealing with civil disorganization and the ravages both of nature and the ever-encroaching Germanic peoples from the north. As a result, a complicated bureaucratic apparatus began to emerge at the papal court that formed the basis for today's *curia*—that is, the bureaus, often headed by a cardinal, that make up the papal government.

Part of the distinctively Roman character of the Catholic Church, then, is its elaborate administrative apparatus, which it developed out of temporal necessity and also as the heir to the legacy of the Roman Empire. In the era of close church-state relations known as the *Middle Ages*, a *Holy Roman Empire* and other Christianized secular powers emerged to reclaim the civic functions that the papacy had foisted on it willy-nilly. Still, the church retained and even continued to expand its internal administrative apparatus and develop its code of *canon* (church) *law*, another heritage from the Roman Empire.

The emergence of a Christian secular power during the so-called Middle Ages, however, did not mark an end to the church's claim to temporal authority. The titles of bishop, abbot, and especially pope carried with them control of wealth and power

that, when challenged, was seldom readily relinquished. It was not until the unification of the modern Italian nation in 1870 that papal control over the "Papal States,"
which ran through the central part of the Italian peninsula, came to a definitive end,
and with it the pope's role as a secular prince. This situation was not normalized
until the signing of a *concordat,* or papal treaty, with Mussolini in 1929. The bitterness of this struggle contributed to the suspicion and sometimes outright hostility
with which the papal government viewed the secular order during the nineteenth
and early twentieth centuries.

Taken together, these elements of a conscious heritage from the Roman Empire—
bureaucratic complexity, an elaborate legal code, and an interweaving of religious
and political authority—have all contributed to the development of the quality of
Romanità, a term often invoked to characterize the distinctive ethos of the Vatican
and the papacy. Another way of characterizing this quality is as the possession of
a sense of history that views with suspicion rapid change and looks at matters *sub
specie aeternitatis*—from the perspective of the ages rather than the standpoint of
the present moment. This attitude, needless to say, is very different from the pres-
ent- and future-mindedness of many Americans, Catholics included. This difference
in perspective has often led to conflict between Vatican authority and the American
branch of the church.

The second feature of Roman Catholicism worth noting is its claim to *catholicity*—
universality and inclusiveness. The Catholic Church has for centuries claimed that
it possesses the fullness of saving truth in its structures, sacraments, and tradition,
and that all of humanity should rightfully find a place within it as the surest guide
to salvation. Some of the church's claims to exclusive possession of such truth were
modified by Vatican II, but the church still regards its goal as universal membership. (The exclusiveness of post–Vatican II Catholic claims on saving truth was emphasized in September of 2000, when two Vatican pronouncements—a note from
then-Cardinal Ratzinger and the document *Dominus Iesus*—declared that Christian
communions without the apostolic succession of bishops should not be referred to
as "sister churches," and that Catholic theologians should refrain from claiming that
there were alternate paths to salvation besides the Catholic Church.) To this end,
it maintains a worldwide missionary effort, conducted principally by members of
religious orders, and coordinated by the Congregation for the Propagation of the
Faith in Rome.

In many ways, the claim of the Roman Catholic Church to be universal is borne
out in reality. It is the largest single organized religious body both in the United States
and in the world, with well over a half billion adherents worldwide. Its members are
spread through every inhabited continent, with the heaviest concentrations in Europe
and the Americas and rapidly growing numbers in Africa. Much of this geographical spread was achieved during the period of exploration and colonization of the
Renaissance, when the Catholic nations of France, Spain, and Portugal established

hegemony throughout virtually all of Latin America and substantial portions of North America and Africa. Even after the age of colonization and the onset of independence in developing countries, the Catholic Church continues to enjoy wide adherence in former colonial areas, though it has been aggressively challenged by Marxism on the one hand and by pentecostal and other evangelical Protestant missionary effort on the other. In recent years, the acute problems of economic inequality and political oppression especially in Latin America have led to the emergence of a new movement in Catholic thought and action called *liberation theology*. Articulated in the work of thinkers such as Leonardo Boff and Gustavo Gutiérrez, this school of thought focuses on the relevance of the teachings of the Gospel to present-day human need in situations of want and oppression. It has been, in both religious and political circles, extremely controversial, provoking censure from Pope John Paul II.

The third element in Catholicism's name is "church," a term that carries with it a variety of levels of meaning. *Church* may refer to a building in which worship is conducted; the congregation that assembles for worship; or the organizational structures that unite a number of local congregations into a larger denomination. In the vocabulary of such founders of the sociology of religion as Max Weber and Ernst Troeltsch, however, the term *church* took on another, more technical meaning that is particularly useful in understanding the significance of the term in this context.

The primary models of religious structure that presented themselves to this generation of thinkers came from the classic pattern of the Middle Ages, which was rapidly breaking up in the Europe of the later nineteenth century. Until the era of the Reformation, one universal church—at least in theory—included the entirety of the population of western Europe within its scope. The only exceptions to this all-encompassing Christendom ruled spiritually by the pope and (at least in wish or theory) temporally by the Holy Roman Emperor were the Jews, who enjoyed an exempt status when times were favorable, and various groups of Christian dissidents labeled by the church as "heretics." These latter people, such as the Waldenses of twelfth-century north Italy or the Hussites of fifteenth-century Bohemia (now part of the Czech Republic), regarded themselves as reformers who rejected on various grounds the claims of institutional Catholicism to authority. The term later given by sociologists to these groups was *sects*, and their adherents were called *sectarians*.

The idea of a sect in practical terms presupposes that of a church, since sectarians receive their warrant for existence in their rejection of what they regard as the inevitable compromises of any church that attempts inclusiveness of membership. This ideal of inclusiveness, which is manifest in the term *catholic* itself, has always been a characteristic of Catholicism. Even after the Reformation had effectively divided Europe into a number of separate and frequently hostile religious spheres, this idea of the "church" as including by definition all of the people in a given political unit remained dominant throughout most of Europe, whether in the form of Anglicanism in England, Lutheranism in many of the German states, or Catholicism, which continued to prevail primarily in the southern parts of the Continent. Even though its actual scope was curtailed, however, the Catholic Church continued to assert its claims to universal inclusiveness, and directed its energies at once to missionary expansion overseas as well as to the reestablishment of its influence in Protestant Europe through such arms of the "Catholic (or Counter) Reformation" as the Jesuit order founded by Ignatius Loyola in 1540.

Although the idea of a "church" in this context carries with it strong political overtones, it also has an important religious dimension. The earliest Christian communities had been more sectarian than "churchly" in the rigor of their requirements for membership and the ever-present danger of martyrdom that confronted them. The Constantinian Revolution then resulted in a radically transformed organization that found itself responsible for the welfare of the entire community. From that time on, the Catholic Church began to regard itself as the institutional means through which God's redeeming grace was mediated potentially to the entirety of humanity. This was not to say that everyone would ultimately achieve salvation; it was, however, to affirm that all people should at least be exposed to the means of saving grace, and provided a warrant for the church's campaign through missionary work and institutional expansion throughout what was then regarded by Europeans as virtually the entire world.

Another aspect of the "catholicity" of Roman Catholicism has been its provision of a wide variety of religious lifestyles to accommodate the wide variety of spiritual types it takes in. The most totally committed men and women have from early on had the option of being called to the monastic life. Many of the most spectacular "spiritual athletes" of the early Christian centuries chose the life of *anchorites,* or hermits living in isolation. St. Benedict of Nursia provided an alternative, and ultimately more viable, model in the community he organized at Monte Cassino in Italy around A.D. 540. Monks who followed this communal style, in which they lived together in work and prayer organized according to a rule, were known as *cenobites* (SEN-oh-bites). This cenobitic monasticism soon displaced the anchoritic style as normative in western Christendom. Religious orders for women as well as men also emerged at an early date.

Monasticism flourished during the Middle Ages, undergoing various high and low periods and frequent reforms, and continues to the present day in a variety of communities with differing traditions. Benedictines, for example, are involved in the world through the maintenance of colleges, such as St. John's in Minnesota, and other educational endeavors, while Trappists live a life of silent contemplation in almost complete withdrawal from the secular realm. Monasticism is now comparatively unusual in late twentieth-century America; however, its popularity received a major boost through the life and writings of Thomas Merton (1915–68), whose autobiographical *The Seven Storey Mountain* (1948) presented the contemplative life as an intellectually respectable and spiritually compelling alternative to what Merton represented as the arid secularity of contemporary American life. Merton's later antiwar activism and death while participating in a conference at a Buddhist monastery further demonstrated that even the most rigorous monastic lifestyle was not incompatible with an engaged participation in the broader concerns of humanity.

In addition to the monastic life, a number of alternative models for living in community developed with the changing conditions of later centuries. The urbanization of late medieval Europe brought about the preaching orders, most eminently, the Franciscans and Dominicans. Members of these orders were not remote from the world but rather engaged to spread the Gospel among the urban dwellers who seemed to be falling through the cracks of the new social order. Later, in the Reformation era, the Society of Jesus was founded by the Spanish ex-soldier Ignatius Loyola in 1540. The Jesuits came into existence to try to halt the spread of Protestant ideas, particularly through the rigorous education of the sons of influential families. In later centuries, all three of these orders turned their attention to overseas missions, education, scholarship, and a wide variety of other tasks. Religious orders of women—known in America more or less interchangeably as "nuns" or "sisters"—had existed from the time of the early church. Like their male counterparts, some of these women retreated from the world into cloistered lives of prayer. As new orders were founded, though, especially during the post-Reformation era, the majority turned their attention, especially in nineteenth- and early twentieth-century America, to the practical tasks of teaching, nursing, and various forms of social work.

Although lay people have always been thought capable of lofty spiritual attainments, the bias of the institutional church until the changes of direction brought about by Vatican II has been toward the special recognition of those men who have been ordained to the priesthood or women and lay brothers who have entered a religious order. A major category used by the Catholic Church to recognize lives of heroic piety, whether led by clergy or laity, is that of *sainthood*. The term *saint* was used in the early church to designate followers of Jesus but gradually began to take on other associations. During the decades of persecution that took place periodically prior to the Constantinian settlement, Christians who remained faithful even to death were acclaimed as *martyrs,* and thus achieved, albeit posthumously, a heroic status in the eyes of the Christian community. After the age of martyrdom had passed, a new preoccupation with the ability of martyrs and other witnesses to the faith— *ascetics,* for example, who lived lives of rigorous self-denial and punishment—to work miracles began to arise. *Cults* devoted to the preservation and veneration of the memories and relics of such miracle workers grew up spontaneously throughout Christendom, and the spiritual heroes who were thought to be so divinely favored as to perform miraculous healings and other events of a supernatural character were acclaimed as *saints.* Eventually, the recognition of saints was routinized by the institutional church, and an elaborate process of collection and evaluation of evidence must now be undergone prior to an individual's being declared—always posthumously—to be among the ranks of the saints. Although the traditional cult of saints receded following Vatican II, Pope John Paul II later labored to revive it by expediting the canonization of a host of new candidates.

Such spiritual heroes, however, were not the only Christians who made up the church. Most individuals, though not capable of such heroic piety, nevertheless could expect salvation through the more ordinary means to that goal provided by the institutional church through the sacraments. Particularly directed toward this expectation of human failings was *Penance*—more recently renamed Reconciliation—which provided a regular means for the confession of and atonement for the lapses into sinfulness into which all humans periodically strayed. After confessing one's sins to a priest, receiving absolution, and performing prescribed acts of penance, one could regularly return to a state of *grace,* or reconciliation with God, and therefore be fit to enter into heaven if death occurred when one had been in the appropriate state. For the ordinary run of mortals, however, one would ordinarily expect to undergo some experience of *Purgatory,* a state of otherworldly atonement for the effects of one's sins prior to admission into Paradise itself.

This worldview, which evolved gradually during those centuries collectively designated the Middle Ages and received definitive expression during the time of Dante and St. Thomas Aquinas (ca. 1200–1300), received a revivification and also a rigidification in the wake of the Reformation of the sixteenth century. The challenge to papal authority begun by Martin Luther in 1517 and carried further by Calvin, Zwingli, and the other reformers, generated a Counter-, or Catholic, Reformation as a response to the questions of belief and practice that these harbingers of a new era raised. On the one hand, most Catholics were prepared to admit that there was considerable failure within the church to live up to its own ideals. Abuses among clergy and hierarchy were rife. On the other hand, the institutional church was not prepared to acknowledge the validity of the claims of Luther and his followers to theological revisionism, that is, the rejection of the Catholic idea of tradition as a valid source of religious authority.

The means through which both an internal housecleaning and a vigorous counterattack against the inroads of the Reformers was carried on was the convening of an ecumenical council at Trent, in northern Italy, in 1545. The Council of Trent, which was in session on and off for the next eighteen years, made great strides in establishing a disciplined, educated, and moral clergy that would be impervious to the accusations of both external and internal critics of the previous decades. In addition, a number of new religious orders, especially Ignatius Loyola's Jesuits, helped to wage a vigorous effort to combat the inroads of the Reformation wherever possible.

The three centuries that elapsed between Trent and the Vatican II coincided almost exactly with that period in England and America that Sydney Ahlstrom has characterized as "the Great Puritan Epoch." For the Roman Catholic Church and the areas in which it remained dominant, this same period might well be called "the Great

Tridentine Epoch." According to the sociologist Max Weber, Puritanism and other forms of Protestantism helped to provide the ideological basis for the transformation of Western society often described as "modernization": the displacement of country by city, agriculture by industry, oral culture by literacy, monarchy by democracy, provincialism by cosmopolitanism, the hold of tradition by the idea of progress. Although the parts of southern and central Europe that remained Catholic following the Reformation were not immune to the solvents of modernity, the coming of its inexorable components was certainly slower than in the Protestant climes of the Netherlands, the British Isles, and those colonies that would become the United States. During these centuries, Catholic hegemony was maintained, often through uneasy compromises with the forces of tradition in European life that continued to dominate especially in Spain, Italy, Austria, and France. When change came, as it inevitably did in all of those regions, the consequences were frequently cataclysmic.

The post-Tridentine Catholic Church may be characterized as authoritarian, traditionalistic, clerical, legalistic, and devotionally oriented. The papacy strove continually to regain its hegemony and enhance its eminence, which it was only periodically successful in accomplishing. With a few major exceptions, such as the work of John Henry Cardinal Newman (1801–90), a convert from Anglicanism, the Catholic theology that emerged in this era was derivative, consisting primarily of extensive commentaries on the work of Thomas Aquinas and other medieval and Counter-Reformation era theologians. The Vatican viewed theological innovation with suspicion, and intellectual venturesomeness was not encouraged by the centralized clerical education mandated by Trent.

The administration of the church grew even more bureaucratic. A legalistic outlook prevailed in the realms of both administration and moral theology, where highly detailed guidelines for individual conduct provided norms for behavior. Creative religious energies were focused on the founding of new religious orders, especially in seventeenth- and eighteenth-century France, which in turn provided the seedbeds for an efflorescence of piety inspired by appearances of the Virgin Mary to members, usually female, of those orders. These devotions consisted of saying prayers; wearing scapulars; venerating statues of Jesus, Mary, and other saints; undertaking pilgrimages to holy sites such as Lourdes, where a particularly important appearance of the Virgin was reported in 1858; and maintaining membership in societies founded to promote these activities.

Although these tendencies were characteristic of most of the Tridentine epoch, their apogee came in the nineteenth century with the pontificate of Pius IX ("Pio Nono") from 1846 to 1878. By the time Pius had ascended to the papal throne, the relationship of the Catholic Church with the parts of Europe that had remained loyal since the Reformation had been undergoing an upheaval as traumatic as the revolt of Luther and his successors itself had been. Although the underpinnings of the new revolt against traditional Catholicism lay in the broad intellectual movement known as the Enlightenment and the economic and demographic transformations that were slowly changing the infrastructure of European life, the decisive historical turning point was the French Revolution. In the minds of the insurgents, the institutional church had been intimately complicit in the political order that had weighed so oppressively on the French people for so long and that now had to be overturned—if necessary, by violence. The result was the wholesale execution of priests and bishops as well as nobles at the guillotine, and the driving of many more into exile.

Not surprisingly, the new ideologies of the eighteenth and nineteenth centuries—Freemasonry, socialism, anarchism, communism, and "liberalism" of various sorts—did not find ready acceptance by the Catholic Church. Pius IX had been regarded as something of a liberal at the beginning of his reign, but the anticlerical character that the movement for the unification of Italy assumed soon soured him on all things modern. One result was the "Syllabus of Errors" of 1864, a series of eighty theses that Pius condemned as erroneous. The last of these was the proposition that "the Roman pontiff can and ought to reconcile and harmonize himself with progress, with liberalism, and with modern civilization." Even allowing for a somewhat different sense of the key terms, especially *liberalism,* in the context of the time, from that to which we are now accustomed, it is clear that this is not a statement of enthusiasm for rapid change.

The other major event associated with the pontificate of Pius IX that has had major ramifications for Catholic life and thought up to the present was his convening of an ecumenical council at Rome in 1869, known in retrospect as "Vatican I." The major agenda item at this coming together of all the bishops of the Roman Catholic world was the formal definition of the infallibility of the pope when speaking on matters of faith and morals *ex cathedra* ("from the chair")—that is, in his capacity as the intentional and ultimate arbiter of orthodox belief. This absolutizing of papal authority, even under clearly and rather narrowly delimited circumstances, was intended to bolster the pope's prestige at a time when it was under attack from a variety of quarters. In the longer run, it came to be a symbol of the propensity of the institutional Catholic Church to draw rigid boundaries between itself and other Christian communions, and continues to prove an obstacle in ecumenical conversations. It is worth noting that only two doctrines have been formally declared in an infallible manner in recent times: the immaculate conception of the Virgin Mary (Pius IX, 1854), and her bodily assumption into heaven (Pius XII, 1950). These, too, have proven problematic in ecumenical discussions with Protestant groups, which have never endowed the Virgin with such supernatural attributes.

Pius and his successors continued on this defensive course for the next several decades. When the Vatican Council was disrupted in 1870 by the Italian occupation of Rome, Pius was faced with the loss of temporal control of the Papal States. He declared himself a "prisoner of the Vatican," a status maintained by his successors until a concordat, or treaty, was negotiated between Pius XI and Mussolini in 1929. Leo XIII (reigned 1878–1903) showed signs of a new appreciation of the unique problems of the modern industrial age in his encyclical letter *Rerum Novarum* ("Of New Things," 1891), but later demonstrated a more traditionalist side in *Testem Benevolentiae,* a response to disputes within the American church issued in 1899. Leo's successor, Pius X, issued a far-reaching condemnation of theological accommodation with contemporary biblical criticism in his encyclical *Pascendi Dominici Gregis* ("Feeding the Lord's Flock," 1907), a move which had a profound impact on the American scene as well. Papal intransigence against modern "isms" was further reinforced by the attacks on the church, its personnel, and its property by both the Right, in the form of Nazism and Italian Fascism, and the Left, as manifested in the virulent anticlericalism of the Mexican and Russian Revolutions as well as the Spanish Civil War.

Signs of change gradually appeared—for example, in Pius XII's endorsement of modern biblical criticism in his encyclical *Divino Afflante Spiritu* ("Inspired by the Divine Spirit," 1943). However, the general posture of the institutional Catholic Church remained firmly conservative until the end of this latter Pius's pontificate in 1958. Upon his death, the College of Cardinals elected a dark horse, Angelo Giuseppe Roncalli, the elderly cardinal patriarch of Venice, for what many assumed would be a brief, "care-taking" pontificate. Roncalli, who took the name John XXIII, surprised almost everyone by convening a second ecumenical council at the Vatican to complete the agenda of the first council and to bring about, in Pope John's word, an *aggironamento,* an "up-to-dateness" of the church with the world around it.

The council, which soon became known as Vatican II, began its deliberations in 1962 and concluded its work under John's successor, Paul VI (reigned 1963–78), three years later. Vatican II was an instant success as a media event, in part because of the enormous personal charm and warmth of its convenor. Its mission was primarily "pastoral" rather than dogma defining, and its ecumenical character was emphasized by the inclusion of Eastern Orthodox and Protestant representatives as nonvoting participants. Its impact was extraordinary, since the council's documents, or "constitutions," provided often dramatically new approaches to a wide variety of issues on which the institutional church had previously taken an uncompromisingly traditionalist stand.

For Catholics, the most visible result of the work of the council was liturgical change and reform, described in the preceding chapter. There were many other results of the council, conspicuous or subtle, that represented major changes in the life and mindset of Catholics throughout the world. Priests and religious women were now encouraged to enter more fully into worldly life rather than trying to emphasize their separation from it. Clerical dress and sisters' habits were duly, and sometimes radically, modified, so that it became difficult to distinguish their wearers from "secular" men and women. This deemphasis on boundaries between the church and the world contributed to the reappraisals that many priests and sisters brought to their "vocations," and large numbers began to apply for dispensations to leave the priesthood or convent to take up a new life in the secular world, including marriage. Although such permission was at first much easier to obtain than it had been, many omitted the formalities and simply left.

This deemphasis on the boundaries between the Catholic Church and the rest of the world also set in motion a chain of new developments. The presence of non–Roman Catholic observers at the council betokened a new receptivity to positive relations with other religions, including the Jewish and Eastern traditions, and even with Marxism and other nontheistic ideologies. The *ecclesiology,* or doctrine of the church, promulgated in the council's documents helped make this possible. The council shifted the governing metaphor from the "Church Militant" to the idea of the "pilgrim people of God" engaged in collectively seeking truth and salvation here on earth.

By admitting that the Catholic Church was not perfect, a way of acknowledging the positive elements in other religions became available. "Dialogue" groups from the parish to the formal international level began to take place, and Catholic clergy and laity were no longer barred from participating in non-Catholic or interdenominational worship. Discussions with other "liturgical" churches such as the Lutheran, Anglican, and Eastern Orthodox have proven particularly fruitful in bringing about agreement by theologians on long-disputed questions such as the nature of justification (salvation), and close relationships between individual local parishes—that is, Roman Catholic and Episcopal or Lutheran—have resulted in "covenants" bringing the congregations together in ways stopping only at intercommunion. However, more "political" issues such as papal infallibility and the ordination of women continue to impede major progress toward full intercommunion or organic union.

An ambiguous consequence of Vatican II was the new perspectives that it brought to bear on the question of *authority* within the Roman Catholic Church. Since the days of Trent, the church had become accustomed to an authoritative, hierarchical, and monarchical system of governance reinforced by the definition of papal infallibility at Vatican I and legitimizing itself on the basis of tradition as well as scripture. Vatican II began to change this. First, scripture was accorded a renewed importance, and was now interpreted through sophisticated historical criticism rather than in the static, propositional categories that Catholic exegetes had shared with their conservative Protestant counterparts. This new historical-critical awareness undermined the ahistorical self-image that the church had for many centuries promoted, in which contemporary systems of belief and practice were projected back into New Testament times. Awareness of the reality of change in the past thus reinforced the idea of the possibility, and even the desirability, of change in the present. As in the Reformation, change was not necessarily seen as innovation, but rather as the *restoration* of the practices of biblical times—that is, in the sharing of authority and of lay participation in the liturgy.

Another challenge to traditional authority was the concept of *collegiality,* or the sharing of power within the church among its various constituents. Pope John convened the council ostensibly to complete the work left unfinished at Vatican I, where papal authority had been definitively addressed but that of the bishops had not been dealt with. According to this idea, all of the components of the church—the papacy, the episcopate, the clergy, and the laity—had an essential and responsible part to play in the church's life, and a model in which authority simply flowed downward from the top was no longer adequate. The council itself, in which bishops, advised by theologians, shared authority with the pope, was a model at one level of this new collegial outlook. Sharing of authority also was implemented at the diocesan level, where priests met in regular assemblies to advise the bishop, and in parish councils, where lay delegates played a similar role for the priest. In practice, these structures did not always work well when a reluctance to share power manifested itself on the part of the bishop or priest, but the idea of absolute and unquestionable authority now was clearly on the defensive.

The major crisis of authority in the post–Vatican II church took place when Pope John's successor, Paul VI, issued his encyclical *Humanae Vitae* ("Of Human Life," 1968) condemning artificial contraception against the advice of the majority of the commission he had assembled to assist him on the issue. Reaction among Catholics of child-bearing age, especially in the developed nations of the West, was overwhelmingly negative, and the papal judgment on the matter was simply ignored by many lay people and their clerical advisors. Dissent at the theological level also continued, with prominent thinkers such as Germany's Hans Küng calling the doctrine of papal infallibility into serious question in his 1971 work, *Infallible?*

Challenges to traditional authority emerged from the right as well as from the left. Political conservatives, especially in America, have taken exception to a whole series of encyclicals by recent popes that made a strong case for peace and social justice, particularly in the context of the emergent developing nations. These began with Pope John's *Mater et Magistra* ("Mother and Teacher") of 1961, and have continued through John Paul II's *Sollicitudo Rei Socialis* ("The Social Concern of the Church," 1988), which attacked exploitation of developing nations by both "liberal capitalism and Marxist collectivism." Also, a "traditionalist" reaction to the substitution of the vernacular for the Latin Mass was led by Marcel Lefebvre. This ultraconservative French archbishop challenged the authority of the church to change, and in 1988 led his followers into a *schism*—that is, a political split not involving doctrine—following years of unsuccessful negotiations with Rome. Lefebvre's movement was a manifestation of the position known as "Integralism" formulated by conservatives early in the century, which affords all papal teachings the same level of authority accorded to the Bible by Protestant fundamentalists. (Integralism has been called "Catholic fundamentalism" by some writers.) The dilemmas arising from papal condemnation of Integralist activities are obvious, as manifested in the abandonment of Lefebvre by many of his followers following his condemnation by the pope. This reaction, however, was an indication that the reforms issuing from Vatican II were not without their cost in terms of Catholic unity.

The death of Paul VI in 1978 ushered in the "year of three popes" when his successor, who took the name John Paul I, died within a few weeks of his election. A second assemblage of the College of Cardinals chose the first non-Italian to the papacy since the Dutchman Adrian VI in the 1520s—Karol Wojtyla, the cardinal archbishop of Kraków in the Communist-dominated but overwhelmingly Catholic nation of Poland. Wojtyla, who took the name John Paul II, was both a scholar and an activist whose career was shaped by the twin hostile forces of Nazism and Communism, and whose interpretation of the role of the institutional church was correspondingly much more aggressive than had been that of his three immediate predecessors. John Paul gained wide exposure through his extensive worldwide travels, including more than one visit to the United States, in which he gained much goodwill through his engaging personality. However, his doctrinal conservatism, his willingness to assert his office's traditional authority vigorously, and his unreceptivity to dissent—themes continued since 2005 by his successor, Benedict XVI, the former Cardinal Joseph Ratzinger—have rendered his pontificate an extremely strong albeit controversial one.

C. The Reformation Era: The Sundering of Western Christendom and the Emergence of the Protestant Traditions

The term *Protestant* is venerable and resonant, but its meaning in practice is so diffuse that it is difficult to pin down very precisely. Negatively, it describes those traditions in Western Christianity that reject the authority of the pope, thus reflecting its origins in Martin Luther's refusal to acknowledge Roman claims to obedience. More positively, it can be interpreted through its roots as meaning a "witness for" something—that something often defined as Luther's doctrine of salvation by faith through grace.

Protestant made its first appearance in the *Protestatio* of the Diet of Speyer in 1529. However, even during that seedtime of Protestantism—the Reformation of the sixteenth century—the varieties of non-Roman Christianity that rapidly took shape during the early and middle 1500s were so diverse that it is difficult to speak meaningfully of them in terms of specifics. John Calvin, for example, accepted many of Luther's basic insights, but developed them in such a way that his theology forms the basis for a distinctive tradition within Christianity. On the other hand, the Lutheran and Anglican traditions are often treated as manifestations of "Liturgical Christianity," with a stress on their affinities with their Roman Catholic origins rather than the distinctly "Protestant" character of, for example, "low" church Episcopalianism and "Eastern" Lutheranism in nineteenth-century America.

For all its difficulties, though, the term *Protestant* remains with us. What is less ambiguous is the fact that, during the sixteenth century, Europe was torn apart by theological ferment, ecclesiastical reform, and political upheaval bent on bringing that reform to life. The following chapters discuss some of the major features of this seminal era, and the enduring traditions that took shape during those years.

CHAPTER 8

The Lutheran Tradition

Martin Luther was arguably the most significant single individual in the history of Christianity between the time of Constantine and the present. The complex of ideas that exploded in the Reformation of the sixteenth century did not all originate with him. It was his genius, though, that combined them into a coherent system of theology as well as a program for action that was able to channel the impulses of his time into a colossal upheaval with consequences that are very much with us to the present day. He ranks with very few other figures in Western history—Alexander the Great, Napoleon, Lincoln—as of "world-historical" stature, however controversial their achievements may have proven.

That the person as well as the work and thought of Luther was a significant aspect of his achievement was evident even to his contemporaries. After his career as a reformer had been firmly established, his friends and followers began to record even his dinner-table conversation, which was subsequently published as the *Tischreden* or "table-talk." Although he himself strongly preferred that the branch of Christianity that he brought into being be known as the *evangelische Kirche*—that is, "Evangelical Church" or "Church of the Gospel"—his own name ultimately displaced that which he had preferred, and his spiritual descendants now proudly call themselves "Lutherans." Even the nomenclature of American Lutheranism, in which names associated with his career such as Augsburg, Wartburg, and Wittenberg are attached to colleges and publishing houses, demonstrates the deep impact his personality had on the movement to which he gave rise.

Perhaps not surprisingly, the details of Luther's life are still the source of controversy. In recent years, as arguments between Catholics and Protestants over the significance of Luther have moved toward an ecumenical convergence, scholars are still attempting to separate the biographical facts from the pious and heroic legends that early became part of his followers' account of his life. For example, Luther is said to have decided to enter a monastery as a result of making a vow to Saint Anne when he became terrified during a thunderstorm. Recent research casts doubt on the literal authenticity of this and similar stories. However, their status as folklore rather than history is significant in what it reveals about the power of Luther to inspire this kind of reverential invention. Such stories are characteristic in Christianity and other religious traditions as a form of *hagiography*—saints' lives as a literary genre—and therefore indicate the awe he was capable of arousing.

Martin Luther was born in Saxony in 1483. After receiving a thorough philosophical education, he entered the Augustinian monastery at Erfurt in 1505, whether as a result of his terror in the storm or more complicated reasons. Although he proved a brilliant student and teacher of theology and scripture, he was never fully comfortable as a monk because he was unable to assure himself of the certainty of his salvation. Luther's psychology was complex; it has been the subject of speculation from the time of his bewildered confessor Staupitz to the theorizing of the eminent contemporary psychologist Erik H. Erikson in his ground-breaking and controversial work of psychobiography, *Young Man Luther,* in 1955. It seems likely, though, that much of Luther's problem stemmed from his troubled relationship with his overbearing father Hans, a Saxon miner who was displeased with his precocious son's forsaking a lucrative secular career as a lawyer for that of a monk. Whatever the reasons, he was a clear example of what the psychologist William James called a "twice-born" person: someone to whom life did not come easily, and who needed to undergo a dramatic resolution of his internal tensions before he could experience peace.

Such a resolution did indeed come to Luther—in a tower, according to tradition—but its details are again shrouded in uncertainty. The occasion of this resolution was Luther's perusal of Paul's letter to the Romans, particularly the phrase "the just shall live by faith." What Luther came of a sudden to realize was that his previous attempts to achieve assurance of salvation through the rigorous monastic routine of prayer, study, and sacramental observance were destined to be in vain in the absence of what he now understood to be the true significance of God's grace and corresponding human faith. In reflecting on his own insight and personal transformation, Luther developed the ideas of *sola gratia* and *sola fide*—salvation "by grace alone" and "by faith alone"—as expressions of this experience. "Salvation by grace through faith alone" has subsequently come to be one of the bywords of the Lutheran tradition and, more broadly, of Protestant Christianity ever since.

Luther was maintaining that the traditional Catholic interpretation of the process of salvation had begun at the wrong end. In late medieval Catholicism, emphasis had been placed on the centrality of the church and its clergy as custodians of the sacraments, the faithful reception of which was the key to individual salvation. Although Luther never rejected the sacraments as such, he did come to repudiate them as a means of achieving salvation. The general problem, which Luther identified as "works-righteousness," lay in the notion that salvation could somehow be achieved through human effort. To rely on pleasing God and thereby attaining righteousness in his sight through "good works"—which included sacraments, prayers, charitable deeds, or anything else that was the result of human striving—was to miss the fundamental point that nothing solely of human origin could appease God and thereby win salvation. Human nature in Luther's view was so far fallen that only God himself could counteract the effects of original sin. To speak meaningfully of salvation, then, one had to begin not with human effort but with divine initiative.

Luther's new account of the dynamics of salvation thus began with the phrase *sola gratia*—by God's grace, or saving power, alone, was salvation made possible. The corollary of this offer of grace was the human recipient's response in faith; "by faith alone" (*sola fide*) was the transaction of salvation completed. This response was not the result of free choice, however, but the work of the Holy Spirit. It was the only way in which one could respond once grace had been proffered. All of this did not mean that the person who had experienced justification had entered into any state of purity or guiltlessness. Rather, Luther used the formula *simul justus et peccator*—"at the same time justified and sinful"—to stress that the impact of original sin itself had not been removed, but rather that the divinely imposed penalty for it had been taken away. To complete this description, Luther added a complementary third term, *sola Scriptura*, to emphasize the centrality of scripture as the only source of saving knowledge. It was in the Bible, God's Word, that the true account of the relationship of God and humanity could be found. Although the church still had its place in Luther's scheme—as the place where grace was experienced—he radically deflated the claims of the Catholic Church as an institution to play an indispensable role in the administration of the sacraments and thereby in bringing about salvation. The implications of this line of thought were, to say the least, subversive of the status quo.

The roots of the transformation of this personal experience and theological insight into a program of institutional reform lay in Luther's earlier visit to Rome in 1510. Instead of being edified by his pilgrimage to the center of Christendom, Luther was instead shocked by the secularism and corruption that he now witnessed at first hand. A whole catalogue of terms had arisen to describe the abuses that characterized the Renaissance papacy: *nepotism,* or the appointment of relatives (sometimes illegitimate) to high ecclesiastical office; *simony,* or the sale of church offices for profit; *pluralism,* or the holding of several profitable church offices simultaneously, usually in an absentee relationship; and *nicolaitism,* or clerical concubinage. Faithful Catholics such as Erasmus of Rotterdam were outraged by such abuses, and the Council of Trent ultimately put a stop to most of them. However, Luther was not content to settle for internal change; he was becoming convinced that the whole structure of Catholic belief and practice was based on fundamental errors as to the character of salvation that he was engaged in refuting.

The specific occasion that launched Luther as a reformer was the coming to Germany of the Dominican preacher Johann Tetzel in 1517. Tetzel had been sent to raise funds for the building of the new St. Peter's basilica in Rome under the sponsorship of Pope Leo X, a scion of the Medici family. His fund-raising focused on the sale of indulgences. An *indulgence,* which had its origins in the time of the Crusades, was a reduction of the penalties imposed by the church for sins. By the time of Tetzel, indulgences had come to be interpreted by the Catholic Church not only as a means of escaping the penalties imposed by the church in this world but also as a release from sufferings in Purgatory in the hereafter. To make them even more attractive, indulgences were presented as efficacious not only for the purchasers but for their departed friends and family as well. To obtain an indulgence, one needed only to make a contribution to the pope's architectural enterprises. When this was done, the "Treasury of Merits" built up by Jesus and the saints could be drawn on by the church for the supernatural benefit of contributors and their kindred.

Luther, needless to say, was outraged by the commercialism of this enterprise as well as by what he saw as the shaky theological foundations on which the whole notion of indulgences was based. For indulgences to be effective, the church on earth had to have some control or at least influence over the supernatural realm. For Luther, this was presumptuous nonsense. The indulgence question was therefore one against which Luther could muster the whole theological arsenal that he had been accumulating since the resolution of his personal religious questionings some years earlier. In Wittenberg on 31 October 1517, in response to Tetzel's slogan that "each time a coin in the coffer rings, another soul from Purgatory springs," Luther publicly posted ninety-five theses, that is, brief controversial assertions directed against Tetzel's claims.

Luther's theses aroused the wrath of the Catholic authorities, who summoned him to a judgment at Augsburg in 1518. Had luck not been with him, he most likely would have met the same fate as his spiritual predecessor, the Bohemian reformer Jan Hus (or John Huss), who had been burned at the stake in 1415 after he had raised many of the same objections against Catholic belief and practice. History, however, now proved to be on Luther's side. Many of the rulers of the German states of the era were annoyed with papal interference in their affairs as well as the outflow of cash that resulted from the hawking of indulgences. Luther found in particular a protector in Elector Frederick of Saxony. After Luther and his teachings had been condemned at the Diet of Worms in 1521, Frederick arranged for Luther to be taken into protective custody at his castle, the Wartburg, until the situation could be resolved.

By the early 1520s it had become clear that no reconciliation was likely to take place between Luther and Rome, and that Western Christianity was to be split irrevocably into mutually exclusive camps. Luther himself, it should be noted, had never seen himself as the founder of a new church; rather, he wanted to reform the church in which he had lived his entire life but which now seemed to offer him no choice except leaving. He later coined the phrase *ecclesia semper reformanda*—"the church always reforming itself"—as an expression of the continuing need for an imperfect, earthly institution to be on the alert for the corruption into which it would inevitably fall. The Roman church was clearly unwilling to adopt this attitude. Luther and his followers, especially Philip Melanchthon, now entered into a long period of negotiation with secular rulers and other religious dissidents to translate his theology into an actual program of reform.

One significant event in this process was the Diet of Speyer in 1529, which confirmed the German rulers' right to regulate religion in their own realms. The Diet of Augsburg the following year resulted in the Augsburg Confession, one of the first definitive summaries of Luther's positions. From the beginning of his protest, Luther had engaged in relentless pamphlet warfare with his Catholic and other opponents, and developed and disseminated his religious and political ideas in such important works as his *Open Letter to the Christian Nobility, The Bablyonian Captivity of the Church,* and *The Freedom of a Christian,* all written in 1520. Luther was an enormously prolific writer during his entire career, and the definitive edition of his collected works fills over fifty volumes of sermons, lectures, tracts, and other religious genres. The development of movable-type printing only a few decades earlier and a rapid rise in the rate of popular literacy facilitated the spread of his writings and those of his opponents, and the Reformation rapidly developed into a continental war of words.

Luther's program of reform was not piecemeal but followed from the central theological principles that had impressed themselves on him through personal experience. Beginning with the premise that God alone brought about justification (that is, salvation made possible through divine remission of the consequences of human sin), he argued that the church should no longer be considered the instrument through which salvation takes place mechanically; rather, it was the fellowship of those united in God's saving love who assemble for the preaching of God's word and the reception of the sacraments, as well as "a mother in which faith is begotten." The sacraments were reduced by Luther from the seven recognized by medieval Catholicism to the two that Luther believed were directly instituted and commanded by Jesus himself: the Eucharist, of which the Last Supper was the prototype, and Baptism, based on Jesus's own immersion in the Jordan by John the Baptist. Luther also spent much time on the question of the meaning of the Eucharist, which he felt had been reduced to a mechanical level in late medieval teaching. Although his own interpretation varied during his career, he continued to maintain that Jesus was genuinely present in the sacrament. In doing so, however, he rejected Thomas Aquinas's concept of *transubstantiation,* that is, the idea that after consecration the bread and wine ceased to be bread and wine but were completely transformed into the body and blood of Christ while retaining the appearances of their old natures. Luther thought that this explanation, derived from Aristotelian metaphysics, was too easily reduced to a kind of magical transformation. Throughout his career, though, he continually affirmed the Real Presence—that the body and blood of Jesus Christ were actually present in the Eucharist.

Luther's enforced leisure at the Wartburg provided him with the opportunity to carry out one of his major campaigns in implementing his new ideas. Drawing on the results of his years spent in the monastery as a teacher of scripture, he prepared German translations of first the New and then the Old Testament from the original Greek and Hebrew. This task would not have been easy for even the most learned scholar, because a collection of dialects, rather than a standard German language, is all that existed at the time. It was a significant part of Luther's achievement that he was able to choose skillfully among these linguistic variants to devise a new idiom that transcended regional particularities and was thus suitable for the communication of the word of God in intelligible, even elegant form to all German speakers. In the longer run, the availability of this new German language forged in the *Luther Bibel* contributed to a sense of German cultural unity that saw fruition only centuries later in the unification of the German states under Bismarck.

A vernacular Bible provided a major part of the equipment that Luther needed to carry out a more thoroughgoing reform of Christian life and worship for his followers. Luther rejected the medieval notion that the clergy were the sole guardians of God's word and worship, which hitherto had been available exclusively in Latin. Luther set about adapting the Eucharistic service, or Mass, into German, which was now to be performed with the celebrant facing the congregation. (Lutherans continued to use Latin as well for the next two centuries, however.) To enhance this program of liturgical democratization, Luther also began to compose hymns in the vernacular, which were set to popular melodies of the time and which could thus be sung by the congregation. Previously, liturgical music was in the form of Gregorian chant, or plainsong, or in complicated polyphony, which could only be executed by trained monks or choristers. Now the entire congregation could participate in lusty renditions of such hymns as "Ein' Feste Burg"—"A Mighty Fortress Is Our God," a roar of defiance against those who dared to deny the rightness of Luther's teachings.

A further course of democratization was articulated in his formula "the priesthood of all believers." Luther, like his Catholic opponents, continued to maintain that a specially educated clergy was necessary as a mark of a true church, along with the preaching of the Word, and the administration of the sacraments. However, Luther did not regard the clergy as acquiring any specially elevated spiritual status by virtue of their ordination. Since Jesus's sacrifice had been effective once and for all in making salvation possible, there was no need to believe that priests repeated this unique sacrificial act in the Mass. This reinterpretation thus went far in depriving their office of much of its mystique. Real priesthood for Luther meant serving as a mediator between God and one's neighbor, a service that any Christian could and should perform. Therefore, the priesthood encompassed all believers, who by virtue of divine grace would be expected spontaneously to perform the good works of Christian witness that flowed from "justification by grace through faith alone."

A corollary to this notion was Luther's reinterpretation of the idea of *vocation*. In traditional Catholic usage, only a small number of Christians received from God a special vocation (from the Latin *vocare,* to call) or calling to the higher religious life as a priest, monk, or nun. Other Christians might well be saved through the faithful reception of the sacraments and perseverance in good works, but their status was somewhat inferior to the specially called. Luther argued instead that all Christians were equal in God's sight both in intrinsic sinfulness and in divinely offered grace, and that spiritual distinctions therefore did not apply. Rather, all Christians had equally valid callings to honorable earthly occupations, whether as preachers, teachers, farmers, princes, or to whatever their special skills and circumstances led them. Luther therefore abolished the institution of monasticism, rejecting what the sociologist Max Weber has called its "other-worldly asceticism" in favor of a responsible and faithful life in this world led for God's honor and glory. Luther followed this counsel not only by leaving the monastery himself but by marrying Katharina von Bora, a former nun with whom he lived happily and who bore him six children. He died in 1546.

From the German states where it first took hold, Luther's "Evangelical Church" spread rapidly northward into the Scandinavian countries, where it has been dominant to the present day. Although specifically "Lutheran" Christianity was confined in Europe primarily to these areas—and a significant part of Germany remained Catholic—the influence of Luther's ideas reached far beyond. Subsequent reformers such as John Calvin built on Luther's beginnings, and no aspect of Protestant thought was unaffected by the basic premises he had established as the starting point for any critique of Roman Catholic orthodoxy. Western Christianity was now irretrievably divided into those loyal to Rome and those who rejected the claims of papal supremacy in favor of the principle of *sola Scriptura*—the authority of the Bible alone.

Despite the radical impact of Luther's movement on the Christianity of his age, the Lutheran tradition today seems more similar to Roman Catholicism, especially in its liturgical focus, than to later manifestations of Protestantism. One significant way in which it differs from other "liturgical" traditions such as Anglicanism and Roman Catholicism is in its lack of a centralized or even a common polity. Luther himself had a functional or instrumental view of church government, and did not care a great deal how churches were administered as long as conditions were proper for the achievement of the hallmarks of a truly Christian church: the preaching of the Word and the proper administration of the sacraments. In the early years, Luther was forced to depend on the goodwill of the German princes for the survival of his

"Evangelical Church," and those very princes often served as heads of the church in their realms, sometimes using the title of "emergency bishop."

Although the title of bishop has been retained in most branches of Lutheranism, it is primarily in the Swedish church that the older Catholic notion of the office as validated by apostolic succession has survived. In other countries the office is primarily functional and does not have a sacramental mystique attached to it. The title is employed by the Evangelical Lutheran Church in America (ELCA), with a bishop, vice-president, and national secretary as its three national officers and a division into regional *synods,* each presided over by a bishop. In addition, it has a number of divisions and commissions, based in Chicago, to serve the denomination as a whole. The second largest American group, the Missouri Synod, uses the term *synod* to refer to the denomination as a whole. A president is elected by a national convention as head of the entire synod, which is subdivided into "districts," each of which is also supervised by a president (rather than a bishop). Traditionally, however, considerable power resides in individual congregations.

Polity has therefore never been a means through which Lutherans could preserve their unique traditions, either in the Old World or the New. No pope or archbishop, no canon law, and not even a commonly agreed on form of organization could be resorted to by all. A different route to continuity, however, lay in doctrine. Personal religious experience has sometimes been valued by Lutherans, but the more dominant concern has been with the objectivity of religious truth. One of the hallmarks of the Lutheran tradition from its beginnings has been an emphasis on correct belief— "orthodoxy" in its strictest sense. The traditional "symbol" of Lutheran orthodoxy has been the *Book of Concord,* compiled in 1580 by Luther's followers to provide a standard of reference for ascertaining correctness of belief. The *Book of Concord* contains the three creeds of the early Christian church (Nicene, Apostolic, and Athanasian); several of Luther's own writings, including his Small and Large Catechisms; and a number of documents drawn up by his followers to set forth the Lutheran position in negotiations with other reformers and among Lutherans themselves. Of these, the most influential has been the "Augsburg Confession," drafted by Luther's lieutenant Philip Melanchthon in 1530 and held by Lutherans over the centuries as a definitive statement of their faith. Lutherans have not always been in accord as to the exact interpretation or authority of these documents, but altogether the *Book of Concord* has served as a revered symbol of the beliefs that transcend the forces dividing Lutherans one from another.

Liturgy is another force which, though productive at times of division or at least diversity, is also a common bond uniting a people that has traditionally followed a formal ritual for its communal worship. Luther himself did not create a new liturgy but rather adapted the late medieval Catholic Mass to fit his reinterpretation of such issues as the character of the sacraments and the relationship of the celebrant and the congregation. During the period of ferment among American Lutherans in the nineteenth century, a wide variety of liturgical practices arose. "Eastern" Lutherans, particularly members of Samuel Simon Schmucker's General Synod, tended to follow the lead of their evangelical neighbors: grape juice was substituted for wine, services were conducted in English, the Eucharist was celebrated as little as twice yearly, and the liturgical year—even Christmas—was not observed. The opposite course was typical of the ethnic synods of the Midwest, where doctrinal sermons were preached in the old languages from side (rather than central) pulpits; wine was used in a communion taken first by men and then women; and the traditional liturgical year was the basis of the cycle of worship.

With the erosion of regional and ethnic particularity in the twentieth century, American Lutherans of all sorts began to converge on a common liturgy. A variety of cooperative endeavors culminated in the formation of an Inter-Lutheran Commission on Worship in 1966 by several American Lutheran denominations. The result, first issued in 1978, was the *Lutheran Book of Worship,* which became standard in slightly different versions for the two major Lutheran bodies (ELCA and Missouri Synod). It reflected the liturgical revival that swept over a number of Christian churches during the mid-twentieth century, and the basic eucharistic service differs only in detail from the Roman Catholic and Episcopal versions. Weekly celebration of the Eucharist is the recommended norm, but individual congregations have considerable latitude in deciding how far they want to accommodate their often diverse practices, rooted in a variety of ethnic traditions, to those outlined in the *Book of Worship.* In 2006 the ELCA replaced the *Book of Worship* with *Evangelical Lutheran Worship,* which contains an expanded selection of worship texts and hymns and uses inclusive language.

The *Book of Worship* and *Evangelical Lutheran Worship* contain not only liturgical texts but musical settings as well, including both chants and hymns. One of the richest aspects of the Lutheran tradition from the time of Luther himself has been a delight in choral music, perhaps reflective of the German ethos from which the *evangelische Kirche* arose. In addition to Luther's own hymnody, of which "A Mighty Fortress" remains the most famous among Christians of all stripes, the choral works of Johann Sebastian Bach and Georg Friedrich Handel have been outstanding in their beauty and universal appeal. Bach wrote much of his work in his capacity as *Kantor* (church musical director): his cantatas were composed to be performed according to the cycle of the liturgical year, and the congregation was expected to participate during Lent in his *Passions*—those according to St. Matthew and St. John. Handel's *Messiah* has, of course, become part of the common musical heritage of the Western world, and is still frequently performed at Christmas and Easter by many religious, and even secular, groups. Hymns in the *Book of Worship* and *Evangelical Lutheran Worship* are drawn from a variety of sources, both Lutheran and others; the former range from the work of German Pietist composers such as Paul Gerhardt and Nicholas von Zinzendorf to Swedish folk melodies.

Despite the divisions that still persist among American Lutherans, bonds that transcend the institutional and even the narrowly theological provide a sense of commonality to the American Lutheran community; surveys have indicated that Lutheran loyalty is more to the tradition as a whole than to any particular branch of it. Part of this loyalty springs from the powerful symbols of Luther's personality, life, and work and that of his followers, and the mystique that the very word "Reformation" still evokes for many. As Jaroslav Pelikan has pointed out, the Lutheran parsonage has served as a potent means of preserving and transmitting the tradition through the remarkably talented families that it has nurtured. The tradition of communal worship and especially of music that dates back to Luther himself has also provided a major vehicle of continuity. Perhaps the concluding verse of "Ein' Feste Burg"—"A Mighty Fortress"—expresses best the deep sense of conviction and loyalty that has characterized Lutherans to this day:

> That word among all earthly powers,
> No thanks to them, abideth;
> The Spirit and the gifts are ours
> Through him who with us sideth:
> Let goods and kindred go,
> This mortal life also;
> The body they may kill:
> God's truth abideth still,
> His kingdom is forever.
> (Martin Luther, 1529; trans. Frederick Henry Hedge, 1852).

CHAPTER 9

The Anglican Tradition

Until the sixteenth century, western Europe was nominally united under the pope and the Holy Roman Emperor as "Christendom." This supposed unity was gradually being undermined by the emergence of distinctively national varieties of Catholic Christianity in those areas of Europe that were beginning to materialize as consolidated nation-states rather than loose feudal social and cultural aggregates. Spain, which would later be regarded as one of the most politically backward parts of the Continent, took the lead in this process with the marriage of Ferdinand of Aragon and Isabella of Castille—"the Catholic Monarchs"—in 1469. This dynastic union made possible the political consolidation of the nation, which was furthered by the expulsion of the Muslims and Jews from the Iberian Peninsula during the 1490s and the aggressive development of the Spanish Empire in the following decades. The Spanish crown received extensive privileges from the papacy in the appointment of bishops and other areas that came close to political independence in the ecclesiastical realm. A similar process was taking place in France at about the same time, where "Gallicanism"—the claim that the French church was virtually independent of the pope—had attracted adherents since the fourteenth century. In neither case did these jealous guardings of national traditions and control lead to a break with Rome. However, both are evidence that the more radical course of events that occurred in England had important parallels on the Continent.

Christianity had existed in the British Isles since early Roman times, and its history of relations with Rome was not that unusual in the context of almost perpetual struggles between church and state for power. By the time of Luther, however, many English had become disenchanted with the role that international church politics had come to play in their national life. Although ideas of reform were beginning to enter academic circles, the real impetus for the decisive break that would begin to take shape in 1531 lay even higher. Independence for English Christianity from Roman control was not the work of scholarly reformers nor an upswell of popular sentiment. Rather, it had its source squarely in the will of King Henry VIII (1491–1547), the second ruler of the Tudor dynasty and one of the most extraordinarily effective sovereigns in his time and country or any other. In this sense, the emergence of an independent Church of England was a chapter in the story of what has been called the "Magisterial Reformation"—reform by action of the magistrate, or civil ruler. Therefore, the English Reformation had much more in common politically with that of Luther in Germany and Calvin in Geneva than it did with the disorganized, decentralized, popular movements—the "Radical Reformation"—that began to sweep the Rhine Valley in the 1520s.

The occasion of Henry's break with the papacy was the refusal of Pope Clement VII to annul the marriage Henry had entered into with his brother's widow, Catherine of Aragon. Henry, who was desperate for a male heir, which his wife had been unable to give him, now claimed that his union was incestuous, even though he had previously received papal dispensation to enter into it. The pope might well have acceded to Henry's request had not Henry's wife been the aunt of Charles V, the Holy Roman Emperor, who exerted powerful influence over the papacy. When the declaration of nullity was not forthcoming, Henry, who had earlier been awarded the papal title of "Defender of the Faith" for a refutation of Luther's teachings, took matters into his own hands and secured from the English Parliament in 1534 an Act of Supremacy declaring that he, as king, was "Supreme Head" of the English church. Although a few influential persons, such as the lord chancellor, Thomas More, refused to accept this new state of affairs, the passage of English Christianity from papal to regal leadership occurred with remarkably little protest or resistance. (More, who was beheaded for his obstinacy, was later recognized as a saint by the Roman Catholic Church.)

Until Henry's death in 1547, the English Reformation remained primarily a political rather than a theological event. Mass continued to be said in Latin, bishops and priests presided over the spiritual life of the church much as before, and the effect of the new regime on the religious life of the average person was scarcely noticeable. The one major change in church life was Henry's suppression of England's numerous monasteries, which created a bounty of wealth that could be used to reward the king's supporters. The existence and magnitude of this very wealth, however, was indicative of the material abundance that had proliferated in late medieval times among the religious orders, which presumably did little to enhance the spiritual qualities of the monastic life. Most of the monks accepted Henry's secularization of their lifestyle with little protest, although a few who resisted came to very unpleasant ends. Henry's motives in suppressing monasticism were probably not deeply theological, but his actions did bring English practice closer to that of the former Augustinian Martin Luther, whose "Evangelical Church" existed without benefit of monastic institutions.

Henry was succeeded by his one son, Edward VI, who had been born of a later marriage and ruled under the tutelage of noble "regents" until his death at the age of sixteen in 1553. It was during Edward's brief reign that impulses toward liturgical and theological reform that had not been able to emerge into the open under Henry now found a more receptive atmosphere. In particular, Thomas Cranmer, whom Henry had made archbishop of Canterbury in 1532, brought his genius to bear on the revision of the church's order of worship. Until now, worship in England had continued to be conducted in Latin, a language that was unintelligible not only to most of the laity but very likely to many of the ill-trained clergy as well. In the two editions of the *Book of Common Prayer* that appeared in 1549 and 1552, Cranmer set about following Luther's example in creating an order of worship that all could understand. In these superb examples of English prose, Cranmer not only translated the medieval Mass into English but substantially altered its character to reflect a new concern for the centrality of scripture as well as a desire to disown a popular and highly literal notion of the nature of the presence of Jesus Christ that was said to take place in the eucharistic sacrifice. Although the wordings of these rites changed somewhat from the earlier edition to the later, and the precise character of Cranmer's theology was never entirely clear, there is little doubt that the ideas of the Continental Reformation were beginning to have an impact on English thought and practice.

Cranmer came to a martyr's end after Edward's death, when Edward's successor and half-sister, Mary I, attempted to restore England to Roman control. Although Mary (reigned 1553–58) had the former archbishop and numerous others who refused to acknowledge the restoration of papal authority consigned to the "fires of Smithfield," her own reign was cut short by her death after six years. Her half-sister, Elizabeth I, then acceded to the throne.

Elizabeth had little use for religious controversy, and attempted to separate the political and theological dimensions of religious observance. Her main concern was that all the people of England acknowledge the royal supremacy over the governance of the church and renounce any loyalty to Roman dominion, which Elizabeth regarded as the equivalent of treason. This policy of "comprehensiveness" aimed at the creation of political uniformity and stability, with little concern for theological disagreements, which could flourish as long as they carried no political implications with them.

This spirit of inclusiveness did generate a theological corollary, however. During Elizabeth's reign a party began to develop in the Church of England at Cambridge University and acquired the nickname "Puritan" for its adherents' concern with the moral, liturgical, and theological purification of the church. For the Puritans, scripture was to be the sole source of religious authority, and all church practices had to be based on scripture to be licit. This desire to make the entire English church conform to one rather rigid interpretation of scripture not only drew political suppression from the government of Elizabeth and her Stuart successors but also evoked an eloquent response on theoretical lines from Richard Hooker, an Oxford-educated country clergymen who composed his *Treatise on the Laws of Ecclesiastical Polity* in response to the Puritan challenge. (The first five books were published 1594–97, the complete work not until the mid-seventeenth century.) Against the Puritan claim that there must be explicit scriptural warrant for every belief and practice of the church, including its governance or "polity," Hooker argued instead that human reason is also God-given, and that humans are capable of knowing a "natural law" that complements the revelations of scripture. Therefore, reason and tradition are also valid grounds for particular church practices—such as "episcopal polity," or government by bishops—in cases where scripture does not explicitly contradict the church's practice. This articulation of a threefold groundwork for religious authority—scripture, reason, and tradition—has come to be the philosophical basis of that distinctively Anglican conception of the Church of England (and its daughter churches) as a *via media*—a "middle way" between the extremes of Roman Catholicism on the one hand and Protestantism, especially in its Calvinistic form, on the other.

The final major component of a distinctly Anglican form of religious expression took place in stages during the sixteenth century. It culminated during the reign of the first of the Stuart monarchs, James I (reigned 1603–25), in the publication of the Authorized or "King James" translation of the Bible into English in 1611. One of the few good things ever to come out of a committee, the King James Version (KJV) represented not only the most advanced biblical scholarship of the era but also one of the masterworks of English prose in an age noted for the flourishing of the written word. This translation built on the work of a series of predecessors, including William Tyndale and Miles Coverdale, who in turn had drawn on the direct access to Greek and Hebrew texts that had been the fruit of the Humanist movement of the Renaissance. Although the KJV is no longer regarded as reliable by scholars, it has in turn formed the basis for subsequent revisions, and has exerted an effect on the rhythms of the English language exceeded only perhaps by Shakespeare. A good example is found in some of the opening verses of the Book of Ecclesiastes, which Ernest Hemingway used as an epigraph for a novel whose title can be found therein:

> One generation passeth away, and another generation cometh: but the earth abideth for ever. The sun also ariseth, and the sun goeth down, and hasteth to his place where he arose. The wind goeth toward the south, and turneth about unto the north; it whirleth about continually, and the wind returneth again according to its circuits. All the rivers run into the sea; yet the sea is not full; unto the place from whence the rivers come, thither they return again. (1:4–7)

The primary purpose of the KJV, however, was not aesthetic. From the time of Cranmer and before, the religious shapers of the Church of England had been concerned with the centrality of scripture in worship, a centrality that had been obscured by the inaccessibility of the Latin Vulgate to all but a handful of appropriately trained clergy. Although Anglican eloquence at times had an elitist slant, as in the sermons of John Donne, Lancelot Andrewes, and others of the great preachers at the Stuart court, that eloquence could also be put to democratic uses. The KJV, for example, uses only some 8,000 words, and was therefore presumably comprehensible to the greater number of readers and auditors. (Shakespeare, in contrast, uses over 50,000.)

As the English from the time of James I began to colonize the New World, a transcontinental Anglicanism began to develop, first in North America and then throughout virtually the entire world in the wake of the British Empire. With it, a new relationship between the Church of England, which was inextricably intertwined with the British monarchy and nation, and the developing religious tradition known as Anglicanism began to emerge. When the Protestant Episcopal Church was created in the newly formed United States in the aftermath of the American Revolution, the political structure known as the Church of England was no longer adequate to encompass those who considered themselves Anglican but could not maintain allegiance to the English monarchy that headed that church. As other former colonies attained independence and other autonomous national churches developed as a result, these several churches began gradually to regard themselves as a worldwide Anglican Communion, sharing a common understanding of worship and theology and regarding one another as fully legitimate heirs of a common tradition, but not exerting any authority over one another other than that of mutual respect.

The principal institutional expression of this Communion is the Lambeth Conference. Beginning in 1867, bishops of the various Anglican churches began to assemble at roughly ten-year intervals at Lambeth Palace, the residence of the archbishop of Canterbury (the spiritual head of the Church of England and one of its two archbishops, the other residing at York). Although these conferences were originally conceived as a means of resolving doctrinal disputes in the manner of the early ecumenical councils, they soon evolved into a less authoritative vehicle for bishops of common heritage to gather from around the world and issue statements on matters of common concern, which had no binding character. In some ways, the Communion is similar to the relationships among the Eastern Orthodox churches, who acknowledge one another's validity while maintaining political independence and traditions that vary according to individual patterns of cultural development. Using the same analogy, the archbishop of Canterbury enjoys a role more similar to that of the patriarch of Constantinople than that of the pope: a primacy accorded respect and serving as a symbol of unity, but not carrying any actual power. (Recent controversies within the Anglican Communion, however, have called into question the whole notion of authority within Anglicanism.)

Contemporary Anglicans, including the Episcopal Church in the United States, have traditionally shied away from both highly centralized political control and mandatory statements of belief, finding unity instead in an order of common public worship. The major document that has united Anglicans since the days of Cranmer has been the *Book of Common Prayer,* which is best defined as a collection of liturgical texts. An examination of the contents of the present American edition, which dates from 1977, gives a useful overview of the Episcopal attitude toward the relationship between worship and belief.

At the core of the *Prayer Book,* as it is usually known, are two alternative versions of the Eucharistic liturgy. In earlier versions—the next most recent dated from 1928—only one rite existed, which was not radically dissimilar from the 1559 edition of Queen Elizabeth I's reign. The 1977 version was intended to make the liturgy as accessible as possible to the contemporary worshiper, a concern anticipated by Roman Catholics in Vatican II. Rite I is modeled on the more traditional usage, employing only slightly modernized diction and eliminating phraseology reflecting a Calvinistic interpretation of the human condition (for example, the phrase "miserable offenders"). Rite II, on the other hand, strives vigorously to be contemporary, and includes a version of the Lord's Prayer recast in less formal English. These attempts at contemporaneity have been the occasion of heated protest, and have been in part the grounds for some of the formal divisions in the Episcopal Church in the 1970s and beyond.

In addition to the eucharistic services, which have become the standard for Sunday worship in most Episcopal churches, the *Prayer Book* also provides the texts of morning and evening prayer. Morning prayer was often used in the "low" church tradition on most Sundays, but this is less often the case today. Both services were originally adapted by Cranmer from the daily monastic offices, that is, orders of worship recited by monks and nuns at seven specified intervals in the course of each day. In Anglican usage, these have been reduced to three—the third being *Compline,* said at the very end of the day—and are now used as supplementary public devotions, primarily on weekdays, for the ordinary worshiper. The order of evening prayer is especially notable for its two readings from the Gospel of Luke, the lyrical *Magnificat* ("My soul doth magnify the Lord") and the haunting *Nunc dimittis* ("Lord, now lettest thou thy servant depart in peace").

Another major component of the *Prayer Book* is a set of rituals for sacramental worship other than the Eucharist. This arrangement reflects a particular ambiguity in Anglicanism. On the one hand, traditional Anglican/Episcopal teaching follows Luther and the other Continental reformers in maintaining that there are only two "dominically"—that is, by the Lord Jesus himself—instituted sacraments, Baptism and the Eucharist. On the other hand, the *Prayer Book* provides liturgical texts for the other five sacraments recognized by the Roman Catholic Church as well—Confirmation, Marriage, Penance, Clerical Ordination, and services for the sick and dying. Still other "rites of passage," such as adoption of a child and the burial of the dead, are included. Thus, there may be only two officially recognized sacraments, but the ordinary cycle of liturgical observance goes far beyond those two occasions.

Another section of the *Prayer Book* is entitled "Historical Documents of the Church," a phrasing studiously chosen to indicate a respect for tradition on the one hand and a reticence to promulgate binding creedal positions on the other. These documents include the creeds of the early church, especially the Nicene, which is recited weekly during the eucharistic service; the "Articles of Religion," an American version of the Elizabethan 39 Articles containing controversial theological statements now probably foreign to most Episcopalians; and finally, a document of considerable interest, the Chicago-Lambeth Quadrilateral of 1886–88.

The latter document received its name from its four principal parts, and from its adoption first by the bishops of the American church, meeting in Chicago in 1886, and then by their English counterparts in session at Lambeth Palace two years later. The operative part of this "Quadrilateral" is so brief as to merit quotation in full:

> As inherent parts of this sacred deposit, and therefore as essential to the restoration of unity among the divided branches of Christendom, we account the following, to wit:
>
> 1. The Holy Scriptures of Old and New Testament as the revealed Word of God.
> 2. The Nicene Creed as the sufficient statement of the Christian faith.
> 3. The two Sacraments,—Baptism and the Supper of the Lord,—ministered with unfailing use of Christ's words of institution and of the elements ordained by Him.
> 4. The Historic Episcopate, locally adapted in the methods of its administration to the varying needs of the nations and peoples called of God into the unity of His Church.

There are a number of interesting emphases, as well as omissions, in this statement of the essentials of the Christian faith and life from the Anglican perspective. First, the emphasis on scripture is presumably acceptable to all Christians, although such an emphasis is traditionally more Protestant than Catholic. Second, the focus on the

Nicene Creed, though held in common with Roman Catholics, may actually indicate more of a sympathy with Eastern Orthodoxy, which emphasizes the creeds and councils of the early church as alone authoritative (in contrast with later ecumenical councils and papal decrees acceptable to Western, or Roman, Christendom alone). The addition of any early creed to scriptures, however, is indicative of a distancing from classical Protestantism. The definition of two (and only two) sacraments is, however, a Protestant characteristic, although the inclusion of rituals in the *Prayer Book* corresponding to the other five Roman Catholic sacraments provides a balance in the opposite direction.

Finally, the concept of the "historic episcopate" is a firm departure from Protestantism in favor of both Roman Catholic and Eastern Orthodox theory in the realm of polity. "Historic episcopate" refers to the idea of the apostolic succession of bishops, held by Anglicans in common with those two traditions as well as with Swedish and Baltic Lutherans, "Old Catholics," and a few other small groups that Anglicans recognize as fully valid communions. This is a theological-historical rationale for the "episcopal" form of governance, that is, by bishops, who are thought to derive their authority by virtue of their standing in an unbroken succession from the apostles themselves. The apostles, who were in this theory the original bishops chosen by Jesus himself, laid hands on their chosen successors, who did the same with their successors, and so on without interruption until the present.

Although the *Prayer Book* which also contains the Psalms in their entirety and a set of weekly scripture readings for liturgical use on a three-year cycle, can be used for private devotions, it is primarily a collection of texts intended for public worship. Anglicans tend to shy away from dogmatic statements on various articles of faith, and prefer to allow a wide latitude to individual interpretation and judgment on such questions as what really takes place during the celebration of the Eucharist. Where Anglicans do converge is in their weekly public coming together for common worship, in which mutual participation in the proclamation of the divine word, its interpretation in the sermon, and the reception of the sacrament of the Eucharist are primary. Individual congregations and even dioceses still vary somewhat on the emphasis placed on "high" (sacramental) versus "low" (scripture- and preaching-oriented) liturgical practice, but these differences have eroded considerably in the twentieth century.

Two other aspects of Episcopal/Anglican worship link it to the practices of the other "liturgical churches"—Roman Catholic, Eastern Orthodox, Lutheran—and are worthy of comment. First, Episcopal worship is visual and tactile as well as verbal, especially where a leaning to "high" church practice is present. Clergy wear appropriate and sometimes rather elaborate vestments during the celebration of the sacraments, and others participating in the worship in specific auxiliary roles—acolytes, choir members, chalice bearers, and lectors—usually wear robes or simple vestments as well. Services usually begin and end with a vested procession, and in "high" churches services are often accompanied by incense. All of the senses, in short, are engaged, in consonance with a sacramental theology in which all aspects of creation can become means for the transmission of divine grace.

Secondly, worship is attuned to the cycle of the seasons. As with the other liturgical churches, the year begins with Advent prior to Christmas, and each season dictates appropriately colored vestments and coverings for the altar. Special hymns are appropriate for specific seasons, and Christmas, as in most Christian churches, evokes a very particular set of music and ritual. A distinctively Anglican event is the "Festival of Nine Lessons and Carols," which has its rather recent origins at Cambridge University and is now popular with many other Christian communities during the Christmas season. In this service, scripture passages beginning with Genesis 1 are read in alternation with the singing of traditional Christmas carols, culminating in a brief prayer service. Other seasonal liturgies such as the Easter Vigil can be dramatic and poignant as well.

Though Anglicanism had its origins in the power politics of the Tudor monarchy, it gradually underwent a transformation from purely national church into a worldwide religious community united by a common tradition. That tradition, which informs the Episcopal Church in the United States as well as the other members of the Worldwide Anglican Communion, balances an emphasis on continuity with the church of the apostles with a decentralized approach to contemporary governance. Although it affirms the traditional symbols of Christianity—Bible, creeds, and sacraments—its followers are united not so much by a common theological interpretation of these symbols as by sharing in their use in common worship. Anglicanism's distinctiveness thus cannot be summarized in one distinctive teaching—for example, the Lutheran "justification by faith" or the Reformed "sovereignty of God"—but rather in a balance of approaches to ultimate saving truth: scripture, tradition, and reason.

CHAPTER 10

Calvinism and the Reformed Tradition

Martin Luther's successor as the major leader of Reformation thought and action was Jean Cauvin (1509–64), better known as John Calvin. Born in Noyon in the Picardy region of France, he was intended for a career in the church, and studied both theology and law. After a conversion to the Protestant understanding of Christianity, he was called to Geneva in 1536 as an assistant to the reformer Guillaume Farel. Ousted two years later, he took up work as a minister and teacher in the French city of Strasbourg, only to be recalled by his former Genevan patrons in

1541. For the remainder of his life, he served his French-speaking Swiss constituency as a religious and moral reformer so determined and so effective that he has often been characterized as a theocratic dictator. Under his leadership, Geneva became a model of reforming ideas and ideals that went far beyond Luther's—which seemed, in comparison, highly conservative.

A comparison between the two reformers is instructive in a variety of ways. Where Luther was outgoing and gregarious, and the details of his life became objects of fascination and even legend to his disciples, Calvin's personality had little to do with the appeal of his ideas. Not a great deal has been recorded about his personal life, which seems to have been exemplary if rather lacking in anecdotal incident. Where Luther's conversion had a momentous impact on his life and character, little is known of Calvin's. Where Luther's collected works consist primarily of ad hoc writings such as lectures, sermons, and pamphlets, Calvin's more usually take the form of systematic treatises. His best known work, the *Institutes of the Christian Religion,* which was published in several editions between 1536 and 1560, has an architectonic character, dealing with the entirety of Christian theology in tightly logical form and buttressed throughout with biblical proof texts. Where Luther seemed always on the brink of overflowing, Calvin presented an image of constraint verging on constriction.

To an even greater degree than Luther's, Calvin's thought was firmly rooted in the writings of Augustine of Hippo, especially his *De Civitate Dei* (*The City of God,* 413–26). Where later medieval Catholic theology, such as that of Thomas Aquinas, had emphasized the continuities between the realms of God and his creation, both Augustine and Calvin stressed rather the infinite discontinuity between "nature" and "grace." His message focused on what the twentieth-century theologian H. Richard Niebuhr has called "radical monotheism": the singularity of God as opposed to all other beings, and a fierce opposition to any religious beliefs or practices that compromised that uniqueness and awesome power.

The major symbol of divine power that Calvin found in Augustine was that of predestination. Predestination was rooted in the belief that human nature had from the beginning of time been radically compromised and estranged from God through the Fall, that is, the primordial transgression of Adam and Eve. Original sin, then, was the operative principle in human nature. However, human beings, whether the "first parents" or their innumerable generations of offspring, did not freely decide either to defy or obey God. Rather, their spiritual characters had been decided in God's mind at least since the time of the Fall, when he had for his own inscrutable reasons decreed that some should be spared from the eternal consequences of inevitable sin and that others—by far the larger part—should be damned for ever.

This doctrine of predestination is certainly one of the least palatable ideas of the Reformers to the twentieth-century sensibility, and few hard-core Calvinists remain in America today. Luther himself had accepted the idea, but had not emphasized it because he thought it might discourage his followers and lead them to fatalism. For

Calvin, though, "the sweet and pleasant doctrine of damnation" was not intended
as an expression of despair in humanity. Rather, he saw it as an acknowledgment of
the depravity that seemed to characterize so much of the human condition and, even
more, of the unutterable and unfathomable majesty of God. "Where were you when I
created the whirlwind?" asked God of Job, and Calvin might have echoed this same
marvel that humans should dare to question the wisdom of God's decrees. God was
by definition the measure of all things, and all that he had ordained was by definition
good. To suggest otherwise was to cast serious doubts on one's own spiritual state.

The nature of the doctrine of predestination was succinctly articulated in 1618–19
by the Synod of Dort, an assembly of Calvinist divines held in the heavily Reformed
Netherlands. These worthies had gathered to refute what they saw as the errors of
their colleague, Jacobus Arminius, who taught that humans could play some positive
role in their salvation. The canons, or decrees, of Dort in response to the teachings
of Arminius are easily remembered through the mnemonic device of the TULIP
formula, invoking the flower of their land of origin:

> *Total Depravity*—the complete lack or absence of any merit in the unregenerate
>   human condition unaided by divine grace, and the all-pervasive effects of
>   original sin on the human character;
> *Unconditional Election*—the calling by God of some to salvation without regard
>   to any merits they themselves might possess;
> *Limited Atonement*—the sacrificial death of Jesus on behalf only of those God
>   had chosen for salvation rather than potentially for the whole of humanity;
> *Irresistible Grace*—the inability of those God had elected to salvation to refuse
>   the divine gift of saving power;
> *Perseverance of the Saints*—the inevitable salvation of God's elect even after
>   doubts and lapses during their earthly lives.

Calvin, like Luther, taught that human nature was hopelessly estranged from God by
original sin and unable to fulfill the demands of God's law. Further, both agreed that
salvation took place through divine action, or grace, to which the chosen believer
inevitably responded in faith. Unlike Luther, however, Calvin made no bones about
the reality and significance of predestination. He believed that it would provide
comfort and courage to the elect while reminding the reprobate and unregenerate
of the hopelessness of their condition, thereby frightening them into obedience if
not salvation. Further, where Luther had taught simply that God had predestined
his chosen to salvation and left the rest to their own devices, Calvin affirmed the
notion of "double predestination," that is, God's active consignment of the reprobate
to damnation as well.

Although God and humanity were radically estranged from one another through
original sin, there was nevertheless one means by which the gap between them
could be bridged and salvation for the elect accomplished. This was God's Word,

the theme of the Gospel of John: "In the beginning was the Word, and the Word was with God, and the Word was God" (John 1:1). "The Word became flesh and dwelt among us" (1:14). For Calvin, the Word of God was preeminently to be found both in incarnate form in Jesus Christ and also in scripture, in which God reveals to humanity that which he wishes to be known. Where Luther had doubts about the credibility of some parts of scripture, such as the letter of James, and believed that the Hebrew scriptures had been in many ways superseded by the New Testament, Calvin recognized the authority of both. The proclamation of scripture in preaching thus became central to his notion of worship, and the Law of God as found especially in the Old Testament assumed a much more positive centrality in his thought and practice than was the case with Luther.

Even though Luther had reduced the number of sacraments to the two he had found specifically instituted by Jesus, he did not object to any number of other religious practices that were without explicit scriptural basis, as long as they did not contradict the Word of God. For Calvin, however, all Christian practice had to be based firmly on positive scriptural mandate. Worship, therefore, was to be a manifestation of the Word of God alone. To implement this, he and his followers gutted the churches of Geneva, such as Calvin's own St. Pierre, and destroyed all altars, statues, paintings, and any other sensual compromises with biblical rigor. Music was similarly confined to songs found in the Bible itself, that is, the Psalms. The complex and formal liturgy that Luther had adapted from Latin into German was abandoned in favor of a simple order of prayer, psalm-singing, and especially preaching, in which the Word was proclaimed and expounded. A more elaborate Reformed aesthetic of worship did not emerge until considerably later.

The sacraments, which all of the Reformers had followed Luther in reducing to two, had a somewhat problematic place in Calvin's scheme. Like Luther, he never articulated a very clear and systematic interpretation of the Eucharist (or Lord's Supper). Like Luther also, he rejected the radical interpretation of Huldreich (Ulrich) Zwingli, the religious leader of Zurich, who taught that only the divine nature of Jesus Christ is present when the Lord's Supper is celebrated. Calvin instead maintained that, for the believer, Jesus really became present, although the exact nature of that presence remained somewhat hazy. Similarly, Calvin's retention of the baptism of infants presented some problems in the light of his doctrine of predestination, but he refused to follow the lead of the radical Anabaptists in the Rhine Valley in permitting only the baptism of adult believers.

One area in which Calvin's reforms were decisive and systematic, going far beyond those of Luther, was in his teaching and practice on the nature of the church. Like Luther, he maintained that the church was present where the Word of God was preached and the sacraments properly administered. Unlike Luther, however, he thought that it was possible and necessary to make some provisional judgments on who should be regarded as full and proper members of the church on earth, that is, as "saints." In redefining this latter term, Calvin applied his policy of basing all usage on scriptural precedent with manifest rigor. In medieval and subsequent Roman Catholic usage, the term "saint" has been reserved for those believers who had led lives of heroic piety while on Earth. These had then died and gone directly to heaven, where they enjoyed a special closeness to God, as demonstrated in their ability to work miracles on behalf of those still on earth who invoked their aid in interceding with God. Calvin, however, employed the term with greater fidelity to early Christian usage, and regarded as "saints" all those who appeared to be followers of God's Word here on Earth and were thus presumably among God's elect.

A major problem for Calvin, and later for many of his disciples, was that of how to know for certain who was a saint. This question was vital not only for determining who might be admitted to full membership in the church here on earth but also for anticipating one's eternal destiny. Calvin perhaps wisely disclaimed the ability to answer such questions with any certainty, but did maintain that for practical purposes some guesses might be made. As a result, those who professed a belief in Calvin's interpretation of Christianity, who were willing to partake of the sacraments, and who lived upright lives in conformity with God's law were accepted as full members of the church. Hypocrisy might triumph in this world, but God would not be deceived in the next. The larger question of knowing with certainty whether one was in fact among the elect was never fully answered by Calvin, and became the subject of greater attention among subsequent generations of his followers, especially in the Anglo-American world.

The question of church structure, or polity, also evoked from Calvin a thoroughly biblical response. Where Luther was largely indifferent to the question of how the church should be organized and governed, Calvin believed that the New Testament, especially the Book of Acts, provided a workable model for the present that had the force of prescription. Calvin saw the church administered by four kinds of officials: pastors, who preached the Word and most nearly approximated what today would be regarded as a minister; elders, or laymen charged with maintaining strict moral discipline; doctors, who were the equivalent of seminary professors and were to instruct the clergy; and deacons, who supervised church finances and cared for the poor.

The two former offices were the most important, and involved clergy and laity together in church governance through the participation of the two orders in the *consistory.* Although this body had control of church matters, it also advised the *council,* that is, the civil government of the city of Geneva. The two bodies thus worked together in different spheres at the common task of the proclamation and enforcement of God's Law. This latter was a major emphasis for Calvin, who saw the law as serving several functions: a rule for civil government, a means of impressing sinners with the depravity of their condition, and a guide for the elect, who despite their favored status were still not exempt from the effects of original sin.

This emphasis on God's law gave Calvin's Geneva a distinctive tone in the annals of the early Reformation. Although other states had rigorous moral codes as well, none was as thoroughgoing in its enforcement as the civil and religious elite of Geneva, working hand in glove under Calvin's direction. Neither sinful behavior nor dissent was tolerated, and the heretic Michael Servetus was burned at the stake in 1553. Such intolerance was hardly unknown in both Roman Catholic and other Protestant states—Servetus had previously been imprisoned by the Inquisition—in the bloody era of religious strife which was now beginning. Geneva, however, became an international byword for either admirable rigor or fanatical intolerance.

Geneva also served as a point of dispersal for that set of ideas advocated by Calvin and kindred spirits that collectively became known as the "Reformed Tradition." As had been the case with Luther, "Calvinism" originally had a pejorative cast to it. "Reformed" was the preferred designation for the movement that originally had its focus in several of the Swiss city-states and other cities in the Rhine Valley such as Strasbourg. Geneva and other Reformed outposts also became places of refuge for those of kindred views seeking asylum from persecution, especially during the reign of Queen Mary in England. Rapidly, the Reformed version of Protestant Christianity took on an international character, linked together by scholars and churchmen in continual communication with one another. By the end of the sixteenth century, it had acquired considerable influence in the English universities, where it formed the basis for the movement known as Puritanism within and outside the Church of England; in Scotland, led by John Knox and leading to the formation of the Presbyterian movement; in the German Palatinate; in France, where its followers were known as Huguenots; and in the Netherlands, where it provided an ideological rallying point in the quest for freedom from Catholic Spain. It is from several of these European bases that the Reformed movement found its way to the American colonies.

The legacy of Calvinism has been a lively topic among historians. For earlier generations, Calvin's theocratic rule over Geneva served as a cautionary example of tyranny and intolerance. More recently, many influenced by Max Weber's thought—especially his *Protestant Ethic and the Spirit of Capitalism*—have seen Geneva and its Puritan offspring in old and New England not so much as bulwarks of latter-day medieval repressiveness but rather as the vanguard of modernity. In this light, Calvin's notions of predestination have been interpreted as the forerunners of modern political ideology, endowing believers not with a fatalistic resignation to God's will but rather with a disciplined confidence in the rightness of their cause and the inevitability of its triumph. Calvin's systematic reordering of Geneva's civic life has also been viewed as a forerunner of modern society, in which all aspects of human life are subordinated to the needs of a rationalized, capitalistic economy. These interpretations, needless to say, are controversial and by no means accepted uncritically and universally. Nevertheless, the rapid advance of Calvinism on the Continent and beyond during the sixteenth and seventeenth centuries was certainly one of the most dramatic religious transformations in Western history.

CHAPTER 11

The Radical Reformation and the Anabaptist Tradition

Many Americans regard "Pennsylvania Dutch Country" as a bastion of quaintness, patronized by the tour-bus trade and romanticized in films such as *Witness*. Few of these "Dutch," however, have ancestors from the Netherlands; rather, the term is a misunderstanding of *Deutsch*, that is, German. Not all Pennsylvania Germans, moreover, are bearded or bonneted Amish. Only about a quarter of the German-descended population of the area belong to sectarian groups such as the Amish and Mennonites; the majority belong to "churchly" traditions, mainly Lutherans and Reformed. There is no doubt, though, that the ethos of the area has been profoundly shaped by the overwhelmingly German origins of the population, as manifested in the culture, from its foodways to the German dialects still spoken by many.

The original German emigration to the American colonies began in the late seventeenth century and took southeastern Pennsylvania as its focus. Among its major sources were two loosely constituted religious communities that had arisen in German-speaking areas of the Rhine Valley and the Low Countries, beginning with the coming of the Reformation. The first of these movements was the Radical Reformation, the followers of which were known as Anabaptists. From this religious upheaval came today's Amish and Mennonites. Toward the end of the seventeenth century, a new ferment arose among the now well-established Lutheran and Reformed state churches of the same parts of Europe. This movement of religious renewal became known as Pietism, and had profound repercussions within English-speaking Protestantism as well. Anabaptism especially attracted persecution, and both movements induced a restlessness that found an outlet in William Penn's eagerness for new settlers in his peaceable kingdom in the New World.

The Radical Reformation was a very loosely allied series of movements that began to break out in Switzerland, the Netherlands, and parts of Germany almost immediately following Luther's break with Rome. The Rhine Valley was a primary channel of communication and served as an effective conduit for the rapid spread of all manner of new ideas. Many of these movements came to rapid ends; notable among these was the millennial kingdom declared at Münster in Westphalia in 1534, which was destroyed by the magistrates "with fire and sword."

The Reformation era was hardly one of widespread religious tolerance, and the challenge of the Anabaptists to the dominant principles of church and state was equally nettlesome to Catholic and Reformer. Luther, Calvin, and the pope were all in agreement with the time-honored principle that each political unit should support, and be supported by, one church, however much they might differ as to which church should hold that position. Opposed to this principle, which underlay the "Magisterial Reformation"—religious change through action of the civil ruler—was the "Radical" principle that church and state were fundamentally incompatible, and that Christians therefore should have as little as possible to do with the government. For Catholic and Protestant alike, this amounted not only to heresy but to anarchy, and their fury knew no bounds in putting such dissenters into prison and subjecting them to torture and death.

"Anabaptism" was the name that arose to describe these radical reformers. It characterizes one of their distinctive practices, that is, "rebaptism" or "believer's baptism." Virtually all other Christians were united in their adherence to the baptism of infants, usually by sprinkling, as an affirmation of their potential growth in faith through membership in a Christian family. Scriptural precedent, however, was on the side of the radicals, who were literalists in their recognition that infant baptism simply could not be found in scripture and was therefore illegitimate. From this position, they saw Luther and Calvin as inconsistent in their adherence to what had become a long-standing churchly tradition.

For the Anabaptists, the baptism of adults seemed mandatory in the first place because Jesus himself had been baptized by immersion in the Jordan as an adult. Secondly, believer's baptism made sense as a symbol of the nature of the true church, which the Anabaptists conceived of in good sectarian fashion as a "conventicle"—a voluntarily assembled group of the like-minded—rather than as an aspect of the broader society in which membership was compulsory and was entered into in the unknowing state of infancy. To belong to the church was thus to repudiate rather than to reaffirm one's allegiance to the world, and "worldliness" became a major offense to the sectarian way of life.

A literal reading of the Bible, especially the New Testament, and an attempt to re-create the early Christian community characterized Anabaptist practice. Luther, Calvin, and other Reformers might have affirmed similar purposes, but only the sectarians were prepared to follow out to the end what they saw to be the consequences of such a path, come what may. Worship was the closest point of resemblance to the Reformed tradition developed by their Swiss neighbors, Calvin and Zwingli, though even here the Anabaptists were more venturesome. The Lord's Supper was an act of remembrance rather than a sacrament (that is, a physical conduit for divine grace), and worship was often conducted in barns, houses, or other secular buildings. Foot-washing was a biblical ordinance—an action mandated by Jesus—which had been virtually abandoned by other Christians but which was revived by the Anabaptists. And, of course, baptism itself—usually conducted by immersion in running water, although this practice varied among different groups—was a key symbolic act.

In carrying out their program of a literal following of the teachings of Jesus, the Anabaptists also focused on a few texts ("Go the second mile" and "turn the other cheek," for example) that they interpreted as repudiations of all force and violence and a call to pacifism. They extended this policy of noncompliance to a refusal to cooperate in any way with a civil government whose legitimacy rested on actual or potential force—which included every known government. Therefore most sectarians refused to pay taxes, swear oaths, or, of course, perform military duty. Needless to say, this made them extremely unpopular with every government they encountered, and many joined the ranks of martyrs when they were imprisoned, tortured, and executed for such civil disobedience. Lists and stories of these early martyrs, usually recorded in German, make up a considerable part of the literary heritage of Anabaptism, and are still read by the Amish and their other descendants today.

Although many of the wide variety of sectarian groups that arose in the Rhine Valley during the middle decades of the sixteenth century disappeared or were exterminated, some did survive, often by seeking refuge further to the east. Most present-day Anabaptists can trace their spiritual descent to the followers of Menno Simons (1496–1561), a Dutch Catholic priest who renounced his former faith in 1536 and became a leader of the new movement. Menno Simons helped articulate a theology and lifestyle that incorporated the major themes of the movement and became the rallying point for many Swiss "brethren" (as they preferred to be called) who shared these ideals. The Mennonites of the present day take their name and most of their beliefs and practices from Menno Simons and his group.

The major break within the movement after its early, anarchic days took place over the issue of discipline. Menno Simons himself imposed strict norms on his followers and insisted that those who persisted in breaking the rules should come under a ban and be shunned by their fellows, especially through a refusal to share meals with offenders. Toward the end of the century, in the midst of a growing laxity of communal discipline, Jacob Amman, a Swiss Mennonite leader, came into conflict with others over his similar insistence on a rigorous application of the *Bann und Meidung* ("banning and shunning"). Reconciliation never came, and Amman's followers, who were committed to a strict repudiation of "worldliness" in all ways, came to be called the "Amish."

The Anabaptist tradition was transmitted to the New World chiefly through the migrations of some of its surviving groups—Amish, Hutterites, and Mennonites—first to Pennsylvania, the colony noted for religious liberty, and later to the Midwest and the prairie provinces of Canada. Its fundamental practice of adult or believer's baptism, though, has been taken up by the far more numerous Baptist churches, whose more immediate origin lay in the left wing of English Puritanism. The broader legacy of the Radical Reformation lay in its witness to a rigorous and highly idealistic reading of scripture, which placed a radical call to perfection above all considerations of earthly comfort and even survival. However much one might agree with these premises or not, one can still appreciate the role that these and other "peace churches" have played in America's ongoing debate between the demands of patriotism and the dictates of a standard of conduct higher than that demanded by any earthly power.

PART II

EARLY AMERICA: EUROPEANS, COLONIALS, AND TRADITIONAL PEOPLES BEFORE THE REVOLUTION

The American colonies were from their beginnings one of the most elaborate laboratories ever devised for the intermixing of peoples, cultures, religions, and social patterns. Native Americans were themselves a highly complex blend of peoples who had already changed and developed over the centuries through continual interaction. Their exposure to hostile colonists and (more or less) benevolent missionaries forced their adjustment to yet another set of cultures—English Protestant and French and Spanish Catholic—which resulted in a wide variety of responses, few if any of which were very successful in the long run. African slaves, who were also the bearers of traditional oral cultures, underwent even more forcible contact with European traditions. These slaves and their free descendants, however, eventually developed a highly creative and long-lasting synthesis of old and new, the story of which will be dealt with as a whole in the next section.

The original European settlers of what would eventually become the United States reflected every possible variation of relationships between religion and society, or church and state, that had emerged in the Old World during the Reformation era. English Anglicans, French and Spanish Catholics, Dutch Reformed, and Swedish Lutherans all represented state-supported, "established" churches, usually involved in their governments' imperial ambitions. British Puritans and Quakers and Scotch-Irish Presbyterians were highly vocal English-speaking minorities who attained considerable power once transplanted to American shores. The fragmented nature of the colonies and the weak hold that England and its established church maintained

during the seventeenth century made it possible for a wide variety of patterns of relationships between religion and society to develop. This would provide an important
context for the ultimate settlement that had to be forged after independence. Also,
it worked subtle, or not-so-subtle, changes in the character of the colonial religious
communities. New England Puritanism, for example, changed, in Perry Miller's
memorable phrase, from a reformation into an administration.

Although it seemed for a while that the fate of North America was up for grabs
among the major imperial powers—England, France, and Spain—only the first of
these that would prevail in the longer run. Roman Catholics, therefore, had no real
chance for hegemony and had to learn to live as a minority community in both the
United States and Canada. Finally, the Dutch and Swedes were so small in number
that any hopes they may have entertained for the acquisition of power rapidly came
to naught.

Still other groups came to the New World seeking not power but refuge. Sephardic
Jews had been forced to flee their ancestral homes in Spain and Portugal in fear of
their very lives, and settled into a comfortable and prosperous, though somewhat
isolated, existence in the seaports of the Atlantic coast. The variety of groups that
are frequently, and mistakenly, lumped together as "Pennsylvania Dutch" represent
still another experience. Some, such as German-speaking Lutherans and Reformed,
were accustomed to establishment status in the Old World. Mennonites, Amish,
and other sectarian groups, however, wanted no part of worldly power. Rather, they
shared the pacific ideals of the Friends (Quakers) who welcomed and even recruited
them to share life in the Pennsylvania colony.

This is not to say that all of these wildly diverse communities lived together in
warmth and harmony. The Puritans, it is said, fell first upon their knees and then
upon the aborigines. Puritans hanged Quakers; Maryland Anglicans overthrew
their Catholic rulers. Aspirations to hegemony and fears of persecution died hard.
By 1700, though, no one church exercised complete dominion even at the regional
level. The competing claims of the various churches and the changing policies of
the British government eventually resulted in a standoff, where ultimate English
domination was becoming assured but in which no one religious community would
either reign supreme or be hounded into extinction. Thus, of necessity, old-world
attitudes became modified over time, and with them the character of each community. The Great Awakening and then the struggle for independence further involved
these peoples with one another in events that transcended religious particularism.
Sometimes enthusiastically, sometimes reluctantly, often unknowingly, all of these
peoples were learning how to be Americans.

Colonial Anglicans

In the beginning, Anglicanism was the established and dominant religion of the English colonies of North America, which extended along the eastern coast of the continent from what are now known as the Maritime Provinces of Canada to the Caribbean islands of Barbados, Bermuda, and Jamaica. Inroads of dissent gradually became established in Plymouth, Rhode Island, Pennsylvania, and other colonies, but even those Puritans led by John Winthrop, who founded the formidable Massachusetts Bay Colony in 1630, still maintained that they were at least technically part of the Church of England. During the entirety of the colonial period, the bishop of London was responsible for the spiritual welfare of the entirety of the Anglican colonists, and the establishment of a bishop on American shores was a possibility dreaded by those concerned with English encroachments on colonial rights. Church and empire marched together, and an uneasiness about the appropriateness of both reached a crescendo as the Revolution began to loom.

The first Anglican service on American soil was held under makeshift circumstances in 1607 in Captain John Smith's Jamestown. During the seventeenth century, the Church of England became the established church of all of the southern colonies and several counties in New York. However, its actual position—as opposed to its nominal dominance—was one of weakness and disorganization. Major problems included the absence of a resident bishop; the low number and quality of clergy; the scattered population; and competition from both Puritan and Presbyterian Calvinists, on the one hand, and the popular Methodists and Baptists on the other, especially following the Great Awakening of the 1740s. In Virginia, which was the strongest bastion of colonial Anglicanism, parishes were organized and churches established around a plantation society, in which wealthy planters served as wardens and vestrymen (lay officials) dominating a weak and scattered clergy. From the beginning, the tone of Virginia Anglicanism was heavily tinged with Puritanism, foreshadowing the "low" church or evangelical ethos that would continue to dominate the Episcopal Church in the Tidewater in later times.

During the eighteenth century, a number of developments bolstered Anglican fortunes to a degree. The founding of the Society for the Propagation of the Gospel in Foreign Parts (SPG) by Thomas Bray in 1701 improved the number and quality of clergy somewhat, and its sister organization, the Society for Promoting Christian Knowledge (1698), also helped firm up the tenor of colonial religious life. The rechartering of the Massachusetts Bay Colony in 1691 following the Glorious Revolution in England was part of a series of events that, for the first time, brought a royal governor to New England shores, and the establishment of King's Chapel in Boston

in 1688 represented a modest Anglican inroad into Puritan dominance. The ordination of Pennsylvania Quaker George Keith to the Anglican ministry in 1700 and the
conversion of several Yale tutors and Connecticut Congregationalist clergy in 1722
established the groundwork for the extension of Anglicanism among the influential
classes in those areas as well.

Any potentially widespread popularity of the Established Church, however, was
undermined on both religious and political grounds. The Great Awakening—America's first religious revival—began in the late 1730s, and a new approach to Christianity
based on emotional conversion spread in its wake. This Awakening, however, had
virtually no positive impact on colonial Anglicanism. George Whitefield, the "Grand
Itinerant" who turned the Awakening into an event that involved the whole Atlantic
seaboard, was a priest of the Church of England. Despite his Anglican orders and
Calvinist theology, though, he was much more closely aligned with his friend John
Wesley in his approach to religion as something to be experienced intensely and
personally. Wesley himself remained an Anglican priest to his dying day, but both
his official and informal representatives in the colonies (following his own dismal
experiences as a missionary in Georgia in 1735–37) worked to spread Methodism
as an entirely new brand of Christianity rather than as a reform movement within
Anglicanism. Therefore, although the Church of England had an institutional base
already established throughout the whole of the colonies and especially in the South
by the time of the Awakening, it was the Methodists, Baptists, and "New Light" Congregationalists and Presbyterians (that is, supporters of the revival) who attracted
countless followers among the many unchurched scattered along the frontier.

On the political side, fear of the establishment of an Anglican bishop on American
shores was one of the complex of actual and potential grievances that began to unite
the colonists after the Awakening had started to instill a sense of their commonality
among them. The Calvinist Puritans of New England and their middle-colony counterparts were opposed to further inroads on religious as well as political grounds,
and helped create a rhetoric of revolution that pictured the whole English apparatus
of church and state as part and parcel of an oppressive design that was set on doing
the will of the Antichrist. On the other hand, Anglicans such as George Washington, who served as a vestryman in Alexandria, and the more theoretically minded
Thomas Jefferson and James Madison, both William and Mary alumni, opposed
religious establishment on "enlightened" grounds that equated it with tyranny and
obscurantism. When the Revolution did come a majority of laity favored the colonial
cause, and Anglican clergy were divided in their loyalties. Many clergy were Tory in
sympathy and fled to the more congenial Nova Scotia and to England itself.

Anglicanism in the colonial and early national periods thus possessed an oddly
ambiguous status. On the one hand, it was the established church in the southern
half of the Atlantic seaboard, and commanded significant prestige in the northern
colonies as well through its association with the English government and many

families of wealth and power. Historians have demonstrated that its constituency was not entirely "genteel," and that the "all sorts and conditions of men" invoked in its *Book of Common Prayer* were represented within its ranks. Nevertheless, such imposing monuments as Boston's King's Chapel, Christ Church in Philadelphia, and Bruton Parish Church in Williamsburg remain as material evidence of the wealth, taste, and prestige it could muster.

On the other hand, its associations with the higher levels of society did not always serve it well. Although George Washington and Thomas Jefferson, for example, were nurtured in the established faith of the mother country, the depth of their ongoing religious attachment to that faith can most charitably be described as questionable, especially in Jefferson's case. The rationalism that dominated much of eighteenth-century Anglican thought and was reflected in its neoclassical architecture coincided well with the spirit that informed the framers of the Constitution, but also eroded their allegiance to formal belief. However, the close association with all things English, which had been the source of much of the church's prestige in the colonial era, also aroused resentments, at first from those who were excluded from the power elite—as in, especially, Virginia—and later from those patriots exasperated with what they saw as British oppression. By the time of Independence, the result was a church cut off from new currents at both popular and elite levels; the task of rebuilding that awaited it was formidable indeed.

CHAPTER 13

New England Puritans

Like the names of many religious groups, the term *Puritan* originated as a term of abuse in Elizabethan England for those who advocated what their enemies saw as an excess of rigor in religious observance. During the reign of Queen Mary (1553–58), many leaders of the Church of England fled to the European continent to avoid either execution or a forcible conversion to Roman Catholic allegiance, and became imbued with the ideas of Calvin and his contemporaries while in exile. After the independence of the English church had been reestablished with the accession of Elizabeth I to the throne in 1558, these exiles began to return to their homeland, and Continental scholars with decidedly nontraditional ideas began to teach at Oxford and Cambridge. These latter seedbeds of theological ferment became the nurseries of a movement for religious reform, often along the lines of Calvin's Geneva, that went beyond the earlier English political break with Rome, which had left worship, theology, and morals largely unaffected.

Scholars continue to argue as to exactly which and how many English people during Elizabeth's reign could be deemed radical enough to deserve the label "Puritan," and whether these really saw themselves as belonging to a distinctive movement. Elizabeth's drive for a loose uniformity of religious behavior made open attacks on the episcopal structure of the Church of England difficult, and not many went as far as calling for the abolition of bishops. Most of the reform-minded, whether clergy, laity, or even bishops, were more concerned with bringing the actual religious practice of the English people into conformity with the lofty standards that they regarded as mandated by scripture (as interpreted by John Calvin). Their complaints about the status quo were numerous: clergy were insufficiently rigorous in their piety and morals, as well as lax in their doctrine; the liturgy as it was celebrated was encumbered with too much of the ceremony of medieval Catholic practice; and the laity lacked discipline and seriousness, preferring to spend the Sabbath in profane recreations rather than in scriptural study and spiritual contemplation.

As the Tudor dynasty yielded to the Stuart with the accession of James VI of Scotland as James I of England in 1603, the party that its opponents had been deriding as "Puritans" began to become more publicly assertive. James would have none of it, denied their petitions, and on occasion had their more vocal advocates imprisoned and mutilated. Some dissenters left in despair for the Calvinist Netherlands or, with longer-run consequences, the nearly uninhabited shores of New England. Those who remained experienced even greater frustration in the early years of James's successor, Charles I (reigned 1625–49). Under Charles, the Church of England polarized still further under the leadership of William Laud, whom Charles appointed archbishop of Canterbury in 1633. Laud carried the banner for the "Arminian" party, that is, those who rejected Calvinist theology in favor of that latter-day Dutch opponent of the Calvinists, Jacobus Arminius. Closer to the Catholic than the Reformed tradition in his views on liturgy as well as theology and polity, Laud worked vigorously to suppress the Puritan party and earned their lasting enmity in return.

The Puritans had the last laugh, at least in the short run. Parliament was coming under the control of the newer mercantile social and economic interests who were transforming English life during the seventeenth century, and these entrepreneurs were strongly attracted by the Puritan call to the disciplined life. Charles governed ineptly, angering many English by his marriage to the Roman Catholic Henrietta Maria of France. When tensions became too strong, he dissolved Parliament in 1629 and attempted to rule without it. War with the Scots and financial difficulties forced him to reconvene it in 1640, with consequences that were not to his liking. Civil war broke out between king and Parliament in 1642, with Charles and his Archbishop Laud ultimately suffering defeat, arrest, and execution. The "Interregnum" which followed under the leadership of Oliver Cromwell and, briefly, his son Richard, was marked by radical experiments in church reorganization and the rise of a bewildering variety of sects, of which only the Society of Friends (Quakers) survived. After years of confusion ranging from dictatorship to anarchy, the English recalled the Stuart dynasty to the throne in the person of Charles II in 1660. From that time, the various forces of religious dissent that included Puritanism were relegated, with Roman Catholics, to a limited role in English life, and the Church of England with its bishops returned to its established status.

While this momentous and sometimes violent drama was playing out in England, a number of Puritans began to think that the future of their vision of Christianity lay across the sea in the colonies the English were beginning to plant along the North Atlantic coast. The first of these groups was among the more radical of the English Puritans in their refusal to acknowledge the legitimacy of the Church of England itself. These "Pilgrims," or "separating Puritans," were committed to a model of church order in which each congregation constituted an independent church with no need of bishops. Ealier, they had left English soil to try their luck in the congenially Calvinist society of the Netherlands. After a few years of life in Leyden, they grew restless in a culture that was religiously appropriate but still alien, and returned briefly to England to ready themselves for a more permanent venture into the unknown.

The subsequent story of these Pilgrims has become an inextricable part of American mythology, even though their role in the actual establishment of the "New England way" was minor in comparison with their larger and more influential neighbor, the Massachusetts Bay Colony. Being first, however, has always been paramount in the popular vision of history, and the Pilgrims were indeed the first to organize a substantive colony on New England shores. Actually, their arrival there was something of a mistake: since they were supposed to sail to Virginia. The *Mayflower*, for whatever reasons, touched land instead at the tip of Cape Cod (now Provincetown) in November of 1620. After some weeks of reconnoitering, they finally alighted at Plymouth, on the mainland to the south of what is now Boston, and named it after their point of departure in England. Even before debarking, however, they entered into the famed "Mayflower Compact," banding themselves together "for the glory of God, and advancement of the Christian faith, and honor of our king and country." (Spelling and punctuation here and in later quotations is modernized.)

Governed for decades and immortalized by William Bradford (1590–1657) in his *History of Plymouth Plantation* (pub. 1856), the "Pilgrim Colony" never grew beyond a few thousand in population, chronically lacked clergy, and ultimately was absorbed by the Massachusetts Bay Colony in 1684. This latter venture was led by the prosperous lawyer John Winthrop (1588–1649), who even before the arrival of his party of "nonseparating" Puritans in 1630 set forth on board their ship the *Arbella* his vision of their enterprise in resounding biblical cadences:

> The Lord will be our God and delight to dwell among us as His own people and will command a blessing upon us in all our ways, so that we shall see much more of His wisdom, power, goodness, and truth than formerly we have been acquainted with.

We shall find that the God of Israel is among us when ten of us shall be able to resist
a thousand of our enemies: when He shall make us a praise and glory, that men shall
say of succeeding plantations: the Lord make it like that of New England. For we must
consider that we shall be as a city upon a hill, the eyes of all people are upon us; so that
if we shall deal falsely with our God in this work we have undertaken and so cause Him
to withdraw His present help from us, we shall be made a story and byword through
the world.

The Massachusetts Bay venture, with its capital at Boston, differed from its predecessor and neighbor at Plymouth in refusing to repudiate completely the legitimacy
of the Church of England (hence their label, "nonseparating"). Geographical isolation from the mother country, however, made this difference moot. Eventually four
"Holy Commonwealths," differing in detail of organization but united in common
purpose, arose in New England. By the mid-1630s, the Connecticut colony arose
out of a migration from Newtown (now Cambridge) led by Thomas Hooker. This
venture eventually merged in 1662 with a settlement at Saye-Brook (Saybrook) on
Long Island Sound and the nearby colony founded at New Haven in 1643 by Theophilus Eaton and John Davenport. These original colonial establishments, by the
end of the century combined into two, were counterpointed by neighboring Rhode
Island—the "sewer" of New England in the minds of the Puritans. "Rhode Island
and Providence Plantations" was founded by and accommodated dissidents such as
Roger Williams, who objected to what they saw as overly close ties between church
and state in the original colonies.

As Winthrop's lay sermon on the *Arbella* proclaimed, the Puritan "errand into the
wilderness" of New England was no ordinary commercial overseas venture. Rather,
it was a systematic attempt with only minor variations among these Holy Commonwealths to emulate the example of Calvin's Geneva in a setting virtually free of
the constraints of the English religio-political establishment and even of the fabric
of medieval churches. Although the New England Puritans made some sporadic
attempts to evangelize the Algonkians and other aboriginal settlers, little of perma-
nence came of these efforts, and most of the Indians either died of European-borne
diseases or were pushed inexorably westward. The Atlantic colonial economy linked
New England with Britain, the West Indies, and even Africa in a system of reciprocal
trade, and lavish natural resources, especially timber, offset the barrenness of the
ground and the harshness of the climate. Although the earliest English settlers faced
stern adversities, such as those chronicled in Bradford's account of Plymouth, the
longer-range future was filled with opportunities for both religious experimentation
and commercial prosperity.

The genius of Calvin's Geneva had lain in an attempt to order simultaneously
all aspects of life—the individual, the church, the political, and the social orders—
according to biblical dictates and prototypes. The New England Puritans took this
plan as their starting point and worked very consciously from the theology of Calvin

as interpreted through his Dutch and English followers, preeminently the Cambridge divines William Ames and William Perkins. Calvin, again, believed that he could find in scripture clear precedents for the organization of both church and state, respectively in the description of the earliest Christian community in the Book of Acts and other New Testament texts and in the history of Israel in the Old Testament. Not all aspects of the latter, such as the cultic and dietary prescriptions of Leviticus, were to be accepted literally, but the general idea of a civil and ecclesiastical polity working in tandem according to God's ordinances and for God's greater glory was common to both Geneva and New England.

What was specifically added to the ideological framework of the New England attempt to establish a series of Holy Commonwealths was the notion of *covenant.* This "federal theology" (from Latin *foedus,* "covenant") had roots in European and British Calvinist thought, as well as in medieval contract theory. It was in New England that the notion, which itself was derived from the Hebrew scriptures, was systematically applied to virtually all areas of life. Through the Covenant of Redemption, the saving act of Jesus made possible the release of the saints from the eternal penalty for original sin. Through the Covenant of Grace, originally established by God with Abraham, the individual saint entered into a personal relationship with God through which his or her salvation was brought about. Similarly, various social relationships were interpreted in the covenantal framework. New churches were established through a covenanting between God and a select group of saints; marriage was no longer regarded as a sacrament but as a covenant; and, at the more complex levels of social organization, each of the Holy Commonwealths was regarded as gaining its legitimacy through a collective covenanting with God.

At the individual level, these Puritans were intensely preoccupied with their spiritual state. One of the conundrums of Calvinism was the question of how to know whether one was in fact among the elect, and the New England "saints" pursued the question relentlessly. The topic was common in the sermons of the day, and countless diaries recorded minutely the daily interior religious experiences of the devout. Gradually, in Edmund Morgan's phrase, a "morphology of conversion" developed, a description of the distinct phases that characterized the religious development of many believers, which could then be used as a guide for those concerned with their own condition. Much of the voluminous theological literature of early New England dealt with the question of "preparation," that is, whether an individual not yet sure of election could do anything actively to prepare the way for God's saving work, or whether he or she could only wait for God to take the initiative as he chose.

The question of knowing whether one was among God's elect had social as well as personal dimensions, because the New England Puritans determined to go a step beyond Geneva in tightening the requirements for full church membership. As opposed to the episcopal polity of the Church of England and the presbyterian system that had developed in Scotland on the Genevan plan, the churches of New England were relentlessly congregational, acknowledging no authority beyond the individual congregation other than God and scripture. As colonization expanded beyond the original Boston area, one of the first acts undertaken by the founders of a new settlement would be the establishment of a church, for which seven adult "saints" who had persuaded one another of their probable election were necessary as a nucleus. These then covenanted with one another and with God to establish a church, and could then proceed to call a minister, admit other members, and get on with their appointed tasks. This and other salient details of church governance were spelled out in the "Cambridge Platform," drawn up by a synod, or gathering, of colonial clergy in 1648 for the purpose of articulating authoritatively the "New England way."

Whereas in Geneva the primary criteria for recognition as a probable saint were external, a new and more profound requirement for full membership rapidly developed in New England. Candidates desiring this status presented themselves to the minister and a select group of church members and delivered an account of their internal spiritual development. If they satisfied their examiners that their experience was in conformity with the Puritan "morphology of conversion," and that they were neither hypocrites nor simply misinformed, they could assume the privileges reserved for "visible saints." These included the taking of communion, voting on congregational affairs, and ordinarily, if male, receiving enfranchisement in civic matters as well. However, this examination was not conducted with excessive rigor and a "judgment of charity" was supposed to be rendered in the favor of the candidate when the evidence was not conclusive.

At the broader level of civil government, the New England commonwealths were conceived, as in Geneva, as dedicated to God's glory through the enforcement of his law. Although they have frequently been characterized as "theocracies," that is, governed by God through his human agents, these commonwealths excluded the clergy from the ranks of the civil authorities. John Winthrop, who served as governor of the Massachusetts Bay Colony for most of the years between his arrival and death, was never ordained to the clergy, despite his eloquent sermon aboard the *Arbella*. Similarly, prominent clergy such as Cotton Mather, the third generation of his family in New England, exercised influence through advice and example but not through the holding of any civil office. Church and state worked together for a common goal, but did not employ the same personnel.

This unity of purpose that underlay the church-state alliance was central to the "New England way," and was manifested in a variety of other social and cultural forms as well. The role of education, for example, was eloquently evoked in *New England's First Fruits,* a promotional pamphlet published in 1643 to create a favorable impression of the New England experiment in the mother country:

> After God had carried us safe to New England, and we had builded our houses, provided necessaries for our livelihood, reared convenient places for God's worship, and

settled the civil government, one of the next things we longed for and looked after was to advance Learning and perpetuate it to posterity, dreading to leave an illiterate ministry to the churches when our present ministers shall lie in the dust. And as we were thinking and consulting how to effect this great work, it pleased God to stir up the heart of one Mr. Harvard (a godly gentleman, and a lover of learning, there living amongst us) to give the one half of his estate (it being in all about 1700 £.) towards the erecting of a college, and all his library. After him another gave 300 £., others after them cast in more, and the public hand of the state added the rest. The college was, by common consent, appointed to be at Cambridge (a place very pleasant and accommodate) and is called (according to the name of the first founder) Harvard College.

Harvard was originally founded for the training of both a learned ministry—an ongoing emphasis in the Reformed tradition—and a literate corps of civil leaders, nurtured on the traditional classical curriculum of the English universities with a good dose of Puritan divinity. The New England colonies also took the lead in promoting nearly universal literacy for the citizenry at large, on the premise that God's saints needed to be able to read if they were to encounter God's word directly in scripture. The *New England Primer* was a widely used text, which, in such verses as the following, at once taught the alphabet and elementary moral, theological, and biblical lore:

> In Adam's Fall,
> We sinned all.
> Job feels the rod
> Yet blesses God.
> Zaccheus he
> Did climb a tree
> His Lord to see.

During the nineteenth century, this Puritan drive for education was continued by more liberal spokesmen such as Horace Mann, the Massachusetts education secretary who crusaded successfully for free and universal secondary education. Education at all levels seemed to follow naturally from the Reformed impulse, and the plethora of colleges founded throughout the entire northern half of the nation from colonial days to the Civil War era was a tangible legacy of the Puritans and their Calvinist allies.

Two areas of Puritan practice that have embroiled subsequent historians in ongoing controversy have been politics and economics. The New England towns of the colonial era, though by no means permitting universal suffrage, did enfranchise considerably more adult males than had been the case in England. Town meetings through which local government was conducted by direct citizen participation were authentic examples of the affinities between Puritanism and democracy. On the other hand, the Puritans looked backward to a medieval worldview in their political philosophy. This was based on the premise, as articulated early in John Winthrop's

Arbella sermon, that God had assigned different estates to men and women in this life, designating some to govern and others to serve. Wealth and social rank helped determine status in a variety of aspects of New England life, from the allocation of land in new settlements to the arrangement of pews at meetinghouses.

Economics was another realm of cultural life in which the Janus-faced quality of Puritanism was apparent. On the one hand, the Puritan commonwealths exercised a careful control over prices and perpetuated the medieval distrust of usury, or lending money at interest. On the other, economic success of a distinctively modern sort was hardly a rarity in colonial New England. One of the most stimulating and controversial documents of modern social science is Max Weber's *The Protestant Ethic and the Spirit of Capitalism* (1904–5), in which the German sociologist argued that an "elective affinity" existed between Puritanism and the "spirit" of the nascent economy of capitalism that was emerging in northern Europe and its American extensions from the sixteenth through the eighteenth centuries. Weber argued that Puritanism fostered capitalism indirectly by encouraging the development of a personality type especially suited to this novel form of economic life, where self-discipline, indefinitely delayed gratification, rational calculation, and systematic reinvestment of surplus funds were the virtues most conducive to success. In addition to self-discipline and Luther's idea of labor for God's glory in a this-worldly vocation or calling, the preoccupation with one's ultimate destiny that Calvinism fostered but never satisfactorily answered gave capitalism yet another religious legitimation. According to Weber, the desire for assurance that one was indeed one of God's elect could receive an indirect satisfaction from external evidences of worldly success, which could be interpreted as signs of divine favor. This syndrome, known most commonly as the "Protestant (or Puritan) work ethic," has certainly continued in secularized form over the centuries as an intrinsic part of American culture—as manifested, for example, in the "Yuppie" drive for success in business and the professions during the 1980s. Although social historians continue to dispute the accuracy of Weber's argument, it remains a richly suggestive insight into the role that Puritan culture played in shaping a latter-day American character and society.

In the realm of literary and artistic culture, the religious core of Puritan society was everywhere apparent and is best illustrated in the character of worship itself. Its setting was not the church, a form of building consciously rejected by the Puritans as implying that God could somehow be confined in earthly space. Rather, they devised a new architectural form, the meetinghouse, based in part on the model of medieval English market-halls rather than on the Gothic churches of the Anglican heritage. These buildings looked like large private houses, forts, or other secular buildings. They were used initially for any number of civil as well as religious functions, because they were not considered sacred in themselves. Seating was allocated according to social rank, with the most prominent families in box pews near the pulpit, and servants and occasionally slaves in the galleries.

The interior of the meetinghouse was dominated by the pulpit, from which the minister proclaimed and expounded the word of God in lengthy sermons during the Sabbath—the Hebrew term the Puritans substituted for the traditional "Sunday"—and occasionally during days of fast or thanksgiving. The sermon was supposed to be clear exposition and application of scripture, without the elaborate literary embellishment characteristic of much contemporary fashionable English preaching. Similarly, the meetinghouse itself was austerely furnished, with no pictorial representations of religious themes (again in the Hebrew tradition of iconoclasm) or ornament, other than perhaps some skillful pulpit carving. Both sermon and meetinghouse reflected the Puritan aesthetic ideal known as the "plain style," that is, an emphasis on a functional simplicity that would promote the execution of a task without sensual distraction from the glory of God himself. Church music was similarly austere: it was restricted to biblical psalms translated into simple, often jangling English verse and sung to equally simple tunes. Most literature other than sermons was in the form of theological discourse and occasionally gifted poetry such as that by Anne Bradstreet and Edward Taylor also followed the dictates of this plain style.

Although the phrase "Puritan synthesis" has frequently been used to evoke this cultural unity that followed from a powerfully articulated set of religious goals, the Puritans were not very successful in maintaining this culture in very pure form for very long. From the beginning, dissent jarred their attempts at a harmonious uniformity. Such challengers of the established order such as Roger Williams, Anne Hutchinson, and various parties of Quaker evangelists were either exiled to Rhode Island, as was the fate of the first two, or variously imprisoned, whipped, or even hanged after repeated offenses, as happened to some of the Friends' representatives.

Anne Hutchinson (1591–1643?) is an especially interesting study in dissent, because a major part of her offense lay in being a powerfully articulate woman in a patriarchal society. However, her teaching itself, which attracted a considerable following among both sexes, was corrosive enough in its own implications. Against the Puritan claim that only a probable knowledge of divine election of an individual was possible, and that this knowledge was available only within the context of the church, Hutchinson instead maintained that God's chosen knew their own status certainly when God enlightened them and were able to discern their fellow saints through intuitive knowledge as well. If this *antinomian* (that is, "against law") heresy had prevailed, the role of the institutional church and its male clergy would have been drastically undermined, and the notion of a godly commonwealth would have collapsed. Hutchinson, who remained unrepentant and defiant through her trial, was not surprisingly consigned to exile.

The first generation was able to deal forcefully and, from its own viewpoint, effectively with such dissidence, which could be blamed on a handful of troublemakers. Before long, though, the clergy were beginning to deliver ritual denunciations of their fellow saints for systematic breaches of the covenant, which, it was argued, led to God's punishment of his "New Israel" through epidemics, Indian attacks, droughts, famines, and various other manifestations of divine displeasure. These denunciations soon took on a predictable, generic form that later came to be known as the "jeremiad," after the prophet Jeremiah, whose condemnations of the earlier Israel provided their prototype. Typically they were delivered by prominent clergy who had been appointed to deliver the "election sermon" on the day that the lower house of the General Court (legislature) met to elect the upper. In such a public setting, these preachers provided an official interpretation of New England's mission, in which the bad news of collective transgressions underscored the underlying good news that God still cared for New England sufficiently to carry on his controversy with it. This theme of collective mission, even when expressed negatively, remained a powerful motif in the self-understanding not only of New England but of the subsequent American nation as well, an ongoing interpretation of Winthrop's image of the "city set on a hill."

Other problems, which in retrospect seem almost inevitable in a society based on such lofty ideals, made these jeremiads and their idealization of the earlier, founding generation seem plausible. One problem that began to chafe after some decades had passed was the question of the admission of the children and then the grandchildren of the original saints to church membership if they had not passed the mandatory test of successfully narrating an account of their religious awakening. The second generation of New Englanders, perhaps because of the relaxation of the pressures and excitements that had inspired their parents, were experiencing fewer and fewer conversions, even though they by and large remained loyal to the "New England way." They were thus relegated to second-class status and could not receive communion or otherwise exercise the rights of full members.

The question became acute when this second generation began to increase and multiply, and to present their children for baptism. As had been the case in Geneva, infant baptism had been retained as an affirmation of the workings of divine grace through the family, even though the theological arguments for it were rather shaky when viewed from the standpoint of predestination. In the early years of New England, the privilege of baptism had been reserved for the children of saints, on the premise that their offspring were more likely than most to be elected as well. Clearly, a major dilemma was at hand, because the formally unconverted now wanted their children to be brought within the familial covenant that baptism symbolized.

A compromise was achieved at a 1662 assembly of divines, which acquired the name of "the Half-Way Synod" because of its results. Here it was proposed that the children of unconverted churchgoers who were otherwise in good standing might be baptized as well. This clearly was a relaxing of the rigor that had characterized the earlier New England conception of church membership. Edmund Morgan has interpreted it as an acknowledgment of the social force of what he has aptly called "Puritan tribalism," that is, the triumph of family loyalty over religious principle.

However, since Puritan polity was rigorously congregational, the synod's decision was merely advisory, and many congregations never adopted it.

By the end of the seventeenth century, a wide variety of events contributed to and reflected the breakdown of the "New England way," revealing it as a lofty but unrealizable ideal. Economic prosperity was widespread though not universal, and many latter-day emigrants were attracted less by the vision of the city on a hill than the economic main chance. (A New Yorker cartoon has one Puritan on shipboard saying to another, "In the short run, my goal is religious freedom, but in the long run I'd like to get into real estate.") More directly corrosive of Puritan dominance was the revocation of the Massachusetts Bay charter in 1684 and its rechartering in 1691 according to imperial rather than religious considerations. A royal governor brought with him a retinue loyal to the Church of England, and Anglican houses of worship such as Christ Church and King's Chapel began to introduce liturgical, theological, and architectural variety into the Boston religious scene. In part as a result, the old meetinghouse form was soon abandoned, and eighteenth-century Puritan houses of worship began to boast steeples and spires. The franchise was now openly granted on the basis of property ownership rather than sainthood. Although Puritan leaders such as Cotton Mather remained influential, their power was seriously diluted. The witchcraft craze and subsequent executions that swept Salem Village in 1692, involving Mather among many others of all ranks, was at least as much an expression of rapid social, economic, and political change and its resulting confusion, as the work of Satan in the colonists' midst.

The events of the Great Awakening beginning in the 1730s further eroded what still remained of the New England "synthesis" of church and state working together for the honor and glory of God, as did increasing religious pluralism and secularization. Three New England states retained an established church, now called "Congregational" rather than "Puritan," for some time after independence: Connecticut (1818), New Hampshire (1819), and Massachusetts (1833). By this time, other churches, especially the liturgical Episcopal and the liberal Unitarian, vied with the Congregationalists for the allegiance of the wealthy and educated, while Jeffersonian democracy and a host of popular denominations undercut the prestige of the Federalists as the political expression of the older Puritan "oligarchy." The term *Puritan* had disappeared as anything but a historical reference by the early nineteenth century, and was more beloved by genealogists than theologians.

Puritanism, however, was by no means spent as a cultural force. Many of the issues raised by latter-day Puritans such as Jonathan Edwards preoccupied later theologians and exerted a particular fascination for intellectuals again in the mid-twentieth century. The broader impulse toward education at all levels continued to be manifest in the burgeoning of schools and colleges of all descriptions in subsequent decades, although the rationale had shifted after independence to the preparation of citizens for an active role in a democratic society. The Puritan concern with moral government also helped shape the political cultures of the northern tier of states to which New Englanders migrated in the nineteenth century. The Puritan ideal of the disciplined individual striving for evidence of election through hard work in a vocation can still be seen in secularized form in the ongoing American "dream of success." The notion of New England as a people specially chosen by God, like Israel of old, similarly became part of a later American rhetoric of nationalism, as exhibited in presidential inaugural addresses to the present day. Even Puritan aesthetics continue to manifest themselves in periodic protests against excessive ornament and ostentatious display, in favor of a simple, utilitarian "plain style" expressed in later years in the slogan that "form follows function."

Puritanism, in short, died long ago as an organized religious impulse, and the New England churches and congregations that had once espoused it are now usually affiliated either with the liberal United Church of Christ or the ultra-liberal Unitarian-Universalist Association. In terms broader than the institutional and theological, however, Puritanism transcended that demise and became in secularized form both Americanized and a force for Americanization. The earliest Puritans had considered themselves to be protesters within the Church of England, seeking a restoration of biblical Christianity. After going into colonial exile, they began to interpret themselves as a New Israel, temporarily on an "errand" into the "waste and howling wilderness" that was New England. Gradually, however, they came to identify with that land that had once seemed so hostile and forbidding, and ceased to think of themselves simply as English saints in exile. Judge Samuel Sewall, a contemporary of Increase Mather, expressed this sentiment vividly when writing of Plum Island off the coast of Massachusetts in his *Phaenomena* of 1697:

> As long as Plum Island shall faithfully keep the commanded post, notwithstanding all the hectoring words and hard blows of the proud and boisterous ocean; as long as any salmon or sturgeon shall swim in the streams of Merrimac, or any perch or pickerel in Crane Pond; as long as the seafowl shall know the time of their coming, and not neglect seasonably to visit the places of their acquaintance; as long as any cattle shall be fed with the grass growing in the meadows, which do humbly bow down themselves before Turkey Hill; as long as any sheep shall walk upon Old Town Hills, and shall from thence pleasantly look down upon the River Parker, and the fruitful marshes lying beneath; as long as any free and harmless doves shall find a white oak, or other tree within the township, to perch, or feed, or build a careless nest upon, and shall voluntarily present themselves to perform the office of gleaners after barley harvest; as long as nature shall not grow old and dote, but shall constantly remember to give the rows of Indian corn their education, by pairs; so long shall Christians be born there, and being made first meet, shall from thence be translated, to be made partakers of the inheritance of the saints in light.

From these lyrical cadences, it is not far to "I love thy rocks and rills, / Thy woods and templed hills" in "My Country, 'tis of Thee" (Samuel Francis Smith, Baptist student at Andover Theological Seminary, 1832), and then to "O beautiful for spacious skies, for amber waves of grain, / For purple mountain majesties, above the fruited plain" (by Katherine Lee Bates [Congregationalist], a professor of English at Wellesley College, in 1893).

As would Irish Catholics, Russian Jews, Swedish Lutherans, and Pakistani Muslims in subsequent generations, the Puritans were becoming Americans.

CHAPTER 14

Presbyterians and Other Reformed Churches

The term *Presbyterian* describes one of several types of polity, or church organization and governance, associated with the Reformed tradition. The term *presbyter* itself is derived from a Greek word for the officials of the earliest Christian churches in Palestine, and has been variously translated as "priest" or "elder." In Calvin's attempt to use the New Testament as a specific model for the church at Geneva, he devised a fourfold ministry: pastors, elders, teachers, and deacons. Of these four offices, the most important were pastors and elders, who periodically met with their counterparts from other congregations as a *consistory*. This sharing of authority between what were essentially clergy (pastors) and laity (elders), both within each separate church and in groups that constituted higher levels of authority, was the nucleus of the presbyterian system as it would be implemented in Scotland and later in America.

It is with Scotland especially that the origins of Presbyterianism as a distinctive strain within the Calvinist or Reformed tradition lie. Here, presbyterian polity took shape in the sixteenth-century reform movements led by John Knox, and has lasted to the present in virtually unchanged form and terminology. The grassroots unit is the *session*, consisting of the clergy and lay elders of an individual congregation. These officials meet at appointed times with similar representatives of other congregations within a specific geographical area to constitute a *presbytery*, which ordains clergy, deals with disciplinary matters, and generally performs collectively those duties that a bishop would carry out in an episcopal system. A group of presbyteries similarly sends elected delegates to a *synod*, that is, a judicial body with authority over a larger region. Finally, a Presbyterian church as a whole—that is, the religious unit that includes an entire nation or similar large political unit—is governed by a *General Assembly* of clerical and lay delegates similarly elected by the groups below it.

These terms may vary somewhat from place to place—for example, Dutch Reformed churches use *coetus* or *classis* instead of *presbytery*—but the idea of a succession of clerical and lay delegates forming hierarchically arranged groups with increasing degrees of authority remains constant.

Although Presbyterianism in the longer run has become a distinctively American denomination on this side of the Atlantic, its heritage has always been as firmly rooted in Scotland as that of Lutherans is inseparable from Germany and Scandinavia. Although its founder, John Knox (1513?-72), is remembered as heroic in his almost single-handed transformation of the Scottish nation during his lifetime, he seems to have shared in his mentor Calvin's lack of personal charisma. The satiric poet Dorothy Parker once observed that "those whose love is thin and wise / May view John Knox in Paradise."

Where pre-Reformation Scotland has been described as something of a Celtic backwater, still torn apart by warring clans, Knox's work in naturalizing the ideals of Geneva on its soil produced a sternly disciplined nation that for a century would be at odds with neighboring England over the future of its religious establishment. A Church of Scotland organized on presbyterian principles was first constituted in 1560, but its success in resisting the attempts of the English to impose an episcopal system varied greatly over the years. When James VI of Scotland became king of England as well in 1603, he and the later Stuart dynasty had little sympathy with the party of Knox's successors and their English Puritan allies. The obstinacy of both parties was an important contributing factor to the outbreak of the English Civil War and the ultimate defeat and execution of Charles I in the 1640s. The principal mode of Scottish organization against what they perceived as English tyranny was the promulgation of successive *covenants,* or pacts, of which the most significant was the "Solemn League and Covenant" entered into with the antiroyalist English "Long" Parliament in 1643. It was not until after the final overthrow of the House of Stuart in the "Glorious Revolution" of 1688 that the Kirk (Church) of Scotland became permanently organized on presbyterian lines.

During this tumultuous century, the Scottish Kirk was also active in defining its doctrines, which were firmly based on the predestinarian teachings of Calvin. Most notable among these documents, which subsequent generations of Presbyterians on both sides of the Atlantic have looked to as a source of religious authority over the decades, has been the Westminster Confession of 1646. Prepared by order of Parliament during the Civil War after the adoption of the Solemn League and Covenant, it consisted of thirty-three chapters that dealt with the entirety of Christian belief from a Calvinist perspective. In addition to affirming predestination, it especially stressed the identity of the Christian Sunday with the Jewish Sabbath, and called for the strictest observance of that institution.

The New England Puritans of the seventeenth century were clearly very similar to the Scottish Presbyterians in their general approach to religion, and by the early eighteenth century the churches of the Connecticut colonies had developed a "consociational" system of governance, affirmed in the Saybrook Platform of 1708, that differed from the presbyterian pattern only in detail. As Scots began to emigrate to the Middle Colonies around that time, their contact with Puritans in Long Island and northern New Jersey was generally congenial, because they scarcely differed on matters of doctrine and polity. It was this contact that formed the nucleus of one of the major factions within the American Presbyterianism that began to emerge during the early eighteenth century.

The first organizer of the scattered congregations that endorsed a presbyterian system of polity was Francis Makemie (mah-KEM-mee) (1658–1708), who served as a missionary in Virginia, North Carolina, and Barbados before settling into a ministry at Rehoboth, Maryland, in 1698. In 1706 he brought together six other similarly inclined ministers to form the first American presbytery at Philadelphia. The following year he was imprisoned briefly in New York for preaching without a license, but won both acquittal for himself and a victory for religious nonconformity in the trial that ensued.

Though of Scottish extraction, Makemie, like many of his compatriots, was born not in Scotland but in northern Ireland, or Ulster. This Scottish presence in Ireland was the result of a colonization policy undertaken by James I to resettle Protestants, mainly from the lowlands of Scotland, on lands confiscated from rebellious Irish leaders. Later British policy, however, worked against the economic and religious interests of Presbyterian as well as Catholic Celts, and a mass migration of "Scotch-Irish," as they came to be known, began shortly after the turn of the eighteenth century. Most of these emigrants were poor but fiercely independent, and provided much of the stock that would produce the typical American frontiersman of later years. Before the move across the Cumberland Gap into Tennessee and Kentucky following independence, the first generations of Scotch-Irish typically arrived in Pennsylvania and rapidly fanned out into that colony's western regions, as well as southward into what is now Virginia, West Virginia, and North Carolina. Although many were only loosely schooled in what by now had become their traditional faith and would become eager converts to the Baptist, Methodist, and other aggressive new frontier denominations, they nevertheless provided one of the major ethnic components of the colonial Presbyterian presence.

It was in fact the loose division of early colonial Presbyterians into a primarily English area in the north and a Scottish–Scotch-Irish zone further south that set the scene for the conflicts that were to divide that community, often bitterly, during the prerevolutionary decades. The issues were versions of those that have over the years plagued almost every religious group that has achieved a critical mass of membership and with it a reasonable diversity of background and outlook. The "Scottish" party to the south was generally inclined toward a rigorous traditionalism and viewed the Westminster Confession as the ultimate test of doctrinal purity. The

"English" party, as those from New England and New York might be called, were less attached to this and similar creeds, and instead regarded the Bible itself as the final standard of orthodoxy. The mutual acceptance of the "Adopting Act" of 1729 marked a temporary peace, with the victory going to the latter, but the underlying issues of rigor and authority still festered.

The second phase of this conflict focused on a new movement that provided much of the impetus for the religious revival that would sweep the entire Atlantic seaboard: the Great Awakening of the 1730s and 1740s. Like other branches of the Reformed tradition, Presbyterian preaching traditionally had focused on the exposition of doctrine, that is, on theological teaching. In the Middle Colonies, however, a remarkable family named Tennent arose that led the way in promoting a new form of preaching, aimed at the emotions rather than the intellect and designed not to instruct but to bring about an emotional awakening or conversion. William Tennent Sr. (1673?–1746) was the patriarch of this line of evangelical preachers, and he prepared his sons and other followers for their calling at a makeshift seminary in Neshaminy, Pennsylvania, that became known as the "Log College." His son Gilbert (1703–64) especially gained a reputation as a firebrand of the later Awakening and alienated many "Old Side" clergy with his attack on their alleged lack of vital faith in his notorious sermon, "The Danger of an Unconverted Ministry." The Tennents and their partisans emerged as the "New Side" of the colonial Presbyterians as the Awakening led to polarization. In 1741 they organized the dissident New Brunswick Presbytery, which in 1745 joined with other prorevival groups to form the Synod of New York. As in earlier disputes, the question of whether Scottish (Old Side) or New England (New Side) influence would prevail was a major issue in this family quarrel.

A reconciliation took place in 1758 after revival fires had cooled somewhat, and the dissident groups united to form the Synod of New York and Philadelphia. The issue of doctrinal rigor versus revival preaching was by no means resolved, but it had retreated into a state of dormancy until frontier expansion began again in earnest in the decades following independence. Two major events now drew attention from the reunited Presbyterians. First, the question of higher education had always loomed large in this tradition, as it did for their New England counterparts. The Reformed ministry was predicated on an educated clergy who could study the Bible in the original languages, and a vehicle for their training in the New World was highly desired. The result, largely the work of New Side initiative, was the chartering under public auspices in 1746 of the College of New Jersey, later to be known as Princeton. Although its earliest presidents, including the renowned New England theologian Jonathan Edwards, seemed to fall under some sort of curse and die shortly after taking office, stability finally came with the arrival of the Scotsman John Witherspoon (1723–94) in 1768, the beginning of a twenty-six-year administration.

Witherspoon served as a reconciling influence among the factions in this tradition, although he himself was of rather conservative bent. His espousal of the Scottish Common Sense philosophy made Princeton a major force in the development of Reformed theology in America during the nineteenth century, and underscored the emphasis in the Presbyterian tradition on the importance of the intellect. At least as important, however, was Witherspoon's role as a delegate to the Continental Congress, where he became the only clergyman to sign the Declaration of Independence. It is something of a paradox in the Reformed tradition that it contained on the one hand a stress on the legitimacy of civil government as a God-given means of enforcing the divine law, while at the same time providing an ongoing support for rebellion against what its advocates perceived as usurpations of that law by established governments. Witherspoon was therefore typical of American Presbyterians, as well as other Reformed churches such as the Puritan Congregationalists in New England, in taking the lead in the ideological battle that ultimately erupted into revolution—a pattern already familiar in Scotland, where resistance to English tyranny had become virtually a way of life.

A related characteristic of Scottish American Presbyterianism was its contentiousness, the willingness of its members to split and form new groupings on matters of principle. At the time of independence, Presbyterians were outnumbered only by Congregationalists. Most of them were organized into four synods consisting of sixteen presbyteries, which combined in 1788 to form the General Assembly of the Presbyterian Church in the United States of America (PCUSA). However, two groups of Scottish derivation demonstrated their traditional principled resistance in refusing to join this new national church. One group was known as Covenanters, who in 1733 had emerged among Scots who had earlier refused to acknowledge the legitimacy of the restored Stuart monarchy. A second group of dissidents were the Seceders, who came together in Scotland in 1743 to resist the practice of clergy being appointed and supported by lay patrons. Many of these American Covenanters and Seceders recognized their commonality and united in 1782 to form the Associate Reformed Presbyterian Synod (later Church). This group divided in 1822 over sectional issues; the northern branch ultimately merged into today's PCUSA, whereas the southern division remains an independent denomination.

The colonial Presbyterian culture of the eighteenth century contained within itself two seeds for future development. On the one hand, Presbyterianism, with its leadership and educational centers based along the eastern seaboard, would emerge as one of the most elite of the new nation's denominations. Although Presbyterians shared many theological emphases with other evangelical groups such as the Baptists and Methodists, they were closer to the Episcopalians in social status, and were characterized especially by the old Reformed emphasis on divine and human law and on social and religious order. On the other hand, much of the most fertile soil for recruitment by popular movements and new denominations from the Great Awakening on were the Scotch-Irish, inexorably moving southward and westward, away from the colonial centers of religious culture and authority. Here was a people fiercely committed to individual liberty of choice—of lifestyle and of belief. They provided the matrix for much of the popular religious enthusiasm that character-ized American development during much of the nineteenth century, especially in the South and West—a story that continues later with that of the Second Great Awakening.

The religious impulse unleashed in the Swiss city-states of the sixteenth century had a profound impact in the English-speaking world, but was by no means confined to that world. Calvinism spread rapidly into the Netherlands, where it became the dominant faith; to France, where it underwent both popularity and persecution until the latter finally prevailed; and throughout central Europe, especially in what are now Germany and Hungary, where it became entrenched in various states as a local majority or national minority of some consequence. Immigrants from all of these areas came to America and brought with them their own variants on the common theme. In most cases, assimilation into the English-speaking Protestant community was more or less rapid and thorough, with one significant exception: the Dutch.

In the British Isles, another Celtic people, the Welsh, became converted in large numbers to a latter-day variant of the Reformed faith known as Calvinistic Method-ism during the eighteenth century. Welsh speakers who came to the farming and mining centers of Pennsylvania and Ohio in the nineteenth century established their own churches, but subsequent generations who spoke mainly English were usually absorbed into the Presbyterian fold. In 1920, most of the congregations of the Welsh Calvinistic Methodist Church formally merged with the Presbyterian Church in the United States, another casualty (or beneficiary) of the Americanization process.

In France, Calvin's native land, his followers became known for obscure reasons as Huguenots (HEW-geh-notts or UE-gay-nose). First organized formally in 1559, they rapidly gained powerful adherents and enemies, and several thousand were murdered in the St. Bartholomew's Day Massacre of 1572. They were granted toleration under the Edict of Nantes in 1598, but their situation was reversed in 1685 by Louis XIV. Some 160,000 were forced into exile, many of whom found refuge in the vicinities of Boston, New York, and Charleston. Although many were commercially success-ful, few managed to maintain any coherent sense of community for long, and most were rapidly absorbed into Anglican, Dutch Reformed, or other congregations.

Among German speakers, the Reformed impulse was most successful in the Palati-nate in the Rhineland, from which many emigrants began to arrive in Pennsylvania in the 1720s and 1730s. Here they mingled with other Germans of any number of other varieties of Christianity, who collectively became known, erroneously, as "Pennsylva-nia Dutch" (a misunderstanding of *Deutsch*, that is, German). In general, the German Reformed in America were more conscious of being German than Reformed; lacking a strong central organization, they were inclined toward cooperative arrangements with other German-speaking churches, especially Lutheran. The first synod of the German Reformed Church was formally organized in Lancaster, Pennsylvania, in

1793, and dropped the "German" from the official name in 1869. The denomination increased about tenfold from its original fifteen thousand members during the nineteenth century. In the twentieth century, the erosion of older ethnic and even theological divisions resulted in a series of ecumenical unions. The Reformed Church absorbed most of what had previously been the Hungarian Reformed Church in 1924, and in 1934 united with the Evangelical Synod of North America, a German Lutheran–Reformed body on the Prussian model, in which doctrinal differences were subordinated to political unity. The resultant merged group was known as the Evangelical and Reformed Church. This new denomination then united in 1957 with the Congregational Christian Churches—the direct descendants of many of the old New England Puritan congregations—to form the United Church of Christ.

German Reformed churches in America never grew very large. Throughout their history they failed to develop a clear identity, and eventually lost their distinctiveness completely as the German language lost its place in American life. However, this community was influential beyond its numbers in its impact on American religious thought. During the middle and later nineteenth century, the tiny seminary at Mercersburg in central Pennsylvania (since removed to Lancaster) attracted two extraordinary professors, John Williamson Nevin (1803–66) and Swiss-born Philip Schaff (1819–93), whose work became known collectively as the "Mercersburg Theology." This school of thought (with two exponents) constituted a "high" church movement within the evangelical Protestantism of the nineteenth century, and stressed the role of the historical church and its sacraments over the dominant revivalism of the era. Later, in the twentieth century, the brothers Reinhold and H.Richard Niebuhr, nurtured at Eden Theological Seminary in St. Louis, became two of the most important voices within the "Neo-Orthodox" movement in American religious thought.

The Dutch have been the one community among the American Reformed that most strenuously and successfully resisted complete Americanization. These sturdy entrepreneurs first came to the Atlantic seaboard in the 1610s, with settlements in the New York City and Albany areas that early came under the control of the Dutch West India Company. The first Dutch Reformed church was established in New Amsterdam (New York City) in 1628, and others were soon founded in the Hudson and Mohawk Valleys, Long Island, and northern New Jersey. These early Dutch settlers were intolerant of other religious groups and managed to retain their privileged status, with an accompanying right to tax support, on an equal basis with the Church of England even after the English acquired the New York colony in 1664. The most notable personage in the colonial Dutch Reformed community was Theodore Jacob Frelinghuysen (1692–1748?), who helped lay the foundations for the Great Awakening through his preaching in New Jersey's Raritan Valley.

Until 1747, the year in which Frelinghuysen and his followers obtained permission to establish a semi-independent *coetus* (that is, presbytery), both Dutch and German Reformed churches in America were largely under the control of the *classis* of

Amsterdam. The subsequent development of the Dutch community followed the pattern of the Presbyterians and other groups. A charter was obtained in 1766 for Queen's College in New Jersey (later known, under secular auspices, as Rutgers); a seminary, still very much extant, was founded in New Brunswick, New Jersey, in 1784; and in 1792, the Reformed Protestant Dutch Church took its formal place in the roster of independent American denominations. (The name was changed to its present form, the Reformed Church of America [RCA], in 1867.)

The New York/New Jersey area has remained to the present day as a major geographical center of the Dutch Reformed community in America, and the RCA still maintains its denominational headquarters in Manhattan. Later immigration during the nineteenth century resulted in sizeable concentrations of Dutch settlement in central Iowa, where Central College is located at Pella, parts of California, and the upper Midwest, especially the western part of Michigan's lower peninsula. In the latter region, Hope College and Western Theological Seminary, both sponsored by the RCA, are located in Holland, and Calvin College, maintained by the Christian Reformed Church, is in nearby Grand Rapids, which is also that denomination's headquarters. The heavily Dutch heritage of the local culture is evident in the proliferation of churches of both denominations, the annual tulip festival in Holland, and bumper stickers that inform the outsider that "If You're Not Dutch, You're Not Much."

The coexistence of two Dutch Reformed denominations, with corresponding educational institutions, in western Michigan is the result of a schism in the Netherlands that had important repercussions in the United States. In 1834 a group objecting to the Dutch government's taking control of the church organized a protest movement that was brought to the United States shortly thereafter by emigrants leaving the Netherlands for economic as well as religious reasons. These schismatics attracted native Dutch Americans who had become discontent with the Reformed Church in America, and led to the formation, beginning in 1857, of what would eventually be known as the Christian Reformed Church (CRC).

Although both groups share a common heritage of Reformed belief and worship and Dutch culture, their division reflects more than anything a differential rate of Americanization. By the twentieth century, the RCA was not distinguishable in most ways from the main stream of American Presbyterianism. The CRC, however, continued to use the Dutch language well into the twentieth century, and objected to what its adherents regarded as the excessive liberalism of RCA practice. Many traditions in America, such as the Campbellites, have experienced similar divisions; probably the most direct analogue in this case, however, is with the Lutheran community, now divided between the more mainstream Evangelical Lutheran Church in America (ELCA) and the extremely conservative Missouri Synod. Like the latter, the CRC insists on purity of doctrine; the importance of creeds or confessions as adequate embodiments of scriptural truths; an emphasis on propositional theology, that is, a highly logical approach to religious truth as capable of being embodied in doctrinal statements; a strict moral code; and a separate school system to socialize the young into a community firmly committed to maintaining its distance from the larger society. Despite these differences, the two groups share many features of their common tradition, including a presbyterian form of polity, and are not radically different in size. (In 2005, RCA membership stood at 270,000, and CRC 187,000; both figures reflect a continuing decline from previous decades.)

The character and fortunes of these various Reformed communities are somewhat puzzling to the outsider, in part because of the low visibility on the American scene. The contrast here is noticeable with other non-English-speaking Protestant groups, such as the Lutherans and Amish/Mennonites, which have been considerably, and usually deliberately, slower in their capitulation to the forces of Americanization. One factor at work was the prior presence of English-speaking religious groups with a similar theological outlook, for example, the Congregationalists and Presbyterians, who provided a ready model for imitation or a vehicle for merger to Continental newcomers.

Another, less tangible factor might lie in the "elective affinities" between the Reformed tradition and the modernization process noted by Max Weber in his *Protestant Ethic and the Spirit of Capitalism* and the work of his followers. For many non-English-speaking groups, assimilation into America was retarded, for better or worse, by a worldview and value system that was at odds with many aspects of American culture. (The Old Order Amish, of course, are among the most radical examples of this.) With the exception of the conservative wing of the Dutch, however, most adherents of Reformed theology were comfortable enough with the modern world, including its American version, to lack interest in maintaining the old ways in the new world. In the case of the Christian Reformed Church, the motives seem to have been a combination of religious and cultural, analogous in different ways to German Catholics on one hand and fundamentalists on the other. To preserve a theology and corresponding worldview significantly at odds with that of the dominant culture, the distance provided by the maintenance of a foreign language was most useful. As a result, the cultural pluralism of the nation was enhanced for several generations by a community that still took Europe rather than America as its point of reference for its own identity. On the whole, however, the cultural transition from the Old World to the new seems to have been fostered more often than impeded by the presence of the Reformed tradition.

The Society of Friends (Quakers)

New religious movements are most likely to arise during periods of social and cultural unrest, and mid-seventeenth-century England had unrest aplenty. Much of the tension that led to the outbreak of civil war and the defeat and execution of Charles I lay in the squaring off between Anglican supporters of the Stuarts—the older landed aristocracy—and the Puritan reformers and their Parliamentary allies, who predominated among the newly wealthy London merchants. Social and economic change thus combined with religious conflict to the point of outright revolution. From 1640, when war finally broke out between king and Parliament, through the beheading of Charles I and the governing of England by the formidable Puritan, Oliver Cromwell, to the overthrow of Cromwell's ineffectual son Richard and the restoration of the Stuart Charles II to the throne—the people of England were caught in the middle of the most bewildering variety of religious options ever to be thrown at them.

Out of this ferment grew any number of usually short-lived movements that can best be called *sects*—intensely fervent small groups of dedicated believers who have fastened on some unusual set of beliefs and practices to distinguish themselves from the ordinary run of Christians. Among those that arose in England at midcentury were the Ranters, a group of pantheists (those who believe the divine can be found throughout all things) who rejected clergy, church, and Bible; the Diggers, who advocated communal ownership of land on religious grounds; the Muggletonians, whose founders claimed to be the "two witnesses" of the Book of Revelation; and the Fifth Monarchy Men, who believed that the Millennium—the return of Jesus and his subsequent thousand-year reign—was about to be inaugurated. Just as all bets were off as to who was actually in charge of England, so were traditional sources of religious authority—Bible and Church—cast into radical doubt by so many contradictory contending claimants to truth.

In the midst of this confusion arose many "seekers." A seeker was a person who did not claim to know the truth but was actively engaged in its pursuit. George Fox (1624–91), the son of a weaver, was a seeker whose spiritual quest attracted a great deal more interest than most. Beginning in 1643, Fox grew impatient with external forms of religion and began to teach that the truth could be found most purely within each individual. He soon attracted followers, who in their early days together in the movement shared the "enthusiasm"—as highly demonstrative, unconventional religious behavior was then called—apparent in Fox's own journal account for 1651:

> And as I was one time walking in a close with several Friends I lifted up my head and I espied three steeple-house spires. They struck at my life and I asked Friends what

they were, and they said, Lichfield. The word of the Lord came to me thither I might go, so, being come to the house we were going to I bid friends that were with me walk into the house from me; and they did and as soon as they were gone (for I said nothing to them whither I would go) I went over hedge and ditch till I came within a mile of Lichfield. When I came into a great field where there were shepherds keeping their sheep, I was commanded of the Lord to pull off my shoes of a sudden; and I stood still, and the word of the Lord was like a fire in me; and being winter, I untied my shoes and put them off; and when I had done I was commanded to give them to the shepherds and was to charge them to let no one have them except they paid for them. And the poor shepherds trembled and were astonished.

And I went about a mile till I came into the town, and as soon as I came within the town the word of the Lord came unto me again to cry, "Woe unto the bloody city of Lichfield!"; so I went up and down the streets crying, "Woe unto the bloody city of Lichfield!" Being market day I went into the market place and went up and down in several places of it and made stands, crying, "Woe unto the bloody city of Lichfield!", and no one touched me nor laid hands on me. As I went down the town there ran like a channel of blood down the streets, and the market place was like a pool of blood. (from Jessmyn West, ed., *The Quaker Reader*, 63–64)

The rhetoric and actions here are clearly those of a prophet, and Fox and his followers—known as "Friends"—became notorious for such extravagant behavior as disrupting church services by running through them naked. Many Friends were imprisoned, and not a few died in England's fetid jails.

The core belief of the "Friendly Persuasion" was that within each human being dwells an "Inward Light" or "Inner Light." This light, which is the Holy Spirit, or spirit of Christ, is the ultimate authority in matters of religious truth, and is to be cultivated and followed by all Friends in the context of their meetings for worship. These meetings were starkly different from ordinary church services. In traditional form, a Quaker meeting for worship—the "first-day meeting"—was conducted in an austere meetinghouse in an unornamented room, with men and women seated separately. (Early Friends rejected the usual weekday names, such as Sunday, as pagan.) Although there was no ordained ministry, officers known as "elders," "overseers," and "recorded ministers" developed to provide administrative continuity. Silence prevailed at meetings until a member felt the promptings of the Inner Light, which would be expressed in a ritualized sort of chanting. Business meetings were held monthly and were also conducted in silence, with no leader as such. Various members would speak according to the promptings of the Light until a consensus was reached; this would be recorded by a clerk. As the movement spread, regional, quarterly, and yearly meetings, attended by delegates from the monthly meetings within their purviews, eventually developed at London and then in the American colonies.

Similar, for instance, to many Anabaptist groups on the Continent, the Friends followed the sectarian pattern in distancing themselves from what they regarded as the ungodly ways of secular society. They were—and many still are—firm pacifists and refuse to engage in any activity involving violence. In the early days in England, their refusal to recognize distinctions among different classes of people manifested itself in a variety of ways. A familiar example was their use of the familiar *thou* and *thee* to all, even those toward whom convention dictated that the more formal and respectful *you* be employed. (This usage continued even after *thou* and *thee* had become archaic.) This refusal to make distinctions resulted in frequent problems with the authorities. Friends refused to remove their hats in court, nor would they swear oaths. When told to tremble before the majesty of the law, as the story has it, they replied that the judge himself ought to tremble before God. This kind of exchange allegedly gave rise to the nickname of "Quakers" which, like many such derogatory nicknames, eventually came to be accepted by the group itself as an informal alternative to its more proper designation, "the Society of Friends."

Because of their refusal to conform to not only religious but civil norms, the early Quakers who escaped overt persecution were nevertheless reduced to second-class citizenship in England. The military and the church, of course, were not options; nor were university educations or the professions, which required religious conformity. The main avenue of worldly endeavor that remained was business. To this the Friends took naturally, and their reputation for complete reliability, together with a strenuous work ethic and a disciplined, frugal lifestyle, resulted in considerable financial success. Much of their gains was redirected into the group for the relief of the suffering of those who were persecuted, and for other philanthropic efforts for which the Friends became well known.

One convert to the Friendly cause was William Penn (1644–1718), the son of a prominent naval officer to whom the Stuart government owed considerable money. After Penn became a convert to the Quaker persuasion, he prevailed on Charles II to settle his debts to the Penn family with a large land grant in the middle Atlantic colonies. This colony was called Pennsylvania, "Penn's woods," and its capital was Philadelphia, "the city of brotherly love." It was here in the freedom of the New World that Fox, Penn, and their followers had their main chance to create, in true American fashion, their own version of a Christian utopia, quite literally from the ground up. Even in its physical arrangements, Philadelphia still reflects this attempt, with a grid of broad tree-lined avenues at its center designed to provide a spacious setting in which a society based on peace and harmony might take root and blossom.

In its founder's own words, Pennsylvania was intended from the beginning as "an example and standard . . . set up to the nations." Its instrument of government included such untraditional provisions as legal marriage without clergy, arbitrators or peacemakers attached to the courts, affirmations instead of oaths, and no militia. Although the franchise—among the broadest in the colonies—was restricted to Christians, freedom of worship was extended to all. In keeping with the Quaker view that the Inner Light potentially dwelt in everyone, Penn's dealings with the Indians were notable for their probity—as efforts not only to avoid conflict but to avoid the exploitation and misunderstanding from which conflict arises. Although various domestic and foreign upheavals interfered with Pennsylvania's immediate achievement of a utopian condition, the founder's plans did achieve several decades of a genuine alternative to the "establishments of religion" and accompanying intolerance that were the norm for most of the colonies.

Penn did not intend his foundation to be restricted only to Friends, but actively sought other colonists of similar inclination through recruiting trips into the areas of the Rhine Valley where sectarians abounded. This resulted in the beginning of the emigration of the "Pennsylvania Dutch" (that is, Germans) into the counties near Philadelphia soon after the colony was launched. The Friends, however, achieved rapid prosperity for reasons similar to those that prevailed in England, and they also kept a benevolent but firm hold on the Assembly, which endeavored to reach decisions by general consent. Problems arose when the British government began to assess taxes to finance the French and Indian wars that erupted periodically through the early and middle eighteenth century. Although the Friends were for some time willing to equivocate and assign moneys "for the King's use," they eventually had to come to terms with the compromises imposed on their principles, and in 1756 finally yielded control of the colonial government to others. (Similar dilemmas were faced by Quakers in Rhode Island, where they constituted a significant segment of the population and frequently held high office, including the governorship.) In Philadelphia, however, their social and financial power remained strong for generations, and some colonial Quaker families continue to enjoy eminence to the present day.

The decades surrounding independence brought about numerous changes within the Quaker community. The outbreak of the Revolution posed a severe challenge to their pacifist ways, and many suffered considerably at the hands of patriots who suspected their loyalty when they refused to take up arms. Another test of principle was raised in the work of the New Jersey Friend John Woolman (1720–72), who argued widely and effectively that slaveholding was contrary to basic Quaker beliefs. Woolman was instrumental in persuading many slaveholding Friends to grant freedom to their human "property," and also played a role in Pennsylvania's early abolition of the "peculiar institution." Many Quakers played active roles in the formation of the first antislavery societies in the new nation, and Benjamin Lundy, the Quaker editor of *The Genius of Universal Emancipation,* helped shape the consciousness of his sometime assistant William Lloyd Garrison, the future editor of *The Liberator.*

Ferment and change were also affecting deeply the very core of American Quakerdom at Philadelphia in the realm of religious practice. Although they had renounced direct political power, many Philadelphia Quaker families had become very prosperous and had established an interlocking set of dynasties through intermarriage. As Frederick Tolles pointed out in his classic study, *Meeting House and Counting House,* these great families remained faithful to the old customs of plain dress, but the quality of the material that went into that dress grew progressively finer as their fortunes accumulated.

As the distinction between these well-to-do urban friends and their poorer rural counterparts increased, the kind of split that frequently affects sectarian groups that have become established on a permanent basis happened. Elias Hicks (1748–1830) arose as a spokesman for the rural group, but his protest was couched in theological rather than socioeconomic terms. Hicks regarded himself as a restorationist, determined to bring Quaker practice back into line with that which prevailed in the age of Fox and Penn. Hicks thus emphasized the Inner Light tradition, which he believed was being compromised by the "churchly" emphasis of the Philadelphia elite on more traditional Christian symbols such as the Bible and Jesus. These latter had been affirmed in 1806 by the Philadelphia Yearly Meeting, whose leadership had come into a cooperative relationship with the Protestant community in many benevolent as well as business activities.

This disagreement resulted in 1827 in an overt split of the Quaker community into "Orthodox" and "Hicksite" factions. This was only the beginning, however. Quakers, like most other Americans, were following the frontier westward, and many Friends who had settled in North Carolina and other parts of the South were beginning to head toward the Midwest as they became alienated from slaveholding society. Richmond, Indiana, near the Ohio border, emerged as a focus for these frontier Quakers, and their contact with the Methodists in particular made them receptive to the evangelical style that their Philadelphia counterparts had already absorbed to a degree too great for the likings of the Hicksites. Before long, Quakers in Indiana and the surrounding region could scarcely be distinguished from their Protestant neighbors in their use of revival preaching, hymns, churchlike buildings, and the equivalent of a professional ministry.

As the issues became more clearly defined, two more leaders arose whose names became identified with the emergent factions. Joseph Gurney (1788–1847) became identified with the evangelical cause, stressing the authority of the Bible and the doctrine of Jesus's sacrificial atonement for the sins of humanity. It was Gurney's teachings that were adopted most eagerly by the Richmond group. Opposed to Gurney were the followers of John Wilbur (1774–1856), who, though "Orthodox" in their emphasis on the divinity of Jesus, also stressed the traditions of the Inner Light and plain speech and dress, which they thought the Gurneyites were abandoning. These Wilburites were strongest in New England, and broke off to establish the Conservative Friends in 1847, as well as in the Philadelphia Annual Meeting, which broke relations with the New England Meeting that had expelled Wilbur. The issue for many was thus becoming whether the distinguishing slogan for the Friends was to be the "Inner Light" or the "Blood of Jesus."

Despite these schisms, American Friends found plenty to unite on during the turbulent decades of the nineteenth century. Their traditional witness for peace was tested especially during the Civil War and, together with other "peace churches" such as the Mennonites and the Brethren, they gradually won recognition for the status of conscientious objector. They were hardly isolated from the events leading up to the war, though, because many Friends, such as Cincinnati's Levi Coffin, played an active role in the antislavery movement and the Underground Railroad. (Coffin was a prototype for the Quaker abolitionist in *Uncle Tom's Cabin*.) Following the Civil War, Friends were also active in philanthropic work among the freedmen in the South. Quaker attempts at penal reform resulted in the first "penitentiary," Philadelphia's Walnut Street Jail of 1796. This involved a building designed not so much to punish but to reform malefactors through providing an opportunity to reflect on and repent of their misdeeds. Quakers were also active throughout the century in any number of other philanthropic activities, all based on the premise of universal human goodness and equality that could be actualized through a drawing-out of the Inner Light in every individual. (Another consequence of this belief was the active role played in the movement by women, who from its beginnings served as preachers and missionaries. Special meetings for women also assured them an active role in communal religious life.)

During the twentieth century, the role of the Friends in American society has undergone some significant transformations, with corresponding realignments within the Quaker community itself. Representative of more recent emphases is the American Friends Service Committee (AFSC), which was founded in 1917 to help conscientious objectors find suitable deployment during World War I. Its work eventually broadened into postwar relief and a wide variety of other humanitarian endeavors, which have attracted support and goodwill from many non-Quakers. A prominent American Friend, Herbert Hoover, gained considerable recognition through his extensive contributions to postwar European relief, although his reputation as a humanitarian was later overshadowed by his unfortunate term as president. (Another president of California origins, Richard Nixon, also came from a Quaker background.) The Wider Quaker Fellowship, founded in 1936 by the influential theologian Rufus Jones, was another vehicle through which non-Friends who were sympathetic with Quaker ideals but not ready to enter into full membership could attain "fellow-traveler" status within the Quaker community. Colleges of Quaker origin, such as Earlham, Haverford, and Swarthmore, also perpetuate Quaker emphases and traditions in many of their practices, even though large numbers of their students have other or no religious affiliation.

At the present, American Friends are divided organizationally into three major groupings and some smaller ones, reflecting both the schisms of the nineteenth century and the circumstances of the twentieth. The Friends United Meeting is largest with about 44,000 members distributed among more than 580 local meetings. The FUM's organizational focus is the Earlham School of Religion in Richmond, Indiana, whose faculty reflect a diversity of theological standpoints but tend toward the evangelical end of the Quaker spectrum. FUM Quakers employ a professional ministry and frown on the use of alcohol and tobacco.

Where the FUM represents the continuation of the Gurneyite tradition into the present, the General Conference of the Society of Friends carries on the Hicksite strain. General Conference Friends are often members by conversion or "convincement" rather than "birthright," and represent the social activist emphasis within the broader tradition. The General Conference does not utilize professional clergy, creeds, or sacraments, and downplays biblical authority. Its roughly 33,000 members and six hundred meetings are divided into four yearly meetings, of which the Philadelphia Meeting, organized in 1681, represents a direct continuity with the beginnings of the tradition in America.

The third branch of present-day Friends with a fairly substantial membership is the Evangelical Friends International, with about 8,600 members, which is based in the Midwest and West. EFI Quakers are the closest to conservative Protestantism and have particular links with the holiness tradition that emerged from Methodism in the late nineteenth century. The Wilburite tradition is perpetuated in the very small Religious Society of Friends, and a few thousand other Quakers belong to meetings that are not affiliated with any larger organization.

Like the Amish, the Quakers have acquired a stereotyped image perpetuated through such media as the smiling visage on the fronts of oatmeal cartons that obscures their ongoing witness to their traditional beliefs. With a few exceptions, contemporary Friends live much like their evangelical or "mainstream" neighbors, depending on the branch of the tradition with which they identify. The most distinctive feature of liberal Quakers is their commitment to peacemaking, which manifests itself not in language or dress but rather in social involvements. Like the Amish and Mennonites, Friends have had to accommodate themselves to the dilemmas of trying to follow idealistic principles in a pluralistic, modernized society that is no longer so much hostile as indifferent to their goals. For those who have taken on an evangelical Protestant identity, the task is perhaps easier. More difficult is the maintenance of the traditional witness of peacemaking and reconciliation in a world in which they are otherwise indistinguishable in their external lifestyle, and in which they are seldom hopeful of growing greatly in number. They remain as a leaven, hopeful that the light they kindle will radiate far beyond their own small community.

John Wesley and the Rise of Methodism

Like most popular religious movements, Methodism arose in the midst of an age of social ferment. When John Wesley, a priest of the Church of England, began to preach out of doors to the coal miners of Kingswood in 1739, he was acknowledging by his deeds that "new occasions teach new duties." England was no longer the "green and pleasant land" lamented by the prophetic poet William Blake in his poem/hymn, "Jerusalem." Rather, it was turning into a nation of "dark Satanic mills," dependent on coal power and child labor to keep their steam turbines fueled. The Industrial Revolution was leading England into the vanguard of the modernization process, and the relevance of a Church of England that still was oriented toward an earlier, agrarian social order was no longer very clear.

In the midst of this disorienting change, a sensitive young clergyman emerged who at first did not seem a very promising candidate for rewinning the hearts of England's developing proletariat to Christianity. John Wesley (1703–91) did, to be sure, come from an environment saturated with religion. His father Samuel was the rector of the Anglican parish at Epworth, and his mother Susanna played a critical role in embuing her large brood of offspring with an evangelical-leaning piety. John and his younger brother Charles both attended Oxford, where they became involved with a group of earnest students, sometimes dubbed the "Holy Club," that met regularly in Pietist fashion for scripture study and the pursuit of the devout life. Another member of this circle was George Whitefield (WHITT-field), who would later become the focus of the dramatic colonial revival known as the Great Awakening.

After leaving Oxford, the Wesley brothers tried their own hands as missionaries for the Society of the Propagation of the Gospel in Georgia in 1735. John became involved in an unhappy romance while on his colonial "errand," handled it badly, and generally went through a low period of ineptness and lack of self-confidence. Once while crossing the Atlantic during this seemingly ill-fated adventure, though, he came into contact with a band of Moravians who were on their way to join the communities that their movement was founding in the New World. During a violent storm at sea—in those days, a life-threatening event—Wesley became profoundly impressed with their hymn singing and calm acceptance of God's will. Here was yet another sign that the Pietist path of devotion was the way to achieve the inner peace he sought but could not yet successfully impress on others.

John Wesley is a good example of someone the philosopher William James would characterize as "twice-born." Although the resolution of his inner doubts was probably not as dramatic as later legend would have it, he nevertheless did not come easily by the sense of spiritual security that his later teaching projected. And, like his fellow "twice-born" reformer, Martin Luther, Wesley's dramatic presence and effectiveness as a mature religious leader gave him a charismatic aura typical of the most dynamic of such men and women. In particular, later Methodists have focused on the experience that Wesley recorded in his journal for 14 May 1738: "In the evening I went very unwillingly to a society in Aldersgate Street, where one was reading Luther's preface to the Epistle to the Romans. About a quarter before nine, while he was describing the change which God works in the heart through faith in Christ, I felt my heart strangely warmed. I felt I did trust in Christ, Christ alone, for salvation: and an assurance was given me, that He had taken away my sins, even mine, and saved me from the law of sin and death."

It no longer seems clear that this "Aldersgate experience" was *the* decisive turning point in Wesley's spiritual journey; however, several aspects of the event are worth noting. First, the meeting on Aldersgate Street was conducted by Moravians, the German Pietists whose serenity of faith had already made such a positive impression on Wesley. Second, the impact on Wesley of Luther's reflections on Romans, which were the occasion of his own conversion experience, establishes a continuity of evangelical orientation between the two. Third, *Aldersgate* in later times became a watchword among Methodists—together with the phrase "my heart strangely warmed"—and Wesley's experience was thus treated as a norm for his later followers. Although recent scholarship has interpreted Aldersgate as one of an extended series of important developments in Wesley's inner life rather than as conclusive in its own right, it proved to be the stuff out of which traditions—like Luther's "tower experience"—are made.

Whatever the importance of Aldersgate, Wesley did overcome his early uncertainties to the point that he could direct his formidable energies and abilities toward the task of introducing a vital religion to what he saw as a spiritually starved England. Like his Continental Pietist predecessors, Wesley was not concerned with founding a new church; rather, he worked within the framework of the established Church of England to enrich its overly formal, impersonal round of worship and obsolete structure that failed to reach the multitudes of laborers and miners who no longer fit conveniently within the medieval parish system. To this end, Wesley began to organize small groups of lay people to meet at times besides those of ordinary worship for biblical study, prayer, and mutual improvement.

There were several noteworthy features to this "connexional" system that Wesley and his followers thus brought to life. First, although it was aimed at making religion accessible to the uneducated masses of workers, control remained firmly in the hands of the Oxford-educated Wesley. Second, although Wesley himself was an ordained priest of the Church of England, the people who made it work—including his "assistants," the preachers—were drawn from the ranks of the laity. Third, the system worked because of Wesley's genius for organization and the firm control he exercised throughout his lifetime on the activities of his followers. Fourth, although

Wesley's evangelical approach to Christianity stressed the emotional dimensions of the religious life, these "affections" were never allowed to dominate those who experienced them, but were rather drawn under tight rein by the regimen of spiritual discipline that had given rise to the movement's name of "Methodism."

What distinguished Wesleyan Methodism from the ordinary worship of the Church of England was its emphasis on personal spiritual growth in the context of a small group of like-minded folk under the supervision of a layman specially designated for the task. The basic unit was the "society," which met for prayer, scripture study, hymn singing, and the like at a time other than regular Anglican church services. Smaller groups known as "bands" and "classes" also developed for more intensive group life. All of these groups were carefully supervised by traveling lay preachers who followed a regular circuit and who met annually at the "conference" presided over by Wesley himself. Methodism was therefore highly "methodical"—rather than "enthusiastic"—both in this tightly coordinated national system of organization and in the rigorous spiritual discipline that the societies imposed on their members.

Although Wesley is best remembered as a preacher and organizer, he was also a theologian of no mean ability, and in his many writings sought to give an informed rationale for his plan of spiritual growth that had attracted so many followers. As opposed to his friend and colleague George Whitefield, Wesley rejected the Calvinism that was still influential in many evangelical circles and taught instead what was then called "Arminianism." This meant that although Wesley accepted the Reformed doctrine of the enslavement of the human will by the power of sin, he rejected the notion that salvation was confined to God's "elect." Instead, he stressed the cooperative role that the individual plays with God in attaining salvation when choosing to take advantage of God's "prevenient" (literally, "coming before") grace.

Salvation, or "justification," was not the end of the individual's spiritual journey on earth, however. For Wesley, a second religious experience was possible, which he termed "entire sanctification." This experience—later known also as the "second blessing"—marked the attainment of a state of "holiness," that is, a transformation of consciousness characterized by a state of freedom from voluntary sin. This state would not necessarily last forever, but had to be continually maintained by the following of the disciplined spiritual and moral life that Wesley prescribed for his followers.

The Methodist way was not as somber as all this talk of "discipline" might make it seem, however. Rather, it stressed very much the cultivation of the emotions, or "affections," so that the ultimate goal of self-control was the attainment of a new and highly pleasant state of consciousness characterized by a personal relationship with Jesus. This "affective" dimension of Methodism can be seen most clearly in the hymns written by Charles Wesley, John's brother and collaborator. Charles was the author of over five thousand such hymns, including such perennial favorites as "Hark! The Herald Angels Sing" and "Love Divine, All Loves Excelling." Particularly popular within the Methodist tradition, though, have been those such as "Jesus, Lover of

My Soul," which stress the personal dimension of the religious experience. Together with Isaac Watts, a near-contemporary English evangelical whose best-selling collections of hymns included "When I Survey the Wondrous Cross" and others that have endured as classics, Charles Wesley helped inaugurate a virtual revolution in Protestant religious music that would have far-reaching consequences for later American practice.

Although John Wesley lived out his long life as a priest of the Church of England, it was hardly conceivable that such an extensive and well-organized movement as his would not generate tension with the parent church. This was in fact the case, and English Methodism finally separated from the Established Church in 1795 after Wesley's death. In America, however, the path to independence took some distinctive turnings. Methodist societies began to form in the Middle Colonies during the 1760s, particularly in the neighborhoods of Baltimore, New York, and Philadelphia. Wesley himself started to send preachers from his own cadres in 1769. The following year, Francis Asbury, who might well qualify as American Methodism's patron saint, made his way to these shores. Asbury would eventually log over a quarter of a million miles on horseback, thus setting the example for subsequent "circuit riders"—mounted itinerant preachers—on the American frontier.

The establishment of a distinctively American Methodist church was not entirely smooth. Wesley, for example, was hostile to the American Revolution, and advised his followers here to remain neutral. The presence of a connection of Methodist societies on this side of the Atlantic also raised organizational problems. Wesley addressed these with increasingly bold measures, especially after American independence had been won. In 1784, he and two of his associates, who were also Anglican priests, ordained two lay preachers, Richard Whatcoat and Thomas Vasey, to the offices of both deacon and elder—titles that would endure in American Methodism as the official designations of clergy. Wesley then "set apart" Thomas Coke (COOK)—one of his colleagues in the previous ordination procedure—to the office of "superintendent" of the American operation, and sent the three men, all elevated to ecclesiastical office outside of the ordinary channels of the Church of England, to America to help organize the ongoing work.

The culmination of this process took place at Lovely Lane in Baltimore in December of 1784. At this memorable "Christmas Conference," the Methodist Episcopal Church was established by Asbury, Coke, and about sixty other American Methodist preachers who had assembled for the purpose of creating an American Methodism. Unlike the parent movement, this New World Methodism was from its beginnings independent both of the Church of England and of its offspring, the Protestant Episcopal Church, which saw its first bishop consecrated that very same year. Although Coke had been commissioned by Wesley to ordain Asbury as superintendent, his American colleagues balked at this violation of the democratic spirit, and both were elected to that office by the assembled preachers. In 1787 Asbury and Coke exchanged the functional title of "superintendent" for the more traditional "bishop," a move that greatly annoyed Wesley. The role of the two as founders of American Methodism has subsequently been honored in the word "Cokesbury," a conflation of their names still used by Methodist book outlets.

The combinations of tradition and innovative adaptation, discipline and emotion, structure and flexibility, democracy and strong leadership that characterized early Methodism both in England and America were powerful sources of appeal in the new nation. Here was an emergent Christian tradition that could easily adapt to the exigencies of frontier life, yet stood in direct continuity with the Anglo-American evangelical experience. Some scholars have attempted to interpret Methodism's rise as a response to a new industrializing, capitalist economic order's need for a work force that had internalized a rigorous self-discipline, such as Wesley had promoted. This is probably too simplistic a view of the matter, especially in the context of the American experience. However, it is certainly arguable that self-discipline enhanced one's "life chances" on the frontier as well as in the mill towns, and that most early American Methodists came from the ranks of farmers and laborers rather than the upper middle classes. In the nineteenth century, for whatever reasons, the spread and growth of Methodism would become one of the great success stories of American religion.

CHAPTER 17

The Great Awakening and the Baptist Tradition

The rise and spread of Pietism and Methodism along both sides of the Atlantic during the eighteenth century were closely related signs of a restlessness within Protestantism that was determined to express itself in new, more vital kinds of religious life. Particularly interesting are the interrelationships among the various aspects of this movement, from Germany and the Netherlands through the British Isles to the North American colonies. German Pietism was a major inspiration for British evangelicals, and the impact of the Moravians on John Wesley was an impressively concrete example of a direct line of influence. The Calvinist George Whitefield was a friend of the Arminian Wesleys at Oxford, and went on to become the catalyst of the Great Awakening in the American colonies. The primary native mover of that Awakening, Jonathan Edwards, wrote an account of what he thought to be God's miraculous work in generating the revival. When published in England by the evan-

gelical hymn-writer Isaac Watts, this account came into Wesley's hands and made a
due impression. In a totally different context, a German-speaking woman who knew
no English was profoundly moved by Whitefield's preaching, of which she could
not understand a word. This new spiritual force knew bounds neither of theology,
tradition, geography, or even language. As such, it was the most powerful—and
diffuse—religious movement since the Reformation itself.

The Great Awakening was the culmination of this intercontinental movement
toward a "religion of the heart." Its sources can be located fairly precisely in smaller,
earlier revivals in the colonies, but its ultimate causes remain obscure. The revival's
adherents included men and women of every region, social class, and branch of
Protestant Christianity in the colonies, so that attempts to impose a simple economic
or political interpretation are ill-advised. The most plausible correlation is geographical. The Awakening was strongest in its immediate appeal and its long-term effects
along such inland waterways as the Connecticut River Valley; conversely, its greatest
opposition arose in more cosmopolitan seaboard regions such as Boston. But this
is a correlation, not a causal explanation. Perhaps the most plausible approach is to
regard such a general outburst of religious "enthusiasm" as a manifestation of the
dis-ease brought about by rapid social change. This took the form, for example, of
British challenges to various colonial privileges, such as the Puritan religious establishment, and a hardening of the fluid socioeconomic patterns of an earlier, looser
society into a more stratified "provincial" order. Even here, though, correlations are
general and direct causality hard to pinpoint.

The Great Awakening was a massive religious revival that swept the entire English-
speaking Atlantic seaboard beginning in the late 1730s. It elevated the personal,
intense religious experience of emotional conversion—the "New Birth"—to a central
role in the process of salvation. Such conversions, of course, were not new in themselves: Augustine and Luther both experienced them, and their accounts inspired
later generations immensely. Such experiences, however, were seldom regarded as
normative by their followers, but rather looked on as the unique stories of spiritual
giants. New England Puritanism had encouraged a minute introspective attention to
the workings of grace within the individual heart, so that a "morphology of conversion" emerged as a guide to the assessment of the spiritual condition of would-be
church members. Here, though, the process was more likely to be gradual than sudden, and firmly located in the context of a patterned, disciplined social nurture.

The forerunners of the Awakening had two primary loci in the earlier decades
of the eighteenth century. One was in the Middle Colonies—New Jersey and Pennsylvania—which were rapidly becoming a Presbyterian stronghold with large-scale
migrations from Scotland and Northern Ireland beginning around 1700. It was in this
context that there arose the remarkable Tennent family—William Sr. (1673?–1746)
the *paterfamilias,* and his three sons, who followed in his footsteps as evangelical
awakeners of this barbaric domain. William Tennent institutionalized this impulse

through his founding at Neshaminy, Pennsylvania, of the "Log College"—a rough-hewn frontier school for the training of evangelical Presbyterian preachers. His son Gilbert (1703–64) especially became active in the later Awakening as one of George Whitefield's chief lieutenants, and helped form the nucleus of the "New Side" Presbyterianism that resulted. A sign of the many-branched roots of the Awakening was the role played in Gilbert's development by Theodore Jacob Frelinghuysen, a Dutch Reformed evangelical minister educated among Pietists, who presided over a series of small revivals in New Jersey's Raritan Valley in the 1720s.

The more immediate forerunner of the Awakening was Jonathan Edwards (1703–58), the successor to his grandfather, Solomon Stoddard, as pastor of the Congregational church in Northampton, Massachusetts. Stoddard had been something of a maverick in the Puritan fold, a reputation gained through his willingness to admit all but the openly scandalous to communion in the hope that the reception of such "ordinances" would be a spur to conversion. In doing so, he openly repudiated the traditional New England notion that the core of the church consisted only of the "saints" who had been able to narrate a persuasive account of their experience of grace. Stoddard also was effective as a revival preacher and counted five "seasons" of revival among his many accomplishments.

It was within this context that Jonathan Edwards carried on his grandfather's pastorate, initially as the latter's assistant and then on his own. In 1734–35, Edwards began to notice a restlessness within his congregation, and increasingly emphasized in his sermons the theme of justification by faith. Conversions soon followed, and Edwards began to think that the results were not simply ephemeral but rather a remarkable—even miraculous—manifestation of God's grace. From then on, his pulpit, and those he exchanged with his colleagues throughout the Connecticut Valley, became bases for the preaching of a revival that soon swept the entire region. When Whitefield later came to tour New England, a visit with Edwards for several days was an important part of his itinerary.

Edwards's role in the revival was crucial in several ways. In the first place, he was one of its most effective preachers. Edwards was steeped not only in traditional Puritan divinity but also in the early writings of the English Enlightenment—those of John Locke and Isaac Newton in particular. Through a combination of theory and practice, Edwards developed a new kind of preaching. His intent was not so much to proclaim scripture and interpret it in the form of doctrine, but rather to bring about a change of consciousness in his listeners. This he attempted to do by appealing not primarily to their reason but to their "affections"—that is, emotions—through the evocation of vivid sensual images. His most famous—or, as it has been presented for generations, notorious—work in this line was "Sinners in the Hands of an Angry God" of 1741. In this now classic piece of rhetoric, Edwards compared the individual to a spider dangled by God over a fiery pit, whose immediate consumption by the flames was prevented only by God's inscrutable but deliberate act. The underlying message was traditionally Calvinist: God was in absolute control of every aspect of the universe, and all humans were incorrigible sinners who were spared, if at all, from the eternal punishment they deserved only by God's mysterious act of forbearance. Edwards's means, however, were novel, and reflected the understandings of the workings both of physical nature and of human psychology he had gleaned from his new learning. The frequent anthologization of "Sinners" in isolation, however, has given Edwards a nasty reputation as a "hellfire and damnation" preacher; his real point, as evidenced in countless other writings, was the majesty and beauty rather than the terror of the divine, at least as experienced by the converted.

Edwards was more than one of the Awakening's foremost preachers: he was also one of its most influential promoters, publicists, defenders, and interpreters. In his classic account, *A Faithful Narrative of the Surprising Work of God* of 1737, Edwards undertook to describe the remarkable stirrings that had taken place among his congregation and to maintain their divine origin. In later works, he would defend the revival against such powerful critics as Boston's Charles Chauncy by attempting to demonstrate that its true fruits were a new life and consciousness in harmony with Christian teaching. Edwards also speculated that these massive stirrings of divine grace among the colonists were signs that America might have a special destiny in God's plan—as the site of the beginning, though not the full extent, of the millennial kingdom. In his later writings, such as the *Treatise Concerning Religious Affections* of 1746 and *Freedom of the Will* of 1754, he developed in classic form a restatement of the essentials of Calvinism in a new philosophical framework that reflected both his thought and his experience and that helped set the agenda of generations of American religious thinkers yet to come.

One consequence of Edwards's reformulation of traditional Puritanism was his rejection of the innovations of his grandfather, and his insistence that only the converted should be admitted to communion. More broadly, he brought an end to an important phase of the long New England tradition of covenant theology. Edwards now focused on the relationship between God and the individual, rather than the broader networks of church and society, as the center of Christian concern. These stern new teachings were far from agreeable to many in his congregation, who had grown comfortable in the easier ways of Stoddard's open communion. Push finally came to shove in 1750 when Edwards attempted to discipline some young people who had been circulating what passed as a naughty book—a manual for midwives. Edwards was dismissed from his long-time pastorate and took up a position as missionary to the Indians in Stockbridge in the far western reaches of the colony. In 1758, he was called to be president of the College of New Jersey, which had some of its roots in Tennent's "log college" and which later grew into Princeton. Shortly after his arrival, Edwards developed complications from a smallpox inoculation and died.

As Jonathan Edwards had been the greatest thinker of the Awakening, there is little doubt that George Whitefield (1714–70) was its greatest preacher. Whitefield, who had been a friend and contemporary of John Wesley at Oxford, illustrated in his own person the multifaceted and even contradictory religious streams that fed into the Awakening. Whitefield was an ordained priest of the Church of England, a Calvinist, and, through his affinity with the evangelical piety of the Wesleys, has frequently been identified as a Methodist. But the primary import of his career lay neither in his institutional affiliations nor his particular brand of theology.

Whitefield gained fame and influence as a traveling preacher throughout the American colonies during his several visits here, the most dramatic of which began in 1739. He soon acquired the nickname of "the Grand Itinerant"—a preacher who is not confined to one particular church and pulpit but who proclaims the Word wherever he can find listeners. Listeners abounded for Whitefield. First they came to the churches of various traditions to which he was invited, and then they assembled in the open air or in the vast tabernacle erected by his admirers in Philadelphia when his audiences grew enormous and the settled clergy became cooler to his presence. Even the eminently rational Benjamin Franklin was moved to the point of emptying his pockets after hearing Whitefield preach on behalf of the orphanage he was sponsoring in Georgia. It was said that he could reduce an audience to tears simply by pronouncing the word *Mesopotamia*.

Whitefield thus served as the catalyst that built on the local revivals kindled by Edwards and the Tennents and transformed them into an intercolonial phenomenon. Virtually everyone in the colonies from Nova Scotia to Georgia had either heard Whitefield personally or knew someone who could deliver a firsthand account. As such, Whitefield might be regarded as America's first celebrity—someone well known if, for nothing else, the fact of being so well known. (Today he would undoubtedly appear on the cover of *People* magazine and on many late-night talk shows.) Whitefield's fame rested on more than such empty renown, however, and his presence gave the scattered colonists a sense of having something profoundly in common with one another: having been participants in, or at least witnesses of, America's first massive revival.

Though Whitefield was not universally welcomed by the colonial clergy, his power and probity won him a respect and influence that brought him invitations from Puritan and Anglican alike. The Awakening only began to become a matter of serious controversy when its cause was taken up by less temperate domestic disciples of the Grand Itinerant. Gilbert Tennent, for example, aroused much ire through his polemical "The Danger of an Unconverted Ministry" of 1739. Here he laid out the common revivalist theme that many of the colonial clergy did not deserve their accustomed authority because they themselves had never been converted. When they continued to come from even less "established" figures than Tennent, such accusations became fighting words.

Tennent's attack on unconverted ministers was an example of *censorious* preaching, which was soon singled out by the established clergy as an intolerable affront.

Out of the Awakening there soon emerged an entire vocabulary of such abuse. Three other innovations stood out especially as signs of either vital renewal or inexcusable perversion, depending on the observer's viewpoint. The first of these was *itinerant* preaching, represented most dramatically by Whitefield. Most of the older religious groups of the colonies—Puritan Congregationalists, Presbyterians, Anglicans, Roman Catholics—were organized according to the timeless geographical order we might call the "parochial principle." This meant that believers were expected to belong to the congregation that served the geographical unit, or parish, in which they resided. These parishes frequently coincided with political units, such as the New England town, and reflected the traditional relationship of church and state as mutually supportive. Itinerancy undermined this principle at its heart, dissolving the bonds between residence, worship, and political allegiance. Some itinerancy was permissible when a guest preacher was specifically invited by a "settled" clergyman, because the latter's authority was thus respected. Those clergy especially who derived their support from the state—as in both Virginia and New England—were not surprisingly alarmed at what they saw as a challenge to their privileged status when itinerants began to invade their turf unbidden and unwelcomed.

Whitefield may have been the grandest of itinerants, but he was, after all, an ordained clergyman with the proper educational credentials and a reasonable amount of discretion. Not so, however, were all his imitators. In addition to being on the move physically, they frequently were not ordained but rather were responding to what they felt to be a personal divine calling. *Lay* preaching was thus the second offense of this new breed. Revival preachers also breached traditional clerical decorum by imitating Whitefield's custom of *extempore* preaching. The Puritan-Reformed tradition especially had prescribed that a sermon should be delivered at length by an ordained minister in a church from a prepared manuscript. Not only was it to be formal but also learned, reflecting the biblical and theological preparation ordinarily available only to the clergy. Extempore preaching violated many of these canons; when it was performed by a layman, all of the rules went by the boards.

The culmination of this growing ferment was the career of James Davenport (1716–57), a minister of good New England stock and Yale training. Davenport claimed special prophetic gifts and gained a following through his extravagantly emotional and censorious diatribes. An amusing account of the climax of Davenport's fevered career is included in the journal of Dr. Alexander Hamilton, an Englishman touring the colonies at the time:

> Sunday, August 16 [New London, Conn.] I went home at 6 o'clock, and Dean Green's son came to see me. He entertained me with the history of the behavior of one Davenport, a fanatic preacher there who told his flock in one of his enthusiastic rhapsodies that in order to be saved they ought to burn all their idols. They began this conflagration with a pile of books in the public street; among them were Tillotson's Sermons, Bev-

eridge's Thoughts, Drillincourt on Death, Sherlock, and many other excellent authors, and sung psalms and hymns over the pile while it was a-burning. They did not stop here, but the women made up a lofty pile of hoop petticoats, silk gowns, short cloaks, cambric caps, red heeled shoes, fans, necklaces, gloves, and other such apparel, and what was merry enough, Davenport's own idol with which he topped the pile, was a pair of old, worn out plush breeches. But this bonfire was happily prevented by one more moderate than the rest, who found means to persuade them that making such a sacrifice was not necessary for their salvation, and so everyone carried off their idols again, which was lucky for Davenport who, had fire been put to the pile, would have been obliged to strut about bare-arsed, for the devil another pair of breeches had he but these same old plush ones which were going to be offered up as an expiatory sacrifice. [spelling modernized]

By this time, the climate of opinion on the Awakening had begun to polarize, and parties emerged among both New England Congregationalists and Middle Colony Presbyterians. Among the latter, the breach between "Old Side" and "New Side" was temporary, and the resultant schism patched up a few years later. In New England, the situation was complex. Davenport's tactics resulted in his arrest and exile after being declared insane. When Whitefield returned to New England in 1744 after his earlier triumphs, he was condemned by the faculties of both Harvard and Yale. What had once been an almost unanimous welcome for the message of the "new birth" now split into a welter of contention.

The most articulate spokesmen for the "Old Lights" and "New Lights" who respectively attacked and defended the Awakening were Charles Chauncy, minister at Boston's First Church, and Jonathan Edwards. Chauncy was the author of the influential tract *Seasonable Thoughts on the State of Religion in New England* (1743), which denounced the revival for its exaltation of emotion at the expense of reason. Edwards, who had earlier defended the revival in a number of occasional pieces, responded in 1746 with one of his systematic masterpieces, *A Treatise Concerning Religious Affections*. Here he argued that "true religion, in great part, consists in holy affections" rather than simply correct belief. From that time on, New England began to divide up into spheres of theological influence. In the more cosmopolitan Boston area, Chauncy and his colleagues Ebenezer Gay and Jonathan Mayhew began to develop the rationalistic emphases that would culminate in Unitarianism, with Harvard as their intellectual center. In the more conservative Connecticut Valley, Edwards and his disciples held the allegiance of most of the clergy, and Yale became the focus for further evangelical development.

Old and New Light Congregationalists managed to remain in fellowship for many decades, however deep the disagreements among them might have run. Another faction, however, was determined that the principles of the Awakening were too radical for a facile reconciliation, and insisted on separating from the established churches entirely. These sectarian "Separate" Congregationalists rejected government influence

on their religious lives and insisted on the strictest standards for church membership. Many congregations split over these issues, though the institutional obstacles
in the way of founding permanent new congregations were too great in most cases
to achieve lasting results. To this day, however, two Congregational churches stand
side by side on the New Haven Green across from the Yale campus. Though today
their differences are minimal and both belong to the United Church of Christ, they
still exist as a mute, material testimony to the powerful disharmony that the revival
could leave in its wake.

A more lasting consequence of the separatist spirit was the rejuvenation of the
Baptist, or Free Church, community, which had lain rather dormant in Rhode Island since the early days of the New England experiment. The Baptist movement,
which had its origins among early seventeenth-century English Puritans, added to
the Calvinist tradition the Anabaptist premise that baptism should be restricted
to believers. This was certainly a logical deduction from the premise that the true
church is a small company of predestined saints who should gather themselves out
from the world. However, it was not acceptable to most Puritans in either Old or
New England, who believed that infant baptism should be retained as a symbol of
God's working his grace in a broader social context. In most ways, however, early
Anglo-American Baptists represented a variation on the broader Puritan theme in
their congregational polity and (often) Calvinist creed; their ties to the Anabaptist
tradition on the Continent were somewhat tenuous except for their one distinctive
shared practice.

In New England, Roger Williams (1603?–83), the minister of the church at Salem,
was exiled to the wilds of Rhode Island for rejecting the Puritan alliance between
church and state on the grounds that the power of the latter would inevitably corrupt
the purity of the former. After founding a new settlement that provided a safe haven
for dissent, Williams espoused the Baptist position and was immersed in 1639. He
soon moved from this to the status of "seeker"—like the young George Fox, whom in
his later life Williams personally engaged in vigorous debate—but is honored as the
founder of the Baptist faith in America. More broadly, the Baptists are the principal
descendants of what became known in England as the "Free Church" movement—
those Puritans who refused to accept the established church's authority. Ironically, the
tables were turned in the New World, where Puritan Congregationalists themselves
became established, and the Baptists were left to carry on the tradition of nonconformity against their sometime allies.

Baptist life for the next century was rather sleepy, confined to the two venerable
churches in Providence and Newport and a few scattered congregations elsewhere in
New England. The Awakening brought it back to a sometimes reluctant vivacity, when
many Separate Congregationalists began to declare themselves to be Baptists. Older
Baptists were not uniformly enthusiastic about the revival; still, they had to respond
to their abrupt shift in status from an isolated sect to a rapidly growing denomination

as individuals and entire congregations began to join their ranks. One of the most remarkable of these Separate Baptist converts was Isaac Backus (1724–1806). As a minister for these dissenters in Massachusetts, Backus became a major spokesman for the rights they felt had long been denied them in New England especially, and later helped lead the fight for official recognition of such rights in the Constitution of the new nation.

Voices of the Awakening and the Baptist cause alike began to be heard in the southern colonies as well. Samuel Davies (1723–61) was sent by the Presbyterians to evangelize Anglican Virginia and eventually won a decree from London that granted toleration to religious dissenters in that colony. The growth of the Baptists in the South was more complicated, since that tradition has always been notable for its resistance to centralization. In 1707 the Philadelphia Baptist Association brought together several early congregations and provided a focus for the subsequent expansion of Particular (Calvinist) Baptists throughout Virginia and North Carolina. Some General (Arminian) Baptist congregations had been founded in this part of the country, but were eventually converted to Particular principles through the superior organization and zeal of the latter party. Separate Baptists, led by New Englander Shubal Stearns, provided another path for an emergent Baptist presence. In 1755 Stearns and his extended family founded a Baptist church at Sandy Creek in North Carolina. Within five years the congregation had become the nucleus for the Sandy Creek Association, the first such organization in the region, which was soon paralleled by similar groups in Virginia. Although the Separates represented a more rough-and-ready, "enthusiastic" approach to the tradition than the more genteel Philadelphia group, the two were fundamentally united in theology. By the end of the century, the two factions had virtually merged, with Philadelphia as the organizational focus.

Although the Awakening had run its course as a visible movement by the end of the 1740s, it by no means disappeared as a factor in American religious life. Whitefield, for example, made several subsequent visits to the colonies in 1764 and 1770. The "New Light Stir" that swept rural northern New England during the revolutionary era launched a new round of sectarian formation—Free Will Baptists, Shakers, and Universalists, all of whom combined enthusiastic religion with a non-Calvinist theology. It has even been argued that the Awakening never really ended at all, but continued here and there on a smaller scale until it melded into the "Second Great Awakening" that swept New England in the 1790s and continued westward along the frontier in newer, more dramatic form. However one might want to categorize such movements, there is no doubt that revivalism was from the time of Edwards and Whitefield established as a mainstay of evangelical Protestantism in America.

Other results were abundant, though some were more subtle than others. On the political scene, religious pluralism and agitation for the legal recognition of minority rights became more and more visible. Similarly, in social terms, the notion of a homogeneous order based on traditional patterns of deference was clearly anachronistic, because religious disagreement both reflected and fostered social division. The various Protestant churches were split into factions, with those favoring a religion of the "heart" squaring off against those who were partisans of the "head." Higher education was stimulated by the new demands for clergy who met the specifications of newly expanding groups. Princeton emerged from early Presbyterian beginnings at Neshaminy and Brown arose in Providence to serve the rejuvenated Baptists. Dartmouth in New Hampshire had similar origins in a new sense of mission among New England Congregationalists to spread the New Light message to Native Americans. The latter attempt was unsuccessful, but another brick had been laid in the Ivy League wall.

Division and pluralism were obvious fruits of the Awakening, but so was a centripetal movement toward a new sort of unity that upset and transcended long-standing barriers of geography and tradition. Although its basic assumptions were Calvinist, the thrust of the revival had been away from an emphasis on theological particulars in favor of an awakening of the affections—in short, conversion. Further, there was a compelling need generated by these conversions to spread the good news as widely as possible—a missionary imperative. New Light and Separate Congregationalists, New Side Presbyterians, General Baptists, emergent Methodists, and sympathizers from various other denominations ranging from a handful of Anglicans to numerous German-speaking Pietists could unite on this program. American religious life would now be characterized for generations by the dominance of a new phenomenon that subsumed all of these communities in the broader religious culture known as evangelical Protestantism.

CHAPTER 18

The Origins of Modern Religious Liberalism

Liberal—like *conservative, orthodox, romantic, puritan,* and any number of others—is a word that may have a very specific or a very general meaning, depending on the context. Liberalism is defined by historical and social setting; one generation's liberal may seem distressingly conservative to the next. Unlike radicals, liberals prefer to work within already established structures, softening rigidities and boundaries that structures impose when they go unquestioned for too long. In its broadest sense, liberalism implies a spirit of openness to change and novelty, and of pluralism—a tolerance, respect, even enthusiasm for the opinions of others.

In religion, liberalism implies a concern with ethics rather than metaphysics; a focus on this world rather than the supernatural; an impatience with rigid barriers separating different groups of people, realms of thought, or categories of being; a confidence in the powers of the individual to discern the ultimate truth, without excessive reliance on revelation, tradition, or other external authority; and a predisposition to stress the positive, the fundamentally benevolent character of humanity, the divinity, and the cosmos in its broadest sense.

The sources of modern religious liberalism, as well as many other aspects of contemporary culture, can be found in the era known as the *Renaissance*. This "rebirth"— of classical culture, in its original form—had its roots in fifteenth-century Italy but rapidly spread throughout Europe to become a genuinely cosmopolitan movement. At the core of the Renaissance was a group of classical scholars who called themselves "humanists." By *humanism* they meant a disenchantment with the scholastic philosophy and the "decadent" Latin of the later Middle Ages. These they rejected in favor of a return to the purer sources of Western culture in ancient Greece and Rome. Although most were Christian, their interpretation of Christianity was strongly influenced by the Neoplatonic philosophy that many of them favored over medieval Aristotelianism. Humanists also tended to be sharply critical of tradition when it could not be defended by the new methods of historical investigation they practiced. An example of the latter was the humanist Lorenzo Valla's exposure as fraudulent of the "Donation of Constantine"—a document that was long believed to be the Emperor Constantine's will, in which he allegedly charged the bishop of Rome with the secular custody of that part of Italy that had come to be known as the Papal States. Although this had nothing to do with church doctrine as such, the spirit of skeptical inquiry that underlay such investigations could hardly help but promote a more broadly critical spirit.

Some of that spirit found its way into the work of Martin Luther, who launched the thoroughgoing attack on Roman belief, practice, and structure that helped precipitate the Reformation and the irreversible sundering of Christendom into mutually hostile spheres. More representative of the spirit of Renaissance humanism, though, was Erasmus of Rotterdam (ca. 1466–1536), who freshly translated the New Testament from the original Greek and also wrote scathing satires on corruption within the Catholic hierarchy. Though critical of the church, Erasmus wished to remain an insider; he accepted the basic premises of the Roman faith while bringing his critical powers to bear on its abuses. This role as a critic from within became harder to maintain as Europe polarized on religious lines, and the Counter-Reformation turned its attention to anyone suspected of disloyalty to the Roman establishment.

It was not a theologian but a scientist, Galileo Galilei (1564–1642), who is best remembered as the object of this campaign to suppress religious dissent. Using actual observations of heavenly bodies through his telescope as evidence, Galileo argued that the traditional system of astronomy taught by Ptolemy was obsolete, and that the Polish astronomer Nicholas Copernicus had been correct in maintaining that the earth and other planets revolved around the sun. Although Galileo's theories were condemned by the Inquisition as subversive of doctrine and authority and he was forced to recant, Galileo has been since remembered for his (perhaps apocryphal) appeal to empirical observation: "And yet it moves." This commitment to empiricism was given formal philosophical expression by Francis Bacon (1561–1626), whose *The Advancement of Learning* (1605) had a great long-range impact on the subsequent development of Anglo-American thought.

Another "heretic" who has often since been cited as an exemplar of religious liberalism was Michael Servetus (1511–63), a Spanish scholar who denied the divinity of Christ and the doctrine of the Trinity. Servetus was one of an informal company of mystics and rationalists that the historian Roland Bainton has characterized as "the free spirits" of the Reformation era. These stout nonconformists lived in a twilight zone between Catholic and Protestant camps, usually detested by both. Servetus fled from the Roman Inquisition to Geneva, where he was charged by Calvin with heresy and burnt at the stake. A more successful proponent of similar ideas was Faustus Socinus (1539–1604), an Italian who found refuge in Transylvania and Poland. It was in these remote outposts that there thus arose the first organized forerunners of unitarian Christianity—that is, one which affirmed the oneness of God and thus denied the deity of Jesus.

These scattered appeals to unfettered scholarship, rationalism, empirical investigation, toleration, and free inquiry began to emerge into a new status by the end of the seventeenth century, after the dust had settled on the long and bloody warfare that had been the legacy of Europe's religious polarization. An international movement, consciously cosmopolitan in outlook, began to take shape on the European continent, in Britain, and ultimately in the New World, and took for itself the evocative name of "the Enlightenment." The cluster of ideas and emphases that dominated the intellectual life of the eighteenth century was propagated by a loose alliance of university scholars, clergy, and "public intellectuals" who saw themselves as the avant-garde of a new era of liberation from the mental and institutional baggage of the past. Taking as their point of departure the scientific and philosophical issues of the Renaissance, the advocates of Enlightenment broadened this range of concern, gave it a new and aggressive cast in the freer, more secular air of the eighteenth century, and expanded its scope to include a critique of the whole range of contemporary thought and institutions.

The core of Enlightenment thought was epistemological: how do we know things to be true? In place of appeals to tradition, authority, and revelation, the leading thinkers of the Enlightenment argued instead that human reason, working with materials provided by the senses through empirical observation, was the surest path to reliable knowledge. The most important spokesmen for this viewpoint in the Anglo-American world were Sir Isaac Newton (1642–1727), who attempted to reduce the workings of nature to an orderly system of physical laws, and John Locke (1632–1704), who argued in his *Essay Concerning Human Understanding* (1690) that the human mind was a blank slate—*tabula rasa*—to which all contents came through the senses. Both Newton and Locke regarded themselves as Christians; both, however, helped to formulate a systematic approach to the investigation of the physical and mental worlds that made both Protestant and Catholic attitudes toward authority and revelation in religion problematic.

The impact of the Enlightenment on religion in the American colonies and the new nation took a number of forms, ranging from the fostering of avowed skepticism to an intellectual reinforcement of orthodoxy. Few went so far as to take the radical position of the Scottish philosopher David Hume (1711–76), who in his *Dialogues Concerning Natural Religion* (pub. 1779) attempted to demonstrate the futility of trying to prove the existence of God through reason and observation. More representative of the religious "left" was the stance known as *Deism* (from the Latin *deus*, god), which took exactly the position that Hume had tried to refute: that all that could and needed to be known about God was knowable through the use of human reason.

In the American colonies, Benjamin Franklin (1706–90) and Thomas Jefferson (1743–1826) were both Deists in their religious positions. They were also the closest American counterparts of the French *philosophes*—intellectuals of broad-ranging interests who turned their attention to practical as well as speculative matters. Franklin's development from provincial Boston Puritan to cosmopolitan man of affairs is narrated in his *Autobiography* (begun 1771), which has been described as a secular version of John Bunyan's *Pilgrim's Progress*. Franklin attributed his astonishing success not to God's favor or election but rather to his disciplined cultivation of the kind of personality that could prove useful in achieving wealth and fame. One well-known passage describes, with more than a hint of self-mockery, Franklin's effort to perfect himself through the systematic cultivation of one virtue after another—for example, temperance and frugality—by the use of a daily checklist. His thirteenth and final virtue is humility; to achieve this, one should "imitate Jesus and Socrates." The *Autobiography* also contains some amusing descriptions of Franklin's encounters with the great itinerant evangelist, George Whitefield. During one of Whitefield's visits to Philadelphia, thousands came to hear his message and be moved to conversion; Franklin, in the meantime, occupied himself with estimating the size of the crowd.

Thomas Jefferson, America's third president and polymath equal in virtuosity to Franklin, was also skeptical of traditional Christian conceptions of religion. As the author of the Declaration of Independence, Jefferson exhibited the philosophical vocabulary of his day in appealing to "truths" held to be "self-evident" to the common run of humanity, who were "created equal" and "endowed by their Creator with certain unalienable rights." Jefferson was here invoking not the judgmental divine Father of the Puritans but rather a more benevolent deity whose existence, character, and wishes could be known through human reason and observation. Jefferson, who had been raised as an Anglican but in his adult life had no formal affiliation, regarded Jesus as a fine ethical teacher but denied that he had any divine status.

Along these lines, Jefferson prepared a work variously entitled *The Morals of Jesus* or *The Jefferson Bible,* in which he presented Jesus's words of moral instruction with all supernaturalistic references—for example, to miracles—carefully edited out. Jefferson stated in later life that his finest accomplishments, in addition to the Declaration of Independence, had been his founding of the University of Virginia, of which a library rather than a chapel was the focus, and his authorship of the Virginia Statute of Religious Liberty (1786), which provided for what would elsewhere be described as a "wall of separation" between church and state.

The larger impact of Enlightenment thought on religion, however, was in more "mainstream" channels. Broad Enlightenment ideals of toleration and church-state separation were widely popular among members of a variety of religious groups, from the small Jewish community to America's first Roman Catholic bishop, John Carroll of Baltimore. Many decades before, however, Protestant thought in the colonies had begun to come under the influence of the movement's emphasis on reason and observation. Jonathan Edwards (1703–58), perhaps the greatest theologian in American history, early came under the spell cast by the writings of Locke and Newton. Instead of becoming a Deist, though, Edwards went on to use their ideas to reinterpret the traditional Calvinist doctrines of original sin and divine sovereignty. He also found Locke's emphasis on direct experience useful in preaching the sermons—such as the well-known but not entirely typical "Sinners in the Hands of an Angry God" of 1741—that helped evoke the dramatic conversions characteristic of the Great Awakening revivals.

More characteristic of the intersection of Enlightenment principles with Christian tradition were a long series of British works such as John Locke's *The Reasonableness of Christianity* (1695); John Toland's *Christianity Not Mysterious* (1696); Bishop Joseph Butler's *Analogy of Religion, Natural and Revealed* (1736); and William Paley's *View of the Evidences of Christianity* (1794) and *Natural Theology* (1802). Although these writers were not uniform in their points of view, the commonality indicated in this series of popular titles is clear. Christianity depended for its credibility not on supernatural revelation but rather on its conformability with the evidence of the senses and the dictates of reason. God himself was no longer an awesomely transcendent mystery but rather the epitome of rationality, rather like a watchmaker who has skillfully crafted his product and now, with amiable detachment, contemplates his handiwork as it runs. Many of these writers were Anglicans, a tradition noted for its emphasis on rationality and toleration, but their influence extended far beyond that community.

The form of Enlightened Christianity that was to have the broadest impact on the American scene was imported not from England but rather its northern neighbor, Scotland. The "Common Sense philosophy" that emerged from the "Scottish renaissance" of the mid-eighteenth century took as its starting point the Enlightenment postulate that the evidences of the senses were reliable. Instead of limiting all knowledge to the physical senses, however, exponents of this position such as Dugald Stewart and Thomas Reid argued instead that all humans possess an innate moral sense that enables them to make responsible choices in their lives. Here was a combination of themes from Bacon, Locke, and many others of the more moderate stream of Enlightenment thought that could readily be reconciled with any number of varieties of Christianity by undergirding the reliability of our everyday knowledge of the external world. John Witherspoon (1723–94), the Scotsman who became president of the College of New Jersey (Princeton) in 1768, was its foremost American exponent.

In the colonial era, liberalism had not yet become institutionalized. Although pervasive mainly among intellectuals, it helped shape the popular movement of Universalism, which rejected the idea of damnation, and was spread in more radical, skeptical form by popular writers like Ethan Allen and, most powerfully, "Citizen" Tom Paine, the revolutionary propagandist. At the elite level, Enlightened thought helped shape the intellectual milieu of a number of highly disparate groups: "Old Light" New England Congregationalists who were turning away from the emotionalism of the Great Awakening to the beginnings of what would later emerge as Unitarianism; Virginia Anglicans—some of whom, like Jefferson, would abandon organized religion altogether; and Presbyterians like Princeton's Witherspoon, who were molding the intellectual foundations for the transdenominational evangelicalism that would dominate American Protestantism during the coming century.

CHAPTER 19

Anabaptists and Pietists in Pennsylvania

The first Anabaptist settlement in the Atlantic colonies took place at Germantown, Pennsylvania, in 1683. This early migration of Mennonites and Amish to Pennsylvania resulted in part from Penn's recruitment along the Rhine and in the Palatinate, and later from older immigrants urging their families and friends abroad to follow them to freer climes. More Amish from various German states arrived in the early nineteenth century during the heyday of German immigration, and Mennonites who had found refuge in Catherine the Great's Russia began to flee the czar's draft in the 1870s for the American and Canadian prairies.

As with the Quakers and other sectarian groups, the American Anabaptist communities began to lapse into arguments and schism once they had become established in the United States (and Canada). The major theme of contention was the degree of accommodation to rapidly modernizing American society permissible within the bounds of their traditional values and practices. Most held firm to their pacifist commitments and often cooperated with Quakers and other "peace churches" to secure legal recognition for their position. Some of the most conservative Amish, however, refused to have anything to do with the legal and political system and urged their draft-eligible young men to accept jail terms rather than seek conscientious objector status.

Contemporary Amish and Mennonites are divided into at least nineteen distinct organized communities, ranging from the ultraconservative Old Order Amish to highly assimilated Mennonites who differ only in a few obvious particulars from other evangelical Protestants. The distinctiveness of the Amish, and the source of their "picturesque" character, is their having given religious significance to the preservation of the traditional agrarian ways their ancestors brought with them from Reformation-era Switzerland. They consequently avoid the use of modern technology, including automobiles, telephones, and electrical appliances, wherever possible, although modifications occasionally take place when the community determines that the use of a modern device will not disrupt the character of their common life. Schisms and court cases, however, have arisen over issues such as the permissibility of brightly colored reflecting tape on horse-drawn wagons when required by state law. Other court tests have taken place on the constitutionality of state laws requiring Amish children to attend secondary school (*Wisconsin v. Yoder*, 1972; an Amish victory) and the legality of a family's enforcing a community ban (*Bann und Meidung*) on association with one of its own members (a defeat). Other distinguishing features are an adherence to old-fashioned peasant-style dress, with beards and plain black clothing for men, and bonnets and aprons for women. Even buttons are looked on as worldly, and hook-and-eye fasteners are used instead. Curiously, modern medicine is accepted.

Estimates in the late 1990s suggest that the Old Order Amish may number about eighty thousand, with three-quarters in Ohio, Pennsylvania, and Indiana. Three other dissenting Amish groups number only a few thousand members each. At the Mennonite end of the continuum, the Mennonite Church USA is the largest—about 114,000 members in 2003—and one of the most assimilated of the Mennonite bodies. Even it, however, maintains a few distinctive practices, such as its pacifist witness, the practice of excommunication, and, among a diminishing number of communities, head covering for women. Unlike most of the smaller sectarian groups of this tradition, for whom the extended family and local community provide most of the organizational structure, the Mennonite Church has developed a denominational apparatus, including national boards (for missions and education), periodicals, a publishing house, a seminary, and two colleges (Bethel in Kansas and Goshen in Indiana). Other Mennonite denominations are very small, and usually stricter on various matters of traditional observance. In addition, more than fifty community "fellowships," many in university towns, are loosely tied in various ways to parent conferences and official bodies.

Worship is an area where Mennonite and Amish practices are clearly distinguishable. The Amish continue the Anabaptist tradition of regarding churches as worldly, and use houses and barns for their services instead. The ministry is divided into three groups—bishops, preachers, and deacons—who are chosen by the small community of families they serve and are self-supporting laity rather than ordained professionals. Two kinds of music, both in German, are utilized in the services, one a traditional, lengthy, slow-moving sort of chant, the other quicker and more tuneful. Mennonite worship, on the other hand, takes place in churches and is not very different from that of Methodists or other evangelical denominations.

A part of Mennonite history reflected in its various independent branches is the migration of a number of its people from Russia and Ukraine in the late nineteenth century after the group had lost such privileges as exemption from military service. These Mennonites followed the general pattern of agrarian emigrants of the time and settled among the still-abundant lands of the American and Canadian prairies and plains, bringing with them their own interpretations of the tradition. The Hutterites were a related group that settled in the same period and area. The Hutterites, also called the Hutterian Brethren, derived their name from their founder, Jacob Hut(t)er (martyred 1536). Their beliefs and practices are similar to those of the more conservative of their fellow Anabaptist heirs with one major exception. Most Mennonites and Amish cooperate closely with other members of their communities in barn-raisings and other activities, but actual property still remains privately owned. The Hutterites practice communal ownership of all goods, including modern farm equipment, which gives them an economic advantage over their more individualistic neighbors and often incurs the hostility of the latter. As of the late 1990s, there were more than forty thousand Hutterites divided among approximately three hundred colonies (family-based settlements) in North America—roughly one-third of them in the United States, primarily in the northern Great Plains, and the remainder in Canada.

The rise of Anabaptism had been the most significant manifestation of popular religious protest during the Reformation era, but the Pietist movement that developed in the late seventeenth century was equally expressive of the religious ferment of that later era. By this time, the Evangelical (Lutheran) Church in the German-speaking states and the Reformed Church in the Netherlands had existed as established institutions for several generations. For the more devout, the result had been an institutional hardening of the arteries. The reaction among those in search of a more vital form of religious expression was not open revolt but rather a quiet reshaping from within. Nor was the movement primarily popular in its beginnings. Just as many Anabaptist leaders had originally been Catholic priests, and were therefore more literate than most of their peasant followers, so were the first Pietists generally well-educated clergy who sensed a need for reform from within. Eminent among these was the Alsatian Lutheran Philipp Spener (1635–1705), whose *Pia Desideria* ("Pious Wishes") of 1675 became a classic text of the movement.

The core of the Pietist impulse was a religion that spoke to the emotions as well as to the reason. Its method was not a lapse into anarchy and "enthusiasm" but rather a disciplined pursuit of spiritual growth within the context of *ecclesiolae,* that is, small groups of the devout who met among themselves for Bible study and prayer. Although the movement was not received with universal enthusiasm by the clergy of the day, it did not usually break with the established churches but rather served as an intensive supplement to the religious fare offered during the ordinary round of worship services. A particular and lasting impact of Pietism on churchly religious life was the creation of a new, devotional hymnody known best in English through the work of the British lyricists Isaac Watts and Charles Wesley.

Although the Pietist tradition had a broad impact on the Lutheran and Anglican traditions—the latter in the form of John Wesley's Methodism—its earliest impact on American religious life came through the sectarian movements to which it gave rise. One of these was the group of churches that has endured to the present under the name of the "Brethren." The earliest of these groups grew up in the German Palatinate in 1708 under the leadership of Alexander Mack, who had been influenced both by Pietism and by local Mennonites. Many of these early Brethren joined the widespread emigration to Pennsylvania then in progress; they established their first church in Germantown in 1723.

The Brethren are also known as "Dunkers" because of their practice of believer's baptism, usually by "trine," or triple, immersion. The early Brethren found a suitable home in Pennsylvania among their fellow German-speaking sectarians, with whom they shared a common ethos of pacifism and biblically based separation from the broader society. Distinctive to this tradition are several features of worship, based on their interpretation of New Testament practice and not often found outside the Pietist heritage. The central ritual is the *agape* (AH-gah-pay) or "love feast," modeled on early Christian services. This includes foot-washing, the exchange of the "holy kiss" among Brethren of the same sex, and a communal meal with wine and unleavened bread.

As was the case among the heirs of the Anabaptist tradition, the Brethren in America were soon overtaken with the contention that inevitably leads to schism in a community without a strong central organization. As a result, the Brethren of today are divided among several independent groups that vary considerably in their openness to modern society and the apparatus of denominationalism. Many of these are very small. The largest, and most directly descended from the original Pennsylvania community, is the Church of the Brethren, with a membership of about 142,000 in the mid-1990s. Like the "mainstream" Mennonites, these Brethren sponsor colleges, missions, publications, and other denominational activities on a national scale. Its membership, and that of the numerous other smaller groups, is made up primarily of Americans of German descent, and is heavily concentrated in areas of eighteenth- and nineteenth-century German sectarian settlement: Pennsylvania, Maryland, Virginia, Ohio, and Indiana.

A Pietist group that has been considerably more influential than its small membership might indicate is the Moravians. The core of the movement was a group of followers of the Bohemian religious leader John (Jan) Huss, who anticipated many of Luther's ideas and was burned as a heretic in 1415. Out of the ferment that he stirred arose the Bohemian Brethren, or *Unitas Fratrum* ("Unity of the Brethren"), who continued a twilight existence in central Europe throughout the next several centuries. The group was revitalized in the heyday of Pietism through the work of the German nobleman Nicholas Ludwig von Zinzendorf (1700–1760), who made his estate available as a home for the community.

These revivified Moravians, as they were now known from the location of Zinzendorf's Herrnhut ("the Lord's House"), exemplified the devotional ideals of Pietism to the extreme and were tireless in attempting to spread their way of life and worship. Most notable among their practices was their devotion to the life and wounds of Jesus, which was expressed in a detailed, convoluted, emotional vocabulary of description and praise especially in hymns. (Music remains an important part of Moravian culture; their trombone bands carried on flatbed trucks still mark the dawn of Easter in their communities.)

Also central to the early Moravian ideal was a semicommunal lifestyle, which was implemented both in Moravia and in their American settlements at Bethlehem, Pennsylvania (1741), and Salem, North Carolina (1753), now part of Winston-Salem. Both the Pennsylvania and North Carolina cities have preserved the original Moravian communal buildings nearly intact. The colonists in these early settlements were divided into "choirs" based on age, sex, and marital status. Different groups (for example, widows or young unmarried women) lived and worshiped together in their own buildings, which formed part of a broader complex of dormitories, stores, craftsworks, and places for worship, surrounded by orchards and farmlands.

As is the usual outcome of communitarian experiments that survive the first generation, however, the Moravians were soon influenced by the example of their less devout and more individualistic neighbors. They abandoned many of their communal practices, such as common property ownership and the "choir" system, and became one denomination among many. Their missions to Native Americans in Ohio and Pennsylvania were notable for their humaneness, but were ultimately unsuccessful. The community has perpetuated itself through descent rather than evangelization. The Moravian Church in America, as it is now known, has a membership of about forty-eight thousand, with its headquarters at Bethlehem, Pennsylvania. It also sponsors Moravian College in Bethlehem and Salem College in Winston-Salem.

Other German Pietist groups emigrated to the American colonies or arose among existing immigrant settlement here. Some, like the Schwenkfelders and the Churches of God, General Conference (Winebrennerians), maintain their independent existence and claim a few thousand members each. Others, such as the monastic Ephrata community in Pennsylvania and the Rappites and Zoarites of Ohio, gradually disappeared. Still others, such as the Church of the United Brethren in Christ, merged with larger, English-speaking denominations—in this case, the Methodists (after an intermediate merger with the Evangelical Alliance). Yet another approach was exemplified by the Amana Colony in Iowa, which in 1932 separated its religious and economic dimensions and transformed its earlier communitarian structure into a secular joint-stock company. Those that have survived the generations have usually taken one of two routes: the maintenance of a combination of religious and cultural (especially linguistic) identity through voluntary isolation, like the Amish and Hutterites, or a gradual accommodation with all but a few crucial aspects of modern English-speaking American society, such as the Mennonites and the Brethren. Collectively, though, they have taken their place with the Quakers in maintaining their distinctive witness against war and violence and have helped to define through a long series of court decisions the potentials, and limits, of religious freedom in America.

CHAPTER 20

Jews and Catholics in Early America

Through much of its history, America has been understood by its citizens to be a Protestant nation, with other religious groups afforded legal tolerance but not a very enthusiastic acceptance. By the 1950s, Will Herberg could argue in his classic study, *Protestant, Catholic, Jew,* that membership in any one of these three communities had become a legitimate mode of being American. For all their differences, American Jews and Roman Catholics have shared a common experience as "outsiders" that has been overcome only in recent years. This experience has colonial roots, and warrants the juxtaposition of the two communities as examples of the introduction of non-Protestant elements into the early American experience of religious blending.

Although some converted Sephardim may have arrived in North America with Columbus himself, the story of the American Jewish community does not properly begin until the arrival of twenty-three Portuguese Jews from Recife, Brazil, in New Amsterdam in 1654. This small group of refugees was the nucleus of the Sephardic community that began to establish small Jewish settlements in the cities of the Atlantic seaboard during the remainder of the colonial era. These settlements constituted almost the totality of American Jewry until the beginnings of the Ashkenazic immigration in the late eighteenth and early nineteenth centuries.

Although Peter Stuyvesant did not care for these newcomers and attempted to expel them, the influence of Jewish shareholders in the Dutch West India Company reflected the role the Netherlands had assumed as a Jewish refuge and assured the continuing Jewish presence in New Amsterdam. From that time on, Jews in the colonies that would eventually coalesce into the United States suffered only the mildest disabilities compared with their European counterparts. The commercial skills they had acquired in the Old World served them well in gaining acceptance in a nascent sea-based mercantile economy. Congregations were organized in New York (formerly New Amsterdam) in 1656; Newport, Rhode Island, in 1677; Savannah in 1733; Philadelphia in 1745; and Charleston in 1750. The Sephardic variant of the traditional liturgy was observed in these lay-dominated communities; advice was sometimes sought from rabbinical leadership in London and Amsterdam on religious matters, because no rabbis permanently resided in North America until the 1840s. The Sephardic community generally kept to itself, married within its own boundaries, and aroused little overt hostility from its dominant gentile neighbors.

Although many colonial Jews faced a difficult choice of allegiance when the Revolution came, the large majority sided with the patriot cause and some, like the New York merchant Haym Solomon, played a crucial role in financing the revolutionary effort. Enfranchisement at the federal level was guaranteed by the First Amendment, but many states proved laggard in extending full rights of citizenship to non-Christians. New York took the lead in its 1777 constitution, but North Carolina, at the other extreme, did not follow suit until 1868.

If there were Jews on Columbus's famed trio of ships, there is no doubt that the vast majority of his crew were Spanish Catholics. Whatever the claims of the Norse, the Welsh, and other European peoples who would like to think that their ancestors were the first to cross the Atlantic, the Spanish—led by their famed Italian navigator—were the first to establish a lasting and significant presence in the New World. Only a few years after Columbus's opening up of the New World for European settlement, they had divided this territory into spheres of influence with the Portuguese through papal mediation. The southern borderlands of what is now the United States marked the northern bounds of the viceroyalty of New Spain, with its capital in Mexico City and the large mass of its population south of the Rio Grande. The Spanish presence was not a long-term major factor in the political and cultural development of those regions until the twentieth century, and what religious impact resulted focused on the attempts of Spanish friars, especially Franciscans, to work with the Native Americans of the Southwest. The subsequent story of a new Hispanic presence—Mexican, Central American, Cuban, and Puerto Rican—will be taken up again in a later section.

As the Spanish settled the southern rim of North America during the colonial period, the French were similarly active to the north. The primary area of French Catholic settlement was in what is now the province of Quebec, where Jesuits, Sulpicians, Ursulines, and "Grey Nuns"—all of them fairly new religious orders—established churches, schools, hospitals, and missions. French-speaking outposts were established along the route of exploration of the Mississippi Valley. With few exceptions,

however, this presence is reflected mainly in place-names now pronounced in grotesquely Anglicized ways: Detroit, Dubuque, Versailles, St. Louis, New Orleans.

Two small areas of continuing French settlement did emerge, however, in northern
New England and southern Louisiana. In 1755, the British expelled several thousand
recalcitrant French settlers from Acadia (Nova Scotia), which had been ceded by
France in 1713. Many of these Acadians, whose story was fictionalized by Henry
Wadsworth Longfellow in his narrative poem *Evangeline,* made their way down to
the bayou country of southern Louisiana, where their name became corrupted to
Cajun. The rest of New France came under British dominion through the Treaty of
Paris of 1763, which provided that the residents of Quebec would be guaranteed the
maintenance of their traditional language, laws, and Catholic religion. The creation
of a francophone (French-speaking) Catholic enclave in the midst of predominantly
anglophone and Protestant Canada led to the French-Canadian church's development of a strategy of *survivance* (suhr-vee-VAHNCE), that is, the maintenance of
the traditional religion and culture through voluntary isolation and perpetuation of
the old ways of pre-revolutionary rural France. As economic hardship encroached
during the nineteenth and twentieth centuries, however, many of these *Quebecois*
emigrated southward into the north of New England in search of employment. In
both cases, the interpretation of Catholicism remained traditional and devotionally
oriented; the French Catholic culture of New England, however, was much more
strictly moralistic than that which developed in the warm land of *zydeco* music and
blackened redfish.

The other, less direct but more far-reaching impact of French traditions on American Catholicism was a consequence of the French Revolution's forcing large numbers
of French clergy and other religious into exile into Ireland and America. In some
cases the result was the temporary defusing of traditional Catholic-Protestant tensions, such as resulted during the tenure of the charming and cultivated Bishop Jean
Lefebvre de Cheverus in Boston during the early 1800s. Many other French clergy
found usefulness as faculty at institutions such as Maynooth seminary in Ireland
and the new Mount Saint Mary's near Baltimore, established by Bishop John Carroll
in 1791, the first institute for the training of clergy established in America. This and
other seminaries were staffed by the Sulpician order, founded in France in 1642, which
became known for specialization in clerical training, especially in the United States
and Canada. Many of these *émigrés,* though staunchly orthodox, had been affected
by the Augustinian emphases of the Jansenist movement of the seventeenth century,
which was ultimately condemned as heretical in its more extreme forms. The ethos
of suspicion of the life of the senses, and especially of sexuality, which it promoted
spread far beyond its inner circle, and colored the character of French and, through
the *émigrés,* Irish and Irish American Catholicism as well. Many of the devotional
practices of the "Baroque" era of the seventeenth and eighteenth centuries that later
became popular in Ireland and America were also of French origin. These resulted

from revelations in visions to the devout, usually nuns. Out of this intense religious culture came a number of religious orders that were to become active in nineteenth-century America, including the Ursulines, the Madames of the Sacred Heart, the Sisters of Notre Dame de Namur, and the Society of St. Vincent de Paul.

The English Catholic presence in the American colonies dated for practical purposes from the arrival on the shores of Maryland of the *Ark* and the *Dove* in 1634. The establishment of a New World colony in which English Catholics could find a suitable locale for settlement was brought about by the Calvert family, especially Cecilius Calvert (1606–75), the second baron of Baltimore. The Maryland colony was based on the principle of broad religious toleration, which was embodied in the "Act Concerning Religion" passed by Catholics and Protestants alike in 1649. In 1654, however, a Protestant faction took control and ended toleration, and later generations of the Calverts reverted to Anglicanism along with the colony itself.

The Catholic presence remained strong throughout the colonial era, through the presence of wealthy English Catholic families and Jesuit missionaries, who adapted themselves to the dominant southern ethos by becoming slaveholders. Public worship was prohibited, so Mass was usually said privately at the Jesuits' residences. One of the most prominent Maryland Catholic families was the Carrolls, who produced by the time of independence two remarkable offspring. Charles Carroll of Carrollton was a wealthy landholder who was the only Catholic signer of the Declaration of Independence. His distant cousin, John Carroll (1735–1815), was to play a more direct role in the forming of the American Catholic community. Educated in Flanders, he entered the Jesuit order and helped to maintain its property and traditions during the period of its suppression by the papacy from 1773 until 1814.

With the coming of independence, the Vatican had to come to terms with the new political realities of North America, where Catholics in the British colonies had previously been under the aegis of the bishop of Quebec. Carroll was first appointed vicar apostolic for the new nation in 1784, then made the first Catholic bishop in the United States in 1789, with his see (place of residence and headquarters) in Baltimore. He was an enthusiastic supporter of the new American spirit of democracy and policy of church-state separation, and had himself been chosen by his fellow priests as their bishop in a rare example of Vatican-sponsored collegiality. Carroll became an archbishop in 1808 when four new dioceses (Boston, New York, Philadelphia, and Bardstown, Kentucky) were created. He spent the remainder of his career organizing governance structures for American Catholic life and promoting education, with the Sulpician-staffed Mount Saint Mary's Seminary (1791) and College (1808) taking shape under his sponsorship. Carroll was also instrumental in the conversion of Elizabeth Bayley Seton, a New York Episcopalian of prominent family, to the Catholic Church. Seton, who would later be canonized as the first native-born American saint, was the founder of the first indigenous American religious order, the Sisters of Charity of Emmitsburg, Maryland, in 1809.

In the Old World, Jews had always lived in a precarious, symbiotic relationship with Christian or Muslim "host cultures," which could not be depended on in the long run. Catholics since the Reformation experienced the extremes of continued establishment and dominance in southern and parts of central Europe, and outlawry and persecution in much of the northwestern part of the Continent. In the Atlantic colonies, neither community numbered more than a few thousand, and neither consequently attracted a great deal of attention, hostile or otherwise. In the meantime, each became assimilated into a distinctively American culture. Sephardic Jews stopped speaking their ancestral Portuguese, while life among English-speaking Catholics—many of them, like the Sephardim, quite affluent—differed little from that of their Anglican counterparts.

This process of assimilation is illustrated graphically in the two most prominent houses of worship these cultures left behind them. The Touro Synagogue in Newport, Rhode Island, was commissioned by the Sephardic congregation as the first such structure in the colonies. It was designed in 1763 by Peter Harrison, often described as America's first professional architect and renowned for works such as King's Chapel in Boston. The Touro Synagogue, which is well maintained today and open to visitors, looks at first glance like the home of a prosperous Newport merchant of the period. Its appearance is not discernibly Jewish or even religious; rather, it is domestic in scale and neoclassical in style. Inside, it contains the usual accoutrements for Orthodox worship—a bema or platform for a reading desk, an ark of the covenant, and seating divided by sex, with a gallery for women. Its message is that it represents a prosperous and sophisticated congregation desiring a tasteful and commodious place for worship, but not wishing to attract undue attention to its presence by anything that might seem indecorous or exotic.

Similarly, the first Roman Catholic cathedral in the United States was intended to signify an active endorsement of and participation in the life of the new Republic. After John Carroll had been named bishop, the prominent (non-Catholic) architect Benjamin Henry Latrobe offered him a choice of designs: an early version of the Gothic Revival and another in the Roman Revival style popularized by Thomas Jefferson. Significantly, Carroll opted for the latter, indicating his solidarity with the republican ideals with which it was associated in the public mind. Later Roman Catholic architecture in America would commonly be in styles more specifically associated with its own heritage; here, though, was a happy combination of Roman and American symbolism. Although it no longer serves as a cathedral, Latrobe's and Carroll's handsomely domed Basilica of the Assumption (1804) still stands in Baltimore as a monument to the best of the period's taste as well as a reminder of the self-conception of English-speaking Roman Catholics before the onset of the great waves of immigration of the nineteenth century.

Houses of Worship: From the Old World to the New

The "Old Ship" meetinghouse in Hingham, Mass. (1681) resembles a private home more than a traditional church. Note later additions such as the Greek revival door frame. Photo courtesy of the Library of Congress, Historic American Buildings Survey, HABS MASS,12-HING,5-20.

The interior of Old Ship features a dominant, centrally placed pulpit from which the Word of God was preached by the minister. Note the box pews, which were allotted on the basis of social standing in the New England town community. Photo courtesy of the Library of Congress, Historic American Buildings Survey, HABS MASS,12-HING,5-26.

Boston's Old North (Christ) Church of Paul Revere fame (1721) introduced the new English style created by Sir Christopher Wren to Boston, which was soon copied by the Puritan Congregationalists for their meetinghouses. Photo courtesy of the Library of Congress, LC-USZ62-102710.

Shaker meetinghouse on Watervliet Shaker Road, Albany County, New York. The meetinghouses of the Shakers were designed in a "plain style" that was also expressed in their distinctive furniture. Photo courtesy of the Library of Congress, Historic American Buildings Survey, HABS NY,1-COL,36-1.

The Quakers of Philadelphia also favored "meetinghouse" over "church," as illustrated in the Arch Street Meetinghouse of 1804. Photo courtesy of the Library of Congress, LC-D4-34757.

Boston's Trinity Church (Episcopal, 1877) was designed by architect H. H. Richardson to showcase the preaching of that "Prince of the Pulpit," Phillips Brooks. Photo courtesy of the Library of Congress, LC-D4-11887.

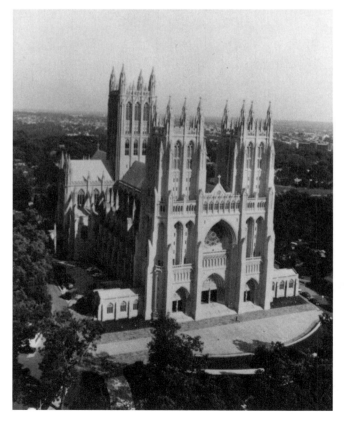

The Gothic revival National Cathedral in Washington, D.C. (1907–90) was intended to serve both the Episcopal Church and the nation as a whole as a "house of prayer for all people." It was the site of President George W. Bush's address to the nation following 9/11 in 2001 and of the funeral of Ronald Reagan in 2004. Photo courtesy of the Washington National Cathedral.

Revival Preaching: An American Protestant Tradition

George Whitefield preaching. Whitefield, known as the "Grand Itinerant," helped spread the revivals known as the "Great Awakening" throughout the Atlantic colonies in the 1740s. Photo courtesy of the Library of Congress, LC-USZ62-75073.

Charles G. Finney became controversial for his "New Measures" revival preaching in upstate New York in the 1820s. Photo courtesy of the Oberlin College Archives.

Dwight L. Moody and his musical director, Ira D. Sankey, brought the revival to the American city in the 1880s. Engraving from *Frank Leslie's Illustrated* 42 (April 15, 1876).

Billy Sunday, depicted in action by artist George Bellows in 1923. Photo courtesy of the Boston Public Library

Pentecostal Aimee Semple McPherson mixed religion and entertainment at the Angelus Temple in Los Angeles in the 1920s. Photo courtesy of The Bancroft Library, University of California at Berkeley.

Billy Graham brought evangelical preaching to American cities during the Cold War years of the 1950s. Photo courtesy of the Archives of the Billy Graham Center, Wheaton, Illinois.

American Catholicism

Baltimore Archbishop John Carroll, painted by Gilbert Stuart (ca. 1805), tried to introduce a democratic style to the newly organized Catholic Church in the United States. Photo courtesy of the Georgetown University Art Collection, Georgetown University Library.

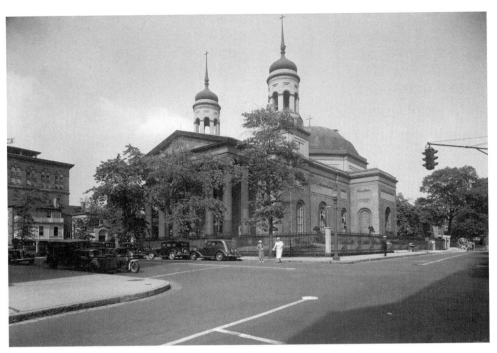

Baltimore Cathedral (1806–18), first Catholic cathedral in the United States, was designed in the Roman revival style for Archbishop Carroll to suggest the compatibility of Catholicism with American democracy. Photo courtesy of the Library of Congress, Historic American Buildings Survey, HABS MD,4-BALT,41-1.

Cartoonist Thomas Nast promoted an anti-Catholic message in "The American River Ganges" (1876), which depicted Catholic bishops as an invading herd of alligators. Photo courtesy of the Library of Congress, LC-USZ6-790.

As Archbishop of St. Paul (1888–1918), John Ireland sought to accommodate traditional Catholic teachings to modern American institutions. Photo courtesy of the Archives of Archdiocese of Saint Paul and Minneapolis.

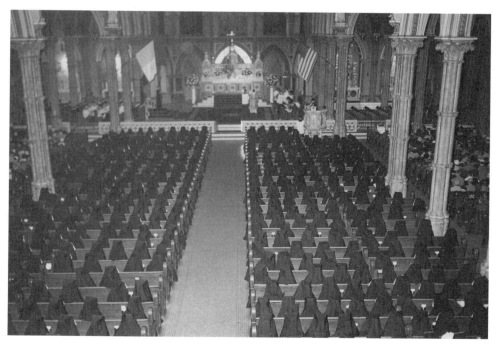

Pews at Holy Name Cathedral are packed with traditionally garbed nuns of the Sisters of Charity of the Order of the Blessed Virgin Mary, as Archbishop O'Brien celebrates Mass marking the 125th anniversary of the Sisters, 1958. Photo courtesy of the Archdiocese of Chicago's Joseph Cardinal Bernardin Archives and Records Center.

Charles Coughlin, Detroit's "radio priest," used mass media to spread a populist political message during the Depression years. Photo courtesy of the Library of Congress, LC-USZ62-111027.

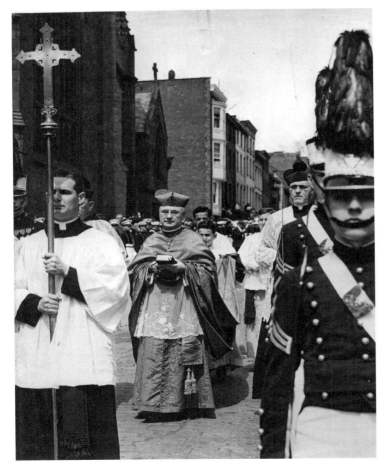

New York's Cardinal Francis Spellman (1889–1967) in the procession leading to a pontifical Mass celebrating the one hundredth anniversary of the Albany Catholic Diocese; Robert E. Wilder, photographer; May 13, 1947. Photo No. 1993.010.4094, courtesy of the Morris Gerber Photograph Collection, Albany Institute of History and Art Library.

Fulton J. Sheen demonstrated that a Catholic bishop could also be a popular television personality in the 1950s. *Herald-Tribune TV and Radio Magazine,* October, 1956; photo courtesy of Karen Fulte, Archbishop Fulton Sheen Communicates, El Paso, Illinois.

Dorothy Day, founder of the Catholic Worker movement, serving soup to Franciscans at Detroit Catholic Worker, ca. 1955. Photo courtesy of the Marquette University Archives.

Marcel Breuer's church for the Benedictine monastery in Collegeville, Minnesota, 1953–61, anticipated changes in church design promulgated at Vatican II. Photo courtesy of the Minnesota Historical Society.

Christian Missions to the North American Indians

Various expeditions of Norsemen may have landed in the northeastern parts of the North American coast during the Middle Ages, but the first significant European presence in the New World began with Columbus's first voyage in 1492. Although it took some time for these newcomers to sort out their cognitive confusions about where they had arrived, the Spanish who followed in Columbus's wake lost little time in subduing and then colonizing almost the entirety of what we now refer to collectively as Latin America. The only significant exception to Spanish hegemony was the presence of the Portuguese, who established the right to a portion of the eastern coast of South America—Brazil—through a combination of papal bulls and the Treaty of Tordesillas, negotiated with the Spanish in 1494. In 1510 the Spanish issued the Requerimiento, a proclamation to the natives spelling out the necessity of conversion and the futility of resistance, even if the listeners had absolutely no idea what the Spanish words meant. The Spanish imperial government was organized into two viceroyalties, at Mexico City and Lima, during the 1530s. A bishop had already been established in Mexico by 1527, a result of the pope's grant to the Spanish Crown of the *real patronato,* or right of virtually complete patronage in appointing the officials of the church in Spain and its rapidly growing overseas empire.

The evangelization of the natives was early identified as a major goal of the Spanish imperial venture, but this was not the primary mission of the *secular* clergy—that is, those who served parishes and answered directly to a bishop as their immediate superior. Introducing the aboriginal peoples to the benefits of Christianity was initially the task of what have been called the "shock troops" of the Spanish church—the religious orders, or *regular* clergy. (*Regular* derives here from the Latin *regula* or "rule"—the set of precepts by which a religious community is expected to live.) The most important of these orders were the Augustinians, from whose ranks Martin Luther was emerging in Germany at about the same time; the Franciscans and Dominicans, both of which had been founded in early thirteenth-century Europe as a response to the need for an effective presence as preachers in the rapidly growing late medieval cities; and the Jesuits, established in Spain in 1534 by the ex-soldier Ignatius Loyola as a means of combating the incursions of Protestantism at the beginning of the Catholic (or Counter-) Reformation.

As the work of conversion was being undertaken, however, a major problem had to be resolved as to the very nature of the aboriginal peoples. The European newcomers had no sure sense of who these aborigines were, and speculated that they might be anyone from the Lost Tribes of Israel to the Welsh. Learned debates raged over the basic question of whether they were even human. This question was hardly academic, since the Spanish Crown entertained genuine reservations about some of the tactics of virtual extermination being waged by the *conquistadores* against natives who did not immediately succumb to their claims of dominion. The climax of this argument took place as a full-dress debate at Valladolid in 1550, when the scholar Juan Ginés de Sepúlveda argued before the Emperor Charles V that the American Indians were brutish and less than fully human, and therefore subject to enslavement according to Aristotle's theory of natural slavery. The opposite side was presented by Fray Bartolomé de las Casas, the Dominican "Apostle of the Indies." Las Casas maintained that the culture of the Indians was hardly inferior to that of the Spanish, and that they should be treated with the full respect due to fellow humans. The result of the debate was inconclusive, but the general tenor of imperial policy thereafter was to forbid the slaughter or actual enslavement of the Indians—injunctions that were not always enforceable across a large ocean.

The attitudes of the missionaries entrusted with the conversion of the Indians varied considerably. Whereas the Franciscans were rather inflexible about reconciling native beliefs and practices with those of Catholicism, the Jesuits of both New Spain and New France were more accommodating in trying to discover and exploit such correspondences. This could vary considerably, however, among individuals and contexts. Throughout Mexico, the Spanish attempted to superimpose the material presence of their religion on the remains of the shrines of the Aztecs and their subject peoples. The cathedral of Mexico City was erected on the site of one of the principal temples of Montezuma's imperial city, and the shrine of the Virgin of Guadalupe stands near the ground sacred to the goddess Tonantzin. Indians were organized into villages under the care of priests, and the rectilinear approach to town planning characteristic of the Spanish Renaissance gave rise to town squares bordered by a church and other public buildings.

The Spanish, in short, were imposing their own version of *cosmos* (order) on what they perceived as the chaos of the aboriginal habitations, a strategy that also had the advantage of creating conveniently organized administrative units and personnel. The Mexican missionaries labored valiantly to master native languages and devise novel approaches to evangelization suited to the situation. These included open-air churches, whose courtyards could accommodate far more people than a standard-sized enclosed structure, and dramas in which Christian heroes inevitably defeated the Muslims or other evil forces. Though more benign than the *conquistadores,* the Spanish clergy regarded the Indians as perpetually dependent, and the order that they imposed on their charges was clearly paternalistic.

As New Spain began to be brought tightly under Spanish control, the secular clergy—the "army of occupation"—took control of the missions from the regulars. The latter were sent to the northern fringes of the empire to deal with the native inhabitants who had thus far escaped the benefits of "civilization." Two major loci of missionary activity by the Franciscans during the middle and late colonial period were among the Indians of New Mexico and California. The stories of these two campaigns are worth rehearsing for the way they reveal the significantly different approaches to the missionary endeavor within the same religion.

The ancestors of the various peoples known collectively as the Pueblo of New Mexico had occupied what is now the American Southwest for some ten thousand years. At the time of the first permanent Spanish presence in 1598, these Pueblo—more accurately known as the Zuñi, Hopi, and Acoma peoples—were united in a loose federation and led a stable, agricultural life centered on apartment-like multilevel dwellings. Their religious life was organized around voluntary societies of priests, which focused on the various significant aspects of earthly existence, such as war, medicine, and hunting. Their most distinctive ritual was conducted in *kivas* (KEE-vahs), or underground ceremonial chambers, in each town's plaza. These kivas represented the earth out of which the ancestors of the human race emerged at the beginning of the world. The priests played the role of masked *kacina* (kah-CHEE-nah) dancers, impersonating the divine figures who had taught the first humans how to live in their new aboveground cosmos.

With the first Spanish in New Mexico came Franciscan missionaries, who relied on their armed escorts for support in attempting to impose Christianity as forcibly as necessary on the Pueblo. They made repeated raids on the kivas, destroying ceremonial apparatus wherever it could be found, and exerted little effort to master the local languages or to understand Pueblo culture. The friars moved frequently from settlement to settlement, and did not make much lasting contact with the local people whom they set to work building their striking adobe churches. They had no interest in trying to translate the abstractions of European theology into the thought and language-patterns of a radically different culture, and insisted that the natives accept the Christian religion and a European lifestyle as an inseparable package. Although some Indians accepted instruction in crafts and Catholicism from the priests, most kept an unbelligerent but skeptical distance.

The failure of the Franciscans to make any significant impact on Pueblo sensibilities became evident in 1680, after a prolonged drought seemed to the natives to disprove the efficacy of the new religion in sustaining even the basics of life. A revolt led by the shaman Popé temporarily drove out the Spanish, and the Pueblo's feelings toward the Franciscans were expressed by killing twenty-one of the thirty-three missionaries stationed in the area. After the Spanish regained control in 1693, the Franciscans returned, but their influence over the natives was circumscribed considerably by the secular power.

Over the centuries, the Pueblo have succeeded more fully than most native peoples in preserving their traditional religious culture while adjusting to the inevitability of the white presence. One reason for this cultural survival may lie in the sophisticated organization of their voluntary societies, as opposed to the greater individualism among religious specialists in other native societies. Try as the Franciscans might to obliterate the traditional patterns, the native priests outwitted them and continued to celebrate their rites in secret. After the Franciscan power had been limited by the Spanish, the Pueblo learned to live in two worlds simultaneously through mental and physical compartmentalization. The Pueblo accommodated themselves to political dominance successively by the Spanish, Mexicans, and Americans, and learned to adapt some of the more useful aspects of modern technology into their lifestyle and to master English as a second language. However, they persisted in maintaining their traditional rituals intact, and resisted blending Christian elements into a native base as many other peoples were to do. (This kind of blending of elements from two or more religious traditions is variously called *hybridity, hybridization,* or, in more recent ethnological usage, *creolization.* The older term *syncretism* is no longer considered appropriate.)

A very different mission campaign by Spanish-speaking Franciscans was launched in *alta* (northern) California in 1768 by Junípero Serra, one of the most remarkable and admired missionaries of all time. Together with his successor, Fermín Lasuén, and their fellow friars, Serra organized a chain of what would eventually become twenty-one mission stations spaced a day's journey (about forty miles) from one another along *El Camino Real*—"the Royal Road"—from San Diego to San Francisco. (It is worth noting the place-names—Saint James and Saint Francis—which have lost their religious connotations in current usage.) The California Indians were not nearly as complexly organized as the Pueblo, and lived a fairly simple life characterized by minimal clothing, brush-covered huts, and seminomadic food gathering (especially of acorns). Their religious system was similarly lacking in complexity.

Serra and his companions approached these "Digger" or "Mission" Indians, as they were later called, with gifts of food and clothing, and avoided any coercion in trying to attract them to Christianity. In a reversal of the roles that had developed in New Mexico, the friars protected the natives from exploitation by the soldiers who had established military bases along the same route and provided the priests with protection. The friars invited the generally friendly natives to help them in the construction of the mission compounds, most of which survive to the present day. These compounds are of considerable interest architecturally, because they incorporate imperfectly remembered Spanish plans with local materials—primarily adobe—and native workmanship. The typical mission was organized around a rectangular patio, with a chapel as the focal point and cloisterlike arcades around the interior rim. Rooms were provided for priests' quarters—Serra's cell may still be seen at Carmel— and for craft workshops, cooking, storage, and accommodations for unmarried native women. Single men and married couples lived in adobe houses nearby.

The compounds were designed to be self-sustaining, and a profitable agriculture flourished around many of them. Under Franciscan tutelage the natives raised cattle, sheep, olives, grapes, and other produce, thus adopting a basically European lifestyle while being instructed in the rudiments of Christianity. Mission priests were expected to master the native language within a year of their arrival, but a language incorporating elements of both Spanish and Indian dialects emerged as a sort of common *pidgin* tongue throughout all of the missions. What resulted can be described in the phrase of Erving Goffman as a "total institution," in which every aspect of the lives of the resident Indians was shaped by the program of mission life developed by the friars. The result was intended as a benevolent paternalism, more European than indigenous in style, but representing a real cultural fusion nonetheless.

Even though the Indians were far more supportive of the California program than had been their counterparts in New Mexico—the largest mission had as many as four thousand people in residence at its peak—the endeavor of Serra and his compatriots to establish a permanent refuge for their charges proved to be only a "brief and shining moment" in the checkered history of North American missions. Secularization of the settlements began to take place under Mexican dominion in 1822, and the subsequent transfer of power to English-speaking Americans accelerated the process further. Mission land and property were sold off, and the buildings began to decay. The Indians dispersed into a disorganized wandering state, never to reassemble. A movement to restore the old compounds was begun in 1891, and some are still used today for Catholic services. The Indians they were built to serve, however, are forever gone as a people.

The California missions at their peak were probably the most comprehensive, sensitive, and, in the short run, successful of the attempts by European Catholics to convert Native Americans to their beliefs—and, almost inevitably, their lifestyle. (Serra, however, was criticized strongly by some Native American groups as having mistreated his Indian charges when he was beatified—the first stage on the road to canonization as a saint—by Pope John Paul II in 1988.) The attempts of the French at the other extreme of North America to conduct similar missions provide an interesting point of comparison. In New France—now known as Canada—the aboriginal peoples lived a more mobile and hunting-based existence than did many of their counterparts in the more temperate climes of the southern parts of the continent. Again, the religious orders rather than diocesan clergy were the agents of evangelization, and the Jesuits were particularly active among the Huron (Wendat) in what is now Ontario.

The Jesuits from early on had distinguished themselves from other Catholic missionaries through their willingness to accommodate their lifestyle and message to those of the peoples they were attempting to convert. Matteo Ricci, for example, assumed the role of Mandarin scholar during his controversial mission in China in the 1580s, and carefully avoided introducing any Catholic teachings that were irreconcilable with traditional Chinese culture. His later successors in Canada were of similarly innovative bent, but their work was seriously impeded both by internal resistance and external obstacles.

The religious life of the Huron was representative of that of the seminomadic native peoples of the north. Religion was not compartmentalized, and ritual or symbolic activity accompanied all important aspects of life. According to their cosmology, the world came into being after the goddess Aataentsic fell through a hole in the sky into the primeval water. The Great Tortoise and other animals came to her rescue, and brought up enough land to provide her with a cushion, which also served as the home for the human race. She gave birth to twin sons, one of whom became the "culture hero" for humanity. For the most part, however, supernatural power diffused throughout the world was much more significant for everyday life than were these rather remote divinities.

Jesuits began to work among the Hurons beginning in 1625, and set about learning the language and immersing themselves in native culture. In the tradition of Ricci, they attempted to equate aspects of Catholic belief with traditional Huron ideas and practices. Their success, however, was limited by the gaps between the mental worlds of the Hurons and the French. The Huron language, for example, lacked abstract nouns, and traditional Catholic theology rested on abstractions such as "atonement." Monotheism made little sense to a people used to seeing supernatural power diffused throughout the natural world. In a society in which shamans were the only religious functionaries, with power based solely on producing tangible results, the more subtle notion of a priesthood ordained for the administration of sacraments did not go very far. Sin and eternal punishment similarly made no sense in the Huron cosmos, and a proper fear of hellfire was hard to drum up. Also, traditional Huron practices such as divorce and the torture of prisoners were irreconcilable with the moral sense of the Jesuits.

The Jesuits had first gained access to and toleration by the Huron because of their connection with French traders and soldiers, who offered both worldly allures and protection. By 1648, however, this presence was insufficient to defend the partially Christianized Hurons and their Jesuit mentors from the fury of their traditional enemies, the Iroquois. The latter launched an attack aimed at the total conquest of the Huron, and the Huron were powerless to resist effectively. In the ensuing battles, several Jesuits, including the now-sainted Jean de Brébeuf, fell into Iroquoian hands, at which they underwent the ferocious tortures traditionally reserved for prisoners of war. As Henry Bowden points out, however, a new element entered the drama that now took place. Brébeuf endured his torments in the stoic fashion of the Indian warrior, refusing to ask for mercy under the most extreme duress. He earned the admiration of his captors (who proceeded to eat his heart), who admired him not for his Christian but rather his Indian virtues. Whether the Jesuits had converted the Hurons or vice versa is an open question.

As a result of this vicious warfare, traditional Huron society was shattered, and the Jesuits who survived were successful in baptizing many of those who still lived. As in the case of Handsome Lake and the Seneca of upstate New York a century and a half later, social disintegration is often a prelude to dramatic religious change. (The story of Handsome Lake is recounted in chapter 39.) Some relocated Huron settlements have survived to the present, but have gradually been transformed by the incursion of modern society. As in the case of the Franciscan missions in California, the goal of an intermediate society—Christian but still distinctively Indian—sought by the Jesuits was doomed to ultimate failure. The heroic legend of Brébeuf and his companion martyrs alone remains as an ambiguous testimony to their endeavors.

The missionary approach of Protestants during the colonial period was generally as inflexible as that of the most rigid Catholics. Missions conducted during the seventeenth century were the work of a handful of Puritan clergy whose Calvinist faith did not easily lend itself to intercultural understanding. The god of the Puritans was not theoretically unwilling to include some natives among the small segment of humankind he had elected for eternal salvation. However, most Puritans simply did not have the inclination to expend very much effort on a people that seemed to them, if not actually hostile, at least an unlikely audience for the message of conversion grounded on intellectual assent to the highly propositional theology they taught. When the New Englanders did address themselves to their aboriginal predecessors, they insisted that the Indians assume their own ways not only of believing but of living. Their success was not extraordinary.

The earliest of the New England Puritans to attempt a mission to the natives was Thomas Mayhew Jr., who in 1642 began to evangelize the Algonkians on Martha's Vineyard in their own language. After his premature death, his work was carried on by both his father and his son, and later by two further generations of Mayhews. Although this family's work was successful in terms of continuity and the mastery of the native language exhibited by the Mayhews, its scope was strictly limited by its literally insular character.

Of broader reach were the endeavors of John Eliot in the Bay Colony, which began around the same time. Eliot produced a dictionary and grammar of the Massachuset tongue, and translated the New Testament and other Christian works as well. He converted considerable numbers of the Massachuset, and organized these "praying Indians" into "praying towns." These settlements, of which Natick was the most notable, were organized within a short distance of Boston. In their heyday later in the century they boasted a total population of about forty-one hundred, perhaps 10 percent of the local native population, which had already been decimated by the introduction by the English of contagious diseases against which the natives possessed no immunity.

These towns, though shaped by Eliot's humane temper, nevertheless reflected the Puritan insistence that a Christian Indian must be a Europeanized Indian. The Massachusets who elected to live in these settlements had to make a decisive choice to reject their entire life patterns, including their kinship ties, to do so. They also traded their seminomadic lifestyle, in which hunting and cultivation both provided food, for one of permanent stability of residence with an agricultural base. Visiting Puritan ministers provided leadership, as did some natives who had been appointed to the status of elder or exhorter (that is, deliverer of homilies). What might have grown into a fairly long-term settlement was disrupted by the outbreak of King Philip's War in 1675. Suspicious Puritans confined all Indians within reach, including Christian converts, in what amounted to concentration camps. Many died as a result, and the praying town experiment went into sharp decline and eventual dispersion.

A few scattered attempts during the eighteenth century met with similarly discouraging results. David Brainerd, whose brief career as an Indian missionary was immortalized by Jonathan Edwards as an exemplary life of heroic piety, converted practically no one. Eleazar Wheelock in Connecticut presided over a charity school that turned out one notable Indian preacher, Samson Occom, who was later ordained by the Presbyterians as a minister to his fellow Indians on Long Island. Occom broke with his mentor, however, after discovering that Wheelock's newly founded Dartmouth College, which had been intended for Indians, had become yet another academy for whites. The few Indians enrolled there had died or left in frustration with Wheelock's regimen, which was intended to break them of their traditional culture as rapidly as possible. (A few Indians had attended Harvard from time to time previously, and most died of the effects.) After leaving Long Island, where he had lived in wigwams and supported himself in various ways while conducting his missionary work, Occom concluded his career in Connecticut.

As the time of independence approached, other religious groups whose theologies and lifestyles differed sharply from the Puritans began work among the Indians as well. David Zeisberger was a Moravian who worked extensively with native peoples in Pennsylvania and then Ohio, where he helped establish three towns of Indians from a variety of tribes. These settlers were forced to migrate to Ontario when the Revolution came, and the better part of them were massacred by suspicious American frontiersmen when they returned to Ohio in 1782 to reclaim what remained of their possessions. The Society of Friends, or Quakers, another pacifist group, early gained a well-earned reputation for fair dealing with the natives through William Penn's early negotiations in the settlement of Philadelphia by his English followers. Quakers welcomed Indians to their meetings but generally did not actively seek to convert them. A group of Quakers working as a sort of "peace corps" among the Seneca in western New York, however, helped to plant some of the ideas that later became incorporated into the movement led by Handsome Lake, which is discussed at some length in chapter 39.

After the establishment of the new nation, federal policy toward the Indians alternated between rather half-hearted developmental assistance called "Civilization Funds," which were usually administered by the churches, and an aggressive policy of military subjugation and forcible removal. The latter was the fate of the Cherokee in Georgia, one of the "Civilized Tribes" forced by Andrew Jackson onto the "Trail of Tears" to Indian Territory (Oklahoma). The Protestant churches, which were the only ones at the time with the resources to attempt much in the way of mission work, channeled their efforts through the interdenominational American Board of Commissioners of Foreign Missions (ABCFM), one of the agencies of the informal "Benevolent Empire" that was attempting to spread evangelical Christianity through a nation in which no established church could legally exist.

The efforts of Protestant missionaries from the beginnings through the nineteenth century were not very productive, largely because of their insistence that Indians adopt not only Christianity as a religion but also the lifestyle that the missionaries believed to be inseparable from it. Robert F. Berkhofer Jr. has demonstrated the primacy of Protestant virtues in the scheme of evangelization. Primary among these was sobriety, which was particularly important in the Native American context because Indians seemed to lack the physiological capacity to partake of even small amounts of alcohol without becoming intoxicated. Other Protestant virtues, such as cleanliness, punctuality, and stability of residence, were not especially alien to the agriculturally inclined peoples, but were unknown to the hunting-based cultures of the Northeast and the Great Plains.

Similarly, private property ownership was a virtue only in the context of an agricultural or commercial society and clashed sharply with the seminomadic attitude of land use for only immediate needs rather than private and exclusive ownership in perpetuity. White and Indian notions of law and order were also at odds; the personalized and traditional patterns of justice practiced by the Indians were not readily reconciled with the abstract, impersonal codes of the Anglo-Americans. Only Indians who had become demoralized over the prospects of continuing in their traditional patterns were likely to be receptive to a message predicated on such a thoroughgoing repudiation of their traditional values. A nature deprived of its supernatural resonances and divided neatly into privately owned farms and house-plots had little intrinsic appeal.

Despite occasional armed outbreaks such as that which resulted in the demise of General Custer at Little Big Horn in 1876, the inexorable movement of the American Indian after the Civil War was toward the government-supervised reservation. Under President Grant, the federal government again chose to share this supervisory work with the churches under what came to be known as the "Quaker Policy" of 1869. (The name referred to the origins of the idea among members of the Friends.) The Indian peoples were thereby divided under the supervision of thirteen different denominations, with little regard to the previous history of work among particular peoples by each group. The Methodists were heavily favored under this scheme. Roman Catholics, who had been involved particularly in missions in the Northwest, came out on the short end, and organized their own mission board in 1874 as a countermeasure. The general policy of the government was first to isolate the Indians collectively on reservations, but the relentless pressure of whites for more land led to a new emphasis on promoting assimilation into the broader society and a concomitant treatment of Indians as individuals rather than members of groups. The Dawes Act of 1887 divided reservation lands among individual Indians, with much of the remainder being sold to whites. Not until John Collier, an anthropologist sympathetic to the preservation of traditional ways, was appointed as commissioner of Indian Affairs in the 1930s did a major reversal take place. Since the New Deal years, federal policy has fluctuated considerably.

In the twentieth century, the newly organized Federal Council of Churches in 1908 took over the coordination of most Indian mission work among Protestants. Its successor, the National Council of Churches, eliminated any specific agency for the supervision of Indian missions, although individual denominations continued efforts. In general, Catholics and more liberal Protestants tended to favor a mission strategy aiming at an accommodation between traditional ways and Christianity, whereas more evangelical Protestants were less hospitable to compromise.

The history of Catholic missionary work among the Lakota Sioux on the Rosebud and Pine Ridge reservations in South Dakota provides a good example of the fortunes of Christian Indian missions during the past century. A regular Catholic presence only became possible in the 1880s, after the Sioux had been forced to abandon their seminomadic ways and settle down on reservations. With government aid, the Jesuits and Sisters of Saint Francis established boarding schools for native children. Despite the long Jesuit heritage of accommodation to traditional customs, however, this particular mission was deeply imbued with the common late nineteenth-century philosophy of "developmentalism." As Harvey Markowitz has pointed out, the developmentalist theory held that native peoples represented an earlier, more primitive stage of development already passed through by European Americans, whose duty was to help their less developed neighbors attain the modern standard as quickly as possible. The Catholic reservation schools therefore attempted to isolate Sioux children from their families, forbidding them to speak anything but English and keeping home visits to a bare minimum. They also considered Sioux medicine men as dangerous and their religion as irredeemably pagan. Their impact on the Sioux was, not surprisingly, rather minimal.

Since Vatican II, however, the atmosphere of pluralism that has spread through the Catholic Church more generally has influenced its *missiology*—philosophy of mission work—as well. Jesuits working on the same missions in the 1980s expressed radically different attitudes toward the Sioux people, regarding their traditions as deserving of respect rather than contempt. Some have gone so far as to participate in traditional Sioux practices such as vision quests and sweat lodge ceremonies. On the whole, however, these modern missionaries express discouragement over their relevance to the Sioux and over the tepid response to their work. This experience may well be typical of the broader range of Christian mission experience among Native American peoples. Though many missionaries are far more sympathetic to these peoples and their traditions than their predecessors, they are almost powerless either to bring about a radical transformation in Indian consciousness or do more than mildly alleviate the collective deterioration of Indian life that has been taking place for two centuries. Like that of the most notable of their predecessors, Serra and Brébeuf, their work can at best be regarded as not entirely unsuccessful.

PART III

RELIGIOUS COMMUNITY FORMATION IN THE NEW REPUBLIC

The decades between the Revolution and the Civil War were crucial in the formation of a new American society and culture. What Sidney Mead has called "the lively experiment" was free to unfold in a nation that had in its very Constitution guaranteed complete religious freedom and that enjoyed what seemed at the time to be endless room for expansion. European visitors from Alexis de Tocqueville to Charles Dickens came in a never-ending stream to marvel at the fortunes and follies of their New World cousins. Natural wonders, utopian societies, frontier cities, black slaves, and even innovative prisons were among the novelties they noted and reported back to their news-hungry compatriots.

Religion was one of those cultural realms where experimentation could and did take place ceaselessly. Without an established church, almost anything short of human sacrifice—or, more relevantly, polygamy—could be tried in the name of God's will. No religious group could count on anything but voluntary membership, but it did not seem difficult to attract new members to the most improbable sorts of religious, reform, and social movements, many of which combined features of all three. Primarily secular utopian experiments, such as Robert Owen's New Harmony or George Ripley's Brook Farm, did not usually last very long. Some, like "Mother" Ann Lee's Shakers and John Humphrey Noyes's Oneida, prospered for several decades, then fell into irreversible decline. Still others, like Joseph Smith and his Mormon followers, laid the foundations of enduring new religious traditions.

For the more "mainstream" groups, the frontier presented new challenges. Social stratification was by no means absent in American religious alignments, and Presbyterians, Congregationalists, and Episcopalians continued to attract the prosperous and educated. The "growth industries" of contemporary Christianity, however, were the popular denominations—Baptists, Methodists, and Campbellites—who knew how to say what frontierspeople wanted to hear. But even these latter groups did not remain static. Just as American social classes have always been porous at the boundaries, denominations changed character with their constituents. As Methodists moved from frontier hamlets into middle-class urban neighborhoods, their circuit riders yielded to a settled clergy, and Gothic churches replaced outdoor camp meetings. Religious revivals settled into the landscape, but changed character as well with the times.

These individual Protestant denominations, though, did not exhaust the religious energies of their members. Cutting across their organizational lines were the agencies of the "Benevolent Empire," a loosely related collection of evangelistic and reform societies led by both laity and clergy. In addition, a common evangelical religious culture developed during the earlier nineteenth century that could easily be shared by almost all who identified themselves as "Protestant." This culture was shaped by denominational and interdenominational agencies, and was spread through Sunday schools, colleges, books, periodicals, sermons, and hymns. If Americans shared a common culture during these years, its character was distinctively religious.

But not all Americans were white evangelical Protestants. Dissent manifested itself within the Protestant camp in the liberalism of the Unitarians and Universalists and the liturgical preferences of many Lutherans and Episcopalians. Although blacks shared many of the religious premises of their white evangelical counterparts, they were often neither able nor willing to worship alongside them. Free blacks in the North formed their own churches, whereas their enslaved kindred developed a distinctive amalgam of Christian and African elements in their frequently surreptitious worship.

Beyond the bounds of Protestantism entirely were Jews and Roman Catholics, whose numbers were being rapidly expanded through immigration from Germany and Ireland. The Irish were confined by circumstance primarily to the eastern seaboard, whereas Germans of all religious stripes began to find new homes in the Midwest. The story of these groups, together with that of later Jewish and Roman Catholic immigrantsfrom southern and eastern Europe, is dealt with in the following unit.

A. Toward Independence

CHAPTER 22

The Revolution and the Constitution

The question of exactly what caused the American Revolution is one of those convoluted problems that historians have wrestled with for generations with successive waves of insight but no definitive answer. In addition to specific political and economic grievances, such as taxation without representation, the momentum to make a definitive break with the mother country emerged from a transformation of consciousness. It was not enough simply to want to become independent *from* England; rather, it was also necessary to be free to *become* Americans as well. During the seventeenth century, such an identity had not yet emerged. Colonists thought of themselves as members of a particular colony—Massachusetts Bay, Virginia, or Pennsylvania—and as English. Communication and travel were far more extensive between individual colonial ports and England than they were between the different colonies. An American identity that transcended regional loyalties was still in the future.

The Great Awakening was in some ways the first major event in *American* history—as opposed to the history of the British Empire. It is ironic that its catalyst was George Whitefield, an Englishman—but symbolic that he was buried in American soil. Although its roots may have lain deep in European Pietism, it was American colonists of all sorts and conditions who experienced the great revival, and few emerged from its fires unscathed. Far more than the French and Indian wars, which were essentially colonial affairs, a truly *national* event had taken place in which all Americans had been somehow implicated. In addition, the challenge of Whitefield and other itinerant evangelists to the various colonial establishments helped mold a new attitude toward authority, in which tradition became challenged by experience and hierarchy by democracy.

The Awakening also helped prepare the way for the Revolution by nurturing a national consciousness that made Americans aware of their commonality with one another and familiarized them with intercolonial cooperation. In addition, it is possible to see the Revolution as a continuation of the revival. Many Anglican clergy opposed both events, and Quakers and the German sects tried to stay neutral. Within the English-speaking Reformed churches—Congregational and Presbyterian—there was little hesitation among either New or Old Lights in lending their support to the coming conflict. Jonathan Mayhew especially among the liberals helped construct a rhetoric of defiance, and countless Puritan preachers took their turns in interpreting the struggle for independence as a religious act.

The basic argument promoted from many pulpits was this: Colonial preachers had already developed a theological framework for interpreting historical events on the premise that the Reformation in general, and the emergence of Reformed Christianity in Britain in particular, was the beginning of a divine plan for the transformation of the entire world. During the French and Indian wars, the French and the papacy—France was a Catholic nation—were depicted in many sermons not just as secular enemies but as agents of the Antichrist in an unfolding apocalyptic struggle. When the Revolution began to take shape, the framework remained steady while the characters changed. The Church of England had long been resented both as religiously corrupt and also as an instrument of political imperial control. The king of England became the embodiment of evil, whereas the French, who sided with the American cause, lost their sinister character. Furthermore, the old Puritan "jeremiad" tradition was invoked in the argument that the sufferings that Americans were undergoing at the hands of the British were a punishment for having strayed from the straight and narrow. If Americans repented and returned to the old ways, God would reward them by delivering them from tyranny. The Revolution, in short, was not just a war but also the occasion for a revival. Beyond that, it was part of the dramatic unfolding of God's millennial plan for transforming the world through an ongoing struggle between good and evil. The Americans were God's agent for good—assuming that they could get their proverbial act together.

On the other hand, it is dangerous to overemphasize the role that religious motives played in bringing about the Revolution. Although clerical zeal for liberty—Christian or political—ran high, the churches over which they presided were generally unable to command the continuing allegiance of the generations following the Awakening, and church membership reached a low ebb during the revolutionary era. The British Whig political thought that helped mold the ideological basis of the Revolution was rooted as much in secular as in religious sources, and Puritans, Anglicans, and Deists had all contributed to the latter stream. As Nathan Hatch, George Marsden, and Mark Noll have pointed out in their cautionary work on viewing the emergent nation as a Christian society, even the arch-Presbyterian John Witherspoon, the Scottish divine who became president of Princeton, abandoned religious claims in the political theory he began to expound at that institution. It is also significant that Witherspoon was the mentor of James Madison, the Virginia Anglican who contributed so much to the theory and practice of the separation of church and state first in Virginia and then in the Bill of Rights.

Illustrative of this interplay between sacred and secular is the emergence during and after the Revolution of a new kind of religious imagery around the nation itself and its leaders—a "civil religion." George Washington emerged as a cult figure, and was identified publicly with both Moses and Joshua as a divinely appointed agent of deliverance from bondage. Thomas Jefferson suggested that the official seal include a representation of Moses leading the children of Israel into freedom. Images from the Old Testament combined with those from the Roman Republic: Washington also became identified with Cincinnatus, the general who refused a kingship after victory and returned to his plow. The seal that still appears on our currency bears two Latin inscriptions: *Novus Ordo Seclorum* ("a new order of the ages") and *Annuit Coeptis* ("He has prospered our undertaking").

What did the victory over the British and the constitution of a New Republic mean? Clearly, two major sources of imagery converged: biblical and classical, sacred and secular. These same two strains also came together in resolving the question of what role organized religion was to play in this "first new nation." On the one hand, Jefferson, Franklin, and other representatives of the Enlightenment tradition feared that any government support for religion would lead to corruption of the state—as the entanglement of the Roman Catholic Church with the Bourbon monarchy indicated only too vividly. On the other, separatist spokesmen such as Isaac Backus of Massachusetts revived Roger Williams's old argument that such support would lead to a corruption of the church—as their experience with the New England "standing order" indicated only too vividly. From utterly different ideological perspectives, then, a solution other than that which had been the norm in Europe and most of the colonies seemed very much in order.

Pennsylvania and Rhode Island had helped pave the way, with laws that had granted broad toleration for generations. The other Middle Colonies—New York, Delaware, New Jersey—had at most limited establishment, and readily opted for pluralism when independence was at hand. Although a plan for the equal support by the state of all Protestant churches was debated in Virginia and briefly tried in South Carolina, the southern states moved rapidly toward disestablishment and religious freedom, in part out of revulsion over the Tory allegiances of many Anglican clergy during the revolutionary struggle.

Virginia, which provided so much of the leadership in both the Revolution and the framing of the new nation, was the scene of one of the most complicated debates over what role religion should play in the emergent commonwealth. It was here that the Church of England had been most effectively established, and here as well that dissenting opposition to that establishment was highly vocal. Presbyterians were especially active in arguing for an end to state support of religion out of fear of the harm that such support might wreak on the church—as, they argued, it so frequently had in the Old World.

The main proponents of disestablishment, however, were the Deist Jefferson and the more moderately "enlightened" Madison: the latter's "Memorial and Remonstrance" of 1785 helped secure passage of the former's Statute for Religious Freedom the following year. After a lengthy introductory section which asserts that "Almighty God hath created the mind free" and enumerates the harm that results from attempting to coerce religious belief, Jefferson's act goes on to state:

> Section II. We the General Assembly of Virginia do enact that no man shall be compelled to frequent or support any religious worship, place, or ministry whatsoever, nor shall be enforced, restrained, molested or burthened in his body or goods, or shall otherwise suffer, on account of his religious opinions or belief; but that all men shall be free to profess, and by argument to maintain, their opinions in matters of religion, and that the same shall in no wise diminish, enlarge, or affect their civil capacities.

The final provision goes on to warn future legislators that "the rights hereby asserted are of the natural rights of mankind, and that if any act shall be hereafter passed to repeal the present or to narrow its operations, such act shall be an infringement of natural right." The enactment of this sweeping declaration of religious freedom was part of a series of state actions from 1776 to 1802 in which payments to the established clergy were suspended, the Episcopal Church was deprived of its incorporated status, and its glebe (revenue-producing) lands were sold off as state property. It is noteworthy that Jefferson later regarded the Virginia statute as one of his three most significant accomplishments.

Although the actions of Virginia were highly influential, most were taken prior to the settlement of the question of relationship of church and state at the national level. This still had to be resolved at the Constitutional Convention in Philadelphia, where James Madison, one of the authors of *The Federalist,* again played a leading role. The practical consequences of de facto religious pluralism in the new states also pointed toward a formal acknowledgment of this situation as a norm. After all, even if it seemed wise for the federal government to support a religion, which one should it support? Too many mutually exclusive claimants were there to satisfy anyone. Furthermore, the pressure for limited central government and the maintenance of states' rights further militated against positive action at the federal level; had the national government attempted to interfere with the various courses individual states were pursuing with regard to religion, the result would doubtless have been rejected. It does not seem, in fact, that any of the delegates was inclined to argue for an establishment, and that the debates that preceded the Bill of Rights dealt only with questions of wording and of scope, that is, should their measure be binding on the states or simply on the national government, or should conscientious objection to participation in war be guaranteed. (The latter somehow seems to have fallen by the wayside, though in later years the courts began to recognize such a right as implicit in the First Amendment.)

It is noteworthy in considering the Constitution that the only direct references to religion are negative: "no religious test shall ever be required as a qualification to any office or public trust under the United States" (Art. VI); and "Congress shall make no law respecting an establishment of religion, or prohibiting the free exercise thereof" (the beginning of Article I of the Amendments, better known as the Bill of Rights). Although the Declaration of Independence invokes the deity several times, albeit in language that is scarcely traditionally Christian, the Constitution makes no such reference; rather, in Glenn Miller's words, "the document was one of the most secular in history."

The First Amendment was adopted in a newly forming nation in which religious establishment had already become severely weakened, and denominationalism was a de facto reality. Moreover, the cultural hegemony enjoyed by Protestantism in its several varieties ensured that anything resembling absolute freedom of religion would be slow in coming. The First Amendment prohibited religious establishment only at the national level, and support of religion by the individual states persisted as late as 1833 in the case of Massachusetts. Nevertheless, the long-term impact of the First Amendment was revolutionary, and its implications are still being sorted out in the courts year by year. Instead of the religious *toleration* practiced in varying degrees in the colonies, religious *liberty* was now the nationally mandated norm. America was now a nation friendly but officially neutral toward the panoply of churches that it sheltered. Whether and how this neutrality could work itself out in practice is a major theme of the story of evangelical Protestantism in the nineteenth century.

B. White Evangelicalism

CHAPTER 23

The Second Great Awakening(s)

The winning of independence and the constitution of the new nation were both exhilarating and threatening for evangelicals. Most had supported the patriot cause, and rejoiced in yet another step being taken toward the unfolding of God's plan for the coming of the millennium here on earth. All of the evangelical denominations had experience in resisting tyranny—sometimes each other's—and all were prepared to join in the task of shaping the new democratic republic. Though some were more enthusiastic about democratic prospects than others, most agreed that the kingdom of God was not simply going to arrive but needed hard human work for it to be ushered in. Challenges abounded in religious freedom, pluralism, and disestablishment, including the expansion of the frontier and the myriads of the unchurched who streamed out to inhabit the new lands opening up for pioneering and settlement; and the multiplication of enemies, real and imaginary, who had to be smoked out and vanquished by the sword of the Lord. The evangelicals, in short, had a full plate.

Who were these "evangelicals"? The word itself had a long history, going back to the "good news" of the Gospels and revived in Luther's *evangelische Kirche*. By the time of independence, "evangelical" as a designation for Anglo-American Protestants had taken on a distinct though broad meaning. It did not refer to a specific new tradition or single denomination, but rather included a wide variety of established and emergent groups—Congregationalists (formerly Puritans), Presbyterians, Methodists, and Baptists. In addition to describing most of the members of those groups, it included "low" church Episcopalians, who were gathering strength in Virginia and other parts of the South, and the Americanizing followers of Samuel S. Schmucker among Lutherans in Pennsylvania and Ohio. Various German-speaking sects and movements of frontier provenance, such as Alexander Campbell's "restorationists," also came under this umbrella.

These various sorts and conditions of Protestants did not all share a formal theology. Like Wesley and Whitefield, the archetypal revivalists, some were Arminians whereas others were Calvinists, and a new "middle way" between them was emerging in New Haven. What they did share was a set of three emphases, however much they might quarrel about other issues. First was a commitment to the Bible as the sole source of revelation and religious authority—the legacy of the Reformation. Second was an insistence on personal, emotional conversion as the hallmark of salvation—the fruit of the Great Awakening. Third was the "missionary imperative," the inexorable internal demand on the converted not to hide their lights under proverbial bushels but to go out and share the good news with others who had not yet experienced its power. This could take the form of revival preaching, missionary work, personal witness, or participation in any of the number of benevolent societies founded to spread the Christian message and, beyond that, help to reshape society according to that message.

The first major problem confronting evangelicals after independence was their legal status. During the colonial era, most of the New England and southern colonies had some form of government support for organized religion. Even the Massachusetts Puritans, though, had been forced to share that support with other groups as they had become hemmed in by Separatist dissent on one side and Anglican interference on the other. The First Amendment to the new Constitution made it illegal from the start for the federal government either to support or to interfere with religion. This injunction did not apply to the states, though many of the latter rapidly followed the precedent of Virginia in refusing to sanction any sort of establishment.

Three of the old Puritan domains refused to follow suit: Connecticut, Massachusetts, and New Hampshire. Lyman Beecher (1775–1863), the staunch Connecticut Congregationalist revival preacher, described the situation in his *Autobiography*:

> The habit of legislation from the beginning had been to favor the Congregational order and provide for it. Congregationalism was the established religion. All others were dissenters, and complained of favoritism. The ambitious minority early began to make use of the minor sects on the grounds of invidious distinctions, thus making them restive. So the democracy, as it rose, included nearly all the minor sects, besides the Sabbath-breakers, rum-selling tippling folk, infidels, and ruff-scuff generally, and made a dead set at us of the standing order. (John Harvard Library ed., I, 251)

After this rather lurid characterization of his opposition, Beecher went on to describe both the complex religious scene and the rapid change in the political situation:

> But throwing [Governor John] Treadwell over in 1811 broke the charm and divided the [Federalist] party; persons of third-rate ability, on our side, who wanted to be somebody, deserted; all the infidels of the state had long been leading on that side; the minor sects had swollen, and complained of having to get a certificate to pay their tax where they liked; our efforts to enforce reformation of morals by law made us unpopular; they attacked the clergy unceasingly, and myself in particular . . . with all sorts of misrepresentation, ridicule, and abuse; and finally, the Episcopalians, who had always been stanch Federalists, were disappointed of an appropriation for the Bishop's Fund, which they asked for, and went over to the Democrats. (Ibid., 251–52)

This combination of forces prevailed in 1818 to bring about disestablishment and the end of the complicated system of state support for various churches. Beecher was at first profoundly depressed, but soon changed his mind as to the implications of this radical act:

> For several days I suffered what no tongue can tell *for the best thing that ever happened to the State of Connecticut*. It cut the churches loose from dependence on state support. It threw them wholly on their own resources and on God.
>
> They say ministers have lost their influence; the fact is, they have gained. By voluntary efforts, societies, missions, and revivals, they exert a deeper influence than ever they could by queues, and shoe-buckles, and cocked hats, and gold-headed canes. (Ibid., 252)

New Hampshire yielded in 1819; Massachusetts held on until 1833, after a bitter court fight granted the new, liberal Unitarian party control over most of the church property that conservative Congregationalists had claimed. This "Dedham decision" of 1820 established the principle that all of the members of a geographical parish, rather than just the full members of the church proper, had legal control over the property. When the conservative faction realized that they had become the victims of their own system, they rapidly abandoned the principle, and eventually saw Massachusetts relinquish its dubious status as the last holdout against disestablishment.

The result of this slow but steady process was the addition of two new words to the American religious vocabulary: *voluntaryism* and *denominationalism.* All organized religious life from now on had to be conducted on a voluntary basis. Informal social pressure might still exist, but no official government action could either support or hinder particular groups. No one church enjoyed any privileged status in the new nation or its constituent states; all, rather, stood equally on their own as *denominations,* sharing a common Christian heritage; differing from one another through particular emphases and practices *denominated* by their names; and alternately cooperating or competing as circumstances dictated. The burden was now on the churches to attract and retain members, and with them their support in energy, time, and money. As Lyman Beecher was ultimately constrained to observe, this turned out to be the best thing that ever happened—not only to the state of Connecticut but to American Christianity itself.

The main engine of voluntaryism had already been set in place by the Great Awakening: revivalism. Revivals became a staple of religious life for a broad cross-section of American Protestants, and after the Awakening of the 1740s they manifested themselves in various, more restricted forms such as Whitefield's later tours, the "New Light Stir" in northern New England, and assorted outbursts throughout the southern colonies. The Revolution diverted attention from religious life in the narrow sense, but itself took on the character of a revival for many of its clerical interpreters and well-wishers. After independence, the familiar postwar phenomenon of a brief decline in religious activity set in while Americans got their bearings and in many cases pulled up stakes and headed west or south.

Although formal church membership was low, Americans were too steeped in various traditions of piety to allow purely secular enthusiasms to prevail for long. By the 1790s, pressure was building for a revival of religion both in New England and the southern frontier. What happened in both these regions, and subsequently in upstate New York and other parts of what was then the "West," have collectively been called the "Second Great Awakening." (Some scholars have identified at least seven such "awakenings" in American history, although only the first two are usually recognized.) The three major phases of this Second Awakening were so separated in space, time, and character that their unity is problematic. However, there is no doubt that the early decades of the nineteenth century were a period of extraordinary religious ferment, notable as much for its disparity as its intensity.

The first phase of this Awakening arose in New England, with its epicenter in Connecticut. The Congregationalist clergy in this most traditional of the sometime Puritan commonwealths was, as Beecher had described it, firmly committed to the established ways and allied itself with the most conservative political faction, the Federalists. Theologically, its most venturesome members were committed to the "New Divinity" developed by Jonathan Edwards and his followers: Joseph Bellamy, Nathanael Emmons, Samuel Hopkins, and Jonathan Edwards Jr. These men attempted

to continue the older Calvinist tradition while at the same time reconciling it with
a New Light defense of the Awakening's revivals. Their thought is too diverse and
highly technical to be summarized easily. Among their principal concerns were a
stress on the moral character of God's government of the world and a backing away
from the doctrine of original sin toward an emphasis on the active role of individuals
who actually do the sinning. Although these men regarded themselves as rigorous
Calvinists, their thought was clearly pointing in a new direction.

The Second Awakening in Connecticut took place almost exclusively in its Congregational churches and at Yale College. Its early agents were the established clergy,
most notably the parish minister Asahel Nettleton (1783–1844) and Timothy Dwight
(1752–1817), the energetic president of Yale. Around 1797, they turned their energies
to the task of conversion, and the results were highly gratifying. Dwight's preaching,
which brought the revival to Yale in 1801, inspired a generation of students such as
Lyman Beecher and his ally, Nathaniel William Taylor. These two and a number of
their contemporaries would together institutionalize the revival as a staple of religious life in New England and its extending sphere of influence for a generation.
This Awakening stood firmly in the tradition of Jonathan Edwards rather than that
of Tennent and Davenport. It was decorous, restrained, engineered by the established
clergy, and very much under their control.

Not so the "Great Revival" of the southwest, which is often regarded as the Awakening's second phase. After independence, sturdy Scotch-Irish pioneers were crossing the
Cumberland Gap and spreading out into the new expanses of Tennessee, Kentucky,
and southern Ohio. The ancestral Presbyterianism that they brought with them was
not readily transplanted into a region where learned sermons and elaborate polity
made little sense. It was in this context that men like James McGready, a Presbyterian
from North Carolina who arrived in Logan County, Kentucky, in 1796, began to labor
for a revival of the religious excitement that he and others had long desired.

Assisted by some Methodist friends from Carolina, McGready launched a new
wave of revivals first at Red River and then at Gasper River, Kentucky, in 1800. These
were followed by the even more dramatic outburst the following year at Cane Ridge,
northeast of Lexington. Cane Ridge is still remembered as the greatest of the "Camp
Meeting revivals"—a new form of indigenous frontier religious life. Here Presbyterians Barton W. Stone and Robert Finley were joined by Methodist and Baptist
preachers in a revival that attracted tens of thousands of isolated, sensation-starved
frontier people. These new in-migrants were rapidly filling up the area, but had little
in their organized social or religious lives to relieve the dangers and privations they
encountered daily.

The Cane Ridge Revival lasted a full week, and was by all accounts a spectacular
success in terms of sheer numbers and enthusiasm. More took place at Cane Ridge,
though, than its promoters had anticipated. In the midst of the excitement, many of
the participants fell into neuromuscular seizures that were soon known as "exercises."

These included "barking," "jerking," "falling," "dancing," "laughing," and other symptoms that might now be regarded as hysterical but were interpreted at the time as potent evidences of the power of the Spirit. On the other hand, the revival provided a chance to engage in more secular recreations, and skeptics observed that more souls were conceived than saved during the proceedings.

The camp meeting rapidly became a fixture of frontier life. At first it manifested itself in the semispontaneous, enthusiastic manner of Cane Ridge; later, it took on a more routinized form devised by the organizationally minded Methodists who appropriated it as their own. Here was a form of religion generated by and uniquely expressive of the needs of the frontier. It was eagerly embraced by the popular denominations, such as Baptists and Methodists, who had a no-holds-barred approach to the challenge of evangelization. On the other hand, the active participation of Presbyterians was strong medicine for their East Coast counterparts who believed that traditional, decorous forms of worship and polity were divinely sanctioned.

Community and authority were unstated but important themes of the Awakening in all its phases. The Connecticut phase built on a society with a venerable history, but one in which authority had been called into question by the upheaval of the Revolution. Timothy Dwight and company thus carried on a movement of social as well as religious revitalization, together with a reassertion of establishment influence. On the Kentucky frontier, there was nothing to reestablish; community had to be built from the ground up, and the initial experience of community was chaotic and ecstatic. Authority was similarly nonexistent, and the remote claims of eastern Presbyterians were hardly compelling. This early phase lasted only a few years, but while it lasted, it contrasted dramatically with the sober rituals of the "land of steady habits."

The third major phase of the Second Great Awakening fell somewhere in between these extremes. Just as Virginians and Carolinians were pouring into the southwest, countless Yankees from the rocky, unproductive farmlands of New England were following the path of the Erie Canal west across upstate New York from Albany to Buffalo. This "Yankee Exodus" continued westward, leaving a heritage of New England–like towns across northern Ohio and southern Michigan; skipping Indiana, which was settled by southerners moving northward; continuing across parts of Illinois, Wisconsin, Minnesota, and Iowa; and ultimately planting settlements in the Pacific Northwest and northern California. This demographic movement can be traced by looking at the spread of Congregational churches, which were usually built in the Greek Revival and "carpenter Gothic" styles popular at the time.

Upstate New York in the decades between independence and the Civil War soon became known as the "Burned-Over District" for the intensity and variety of the religious life that it generated. Here, the Shakers created their distinctive communities; John Humphrey Noyes and his followers sought perfection; and Joseph Smith claimed to have encountered the angel Moroni, who made known to him a set of mysterious

golden plates containing a new revelation. The followers of these new spiritual directions came from a wide variety of social and educational strata but had in common
a long familial nurture in New England piety. In this bustling environment they
were free to seek new kinds of salvation as well as temporal fortunes. Lurking in the
background, though, was the ancestral Puritanism that Charles Grandison Finney
(1792–1875) set out to revive.

If there is any truth to Emerson's notion that each age generates its own characteristic "representative men," then Finney was certainly one of Emerson's own era. Born
in Connecticut, he was raised in upstate New York, and became first a schoolteacher
and then a lawyer. After his conversion, he abruptly forsook his law practice to take up
"a retainer from the Lord Jesus Christ to plead his cause." Although lacking in formal
theological education and a bit vague on certain doctrinal matters, Finney managed
to inveigle a local presbytery to ordain him and began a new life as a preacher.

Although sponsored by the Presbyterians, Finney's course was much too independent to be restricted by any denomination. He preached wherever he could,
focusing on the Burned-Over District he already knew well. Finney soon attracted
attention through his employment of "New Measures Revivalism," which was largely
of his own devising. One of these new measures that raised many eyebrows was the
"anxious bench," a seat placed near the revivalist on which those who appeared to
be on the brink of conversion could be placed and worked on intensively. Pressure
for conversion was intensified by another measure, the "protracted meeting," which
stretched on for hours at a time and often was continued on succeeding days. Women
openly testifying at meetings and Finney's praying by name for his antagonists were
still other innovations that were less than universally welcomed.

Among those who conspicuously withheld their approval for the new measures
was Lyman Beecher, who confronted Finney at a dramatic meeting called at New
Lebanon, New York, in July of 1827. Beecher at the time was serving a church in
Boston, where he gained fame as a revivalist and vocal antagonist of both Unitarians and Catholics. Although Beecher vowed to fight Finney every step of the way
east, Finney refused to compromise and went on to conduct triumphal evangelistic
tours in Boston and New York. What was really happening here was an example
of what Sigmund Freud has called "the narcissism of minor differences." Beecher
and Finney were so similar in approach to the question of evangelization that the
flare-up between them was more an indication of closeness than distance. Beecher,
that diehard defender of establishment in Connecticut, would simply not yield the
authority of the East to the upstart from the West. Ironically, Beecher was shortly
thereafter called to be president of the new Lane Seminary in Cincinnati. He soon
found himself in hot water, charged with heresy and hypocrisy by a local minister who
found Beecher's views far too radical. Although Beecher was acquitted, the proceedings helped set in motion the split between Old and New School Presbyterians—in
part over revivalism—that took place in 1838.

Neither Finney nor Beecher was preaching primarily to the utterly unchurched but rather seeking to revive religion and community among those who had left them behind. Finney went on to a career as professor of theology and later president of Oberlin College, located in the Western Reserve lands of Connecticut in northeastern Ohio. In addition to his *Memoirs* of 1876, he produced two notable works. One, a systematic theology, developed the ideas of holiness and perfection that he had absorbed from the Methodist tradition. The other, which is still kept in print by evangelical publishing houses, was far better known: the *Lectures on Revivals of Religion* of 1835. These *Lectures,* which were exactly that in their original form, constituted a how-to-do-it manual for would-be revivalists. In careful detail, Finney explained just how to go about organizing, promoting, and carrying out a revival campaign guaranteed to win souls. Finney was nothing if not practical, and was hardly concerned with holding on to trade secrets.

In his first lecture, Finney made it clear that a major theological shift had taken place from the time of the first Great Awakening. Jonathan Edwards had maintained that revivals were the work of God, and that preachers such as himself were simply God's instruments. Not so for Finney: "*Religion is the work of man. It is something for man to do* . . . A REVIVAL OF RELIGION IS NOT A MIRACLE. A miracle has been generally defined to be, a Divine interference, setting aside or suspending the laws of nature. All the laws of matter and mind remain in force. They are neither suspended nor set aside in a revival. . . . [A revival] is a purely philosophical result of the right use of the constituted means" (John Harvard Library ed., 9, 12, 13).

It is clear from Finney's words that the Calvinism of Edwards now lay far in the past. The emphasis here is clearly not on depravity and the bondage of the will by original sin; rather, it is on human ability to do what God wants. This is not to say that humans act autonomously; rather, it is to assert the presence of a God-given ability to exercise one's faculties to do the right by choice. Similarly, Lyman Beecher depended heavily for his theology on his old Yale comrade, Nathaniel William Taylor (1786–1858). "Taylorism," as his thought came to be known, advanced some of the directions taken by the "New Divinity" into a theological stance compatible with the activist spirit of revivalism. Instead of stressing God's sovereignty, Taylor stressed the theme of God's "moral government" of the universe. Instead of stressing total depravity, Taylor pictured humanity as theoretically free to do good. In practical terms, all would sin and therefore need redemption; however, there was no metaphysical necessity lying behind this irresistible tendency. Although Taylor claimed to be faithful to the Calvinist tradition, he and Finney both were working out an essentially Arminian position consistent with the revivalist spirit. "Taylorism" also became known as the "New Haven theology," after Taylor's position as minister at that city's First Church and his professorship at Yale Divinity School.

Although the Second Great Awakening began in a revival of piety in New England, it is clear enough that its main arena was the expanding frontier. Revivalists were the shock troops of this initiative, and the revivals helped to secure beachheads—much like the role the religious orders played in the "spiritual conquest" of New Spain. The task for both old and new evangelical denominations then became the consolidation of the gains won by the vanguard of preachers. In this effort, Presbyterians and Congregationalists took a major step toward ecumenical cooperation through their "Plan of Union" of 1801. Engineered by Jonathan Edwards Jr., this plan provided that no church of one denomination should be established within five miles of one of the other, that ministers of either denomination could be called by any of these churches, and various other provisions for interdenominational cooperation. The Presbyterians were the major beneficiaries of the plan, because they were closer to the frontier and better able to mobilize their resources. The plan finally was abrogated in 1837, as one of the issues that precipitated the schism between Old and New School Presbyterians.

For the Methodists and Baptists, who had less of an established base from which to work, the task of evangelization and the establishment of order was more compressed. The exemplary Baptist figure was the "farmer-preacher," who felt a call to the ministry and preached to whomever he could gather to hear him on Sundays. Since Baptists traditionally resisted centralization, the movement spread primarily from these grassroots foundations. Methodists, however, loved organization, and "circuit riders" were their answer to the same set of challenges. Circuit riders were young men endowed with little education but enormous energy and dedication. Equipped with a horse and saddlebags filled with Bibles, hymnals, and the Methodist *Discipline,* they followed regularly assigned routes around the frontier, stopping to preach wherever an audience of a few could be found among scattered cabins, farmsteads, and hamlets. When possible, a small "class" of lay people would be gathered, who could continue the spiritual life on their own until the rider came round again. As settlement increased, these classes often grew into churches, and the circuit riders who had not yet died young from exhaustion yielded to a settled clergy. Peter Cartwright (1785–1872), one of the greatest of the breed, lamented in his classic *Autobiography* of 1856 the passing of this rugged frontier piety into what to him seemed a namby-pamby gentility.

The Second Great Awakening was clearly not a unified sequence of events like the first, in which a direct cause-and-effect relationship could easily be traced. The discreet preaching of Nettleton and the barking and jerking of Cane Ridge were worlds apart, based on a common premise but executed in drastically different contexts. None of the loosely connected components of the Second Awakening can be simply described as revivals of religion, though. Each was firmly rooted in deeply felt social needs, reflected those needs, and helped bring about a transformation of community in a profound sense. Beecher and Finney, who emerged as giants in the Awakening's later phases, helped provide a continuity between East and West, Calvinism and Arminianism, civilization and frontier, old and new. As such, they were harbingers of a new social order, which started with revival, went on to reform, and ultimately shaped a culture that would endure for decades.

CHAPTER 24

Moral Reform, Antislavery, and Civil War

During the first Great Awakening, Edwards, Whitefield, and their fellow revivalists focused their efforts on the saving of individual souls. The revival influenced and was affected by society, but few were concerned with or even much aware of this. One of those long-range social effects was an undermining of the "parochial principle"—the notion that religion, geography, and politics shape and reinforce one another, and that one's religious allegiance is a function of where and under what authority one lives. Akin to this was the idea of freedom of religious choice, which ultimately had vast implications for the role of religion in the New Republic: America was the first country where one could elect a "community of memory"— in effect, where one could choose a past in the form of affiliation with a religious community. By the time of the Second Great Awakening, church membership was well on its way to becoming a voluntary matter. Revivals were needed again, to stir up the enthusiasm that would make voluntarily supported churches work.

During the colonial era, the institutions of society were in theory maintained through an alliance of church and state. The family, the church, and the town or parish were the primary units of social organization, and it was through some combination of their work that children were educated, criminals punished, and the poor and disabled cared for. Relative at least to postcolonial times, society had an organic character, and everyone within its purview was simultaneously supported and supervised through its network of resources. The benefits of this arrangement were a psychological security of knowing one's place and having someone to rely on in bad times. The negative side was an insistence on conformity and subordination; deviance, especially in the form of challenging society's norms, simply could not be tolerated.

With the disestablishment of the churches and the growing mobility and pluralism of the broader society, whatever reality had existed in this "ideal type" of an "organic society" came into serious jeopardy. The state churches were gone, or rapidly going; people were no longer forced to dance to their tune and became inclined to turn to the secular government for whatever needs they could not supply for themselves. For the likes of a Lyman Beecher, this situation might have benefits; however, those benefits would not simply fall into American Protestant laps but had to be actively cultivated. The obvious conclusion was that revivalism simply as a means for soul-winning was necessary but not sufficient. To bring about a "Christian America"—Christian in practice, if not by statute—revivals had to be hitched to a new idea: reform.

Reform became the byword of early nineteenth-century America. Its roots lay in almost all of the major traditions of the colonial era. Quakers derived from their notion of the "inner light" the doctrine of the radical equality of all of humanity, which meant for them the promotion of peace, the active participation of women in society, the abolition of slavery, and humane treatment of the imprisoned and other unfortunate classes. Although Puritanism was never quite utopian, Winthrop's vision of the "city set upon a hill" had powerful implications for a vision of a society ordered according to God's wishes. The Enlightenment, which shaped the thought of the Founding Fathers, took as one of its premises the notion that human progress was inevitable and illimitable if reason was the basis for social organization. Finally, John Wesley's Arminianism and his teaching that "entire sanctification" was within human reach provided yet another impetus to the broader idea that society could and should be changed for the better. For many evangelicals of the day, God's millennial kingdom emerged as an ultimate, achievable goal.

The Second Great Awakening was a high tide of reform as well as revival—the two simply would not be separated. Not only evangelicals took on the reform mantle—the activities of Unitarians, Quakers, and various utopians were all significant parts of the "Lively Experiment" of "Freedom's Ferment," and are discussed elsewhere. (Conversely, however, not all evangelicals—including many Lutherans and Old School Presbyterians—were especially keen on tinkering with existent social arrangements.) But just as the Awakening itself was complex and even contradictory in its various phases, so was reform.

The New England revivals that began in the 1790s and continued on for many years were rooted firmly in an established social and religious order. The defenders of this order felt a pressing need to reestablish its legitimacy against threats from Jeffersonian democracy and the perceived forces of "infidelity." In addition to rekindling individual religious enthusiasm through the revivals of Dwight and Nettleton, Lyman Beecher especially saw the need for a more general program of evangelical outreach to keep New England and the whole new nation from falling into the coils of sin and disorder. Beecher rapidly became involved in a whole array of reform endeavors that were springing up around him. Dueling, which had taken the life of Alexander Hamilton, was one evil against which he took up the (figurative) sword. Soon came campaigns against excessive drinking, the profanation of the Sabbath, and other signs that the New Republic stood on the brink of moral chaos unless rescued by evangelical vigilance.

The result of this organized vigilance was a whole network of independent but interrelated societies that soon became known as "the Benevolent Empire." The societies usually were organized first at the local and state levels; by the 1820s, these had multiplied sufficiently that they began to coalesce into national organizations.

Although most of their members were Congregationalists and Presbyterians, who were also collaborating in the Plan of Union, the societies themselves were interdenominational, and a fair number of Methodists and other evangelicals also became involved. Unlike the colonial period, in which the clergy and civil leadership were expected to take primary responsibility for religion and order, these societies were often led by laymen, though clergy such as Beecher were active participants. Also, as Beecher's career illustrates so well, many of the same men were active in a variety of organizations, thus creating an informal system of "interlocking directorates" binding the work of the "Empire" together. Crucial to the success of these societies was the lavish support of wealthy evangelical businessmen such as the brothers Arthur and Lewis Tappan. Finally, there was throughout this era a continual interaction between British and American evangelicals. Frequently, as in the beginnings of the Sunday school movement and the emancipation of slaves in the British West Indies, events in the parent country had major reverberations across the Atlantic.

As Robert Kelley has pointed out, the reform impulse also correlated significantly with the fortunes of the Whig party, which favored a strong federal role in promoting economic development and middle-class interests, and which in turn was strongly related to regional, ethnic, and religious factors. As he observed in *The Cultural Pattern in American Politics,* "Wherever Yankee Whigs went in their westward migration, they carried with them a righteous and confident urge to use the secular government to create a morally unified society" (166). From southern New England especially this cultural impulse spread along the paths of the "Yankee Exodus" across upstate New York, northern Pennsylvania and Ohio, southern Michigan, and on westward, and was conspicuous by its absence in such areas as the "Egypt" region of southern Illinois settled primarily by southerners. Democrats, who generally opposed interference by the federal government in matters of religion and morality, found much of their support among outgroups who resented the pretensions to hegemony by the upwardly mobile, evangelical Protestants of English background who formed the core of "Whiggery." Therefore, Irish and French Catholics, German Lutherans and Reformed, urban freethinking intellectuals and—until the advent of large numbers of Irish Catholics altered the demographic balance—Scotch-Irish Presbyterians rallied in large numbers behind the banners of Jacksonianism. Similarly, in the South, slaveholders usually resented moralistic Yankee interference and supported the dominant Democratic Party, whereas Whigs such as Kentucky's Henry Clay were strong in upland regions where slavery was of less economic importance.

The reform societies that constituted the Empire had a variety of intersecting and overlapping goals. One was the fostering of true religion, the basis of all genuine reform. This was the work of the American Bible Society (1816), which grew out of a network of state societies founded a few years earlier. The purpose was quite simply the printing and distribution of Bibles, especially among the unchurched, so that they could encounter the divine word directly. Closely related were the tract societies, which similarly merged into the American Tract Society in 1825. Tracts were brief pamphlets that presented an argument or appeal for religious truths or reform causes, such as temperance. Similarly, the American Sunday School Union (1824) built on the work of an earlier British prototype, which directed its efforts mainly toward fostering literacy among poor children. In America, the emphasis soon shifted toward direct evangelization, both of the unchurched and, eventually, the children of churchgoers. By some estimates, the latter two organizations had distributed some seventy-three million pages of print by 1836.

The missionary impulse was another vital part of the Awakening. This was vividly exemplified in the "Haystack Prayer Meeting" of 1806, when a group of Williams College students was overtaken by a commitment to foreign missions while taking refuge from an outburst of rain. The American Board of Commissioners for Foreign Missions (1810), the American Home Mission Society (1826), and the General Convention of the Baptist Denomination in the United States of America for Foreign Missions (1814) represented some of the aspects of this movement, which sought the conversion of infidels at home and abroad. The Burma mission conducted under Baptist auspices by Adoniram Judson (1788–1850) and his succession of three wives was the inspiration for a flood of edifying literature, in which these intrepid souls were presented as Protestant saints. Despite the hardships endured by these and myriad other missionaries, especially in the Pacific, the Middle East, and Asia, American evangelicals were infused with enormous enthusiasm for the prospects of rapidly evangelizing the entire world—another harbinger that the millennium might be at hand.

The further objects of benevolence were legion. Societies arose to minister to sailors, rescue prostitutes, and reclaim drunkards. However vast and complex the Empire might become, though, some underlying premises always remained clear. Because the United States could not and would not support religion directly, it was incumbent on the evangelical churches to carry on their work though voluntary effort. This included both the conversion of individuals and the reform of institutions. Lobbying the government was not out of the question, as evidenced in the campaign of the General Union for Promoting the Observance of the Christian Sabbath to end Sunday mail delivery and other profanations of the Lord's Day. The net result of this concentrated, coordinated campaign was to be the eventual achievement of a Christian America, where evangelicalism had won the day not so much by legal coercion as through moral suasion. When this had been achieved, the millennium might well have been ushered in—in part through human effort.

Though far more optimistic about human possibilities than their colonial predecessors, the promoters of the Benevolent Empire remained conservative when compared with their brethren further west. Alike as Finney and Beecher may have been in the general shape of their careers, there was still a significant difference in the thrust of their ideas and actions. Although Beecher had come closer and closer to an Arminian position, Finney outdid him in espousing perfectionism. No matter how aggressive in their posture toward reforming society in their own image, New Englanders such as Beecher generally retained a Puritan caution in their expectations as to how far society could, or should, be fundamentally altered.

Whether interpreted by Beecher or Finney, though, the reform impulse up until the mid-1830s was hardly intended to bring about any fundamental realignments in American society. The moral reforms advocated by the Benevolent Empire, such as temperance and Sabbatarianism, were clearly not attempts to bring about something new but rather to adapt something old to a very new context. That their advocates thought a vigorous campaign necessary reflected the rapidly changing social structure of Jacksonian America, in which one had to run faster than ever simply to stay in the same place.

Paul E. Johnson, in *A Shopkeeper's Millennium*—his study of the social background of Finney's revivals in Rochester, New York, in 1831—concluded that the city in which these revivals had such an extraordinary effect, especially among the merchant classes, was in the midst of a profound transformation. Previously, employers had followed the colonial pattern of taking in many of their employees as boarders, sharing much of their everyday life with them—including a frequent tipple or two—and generally being in a position to supervise their behavior and bring them gently back into line if they deviated too much from informal societal norms. In the 1820s, however, employers and workers rapidly began to segregate themselves into separate communities, so that such "social control" was no longer possible or desired. The revivals had the incidental but important side effect of re-uniting a merchant class that had become badly divided over religious and political issues, and creating a new cultural ethos in which conversion, followed by voluntary temperance and self-discipline, characterized management and the "right sort" of labor alike. Virtuous merchants now hired only temperance men for their help. Max Weber, who had postulated an "elective affinity" between the "Protestant ethic" and the "spirit of capitalism" in the Puritan era, would doubtless have felt vindicated by Johnson's findings.

That not all reformers were so committed to the interests of classes already entrusted with wealth and power is illustrated vividly in the unfolding drama over the "peculiar institution" of slavery, which exemplifies the stakes for which the game of reform could be played. Quakers—never, at least in theory, respecters of persons and status—were the earliest activists in the crusade against slavery. In the eighteenth century, Anthony Benezet and John Woolman led the rise among slavery's opponents. William Lloyd Garrison (1805–79), who had gained experience working with the Quaker abolitionist editor Benjamin Lundy, rapidly emerged as the irrepressible spokesman for a new idea: immediatism. In his *Liberator*, which he began to publish in Boston in 1831, Garrison took an uncompromising position not only on the evil of slavery but also on the necessity of abolishing it immediately. If the Constitution sanctioned slavery, then the Constitution was evil and must be discarded: it was, according to Garrison, "a covenant with Death and an agreement with Hell."

Garrison thus served as the "point man" for radical abolitionism, and combined his concern with ending slavery with other "ultra-ist" causes. Chief among these were pacifism and the rights of women, concerns that up until then had been maintained steadily only by the Quakers. The Garrisonians first broke with the American Peace Society, which they did not consider radical enough in its acceptance of a government that was ultimately based on force. A more important division came in 1840 when the American Anti-Slavery Society split on the issue of whether it was proper for women to speak publicly to audiences not wholly composed of other women (as in the various Female Anti-Slavery Societies). The more conservatively inclined, including most of the clergy, withdrew from the Garrisonian-dominated group to form the American and Foreign Anti-Slavery Society, in which the role of women was more restricted. Whatever the implications for abolitionism, these events gave a clear boost to organized feminism. Anti-slavery and other reform societies were among the first occasions women received in the nineteenth century for acquiring political and organizational skills. These skills soon found expression at the historic Women's Rights Convention held in Seneca Falls, New York, in 1848 under the leadership of Elizabeth Cady Stanton and Lucretia Mott. (Mott was a Quaker who helped Stanton abandon her childhood Presbyterianism. Stanton did this so decisively that she later became friends with the agnostic Robert Ingersoll, and wrote in 1895 *The Woman's Bible* a harsh critique of the portrayal of women in scripture.)

The role of Garrison and his radical followers in helping or hindering abolition has been much debated; whatever the verdict, they certainly helped bring the issue to the forefront of public attention through their relentless activity. Another aspect of the "perfectionist" wing of the movement was focused in Ohio and led by Theodore Dwight Weld (1803–95). ("Perfectionism" was the Wesley-inspired belief that individuals could attain a state of freedom from sinfulness.) Weld had been converted by Finney, and after a career as a revivalist and temperance advocate enrolled in 1832 at Lane Seminary in Cincinnati for more formal ministerial training. Weld rapidly converted most of the student body to abolitionist principles, and together they began to work with the Cincinnati black community. While Lane's president, Lyman Beecher, was back east raising funds, the Lane trustees ordered Weld and his followers to end their activism, which they refused to do.

As a consequence, the "Lane rebels" picked up stakes and left for Oberlin, where Finney was teaching theology and the sturdy abolitionist president Asa Mahan welcomed them. (Oberlin, founded in 1833 by New England Congregationalists, was known as a center for social radicalism, and was soon to become the first coeducational and interracial American college.) Weld went on to a career as an organizer and publicist for the antislavery cause, and his followers—the "Band of Seventy"—tirelessly and at great personal risk set about organizing antislavery societies in New York, Ohio, and environs. The pressure that these groups were able to bring to bear on the federal government played a major role in turning around northern opinion on slavery.

No one factor was decisive in bringing about this shift. Northern opinion was swayed by moral revulsion against slavery, fear for white civil rights after the Dred Scott decision, dislike of the South, and attachment to the Union. Most northerners probably shared to some degree the southern argument that blacks were an inferior people needing paternal protection. However, the question of whether that protection was being provided received a resoundingly negative answer in Harriet Beecher Stowe's epoch-making *Uncle Tom's Cabin,* published as a book in 1852 after previously appearing in serial form. Stowe had lived in Cincinnati for many years with her father, Lyman Beecher, and had the opportunity to gather many firsthand impressions of slavery in bordering Kentucky. Stowe's heroes were the weak, the oppressed, and the peaceable: women, children, blacks, and Quakers. Notable among these heroes was Little Eva, a white slaveowner's child who dies in a wash of sentimentality. Most memorable, though, was Uncle Tom himself, whose death at the hands of the Vermont-born overseer Simon Legree transfigures him into a black Christ. Stowe ends the novel on an apocalyptic note:

> This is an age of the world when nations are trembling and convulsed. A mighty influence is abroad, surging and heaving the world, as with an earthquake. And is America safe? Every nation that carries in its bosom great and unredressed injustice has in it the elements of this last convulsion.
>
> Christians! every time that you pray that the kingdom of Christ may come, can you forget that prophecy associates in dread fellowship, the *day of vengeance* with the year of his redeemed? A day of grace is yet held out to us. Both North and South have been guilty before God; and the *Christian Church* has a heavy account to answer. Not by combining together, to protect injustice and cruelty, and making a common capital of sin, is this Union to be saved,—but by repentance, justice and mercy; for, not surer is the eternal law by which the millstone sinks in the ocean, than that stronger law by which injustice and cruelty shall bring on nations the wrath of Almighty God! (Signet Classic ed., 476–77)

The slavery issue took its toll on the organized Christianity that Stowe thus indicted. Biblical defenses of slavery, including God's curse on Noah's son Ham as the origin of the black race, began to be propounded by southern divines and soon became common ideological currency in a region where religion was as ensconced as the "peculiar institution." Among the "liturgical churches"—Roman Catholic, Episcopal, Lutheran—antislavery sentiment was limited or regional, and no lasting schisms occurred. Congregationalists and Unitarians were scarce in the South, so were barely affected organizationally. It was the three great national evangelical denominations—Baptist, Methodist, and Presbyterian—that were rent asunder by the growing debates. The Baptists were traditionally decentralized, so that the formation of the Southern Baptist Convention in 1845 created little turmoil. North and south went their own ways, and in the twentieth century grew so far apart that no reunion seems even remotely possible. Early Methodism had been steeped in John Wesley's antislavery teachings, and slaveholding was forbidden among early American Methodists. As the movement grew popular, though, it began to make its peace with the dominant mores of the South, so that slaveholding bishops began to appear by the 1830s. It was over this issue that the denomination finally split in 1845—a rift that was healed nearly a century later.

The situation among the Presbyterians was the most complicated. The trial of Lyman Beecher and other "liberals" in the 1830s was a sign that trouble was at hand, although the slavery issue was not yet a major factor. At stake was tradition versus innovation, and Beecher, for all his timidity on some questions, was clearly on the latter side in the denominational context. "Old School" Presbyterians gained the upper hand over the "New School" in the General Assembly of 1837, and two churches thus came into being. As slavery emerged as a decisive issue, both of these "Schools" were to split yet again. The New School, which had a firmer base in the North, divided in 1857 after taking a series of increasingly stronger antislavery positions. The Old School, always more conservative and southern-based, held together until the war erupted in 1861. After the war, the various factions reformed on sectional lines, creating northern and southern Presbyterian churches that lasted until the merger of 1984.

Like most wars, the Civil War was viewed by many Americans as a religious event—or at least a political and military event with profound religious dimensions. Shortly before the war, a "third great awakening" had taken place in a series of urban revivals, or union prayer meetings, following the panic of 1857. Preachers from many denominations on both sides invoked divine sanction on the struggle. Many clergy, laity, and nuns served as chaplains, nurses, or in other humanitarian roles, such as those provided by the evangelical Christian Commission and the Unitarian-led Sanitary Commission—the predecessor of the Red Cross. It was on a visit to the nation's capital while working for the Sanitary Commission that Julia Ward Howe, a radical Unitarian from Boston, was inspired with an apocalyptic vision most out of keeping with her immediate theological convictions. The "Battle Hymn of the Republic," published in 1862, was immediately set to the tune of "John Brown's Body"—memorializing the antislavery martyr of Harper's Ferry—as an anthem of the Union army. Its rich biblical cadences not only stirred the war effort but provided it with a theological interpretation:

> He has sounded forth the trumpet that shall never call retreat;
> He is sifting out the hearts of men before his judgment seat;
> O be swift, my soul, to answer him; be jubilant, my feet!
> Our God is marching on.

Perhaps, in retrospect, the most interesting interpretation of the war's religious meaning came in President Lincoln's brief Second Inaugural Address of 1865. Such addresses have almost invariably contained some reference to God and his providential wishes for America, though usually not of a very imaginative sort. Lincoln himself came from a Baptist background but later in his career maintained no regular church affiliation. (Allen Guelzo, in his 1999 study, maintains that Lincoln was not a believer in any traditional Christian sense.) Obviously, though, he was deeply steeped in scripture and demonstrated a remarkable talent for critical theology: he at one time characterized America as "this, His almost chosen people." Near the end of the war, he publicly offered these startlingly original and complex reflections on the drama in which he himself was a principal:

> Neither party expected for the war the magnitude or the duration which it has already attained. Neither anticipated that the cause of the conflict might cease with or even before the conflict itself should cease. Each looked for an easier triumph, and a result less fundamental and astounding. Both read the same Bible and pray to the same God, and each invokes His aid against the other. It may seem strange that any men should dare to ask a just God's assistance in wringing their bread from the sweat of other men's faces, but let us judge not, that we be not judged. The prayers of both could not be answered. That of neither has been answered fully. The Almighty has His own purposes. "Woe unto the world because of offenses; for it must needs be that offenses come, but woe to that man by whom the offense cometh." If we shall suppose that American slavery is one of those offenses which, in the providence of God, must needs come, but which, having continued through His appointed time, He now wills to remove, and that He gives to both North and South this terrible war as the woe due to those by whom the offense came, shall we discern therein any departure from those divine attributes which the believers in a living God always ascribe to Him? Fondly do we hope, fervently do we pray, that this mighty scourge of war may speedily pass away. Yet, if God wills that it continue until all the wealth piled up by the bondsman's two hundred and fifty years of unrequited toil shall be sunk, and until every drop of blood drawn with the lash shall be paid by another drawn with the sword, as was said three thousand years ago, so still it must be said "the judgments of the Lord are true and righteous altogether."

CHAPTER 25

The Culture of Antebellum Evangelicalism

Revivalism and reform were two major components of a broader set of institutions, practices, literature, ideas, and viewpoints that together can be seen as a *culture*. This culture not only shaped the lives of evangelicals themselves but became so pervasive in national life that all Americans had to come to terms with it in one way or another. Given the realities of religious pluralism and the need for cooperation, this culture could not be based on a hard core of commonly held theological assumptions, because evangelicals themselves had never reached such a consensus. In more diffuse form, though, they worked together from a common set of assumptions toward the achievement of the goal of creating a "Christian America" in which this culture would reign as normative.

Evangelical theology had two primary sources, Calvinism and Wesleyan Arminianism. Princeton emerged early in the century as a bastion of the former, and would later play a major role in forging the intellectual groundwork for a new movement, fundamentalism. The rapidly growing Methodist denomination, of course, was the main repository of Wesley's thought. Beecher and Finney exemplify the middle ground toward which the two began to move. The "New Haven Theology," which claimed to continue the Calvinist tradition but in fact pulled out its predestinarian props, was vigorously promoted by Beecher among Congregationalists and Presbyterians. Finney in turn was equally vigorous in developing the implications of the "perfectionism" that arose from Wesley's idea of entire sanctification.

Meanwhile, in Hartford, the Congregationalist preacher Horace Bushnell (BUSH-n'l) was moving in yet another direction. Under the influence of the Romantic movement, Bushnell was working to undermine revivalism itself through his downplaying of the boundaries between the divine and the human and his promotion of the idea of "Christian nurture." The memory of Jonathan Edwards still commanded great prestige, but those who actively continued in his tradition grew fewer as the century wore on. Eventually, evangelical ranks would find themselves split by those pulled first in the direction of liberalism, and then others attracted by the hard line of opposing fundamentalism.

For much of the century, though, evangelicals of a wide variety of particular theological persuasions—and even moderate Unitarians—agreed on the basic assumptions of the Scottish Common Sense philosophy that had been a major legacy of the Enlightenment. This philosophy declared that God had created humans with the ability to perceive reality accurately through the senses; further, he had endowed them with an innate sense that enabled them to make accurate moral judgments. This philosophy placed a great deal of confidence in the human ability not only to know the truth but to do the good, a step decidedly away from the Calvinist notion of total depravity.

The Scottish philosophy became the staple of much of the curriculum at the colleges that were in a seemingly continual process of foundation throughout the century, many under evangelical sponsorship. At Brown, which had been established under Baptist auspices in the aftermath of the first Awakening, Francis Wayland (1796–1865) exemplified the crucial role that this system of ideas played in the curriculum. In his teaching, his preaching, and his popular textbook *The Elements of Moral Science* (1835), he helped to develop and propagate a unified view of the world echoed in countless pulpits and classrooms. By early in the century, it had become a standard part of the college curriculum for the president to teach a "capstone" course in moral philosophy for seniors. "Moral philosophy" included a great deal more than what might now be offered under the title of "ethics." It encompassed almost everything that would in the twentieth century be regarded as "social science": economics, political science, sociology, and ethnology. The approach, though, was hardly "scientific" in the modern sense; rather, it was highly prescriptive, and its practitioners attempted to interpret the entirety of human social activity under "common sense" evangelical guidelines. In Wayland's case especially, Protestant ethics were enlisted in the defense of the doctrine of the laissez-faire capitalism that another redoubtable Scot, Adam Smith, had introduced into the Anglo-American sphere a few decades earlier.

The college was thus an important part of the comprehensive educational system that was emerging during the antebellum decades under evangelical auspices. This is not to say that secular institutions, such as Jefferson's University of Virginia; bastions of theological liberalism, such as Harvard; and Georgetown and other Roman Catholic colleges were not also doing well. Evangelicals, as their name implies, had a particular sense of mission in this regard, and colleges blossomed in their wake as they set about to win the West for Christianity. Higher education in Ohio, a major state in the early frontier era, still stands as a microcosm of this process:

Marietta (Congregationalist, 1797)
Kenyon (Episcopal, 1824)
Denison (Baptist, 1831)
Oberlin (Congregationalist, 1833)
Ohio Wesleyan (Methodist, 1841)
Wittenberg (Lutheran, 1842)
Baldwin-Wallace (Methodist, 1845)
Otterbein (United Brethren, 1847)
Heidelberg (German Reformed, 1850)
Capital (Lutheran, 1850)
Hiram (Disciples, 1850)
Wooster (Presbyterian, 1866)

Miami University (1809), like Indiana University in Bloomington, illustrated a parallel pattern of receiving state support while in fact remaining under Presbyterian tutelage. Women's colleges, or "female seminaries," also flourished during this era, such as the Western College for Women (1853; later absorbed by Miami), and Lake Erie College (1856). Both began as daughter schools of Mt. Holyoke in Massachusetts, founded under Congregationalist auspices by Mary Lyon in 1837 as a bastion of evangelical piety. In addition to these three, which have survived in one form or another, many others were established that did not survive. In other states in which northern evangelical influence was also strong, especially in the Old Northwest, the same pattern predominated. Southern culture, though also strongly evangelical, went in a different direction on education, which was confined largely to a few elite private colleges and an early system of state universities.

The Reformed tradition, especially in its New England Puritan form, had stressed literacy as an essential prerequisite for the systematic cultivation of piety. All of the laity were expected to be able to encounter the Bible directly, and the ability to read other forms of religious writings was a valuable side benefit. Well into the nineteenth century, a core of religious literature persisted that was supplemented but not superseded by later writings. The King James, or Authorized, version of the Bible (1611) was central and became an icon of Protestant identity and was even thought to be specially inspired. Perennially popular as well were John Foxe's *Acts and Monuments* (or *Book of Martyrs*, 1554, 1563); John Bunyan's allegory of the individual's spiritual journey, *The Pilgrim's Progress* (1678); Richard Baxter's devotional classic, *The Saints' Everlasting Rest* (1650); and the eighteenth-century hymns of Isaac Watts and Charles Wesley. This Puritan-Pietist devotional tradition was continued in America in such works as Jonathan Edwards's edifying biography of his daughter's missionary fiancé, David Brainerd, whose premature death gave him a posthumous near-saintly stature in Edwards's account of 1749. This latter was widely reprinted, in such formats as the multivolume *Evangelical Home Library* of Anglo-American classics distributed by the American Tract Society. In addition to books, countless periodicals, benevolent society reports, tracts, and other publications made clear that the ability to read was central to active participation in this emergent culture.

Literacy, then, had religious as well as practical uses, and had to be taught systematically. By the nineteenth century, both evangelicals and liberals, such as Massachusetts's secretary of education Horace Mann, agreed on its value not only on these grounds but also as a necessity for an informed electorate in a burgeoning democracy. Universal elementary education thus became a widespread goal especially in the northern states. Although this education was to be publicly supported, Protestants of most stripes agreed that the "common schools" could nevertheless serve as a conduit for nondenominational moral training. School boards thus commonly came to resemble local branches of the Benevolent Empire, with prominent evangelical laymen and clergy dominating their activity. Reading in class from the King James version of the Bible was a common practice, and many textbooks were very clear on the superiority of Protestant culture over that of Roman Catholics and non-Christians. Needless to say, Catholics were sufficiently indignant about these assumptions both to erect their own parallel system of parochial schools and also, eventually, to challenge evangelical domination of the common schools in court. A landmark decision was that of the Ohio Supreme Court, which in 1870 upheld the protest mounted by a coalition of Catholics, Jews, and freethinkers in Cincinnati against such use of the King James Bible. Other cultural forces soon joined with this legal hindrance to deflect public school curricula into more secular directions in the decades to come.

Among the classics of the didactic literature of this era were the series of graded readers edited by the Presbyterian divine and educator William Holmes McGuffey (1800–73) with the help of his brother Alexander. These *Eclectic Readers* pervaded the Midwest and beyond well into the twentieth century, and sold in aggregate in excess of 122,000,000 copies. In addition to teaching reading, spelling, and pronunciation, the more advanced of these readers served as literary anthologies as well as not-so-subtle tools of moral edification. Although they did contain extracts from the King James Bible, no overt theology was included. Rather, many of the selections were exemplary stories demonstrating how respect for the Sabbath, temperance, punctuality, honesty, and other evangelical virtues were rewarded, often in very material terms. Conversely, vices, especially those of the young, were severely punished by divine intervention or human device. Not all of their contents were so explicitly didactic: selections from the Unitarians Hawthorne and Longfellow were also included, and many readings reflected a romantic, even sentimental appreciation for rural life and nature. The net impact, though, was clearly moralistic, though scrupulously nondenominational.

In addition to the common school and the liberal arts college, other forms of education arose under evangelical purview during these years. In the colonial period, would-be clergy usually acquired their basic preparation at the collegiate level, then left to read divinity under the tutelage of a parish minister. By the early 1800s, such on-site training began to be displaced by the divinity school or seminary, devised to provide formal postgraduate education for the ministry among those denominations that valued such training—Congregationalists, Episcopalians, Presbyterians, and Roman Catholics. Colonial colleges such as Harvard and Yale established such schools respectively in 1811 and 1822. Harvard's liberalism spurred the founding of the more orthodox Andover Academy in Massachusetts in 1808. Presbyterians did likewise at Princeton Theological Seminary in 1812. Before too long, Methodists and then Baptists began to abandon their distrust of formal learning. Methodists especially became active in establishing a network of seminaries that would attain particular distinction in the twentieth century, especially in the South. After the Civil War, the proliferation of education beyond the collegiate level helped nurture a more research-oriented approach at some schools. Many of the best of these—Harvard, Yale, Union (New York), and the newly founded University of Chicago—distanced themselves from their earlier affiliations, and took on an interdenominational identity.

Although most evangelicals were content with the cultural fare offered by the public schools at the primary and secondary levels, they nevertheless desired a specifically religious supplement to this general academic and moral training. One answer lay in the Sunday school, which had its origins in British evangelical outreach to the poor in the late eighteenth century. The Sunday school was introduced in America at Philadelphia in 1790. It soon became less oriented toward providing the poor with a basic education, as had been the intent in Britain, and more concerned with the religious education of the children of the middle classes. In 1824 the American Sunday School Union joined the ranks of the Benevolent Empire. This union soon produced a vast instructional literature, and a majority of antebellum American libraries began in Sunday schools. Individual denominations soon founded their own educational bureaus, paralleling the break-off of mission societies and other agencies from interdenominational auspices as the Empire began to founder. After the Civil War, a nationally coordinated interchurch effort, featuring a standardized Uniform Lesson Plan taught across the entire country, gave the movement a new, national, and bureaucratic character on an unprecedented scale.

Central to evangelical culture, then, were literacy, learning, and the network of institutions designed to promote them. Theology was not yet restricted to research scholars at graduate-level institutions but was intimately enmeshed in the work of college teachers and parish ministers. One important implication of the pervasive commonsense philosophy was its stress on the availability of saving knowledge to all. Virtually every individual had the God-given faculties to arrive at truth. For most evangelicals—at least those that were no longer immersed in the raw culture of the frontier—the pursuit of this truth was aided by the network of churches, schools, religious publishing, and other institutions created to foster the quest. Common sense and common schools went together. They were twin forces of evangelicalism in developing an ethos at once Christian and democratic—one, in short, that was highly appropriate for the citizenry of the New Republic, in which church and state had a separate but cordial and cooperative relationship.

In addition to common and Sunday schools, the family home also received a new religious significance in the religious culture of the age. With the social, economic, and geographical changes of the mid-nineteenth century, middle-class women found themselves for better or worse cut off from the workplace and isolated with their children in genteel neighborhoods far removed from urban turmoil. Although usually barred from the ranks of the clergy, women had always been stanch supporters of religion, and played any number of active roles ranging from the multi-dutied minister's wife to missionary to Sunday school teacher to faithful attender at worship. With the advent of widespread middle-class status, by the 1830s a new "cult" of "domesticity" or "true womanhood" began to emerge among American Protestants that provided yet another link between women and the religious sphere.

As Colleen McDannell has demonstrated, the middle third of the nineteenth century witnessed a flourishing of the notion that the family home should be regarded as a Christian shrine, with the woman who presided over it a sort of secular priestess. The Gothic cottage, born of the Romantic movement in architecture, became popular among prosperous suburbanites not only for its picturesqueness but also for its associations with Christianity (even if in its medieval incarnation), and crosses sometimes appeared atop gables. (Lyman Beecher's daughters, Catharine Beecher and Harriet Beecher Stowe, promoted houses of this sort in their *The American*

Woman's Home of 1869.) Inside the house, samplers, bookmarks, Bibles, and even pincushions could be used to illustrate religious themes, often of the ornate and sentimental sort characteristic of the era. Although the paterfamilias would usually preside over family prayer, it was the mother who was primarily responsible for the maintenance and decoration of the home as well as the moral and religious nurture of the children. This sort of domestic piety, popularized in *Godey's Lady's Book* and innumerable other books and periodicals, had a profound influence on American Protestant piety, and manifested itself also in the devotionally oriented Catholic culture that began to spread widely in the century's latter decades.

Another aspect of evangelical culture in which the easy relationship between sacred and secular was evident was that of worship. A widespread consensus emerged during the early nineteenth century that the most appropriate architectural forms for the new nation were revivals of the styles of the ancient Greek and Roman republics. Just as George Washington was identified with Cincinnatus, so should the public buildings—banks, state and national capitols, and the like—be modeled on classical temples, with columns, domes, and other features evocative of democracy in antiquity. Interestingly, the nation's churches were among the most enthusiastic in joining this trend, and countless houses of Christian worship began to arise in the form of pagan temples. Evangelicals of all stripes participated in what was significantly known as an architectural *revival*—as did Jews and Christians of other traditions as well.

The form of worship varied considerably, ranging from the anything-goes spirit of the early camp meetings to the decorous services of New England Congregationalism. Revival preaching, of course, was widely accepted within the evangelical spectrum and had been domesticated by Finney into a predictable routine. Revivals, however, could only be infrequent if they were to be effective. Worship in most evangelical churches followed a pattern developed in the colonial era. It consisted of prayer, which could best be described as "occasional"—composed for the occasion—rather than spontaneous; preaching, which could become highly dramatic; and singing. Isaac Watts and Charles Wesley had broken down early Puritan resistance to the use of hymns of human composition, as opposed to strictly scriptural psalms. An American hymnody began to augment British staples by the late eighteenth century. These hymn styles varied in nature according to region and tradition. In the South, for instance, "shape note" or "fasola" singing developed, with notes indicated by easily recognized, distinctive symbols. Finney's revivals drew on a somewhat more sophisticated native school based on the work of the prodigious Lowell Mason, together with Thomas Hastings and William Bradbury. Characteristic of this school was Hastings's music for Toplady's "Rock of Ages," the lyrics of which contain a distinctively perfectionist sentiment: "Be of sin the double cure, Save from wrath and make me pure." In addition to such explicit reference to the Wesleyan doctrine of "entire sanctification," "Rock of Ages" is also typical of the era's preference for devotional themes: "the water and the blood, from thy wounded side which flowed"; "In my hand no price I bring, Simply to Thy cross I cling." Many of these lyrics—including this one—were actually composed in eighteenth-century England and received new music and an enthusiastic reception in evangelical America.

Theology, literature, organizational and educational networks, revivals and more routine worship, church buildings, and hymnody were all important components of this culture, at once evangelical and republican, that was being fashioned during the decades between independence and the Civil War. To conclude this survey, we should note a few distinctive elements of the evangelical worldview that prevailed at the time. In terms of place, there is little doubt that America itself occupied a preeminent position in the evangelical imagination. Literal and figurative peace had been made with England, and continual trans-Atlantic interaction reminded Americans of their British spiritual heritage. Nevertheless, since at least the time of Edwards, there was a growing conviction among Americans that it was their own country that was specially chosen by God for great things. It is no accident that one of the most enduring hymns of the "civil religion" was composed in 1832 by a young New England Baptist minister, Samuel F. Smith. "America" or, as it is better known, "My Country, 'tis of Thee," clearly celebrates the *American* landscape in its evocation of "thy rocks and rills, thy woods and templed hills" as God's presumed country.

God's special choice of America leads from space to time. When Jonathan Edwards had speculated that the millennium might well take place in America, he was preparing the conceptual groundwork for a view of time—or, more specifically, of history—that would become pervasive among antebellum northern American evangelicals. This was the notion of "postmillennialism"—that is, the belief that the thousand-year kingdom described in the Book of Revelation would unfold gradually, and be climaxed at the end of the millennium by the Second Coming of Jesus. The other version of this teaching—"premillennialism"—was a minority position at the time. Premillennialists believed instead that the thousand years of peace and prosperity could not begin until Jesus had made his second appearance. This would be accompanied by wars and cataclysms, and throw the whole earth into convulsion. This latter position took a dim view of human possibilities in the present historical dispensation. It did enjoy occasional currency, for example, among the followers of William Miller, who calculated that the Second Coming would take place in 1844. Postmillennialists, on the contrary, saw the United States gradually turning into a wondrous millennial kingdom, in part through concerted evangelical effort.

The ushering in of the thousand years, though, was not to come easily. History was not a smooth flow but a turbulent drama in which the forces of good and evil, of God and the Antichrist, were locked in mortal combat. Though the eventual outcome was sure, the precise course of events leading up to that end was revealed only in its unfolding. Already a tradition had developed among American preachers of interpreting historical events providentially, as part of this unfolding plan. The English

Reformation, the coming of Protestantism to the New World, the wars against the French and Indians, and the Revolution had all revealed successively new aspects of the drama, and the Civil War now promised victory over yet another set of foes: slavery and the sinful, decadent slaveholders. As Julia Ward Howe proclaimed in the "Battle Hymn of the Republic," God was powerfully at work in our very midst.

Evil did not exist as an abstract force but in very this-worldly personifications. The "slavocracy" was its most current embodiment, and the contemporary literature of what David Brion Davis has called "countersubversion" depicted with outraged relish the combination of sadistic and sexual gratification the "lords of the lash" derived from their helpless black charges. Although the French alliance during the Revolution temporarily brought about a rapprochement with Catholicism, the Irish immigration that reached a flood tide by the 1840s revived this, the most ancient and enduring denizen of the evangelical demonology. The subliterature of anti-Catholicism mythologically identified the Catholic Church and its pope with the "Scarlet Woman" and the "Whore of Babylon" of the Book of Revelation—a representation of the Antichrist. Especially popular were bogus tales of nuns escaped from convents, where they had been held captive and sexually abused by priests. The all-time best seller of this genre was Maria Monk's *The Awful Disclosures of the Hotel Dieu Nunnery of Montreal* of 1836. Ms. Monk claimed that priests had regularly cohabited with the nuns of this Gothic institution; when children arose from these blasphemous unions, they were immediately baptized and then strangled and buried. Subsequent investigations in America and Canada of these and similar stories yielded no substantiation, though they never lacked a ready audience of eager believers. Maria Monk, whose mother attributed her vivid imagination to a pencil's having been stuck in her head as a child, eventually died in prison after picking the pocket of one of her clients in a brothel.

Such stories continued not only to attract a wide readership but to help shape a climate of opinion and action. Lyman Beecher was a somewhat more respectable actor in this drama. His *Plea for the West* of 1835 was a fund-raising effort on behalf of Lane Seminary. Beecher argued for such support on the grounds that Protestant bulwarks were needed in what was then the west to combat the growing Catholic menace. According to this line of argument, Beecher and others maintained that the pope, through the Jesuit order, was attempting to subvert American democracy and possibly to prepare a future papal headquarters in the Mississippi Valley. To this end, Protestants must raise up a vigilant clergy to prevent the mass conversions that would undermine the Republic. Although Beecher was not directly responsible, his preaching in this vein in Boston helped prepare the climate that resulted in the burning of the Ursuline convent in Charlestown, Massachusetts, in 1834. Anti-Catholic riots later erupted in Philadelphia and New York, in part as a reaction to increasing Irish immigration and economic competition. By 1849 a political party, the Know-Nothings, had formed around an anti-immigrant, anti-Catholic platform. For a few years they scored some remarkable electoral victories, but rapidly faded as the "impending crisis" of Civil War began to divert popular attention.

Evangelicals thus had a cosmic map: a sense of origin in the English Reformation; a promised land, in which the millennium was actively awaited; a destiny, to help usher in that millennium; and a demonology, which focused alternatively on Catholic immigrants and slaveholders. Following the Civil War, the rise of the city would present new challenges, and the antipathy toward the non-Protestant and the foreign-born would if anything grow still stronger. And a familiar but newly potent demon loomed on the horizon—"demon rum."

C. Alternative Protestant Patterns

CHAPTER 26

Liturgical Protestantism: Lutherans and Episcopalians in Changing Worlds

Among the array of denominations which took shape under the terms of the American experiment, Lutherans and Episcopalians occupied an ambiguous position in the emergent Protestant spectrum. Both had emerged in the vanguard of the "Magisterial Reformation" as state churches, so that democracy was hardly part of their formative experience. For Anglicans, the close relationship between the Church of England and the overseas regime against which the colonists—including many Anglicans—successfully revolted was a major factor in their problematic accommodation with the new order. For Lutherans, language—various German and Scandinavian tongues—and culture were more potent barriers to assimilation. For both, moreover, the relationship of their traditional, liturgically formal worship with the pressures of the emergent evangelical norm, which focused on revivalistic preaching, was also a source of considerable contention. The ways in which each tradition attempted to come to terms with these issues provide two interesting case studies in the problems of adjusting to the American denominational pattern.

The first Lutherans to arrive in the American colonies came from Sweden and settled in what were originally known as New Netherlands and New Sweden. In the latter territory, the Lutheran Church was officially established, as it was in the homeland. The Dutch, however, prohibited public Lutheran worship until their hegemony yielded to that of the English, and the first Lutheran congregation was established in 1669. Growth was slow until the following century, when a larger-scale emigration from the German-speaking Rhineland brought thousands of Lutherans among other Germans to the hospitable colony founded by William Penn. It was thus Pennsylvania that became the center of colonial Lutheranism, and it was there that the German-born Henry Melchior Muhlenberg (1711–87) organized the Pennsylvania Ministerium in 1748. This regional alliance of clergy represented the beginnings of organized Lutheranism in America and was strongly influenced by the Pietist movement that came with the early ministers from Europe. Pietism, which had its origin at the University of Halle in Germany in the late seventeenth century, stressed personal devotion and spiritual cultivation over formal theology in the practice of the ministry, and conditioned early American Lutherans to be receptive to similar emphases in Anglo-American Methodism. The scarcity of clergy among the early Lutheran immigrants also contributed to the dilution of specifically Lutheran traditions.

The achievement of American independence, on which Lutherans took no formal or united stand, raised new questions for the identity of this heavily German-oriented community in the new nation similar to those that Jews, Catholics, and others who were not English-speaking Protestants had to confront. Leadership in accommodating Lutheranism to American Protestant norms was provided by Samuel Simon Schmucker (1799–1873), who was instrumental in the early life of the General Synod (1820) and the Lutheran Seminary at Gettysburg (1826). Schmucker maintained that the best course for Lutherans in America was to become English-speaking and to conform their worship and piety to the practice of local Methodists, Presbyterians, and other evangelical Protestants. This program for "American" or "Eastern Lutherans," as his followers have been variously known, deemphasized formal liturgy and the importance of the sacraments, advocated strict Sabbath observance, promoted the cause of temperance, maintained Sunday schools, supported missions, and sympathized with revival preaching. Schmucker's agenda was simultaneously to convert American Lutheranism into a denomination similar in ethos to its evangelical neighbors and to provide an institutional framework for a loose union of the various Lutheran groups that already existed.

Schmucker's vigorous Americanizing met resistance among many Lutherans who had come under the influence of the "Old Lutheran" movement in Germany. This had emerged out of a resistance to Rationalism and to the enforced merger of the Lutheran and Reformed (that is, of Calvinist heritage) churches brought about through Frederick William III's "Prussian Union" of 1817. The movement's American offshoot, which found a theological spokesman in Charles Porterfield Krauth (1823–83), expressed itself institutionally through the General Council (1867) and a new seminary founded at Philadelphia in 1864. Originally it had appealed to doctrinally conservative midwestern groups because of its vigorous adherence to the tenets of early Lutheran belief as outlined in the Augsburg Confession of 1530, which Schmucker had wanted to modify. Soon, though, it met resistance from that same quarter for its willingness to tolerate worship practices, such as open communion, which deviated from its avowed theological commitments. As a result, conservative groups in Ohio, Missouri, and other parts of the Midwest withdrew and organized a Synodical Conference in 1872, although even this alliance was doomed to failure because of the proverbial American Lutheran penchant for doctrinal infighting.

The General Council thus represented a middle though not a mediating ground in the nineteenth-century spectrum. Though theologically conservative in its stress on the objective truth of the doctrines formulated by Luther and his followers, it nevertheless was heavily English-speaking and accommodating to a wide range of practice. In contrast, the Lutheranism that was developing in the upper Midwest during and after the Civil War years had its origins in a mass immigration from northern Germany and the Scandinavian countries, often through whole communities leaving the Old World and resettling themselves as a bloc in the new. The availability of farmland in the unsettled stretches of Minnesota, Wisconsin, Iowa, and the Dakotas permitted a continuation of old-world language, customs, and religious practices in isolation from "Yankee" influence, so that the Americanizing forces promoted by Schmucker, which had resulted almost inevitably from enforced intermingling with English-speaking Protestants, were effortlessly resisted for decades.

The coming to the Midwest of Danes, Swedes, Norwegians, Finns, Icelanders, and Germans of all sorts resulted in unprecedented organizational confusion: sixty new Lutheran church bodies (usually called "synods") were organized between 1849 and 1875, though many did not last long. Geography, ethnicity, and doctrine all combined in various ways to produce this proliferation, and attempts at unity or even cooperation were not likely to encounter a favorable reception until the passage of generations, restrictions on immigration, and the anti-German hysteria that World War I brought about began to take their toll on differences based on old-world themes. The most durable result of the nineteenth-century midwestern ethos of doctrinal combativeness and separatism was the Missouri Synod, founded primarily by Saxon immigrants in 1847 and led most notably by C. F. W. Walther (1811–77). The Missouri group had been a major force in the organization of the unsuccessful Synodical Conference, and continued into the twentieth century as a bastion of ultraconservative theology and partial cultural separatism (as manifested particularly in its comprehensive school system). On the other hand, its development of a congregationally based polity differentiated it from other Lutherans in both the Old and New Worlds, and indicated an American pragmatism even in this most traditional of denominations.

The American Lutheran experience during the formative decades of the eighteenth and nineteenth centuries paralleled that of many other immigrant groups from Continental Europe. Both Roman Catholics and Jews, for example, were disadvantaged in the New World by their lack of knowledge of the English language and American mores. Each also represented a religious community that incorporated a variety of cultural and linguistic diversity. However, the Lutherans *were,* after all, Protestants, which was at least generically the dominant religious persuasion in the new nation. One of their main dilemmas, however, was the choice which faced them as to *how* they were going to express this Protestantism: through the liturgical worship and cultural traditions of the Old World, or by adopting the methods and mores of American evangelicalism. Their ethnic diversity and lack of centralized leadership precluded a definitive solution. It was not until the twentieth century that the process of Americanization had proceeded far enough on all fronts for something approaching a common identity to emerge.

For American Anglicans, the impact of the Revolution and independence was traumatic. Disestablishment rapidly took place at the state level, and the First Amendment to the federal Constitution precluded any privileged status in the nation at large. Thus, they could no longer enjoy whatever benefits may have accrued from their established status in several of the colonies. To the left, many of the best lay minds were lost to Deism, the religious offshoot of the Enlightenment, which scorned tradition and supernaturalism. On the right, the postrevolutionary taint of disloyalty put what had now become one among many "denominations" under a continuing cloud when many of its clergy remained loyal to tradition and the mother country, and left for England or Canada. Nevertheless, a number of able men began the task of reconstruction, many of them being simultaneously involved during the 1780s in the fashioning of a secular government. William White (1748–1836), a member of the Philadelphia clergy, was especially active in this process of bringing Anglican traditions into conformity with American realities. The first General Convention, held in Philadelphia in 1785 after a series of regional meetings, began to deal with the vital issues of a revised *Book of Common Prayer,* a means of obtaining consecrated bishops, and a plan of governance.

The first major breakthrough in the establishment of ecclesiastical independence took place in 1784, when Samuel Seabury (1729–96) of Connecticut became the first American Anglican bishop. The obstacles here had been formidable. On the one hand, the principle of the apostolic succession of bishops central to Anglican polity necessitated the laying-on of hands by at least three proper bishops in the consecration of a new one. On the other, bishops of the Church of England were required to swear allegiance to the English monarch as officers of a state church. Clearly, a citizen of the new nation could not take such an oath—even a curmudgeonly Tory like Seabury, who persisted in remaining in Connecticut after his politics had rendered him highly unpopular during the revolutionary years.

The solution in this dilemma lay in a curious twist of church history. Following the overthrow of the House of Stuart in England's Glorious Revolution, a number of Scottish bishops refused to acknowledge the new dynasty and swear allegiance to it. These bishops and their successors came to be called "non-juring," and the issue of oath-taking by candidates for consecration at their hands was thus moot. Seabury thus journeyed to Scotland after being turned down by the English, and paved the way for the apostolic succession, or "historic episcopate," to continue beyond the political confines of England and its established church. The latter, however, soon came to see the futility of continued resistance to the acknowledgment of American independence, and the next set of candidates in 1787 did not need to make the trek to Aberdeen. After the initial set of consecrations under British auspices, a critical mass of an American episcopate was able to become self-perpetuating.

The remainder of the task of establishing an "infrastructure" took place at the Second General Convention in 1789. After some initial compromises, previously aloof Massachusetts and Connecticut sent delegates, and a truly national Protestant Episcopal Church in the United States of America came into being. Like the new nation itself, this church was bicameral in governance. Its polity at the national level consisted of a House of Bishops, in which the senior member took the title and function of presiding bishop; and a House of Delegates, consisting of elected members of both clergy and laity. The convention's accomplishments also included the adoption of a code of canon (that is, church) law and a version of the *Book of Common Prayer* adapted to American usage, for example, in the substitution of prayers for the president for those for the English monarch.

Despite this impressive set of accomplishments, the newly re-formed Protestant Episcopal Church proved unable or unwilling to join effectively in the competition for the allegiance of the multitudes of unchurched in the decades following independence. The revival spirit of the Second Great Awakening was uncongenial to most "Churchmen" (as Anglicans have often called themselves), and the challenges of the evangelization of the frontier were not seized upon with great enthusiasm. Membership, therefore, remained very low for almost half a century, and the demoralization brought about by the exodus of clergy and the suspicions of lingering Toryism did not abate until the advent of a new generation of leadership in the 1810s and 1820s.

Episcopal revival, when it came, followed two loosely coincident principles, theology and geography. The church in the southern states found leadership in Virginia bishop Richard Channing Moore (1762–1841), and the seminary established in Alexandria supplied southern dioceses with clergy immersed in the "low" church or "evangelical" tradition that Moore espoused. Moore and other "low churchmen" regarded the Episcopal Church as fundamentally Protestant, different from the other evangelical denominations of the day not so much in doctrine as in polity and liturgy. As a consequence, Anglican worship in Virginia and many (though not all) of the southern states commonly utilized the service of Morning Prayer for Sunday worship, with only a quarterly celebration of the Eucharist. Scriptural proclamation and preaching tended to be emphasized over the sacraments, and preaching was frequently oriented not so much toward instruction and edification but rather to the personal experience of conversion that was the common goal of evangelicals of all stripes.

The other focus of early nineteenth-century Episcopal strength was New York City, where Bishop John Henry Hobart (1775–1830) and the General Theological Seminary promoted a style of "churchmanship" dramatically at odds with that of Moore and Alexandria. The "high" church movement in Anglicanism had its roots in the era of the early Stuart dynasty in England (1603–40) and emphasized the Catholic (though not Roman) aspects of the Anglican heritage. Central to the high church party was a theology that was at once historical and sacramental. The continuity of the life of the church was symbolized in the apostolic succession of bishops, and the integrity of doctrine and the sacraments had thus been maintained even during medieval times. Although scripture and preaching were by no means rejected, emphasis instead was placed on the sacraments—the Eucharist and Baptism—as primary channels of divine grace. As in the Roman tradition, the church itself was recognized as sacramental in character—"the Body of Christ"—rather than simply a pragmatic necessity.

Forces external to the Episcopal Church reinforced both of these tendencies. The evangelical understanding of Anglicanism was not new to America, but had strong roots in eighteenth-century English piety, including John Wesley's Methodist movement. In the new nation, however, the Second Great Awakening in its various phases gave the evangelical cause considerable aid and comfort, and a number of Episcopal clergy were active in the agencies of the Benevolent Empire and parallel denominational structures aimed at the distribution of religious literature, moral reforms, and other common concerns of evangelicals of all denominations during the early decades of the nineteenth century. In the Tidewater South and in some of the early western missions, to which Episcopalians were gradually beginning to turn, the evangelical party was in the ascendant, and was in many important ways more aligned with its Presbyterian and Congregationalist contemporaries than with its fellow "churchmen" to the north.

The great stimulus to the high church party came during the 1830s and 1840s from the tumult that overtook the Church of England itself during those years. The beginning of the Oxford Movement as a distinct force in Anglicanism came with the publication of John Keble's sermon on "National Apostasy" in 1833. Keble was one of a group of Oxford dons concerned with the threat to the integrity of Anglican Christianity from an overly close dependence on the state, since the church was (and still is) subject to king and Parliament in any number of questions of policy and governance. Keble and his colleagues, who included Richard Hurrell Froude, Edward B. Pusey, and John Henry Newman—later to become a Roman Catholic convert and ultimately a cardinal—had broader concerns. These were rooted in the older tradition of high church Anglicanism, which they began to make known in a series of "Tracts for the Times," ninety of which appeared between 1833 and 1841. In this series, these "Tractarians" set forth a thoroughly "Catholic" understanding of Anglican Christianity, stressing the sacramental function of the institutional church and its priesthood and hierarchy.

The manifestos of the Oxford Movement found a ready following in the Diocese of New York and the General Theological Seminary, which earlier under Bishop Hobart had maintained the high church tradition in America. Throughout the decades to come, the lines were drawn for a viciously partisan division within the House of Bishops. Evangelicals expressed alarm over a small but significant defection of high churchmen to Roman Catholicism, including North Carolina Bishop Levi Silliman Ives (1797–1867). Over the years much of the original theological and spiritual focus of the high church party became channeled into a preoccupation with highly elaborate, medievally inspired liturgical practices involving clerical vestments, processions, and the use of incense and bells during the Eucharistic service. This "Anglo-Catholicism" still manifests itself in a few, usually urban, parishes to this day, for example, St. Mary the Virgin in New York City and the Church of the Advent in Boston. (Irreverent nicknames such as "Smoky Mary's" and "Smells and Bells" are often attached to such churches by skeptics.)

These party lines were never absolutely correlated with geography—Tennessee, for example, was a high church enclave in the South, and various low church clergy were to prove thorns in the sides of a number of New York bishops. As the Episcopal Church moved slowly westward, countervailing forces followed. Even in comparison with other "elite" denominations such as the Presbyterians, the "home missions" (that is, in the United States itself) force was slow in developing. A popular saying had it that, in the settlement of the West, "the Baptists came on foot, the Methodists on horseback, and the Episcopalians in parlor cars." This saying, though, is belied by the vigor with which some Anglican pioneers undertook the task of frontier evangelization. The first major leader in this effort was Philander Chase (1775–1852), who converted to Anglicanism while a student at Dartmouth and set about aggressively to bring a distinctively low church brand of his adopted faith to the frontier. He had the distinction of founding two new dioceses (Ohio in 1818 and Illinois in 1835) as well as a church-sponsored college, Kenyon and Jubilee, in each. On the other hand Jackson Kemper, the first missionary bishop appointed for service in the West in 1835, was of the high church persuasion, reflecting an informal agreement that the evangelical party would have foreign missions as its domain whereas its rivals would be entrusted with the task of evangelizing the American frontier. The upper Midwest soon became one of the bastions of the high church movement, with the Nashotah House seminary (1840) providing an institutional basis for training clergy for service in the "Biretta Belt" (a nickname again indicating the high church propensity for emulating Roman Catholic practices). Missionary work on Indian reservations attracted some dedicated individuals such as William Hobart Hare, but western growth of any sort was based more on the development of an indigenous white upper middle class than on sporadic and undersupported missionary endeavors.

In the South, the once powerful position of the church as that of the upper classes was undermined both by the rapid growth of the Baptists and Methodists on the southern frontier as well as by the emergence of the Presbyterians as a rival for the allegiance of the elite. Nevertheless, many of the most powerful and respected leaders of the Confederacy—Robert E. Lee of Virginia and Jefferson Davis of Mississippi—remained in the fold. One representative figure in the relationship between the Episcopal Church and the Old South was Leonidas Polk (1806–64), a North Carolinian educated both at West Point and the seminary in Alexandria. In 1838 Polk was consecrated missionary bishop with responsibility for what was then the entire southwestern corner of the nation. His subsequent activities included unsuccessful management of a Louisiana sugar plantation and service as bishop of Louisiana. Most notably, Polk led the drive for the founding of the University of the South (1856–60) high on a mountaintop in Sewanee, Tennessee, as an indigenous means of education for a regional elite. After the war broke out, Polk was commissioned a general in the Confederate army and died in battle near Pine Mountain, Georgia.

During the decades leading up to the Civil War, individual Episcopalians both attacked and defended the institution of slavery, but the denomination as a whole never took an official stand on the issue. Some southern blacks, especially in the older Tidewater area, belonged to the church—an estimate for the early nineteenth century is thirty-five thousand—but, as with whites, the less formal and more emotional worship of the Baptists and Methodists was far more attractive to the slave and free black population. When the war finally came, the southern dioceses collectively withdrew from the national church and convened instead as the Protestant Episcopal Church in the Confederate States of America. This division lasted only for the war's duration, and the 1866 General Convention drew representatives from all of the dioceses of the reunited body. (The 1862 convention was the only one from which southern delegates were absent.)

The course of the Episcopal Church in the postbellum South continued to be conservative in tone, with segregation the norm in church life as elsewhere. A number of black colleges were founded under denominational sponsorship, some of which, such as St. Augustine's in Raleigh, North Carolina, are still in existence. Some blacks did enter the priesthood, and the Bishop Payne Divinity School was founded in Petersburg, Virginia, in 1887 to provide them with an education similar to but physically separate from that of the all-white parent institution in Alexandria. (The two finally merged in 1953.) The church in general did not play a very active role in promoting desegregation until the 1950s, when the faculty at the School of Theology at Sewanee successfully forced positive action on racial integration in 1953 and blacks began to acquire full enfranchisement in the church as a whole.

The experience of the Episcopalians in the nineteenth century was, like that of all other religious traditions of European origin, one of continual adaptation. The Episcopal Church, with the Congregational, was the most reluctant to come to terms with the rapidly changing circumstances of a vibrant democracy with no established church, and it was even slower than the Congregationalists to respond to the inexorable fact of the frontier. The emergence of a new, urban frontier in the century's latter decades proved a more congenial challenge, and its manifold responses to social and cultural change—ranging from monasteries to institutional churches—restored its standing as a major presence in the American religious spectrum. By the end of the nineteenth century, it had emerged as perhaps *the* church of the American urban elite, a status—or stigma—that would last until well into the twentieth.

CHAPTER 27

Religion in the Slave Community

African slaves began to arrive in the American colonies beginning in 1619 in Jamestown, Virginia. Specific statements about the religious life of these earliest African Americans are difficult to make, given the sparsity of reliable evidence. Whatever may have happened to the traditions they brought with them, few were converted to Christianity because of the reluctance of whites to permit their evangelization. The southern colonies, where slavery flourished, were also largely outside the bounds of effective organized religion, so that clergy and missionaries were not widely distributed among the population in general, and many whites had no active religious life themselves. In the case of slaves, however, whites were further leery of spreading the Christian gospel for fear that black converts might acquire legal rights if baptized, and that notions of freedom suggested by various scriptural passages might give them dangerous ideas.

The eighteenth century brought about a number of developments that worked in the opposite direction. As slavery became more routinized, families began to develop among African Americans. This provided a setting more conducive for the development of religious life than was usually possible for newly arrived, single, and unacculturated individuals. Colonial legislatures took measures to ensure that baptism did not guarantee liberation in any legal sense. The Church of England began to take a more serious interest in missionary work, as manifested in the founding of the Society for the Propagation of the Gospel in Foreign Parts in 1701. Its success, however, was less than complete, as its missionaries found work with whites easier and more productive than with slaves. Catholics in Louisiana and Maryland, including slaveholding Jesuits in the latter colony, were more conscientious than most in providing religious instructions for blacks.

The most important development in the eighteenth century for the shaping of African American religious life was the Great Awakening of the 1740s. This first great American revival spread a new version of the Gospel among blacks and whites alike along the entire eastern seaboard, and stressed personal religious experience and conversion over theological learning and liturgical worship. The Awakening, which gave a great boost to the emergent Baptist and Methodist movements, also generated lay preachers with little formal education and no specific credentials other than their own claim to have been called by the Holy Spirit. This religious "enthusiasm" appealed greatly to the unlettered slaves, who identified with the kind of direct experience involved and who were now permitted to be exposed to Christian teachers by masters who themselves had been converted for the first time.

In the 1830s the Methodist preacher Charles Colcock Jones and others from several denominations launched an intensive campaign known as the "Mission" for the conversion of blacks on a larger scale. Since the not-so-hidden goal of much of this effort was to produce a more docile slave community, its lack of conspicuous success is perhaps not very surprising. The more authentic, indigenous Christianity that emerged among the slave communities in the century or so between the Awakening and the Civil War is frequently described as the "invisible institution," since the social and legal status of its clientele made all but the most minimal organization impossible. Baptist preachers and Methodist exhorters required little if any formal training. These two traditions therefore spread rapidly among black and white alike, although slaveholders generally exercised supervision over any black worship meetings. In a few cases, such as the Silver Bluff Baptist Church in South Carolina, independent black churches managed to emerge, but their autonomy was usually precarious and short-lived.

The religious lives of plantation blacks frequently exhibited a split quality, reflecting in public the desire of whites to utilize Christian teachings—especially certain texts of Paul enjoining slaves to obey their masters—to reinforce a spirit of obedience and docility in the services that they themselves attended or supervised. It was in private, however, that the "invisible institution" developed its particular character. When opportunities presented themselves, slaves would assemble surreptitiously wherever they might—for example, in wooded areas known as "hush harbors" where worship could be conducted in secret. Spirituals, the unique musical expression of slave Christianity, sometimes conveyed coded messages, and "Steal Away to Jesus" was often a call to steal off quite literally for an impromptu service.

The kind of Christianity that developed along these lines was a folk religion that combined elements from both the African and European heritage in a unique social and cultural context that gave it an identity of its own. Black preachers enjoyed a special status within the slave community, based on charisma rather than any formal education or even literacy. Slaves were forbidden to learn to read, so that their knowledge of the Bible and Christian tradition was acquired entirely from hearing it preached. Folk preaching, which continues in modified form to this day, was formulaic, consisting of set phrases that could be inserted at various points in the narrative. It was also participatory, following a call-response pattern, possibly of African origin, in which the congregation would actively answer the preacher's words and injunctions. (This active participation still characterizes much black worship today.) Further, worship was not simply verbal but also enacted. The "shout" or "ring shout" was a familiar style of acting out the religious impulse. It consisted of a highly rhythmic counterclockwise shuffle-dance in which the whole body participates in the movement, again possibly echoing the rhythms of traditional African worship, which were beaten out on drums forbidden to American slaves.

One of the most enduring aspects of the tradition of slave Christianity is the "spiritual," a distinctive musical genre derived from the fusion of the Anglo-American style of hymnody founded by Isaac Watts with the distinctive rhythms and concerns of the slave community. (Southern white folk-hymns, such as those found in the "Sacred Harp" or "shape-note" tradition, have a similar origin, but reflect different cultural emphases.) Lyrics developed through oral adaptations of original Watts-style hymns became simplified and transformed to reflect black concerns, such as the pervasiveness of suffering and the longing for deliverance. Among the better known are "Go Down, Moses," "Joshua Fit de Battle of Jericho," "Roll, Jordan, Roll," "Were You There When They Crucified My Lord," and "Nobody Knows the Trouble I've Seen." Many of these titles reflect biblical themes, focusing especially on figures of deliverance: Moses and Joshua in the Old Testament, Jesus in the New. Musically, spirituals are usually in the African pentatonic or five-note scale, often with a "flatted seventh" that adds a note of melancholy. Spirituals have long outlasted slavery, having been adapted into modern choral settings and also providing the basis for later black gospel music.

The actual meaning of the spirituals has been the subject of considerable debate in recent years. At one level, they express a yearning for deliverance from the woes of this world into a supernatural realm. More recently, they have been interpreted as more subversive of the social order, conveying a desire for a very this-worldly redemption involving escape to freedom in the northern states or Canada. Most probably, as Eugene Genovese has suggested, the distinction between the two was not as clear-cut as this dichotomy suggests. What they in fact express is an undifferentiated desire for deliverance, at times emphasizing the supernatural, at others the natural. Moses, Jesus, and Lincoln similarly were not always clearly distinguishable in the imagery of slave worship, but all represented figures of redemption at one level or another.

The broader question of the interpretation of slave religion was originally posed some years ago in a heated debate between the anthropologist Melville Herskovits and the black sociologist E. Franklin Frazier. Herskovits, who had started the exchange in his *The Myth of the Negro Past* (1958), had been concerned with refuting commonly held ideas about the inferiority of American blacks. He argued that African customs such as rituals involving rivers and certain burial practices had been carried over directly into African American religion, for example, in the popularity of baptism by total immersion in the Baptist manner. Frazier took the position in such works as *The Negro Church in America* (1964) and *The Negro Family in the United States* (1966) that the numerical dominance of whites and the policy of systematically splitting up slaves of similar linguistic backgrounds had virtually obliterated all vestiges of African culture in North America.

Herskovits's position was strongly advocated by many militants during the 1960s, who felt that it enhanced black claims to respect on the basis of cultural continuity. More recent scholarship tends to side with Frazier's argument that it is very difficult to establish any direct continuities, such as are frequently apparent in the case of Latin American syncretistic cultures, between African American and traditional African practices. This is not to say, however, that all continuity with Africa had been obliterated; rather, it manifested itself indirectly, for example, in the rhythms of the ring-shout and the call-response pattern of slave worship. The overt content of slave religion may have been derived from English-speaking Protestant Christianity, but the underlying pattern of nonverbal expression was quite clearly evocative of the African past. The result, however, was not simply a fusion of the two but a *tertium quid*, a new synthesis invoking elements from each tradition but blending them with the unique concerns and experiences of the African American slave community.

Although African American slave religion was most often manifest in this synthesis of African patterns and evangelical Protestantism, especially in its Baptist and Methodist forms, it was not confined to this. Many slaves in Maryland and Louisiana were converted to Roman Catholicism, though they were barred from ordination to the priesthood until late in the nineteenth century. At the other end of the religious spectrum, New Orleans was the focus of the Voodoo (Haitian *Vodun*) cult, one of the most direct descendants of African practices present in North America. As its practices spread throughout the South, however, they lost their explicit religious forms and were practiced as "Hoodoo" or "rootwork" by "conjuremen," who enjoyed a following among both rural blacks and whites for their magical and curative powers. Slave Christianity tended toward a protean character, open to taking new shapes and elements because of its lack of formal organization. It thus could blend at the edges with this underground folk world of charms and curses that evoked the African world picture of a cosmos filled with diffuse power that could be harnessed, with the proper knowledge, for personal good or the harm of others. In this world, skill, fate, and luck challenged the Christian notions of good and evil, freedom and responsibility, grace and sin. The results were a twilight region of folklife: part Christian, part African, distinctly African American.

D. "Freedom's Ferment": New Religious Movements

CHAPTER 28

Unitarianism, Transcendentalism, and Universalism

Religious liberalism by its very definition is resistant to institutionalization. Openness to novelty and change is one of its major characteristics; it is not easily tied down by creeds, structures, and the apparatus that develops when a group establishes itself as a denomination. On the other hand, even a liberal religious impulse has to take on concrete social and intellectual form if it is to transcend the impulses of the moment, achieve a continuity of expression, and exert itself as an active influence in the broader community. Two parallel liberal movements emerged in the revolutionary era, which later were forced to take on denominational form and which after nearly two centuries merged to form the Unitarian-Universalist Association. Of the two, Unitarianism has always overshadowed its "country cousin," Universalism—an illustration primarily of the differences that social class can make even when theological beliefs are remarkably similar.

American Unitarians have traditionally traced their religious roots to Reformation-era "free spirits" such as Servetus and Socinus and the movements they inspired in Transylvania, Poland, and other areas of central Europe. Another, more immediate source of influence was the emergence in England beginning in the seventeenth century of a small group of Christians who denied that God existed as three persons—a Trinity—and was instead solely one—hence the name "Unitarian." Later English Unitarians such as the renowned chemist Joseph Priestley found their way to America and helped spread such ideas in this country in the postrevolutionary era. English Unitarianism, however, was rooted in a philosophical materialism that did not find widespread acceptance in America, where a very different approach to the question of liberal religion had already begun to take shape.

One of the important results of the Great Awakening of the 1740s was the polarization of the Congregationalist clergy of New England into the revival's defenders, or "New Lights," such as Jonathan Edwards, as well as opponents, or "Old Lights," who were concentrated in the Boston area. Prominent among the latter were a trio of ministers—Charles Chauncy (1705–87) and Jonathan Mayhew (1720–66) of Boston, and Ebenezer Gay (1696–1787) of nearby Hingham. Working informally among themselves and like-minded allies, they developed a critique not only of the "enthusiastic" preaching of the revivalists but of traditional New England Calvinism as well. The most conspicuous teaching of the movement that thus took shape was the denial that God was a trinity. More important was their equally determined assault on the Calvinist stress on the all-pervasive corrupting power of original sin and its corollary, God's predestining of all humanity for salvation or damnation. American Unitarianism was fundamentally an attack on Calvinist doctrine from the *Arminian* point of view—a theological outlook that stressed God's benevolence rather than his awesome power, and human potential rather than depravity.

The first open expression of Unitarian sentiments by a congregation took place at King's Chapel in Boston, an Anglican church that in 1785 adopted a version of the *Book of Common Prayer* from which references to the Trinity had been omitted. It was among the Puritan Congregational churches, however, that the movement had special appeal. Although these early liberals wanted to avoid an open break with their more "orthodox" contemporaries, a number of the latter were sufficiently alarmed with the spread of these new ideas that they began to force the issue. One of the first skirmishes in this battle was over control of the Hollis Professorship of Divinity at Harvard, a crucial institution for shaping the future of the New England ministry. When the liberal faction prevailed, the battle lines were set for what would later be called the "First Unitarian Controversy."

This battle between liberal and orthodox Congregationalists took the form of a bitter pamphlet warfare led by Jedidiah Morse (1761–1826), a conservative clergyman who also had achieved renown as a geographer. The most eloquent spokesperson for the liberals was William Ellery Channing (1780–1842), who in 1819 preached a memorable ordination sermon at Baltimore that set forth the liberal movement's emphases. Prominent among these were the unity of God and his parental character; the single, human nature of Jesus; individual free will; and the moral and ethical character of the Christian religion. A few years later, in 1825, the liberal clergy of the Boston area met to form a loose alliance to promote their common interests. The result was the American Unitarian Association, the first formal institutional expression of this emergent branch of liberal Christianity.

Unitarianism had already triumphed in the Boston area, and eighty-eight of the hundred oldest churches of eastern Massachusetts aligned themselves with the liberal cause. The triumph was not to go unchallenged: the perils of structure for liberalism were now appearing. The first important sign that the Unitarians were themselves hardening into an "orthodox" position was provoked by the address delivered to the graduating class of the Harvard Divinity School by Ralph Waldo Emerson (1803–82) in 1838. Emerson had several years earlier renounced his ministry in Boston because he had difficulties with what he saw as too much of traditional Christianity within Unitarian belief and practice. His "Divinity School Address" came as something of a bombshell to the Unitarian community, for which Harvard and its Divinity School were the major educational vehicle.

The focus of this "Second Unitarian Controversy" was the question of the miracles attributed to Jesus in the Gospels. "Orthodox" Unitarians such as Harvard's Andrews Norton (1786–1853), who earned the nickname of the Unitarian "Pope," took the position that such miracles had been necessary to establish Jesus's authority as a divinely inspired teacher and prophet, even though he himself was not actually divine. Emerson refused to go even this far and denounced such miracles as "monster" on the grounds that they contradicted his own belief that ultimate religious truth was eternal and potentially present everywhere; to constrict it with miracles and specific historical figures was to limit and thereby distort it beyond recognition.

Emerson was the most publicly successful of a band of Boston-area intellectuals who were attracted to one another through their collective interest in the "transcendental" philosophy that was filtering through to America from Germany through England during this "romantic" era of religious thought. These American "transcendentalists" fiercely resisted being pigeonholed as an organized movement; still, their mutual enjoyment of one another's conversation, their collective dissatisfaction with even liberal "orthodoxy," and their involvement in various common endeavors makes it useful to consider them together as a short-lived but uncommonly influential force in American religious and cultural history.

Unitarian theology, like its more conservative evangelical counterparts, was firmly based on the affirmations of the Scottish "common sense" philosophy, which taught that all knowledge was accessible to humans through the senses. The central emphasis of transcendentalism was on the human ability to enter into a deeper, more "original" relationship with the ultimate reality that underlies appearances and that is present everywhere in nature. Human history, customs, and institutions, including organized religion, hindered rather than helped this quest, so that the burdens they imposed had to be cast off if a search for pure and authentic truth was to be pursued successfully.

Emerson's extremely popular essays and lectures, such as those on "Nature" and "Self-Reliance," emphasized the cultivation of this pursuit in the course of everyday life. More radical was Emerson's friend at Concord, Henry David Thoreau (1817–62), whose Walden of 1854 was a chronicle of his attempt to slough off the baggage of civilization and live by himself at the shore of a rural pond in pursuit of an original and essential relationship with Nature. At the other extreme of transcendentalist innovation was the Brook Farm community, established by George and Sophia Ripley in 1844 near West Roxbury, Massachusetts. This experiment in communal living directed toward the cultivation of the higher faculties proved impractical and disbanded within a few years. In the long run, though, Brook Farm stood as an expression of faith that humanity need not be confined forever to the hopeless round imposed by materialistic urban and industrial civilization.

Although it resulted in some significant experiments in church organization, transcendentalism was primarily a literary and intellectual movement. Its major organ was the *Dial,* an influential journal edited by Emerson and Margaret Fuller from 1840 to 1844. The massive output of this band of perhaps three dozen writers was part of a larger efflorescence of literary productivity that has been character- ized variously as the "flowering of New England" or, more broadly, as part of the "American renaissance" of the pre–Civil War decades. At one end of this spectrum of writers was Nathaniel Hawthorne (1804–64), who provided a profound reflection on his own Puritan heritage in *The Scarlet Letter* of 1850. Although Hawthorne had been raised in the Unitarian fold, his own writings reflected a preoccupation with the traditional themes of Calvinism, and he more than once provided biting critiques of what he saw as the follies of his transcendental contemporaries (for example, in *The Blithedale Romance* of 1852). Like his friend Herman Melville, Hawthorne was not an active participant in organized religious life and preferred to reflect on eternal themes from his own detached and individualistic perspective.

More typical of the culture that Unitarianism nurtured was the work of the "Fire- side Poets"—Henry Wadsworth Longfellow, James Russell Lowell, Oliver Wendell Holmes Sr., and William Cullen Bryant. Their writings, which became extremely popular during the middle decades of the nineteenth century, reflected a greater optimism about human possibilities within more conventional bounds of society and thought. Also popular among the cultivated reading public was the North American Review, a literary journal founded in 1815 that dealt with a broad range of issues of the time and eventually left its Boston origins for a New York base. More generally, Unitarianism became the accepted faith of the academic and professional classes of Boston and Cambridge, and taught what was becoming a rather comfortable faith in the possibilities of individual growth and social progress through the church, the schools, and other institutions of society.

Although some Unitarians, like Channing, eventually lent their voices to the grow- ing protest against slavery, it was nonmainstream spokesmen such as Theodore Parker (1810–60) who played the most significant roles in that struggle. Parker also aroused the wrath of the more conservative clergy with his address on "The Transient and Permanent in Christianity" in 1841, which mounted a critique of traditional religion that if anything was even more radical than Emerson's. Perhaps not surprisingly, Parker was ostracized by his fellow Unitarian clergy and went on to take his congre- gation in an independent direction.

The question raised by the positions of Emerson and Parker continued to haunt the Unitarian movement, which was sorely divided between those who saw themselves as the exponents of a liberal but still explicitly Christian faith and others who did not want any restrictions placed on free religious inquiry. One expression of this tension was the formation in 1867 of the Free Religious Association by a small group of dissident New England ministers. More significant over the longer run was a split that followed sectional lines. Unitarianism has always been based in eastern Massachusetts, where its adherents are said to believe in "the fatherhood of God, the brotherhood of Man, and the neighborhood of Boston." Nevertheless, the movement slowly and cautiously followed the frontier westward during the nineteenth century, and those who founded churches in the Midwest and beyond were frequently opposed to any creedal statements that defined Unitarians as Christians. It was from this western matrix that the association of Unitarianism with "humanism"—ethics and human values divorced from theology or even a belief in God—began to develop in the twentieth century.

Whereas Unitarianism had its American roots in a reaction against the Great Awakening, Universalism arose in the religious and cultural ferment that those revivals left as their heritage. It was especially in the northern, rural stretches of New England that were settled by Yankee in-migrants in the decades around the Revolution that a popular dissatisfaction with Puritanism began to stir. Universalism was from the beginning a faith not of the social elite but rather of ordinary people, neither blessed nor burdened with higher education, among whom a number of prophets of liberalism began to arise in the years in which the new nation was taking form.

The core of the Universalist message was that the entirety of humanity would ultimately be saved, a distinct repudiation of Calvinist predestination. Its theological sources were varied. Its exponents in America were influenced chiefly by the writings of the German George Klein-Nicolai, who wrote under the pseudonym Paul Siegvolck, and the Welsh Methodist James Relly. Two Americans in particular came under the spell of these new ideas about universal salvation and began to spread their message far and wide. The first was John Murray (1741–1815), who was English-born but labored primarily in Gloucester and later Boston in Massachusetts. New England–born Elhanan Winchester (1751–97) preached in the Philadelphia area, where his "Society of Universal Baptists" attracted the eminent scientist Benjamin Rush.

From these scattered beginnings, like-minded Universalist congregations began to overcome their aversion to organization in response to needs for legal standing. An early, nonbinding creedal statement was drawn up in Philadelphia in 1790, which was in part the work of Rush. Of more lasting impact was the so-called Winchester Profession of 1803, named after the New Hampshire town where it was composed, which emphasized that all of humanity would ultimately be restored through Jesus to a state of "holiness and happiness." A national spokesperson also emerged: Hosea Ballou (1771–1852), who began life as a Baptist farmer-preacher in New Hampshire and eventually settled into a career as a Universalist minister and leader in Boston in 1817. In such works as his *Treatise on the Atonement* of 1805, Ballou articulated a systematic theological rationale for the Universalist movement and aligned it more clearly with Unitarianism in his rejection of the Trinity.

By 1833 Universalists had developed a formal if rather loose denominational structure, which took the name of the Universalist Church of America. Like their Unitarian counterparts, the Universalists were firmly congregational in polity and were based in New England. Unlike the urban Unitarians, however, Universalists were more likely to be located in the smaller towns of the Northeast and, eventually, throughout the South and other parts of the nation as well. In 1850, roughly 90 percent of the 246 Unitarian churches of the day were in New England; among Universalists, the figures were about 55 percent of 529. A century later, the figures were 145 of 357 for the Unitarians, and a resounding 200 of 300 Universalist. Membership peaked around the turn of the century at approximately 6500, and remained stable until the merger of the two denominations in 1961.

The ethos of Universalism from the early days under Ballou's leadership until the time of the merger was probably more similar to that of the Northern Baptists than of Unitarians, although numerical growth was more similar to the latter than the former. Universalists moved from frontier farmer status to that of middle-class townsfolk, and turned their attention to the development of colleges such as Tufts and St. Lawrence—the two that have survived to the present—and accompanying theological schools. Universalists became involved in the message of Social Christianity toward the end of the nineteenth century, and to some extent in the Humanist movement in the twentieth. Like the Unitarians, they engaged periodically in ecumenical discussions of merger with several like-minded groups.

The natural and ultimately fruitful partner for such discussions was the Universalists' New England counterparts, the Unitarians. Thomas Starr King, who moved from a position as Universalist minister in Boston to Civil War–time Unitarian in California, observed that the real difference between the two groups was that the Universalists considered God too good to damn anyone, while the Unitarians considered themselves too good to be damned. After World War II, it became clear that neither group was destined for continued expansion; that the maintenance of parallel bureaucracies and institutions was a wasteful duplication of effort; and that the differences that had historically separated the two were far more sociological than theological. As a consequence, the Unitarian-Universalist Association was formed by mutual consent in 1961.

New World Space and Time: Restorationist, Millennial, and Communitarian Movements

From the moment that Europeans first arrived on New World shores—or perhaps even from the time they began to imagine lands across the vast ocean—America has had a special role in the Western imagination. Giles Gunn has described this speculation on the ultimate significance of America as "New World Metaphysics"—the attempt to find transcendental meaning in the American experience of time and space. The Spanish quested after the fountain of youth and cities of gold, whereas their more austere English counterparts saw their sojourn in New England as a recapitulation of the biblical wilderness. In later colonial times, Jonathan Edwards became convinced that the Second Coming was likely to take place in the New World. The notion of God acting in American history, and the imminence of the millennium, began to inform American thought patterns over these decades, and to infuse what was becoming a national experience with an import beyond the merely political.

Two themes have especially dominated the quest for the meaning of America: limitless space and a new beginning in time. Though the trauma of depressions and world wars, Holocaust and Hiroshima, and potential ecological disaster has sobered Americans of the early twenty-first century, these powerfully optimistic themes have never died out entirely in our culture. Certain times and places have been especially susceptible to the rise of cultural trends and new religious movements, in which these themes of the transcendence of ordinary time and space have become particularly potent. California, for example, has become legendary as a source of new and exotic social and religious expression from early pentecostalism to the "New Age." The "New Light Stir" in New England during the revolutionary era was an incubating ground for Shakers, Universalists, and Free Will Baptists. Periods of rapid social change and demographic movement seem especially apt times for religious innovation to flourish.

The Kentucky frontier in the decades following the Revolution was one of those places. English and Scotch-Irish pioneers eagerly followed Daniel Boone's lead through the Cumberland Gap westward across the mountains. The unprecedented excitements that took place at Cane Ridge and other sites of the "Great Revival" marked a protean phase of American religious history. The "Burned-Over District" of upstate New York in the 1820s and 1830s was another. The area made accessible by the Erie Canal, from Albany to Buffalo, was rapidly populated by emigrants from the rocky farm country and mountains of New England—the "Yankee Exodus"—seeking a better chance in life. Andrew Jackson's challenge to traditional notions of the relationship between government and society coincided with a rapidly changing economic order in which individualism was displacing kinship networks. Excitement over the nation's seemingly endless possibilities was balanced by apprehension over the loss of familiar patterns of life and work. If religious development in some way reflects cultural change, it would certainly have been reasonable to have expected new religious movements in these volatile settings.

Although it is difficult to find *any* period of American history not characterized by rapid social change, the early decades of the nineteenth century and the area from the Hudson to the Mississippi are particularly fertile for our purposes. This was frontier country—the boundary between intensely settled land and that which was virtually uninhabited, at least by Europeans. As opposed to the later settlers of trans-Mississippi America, the in-migrants who flocked into New York, Ohio, and Kentucky came in large numbers and remained fairly close to their points of origin. Before long, this land was thickly settled and on the way to urbanization. It was this brief period of transition that was ripe for the excitements that seemed to be springing up continually. One theme that was common to a wide variety of highly disparate new religious movements of this era was the suspension of normal, historical time—what, in short, these settlers were experiencing in their own secular lives.

One of the moving spirits of the great revival of 1801 was Barton Warren Stone (1772–1844), a Presbyterian minister who crossed the Alleghenies to take charge of the church at Cane Ridge in Bourbon County, Kentucky. In the aftermath of the Cane Ridge revival, Stone and several of his associates became estranged from the Presbyterians back East who frowned on what they saw as the excesses of the frontier spirit in religion. After they were expelled from the Kentucky Synod in 1803, they organized the short-lived Springfield Presbytery, which they dissolved the next year in a dramatic "Last Will and Testament." Thereafter they preferred to call themselves simply "Christians" rather than taking the name of a particular denomination of Christianity.

Another source of Presbyterian divisiveness was the ongoing quarrels among those still in Scotland and northern Ireland (Ulster) over the relationship of church and society that had resulted in the Seceder and Covenanter movements. From the former faction came Thomas Campbell, an Ulster minister who emigrated to Pennsylvania in 1807 and almost immediately got into trouble with his coreligionists there. He and his sympathizers soon formed a new group known as the "Christian Association," a name significantly similar to that chosen by Stone. Campbell was joined by his son Alexander (1788–1866), who soon took over the leadership of the emergent movement which for a while identified itself with the Baptist cause.

The moving ideas that underlay the Campbells' quest for a new Christianity, though, were really much closer to those of Barton Stone and other contemporaries such as Ohio's Walter Scott, who joined forces with Alexander in 1821. At Christmas in 1831, representatives of the Campbell-Scott and Stone forces met in Lexington, Kentucky, and consummated a union of the two movements whose principles were so clearly harmonious. Campbell's "Disciples of Christ" and Stone's "Christians" were now joined in a new campaign to rid American Christianity of its confusing welter of denominations and to restore instead the pristine, primitive church of New Testament times. Deliberately they avoided any restrictive denominational name, preferring to be known variously as "Christians," "Churches of Christ," or "Disciples of Christ." In the longer run, they inevitably succumbed to division and a measure of institutionalization. At the beginning, however, they were filled with optimism that they could transcend the factionalism of contemporary Protestant Christianity and return to the beginning.

Key to this nascent Stone-Campbell tradition was the assurance that the Bible could be taken as an unambiguous road map for contemporary belief, practice, and organization. "Where the Scriptures speak, we speak; and where the Scriptures are silent, we are silent" was an early motto of Thomas Campbell that became authoritative for the whole movement. Their desire was to escape from "man-made" devices such as creeds and denominational structures, and literally restore the ways in which Jesus and his disciples lived and worshiped. After some initial disagreement among the merged factions, baptism by immersion also came to be a distinctive practice, on the New Testament model, as did the weekly administration of the Lord's Supper.

What differentiated these "restorationists" from the other popular denominations of the frontier, such as the Baptists and Methodists, was the rationalistic tone that characterized their approach to religion. Whereas others were highly emotional and experiential in their pursuit of salvation, the Stone-Campbell followers instead viewed scripture as a text to be approached rationally, even legalistically. Despite the roots of part of the movement in the Great Revival, they came to reject dramatic conversion, and were much closer in spirit to the Scottish Common Sense empiricism espoused by John Witherspoon and the traditional Presbyterians of the East Coast. Alexander Campbell's renown as a public debater was one aspect of this confidence that truth could be arrived at through proper textual interpretation, and salvation through proper belief and action growing out of that interpretation. Consonant with this deliberate mood was an optimistic *postmillennialism* promoted by Alexander Campbell—the confidence that the millennial kingdom was gradually being ushered in through human discovery and application of God's law.

Like that of the Baptists, who also eschewed central organization, the Disciples/ Christian message spread south and west by the work of farmer-preachers and newspapers such as Alexander Campbell's Millennial Harbinger. Though they avoided formal denominational structures, the "Campbellites," as they have sometimes been called, founded schools, colleges, and a missionary society. A network of colleges and publications in the longer run emerged as a substitute for a centralized administrative apparatus in shaping an informal consensus of opinion, especially within the movement's conservative wing. Eventually, the division that emerged following the Civil War between the more liberal, urban "Disciples" and the stricter, rural "Churches of Christ" reached the breaking point, and resulted in the schisms that began to take place early in the twentieth century.

Although caution must be used in making a sharp distinction between the two, the terms "premillennialism" and "postmillennialism" have become so common that they necessarily provide a starting point in looking at religious movements that take a radical view of historical time. The Stone-Campbell tradition in its earlier years has been called "postmillennial," that is, characterized by the belief that the thousand years of peace and harmony of earth allegedly foretold by the Book of Revelation will be climaxed, rather than inaugurated, by the Second Coming (or advent) of Jesus. "Postmillennialism," as evidenced in the title of Campbell's *Millennial Harbinger,* was not so much a strict theological tenet as a climate of opinion, of expectation, that was pervasive throughout nineteenth-century America. In its more secular forms, it was expressed in phrases such as "Manifest Destiny"—the divinely given right of America to expand its boundaries from coast to coast—and in the idea of "Progress" that so dominated the Victorian imagination. ("Progress is our most important product," as Ronald Reagan reminded Americans weekly as host of television's "GE Theater.")

Premillennialism is the belief that the Second Coming of Jesus will come *prior* to the millennium, usually accompanied by great upheavals here on earth and an apocalyptic struggle between the forces of good and evil (see Revelation 20). The Civil War was frequently interpreted as this sort of apocalyptic struggle, as in Julia Ward Howe's stirring "Battle Hymn of the Republic" ("He is trampling out the vintage where the grapes of wrath are stored / He has loosed the fateful lightning of His terrible swift sword"). Beginning in the 1840s, though, the idea that Jesus was about to return, literally and soon, provided the inspiration for a series of religious American movements. It continues to this day, among fundamentalists of various denominations, as well as in distinctive sectarian groups such as the Jehovah's Witnesses.

William Miller (1782–1849) has achieved historical notoriety as one of the best-known and least successful millennial prophets in American history. Like many before and since, Miller approached the apocalyptic writings of the Bible—especially Daniel and Revelation—as containing a numerical code that could be cracked with the appropriate mathematical calculations. Using the widely accepted chronology of the seventeenth-century Irish archbishop James Ussher, who had attempted to demonstrate that the world had been created in 4004 B.C., Miller calculated that the Second Coming was due in March 1843. Ordained as a Baptist and aided by the publicist Joshua Himes, Miller began to attract a wide following during the early 1840s through his speaking tours and publications such as *The Midnight Cry.*

Jesus did not appear in March of 1843, nor, after Miller had made some recalculations, the following March. Finally, he fixed 22 October 1844 as the definitive time for the Second Coming. This nonevent soon became known as the "Great Disappointment," and forced the many thousands who had believed in Miller's predictions to come to terms with the question. A gathering of those who remained faithful met the following year in Albany and set in motion an organizational plan to keep the movement alive. This did not prove very successful in the long run. Factions developed among the remaining adventists, but only one was destined for enduring success.

Ellen Gould Harmon White (1827–1915) was a follower of Miller who subsequently married the adventist minister and writer James S. White. Of perpetually delicate health, Ellen White was also subject to visions and claimed to have experienced some two thousand in the course of her lifetime. The milieu of folk religion of the rural northern New England in which she lived her early life was in many ways similar to that which had produced Joseph Smith and would later shape Mary Baker Eddy's "discovery" of Christian Science. Prominent in White's experience were Methodist camp meeting revivalism, which led to her conversion in 1841; faith healing, which she continuously sought as a relief for her various distresses; dramatic visions of the supernatural realm, which critics attributed to Mesmerism (hypnotism); and her involvement in the Millerite excitement of the early 1840s. Here was a religious culture that provided a rich mixture of dramatic symbols, together with a troubled personality with the need for healing and the gift of leadership.

Around the prophetic leadership of White there began to coalesce a new movement that built on the unfulfilled adventist message of William Miller but that added a number of new emphases and refinements. This new adventism was based on a reinterpretation of Miller's prophecy developed by Hiram Edson, who argued that Jesus had in fact cleansed the Temple, as was supposed to have taken place on his return, but that this had happened in heaven rather than on earth. The subsequent, earthly cleansing was yet to take place, and these postdisappointment adventists perhaps wisely refrained from being too specific about the date. To this reconceptualized millennial message was now added a reappraisal of the way in which the Sabbath was observed by Christians. White confirmed through one of her visions the arguments of a contemporary movement known as the Seventh-Day Baptists, who maintained that Saturday rather than Sunday—in the manner of the Jews—was the proper day for worship. This combination of teachings led to the name "Seventh-Day Adventist Church," which she and her followers adopted when they organized into a distinct denomination in 1860.

Another theme that has continued to this day to be a major emphasis among Seventh-Day Adventists is that of health and bodily purity. As the anthropologist Mary Douglas has pointed out, the integrity and wholeness of the human body often serves as a symbol for other sorts of wholeness, whether that of society or of the cosmos. From at least the time of Leviticus, Western religion has frequently incorporated this symbolism into its beliefs and practices. Further, a preoccupation with bodily health and wholeness emerged as an important theme in American culture during the middle and late nineteenth centuries. This may have been a reflection of the fragility of the rapidly changing society of the time and the anxieties it aroused. It also may have sprung from the rising expectations that science and technology were encouraging and that the absurdly primitive medical knowledge and practice of the time were unable to fulfill. Yet another aspect, which was expressed forcefully again in the career of Mary Baker Eddy, was the problematic role of women at the time, and the frustrations that intelligent but poorly educated women like White experienced and channeled into symbolic expression. None of these sorts of explanations can ever be definitively "proven" or regarded as a final explanation of any particular religious behavior, but together they help to provide a context in which the rise of new movements such as Seventh-Day Adventism can be understood.

In any case, White, on 5 June 1863, experienced a vision in which she learned that meat, alcohol, and tobacco were not to be consumed; that doctors and the drugs on which they relied were similarly to be avoided; and that her disciples were to rely for their health on air, sunshine, rest, exercise, and a proper diet. Masturbation, a means of sexual pollution, was also condemned. Some of these tenets had already appeared in her earlier teachings; further, as White's biographer, the historian of science Ronald Numbers, has demonstrated, many were commonplace amid the reformist enthusiasm of the day. Temperance, of course, had already become a popular evangelical cause. Sylvester Graham, whose name has survived in that of a popular cracker, originally developed this tasty product as part of a comprehensive scientific and philosophical scheme for promoting health and well-being at a time when the diet of many Americans was notoriously heavy and unhealthy. Alternative medical systems to the unreliable "orthodox" practice of the times also flourished, as in the practices of homeopathy and hydropathy, and probably did at the least no more harm than their more socially respectable rivals. (Homeopathy is based on the principle of curing by giving patients small doses of substances which would produce symptoms similar to their own in a healthy patient; hydropathy aims at cures through the internal and external use of water.)

This preoccupation with health and diet received some of its most explicitly religious expression in Seventh-Day Adventism. At the denomination's headquarters in Battle Creek, Michigan, where the Whites had earlier settled, considerable attention was turned to medical and dietary reform. Hydropathy was especially favored, and the Western Health Reform Institute opened in Battle Creek in 1866. White and her followers—most notably John H. Kellogg—also turned their attention to developing a wholesome diet based on fruit, grain, and vegetables. Out of this developed the modern cold breakfast cereal, although it is doubtful that White and Kellogg would endorse products such as Froot-Loops or Count Chocula with the same enthusiasm bestowed on the early corn flake. A later rift between White and Kellogg resulted in the latter's disfellowshipping, and the movement did not benefit from the enormous future profits of Kellogg's products. Over the years, however, the Adventists have remained true to their commitment to bodily wholeness. In addition to continuing to condemn the use of alcohol, tobacco, and unnecessary drugs (vegetarianism is optional), they maintain numerous medical centers and schools in America and abroad.

Closely related to the idea that a new era of time had begun was the notion that a new beginning in history could be achieved through the formation of an ideal community in space. The Puritans, though not utopians as such, certainly came to view New England as a providential opportunity for the creation—quite literally from the ground up—of as ideal a society as could be fashioned through human effort in a fallen world. German sectarian groups such as the Moravians experimented with a reorganization of society on semicommunitarian lines, though their effort had been abandoned by the time of independence. Other German Pietists experimented with communal living into the nineteenth century and even beyond, as in the cases of Ohio's Zoar and Iowa's Amana. At the other end of the theological spectrum, New England transcendentalists had a go at communitarianism at Brook Farm, which later turned into an unsuccessful experiment in utopian socialism on the principles of Charles Fourier, and on a tiny scale at Bronson Alcott's Fruitlands. Beyond the confines of religion altogether was the secular, socialist community of New Harmony, established by the Englishman Robert Owen in Indiana in the 1820s. Even the Mormons tried communal ownership of property during their stay in Kirtland, Ohio, during the following decade, in the short-lived "United Order of Enoch."

Two of the longest-lived utopian communal ventures were founded explicitly on versions of the millennial theme: the Oneida Community and those of the Shakers. Oneida was the inspiration of John Humphrey Noyes (1811–86), a Vermonter who was educated for the ministry at Yale Divinity School. While still at Yale, Noyes got into trouble for maintaining that he had entered into a state of perfection, completely free from sin. Unlike the more traditional John Wesley, who also espoused a sort of perfectionism, Noyes maintained that sinlessness was possible because Jesus had in fact already come again, in A.D. 70. Although this second advent had been spiritual, it made possible the attainment of perfection by all people, including Noyes.

Since Noyes could not hope for a career in the "orthodox" churches of the day, he decided to implement his ideas by founding a community of his own. An initial venture in Putney, Vermont, which he began in 1836, eventually came to an end because of the hostility of the neighbors to Noyes's extreme ideas in the realm of sexual relations. Noyes thus moved the community to Oneida, New York—in the heart of the "Burned-Over District"—in 1848. Noyes advocated the practice of "complex marriage," in which sexual partners were delegated through group mediation and children raised communally. When children were not desired, *coitus reservatus* was promoted as an effective preventative and discipline, and the pursuit of carefully regulated reproduction that resulted—a form of eugenics—was known as *stirpiculture*. Actually, these seemingly scandalous practices were an aspect of a common life tightly regulated through communal ownership of property and mutual criticism sessions. Life at Oneida may have been eccentric but it was hardly orgiastic.

The Oneida experiment was for a time a considerable success, and centered on the massive Mansion House at the heart of the community. Unlike many such communities, which foundered for lack of a firm economic basis, Oneida thrived through the manufacture and sale first of steel traps and then of silver-plated flatware (which continues to sell well). However, the religious perfectionism that had been the community's original inspiration had begun to flag even within Noyes's own lifetime. The community had never attempted any rigorous isolation from the external world, except for self-protection, and secular ideas and culture had always been welcome. As Noyes yielded control of the community to his son, Pierrepont, the religious trappings began to fall away, though much of the group—many of them Noyes's own descendants, courtesy of stirpiculture—elected to continue to live semicommunally together. Finally, by the 1930s, even the family aspects of Oneida had eroded, and control of the manufacturing enterprise passed into outside hands.

The other communal society based on millennial principles that enjoyed a long-term (though not indefinite) success was the United Society of Believers in Christ's Second Appearance, better known as "Shakers." The Shakers came into being through the life and work of "Mother" Ann Lee (1736–84), an Englishwoman of the working class who had experienced considerable anguish through the death of all of her children. In part, no doubt, as a result of her distressing and unfruitful marriage, she became convinced that sexuality was the root of sin and evil. She also became associated with a group of ecstatic "Shaking Quakers" in England, and then began to have visions of her own. After she and her followers were harassed in England, they emigrated to New York in 1774.

Although "Mother Ann" herself died within a decade of her arrival in America, her example and teachings inspired a movement that has survived, if only vestigially, into the present day. Shaker theology was unique in regarding Ann Lee as the second coming of Christ, in the form of Holy Mother Wisdom. Her teachings thus acquired an authority far greater than those, say, of Noyes. Like Oneida, however, the consequences of these new revelations involved a millennial perfectionism based on the regulation of sexuality and sex-roles. At the approximately two dozen Shaker communities that were functioning during the movement's heyday in the years before the Civil War, celibacy was the rule. Men and women lived, worked, and worshiped in close proximity, but all erotic contact was strictly prohibited. The communities perpetuated themselves through the conversion of outsiders and the rearing of adopted orphans, many of whom elected to remain after reaching adulthood. In addition, communal life was based on a strict equality of the sexes, with two male and two female leaders in charge of each "family" (that is, grouping within each settlement).

Although the fundamental impulse behind Shaker life was religious, the group has come to be known best for its aesthetics and craftsmanship. The handsome, simplelined Shaker furniture that now commands premium prices on the antique market was not radically different from contemporary New England crafts. Neither were the symmetrical buildings the Shakers raised for living, working, and worship. The distinctiveness of these artifacts lay in the combination of devotion, skill, and desire for efficiency that inspired their design and execution. Brooms, washing machines, herbs, and the rows of pegs on every wall all reflected a desire to honor God through an ordered, industrious life. The Protestant ethic and "plain style" of the Puritans had combined with the celibate imperative of medieval monasticism to produce a uniquely Yankee religion.

The seemingly ubiquitous communal societies of early nineteenth-century America attracted a never-ending stream of foreign observers, and the Shakers were no exception. The particular fascination they exerted for Americans and Europeans alike was their worship, which was frequently open to the public. Shaker meetinghouses were their only buildings painted pure white, part of a color-coding scheme reflecting a correspondence here on earth with the heavenly sphere beyond. In the Puritan-Quaker tradition, the meetinghouse interior was plain and white, with no ornamentation. Spectators were seated on movable benches while the worshipers faced one another, men on one side, women on the other, and engaged in dancing and singing that often became ecstatic—hence the nickname "Shakers." Even here, though, this ecstasy, or *anti-structure*, was expressed through rehearsed and stylized dancing rather than undisciplined, individualistic frenzy. Potentially chaotic emotion was thus channeled into the purposes of a higher order of social structure—what the anthropologist Victor Turner has called *communitas*, the absorption of the individual into a larger social whole.

The spiritual and social health of the Shaker communities depended on a strict external organization and a firmly internalized commitment of each believer to the demanding regimen the life demanded. Although the communities welcomed visitors and generated considerable income through the sales of seeds and crafts to outsiders, their physical isolation reinforced their distinctiveness and helped maintain morale. Despite all of their means of reinforcing loyalty and discipline, however, the system on occasion showed signs of strain. One manifestation of this stress was the appearance in the 1830s and 1840s of "Mother Ann's Work," in which individual spirit possession threatened to undermine the collective emotional worship that reinforced rather than sundered community ties. It was during this period of shaky leadership as well that "spirit drawings," such as the popular "Tree of Life" motif that now appears frequently on posters and greeting cards, began to take place.

The heyday of the Shakers was the effervescent period prior to the Civil War, when their numbers reached some six thousand distributed over eighteen to twenty-four communities, depending on one's system of reckoning. With the changes in society that took place during the subsequent era of urbanization, new converts became scarcer, and natural reproduction was, of course, nonexistent. Communities began to decline and were ultimately abandoned. Two survived into the late 1980s—at Sabbathday Lake, Maine, and Canterbury, New Hampshire. At the latter, the handful of elderly members refused to recognize the legitimacy of the former, since the men who belonged to the Maine community had entered after the last males in the original succession had died. Tradition required that new converts confess their sins to a member of the same sex, which had been impossible in their case. In neither community, however, was there enough of a critical mass of membership to make chances of future survival appear very promising, and the New Hampshire group had simply decided to regard the venture as nearing its final end. (Its last member died in 1992.) In both cases, many outsiders have become involved as volunteers and interns, helping maintain the communities through tours, gift shop sales, and the like. A perilous balance is thus maintained among a few surviving Shakers, scholars, and volunteers trying to preserve their heritage, and the diffusion of that heritage into popular culture and commercial exploitation. The revival of the Shaker hymn "The Gift to Be Simple" by the folksinger Judy Collins in the 1960s, and its metamorphosis into "Lord of the Dance" in the mainstream churches, are ambiguous signs of the tradition's penetration into the broader culture. The handful of Shakers who still survive, however, are determined that their community will endure.

CHAPTER 30

New World Revelation: Joseph Smith and the Rise of the Mormons

The "Burned-Over District" of upstate New York was one of the classic sites of social ferment that provided an ideal matrix for the emergence of new religious movements. The career of Joseph Smith Jr. reflected in a particularly intense way this volatile combination of social and cultural forces. Smith's family came from respectable old New England stock but had not been overly blessed with worldly success. His father was skeptical and restless in religious matters, constantly exploring new alternatives and at times embracing the New England tradition of popular Deism. His mother identified more with the evangelical tradition launched by the Great Awakening and its aftershocks, and joined the Presbyterian church after the family's move from the Vermont mountains to Palmyra, New York, in 1816. The family was also deeply involved with the rural tradition of folk magic, in which divining rods, astrology, and other mild forms of the occult promised access to knowledge and wealth not easily acquired through natural means.

Joseph Jr. was raised in this uncertain world of marginal social status, religious experimentation, and magical investigation. From the beginnings, the details and significance of his later, remarkable career are inevitably colored by these origins and the possible meanings. Mormons (or, more properly, Latter-day Saints), continue to regard him as a divinely appointed prophet, and the events of his brief, vivid life as fraught with sacred meaning. Skeptics, such as the irrepressible Mark Twain, and former Mormons like the late historian Fawn Brodie have seen him as at best an amiable fraud who managed to delude even himself into accepting his extravagant claims to latter-day revelation. Serious "Gentile" (that is, non-Mormon) students of his life and the movement it launched have tried to avoid these extremes, interpreting his career as the coincidence of a remarkable personality with an unusually protean set of circumstances.

There seems little question that the younger Joseph Smith engaged as a boy in the traditional "white magic" practices such as divination and treasure hunting that were part of his family folk heritage. The relationship of this innocent occultism with the unusual series of events that followed is more problematic, and probably not resolvable to everyone's satisfaction. The "sacred history" of Joseph Smith began at age fourteen (1820), when a vision of "the Father and the Son" appeared to him and cautioned him against joining any of the competing denominations of the age. (Compare this with the desire to transcend "man-made creeds" that was motivating Thomas and Alexander Campbell at the same time.) Smith had now clearly ascended to a higher level of interaction with the supernatural: his career as a visionary and prophet had been launched.

Three years later, on 21 and 22 September 1823, Smith went into a trance in which the Angel Moroni appeared to him. Moroni had been the last survivor of an ancient American people descended from the Hebrews, who were ultimately destroyed by a rival tribe of similar origins. His father, Mormon, had entrusted him with his people's history, which was inscribed on golden tablets, the existence of which was now revealed to Joseph (as Mormons still refer to him). These plates were concealed nearby in the hill Cumorah. With them were two stones, the "Urim" and "Thummim," which were the means through which these plates might be translated from the "Reformed Egyptian" in which they were written. (*Urim* and *Thummim* are Hebrew words that originally designated stones used by high priests for casting lots.)

It was not until four years later that the plates themselves were given to Smith in another epiphany. From this critical moment in 1827, he now embarked on a full-time career as translator of these supernatural treasures—a task that culminated in their publication in 1830. During these three years of toil, Smith was aided by Emma (née Hale), his new wife, and by other followers he had begun to attract. In 1829, Smith and Oliver Cowdery received together a new revelation announcing the restoration of the Aaronic priesthood of the ancient Hebrews, as well as baptism under a "new and everlasting covenant." As the historian Jan Shipps has demonstrated, the nascent religion that would come to be known as Mormonism had three central elements in place at this point that constituted it as a potentially new and distinct religion, rather than simply as another denomination of Christianity. These elements were a *prophet,* namely, Smith himself; a *church,* called initially "the Church of Jesus Christ," in which restored Old Testament priesthoods such as the "Aaronic" would play a major role; and a *scripture,* the *Book of Mormon.*

The *Book of Mormon* is one of the most controversial works ever published in the United States. It is also widely disseminated, for example, by Mormon missionaries and in Mormon-owned enterprises such as the Marriott hotel chain, in each bedroom of which is a *Book of Mormon* and a Gideon Bible. In format it resembles closely a standard Bible, and is divided into books, chapters, and verses. Its diction is very similar to that of the King James (Authorized) version of the Bible; the proper names that appear throughout are frequently identical or very similar to many of those in the Bible, and a considerable number of verses begin with the phrase "And it came to pass."

The story it tells is that of the Hebrew patriarch Lehi, who left Jerusalem just before the Babylonian conquest of 587 B.C. He and his family crossed the Atlantic and landed in the New World, where they began a new life together. His descendants divided into the Nephites and the Lamanites, who were often in conflict with one another. A break in this conflict came when the resurrected Jesus appeared among these people. This event inaugurated a millennial-like reign of peace that lasted for two hundred years. Conflict then erupted again, with the Lamanites destroying the Nephites. Moroni was the last surviving Nephite. As such, he added a concluding section to the account of this history written by his father, Mormon, and concealed the plates on which it was written in the hill Cumorah. It was only with the reappearance of his spirit to Joseph Smith several hundred years later that these remarkable documents would come to light as part of the divine plan of revelation. In the meantime, the surviving Lamanites, who lacked written records, lost all memory of their early history, and their descendants were encountered by later-arriving Europeans as American Indians. To this day, Mormons regard Native Americans as a people with a special religious significance, and have made particular efforts to enlighten them as to their true spiritual destiny.

Because the *Book of Mormon* is regarded as divine revelation by a considerable number of people, and as arrant imposture by many others, it is difficult to assess its character neutrally. Thomas F. O'Dea, the Catholic sociologist of religion, was the author of one of the most successful attempts at this perplexing task in his classic work, *The Mormons* (1957). As a scholarly outsider, O'Dea interpreted Smith's narrative skeptically but sympathetically as an "almost completely neglected primary source for the intellectual history of the common man." Behind the saga of the Nephites and the Lamanites could be found the social, political, and religious themes that preoccupied the inhabitants of the Burned-Over District in Smith's time: religious revivalism, Calvinist versus Arminian theology, virtue leading to prosperity that then begets pride and sin, distrust of secret societies, egalitarian political sentiments, and other preoccupations of Jacksonian Americans. Whatever else it may be, the *Book of Mormon* can be read as a document of its times.

The publication of the *Book of Mormon* signified for Smith's followers a reopening of the canon (that is, authoritative list of contents) of scripture. Such was an act of religious radicalism only hinted at by the Quakers, who regarded the promptings of the Inner Light as continuing (but not written) revelation. Even the Shakers, who saw Mother Ann Lee as a redemptive figure, did not regard any new body of religious writings as authoritative. The most direct parallel in the history of Western religion is the Qur'an, revealed many centuries before to the Prophet Muhammad, which stands together with Hebrew and Christian scripture as the foundation of the religion of Islam. However, Islam was virtually unknown in America during the 1820s, so there is no reason to believe that Muhammad and the Qur'an offered Smith any sort of model.

As noted by Shipps, this prophet, scripture, and church betokened a new religion with an extremely complex relationship to the past, present, and future. Christianity had lost its original promise as the agency of redemption with the "Great Apostasy," which took place in the apostolic age itself and left a gap of centuries until the coming of a new prophet. Smith's new "Church of Jesus Christ" (later, "of Latter-day Saints") had been divinely established in "the last days" as a preparation for the Second Coming of Jesus. This was expected to take place soon—a reflection of the millennial enthusiasm characteristic of the age. The church's adoption of baptism by immersion and foot-washing, together with the institution of a new "Twelve Apostles," were indicative of its self-conception as a revival of primitive Christianity. Similarly, the divinely mandated restoration of first the Aaronic and later the Melchizedek priesthoods was an aspect of Smith's notion that his followers were quite literally reconstituting the ancient people of Israel. Further revelations over the next decade or so introduced new "ordinances" (rituals) not recorded in the Old or New Testaments, and added the *Doctrine and Covenants* and the *Pearl of Great Price* to the canon of latter-day scripture. "Mormonism" was to be all of these things—Israel and Apostles—and yet more.

Smith and his followers soon abandoned the Burned-Over District for Kirtland, Ohio, a town near Cleveland where the recent convert Sidney Rigdon and his congregation prepared the way for them. These new disciples had earlier embraced the message of Thomas and Alexander Campbell, who had called for the abolition of all creeds of human origin and a return to New Testament ways as the exclusive form of pure Christianity. This "restorationism" was also clearly part of Smith's message and presumably was a major element in Rigdon's conversion. The move en masse to Kirtland in 1830–31 was the first in a series of relocations by Smith and his followers, who now began to think of themselves in Hebrew fashion as engaging in a "Gathering"—a coming together as a distinct people. The westward moves they made during the next two decades reflected the pioneering spirit abroad in the land, which here was acquiring a unique religious rationale.

At Kirtland, Smith and his followers for the first time set about creating a coherent community—not simply of belief and worship but of the whole of their lives. Here they built their first temple, an eclectic combination of architectural elements with the frame of a New England meetinghouse. (The Kirtland Temple is still preserved as a museum.) This monumental structure, built by the community's pooling of resources and effort and sited high on a hill, provided a physical setting for the new rituals, or "ordinances," which were progressively being revealed to Smith. On the two main floors, for example, were two complete sets of pulpits facing one another at either end, which were designed for use by the newly restored Aaronic and Melchizedek priesthoods. The "patriarchal blessing," clearly based on the Old Testament, was introduced during the sojourn at Kirtland, as was—surreptitiously and controversially—polygamy. Another indication of the eclectic and sometimes exotic combination of elements that was contributing to the new religion was the display at Kirtland of Egyptian mummies and a papyrus scroll, which Smith translated as the *Book of Abraham* (later part of the *Pearl of Great Price*). Biblical, ancient Near Eastern, and Masonic themes were thus incorporated into Mormonism through a process of *syncretism*—that is, borrowing from diverse sources to form a new whole.

The Mormons at Kirtland were becoming not just a new religion but a society—even a people—bound together by a common set of beliefs and practices that differentiated them from their gentile neighbors. This goal of developing an entire culture grounded on religious values and symbols extended into the economic realm as well. While at Kirtland, Smith instituted the "United Order of Enoch," a system of communal property ownership with control in the hands of the church. Although this radical deviation from economic individualism did not last long, the principle of economic cooperation again proved valuable in the critical early years at the Great Salt Lake and has persisted to the present day in the Mormon requirement of tithing and the provision of relief by the church rather than the secular government. In addition, Smith founded an "Antibanking Society"—called such in an attempt to circumvent requirements for a regular bank charter—which issued currency and engaged in other financial activities. Its collapse helped precipitate the Mormon departure from Kirtland in 1838.

During the Kirtland years, Mormon geographical horizons were expanding in several directions. On the one hand, missionaries were sent to northwestern Europe, particularly the British Isles and Scandinavia, where they were soon successful in recruiting converts willing to emigrate to America. On the other, Smith launched a series of attempts at settlement in Missouri, where he believed the Garden of Eden had originally been located. As in Kirtland, non-Mormon hostility contributed to the rapid failure of these ventures. However, they helped set expectations for further westward movement, and contributed to the growing belief that the history and destiny of America itself were an intimate part of a grand divine design now on the brink of fulfillment.

After the failure of the settlement at Far West, Missouri, in 1838, Smith and his followers moved back eastward to the town of Commerce, Illinois, on the banks of the Mississippi. They obtained a charter from the state granting semiautonomy, and Smith gave the city the new name of Nauvoo—"a beautiful plantation" in the "revised Hebrew" language to which Smith was privy. As were many of the new cities that were arising in America at the time, Nauvoo was carefully platted for planned growth on a rectangular grid. What differentiated it from others was Smith's intention to make it the symbolic and actual capital—the new Jerusalem—of the new Zion he envisioned in the American heartland. One of its two foci was the "Nauvoo House," which was to serve as Smith's residence and a hotel for visitors. The other, and more important, was the second of Mormonism's temples. The Nauvoo temple was an imposing neoclassical structure that incorporated explicitly the new set of visual symbols, such as suns and moons with human features, that Smith was working out to express his continuing revelations. Inside were the system of dual pulpits first used at Kirtland, and a massive pine tub, supported by twelve wooden oxen, for the newly introduced ritual of baptism of the dead. Nauvoo, in short, was the scene of the continuing development of Mormonism as both a religious and a social system.

Smith's identification with America as the new Jerusalem—the millennial kingdom—was further promoted with his announcement of his candidacy for the American presidency in 1844. (American secular titles such as "president" are mixed with traditional ecclesiastical titles such as "priest" and "bishop" in Mormon usage.) Smith also cracked down on an opposition newspaper that was being published in Nauvoo, and had its presses destroyed. What was perceived as the beginnings of a dictatorship aroused the already potent hostility of local Gentiles. The governor ordered Smith to surrender himself to face the charges that developed from this incident. A mob burst into the jail at Carthage, Illinois, where Smith and his brother Hyrum were awaiting trial, and shot them and other leaders of the group to death.

The Mormons at Nauvoo now had a martyr but no leader. Contention over the succession to Smith's position led to the departure of Sidney Rigdon and other unsuccessful aspirants to the title, several of whom founded rival churches. Brigham Young (1801–77), an early follower of Smith and a fellow Vermonter, had been president of the Twelve (Apostles) at the time of Smith's death and was rapidly acclaimed as his de facto successor. Growing pressure from the gentile community made it clear that a further—and final—move west was now called for. While working strenuously to complete the temple, the Mormons began preparations for one of America's epic *Völkerwanderungen*—the trek of a whole people, their numbers swelled by immigration, hundreds of miles over desolate territory to found a new Zion in the Utah desert.

It was Brigham Young who presided brilliantly over this "exodus," which added yet another opportunity for the Mormons to recapitulate the Hebrew experience. Beginning on 4 February in 1846, the first contingent arrived at the Great Salt Lake—its ultimate resting place—by late July. In rapid succession, a site for a temple was staked out, Young was confirmed as the new president as well as "Prophet, Seer, Revelator"—and, thereby, as Smith's full and official successor—and a provisional State of Deseret was established. (*Deseret* was a word from the *Book of Mormon* meaning "honeybee." A short-lived experiment with a Deseret alphabet, however, was unsuccessful, and Mormon culture has never generated more than a few such exotic terms.)

In 1850 this provisional state was recognized by the government as Utah Territory, and Brigham Young was appointed governor. The road to full statehood, however, was to be anything but straightforward. As the anthropologist Mark Leone has pointed out, the "Great Basin Kingdom" that Young and his followers established in the Utah desert was considerably more than another frontier outpost of American society. Rather, the Mormons were attempting to establish a "counterculture," which repudiated many of the values and practices that informed the lives of other Americans and substituted other alternatives that seemed radical in the context of Victorian America.

One deviation from standard American practice was the cooperative economic scheme that, under Young, literally made the desert blossom. To make the salt flats of Utah habitable, a massive and sophisticated system of irrigation had to be designed and constructed, a task clearly beyond the scope of any individual pioneers. The entire colonization of Utah and parts of adjoining states was centrally directed, with as little as possible left to chance. Land was distributed, infrastructure built and maintained, and need alleviated under the firm direction of the First Presidency at Salt Lake City. Utah thus rapidly became a *theocracy*—a government by divine will, as interpreted and implemented by the Prophet, Seer, and Revelator. Not since the Holy Commonwealths of seventeenth-century New England had America seen such a thoroughgoing attempt at governance according to God's plan. Probably never has it seen such a unified and successful attempt, at least for the "brief and shining moment" that the Deseret experiment was to survive.

Its survival was not really endangered by Young's unorthodox politics and economics, nor by his even less orthodox theology—manifested visually in the massive Salt Lake City Temple undertaken under his own supervision in 1847 and completed only after his death. The symbolic focus of Mormon "differentness" was the practice of polygamy, or plural marriage, that first came into the open at Salt Lake City. It was this oddly potent issue that would lead to decades of legal and political controversy, and even violence. When the controversy was finally resolved in 1890, the relationship of this gathered people and their kingdom with the rest of America would be irreversibly and radically transformed.

PART IV

THE END OF THE FRONTIER AND THE RISE OF THE CITY

The decades between the Civil War and World War I were a time of rapid growth and major demographic change. The issue of national unity had been definitively resolved, but the abolition of slavery only changed rather than settled the question of the status of blacks. Southern whites eventually rid themselves of hostile northern tutelage, developed segregation to a veritable science, and worked out variations of the tradition of evangelicalism to produce an insular and distinctively southern form of Protestantism. As southern blacks began to flee their tenant farms for the promise of urban jobs precipitated by the "Great War," they began to work variations on their own evangelical traditions, and to generate remarkable new religious movements as well.

The movement of blacks to the great cities of the Northeast and the Great Lakes region was by no means the only facet of urbanization. In 1890 the Census Bureau announced that the great American frontier could now be regarded as closed; no more unclaimed arable land existed in sufficient quantity to attract new settlers. Meanwhile, technological change generated commercial and industrial employment in the burgeoning cities, and inventions such as the elevator and steel-frame construction gave those cities a new look and a new density. Their need for low-wage, low-skill workers was filled only later by southern blacks. Before the arrival of these blacks in great numbers, the social and economic upheavals that were similarly transforming the face of Europe were pressing Italians, Greeks, Poles, Bohemians, Ukranians, and others from the less developed parts of that continent to seek their fortunes overseas. Most of these "new immigrants" found employment—brutal as it may have been—in the teeming cities, where they settled into ethnic neighborhoods. With amazing speed, they erected Roman Catholic and Eastern Orthodox churches and Orthodox Jewish synagogues to serve their needs and mark their presence. Americans of older stock and Protestant faith often recoiled in fear and amazement at this exotic transformation of their land.

The city was the frontier of the late nineteenth and early twentieth centuries in America. In Victorian Boston, Mary Baker Eddy turned her vision of Christian Science into an institution. In Chicago, Dwight L. Moody and Ira D. Sankey launched a new form of urban revivalism. In Detroit, New York, and Philadelphia arose the "black gods of the metropolis" that Arthur Fauset studied. Father Divine, Sweet Daddy Grace, W. D. Fard, and Elijah Muhammad were all prophets of new black religions that repudiated Christianity entirely. The black ghettoes of the great cities continued to be a frontier for blacks and more recently arrived minorities—Puerto Ricans, Mexicans, Central Americans, Cubans, Syrians, Lebanese, Vietnamese, and Laotians—as the twentieth century continued. It is among many of these people that the "storefront" church—usually pentecostal, holiness, or fundamentalist—has continued to thrive.

These latter movements would also prove crucial for the development of white Protestantism throughout the century. For decades, a liberal theology that transcended denominational lines gained a stronghold among many of the most influential pulpits and seminaries. Its offshoots—the Social Gospel and, later, Neo-Orthodoxy—added new elements of social concern to the liberal message and continued to permeate elite circles of denominational leadership as the century progressed. Early on, however, a reaction began to set in, which had its roots at least as much in the cities of the North as in the rural hinterlands with which it became so strongly associated in the popular imagination. Elements of the old evangelical consensus now hardened into a fundamentalism that was dead set against the liberal challenge. From another direction, the holiness movement arose out of the older Wesleyan matrix to add a new element of experiential emphasis to the emergent conservative Protestant movement. Still another and even more potent force, pentecostalism, rapidly emerged from holiness traditions, with nearly simultaneous origins in the Los Angeles ghetto, the Kansas heartland, and the southern piedmont. It was in this latter area that the great drama of the Scopes "Monkey Trial" would play itself out in the 1920s, bringing into national prominence the contrasts and conflicts between religious cultures.

Urban expansion and rural reaction thus set in motion many of the forces that have dominated American religious life throughout the twentieth century. The American people were at once becoming more numerous, more ethnically diverse, and more geographically concentrated. Among some, the oldest religious traditions of the West—Roman Catholicism, Eastern Orthodoxy, and Orthodox Judaism—were experiencing a new vitality and dramatic expansion in the New World. For others, new religions were arising, with urban prophets appearing seemingly out of nowhere. Within what had been the evangelical "establishment" of American Protestantism, tensions erupted that proved uncontainable, and liberals and conservatives set in for a long, inconclusive struggle for cultural hegemony that is still unresolved—after many twists, turns, and realignments—at the beginning of the twenty-first century.

A. The Adjustments of Protestantism

CHAPTER 31

Victorian Evangelicals

Rarely has the name of one person captured so thoroughly the ethos of an era as that of Queen Victoria—in America as much as in England. The name conjures up the staid, censorious image of the queen, in perpetual mourning for her lost Prince Albert, maintaining an aura of serene unamusement at the antics of her times. The Victorian decades in America saw a resurgence of many aspects of antebellum evangelicalism, especially its determination to form or reform the morals of a nation. Temperance in particular became the focus for this new Protestant crusade; the saloon and demon rum were the embodiment of moral evil. Carry Nation's hatchet and Anthony Comstock's blue laws came to symbolize a spirit of repression and censoriousness in which pleasure and sin were regarded as synonymous.

Or so, at least, the story goes—the story fashioned by the *Baltimore Sun's* H. L. Mencken and other "debunkers" of latter-day "Puritanism" in the 1920s and beyond. It was in this school of journalism—and sometimes even scholarship—that the image of the American Puritan became conflated with the Victorian evangelical, and the more extreme representatives of the latter breed equated with the whole of a complex and often contradictory era. Whatever the excesses of some of its celebrities, Victorian America was anything but a sober, repressed, unchanging society when viewed as a totality. The decades between Reconstruction and World War I were the most tumultuous in American history. Immigrants by the hundreds of thousands poured into the burgeoning industrial cities of the East and Midwest, transforming the country almost overnight from an agricultural to a predominantly urban society. Cities are almost by definition anything but decorous and orderly, and the exaggerated moralism of some Victorian reformers reflected the similarly exaggerated tumult of contemporary urban life.

Nor was moral reform the exclusive preoccupation of beleaguered defenders of the Old Order. Prohibition, which came to symbolize Victorian repressiveness to later generations, was in its day a progressive cause. It was actively promoted not only by Bishop Cannon and his Southern Methodist flock but also by the leaders of the Social Gospel, ardent Progressives, and crusaders for women's suffrage. To understand this era in its complexity, we need to disburden ourselves of the legacy of caricature and reaction that has attached itself to these times, and try to see their real, and sometimes surprising, contours and alignments.

The moral energies of the antislavery movement outlasted the Civil War for a few years, rallying themselves during the era of Reconstruction to assist in the task of aiding the "freedmen"—freed slaves—to adjust to their new circumstances. Just as the federal government under Ulysses Grant would turn much of the apparatus of Indian welfare over to the various Christian denominations, so was General Oliver Howard of the Freedman's Bureau more than willing to assist evangelical groups in the task of educating—and, if possible, converting—the former slaves. A wide variety of groups arose to take up this challenge, and the focus of home missions briefly turned toward the South. The typical teacher of the freedmen was evangelical, Congregationalist, female, and from New England. Much was accomplished during these years in developing an educational infrastructure for southern blacks, ranging from elementary public schools to normal schools to much of today's network of "historically black colleges" such as Fiske, Spelman, and Tougaloo. The failure of Reconstruction, the passage of Jim Crow laws, the imposition of rigid patterns of segregation, and the accommodationist stance advocated by Booker T. Washington all prevailed over the ambitious visions of the abolitionists. Blacks throughout the country generally retreated into their own Baptist and Methodist denominations and only slowly laid the foundations for what would decades later emerge as the Civil Rights movement. In the meantime, most white evangelicals turned their attention elsewhere.

The Victorian woman is typically represented as confined to a pedestal in restrictive clothing and unnaturally preoccupied with the repression of sexuality. However, the impact of women on American culture in general and on religion in particular during these years is only now becoming clear to scholars. There is no question that a major change had been taking place for some decades in the American economic and social structure, with profound implications for gender roles. With the rise of a national economy and the displacement of small-scale commerce and manufacture, as well as agriculture, by increasingly complex enterprises, the role of middle-class women and children in economic life grew constricted. A series of parallel dichotomies became sharply etched in the American consciousness: male/female, work/home, power/purity, profane/sacred.

A middle-class mythology rapidly developed in which women were divinely entrusted with the sacred functions of the care of home and hearth and nurture of the family. Men, correspondingly, were expected to cope with the harsh, secular realities of the world of business and the professions. This division was further reinforced by changing patterns in land use. The development of the streetcar made it possible for middle-class families to live in residential suburbs far away from the clamor of commerce, while breadwinners could make the daily commute to serve Mammon. The poor of both sexes were still consigned to hard physical work, while the honor of the pedestal became more and more common for women of the wealthier classes—usually native-born, white, and Protestant.

The church was one area in which these boundaries became somewhat blurred. Throughout the century, the majority of churchgoers were women, and it was the time and effort of women that was the mainstay of much of church life and work. On the other hand, church leadership was almost exclusively a male province. Aside from the Friends, who for the most part rejected a formal ministry, it was the small, decentralized, liberal New England denominations—Congregationalists, Unitarians, Universalists—who took the lead in ordaining women. Similarly, women were barred from voting roles in most denominational bodies, and the schism within antebellum antislavery ranks over the question illustrates the pervasiveness of this pattern within voluntary societies as well. Women did found their own missionary, reform, and other benevolent societies, but were themselves divided as to whether they should be permitted to take a more active role in the governance of the broader organizations they themselves sustained.

On the other hand, the role of organized religion within American society was becoming confused in terms of the dichotomies that were shaping the way many church-goers organized their perceptions of reality. If society could be divided into dichotomous zones, what was the place of the church? The active role of the colonial and antebellum clergy had been straightforward: they were men who exercised a position of leadership not only in the churches but frequently in the wider society as well. Whatever Beecher and Finney may have been, their images were clearly masculine.

During the Victorian decades, however, this role for the clergy and the churches became blurred. One of the most influential religious figures of the era was its greatest evangelist, Dwight L. Moody (1837–99). Moody's career is the embodiment of the American success story. Like Finney, he emerged from the matrix of New England evangelicalism into a secular career, as a shoe salesman in Boston. Seeking the main chance in Chicago, he experienced even greater success in the realm of soul-winning than in business, and became immersed in the YMCA and other evangelistic work. Moody then teamed up with Ira D. Sankey, a talented musician and songwriter, and went on to adapt the well-established tradition of revivalism to the new urban context of late nineteenth-century America—after an initial, triumphant tour of the British Isles.

The Moody-Sankey revivals were in some ways the epitome of the new business civilization harnessed to the evangelical impulse. Before staging an interdenominational revival in a city, Moody insisted that a committee of clergy and laity make preliminary arrangements to ensure success. A vast "tabernacle" would be erected to accommodate the multitudes expected to "hit the sawdust trail"—that is, come forward to shake hands with the evangelist and thereby accept Jesus and his offer of salvation. Modern methods of advertising and publicity were lavishly employed, as were careful provisions made for financial management and physical arrangements. Among Moody's admirers and generous patrons were some of the wealthiest businessmen of the day, including George Armour, Cyrus McCormick, and John Wanamaker. Moody's presentation of the Christian message was thus very much in harmony with the masculine world of commerce and industry—and served the latter's interests in its lack of disturbing social and political implications.

It was Moody's message rather than his means that confused the issue as to where his revival campaigns fit into the cultural matrix of his day. The god of Edwards and Beecher—and even of Julia Ward Howe—had been a masculine god, "trampling out the vintage where the grapes of wrath are stored." In *Uncle Tom's Cabin,* though, a shift of focus was clearing taking place. The agents of the divine were not aggressive clergymen but rather "the meek and lowly"—little children and nonviolent, elderly slaves. Redemption came not through the active mastery of the external environment and the aggressive conquest of sin but through a passive, exemplary role exerted by the saintly. Stowe may not have been a formal theologian, but her powerful images affected far more readers than the learned disquisitions of scholars like her husband Calvin.

Moody's preaching was not complex. Its theological content, in fact, was almost nonexistent, and could be reduced to the proposition that salvation was available for the asking. All the sinner had to do to attain salvation was make a simple decision, symbolized in "hitting the sawdust trail." Instead of theological reflections, Moody's sermons were anecdotal—usually pathetic stories invoking premature death, longing for mother, and a gentle Jesus whose message of redemption was open to all. Judgment was gone, and mercy was everything. Sentimentality—the appeal to the heart, even in contradiction to the dictates of the head—had been raised to an ultimate principle in a way having little to do with Edwards's cult of the "affections." And sentimentality was the province of woman.

Nor was Moody the whole show. Sankey, too, played an active role in the success of the urban revivals, which were the first to use music on a systematic basis. Warming up the audience before Moody's appearance was one role of the music director; so was the provision of suitable accompaniment for later parts of the service, such as the "altar call." The latter event was the climax of a Moody-Sankey revival, in which the preacher would invite all present to hit the trail to indicate that they had made what Billy Graham would later call a "decision for Christ." Sankey and his contemporaries, such as the blind but enormously productive Fanny J. Crosby, devised a whole new genre of religious music for these occasions, known as the "gospel hymn."

(This should not be confused with black gospel music, which has a very different character.) The imagery of these songs could be powerfully visceral, as in "There is a fountain filled with blood, Drawn from Emmanuel's veins." Just as typical of the genre was the vintage altar call hymn of Will H. Thompson:

Softy and tenderly Jesus is calling,
Calling for you and for me;
See, on the portals He's waiting and watching,
Watching for you and for me.
Come home, come home,
Ye who are weary, come home,
Earnestly, tenderly, Jesus is calling—
Calling, "O sinner, come home!"

Similarly, in Charlotte Elliott and William Bradbury's "Just As I Am"—still a popular altar call hymn—Jesus is the "lamb of God" whose blood was "shed for me." The Jesus through whom redemption comes is closer to Uncle Tom and Little Eva—the helpless sacrificial victim—than the god of Edwards, who dangled sinners over the fire like loathsome spiders.

Successful revivals conducted according to modern business methods, then, were very acceptable when the message they conveyed was relevant only to the hearth and not the marketplace. In this vein, Ann Douglas has argued in her provocative study, *The Feminization of American Culture,* that middle-class women and Protestant clergy of the Victorian era found themselves in an implicit alliance in developing strategies to capitalize on their own powerlessness. Women, children, home and hearth, religion—and the ministry—all found themselves on the "sacred" side of the cultural divide and were not expected to exert influence beyond their proper sphere. Douglas argues that a cult of powerlessness—expressed in sermons and popular sentimental fiction—emerged from this "holy alliance," in which claims to moral hegemony served as a rather poor substitute for genuine influence on society.

Not all Victorian women, though, were content with this trade-off. The reform crusades of the antebellum era, and antislavery in particular, had provided women with an opportunity to gain exposure to the world of politics and public life, however constricted their roles may have been in some cases. After slavery had ceased to be an issue, and the subsequent plight of black Americans receded from public consciousness, the possibilities for sweeping moral reform took on new dimensions. From the early days of the Benevolent Empire, the cause of temperance had caught the imagination of many evangelicals. Alcohol had not always been a symbol of evil or pollution in the Protestant imagination; in fact, ordination celebrations in the eighteenth century often ended as drunken carouses. Perhaps reflecting the demands of a new business culture, as against the laxer needs of traditional agrarian society, a revulsion began to set in against such indulgences beginning early in the nineteenth century. "Temperance" at first meant what it in fact denotes—moderation in the use of alcohol, and avoidance of hard liquor as opposed to beer or hard cider. This more balanced approach soon yielded to an absolutist position, and the temperate were only those who had "taken the pledge." By 1826 the American Temperance Society had been founded to promote this gospel of "teetotalism."

Opposition to the indiscriminate use of alcohol in the antebellum era was by no means a sign of fanaticism. According to W. J. Rorabaugh, male citizens of what he calls "the Alcoholic Republic" between 1790 and 1840 drank on the average a half a pint of hard liquor a day—presumably with some adverse consequences. Before long, temperance strategy shifted from the promotion of voluntary abstinence to legal co-ercion. In 1846, the "Maine Law," passed with the aid of abolitionist support, became the model for legislative prohibition of the manufacture and sale of intoxicants at the state level. Though it was soon emulated by other states, most of these laws were of brief duration, and it was not until the postwar period that temperance would again emerge as a major political force. This is not, however, to downplay its role in the antebellum era, when the cause attracted countless adherents among men and women, drunkards and paragons of sobriety, abolitionists and slaveholders, and any number of others regardless of rank and station. It was, in short, the quintessential American reform movement, which could link itself to anything from radical social transformation to revenge against the male sex to the desire for personal respect-ability and success.

After slavery had disappeared from the national scene as an object of reform-ing zeal, temperance returned to prominence in the new social context of postwar urban America. The old argument, dramatized in such popular melodramas as T. S. Arthur's *Ten Nights in a Barroom* (1854), was the destructive effect of alcohol on not only individuals but also families. (Arthur had been strongly influenced by the Washingtonians, a secular temperance movement aimed not so much at committed evangelicals but at drunkards, Catholics, and other groups given little attention by the Benevolent Empire.) In the sentimental imagery of the day, the pathetic child vainly calling for her father at the door of the saloon captured the growing popular appeal of the movement. It was, in short, potentially a women's movement—uncontrolled drink cut right to the heart of women and children as well as the broader social fabric. And women began to organize.

The organization that captured the spirit of the age most fully was the Women's Christian Temperance Union. Founded in Cleveland in 1874, the WCTU began as a single-issue organization under the rather conservative leadership of its first presi-dent, Annie Wittenmyer. In 1879 Wittenmyer was defeated by the formidable Frances Willard (1839–98), whose philosophy of "Do Everything" gave the union both a more activist and a more feminist dimension. Willard more than anyone illustrated the fu-sion of religious and political zeal that characterized Victorian reform as she showed that a woman could and would make herself heard. Significantly, this woman who dared to challenge both church and civil politics as a male preserve chose a white ribbon, for the purity of the home, and the slogan "Home Protection" as the union's symbols. Her concerns included not just shutting down saloons but an activist drive for women's interests in the areas of labor, prisons, prostitution, drugs, health, welfare, racial issues, and virtually every area of society in which women were involved. Most controversially, this included the suffrage, for which Willard was an ardent campaigner, and on behalf of which a "Department of Franchise" was added to the WCTU's structure in 1882. Like Garrison before and Martin Luther King afterwards, Willard saw reform as holistic and never feared compromising the central issue by taking aim at a host of other concerns affected by the underlying problems.

The WCTU was resoundingly successful in its campaign of propaganda and organization, but considerably less so in the realm of legislative and electoral politics. Willard's support for the Prohibition Party presumably helped it achieve some minor victories, and it may have influenced the outcome of the 1884 election. Third-party politics, however, has never been very successful in the American scheme of things, and Willard's later conversion to socialism deflected her potential impact further. By the 1890s the WCTU had been overshadowed by a new group, the Anti-Saloon League, which was founded in Oberlin, Ohio, in 1893. The league was in many ways the legitimate successor to Theodore Dwight Weld and his "band" in its combination of evangelical fervor and grassroots lobbying. Unlike Willard's WCTU, it was strictly a single-issue movement, ready to support any candidate who pledged to vote "dry."

Just as the WCTU's name clearly revealed its identity, so did the League's. Today, *saloon* has become a quaint word used primarily by bars trying to evoke a "wild west" atmosphere. In the late nineteenth century, the term was particularly associated with an establishment that not only sold strong drink but also served as a meeting place for the worst elements of society: prostitutes, crooked politicians, and immigrants. Together with the Catholic Church, the saloon had developed into a uniquely urban institution representing all of the social forces that stood against everything that rural evangelicals and urban Progressives had in common. The saloon helped perpetuate immigrant culture and reinforced Catholic mores; it robbed the workingman of his wages, sobriety, health, and usefulness to his family—and his employer; it served as a den for crime of all sorts; and it provided a convenient basis for corrupt urban machine politics. It was, in short, a symbol of everything that the "better" classes feared might undermine American morality and democratic culture.

The supporters of what was now shaping up as a drive for nationwide prohibition included, but were by no means confined to, evangelical churchpeople. Bishop James Cannon, the "Dry Messiah" of the Methodist Episcopal Church, South, was certainly an influential leader for that constituency. Cannon, though, was joined by such unlikely bedfellows as Archbishop John Ireland of St. Paul, Social Gospel spokesman Washington Gladden, and former president Theodore Roosevelt. The campaign dovetailed neatly with Progressive concerns for clean government and against trusts, including the liquor industry. At the core, though, were the League and the major evangelical denominations—Baptist, Presbyterian, and preeminently Methodist—who were persuaded that the imposition of a national prohibition on the manufacture and sale of alcoholic beverages would be a major step in ushering in the Kingdom of God and a Christian America. The crusade for prohibition thus took on the character of what Joseph Gusfield has called a "symbolic crusade." Its ultimate message was a major victory for a Protestant culture accustomed to deference but now beleaguered by the combined forces of the city, the immigrant, the political boss, an elite of new wealth, and the intellectual forces represented by Darwinism and the "new" biblical criticism.

The grassroots organizational work of the WCTU and the League were doubtless crucial to the movement's ultimate success, but it took a world war to win the final victory. Nativism—the fear of the foreign—had emerged as a potent aspect of the mythology of the prohibitionists; the saloon and its immigrant patrons were a symbol of the erosion of the fabric of traditional Protestant America. War with Germany mobilized nativism to the extent that the teaching of German was forbidden in the public schools and speaking it on the streets invited lynching. In the minds of many, Germany was simultaneously linked with militarism, beer brewing, and the new biblical criticism; revivalist Billy Sunday remarked that if hell were turned upside down, one would find "Made in Germany" stamped on the bottom. Catholics and Lutherans, who maintained the "Continental Sabbath" tradition of relaxation as well as worship on Sundays; who utilized wine in their communion services; who for the most part saw nothing wrong with the recreational use of alcohol in moderation; and who frequently were of German descent were unenthusiastic, to say the least. Their objections were overrun by a public opinion that at times bordered on hysteria. The arguments for prohibition were further bolstered by the patriotic argument that the grain used in brewing and distilling was needed to support the troops.

In December 1917 the House passed the Eighteenth Amendment, which was speedily ratified by all but two states. "The Noble Experiment" of national prohibition took effect on 16 January 1919. Interestingly, the Nineteenth Amendment, guaranteeing women's suffrage, was ratified in August of the following year. As Edward R. Murrow later observed, it was now as illegal to take a drink as it was to deny a woman the vote. Frances Willard would have felt vindicated.

The victory, however, soon proved hollow. The Eighteenth Amendment and its enforcing legislation, the Volstead Act, were widely ignored by upper and lower classes alike, however much the evangelical middle might remain committed. Organized crime, symbolized in Chicago's Al Capone, added a new and noxious dimension to the American urban scene, and owed its existence almost exclusively to the demand for illicit liquor. Public opinion more generally swung away from the crusading zeal that Prohibition represented. Evangelicalism in its new and extreme form of fundamentalism was heaped with public scorn through the Scopes "Monkey" Trial of

1925, where Darwinian evolution was unsuccessfully attacked by William Jennings Bryan—the "beerless leader" of the Populist movement who had served as Wilson's secretary of state. Revivalism had been turned to vaudeville by Billy Sunday, who now found himself eclipsed by new, secular celebrities—Babe Ruth, Rudolph Valentino, Gertrude Ederle, and Charles Lindbergh. H. L. Mencken, the acerbic and agnostic journalist who had covered the Scopes Trial for the *Baltimore Sun,* made relentless fun of the benighted denizens of what he called the "Bible Belt." Despite the relentless efforts of the legendary enforcement agents Eliot Ness and Izzy and Moe, the victory of Prohibition had proven to be, indeed, largely symbolic.

The Twentieth Amendment, which repealed the Eighteenth, was ratified in 1933, shortly after the election of Franklin Delano Roosevelt. The Catholic "wet" Democratic candidate, Alfred E. Smith, had been solidly defeated four years earlier in part through the opposition of southern evangelicals and other supporters of Prohibition. Roosevelt, however, represented a new coalition. Himself an Episcopalian of patrician stock, he mobilized the support of Catholics, Jews, blacks, and other minorities—as well as traditional Democrats and those afflicted with the Depression. The New Deal thus marked the end of the laissez-faire economics that had been a staple of much of evangelical moral theology in the past, as well as the political dominance of the Protestant middle classes and evangelical moralism.

So thorough was the reversal of evangelical fortunes in the 1920s that this era is sometimes spoken of as the "Second Disestablishment"—a spiritual successor to the dislocation that Lyman Beecher had lamented in Connecticut a century earlier. Its symptoms were many. One heretofore unmentioned aspect of Victorian evangelicalism was its stress on world missions. This impulse was tinged with a sense of Anglo-American imperialism especially manifest in the war against Catholic Spain and the subsequent assimilation of the Philippines as a part of an American mini-empire. Following the successful fund drives to support the war effort, a vast campaign to promote home and foreign missions and bring about a general spiritual revival through a unified Protestant effort took shape as the Interchurch World Movement (ICWM). Launched in 1920 in an outburst of optimism, it finally announced a goal of raising one billion dollars. It didn't—and could not even raise enough to pay its debts. The era of interdenominational Protestant crusading had come to an end.

Part of the problem that underlay the ICWM's failure was the division of Protestantism into two mutually hostile camps. Those who saw the emergence of evolutionary biology and "scientific" biblical criticism as healthy challenges to Christian self-understanding became known as "liberals" or "modernists," and they gained a great influence on seminary faculties in particular. Others who saw these intellectual movements as radically corrosive of the traditions they represented coalesced into the "fundamentalist" movement, with modernism as the chief enemy within the ranks. Baptists and Presbyterians in the North were especially torn by the conflicts this split engendered, and heresy trials and internecine politics abounded till most fundamentalists were forced to withdraw into their own groupings. Prohibition had been the last public issue on which Protestants of a variety of theological stripes had been able to unite; by the 1920s the victory was proving hollow, and theological conflict had accelerated to such a degree that future united effort would never again be possible among the contending parties. The quest for a Christian America would resurface again in the 1970s and 1980s, but strictly under fundamentalist (or, more broadly put, militant conservative evangelical) leadership.

Besides this internal division, the "second disestablishment" was precipitated by the rise of powerful external forces already hinted at—pluralism and secularism. Vast numbers of "new" immigrants from southern and eastern Europe had transformed the American urban scene, and had indirectly been the target of the prohibitionists. Their entry into politics, and the shift of population from a rural to an urban majority by 1920, helped make possible the Roosevelt coalition victory of 1932. From this point on, Jews and Catholics were to play an active role in determining the course of American life. On the other hand, Billy Sunday's eclipse by sports and entertainment figures illustrated the power of secular mass culture—radio, tabloid newspapers, and film.

At another level, many social functions that had previously been dominated or strongly influenced by evangelical religion—education and social work in particular—were now coming under governmental or other secular aegis. Many women, for example, who might earlier have devoted their energies to the missions movement now could follow the example of Jane Addams at Chicago's Hull-House and enter a career as a settlement worker. Social workers were now secular "professional altruists," as were teachers, nurses, administrators, and representatives of the other limited number of professions open to women.

The Victorian era had been one of ferment, change, and ultimate irony. Evangelicals had continued fervently in their quest of a Christian civilization, with Americans in its vanguard. Their numbers, however, had become so fraught with internal contradictions that their center could not hold for long. Questions of sexuality and sex roles preoccupied middle-class women and considerable numbers of men; some of the latter became so uneasy about their status that a cult of "muscular Christianity" ranged from elite prep schools to urban YMCAs. New extremes of wealth and poverty led many of the *nouveaux riches* into the arms of the Episcopal Church, strengthened the Roman Catholic presence, and gave rise to the Social Gospel, which applied Christian teachings to contemporary social problems, among reform-minded Protestants. The immigrant influx revived nativist fears, enhanced the contrast between "us" and "them," and led to a demand for immigration restriction among the influential, and also led to the resurgence of the Ku Klux Klan in the 1920s among the disenfranchised. Temperance and then national prohibition became the panacea for these many, mingled anxieties. The result was a temporary triumph and an ultimate defeat. Much of the subsequent history of American Protestantism deals with the breakup of this uneasy evangelical alliance into "liberal," "conservative," and "mainstream" camps in an ongoing struggle that remains both fierce and unresolved at the beginning of the twenty-first century.

CHAPTER 32

Protestant Liberalism and the Social Gospel

Although liberal religious thought had been in the air at least since the time of the Renaissance, it did not begin to take institutional form until the time of American independence. We have already discussed the problems of institutionalizing liberalism, since by definition it resists such confinement. The strains that were manifesting themselves within the Congregational churches and Harvard College by the year 1800, though, had grown so powerful and irreconcilable that a split seems in retrospect to have been inevitable. The American Unitarian Association had become a full-blown political entity by 1825, and its Universalist cousins had similarly taken steps toward denominational status by that time.

Among the sources of later Protestant liberalism in America, Unitarianism was a major influence. These liberal congregationalists had already enunciated the themes of a benevolent deity, a humanity open to growth through religious nurture, and a stress on the ethical rather than the metaphysical. Transcendentalism was also an important intellectual precursor through its emphasis on the continuity among the divine, the human, and the natural. European Romantic thought, such as the ideas of the German theologian Friedrich Schleiermacher, also exerted a strong influence in America through a stress on continuity, process, and feeling rather than judgment, dogma, and abstraction.

One figure, however, among the evangelical denominations in antebellum America stands out especially as a harbinger of new lines of thought: Horace Bushnell (1802–76), a Hartford Congregationalist minister whose writings helped create a whole new climate in American theology. Like his transcendentalist contemporaries, Bushnell recognized that human language was by its nature imprecise and suggestive, like poetry, rather than expressive of hard-edged, unchanging facts. This approach to language and, more broadly, the whole of reality stood in sharp contrast with that of evangelical Protestantism as well as more conservative Unitarianism, which both subscribed to the Scottish Common Sense philosophical position that impressions received through the senses are accurate representations of external reality. Bushnell's approach undermined the traditional Christian assumption, both Catholic and Protestant, that essential truths about the nature of God and religion could be expressed in precise propositional form in creeds and other verbal statements of faith.

Bushnell's best-known and, in the long run, most influential work was *A Discourse on Christian Nurture* of 1847. Here Bushnell sought to undercut the evangelical assumption, which reached its strongest form in revivalism, that all Christians must experience an emotional conversion to be assured of salvation. The necessity for conversion was based on the radical influence of original sin, which had corrupted the human condition so thoroughly that a sharp break had to occur in an individual's life through the operation of divine grace. Even though the theology of contemporary evangelicals such as Lyman Beecher and Charles Finney had undercut the notion of human helplessness in bringing about such a conversion, most Protestants of the era nevertheless believed that an abrupt shift in direction had to take place in each life for the saving "new birth" to be effectual.

In attacking this premise, Bushnell posited a fundamental theme of subsequent liberalism in his denying the existence of sharp boundaries among the supernatural, natural, and individual worlds. The divine and human thus stood not in a contradictory but rather in a complementary relationship, with God's grace permeating and redeeming the imperfect realm of creation. Similarly, redemption need and should not be marked by an abrupt change in consciousness but rather should come about gradually and imperceptibly in the development of a child through the influence of what Bushnell called "Christian nurture." This nurture was not confined to the church but was also carried out in the divinely ordained realms of the home, the school, and society at large. Thus, instead of pointing to a precisely datable moment of conversion, properly raised Christians should never be able to remember a moment when they had not lived within the realms of the operations of grace.

The theme of gradual growth and change was central to much of the thought first of Romanticism and then of other aspects of nineteenth-century intellectual life. The most important manifestation of this emphasis for Protestantism was the new approach to biblical studies that had been developing in German universities during the earlier decades of the century. Sometimes known as the "higher criticism," this school regarded the Hebrew and Christian scriptures not as a homogeneous, unified, divinely revealed pair of documents but rather as a collection of religious texts that had been written, edited, and collected within their respective communities over many centuries. In some cases, such as Isaiah, biblical books that had been regarded as the work of a single divinely inspired scribe were now through textual analysis believed to be the work of two or more hands. More dramatically, the Pentateuch, which had traditionally been attributed to Moses, was now thought to be of extremely complex composition through the hands of the various redactors who had each given it a distinct emphasis representing their own concerns and those of their age and social setting.

Although the use of "form criticism" remains controversial in some circles even to the present day—and although biblical scholars who accept its basic premises are by no means in agreement on their conclusions—its implications were regarded by incipient liberals of the time as a promise rather than a threat. Liberals did not regard the idea that the scriptures were of human authorship as an act of debunking; instead, they read this approach as an affirmation that God's message had not been revealed in static, propositional form but in a progressive, dynamic act of communication though human intermediaries. As the controversy over biblical criticism grew in the later decades of the century, controversies began to rage within the major denominations and their seminaries, and by the early twentieth century an organized reaction had emerged in the countermovement that took the name of *fundamentalism*.

Related to the development of biblical criticism were the changes that were also taking place in the world of learning in general and the sciences in particular. Again, Germany took the lead in developing the seminar method of advanced instruction and the university as an institution for research on a rigorous, scientific model. Until the 1860s, Americans seeking doctorates in any field of investigation, including theology and biblical studies, were obliged to spend some time in Germany, where they could scarcely remain unaffected by the new scholarly ethos. When indigenous advanced degree programs in religious fields emerged at Harvard, Yale, and the newly founded University of Chicago, they modeled themselves, much like their secular counterparts, on the German prototype, and controversy frequently abounded. Notable among these was the heresy trial of Charles Augustus Briggs (1841–1913), a distinguished professor of Old Testament at New York's Union Theological Seminary. Even though Briggs was convicted by the Presbyterian General Assembly in 1893 of false teaching and deprived of his ministerial status, he retained his post at Union for many years and later became an Episcopal priest. In supporting Briggs, Union also demonstrated a commitment to another German concept, *Lehrfreiheit* (academic freedom), which was now rivaling the preservation of orthodox teaching as a value in all realms of higher education.

To conservatives, the findings of the sciences themselves could be as threatening as the application of their methods to religious research. The classic challenge came in 1859 when the English naturalist Charles Darwin first published *The Origin of Species,* followed by *The Descent of Man* in 1871. Although the Civil War diverted American attention from these developments for some time, Darwin's argument that all varieties of life came into being through a gradual process of natural selection rather than a specific act of divine creation eventually forced American Protestants to come to terms with this "Copernican revolution" in biological thought.

Not all Protestants agreed on the implications of Darwinism, however. Conservatives protested that the theory of evolution deprived humanity of its unique character and God of his special creative power. Further, it seemed to repudiate the literal accuracy of the opening chapters of Genesis, which were read by conservatives as an account of the distinctive, specific creation of humanity as opposed to other forms of animate life. On the moral plane, it reduced humanity to the level of beasts, engaged in a continual struggle for the "survival of the fittest."

Some thinkers, such as Yale's William Graham Sumner, welcomed the implications of Darwin's theories as a refreshing new model for the realm of human activity. Sumner, an Episcopal priest who had lost his religious faith and become a sociologist and social philosopher, coined the still-popular phrase "Social Darwinism." This characterized his view of the ideal society as one in which natural selection was left free to operate, rewarding those who exhibited human ingenuity and hard work to an elevated status and condemning the "unfit" who did not merit social survival to a deserved oblivion. Social Darwinism, which carried with it a burden of philosophical determinism without the benefit of a personal god, came into favor among many political conservatives who saw in it a metaphysical justification for laissez-faire capitalism.

Protestant liberals tried to steer a mediating course between these extremes, and attempted to reconcile a belief in a benevolent, personal deity with an acceptance of evolution as a part of that deity's scheme for ultimate human betterment. The "higher criticism" of scripture could thus be accepted optimistically, as a demonstration that God revealed himself progressively and that a fuller knowledge of God was an indication of progress in the most comprehensive sense. This optimism was part of a broader mood of inevitable progress that was pervasive among much of Victorian America's intelligentsia. James Freeman Clarke, the Unitarian clergyman and scholar, captured this mood in his memorable phrase celebrating "the progress of mankind, onward and upward, forever."

Early Protestant liberalism was thus characterized not so much by a specific, rigid creed as by a set of interests, emphases, even moods. These included a stress on growth and development in all realms of existence, from divine revelation to the individual character; a confidence in benevolent divine guidance of these growth processes; a stress on the fundamental goodness of humanity, which could emerge through nurture in proper Christian institutions; a positive attitude toward secular learning, including the sciences, as instruments of progress; and a tendency to downplay the boundaries distinguishing various realms of being, such as the sacred and the secular or the divine and the human. God did not stand against humanity and the rest of creation, but rather worked with and through it to achieve his ultimate purposes. Liberals disagreed among themselves on specific theological formulations, but, as liberals, tended to regard such disagreement as potentially fruitful rather than disruptive.

The vanguard of early liberalism was not the seminary or the university but the pulpit. Victorian America was host to a golden age of preaching, and a galaxy of "princes of the pulpit" drew thousands of often newly prosperous urbanites to hear their optimistic rhetoric. These "princes" represented the spectrum of what had hitherto been primarily evangelical denominations, and frequently had handsome, capacious, theater-like downtown churches erected by their congregations to enhance their stature. Especially prominent among this clerical elite were Phillips Brooks (Episcopalian), of Boston's Trinity Church; George Angier Gordon (Congregational), of New Old South across Copley Square from Trinity; and Henry Ward Beecher (Congregational), and his successor, Lyman Abbot, of Plymouth Church, Brooklyn. Many of these preachers were also prolific writers in an age when theology had not yet split into academic and popular fragments, and their essays and printed sermons found a wide readership among the American urban Protestant middle class.

The message of this generation of preachers, who flourished during the last quarter of the nineteenth century, as well as that of their successors such as Harry Emerson Fosdick of Manhattan's Riverside Church, has sometimes been characterized as "evangelical liberalism." Although they rejected much of the baggage of both Calvinism and revivalism, they nevertheless remained faithful to the traditional Protestant focus on the Bible and Jesus as sure paths to salvation. Their Bible might no longer be literally infallible, and their Jesus more of a friend and example than an atoning savior, but the familiar symbols were still central.

A closely related form of liberalism that shared these premises but added some other crucial concepts was the Social Gospel that began to attract adherents in the midst of the massive transformations that American society was undergoing during these same decades. Where the "princes of the pulpit" tended to stress personal growth through adherence to a properly understood Christian Gospel, ministers such as Baptist Walter Rauschenbusch (1861–1918) brought Jesus's teachings to bear on a different aspect of human experience. Rauschenbusch began his ministerial career in the part of New York's Lower East Side known evocatively as "Hell's Kitchen." Here he came into firsthand contact with the squalor and violence of immigrant slum life that was beyond the experience of most native-born middle-class Protestants. Instead of blaming the immigrant poor for their own misery, Rauschenbusch began to realize that other factors might be more responsible for their condition and that Christianity had resources to illuminate both the causes and cures of contemporary social disorganization.

The core of Rauschenbusch's teaching was that the message of Jesus had not been directed solely to the salvation of individuals but addressed the entire social dimension of human existence as well. The goal of Christianity was consequently the realization here on earth of the Kingdom of God, a biblical concept that had recently been emphasized by the German theologian Albrecht Ritschl. Later in Rauschenbusch's career, his earlier optimism became balanced by a stress on the objective reality of a Kingdom of Evil as well. In both cases, however, religious significance existed not simply in the soul of the individual believer but in the social realm in which all individuals are inextricably involved.

Rauschenbusch's ideas received a wide circulation through his lectures, his teaching at the Baptist seminary in Rochester, and such books as *Christianity and the Social*

Crisis (1907) and *A Theology for the Social Gospel* (1917). However, his was by no means the only voice in the growing Social Gospel movement, which was attracting more and more attention as urban poverty, crime, and labor unrest caught the reluctant attention of middle-class Americans. The other most important publicist of the movement was a Congregationalist minister who became involved in such issues in parishes in Springfield, Massachusetts, and Columbus, Ohio. Washington Gladden (1836–1918) was not, like Rauschenbusch, primarily a theologian but rather an articulate activist clergyman who possessed a gift for theologically literate advocacy. Gladden, sometimes called "the father of the Social Gospel," was especially sympathetic with the emergent labor movement, and called for a spirit of cooperation to replace the growing antagonism between workers and capitalists. Gladden also was a strong supporter of interdenominational and interracial fellowship, was an early advocate of the cause of black rights, and regarded Jews and Catholics as potential allies rather than antagonists. Similar ideas were soon taken up by Catholic social thinkers such as Msgr. John A. Ryan, who used his position at Catholic University to advocate the "just wage" theory that echoed many ideas earlier developed by Gladden and other Protestant activists.

The Social Gospel movement, which Gladden and Rauschenbusch did so much to launch, articulate, and promote, rapidly found other channels as well. Just as the German model had influenced biblical studies, so did the emergent American research universities of the era apply the same "scientific" approach to the social realm. Whereas in earlier decades sociology, economics, and political science had been treated as topics within moral philosophy, the term *social science* now emerged to set them in a more empirical context. Many of the first American social scientists, however, were by no means content to regard these pursuits as morally neutral. Richard T. Ely, for example, was an Episcopalian layman who received a German doctorate in economics, taught at Wisconsin and Johns Hopkins, and was instrumental in the founding of the American Economic Association in 1885. His study of economics was motivated by an ethical concern for what he saw as the destructive consequences of classical laissez-faire capitalism. W. D. P. Bliss, another Episcopalian, helped to put social work on a more scientific basis through his massive compilation of data in his *Encyclopedia of Social Reform* (1898). In the seminaries and universities, an alliance between theology and social science began to take shape in the new field of social ethics, which the Unitarian Francis Greenwood Peabody (author of *Jesus Christ and the Social Question* in 1900) introduced at Harvard and which was widely imitated elsewhere. Throughout the twentieth century, such courses became standard parts of the curriculum at many seminaries, and a ministerial awareness of the complexity of the social realm and its problems is a major legacy of the Social Gospel among most "mainstream" Protestants and Catholics.

In addition to education and advocacy, the Social Gospel made its impact on American Protestantism in a variety of other ways. A distinctive innovation of the era was the "institutional church," of which the Episcopal St. George's and St. Bartholomew's in Manhattan were important prototypes. These were churches that not only offered weekly congregational worship but extended their professional staff, program, and physical plant to promote a wide variety of outreach endeavors for the broader community. These efforts did not exclude religious activity but focused more on such basic matters as day care, summer outings for poor urban children, and educational and training programs for the dispossessed of all ages. As such, they were closely related to the settlement house movement, pioneered by the more secular work of Jane Addams at Chicago's Hull-House. Besides the institutional churches and other urban outreach programs, whole denominations responded by creating social service divisions in their emergent national bureaucracies. Beyond the denominational level, the ecumenical Federal Council of Churches of 1905 grew primarily out of a concern for a coordinated Protestant response to national social issues. Its Commission on Church and Social Service, led by Presbyterian Charles Stelzle, rapidly attracted attention with its investigation of the Bethlehem steel strike of 1910, which condemned such then-common practices as the twelve-hour day and the seven-day week.

The Social Gospel was a central part of a broader late nineteenth-century phenomenon known as "Social Christianity," but it did not exhaust that category. To the right should be mentioned such evangelical responses to social problems as the YMCA/YWCA movement (with Catholic and Jewish counterparts), urban gospel missions, and the Salvation Army (with its schismatic offshoot, the Volunteers of America). All of these efforts recognized that new, sometimes even drastic responses were needed to reach the destitute, but all were premised on the evangelical assumption that the key to the redemption of the body was the prior salvation of the soul through conversion. In their early days in America, however, Salvation Army members often mounted a harsh attack against the excesses of capitalism and sympathized with radical secular reformers such as Eugene V. Debs.

In addition, it should be noted that advocates of Social Christianity were by no means homogeneous in their political and social inclinations. Gladden and Rauschenbusch, like the "mainstream" of the Social Gospel movement, would best be described as left-leaning reformers, who allied themselves with the Progressive movement in American politics and who advocated a significant modification but not a radical upheaval in America's social and economic institutions. Bliss, who had been influenced by the Anglican socialists F. D. Maurice and Charles Kingsley, openly aligned himself with a more radical approach to politics and helped organize the first Christian Socialist Society in 1889. Congregationalist George Herron, who was later deposed from the ministry in part for his radical views, was an influential spokesman for an explicitly socialist perspective and campaigned for Socialist presidential candidate Eugene V. Debs. Toward the other end of the spectrum, Congregationalist Josiah Strong was an impassioned advocate of Social Gospel reform principles, but manifested in his widely read *Our Country* (1885) a strong sense that American destiny was inextricably tied to the genius of the Anglo-Saxon race and the necessity of its triumph.

Though the Social Gospel at the time seemed to present a startling new paradigm for American Protestantism in its shift of emphasis from individual salvation to the Kingdom of God, later observers such as Martin Marty have noted the ambiguities that underlay the emphases of its leaders. The movement, for example, had little sympathy for the nascent feminist movement, and Vida Scudder of Wellesley was one of the few women to play a noticeable role in its development. Similarly, Rauschenbusch and his fellows had little sympathetic understanding of the aspirations of the black community and other minority groups, and accepted with little criticism the intellectual commonplace of the times that "Teutonic" peoples were inherently superior to others. Finally, as Marty notes, the movement was "vague on program, weak on detail, generally out of touch with laborers [and] inept at politics" (*Modern American Religion* [1986], 290). For all its inherent paternalism, however, the Social Gospel introduced systematic concern with human suffering in the context of an unjust social order into the vocabulary of American Protestantism, a heritage that can be measured in the "outreach" committees and humanitarian endeavors of countless churches to this day.

Whereas the Social Gospel was based on a direct involvement of the Christian churches in the everyday experience of Americans, another variety of Protestant liberalism took its stand on experience of a very different sort. Loosely known as "modernists," religious thinkers at several major universities and interdenominational divinity schools turned to constructing a theology that was based not primarily on revelation or reason but directly on human religious experience. Harvard's William James (1842–1910), often called the founder of American psychology, helped lead the way in *The Varieties of Religious Experience* of 1902 to a scientific study of religious experience that had as its goal not the destruction of supernatural faith but rather an appreciation of the positive good that religion can effect among people from a purely this-worldly standpoint. James was also a founder of the distinctively American philosophical school known as "Pragmatism," which held that the truth of an idea lay not so much in its logical consistency but in its "cash value"—not its literal material worth but rather its usefulness to real people in dealing with everyday life. Needless to say, James's approach, which stated that most religious experience generated "overbeliefs"—theological formulations that could not be empirically proven or disproven—was conducive toward tolerance but was hardly compatible with any tradition's claims to normative or exclusive truth.

James, however, was a philosophical psychologist and not a theologian. A number of the latter emerged during the World War I era to apply James's leads to their specific purposes. Prominent among these "modernists" were Yale's Douglas Clyde Macintosh, the University of Chicago's Shailer Mathews and Henry Nelson Wieman, and the school of "Christian Personalists" that developed around Boston University's Borden P. Bowne. Although their individual formulations and their allegiance to traditional Christianity varied considerably, they were united in a common quest to put the analysis of religious truth on a firm empirical basis. Their systems, which were usually highly technical, affirmed that the universe was not starkly impersonal but rather was infused with a dimension that was conducive to the evocation of the moral dimension in human life. With Wieman especially, however, this dimension bore little resemblance to the personal God familiar to most believers, and the long-term impact of the movement was considerably less direct than that of other varieties of liberalism.

Liberalism in its various forms continued to find eloquent defenders throughout the 1920s such as Harry Emerson Fosdick. Fosdick came under attack in conservative Presbyterian circles, and eventually resigned his denominational pulpit to accept a call to New York's interdenominational Riverside Church. Fosdick had aroused anger in his 1922 sermon, "Shall the Fundamentalists Win?" in which he took to task the coalescing conservative opposition to liberal positions that was rallying under the banner of fundamentalism. But fundamentalism, which suffered a major defeat in the realm of public opinion during the Scopes "Monkey" Trial of 1925, was not to play the most important role in bringing liberalism's dominance over much of the life and thought of Protestant churches, seminaries, and denominational activity to an end. Rather, the impact first of the world war and then the Depression called into practical question for many Americans the resolute optimism that had character-ized the spirit of liberalism in all of its forms. Among many erstwhile liberals, a new movement called Neo-Orthodoxy seemed attractive in its combination of major liberal premises such as biblical criticism with a reappropriation of such traditional Christian emphases as the power of sin and the judgmental character of God.

Because of its protean character, liberalism did not simply disappear; rather, its more viable impulses were channeled into new directions. Such emphases as a critical approach to the interpretation of scripture; a concern for the ethical dimensions of the Gospel in the social, political, and economic realms; a rejection of the demand for an emotional conversion and a corresponding emphasis on benevolent nurture in the faith, in part through the Sunday school movement; and a concomitant stress on the role of Christianity in promoting the development of a mature, responsible personality throughout life; all remained staples of pulpit preaching, seminary and Christian education curricula, and denominational programming. Further, those denominations that in the twentieth century became known as "mainline"—Meth-odist, Presbyterian, Episcopal, and others—remained open to the advocacy of a wide variety of causes, both intellectual and social, for which liberalism in general and the Social Gospel in particular had prepared them. This was especially true in the 1960s and after, when the churches, their clergy, and many concerned laity became involved in the civil rights, antiwar, and other movements of the era. Although, at the beginning of the twenty-first century, there is by no means a consensus on either theological or political matters in these denominations, the spirit of tolerance and the rejection of creedal tests that this pluralism betokens is in itself a sign that liberalism has been one of the most important constituent forces in the shaping of contemporary American religious life.

CHAPTER 33

Anglican Renaissance

The Victorian Episcopal Church flourished especially in the established metropolitan areas of the Northeast—most notably New York and Boston—as well as in newly thriving cities such as Chicago. These areas were in the vanguard of the social and economic changes that were rapidly transforming the nation into an urban, industrial, and polyglot society. On the one hand, many of the newly rich—and a number from backgrounds of more established wealth as well—were being attracted to a denomination that represented in visible form the allure of English customs and traditions. Unitarians in Boston and Quakers in Philadelphia both contributed converts, and New York City especially manifested the impact of new wealth and enthusiasm in an outburst of church and cathedral building northward along Fifth Avenue and in other prestigious locales.

This situation evoked a number of institutional responses. For the wealthy families of the Northeast, a complex of "prep" schools modeled on the English church-related public school began to flourish, particularly in New England. These schools, of which Endicott Peabody's Groton (founded 1884) was among the best known, were frankly dedicated to the cultivation of a future elite nurtured on the "muscular Christianity" that had become popular in the England of the time. (Louis Auchincloss's effective novel, *The Rector of Justin* [1956], was based on Peabody's career.) The movement toward the church's playing an active role in secondary education was contemporary with another English import, the revival of both male and female Anglican religious orders. The Society of Saint John the Evangelist, usually called the "Cowley Fathers," is one of the better known of these orders that still exist today. The complex of schools sponsored by religious orders that arose in conjunction with the University of the South at Sewanee are good examples of the interplay of the two impulses. (The novelist James Agee was a product of St. Andrew's at Sewanee, and his correspondence with his mentor Father Flye is a significant literary document.)

Whereas the demands of wealth created one kind of institution, its widespread and conspicuous absence brought forth others. One of the most important innovations of the era was the development of the "institutional church," a manifestation of "social Christianity" directed toward the alleviation of suffering and social disorder brought about by the deluge of "new immigrants" engulfing New York and other major cities. The prototype of the institutional church was St. George's in Manhattan's once-fashionable Gramercy Park. Under the leadership of Irish-born William S. Rainsford (1850–1933), the parish resisted the temptation to follow its wealthy clientele uptown, and instead set about developing a comprehensive set of ministries to the poor: slum missions, trade school classes, fresh-air camps, and a wide variety of activities to involve all attendants. Rainsford's mission was possible in large measure through the unwavering sponsorship of his senior warden (head lay official), J. P. Morgan—one of the "robber barons" whom another New York State senior warden, Franklin Delano Roosevelt, would later characterize as "malefactors of great wealth."

Other Episcopal responses to the challenge of the "Social Gospel" were the founding of the Church Association for the Advancement of the Interests of Labor (CAIL) in 1887, the work of which was continued in a more official denominational context by the Church League for Industrial Democracy (1919) and other agencies. Prominent among Episcopal leaders for social justice in the context of the Christian Gospel were W. D. P. Bliss (1856–1926), a clergyman known for founding the Christian Socialist Church of the Carpenter in Boston (1890) and compiling the *Encyclopedia of Social Reform* (1898); Richard T. Ely (1854–1943), economist at Johns Hopkins University and later the University of Wisconsin, who founded the American Institute of Christian Sociology and cofounded the American Economic Association and, with Bliss, the Christian Social Union; and Vida D. Scudder (1861–1954), who while teaching English at Wellesley College engaged in settlement and labor work, entered the semimonastic Companions of the Holy Cross, and wrote extensively on both the Middle Ages and the highly contemporary social reform ideas they inspired in her and her English predecessor, John Ruskin.

The other major challenge of the later Victorian age was on the intellectual front, in the impact of scientific and especially evolutionary thought on theology and biblical interpretation. One rather mild form of the religious liberalism that spread through the spectrum of denominations at the time was that of Phillips Brooks (1835–93), known as one of the "princes of the pulpit" for his rhetorical performances at Trinity Church, Boston, and later as bishop of Massachusetts. His thought was not systematic or complex, but his spoken and published sermons were extremely popular in their stress on Christianity as a means of helping individuals realize their full innate possibilities. This stress on growth and potential rather than on depravity was a common theme in the liberalism of the day.

Brooks formed part of a new, loosely constituted "party" in both American and British Anglicanism known as the "Broad Church" movement. This movement, which hoped to transcend the internecine strife that had been generated by the factionalism of the nineteenth century, was anticipated in the career of William Augustus Muhlenberg (1796–1877), whose "Memorial" movement—stemming from his petition, or memorial, to the 1853 General Convention—urged the church to take the lead in transcending theological particularities and promoting Christian union. Although little concrete came from this ecumenical thrust, Muhlenberg helped pave the way for an outlook that would eventually smooth the road for later Episcopal encounters with modern thought and society in a positive rather than defensive manner. The church's seminaries embraced the new biblical criticism of the latter part of the century with little resistance, and the fundamentalist movement that was to plague the Baptist and Presbyterian communities had little impact on a church that was never strongly given to precise theological formulations. The only casualty was Algernon Sydney Crapsey (1847–1927), an advocate of the Social Gospel in Rochester, New York, who was deposed from the ministry in 1906 on charges of his denying not the Bible's accuracy but rather that of the creeds of the early church.

What may be called the "Episcopal Renaissance" of these (in Lewis Mumford's phrase) "Brown Decades" did not focus on theology, which was enhanced far more by contributions from heirs of the Reformed and Wesleyan traditions. With a few possible exceptions such as William Porcher DuBose (1836–1918) of the University of the South (Sewanee) and the twentieth-century process theologian Norman Pittenger, whose active career was spent chiefly in England, Episcopalians have not generally been leaders in American religious thought. Because the Anglican tradition has emphasized worship over doctrine, it should not be surprising to find that the most distinguished contribution of the Episcopal Church to the arts has been in the area of ecclesiastical architecture. Many colonial Anglican churches still survive along the eastern seaboard, reflecting the Georgian (neoclassical) style dominant in England and the wealth and social and political prominence of the church especially in the earlier eighteenth century. Some of particular note include Bruton Parish Church, Williamsburg, Virginia (1711–15); Old North (Christ) Church, Boston (1723), of Paul Revere fame; Trinity Church, Newport, Rhode Island (1725–26); Christ Church, Philadelphia (1727); and St. Paul's Chapel, New York City (1764–66), Manhattan's only surviving prerevolutionary building (and the base of rescue operations following the September 11, 2001, disaster, commonly referred to as 9/11).

The architectural mode most closely associated with the Episcopal Church in America, which was to have a profound influence on American church building more broadly, was that of the Gothic Revival—part of a broader revival of appreciation for medieval culture manifested in the resurgence of religious orders, boarding schools, social reform, and other aspects of "organic" community. Interest in medieval churches as the most appropriate prototypes for liturgical worship was encouraged by the Cambridge Camden Society in England, a development coordinate with the Oxford Movement in theology, and spread in the eastern United States by a similar group in New York City. Richard Upjohn (1802–78), an English emigrant, was most influential in adapting the Gothic to American purposes. In addition to Manhattan's monumental Trinity Church (1839–46) at Broadway and Wall Street, Upjohn designed countless wooden small-town and rural churches around the country in the board-and-batten ("Carpenter Gothic") style that became an instant success among American Christians of all sorts and added an important new element to the religious landscape.

Later phases of American medievalism were contributed by Henry Vaughn, also an English-born Anglican who designed both Episcopal churches and "prep school" chapels, and Henry Hobson Richardson, who employed the Romanesque mode in Boston's epoch-making Trinity Church (1872–77), from the pulpit of which Phillips Brooks held forth. Together with the near-contemporary Boston Public Library and New Old South Church (Congregational), Trinity helped demarcate Boston's Copley Square as a quintessential public urban space of the Victorian era—a fitting platform for Brooks, the quintessential Victorian clergyman. Trinity served to display not only Brooks's preaching but also other arts that were undergoing a revival at the time, for example, the sculpture of Augustus St. Gaudens and the murals of John Lafarge. Clergy of other denominations, such as New York's literary Henry van Dyke at Brick Presbyterian, were also encouraging the visual and plastic arts as aids to worship in a land where centuries of dominance of the iconoclastic Puritan spirit had heretofore acted as a damper. The Episcopal Church, though, provided the most effective leadership, in part through the wealth and prestige at its command, but also through its long-standing emphasis on the sacramental role of the arts in liturgical worship.

One of the most influential American church architects, whose career spanned the later Victorian age and the early twentieth century, was Ralph Adams Cram (1863–1942), a New England Unitarian who converted to Anglicanism as a young man and became one of the tradition's foremost apologists as well. Cram's best-known design was that of the monumental (and still unfinished) Cathedral Church of Saint John the Divine (begun 1892) in New York City. Saint John's, however, was only the most spectacular of dozens of other churches, mostly Episcopal, that were conceived by Cram and his partners. In addition, Cram's voluminous writings attempted to provide a philosophical rationale for the role of Gothic in modern society, a role based on the alleged superiority of medieval culture and religion to that of the present.

Cram also played a peripheral role in the design of one of the most splendid ecclesiastical monuments of his era, the Cathedral Church of Saints Peter and Paul in Washington, D.C. The National Cathedral, as it is generally known, was intended by its founder, Washington Bishop Henry Yates Satterlee, to be "a house of prayer for all people," serving the nation as a whole as well as its diocese and denomination. For some Episcopalians of the era, this project was part of a desire to see their church become a de facto national church. Although this goal was never achieved, the Cathedral has often functioned as a venue for solemn national occasions, such as Ronald Reagan's funeral and President George W. Bush's address to the nation following 9/11. (It also was the scene of a memorable episode in the television series *The West Wing* in which Martin Sheen, playing President Jedediah Bartlett, argues with God in Latin.)

The leadership of the Episcopal Church in promoting the arts did not last indefinitely. Resistance by other denominations to the uses of material and visual beauty had dissolved by the turn of the twentieth century, and the Gothic began to appear in such disparate churches as the Duke University Chapel (Methodist) and New York's Riverside Church (Baptist/interdenominational). The graduated income tax, the Depression, and then World War II reduced the once enormous resources available for church construction, and other liturgical denominations, especially the Lutheran and Roman Catholic, began to exert leadership in the design of architecture for worship.

Nevertheless, the association of the Episcopal Church with both the arts and social concern continues to be strong to the present. The Cathedral Church of St. John the Divine, for example, resumed for a period in the 1980s its once-suspended building program to provide training in the crafts for neighborhood youth hired to work toward its completion. The cathedral also sponsors a wide variety of artistic and other community events, ranging from a chapel set aside for the remembrance of AIDS victims to a "poets' corner" on the model of that in Westminster Abbey to an annual "blessing of the beasts" on St. Francis's day in which creatures from elephants to gerbils are brought in for a celebration of the orders of creation. Grace Cathedral, which stands high atop San Francisco's Nob Hill, boasts two labyrinths— one outdoors, one within the nave—that promote a "New Age" style of ecumenical spirituality that had originated in the plans of medieval cathedrals.

In a literary mode, Madeleine L'Engle, a leading author of what might best be described as Anglican metaphysical fantasy, has lived on the grounds of St. John the Divine as artist in residence. Her writings, such as *A Wrinkle in Time* (1962), have been popular with teens as well as adults, and combine adventure with spiritual dimensions in the manner of C. S. Lewis, an English Anglican writer also popular with many Americans of various ages. (The 1993 film *Shadowlands* featured Anthony Hopkins as Lewis with Debra Winger as his improbable American love, and some of Lewis's fiction, such as *The Lion, the Witch, and the Wardrobe* are being made into major motion pictures [2005].) Nora Gallagher's 1998 *Things Seen and Unseen* provides a personal account of a year spent involved in the life of a California parish, including its soup kitchen and AIDS ministry. In a very different key, the novels of Jan Karon, set in the small North Carolina town of Mitford, feature an unpretentious middle-aged Episcopal priest who provides his parishioners with an example of unassuming spirituality, and have inspired discussion groups and Web sites among their many enthusiasts.

In a low-key way, the American Anglican blend of public worship, personal spiritual growth, aesthetic expression, and social outreach has outlived the excesses of the Gilded Age and offers a religious path no longer intimately tied to the culture of a ruling elite. Though Episcopalians are usually classified among the "mainline" denominations, their religious culture, which derives as much from Eastern Orthodox, Celtic, and medieval Catholic spirituality as from Reformation traditions, is quite distinct from that of other, more explicitly Protestant groups. In the New World as in the Old, Anglicanism remains a tertium quid—a "third path" that defies the usual dichotomies of classification.

CHAPTER 34

Reactions to Modernity: Fundamentalism, Holiness, Pentecostalism

Historians such as William G. McLoughlin have argued that American religious history can be read as a series of revivals. Some of these, like the two Great Awakenings, have been explicitly religious in character, and also recognized by their participants as dramatic turning points in our collective religious life. Wars which have involved the whole nation in a protracted struggle—especially the traumatic Civil War, in which Americans killed and maimed one another and died on a scale unequaled before or since—have also been interpreted as religious awakenings, often by the clergy of the time.

Although rapid social change has been a constant in the American experience, particularly intensive periods of such change have been fertile incubators for religious excitement and innovation. The two Great Awakenings were good examples of such periods, and corresponded first with the emergence of a national consciousness and then with the settlement of the eastern reaches of the frontier. The simultaneous exhilaration and insecurity generated by these wide-ranging changes affecting such large numbers of Americans led to the generation of new, experientially oriented and doctrinally innovative movements, as well as reactions against them by those with stronger stakes in the status quo.

The period that ran roughly from the Civil War to the Depression was characterized by equally intense social change manifested in large-scale immigration, urbanization, and industrialization. In addition to the inpouring of immigrants from southern and eastern Europe into America's burgeoning industrial cities, countless other Americans, first white and then black as well, began a vast in-migration from the nation's farms and small towns into these same cities, always seeking "the main chance." The periodic economic upheavals of the era hit farmers especially hard, and the Populist movement filled much of the South and Midwest with deep suspicion of the ways of urban financial magnates whose machinations seemed to be putting a timeless way of rural life at risk. The foreigners who competed for the jobs generated by this new order themselves seemed a threat to the established ways in their exotic languages, religions, and cultures, and a new upsurge of nativism at both popular and elite levels also colored the political life of the times.

By the turn of the twentieth century, three broad-based new religious movements had emerged from this cultural ferment, which were to transform the character of American Protestantism dramatically during the following decades: holiness, fundamentalism, and pentecostalism. Though all would eventually generate a number of independent denominations, each began more as a climate of opinion within a Protestant community that was finding itself profoundly divided over the challenges posed by evolutionary thought, biblical criticism, and theological "modernism," as well as the inevitable pressures toward institutional routinization that came with the achievement of middle-class status.

The crucible in which the ingredients of this new evangelical realignment were forged was the Second Great Awakening. It was in this period that the two major theological strains of evangelicalism, the Reformed and the Wesleyan, entered into an ongoing working relationship in the contexts of such broader endeavors as revivalism and moral reform campaigns that often required cooperation as well as the more usual denominational competition. Cross-fertilization also took place in these years between popular outbursts of "enthusiasm" such as the Great Revival and the more sophisticated revivalist enterprises of such stalwarts as Lyman Beecher and Charles G. Finney.

It was Finney especially who during his lengthy career brought together a number of disparate elements that would prove exemplary for the future. Although ordained a Presbyterian, Finney was never very firmly grounded in Reformed theology, and in his later years became converted to a "perfectionist" position similar to that developed earlier by John Wesley. It was especially during his years in the 1830s as professor and president at Oberlin College that he and his colleague Asa Mahan became convinced that it was possible for Christians to become perfect followers of Jesus, thus attaining a spiritual state free from sin. Though they may have differed in detail from Wesley, this idea, expounded in the *Oberlin Evangelist,* was fundamentally identical with the notion of "entire sanctification" propounded by Methodism's founder.

In addition to moving toward a rapprochement between Reformed and Wesleyan ideals, Finney was also a "bridge" figure in the equivocal position he occupied within the domain of ecclesiastical structures. Though ordained, in spite of questionable preparation, by a major denomination, Finney functioned much more as an independent religious entrepreneur than as a traditional parish minister, and his "New Measures" reflected aptly his freedom from the constraints of tradition. His enthusiasm for reform causes such as antislavery also indicated that he was open to the application of religious ideas to a rapidly changing social order as well.

If Finney could have been Emerson's "representative man" for the antebellum era of evangelicalism, his postwar counterpart was certainly the remarkable Dwight L. Moody. Moody could claim even less formal education than Finney, who had been trained as a lawyer, but was equally entrepreneurial as well as sensitive to the needs of another age of rapid social transformation. Further, like Finney, Moody did not operate under denominational aegis but rather acquired the active support of the gamut of evangelical denominations for his urban revivals. Moody's prime constituency was not the unchurched, at whom his revivals were overtly aimed, but rather the displaced rural folk who made up much of the mass in-migration to the cities of Victorian America. In addition to the innovative techniques he and his music leader, Ira D. Sankey, were continually devising, Moody was also receptive to a wide variety of new theological ideas that were developing in the ambit of Anglo-American evangelicalism. Among these were John Nelson Darby's dispensational premillennialism, a major doctrinal undergirding of the nascent fundamentalist movement, and Keswick (KEZ-ick) holiness, an interdenominational variety of the perfectionism earlier espoused by Wesley and Finney.

Ideas, however, were subordinate to the anecdotal character and emotional appeal of Moody's presentations, which were aimed more at the heart than the head. Furthermore, Moody developed a widespread institutional network, based at the Moody Bible Institute in Chicago and the Northfield and Mount Hermon schools in western Massachusetts, through which his successors could mobilize rapidly in the cause of the new movements they were so well prepared to espouse.

It is important further to note that the holiness and fundamentalist movements, though frequently regarded as arising from among the poorer classes, had solidly middle-class social and intellectual origins. Holiness was nurtured in the highly respectable Manhattan parlor of Phoebe Palmer and similar domestic and ecclesiastical sites, and fundamentalism had many of its roots in Moody's sentimental appeals to middle-class sensibilities and the respectably learned though extremely conservative ruminations of the Presbyterian divines at Princeton Theological Seminary. It was only in the social crucible of the latter days of the Victorian era and the dislocations attendant upon World War I that this potent mixture of forces coalesced into popular movements of extreme power and frequent volatility.

Of the three movements, holiness was clearly the oldest, and emerged directly from the teachings of John Wesley. Though the attainment of Christian perfection was for Wesley a long-term process, it was nevertheless characterized by a discrete, instantaneous religious experience, known in Methodist lore as the "second blessing." This state of holiness pertained to the will of the believer, which was now free from voluntary sinful impulses and behavior, but was not necessarily permanent; continual discipline and vigilance were needed to sustain it indefinitely.

Although American Methodists continued to subscribe to this distinctive feature of Wesley's teaching, the doctrine of "entire sanctification" was not always accorded a central place in the denomination's practice as its members began to attain middle-class status. Beginning in the 1830s, a coterie led by Phoebe Palmer of New York founded a "Tuesday Meeting for the Promotion of Holiness," which was premised on the centrality of the personal experience of entire sanctification. The Tuesday Meeting acquired a dedicated following among a gamut of evangelical leaders from a variety of denominations, including Bowdoin professor Thomas C. Upham, a Congregationalist; Asa Mahan, Finney's Oberlin colleague; Hannah Whithall Smith and David Updegraff, Quakers with evangelical leanings; and a variety of influential Presbyterians, Baptists, and, especially, Methodists. Palmer's *The Way of Holiness* (1843) and other books, journals, and spin-off meetings, which numbered some two hundred by the 1880s, helped spread this preoccupation with holiness across the country. Though this interdenominational movement differed in details from Wesley's earlier theological formulations, it resembled his own movement in its origins not as a new church but rather as a religious climate of opinion promoted by a powerfully effective network of parachurch structures.

Following the Civil War, the holiness impulse began to assume new forms, which enhanced its efficacy as an informal institutional network especially within the broader Methodist ambit. A distinctive innovation was the holiness camp meeting, which had its origins in the frontier gatherings the Methodists had domesticated and routinized during the later antebellum decades. The lead in the further transformation of this institution was taken by John S. Inskip, a New York Methodist minister who had been converted to holiness principles through his wife's example and who now directed his efforts to the movement's promotion. In June of 1867, Inskip convened a camp meeting at Vineland, New Jersey, from which emerged the National Camp Meeting Association for the Promotion of Holiness.

The holiness camp meeting enjoyed extraordinary and rapid success through its fusing of a powerful religious impulse with the changing lifestyles of the middle class. During the Victorian era, summer vacation resorts were becoming financially accessible to members of this middle class, many of whom remained firm in their evangelical piety despite their newly enhanced social status. Summer camp meetings began to be held regularly at picturesque locales at Vineland, New Jersey; Wesleyan Grove on Martha's Vineyard off the Massachusetts coast; and other sites usually situated on an ocean or lake shore. Originally housing participants in tents, many of these holiness camp meetings soon upgraded to colorful wooden cottages for annual family use. In the center was a cleared area of several acres, in which elaborate wooden tabernacles for daily worship services were constructed. Architectural historian Ellen Weiss has described Wesleyan Grove as a "city in the woods," a fusion of the rural camp-meeting form with the "garden suburb," residential areas emerging rapidly on the outskirts of the cities of Victorian America. Owners of these cottages entered into formal associations with strict rules of conduct spelled out. The camp meetings also developed rituals and even a hymnody of their own, of which the ever-popular "Beulah Land" remains a good example.

Another phenomenon of the era with ties to both holiness and fundamentalism was the "Higher Life" movement, which was closely associated with the Keswick Conventions, held annually at St. John's Keswick Anglican parish beginning in 1875 after an initial gathering at Oxford. Like much of nineteenth-century evangelical activity, Higher Life was Anglo-American in scope, and British and American participants intermingled readily. American holiness advocates from a variety of denominations participated actively. Following the Reformed rather than the Wesleyan theological formulation, the movement stressed a practical emphasis on the achievement of personal holiness in which sinfulness was suppressed rather than completely eradicated. This notion was popularized by Moody and Sankey in America in the slogan "power for service," an idea with a broad interdenominational appeal. At the same time, however, the Keswick movement was planting some of the seeds of nascent fundamentalism in its premillennial teachings of Jesus's imminent return and, in its emphasis on faith healing, was anticipating a major theme of pentecostalism as well.

By the 1870s, tension began to mount within American Methodism over the centrality of holiness doctrines, and a number of the more committed holiness advocates began to go their own way. Methodist bishops in both the northern and southern branches of the church denounced the growing independence of holiness associations, and ferment at the grassroots level was sufficient for a new era of reorganization reminiscent of that of Methodism itself having broken its Anglican ties a century earlier. Among the first group to forge ahead on its own was the Church of God (Anderson, Indiana), founded by Daniel S. Warner in 1880. (Today it remains a leading holiness denomination, with a membership of about 230,000 at the end of the twentieth century.)

Although Warner's Church of God was typical of early holiness schisms in its rejection of denominational identity, it, like the earlier antidenominational Campbellites, would ultimately coalesce into typical Protestant organizational status. Even more typical of the transition from sectarian "come-outer" beginnings to full denominational status are the Church of the Nazarene and the Wesleyan Church, with membership at the end of the twentieth century of 608,000 and 118,000, respectively. The origins of each lay in the decision of the charismatic leaders Phineas F. Bresee of Iowa and Martin Wells Knapp of Michigan to "come out" from the Methodist Episcopal Church and found holiness-centered movements of their own. After a complicated series of mergers with like-minded groups, the two had achieved a degree of institutional stability by the 1920s under the names of the Church of the Nazarene and the Pilgrim Holiness Church. The latter merged in 1968 with the like-minded Wesleyan Methodist Church of America to become the Wesleyan Church.

As opposed to the highly institutionalized Methodist Episcopal Church in both its northern and southern branches, these early holiness movements were distinctly popular in leadership and outreach. Although they differed slightly in details of belief and organization, they were united in an emphasis on direct religious experience and a strict code of personal morality, including the by-now-standard evangelical bans on smoking, drinking, and various forms of "worldly" amusements. Though rigid in these matters, they also embodied some of the more radical social emphases of their heritage, such as according women a major role in church life. (One holiness denomination, the Pillar of Fire, was founded by a woman, Alma White, in Denver in 1901.)

Holiness churches were also active in the urban mission field, though varying in emphasis from advocacy of social reform to bringing the latter about through the conversion of individuals. The Salvation Army and its American split-off, the Volunteers of America, had their origins in the British holiness movement and the work of "General" William Booth (1829–1912) and his family. Their colorful street-corner musical evangelism was brought to America in the 1880s. A disagreement with his father led to the formation of the Volunteers of America by Ballington Booth and his wife in 1896. His sister Evangeline Booth took over leadership of the Army proper in the United States during the following decade. The two groups have continued their parallel courses to the present, organized in military fashion with corresponding titles, emphasizing a simple holiness theology and intensive outreach to those who have slipped through society's "safety net."

Another movement of middle-class Protestant origins that took on an astonishingly vital life of its own during these years was fundamentalism. Fundamentalism represents a continuation of the major emphases of the Reformed strain of nineteenth-century evangelicalism, with some distinctive doctrinal innovations and a combative nature honed in its origins as an adversary of the Protestant liberalism that was rapidly gaining momentum late in the nineteenth century. From an interdenominational movement at the conservative end of the evangelical community, it rapidly acquired momentum as a force in the struggle that emerged by the 1920s within the northern branches of the Baptist and Presbyterian denominations for theological dominance. When these attempts proved unsuccessful, the movement withdrew into alternative institutional channels until its dynamic reemergence as a national religious force in the 1970s and 1980s.

Unlike the holiness and pentecostal movements, which stressed religious experience over the finer points of belief, early fundamentalism demonstrated its Reformed roots in its emphasis on doctrine. Central to its emergent identity as the scourge of liberalism was its insistence not only on the authority but also the "inerrancy" of the Bible in all points, including matters of history and natural science. The intellectual origins of this aspect of the movement lay squarely within the faculty of the Princeton Theological Seminary, which had long since gone its own way after the adjacent university had lost its Old School Presbyterian identity earlier in the century. Rooted in the Scottish Common Sense philosophy expounded by their forerunner, John Witherspoon, latter-day Princeton conservatives such as Charles Hodge and, in the following generation, his son Archibald Alexander Hodge and Benjamin Warfield, provided an intellectual formulation for the new assault on advocates of the "higher criticism" being imported from Germany. This stressed the "inspired Word [of God] . . . is without error" in its "original autographs"—that is, as it was originally "dictated" by God to the authors of scripture, who were really scribes more than original writers. Scriptural inerrancy was one of the "five points" adopted by the General Assembly of the Presbyterian Church (northern branch) on several occasions between 1893 and 1910 as key doctrines.

These "points" would later become a widely accepted canon of fundamentalist belief; they also included, with some variation, the Virgin Birth, which emphasized the miraculous origins of Jesus; the "Satisfaction Theory" of the Atonement, which gave the process of salvation a legalistic cast; the Resurrection of Jesus "with the same body," and the literal character of the miracles attributed to Jesus, both reflecting the "common sense" tendency to take a very concrete and literal approach to scriptural narrative.

In other versions of the basics of fundamentalist doctrine, the imminent Second Coming of Jesus was added to or substituted for one of these basics. This was the notion of "premillennialism," the belief that Jesus was about to appear again on earth in the near future to inaugurate the series of events that would culminate in the millennium. (Because in this view the Second Coming is to precede the millennium, rather than to follow it as in other interpretations, the idea has come to be known as "premillennialism.") This vivid eschatology had its roots in the worldview of the earliest Christian community, and came to the forefront of belief at various intervals during the intervening centuries, including the Millerite movement of the 1840s. Since the time of Constantine, however, expectations of Jesus's imminent return had remained in the background of the belief system of most Christians, whether Catholic or Protestant.

The intellectual roots of modern premillennialism were formulated in England beginning in the 1820s in a wave of prophetic enthusiasm. John Nelson Darby (1800–82), was the leader of a contemporary sect known as the Plymouth Brethren. (Also known as "Christian Brethren," they numbered some one hundred thousand in the U.S. in the mid-1990s.) Darby formulated a method for interpreting the entirety of scripture known as "dispensational premillennialism," in which the whole of salvation history from God's covenant with Abraham to the present and on to the end of time are divided into seven epochs known as "dispensations." Based mainly on the Book of Daniel (a perennial favorite for the prophetically inclined), Darby's scheme postulated that God was following different plans for two different peoples: Israel, his earthly people, and their heavenly counterparts, the (Christian) Church. When the Jews rejected Jesus as their Messiah, the Second Coming of Jesus, which was originally intended rapidly to follow his first, was postponed, and what Timothy P. Weber has called "a mysterious, prophetic time warp" or "great parenthesis" resulted.

In order for God's original plan to be fulfilled, the Darbyites postulated two supernaturalistic occurrences, which were expected to be imminent. First, the current and parenthetical dispensation—"the church age"—is nearing an end, as evidenced in widespread apostasy among the churches. (Each previous dispensation had also ended with a collective failure to fulfill God's demands.) Soon, however, those Christians who have remained faithful will be bodily translated into heaven in an event known as the "Rapture." (Bumper stickers in recent years have proclaimed, "The Rapture—What a Way to Go!") After the saints have been thus cleared from the picture, a period of several years known as "the Tribulation" will take place, in which those who have been left behind will undergo terrible ordeals during the reign of the Antichrist, a figure of cosmic evil. At the end of this period, in the midst of a great battle being fought by the world's armies at Armageddon in northern Israel, Jesus and his saints will appear in glory to overthrow the Antichrist and inaugurate the millennial kingdom—a thousand years on earth of peace and prosperity. At the end of the thousand years, Satan will be briefly loosed and defeated, the dead will be resurrected and judged, and this world shall give way to "a new heaven and a new earth" (Revelation 21:1—Revelation, like Daniel, is a major source of premillennialist imagery and interpretation).

One additional feature of this elaborate prophetic scheme is the role played in it by the Jewish people. During the Tribulation, many Jews will become converted to Christianity and suffer for it under the Antichrist. When Jesus returns, he will preside as the Messiah over a Jewish kingdom with a complete restoration of the Temple, its priesthood and sacrifices, and the whole panoply of observances of Israel during its heyday in the time of the monarchy. Because the dispensationalist scheme is based on a belief that all of these events will take place in a very literal way, the restoration of an independent nation of Israel thus became a major item of faith. As its fulfillment began to take on a new plausibility with the emergence of modern Zionism at the turn of the century and Britain's Balfour Declaration during World War I, dispensationalists became reinforced in their beliefs through this seeming external confirmation of their predictions. Support for Israel has emerged in recent years as a major foreign policy commitment of latter-day fundamentalists such as Jerry Falwell as a consequence.

As fundamentalism began to grow into an organized movement, dispensationalism no longer was the property of a few isolated sects, and moved into the mainstream of the new belief system that was being forged from an amalgam of the teachings of Darby with those of the Princeton theologians and the "Victorious Life" theme of the Keswick Movement. Dwight L. Moody again was a potent catalyst, and his Moody Bible Institute and its dozens of imitators soon provided a communications network through which these ideas attained a wide currency. A series of annual Niagara Bible Conferences, begun in 1876 and attended by an interdenominational assortment of sympathetic clergy and lay people, also popularized this core cluster of ideas. A further effective means of propagation was a series of twelve collections of essays expounding the themes of fundamentalism, written by a wide variety of scholarly advocates of the movement. Known, appropriately, as *The Fundamentals,* these brief works were distributed to a large audience at no cost through the beneficence of a pair of wealthy brothers from Los Angeles. Their advent was a turning point in fundamentalism's emergence as a coherent movement rather than a loosely related collection of ideas, events, institutions, and spokespeople.

Whereas dispensationalism became a major doctrinal component for what we might (perhaps with some irony) call the "mainstream" fundamentalism that flourished especially within the Baptist and Presbyterian folds, other forms of millennialism continued beyond the great Millerite excitement of the 1840s in more sectarian form. In addition to Seventh-Day Adventism, which has already been discussed, the Jehovah's Witnesses have been an enduring element in the American religious spectrum since their founding as the International Bible Students' Association by a Pittsburgh haberdasher, Charles Taze Russell, in 1872. Russell taught that Jesus had inaugurated a "Millennial Dawn" with his return in the "upper air" in 1874, and expected the millennial consummation of the worldly order in 1914. Russell himself moved the date up four years before his own death in 1916, and his successor, Judge J. R. Rutherford, continued to adjust it as the anticipated inauguration of a new world order failed to materialize.

Despite repeated "disconfirmations," the Witnesses, as they have called themselves since 1931, have continued to flourish, in part through their aggressive door-to-door evangelism and sales of *The Watchtower,* published at their Brooklyn headquarters. Their distinctive teachings, such as the restriction of full sainthood to 144,000 (Revelation 14:1–3) and their denial of a traditional interpretation of the Trinity, as well as "deviant" practices such as refusing blood transfusions (based on a unique reading of Psalm 16), have rendered them an archetypal example of a sect in modern society. Although they have been consistently attacked by conservative Christians as a "cult," their major societal difficulties have stemmed from their alleged lack of patriotism in refusing to serve in the military and to salute the flag. These refusals result from their sense of constituting a "theocracy" in which all members are ministers, and their concomitant rejection of the religious and political order of the broader world when that order goes against their beliefs.

The sometimes violent persecution this "deviant" behavior has incurred, especially in wartime, has only strengthened their sense of rightness, and has also broadened First Amendment protection for such stances through the 1943 Supreme Court decision in *West Virginia State Board of Education v. Barnette.* (The courts have generally sustained their refusal of blood transfusions for adult believers, but not for children.) By the end of the twentieth century, Jehovah's Witnesses in the United States claimed nearly a million members, having benefited from the general resurgence in conservative religion of the period. They are organized into over ten thousand local congregations which meet in "Kingdom Halls," with headquarters in Brooklyn.

A third movement of great power that had its roots in both the early holiness and fundamentalist movements was pentecostalism. As its name implies, it was a movement of restoration, predicated on the belief that the gifts of the Holy Spirit bestowed on the Apostles on the day of Pentecost were now descending on contemporary Americans as the "latter rain" spoken of in the prophetic book of Joel (King James Version, 2:23; see also I Corinthians 12 and 14 on the "gifts of the Spirit"). As Grant Wacker has pointed out, the worldview of the early pentecostals was radically ahistorical; they believed that a new Apostolic Age was bursting into the world, which was negating the significance of all history since the time of the first Apostles. Since they were not receptive to newer, more historical approaches to biblical interpretation, they were inclined to believe that the Bible "dropped from heaven as a sacred meteor," and was therefore to be read with the same literalism that characterized the emerging fundamentalist hermeneutic (method of interpretation). Not surprisingly, they also readily adopted the tenets of dispensationalism and eagerly awaited the Second Coming with their fundamentalist contemporaries.

Though belief was important for pentecostals, experience was central. They accepted the basic premises of holiness, but took them still further. Whereas holiness advocates had equated the experience of entire sanctification with the "baptism of the Holy Spirit" (and sometimes used the term *pentecostal* in self-description), the new movement that emerged near the turn of the century out of the holiness matrix insisted that this "baptism" was manifest in the experience of the gifts of the Spirit enumerated in I Corinthians. The most prominent of these gifts was the ability to speak in "tongues," as had the Apostles on the day of Pentecost itself (Acts 2:3–4: "And they were all filled with the Holy Spirit and began to speak in other tongues").

This phenomenon of speaking in tongues—*glossolalia*—which is central to pentecostalism, has been the subject of considerable study and speculation, with no definitive conclusions as to its ultimate character. Whether it presupposes an altered state of consciousness is a matter of continued speculation and disagreement. The free flow of speech that results is linguistically distinctive and is not readily confused with actual languages. In the movement's early days especially, however, many practitioners claimed that they and their fellow tongues speakers had spoken actual foreign languages with which they had no previous familiarity. This phenomenon, known as *xenoglossia,* is still occasionally reported, but documentation is elusive enough that researchers have difficulty coming to any firm conclusions. What is undeniable, however, is that pentecostals do participate in a form of out-of-the-ordinary linguistic behavior to which they attribute vital religious significance.

Although speaking in tongues is one of the most distinctive aspects of pentecostal practice, and is regarded by most believers as a necessary sign of Spirit baptism, it is not the only spiritual gift. Of great importance also is healing through religious faith, a phenomenon by no means confined to pentecostals. (In recent years it has become a central concern for many "mainline" congregations, such as Episcopalians, who may incorporate it into their regular Sunday-morning worship or hold special services aimed at those in physical or emotional distress.) Still other gifts, such as the interpretation of tongues and prophesying, are less crucial though also recognized. The snake-handling practices found in a few Appalachian pentecostal churches represent an extreme interpretation which, though widely publicized, is very uncommon.

Occasional *glossolalia* may have taken place in the Shaker communities of the earlier nineteenth century and among "enthusiastic" sectarians in Europe before that. These phenomena were scattered and evanescent, and the origins of modern pentecostalism can be found in the volatile cultural matrix of the American South, Midwest, and Far West of the turn of the century. Whereas both holiness and fundamentalism had their origins in the respectable middle-class environments of the Wesleyan and Reformed traditions, pentecostalism, with debts to both earlier movements, was much more clearly a popular movement in its beginnings. Like the Radical Reformation and the Great Awakening, its origins were multiple, with foci in Los Angeles, Kansas, and central Tennessee, as well as a number of similar areas long familiar with revivalistic religion and often subject to troubling social change and conflict.

Although the origins of the movement remain shrouded in the realm of folklore, the movement's recorded history begins in Topeka, Kansas, at the beginning of the twentieth century. Here an erratic "come-outer" preacher named Charles Fox Parham founded a Bible institute where, according to a disputed tradition, "fire fell" among the students and faculty on New Year's Day in 1901. The tongue speaking that then took place generated a brief flurry of revivalistic excitement in the region, which soon cooled down until Parham tried to revive it in 1903 through taking up a career as a faith healer.

In 1905 a school for the promotion of this "Apostolic Faith" which Parham was conducting in Houston attracted the attention of an itinerant black holiness preacher named William J. Seymour. The next year Seymour introduced Parham's teachings and practices into a black congregation on Azusa Street in Los Angeles—the "Midwest raised to flashpoint," as Reyner Banham has described that city. Soon he had a genuine phenomenon on his hands. Azusa Street lives in pentecostal lore as the first real explosion of the Spirit. For three years, blacks, whites, Hispanics, Asians, and the whole spectrum of Los Angeles's diverse population became involved in an ecstatic revival, much like Cane Ridge, only now with the gift of tongues as an added feature. The Azusa Street revival attracted attention from around the nation, and visitors left with a new message to take back to widely scattered parts of the South and Midwest in particular, where the ground had been well prepared by the holiness enthusiasm of the preceding decades.

The early history of pentecostalism resembles closely that of the holiness movement from which it sprang. Founded by unpredictable leaders like Parham and Seymour and characterized both by the radical "come-outer" sectarian spirit and intense religious enthusiasm, new groups arose, merged, feuded, split, and recombined over and over again before reaching institutional stability in the 1920s. The Church of God in Christ, today a large and primarily black denomination based in Memphis, was founded by two holiness Baptist black preachers in Mississippi in 1897, who split a decade later over the issue of speaking in tongues. The Church of God (Cleveland, Tennessee) arose from a white holiness group through the leadership of Ambrose Jessup Tomlinson (TOOM-lin-s'n), a volatile leader of Parham's stamp. Several schisms have led to a proliferation of churches tracing their lineage back to this founding, due in part to the volatility of later generations of Tomlinsons. The Church of God (Cleveland, Tennessee) has been numerically the most successful of these groups, with a membership of about three quarters of a million in the mid-1990s; the Church of God of Prophecy, the only other sizeable branch, had about seventy thousand members at that time.

These two earliest pentecostal foundings are representative of the excitement and confusion of those early years, and were followed by a host of other new churches, some of which eventually grew into denominations of considerable size. Foremost among these today is the Assemblies of God, which arose out of a 1914 merger of like-minded groups in Texas, Alabama, and Illinois who wanted to distance themselves from the Wesleyan character of much nascent pentecostal belief and align themselves more clearly with the Reformed theological tradition. This they did by conflating the experiences of conversion and sanctification into a single event, followed by a discrete baptism by the Holy Spirit. By the 1990s the Assemblies of God had attracted a national constituency, with a membership of nearly two and a half million. The Pentecostal Holiness Church arose from a North Carolina holiness group of that name's merging in 1911 with the Fire-Baptized Holiness Church of South Carolina. (The names of pentecostal denominations vary from the highly routinized to the vividly evocative.) Foundings continued well into the 1920s, when the colorful Los Angeles evangelist Aimee Semple McPherson—"your sister in the King's glad service"—incorporated her Church of the Foursquare Gospel in 1927. (The name is derived from the symbolism of Ezekiel 1:4–28.)

Following these initial years of effervescence, these three upsurges of Protestant religiosity, at once conservative and radical, entered into a period of eclipse. They by no means disappeared, and continued to gather adherents, especially in the "Bible Belt" of the South and parts of the Midwest and Southwest. By this time they had acquired a reputation no longer as revitalization movements within the mainline of Protestantism but rather as marginal religions, attracting both poor and middle class, both black and white, in the areas of the country least affected by the forces of modernization. The foibles of some of the early pentecostal leaders, and the occasionally bizarre claims made by the itinerant faith healers of the middle decades of the century, removed them from the center of national religious life until a new era of cultural shock in the 1960s and 1970s changed the American scene irrevocably and catapulted them into a new prominence.

The one movement among these three that actively strove to retain a role as a major force in the nation's religious life was fundamentalism. Whereas holiness and pentecostal leadership arose from the come-outer margins of the denominations, that of fundamentalism came from the powerful right flanks of the northern Baptists and Presbyterians. (The southern churches were largely unaffected since Protestant liberalism made few inroads in the region.) The fundamentalist cause was disseminated in a number of highly effective ways: the colorful, aggressive evangelism of Billy Sunday and other, contentious followers along the "sawdust trail" blazed by Moody; the network of Bible schools modeled on Moody's institute, which generated a vast number of lay workers, teachers, and evangelists; denominational groups, such as William Bell Riley's Baptist Bible Union; and a vast outpouring of books and periodicals. The movement was also promoted by a new generation of urban preachers who turned their churches into powerful centers of influence. Conservative successors to an earlier, liberal generation of "princes of the pulpit" included men like John Roach Straton at New York City's Calvary Baptist and William Bell Riley, who presided for forty-five years at his First Baptist Church in Minneapolis. These urban preachers often attracted church memberships in the thousands, and were able to build enormous physical plants and employ the new medium of radio to broadcast their message and consolidate their influence. The congregational polity of the Baptists made it still easier for charismatic leaders of this stripe to acquire independent positions of religious power. The first wave of "megachurches" of the later twentieth century, often Southern or Independent Baptist in affiliation and with membership running into the tens of thousands, was the direct heir of this tradition.

By the 1920s liberals and fundamentalists had polarized sufficiently to have generated an ongoing public struggle for the control of their denominations, especially the Baptists and Presbyterians. (Other primarily northern groups, such as the Methodists and Episcopalians, were not seriously affected by the controversy, in part because of the Methodist "leakage" into the new holiness and pentecostal groups.) Moderates, however, were inclined to defend the rights of liberals to freedom of theological expression, and the fundamentalists were unsuccessful in their attempt to impose their version of orthodoxy on their respective traditions. The results in some cases were schisms, such as the founding of the Orthodox Presbyterian Church in 1936 and the Bible Presbyterian Church the following year.

The symbolic event that marked the eclipse of religious conservatism from the 1920s until the 1970s was, of course, the Scopes Trial held in Dayton, Tennessee—not far from Cleveland—in 1925. The story of the prosecution of a small town high school biology teacher, John Scopes, for deliberately and publicly helping to precipitate a test case on the Tennessee statute that forbade the teaching of evolution in the public schools has become part of the nation's folklore, and has been lightly fictionalized in the play *Inherit the Wind* (subsequently rendered in motion picture and television form as well). The trial took on the dimensions of a cosmic drama of confrontation, with the famous agnostic defender of unpopular causes, Clarence Darrow, as Scopes's attorney, and former secretary of state and Democratic presidential candidate William Jennings Bryan aiding the defense as a spokesman for the fundamentalist attack on Darwinian evolution as incompatible with a literal reading of the account of creation presented in the beginning chapters of Genesis. Comic relief was added by the sideshows this "media event" generated, such as the display of chimpanzees, as well as by the press coverage of the *Baltimore Sun's* ace reporter, the acerbic and skeptical H. L. Mencken. (Mencken had gained notoriety through such coinages as the "Booboisie," the "Bible Belt," and the "Sahara of the Bozart"—that is, beaux arts or fine arts—as characterizations of middle-class Babbitry, the fundamentalist heartland, and the South respectively.)

Scopes's subsequent conviction was overturned by an appeals court on a technicality, though the law in question was not repealed until the 1950s. Regardless of the legal outcome, the hostile media attention generated by the trial damaged the fundamentalist cause badly, and it soon became relegated in the middle-class mind to the backwater status into which pentecostalism and holiness had already slipped. The eclipse of fundamentalism, however, did not mean more than a temporary victory for its liberal antagonists, because religion in general was sliding into what Robert T. Handy has called "the second disestablishment." The rampant secularism of 1920s urban culture and the ensuing turmoil of the Depression both contributed to the sense of irrelevance with which many Americans were inclined to regard organized religion. It was not until the 1950s that "religion in general" enjoyed a widespread new popularity. One of the most visible figures of that era was William Franklin "Billy" Graham, who helped launch the conservative resurgence that would emerge as a major characteristic of American religious life in the ensuing decades.

CHAPTER 35

Religion in the South

In the study of American culture, it is the South that has given particular importance to the question of *regionalism*. Other parts of the country still possess a certain measure of distinctiveness in their ethnic composition, voting habits, economic activity, religious makeup, and other components of regional variation. In terms of regional *culture*—or, perhaps more accurately, *subculture*—it is difficult to find any extended area of America, even New England, where ways of looking at and living in the world are as profoundly affected by the distinctive ethos of the region. California today has acquired some of this distinctiveness, based on its inhabitants' reputed contempt for tradition and openness to the future. In the South, the past—as historical reality and as cultural construct—continues to make heavy claims on the present.

Geographically, the South is roughly coextensive with the eleven states that seceded in 1861 to form the Confederacy, in large part over the continued existence of slavery. One traditional point of demarcation was the Mason-Dixon line that resulted from a major survey of 1763–67. More recently, cultural geographers have argued that the old U.S. Route 40—which cuts across Columbus and Dayton in Ohio and parallels the newer I-70—is a more accurate dividing line. Most of Indiana as well as parts of southern Illinois, Missouri, Oklahoma, and Texas are often regarded as basically southern in ambience; conversely, peninsular Florida, which was not developed until the twentieth century by "Yankees," has little distinctively southern about it other than intense heat. Similarly, southern Louisiana, colonized by French-speaking Catholics, and the mountain South of the Appalachians and Ozarks constitute distinctive subcultural areas that can only be included as parts of the broader South with some qualifications.

Being southern in a cultural as well as a geographical sense involves a number of social conditions and patterns of outlook. Although white southerners often represent a mixture of national origins, the largest number trace their ancestry to the various components of Great Britain. Historians Forest McDonald and Grady McWhiney have even argued that the Celtic strain has been culturally more influential than the Anglo-Saxon English in molding distinctively southern attitudes toward, for example, warfare and violence. (It is worth noting that Scarlett O'Hara bore an Irish name.) In any case, the basic white ethnic stock that made up the core of American southern society was predominantly English, Irish, Scottish, and Scotch-Irish. The emigration of the latter during the eighteenth century, at first to Pennsylvania and Virginia, then south and west into Kentucky, the Carolinas, and beyond, was a demographic factor of the greatest importance. The "new immigration" of the later nineteenth century largely bypassed the South, which was neither sufficiently urbanized nor culturally receptive to such outsiders; even the growing cities of the "New South" failed to attract many who altered so dramatically the social complexion of the North.

The other major ethnic background of southerners, of course, was African. The term *ethnic,* in fact, sounds slightly odd in this context, because the word *race* has been used so extensively to describe the cultural line between black and white. Anthropologists today shy away from the word *race,* because the physical reality of what it has usually been used to denote is so imprecise. For better or worse, however, American life in general and southern life in particular has been inescapably intertwined with the notion that humans can be divided along a color line, on one side or the other of which each person must be classified. Distinctions based on physical as well as cultural characteristics are by no means unknown in other societies. However, even in Hawaii and Brazil, two cultures that can both be designated as "American," the coexistence of members of two or more racial groups has led to extensive intermarriage and a social system in which racial distinctions are real but matters of gradation. In the United States, they are all or nothing; they are, so to speak, a matter of black or white.

Although racism has been endemic among white Americans since the beginnings of the nation, the situation in the South was compounded by its institutionalization in the form of chattel slavery. Black people were by their nature subject to enslavement by whites, and virtually all Africans prior to the Civil War entered America in that condition. Until the transformations brought about by the Civil Rights Movement of the 1960s, even free blacks in the South lived under serious disabilities, whether sanctioned by law or simply by the weight of social custom, economic leverage, and the ever-present threat of violence. On the other hand, as southerners have always been quick to point out, whites and blacks in the South have always lived in close social contact—not as equals, but often as intimates. This reality of genuine, if unequal, contact between the races has distinguished the character of the South from that of other parts of the country, where physical separation and economic inequality more than legal constraint have resulted in what social psychologist Joel Kovel has called "aversive racism."

In addition to the inescapable fact of a distinctive pattern of racial relations, the South has also generated a set of cultural attitudes that have reinforced its difference from the rest of the country. Sociologist John Shelton Reed has identified several such traits that he has claimed can be verified quantitatively. These include *localism,* that is, taking one's immediate social context as one's point of reference and departure, rather than the context of the broader society. Related to localism is a heightened importance placed on the role of the *family,* so that ties of kinship have traditionally taken precedence over those formed through various sorts of voluntary association. *Violence* has for centuries enjoyed a legitimacy in southern culture which has shocked and baffled outsiders, as expressed in such forms as dueling, lynching, or even overly aggressive stock-car racing.

The final distinctively southern emphasis Reed has identified is *religion.* Since at least the early nineteenth century, black and white southerners have been more deeply and visibly committed to religion—especially several varieties of evangelical Protestantism—than residents of any other extended part of the nation. Religious commitment has coexisted, perhaps symbiotically, with other sorts of cultural expression, such as violence and racism, which outsiders have again found alternately perplexing and appalling. Southern religion has also reflected the fundamentally bi-ethnic—British and African American—character of southern society in its relative homogeneity. As a consequence, nothing outside the evangelical spectrum has stood much of a chance for widespread popular acceptance except in those areas that are southern only in a geographical sense, such as metropolitan Miami and New Orleans. Religion, in any case, is an intrinsic component of the culture of the American South, and the course it has taken there has shaped it in a way significantly different from the patterns even its evangelical cousins have taken elsewhere in the nation.

From the beginnings of the colonial era, the Church of England was brought to the South, first at Jamestown and then in the ensuing decades of plantation development. Theoretically, at least, Anglicanism enjoyed the same status as an established religion as it did in England. As Donald G. Mathews has pointed out, however, the dispersed nature of Virginia society, the scarcity of qualified clergy, and the absence of a bishop militated against its functioning as a very effective presence. In the vacuum that ensued, the wealthy plantation aristocracy that dominated the civil realm took control of the sacred realm as well through their dominant role on the vestries, or lay governing boards, of the local churches.

This association of the Church of England with the plantation aristocracy did not in the long run serve it very well, because the unfolding American experiment was not conducive to the unquestioning acceptance of a stratified society based on the principle of deference of inferiors to superiors. Even before the Great Awakening began to challenge the prestige of religious establishments throughout the colonies, evangelical missionaries such as the Presbyterian Samuel Davies began to seek converts and to secure legal rights for religious dissent. The insurgence of Baptists that followed the awakening added new dimensions of size and energy to this challenge to the established order, which involved a radical critique of Virginia's social and political structure as well as a rejection of Anglican belief and worship. As Rhys Isaac has pointed out, the close identification of the colonial version of the Church of England with the plantation aristocracy and what dissidents perceived as their rather loose morals was the subject of what amounted in the prerevolutionary decades to a thoroughgoing social and religious revolution.

In other parts of the colonial South and even in relatively civilized Virginia, however, the Anglican establishment was not the only target of evangelical protest, of which the Separate Baptists constituted the vanguard. As Bertram Wyatt-Brown has demonstrated, the colonial South prior to the Great Awakening was an extension of traditional English folk culture, governed by an ethos hardly touched by the values of either Anglican or evangelical Christianity. Privacy was scarcely thought of, magical practices mingled freely with what formal religion was known, and *honor* was the overriding cultural value. Anglicans and Baptists alike strove to impose order on what they thus perceived as social and moral chaos, though their visions of that order differed irreconcilably from one another.

The First Amendment and corresponding provisions in the constitutions of the several states brought an end to Anglican dominance and the harassment of dissenters, and the latter found the postrevolutionary South ripe for their energies.

The challenge was formidable, because the social critique mounted by the evangelicals was scarcely compatible with the institutions and values that characterized the dominant classes in the South. The first Baptists and Methodists were adamantly opposed to slaveholding, which they associated with aristocratic self-indulgence. As evangelicals gained more of a foothold on the social ladder, and as the South as a region became more and more irrevocably committed to the "peculiar institution," however, a dramatic shift in attitude was in the making.

By the 1840s, as the abolitionist movement began to gain strength in the North, southern evangelical churches had largely made their peace with a social system which was itself undergoing change in response to external challenge and internal development. By now the Baptists and Methodists had become major religious forces, challenging the prestige and influence earlier accorded first to Anglicans—now the Protestant Episcopal Church—and then to Presbyterians. Clerical opposition to deeply rooted southern practices such as the distilling of spirits (which proved an economical way of utilizing grain), dueling and other forms of ritualized violence, and slavery itself waned as evangelicals now were choosing to join what they could not beat. Clergy became active in defending slavery on biblical grounds—for example, by reading God's curse on Noah's son Ham and his descendants as condemning the black race to a perpetually inferior status (Genesis 9:25). Southern apologists such as George Fitzhugh also developed powerful moral critiques of the nascent industrial society of the North, which they claimed, with some plausibility, reduced nominally free factory workers to a social and economic status inferior to that of paternalistically protected slaves.

By the time of the Civil War, the southern clergy had with virtual unanimity rallied to the cause of the Confederacy and were instrumental in promoting morale among both troops and civilians through their religious justifications of their region's cause. Beginning with the Baptists and the Methodists in 1845, the most powerful of the South's Protestant denominations began to break from their northern counterparts and found alternative regional churches. The Old School–New School Presbyterian schism of 1837 had involved slavery as a peripheral issue, and both sides split further along explicitly regional lines as the war grew imminent. (The New School divided in 1856–57, and the Old in 1861). The Protestant Episcopal Church in the Confederate States of America lasted only for the duration of the war, and Roman Catholics, Lutherans, and other denominations without a firm stand on slavery or little southern representation were not seriously affected. The three major evangelical churches, however, were deeply scarred by these events: Methodists reunited in 1939, Presbyterians not until 1984, and Baptist reunion seems highly unlikely in the foreseeable future.

Although important differences of belief, worship, and social class continued to separate the southern branches of these denominations following the Civil War, their common identification with their region's culture was far more important than any such divisions. The consensus that had developed on the slavery issue now continued with a slight adjustment in focus. One key notion helping shape the ethos of postbellum southern Protestantism was the Presbyterian James Henley Thornwell's doctrine of the "spirituality of the church." By this, Thornwell meant that the concern of organized Christianity was with the salvation of the individual rather than with the social realm. The conservative political and cultural implications of this idea were profound, and mightily reinforced the social outlook that the dominant classes were in the process of formulating.

Although the "spirituality of the church" inhibited the southern Presbyterian Church (PCUS) from taking public stands on social issues of any sorts, Presbyterian attitudes did not differ substantially from those of most white Baptists and Methodists. Although the Social Gospel made some scattered inroads on the still largely rural South, the dominant cultural consensus favored the moral reform of the individual, preferably through religious conversion rather than through religiously sanctioned social engineering. Prohibition was an exception, and Methodists such as Virginia's Bishop James Cannon Jr. (1864–1944) energetically promoted its adoption and enforcement. Cannon's leadership in opposing the candidacy of the "wet" Roman Catholic Democrat Al Smith in 1928 further demonstrated the array of political commitments characteristic of southern evangelicals prior to the 1960s. Apart from political activism, most evangelicals were also united in their endorsement of a strict code of personal moral behavior, which forbade smoking, alcoholic beverages, gambling, theater- and, later, movie-going, and even, especially among pentecostals, the wearing of neckties for men and the use of cosmetics or bobbing one's hair among women. The contrast with the ongoing propensity in the same parts of society for "corn likker," cock-fighting, and other rural amusements indicates the extremity of the tensions that characterized much of southern life, which cultural analyst W. J. Cash saw as rooted in the region's tradition of "orgiastic religion." The violence generated by this tension between repressiveness and exuberance has supplied much of the stuff of both popular and "high" cultural interpretations of that life, from Flannery O'Connor's grotesques to *Smokey and the Bandit*.

Racial relations, of course, continued to play a major, even dominant role in southern life in the decades following the Civil War. Black worship was now freed from white supervision, and denominational organization began to flourish. In addition to joining the African Methodist Episcopal and AME Zion Churches, which were imports from the North, southern blacks also organized the Colored (now Christian) Methodist Episcopal Church as an alternative to the segregated Methodist Episcopal Church, South. The National Baptist Convention, U.S.A., Inc., was organized in Atlanta in 1895, and later split twice into sizeable factions. Black as well as white Baptists also gathered into many independent local congregations, as did the "sanctified" holiness and pentecostal churches that emerged around the turn of the century among both races—and, in the early days of pentecostalism, sometimes took biracial forms. The distinctive character of southern black religion is discussed more fully elsewhere; however, it certainly emerged from the same evangelical ethos that shaped much of the South's white Christianity, and the reciprocal influence of each on the other—for example, in patterns of worship, music, and personal experience—has only of late begun to be appreciated.

If black and white influenced one another in religion, they were held apart in other aspects of life by informal custom as well as, beginning in the 1880s, the "Jim Crow" laws, which converted the South into a formally segregated society. Blacks were barred from sharing public facilities with whites and actively discouraged from voting, while many were effectively relegated to a condition of peonage through the practice of sharecropping. This color line was supported by most white churches as well, and the Ku Klux Klan reemerged in the 1920s as a vigilante group dedicated to keeping blacks, as well as Catholics, Jews, and immigrants, in their alleged places. One interesting aspect of the social activism of the era was the formation of the Association of Southern Women for the Prevention of Lynching by Jessie Daniel Ames in 1930, a crusade against one of the Klan's most notorious practices, which grew out of the work of the Woman's Department of the Commission on Interracial Cooperation.

However important a role social issues may have played in southern religious life, the core of the region's religiosity has traditionally been intensely individualistic. As Samuel S. Hill has pointed out, the evangelical Protestantism that has been dominant since the days of the Great Revival at the beginning of the nineteenth century differs in some significant ways from its northern counterparts. Central to its message is the devastating reality of sin and guilt, and a corresponding need for redemption through personal, often dramatic and sudden, conversion. Hill postulates that the burden of guilt southerners have consciously or otherwise carried over the region's implication in slavery and racism may be a major constituent in this preoccupation with guilt. The distinction between worship and revival services became blurred as a result of this focus on conversion, and revivalistic preaching aimed to bring about a change of heart has become a staple of Sunday morning life at many of the region's numerous churches.

During the post–Civil War decades, the level of church membership rose dramatically throughout the South. Baptists and Methodists benefited especially; Presbyterians and Episcopalians continued their role as high status churches; and the holiness and pentecostal churches, as well as the Churches of Christ in the Campbellite/Restorationist tradition, began to acquire momentum after the turn of the century. As Hill also notes, church membership became during these years a virtual requirement for community acceptance and success. Religion and culture were thus more inextricably intertwined than in any other extended region in the country, with the possible exception of Mormon Utah.

In these same years, though, southerners began as well to develop a parallel strain of religiosity that related to the Christian churches in roughly the same way that Buddhism and Shinto have coexisted in Japan. This "civil religion" that emerged from the experience of massive defeat during the Civil War has been dubbed "the Religion of the Lost Cause" by historian Charles Reagan Wilson. Growing out of a propensity during the war years to regard that epic conflict as a "baptism in blood," this postwar regional cult built on the earlier notion of the moral superiority of the South which now had been purified by a fiery baptism. The cult that resulted expressed itself, among other ways, in the building of statues and other public monuments to the war's heroes, such as Robert E. Lee. (Richmond, Virginia, the capital of the Confederacy, particularly abounds in such statues.) Patriotic societies, veterans' groups' reunions, sermons, orations, and other public activities helped to ritualize what amounted to a cultural religion, a latter-day version of which is still perpetuated by means ranging from visits to historical sites such as Chickamauga battlefield and Stone Mountain to bumper stickers reading "Forget, Hell."

Yet another aspect of the multifaceted character of southern regional religion is the spectrum of popular and folk religion that still maintains a strong hold especially in rural areas, including the mountain subcultures of the Appalachians and Ozarks. A wide variety of Baptist churches, together with holiness and pentecostal groups, are dominant in shaping this aspect of religious culture much more than the more organized and urban United Methodist and Southern Baptist denominations. One aspect of a folk heritage that has endured to the present is manifest in the tradition of "shape-note" or "fasola" hymn singing, which originated early in the nineteenth century out of the necessity of providing a semiliterate people with a means of sight-reading. Instead of standard musical notation, triangles, squares, circles, and diamonds were used to indicate the notes to be sung. Spread widely through such works as *The Sacred Harp* of 1844, shape-note singing remains alive today through many parts of the rural South, though its appeal may be based increasingly on nostalgia. Many of the songs performed in this manner date back to the Wesleys of the eighteenth century and the American composer Lowell Mason of the early nineteenth, and include other perennial favorites such as "Amazing Grace" and "Come Thou Fount of Every Blessing." The "gospel hymns" of the era of Fanny J. Crosby and Homer J. Rodeheaver have also remained popular, and "gospel quartets," both black and white, frequently attain widespread regional reputations through traveling performances at many churches.

Another distinctive aspect of popular southern religious life is the *homecoming*. Homecomings are reunions, which can be held by families, school classes, and other groups but are frequently sponsored by churches. Church homecomings are held on their own grounds, which often have permanent picnic tables for the purpose, or at cemeteries or camp meeting grounds. They usually take place on the date of the church's founding and involve the return to the community of members of the extended families of the church's founders as well as those of current members to reminisce and socialize. Flowers placed on graves are often part of the ritual as well, and vast numbers of such decorations can be seen on drives through the rural South in the summer on Decoration Day. The homecoming illustrates vividly the intimate relationship that religion in the South has with other aspects of culture, especially its role as a point of reference for the identity and solidarity of an entire community, now in danger of being scattered through the forces of modernization. (As Jack Temple Kirby has pointed out, participants in many of today's homecomings are urban dwellers returning briefly to their rural roots.)

The religious life of the mountain South also has some characteristics that distinguish it from even the folk aspects of religion in other parts of the region. Unlike the Tidewater and Piedmont areas, many parts of the Appalachians and Ozarks have remained racially as well as ethnically homogeneous; since slavery was unprofitable in mountainous terrain, blacks seldom were brought to the region as slaves and, later, did not often come voluntarily. The isolation of these regions has also inhibited the modernizing forces of the "New South" movement that began to promote industrialization and urbanization in the late nineteenth century; rather, the outside world has been experienced most intensely in the form of exploitative coal companies engaged in strip mining.

The religious consequences of this cultural homogeneity and isolation are manifested in independent, individualistic, and highly expressive variations on the Baptist and holiness-pentecostal basic themes. Primitive, United, and Old Regular Baptists are three varieties of the former tradition that have found in Appalachia a far more congenial home than almost anywhere else. United by an adherence to one form or another of Calvinist theology, they reject activities such as missions or Sunday schools, which contradict their predestinarian beliefs. Their worship is often traditional, featuring a capella shape-note singing and a preaching style that sounds more like a chant or whine than ordinary spoken discourse. Yearly sacramental services feature the Lord's Supper and the ordinance of foot washing, practiced only by members of the same sex, which is also being revived in some parts of the country by liturgical churches. Free-will and other Baptists also abound, and mix such traditions as foot washing with more "modern" innovations such as instrumental music and gospel singing.

Pentecostal and holiness churches also abound in the mountains, and the area around Cleveland, Tennessee, which houses the headquarters of two branches of the Church of God, has sometimes been referred to as the "Burned-Over District" of these movements. It was rural pentecostals who gave rise to such an extremely expressive form of public worship that they became known derisively by outsiders as "Holy Rollers." An extreme but very rare form of mountain pentecostal practice that has attracted an exaggerated notoriety in the broader world is the phenomenon of "snake-handling." In a few churches, mainly in Appalachia, traditional pentecostal worship forms such as *glossolalia* are intermingled with the introduction of live rattlesnakes into the midst of the worshiping assembly as a test of faith. This practice

and related phenomena such as the "salvation cocktail"—a thimbleful of strychnine—
are tests for the faithful of the literal accuracy of Mark 16:17–18 ("And these signs
will accompany those who believe: in my name they will cast out demons; they will
speak in new tongues; they will pick up serpents; and if they drink any deadly thing,
it will not hurt them; they will lay their hands on the sick, and they will recover").

The South was irrevocably transformed by the Civil Rights Movement and accompanying legislation of the 1960s. The color line could now no longer be maintained
legally, and the integration of public high schools and colleges supplied some of the
most dramatic movements for the new "Lost Cause." In addition to southern blacks,
represented most eloquently by Martin Luther King Jr. and civil rights workers from
the North, a small but significant number of white southern clergy banded together
to form the Committee of Southern Churchmen in 1964 to promote the movement
themselves. Will Campbell, a Baptist minister who has served both as director of
religious life at the University of Mississippi and, in an effort at reconciliation, as a
Ku Klux Klan chaplain, is a representative of this alternative consciousness in the
recent South. His experiences have been memorably recorded in his autobiographical
Brother to a Dragonfly (1977).

Irresistible forces toward change from outside have combined with internal social
and economic development to produce a "New New South," as exemplified in such
thriving, cosmopolitan urban centers as Atlanta and Charlotte. On the other hand,
though, the South has undergone a simultaneous religious and political transformation, beginning in the 1960s, which has not been in either a liberal or a "Lost Cause"
direction. With the exception of 1976, when the self-avowed evangelical Jimmy Carter
carried his region in his successful bid for the presidency, the once monolithically
Democratic "Solid South" now tends to vote Republican in national elections and,
less reliably, in congressional, state, and local contests. (South Carolina senator Strom
Thurmond's conversion to Republicanism was a conspicuous sign of this shift.) Although racism is no longer a staple of what was once called the "Gothic politics" of
the region, conservatism in economics, foreign policy, and "social issues" such as
abortion and pornography now attract widespread popular support.

In the religious realm, urban areas in the South now attract a wide variety of
religious congregations, from Unitarians to Hindus, reflecting an accelerating integration of such areas into the national culture. Rural areas continue to be heavily
Baptist, holiness-pentecostal, and, among the middle classes, Methodist. A dramatic
increase has taken place during the same years among Southern Baptists—now by
far the largest American Protestant denomination, with over fifteen million members at the end of the twentieth century—and their cousins, the Independent Baptists, such as Jerry Falwell of Lynchburg, Virginia. These are by no means churches
of the "disinherited," as their rural and small-town counterparts have sometimes
been characterized in the past. Rather, they can be viewed as churches of those in
transition—ascending, slowly or rapidly, the ladder of worldly success, often at the

price of jarring cultural dislocations such as those occasioned by a move from town to city, or from the working class to the middle class.

At the same time that these churches have been growing numerically in the South, their constituencies have been expanding geographically into other parts of the country, especially the Midwest and West, where Southern Baptist and pentecostal congregations of considerable size can often be found today. Similarly, leading "televangelists" such as Baptist Jerry Falwell, pentecostal-turned-Methodist Oral Roberts, and pentecostal Pat Robertson became national rather than simply regional figures during the 1980s. At the same time, country music, which has incorporated much of the gospel tradition into its repertoire, has become a national phenomenon, and figures such as Willie Nelson, Loretta Lynn, Garth Brooks, and Shania Twain have followings all across the nation and at all social levels. Just as the South has been inexorably transformed by an enforced or sought-out interaction with the rest of the nation, so now its distinctive culture and religion are becoming "export goods" as well.

B. Traditions in Transition: European Immigrants

CHAPTER 36

American Catholicism: From Ethnic Pluralism to Institutional Unity

The relationship between religion and *ethnicity* in America has been an extremely complex one. In some cases, as in Anglicanism until fairly recently, the relationship has been quite simple: most Episcopalians were of British, and particularly English, birth or descent. Lutherans have been ethnically diverse, but the European stocks that have been associated with that faith have been linked together to some extent through geographic (German, Scandinavian, Baltic) and linguistic (Germanic) proximity, though not identity. The Jewish people, scattered throughout the world and manifesting many cultural and linguistic variants, have been held together by a common historical and at least vestigial religious experience. In America, moreover, the experience of the "melting pot" often takes its toll after two or three generations, and the relationship between linguistic, cultural, and historic experience on the one hand and religious identity on the other becomes increasingly problematic.

The story of the development of American Catholicism, especially to the time of World War I, is intimately bound up with the interaction of three kinds of forces. First, Rome has made its presence felt periodically, as both a unifying and also a divisive power. Second, American culture, dominated first by evangelical Protestant and then by predominantly secular forces, has provided another context, sometimes welcoming, sometimes threatening, in which American Catholics have had to work out a distinctive identity. Third, Catholics in America have represented the most diverse and pluralistic amalgam of ethnic identities imaginable. Irish, Polish, Lithuanian, French, Italian, Croatian, Slovenian, Portuguese, and Hispanic immigrants have been overwhelmingly Catholic, although their interpretations of their common tradition have differed from one another in very important ways. But English and other British, Czechoslovak, German, Hungarian, Middle Eastern, east and southeast Asian, and African American immigrants and their descendants have also adhered to the Catholic Church in significant numbers, simultaneously enriching and complicating the story still further. The story of American Catholicism during the nineteenth century can be understood best by looking first at the ethnic diversity that continuing immigration brought with it, and then at the impact of countervailing drives for uniformity and centralization that came to prevail against this diversity.

The majority of the handful of Catholic clergy and bishops in this early national period were native-born Americans of English descent and French émigrés. For the most part they were well educated and aristocratic in outlook, and sympathized with the aspirations of the new nation, in which they were still too few to come under serious suspicions of being an alien and subversive presence. The complexion of the American Catholic community began to change rapidly in the 1820s, with the arrival of the first waves of the people who would rapidly come to dominate its life for decades to come.

The major spur to the immigration of Catholic Irish to America was the blight that induced the great potato famine. The "Great Hunger" that ensued devastated the Irish nation from the 1820s through the following two decades. Ireland had since the time of Oliver Cromwell in the 1650s been under the oppressive domination of the English, who regarded this Celtic people as simian-like barbarians and their Catholic faith as superstitious and treasonable. The transplantation of lowland Scottish Presbyterians through English encouragements sowed the seeds of future ethnic strife that has lasted to the present day, and the ownership of much of the Irish land by English absentees further exacerbated the plight of the native people. When the blight began to devastate Ireland's major subsistence staple, the potato crop, starvation and disease ravaged the population. The English for once were eager to encourage the Catholic Irish—to emigrate.

The Irish who were able to leave came to America as best as they could, often as ballast in the holds of timber ships returning from the British Isles to Canada. These newcomers sought refuge in America as they were able, and the seaports of the Northeast, especially Boston, provided the most convenient locales for settlement. Many of the Irish were poor and illiterate but spoke English; their competition for available work at what seemed to the indigenous, Protestant working class as intolerably low wages created a resentment that was a major spur to outbreaks of *nativism*—hostility to the foreign-born. Early American nativism was inextricably bound up with anti-Catholicism, because the vast majority of these immigrants were Roman in their allegiance and popular Protestant mythology going back to the days of Queen Mary in England associated the Catholic Church and the pope with the devil and the Antichrist. Anti-Irish nativist riots broke out in Boston, New York, and Philadelphia beginning in the 1830s, and political movements such as the Know-Nothing Party, which briefly gained some state and congressional electoral victories in the 1850s, gave institutional expression to this anti-immigrant impulse.

Work on the railroad and canal systems that were providing America with a new infrastructure of transportation and communication provided many Irish with opportunities to earn a minimal living. Further, the nature of the work made it possible for them to venture further inland than their earliest circumstances had made possible. The best opportunity for upward mobility within the Irish American community, however, was a career in the church. The priest had usually been the only member of Irish peasant communities who had the education necessary to serve as a communal spokesman, and an extraordinary prestige was accorded the religious life in Irish culture. In America the chronic shortage of priests and sisters during the heyday of immigration—virtually the entire nineteenth century—forced a reliance on the recruitment of clergy abroad, and increased the pressure on Irish American Catholics to encourage "vocations" to the religious life among their children. A vast number of Irish entered America during these years: a million were resident in 1850—one out of twenty-three Americans—and one and a half million more arrived between 1870 and 1900. From the ranks of these immigrants and their offspring came by far the largest part of the clergy and hierarchy who were to chart the path for American Catholicism well into the twentieth century.

The Irish American Catholicism that thus became normative in America during the middle and later nineteenth century had a number of distinctive characteristics that set it apart from the earlier religious cultures of the English and French as well as from that of the Germans and eastern and southern Europeans who were also beginning to arrive in significant numbers. In the first place, the institutional church and clergy enjoyed great prestige in the Irish American community. Though this prestige was sometimes mixed with ambivalence and even resentment, there was seldom any question as to the final authority of the church in matters of faith and morals. The role of the church as a means of education and advancement for the children of a people who had been quickly transformed from a rural peasantry to an urban proletariat reinforced clerical prestige as well. The impact of the French on clerical education in Ireland and America shaped an ethos in which clerical celibacy, marital fecundity, and a general distrust of sexuality were prevailing emphases. Temperance was one value that Irish clergy shared with American evangelical Protestants; alcohol was viewed as a far greater social and moral danger by Irish Americans than by most other Catholic communities. Finally, a "devotional revolution" took place in Ireland during the nineteenth century in which localized cults of saints were displaced by universal pious practices, such as saying the rosary. This "revolution" was part of an attempt by both Rome and the Irish hierarchy to strengthen the institutional church. This piety gained rapid popularity in America as well during the later years of the century as a heavily parish-oriented culture began to prevail.

The other Catholic people who began to arrive in America in significant numbers contemporaneously with the Irish were the Germans. The social and cultural orientation of these German Americans was significantly different in many ways from that of the dominant Irish. In the first place, Germany, which did not achieve national unity until 1870, was a religiously divided society in which Catholics, Jews, freethinkers, and Protestants of a wide variety coexisted more or less amicably. (Bismarck's *Kulturkampf*—"cultural war"—against the Catholic Church later in the century would strain Germany's pluralism severely, though.) This was very different from the Irish context, in which allegiance to the Catholic faith was a major aspect of anti-English nationalistic sentiment. Second, most German Catholics who came to America, though seldom wealthy, were not as near destitution as the Irish frequently were. As a result, these newcomers were able to secure inexpensive farmland in the "German Triangle" delineated by Milwaukee, St. Louis, and Cincinnati, which emerged during the middle of the nineteenth century. Whether settled as farmers or urban artisans, the Germans tended to keep to themselves, preferring that their children be raised in the midst of a German-speaking environment.

It was this desire to perpetuate the old ways in the New World that helped precipitate one of the major struggles for religious and cultural self-definition among America's Catholic peoples during the latter part of the century. German-speaking Catholics in both Europe and America were fearful that the program of Americanization favored by many Irish American church leaders would lead not only to the loss of the old language and folkways (such as the *Biergarten*) but of the traditional religion as well. Anton Walburg, a Cincinnati priest, articulated this argument in 1889. *In The Question of Nationality in Its Relation to the Catholic Church in the United States,* Walburg argued that language, culture, and faith together formed the only effective bulwark against the inroads of American secularism and materialism. In 1886 Peter Abbelen, the vicar general of the heavily German Milwaukee archdiocese, presented a petition to the pope arguing for parishes based on nationality rather than geography for similar reasons. A cognate argument was formulated in Germany and presented to Rome by Peter Paul Cahensly of the St. Raphael Society, which he had earlier organized to protect the interests of German emigrants and encourage missions to them. Cahensly argued in 1890 that vast losses to the church were occurring among German Catholics, and went even beyond Abbelen in arguing that a whole network of German-speaking institutions, including dioceses and seminaries, be established in America for the preservation of the faith. In fact, the German language was frequently used in churches, parochial schools, and other religious contexts among German American Catholics, but its proponents were fearful that these temporary arrangements would not prevail in the face of concerted Irish American hierarchical opposition.

Similar aspirations and fears characterized Polish Americans, who constituted the largest and most articulate group of central and eastern European Catholics who were swelling the ranks of the "new immigration" that had begun around 1870. The Polish experience in Europe had been in some ways closer to that of the Irish than of the Germans, due to Poland's disappearance as a nation in the partitions of its territory between Prussia, Russia, and Austria-Hungary at the end of the eighteenth century. A strong sense of nationalistic zeal thus combined with fervent Catholic allegiance in the American "Polonias"—Polish enclaves—that grew up in the industrial cities around the Great Lakes during the later nineteenth century. Also similar to Irish American piety was Polish devotion to the Virgin of Czestochowa (ches-tuh-HOE-vah), whose image took on nationalistic as well as spiritual connotations. Like the Germans, however, the Poles desired to perpetuate their faith, language, customs, and sense of traditional identity as a unity in the New World, and resisted pressures toward assimilation with similar tenacity.

The rallying cry of Polish Catholics was *rownouprawnienie* (ROOVE-noe-oo-prahv-NYEH-nyeh), a call for parity of representation within the American hierarchy, which was by this time almost totally dominated by the Irish. A partial victory was achieved in 1908 when Polish American Paul Rhode was appointed auxiliary bishop of Chicago, whose Polish community had by this time become the largest in the world outside of Warsaw itself. Rhode's appointment was more of a symbolic than an actual victory; Poles and other Catholic "minority" groups, such as the like-mindedly nationalistic Lithuanians, continued to enjoy only token representation at the higher levels until late in the present century. It was only in the 1960s and 1970s that archbishops with names like Pilarczyk (Polish, Cincinnati), Bernardin (north Italian, Cincinnati and Chicago), and Medeiros (Portuguese, Boston) began to appear in the higher reaches of American Catholicism's elite of leadership.

One offshoot of the Polish struggle for parity of representation was the formation of the Polish National Catholic Church by Francis Hodur in Scranton, Pennsylvania, in 1897. Despite the ferocity with which many of these interethnic battles were conducted, it is remarkable that the PNCC was for practical purposes the only even moderately successful schism from the Catholic Church in American history. In 2006 it claimed 126 parishes and about 60,000 members, down from some 280,000 members in 1960.

Another component of the "new immigration" with an experience significantly different from any so far discussed was that of the substantial number of Italians who were processed through Ellis Island with their counterparts from eastern and southern Europe during this flood tide of population movement. Although Italy had been the seat of Catholicism for centuries, it was by no means a culturally or, until 1870, a politically united nation. In cultural terms, the main division was between the north, which had for some centuries been in the vanguard of economic development, learning, and sophistication—the land from which popes had traditionally been chosen—and the southern part of the peninsula and Sicily, which continued to be enmired in a semifeudal economic and social structure that severely retarded the modernization process. The result of this cultural bifurcation was a suspicion of the institutional church, which was dominated by northern Italians, on the part of the Sicilians and other southerners, whose version of Catholicism was richly infused with folk elements such as the *festa*—a street festival honoring a local patron saint— and belief in the *malocchio* or "evil eye."

It was primarily the Sicilians, Neapolitans, and other southern Italians who chose to leave Italy for the United States and other New World destinations. Sometimes they embarked on temporary money-making forays, but often they left Italy behind forever, rather than continue to endure the bleak future the regional economy foreboded. Once in America, these Italians found themselves in a religious situation similar to the one they had left behind, with an unsympathetic Irish American clergy in place of the north Italians. The result of this cultural clash was an alienation of many Italians from the institutional church. Some defections were brought about by aggressive Methodist and Baptist proselytizing, but a simple absence from the church except at rites of passage—marriages, baptisms, funerals—was more the norm. The old pattern of street *feste* re-created itself in neighborhoods with a heavily concentrated Italian population such as Boston's North End, South Philadelphia, and Italian Harlem in New York City. Also, the work of religious orders such as the Scalabrini Fathers and the Missionary Sisters of the Sacred Heart—the latter founded by Mother (now Saint) Frances Cabrini (1850–1918)—helped create an ethos more sympathetic to Italian customs.

Given this vast inpouring of Catholic peoples into the United States during the nineteenth century, much of the attention of the institutional church was directed toward accommodating their needs. These needs were material as well as spiritual, so that much of the church's resources went not only into the conduct of worship but into the relief of the exigencies of everyday life as well. The assumption by the government of responsibility of the manifold needs of the population was not nearly as developed as it has since become. Priests and sisters therefore had to concern themselves extensively with education, medical care, emergency relief, and provision for the needs of society's many marginal members, such as the multitude of orphans created by periodic cholera epidemics. The shortage of indigenous clergy and religious women prompted frequent recruiting campaigns by American bishops in Europe, where they sought both financial support and personnel. As a result, the clergy and sisters of the nineteenth-century American Catholic Church were nearly as polyglot as the laity, and it is not surprising that centralized controls of the church's manifold institutions remained fairly loose until some stability could be achieved.

The first organizational problem with which the American church had to deal was the result of the new nation's refusal to sanction either religious establishment or persecution, as provided by the First Amendment. This created a situation unprecedented in the Catholic Church's experience, because it had become used to one or the other of these alternatives since the time of the Reformation. The Vatican's acquiescence in the election of the first American bishop directly by the clergy was a sign of tentative openness to the new situation, as was Bishop Carroll's involving of his priests actively in the governance process.

Carroll's enthusiasm for democracy, however, was soon challenged by the emergence of the "trusteeism" question. This situation, in which parish property was owned and affairs managed by a group of elected laymen called "trustees," arose from a combination of reasons: the character of early state laws regarding church property, the scattered and unsupervised origins of the first Catholic parishes, the *congregational polity* that characterized the governance of many of the Protestant denominations, and the general ethos of democracy in the new nation. Still another complicating factor was the presence of a number of priests in these early decades who had left Europe—especially Ireland—because of the ill repute in which they stood with the hierarchy at home. The result was a number of instances of conflict between the early American hierarchy and individual parishes in Boston, New York, and Philadelphia. In the latter case, the Irish-born pastor William Hogan virtually waged war with his bishop for three years until his excommunication in 1822 and a subsequent papal condemnation of the whole system. Eventually, a new legal arrangement in which each bishop was recognized as a *corporation sole* vested property rights directly in the church, and made such challenges to episcopal authority more difficult in the future. Together with nativism, trusteeism presented the antebellum Catholic Church in America with one of its first major challenges in adapting to a significantly new political arrangement and cultural ethos.

The middle decades of the nineteenth century were preoccupied mainly with the tasks of institution building, the challenges of Irish and German immigration, and the fending off of nativist hostility. As the Civil War approached, American Catholics were divided over the issue of slavery, with both lay and clerical defenders of the "peculiar institution" emerging in the South. The lack of any doctrinal issue at stake and of any official Catholic teaching against slavery as such militated against the sorts of schisms that afflicted many Protestant denominations. Northern Catholics were hardly unanimous in their enthusiasm for the abolitionist cause, because many Irish saw the possibility of a larger free black community as a challenge to their own economic prospects. When the war came, however, most rallied to the cause of the Union, and the distinguished service of German and Irish units in battle, as well as the heroic role played by Catholic sisters as battlefield nurses, helped temporarily to allay nativist accusations of disloyalty. Sister Anthony O'Connell of Cincinnati's Sisters of Charity, "the angel of the battlefield," was representative of the role women frequently played not only under wartime stress but in the longer-term tasks of developing medical and educational facilities with minimal resources.

The postwar years saw the coming of the "new immigration" on an even more massive scale than that of the old. Sheer numbers were exacerbated by the less ready adaptability of many of the later newcomers, whose linguistic and cultural differences from native Americans were far greater than those of the Irish and Germans. A major response of the institutional church was an increasing emphasis on church-sponsored education as a means both of assimilating the immigrants and their children and of insulating them from the threats presented by the Protestant- or secular-dominated "common" (that is, public) schools. The Third Plenary Council of Baltimore, at which the American bishops convened in 1884, mandated all Catholic parishes to provide an elementary school as soon as possible, with construction of the school taking priority over the church edifice itself. The question of whether Catholic parochial education was to be polyglot—as it was in many predominantly German and Polish communities—or whether it was to further the assimilation process by promoting the universal use of English was one of the issues that were beginning to create some serious strains within the American church.

By the last decade of the nineteenth century, three distinct schools of thought had emerged within the American Catholic community on the question of what was to be the preferred attitude of the church toward American society. The most conservative faction, whose spokesmen were usually German speakers such as Abbelen, Cahensly, and Walburg, was hostile to the whole notion of Americanization and maintained that the faith could best be preserved as a unit together with the traditional languages and cultures of Europe. Catholic Americans would participate in the American economic and political systems but insulate themselves from the broader society and culture. For them, America was welcome as a political and economic refuge, but the Protestant and secular elements in its culture were hostile to the nurture of the traditional faith as it had developed for centuries in the more hospitable climes of central Europe. Old-world culture maintained on new-world soil could combine the advantages of American prosperity and religious freedom with the traditional piety of Germany or Poland.

A second influential group, led by Irish American Bishop Bernard McQuaid of

Rochester and Archbishop Michael A. Corrigan of New York City, advocated a similar caution about overly extensive involvements in the social and educational networks of American society but nevertheless maintained that Catholic solidarity could best be preserved by the uniform use of the English language. For them, the Catholic Church had a parental mission to shelter its family—many of whom were recent immigrants—from the spiritual as well as the material hazards of American life. The decentralization implicit in the German and Polish positions, however, worked against their vision of a centralized church that could only emerge as a significant force in American life through mastery of the social and political tools—for example, the English language—necessary to survive and even provide an alternative to secularizing Protestant culture.

The third major faction among the American Catholic leadership became known as the "liberals," who were represented most forcefully by St. Paul's Archbishop John Ireland (1838–1918), "the consecrated blizzard of the Midwest." Ireland was backed by other midwestern bishops such as John Keane of Dubuque and John Lancaster Spalding of Peoria, and had the behind-the-scenes support on many issues of the archbishop of Baltimore, James Cardinal Gibbons (1834–1921), whose stature elevated him to the informal role of spokesman for the American church. Ireland and his like-minded colleagues viewed American society as fundamentally benign, and saw its democratic ethos and policy of church-state separation not simply as a tolerable option but as a positive good. Their inclinations, therefore, were to cooperate with other Americans in as many progressive endeavors as they could, as long as matters did not involve actual hostility toward the church or contradiction of fundamental Catholic teaching.

Among these causes were public education, which the liberals saw as fundamentally neutral and perfectly acceptable as long as it was supplemented by appropriate religious instruction under Catholic auspices. Release-time programs in which children were excused for a few hours a week to receive such instruction were experimented with in Faribault and Stillwater, Minnesota, under Ireland's aegis, as well as in Poughkeepsie, New York. The founding of the Catholic University of America in Washington, D.C., in 1884, with John Keane as rector, was another liberal enthusiasm opposed by the conservatives on the grounds of its potential for indoctrinating clergy in suspect teachings and attitudes. Ecumenical undertakings, shunned by the more cautious, were also a favorite liberal pursuit. Bishop Keane, for example, was delighted to deliver in 1890 the Dudleian Lecture at Harvard, which had been established during the colonial era for "the detecting and convicting and exposing the idolatry of the Roman Church," together with other Catholic offenses. (Needless to say, Keane did not fulfill these objectives.) The active participation of the liberals in the World's Parliament of Religions in 1893, which they regarded as an opportunity to put the Catholic cause sympathetically before the world, was equally obnoxious to conservatives who saw such activities as an acknowledgment that Catholicism was no better than one religion among all of the rest of them. Finally, Cardinal Gibbons's success in persuading Rome not to condemn the Knights of Labor as a "secret society" also irritated those who saw labor unions in the same light as the secret anticlerical organizations such as the Freemasons who were out to subvert true religion and good order.

The unlikely event that brought these tensions to a head was the publication in France in 1897 of a translation of Walter Elliott's *Life of Father Hecker,* with an introduction by Archbishop Ireland and a preface by a like-minded French prelate. Isaac Hecker (1819–88) was a German American Methodist who, after a spiritual pilgrimage through the experimental communities of New England transcendentalism, had converted to Catholicism and joined the German-based Redemptorists. Chafing under that order's old-world piety, Hecker left to found a new American group known as the Paulists, whose special mission was the evangelization of American Protestants. Hecker developed an apologetic that stressed the singular compatibility of Catholic and American values, and this was promoted in his books as well as in the order's journal, *The Catholic World.* The activist, pro-American bias of Hecker and his followers that was lauded so highly in Father Elliott's hagiographic account of Hecker's life alarmed French conservatives who happened upon it, and brought about their complaint to Rome that the whole affair smelled of heresy.

The result of the controversy that ensued over Elliott's work was the encyclical (papal letter) issued by Pope Leo XIII in 1899 with the title *Testem Benevolentiae* (that is, a testament of goodwill). In it Leo, whose earlier *Rerun Novarum* had seemed to put him on the liberal side of contemporary issues, declared that the "Americanism" denounced by Elliott's accusers—a collection of highly technical theological propositions—was indeed unorthodox, and its teaching should be stopped if it were being taught. Leo did not, however, assert that it was in fact being taught by anyone.

This omission prompted American liberals to declare that the whole matter involved only a "phantom heresy" that no one was really guilty of promulgating. Although the issues involved and the facts of the matter were extremely convoluted, the upshot of the affair was a victory for the Irish American conservatives (Corrigan, McQuaid, and their sympathizers) in their probably correct reading of the encyclical as a Roman caution to American liberals to dampen their conspicuous enthusiasm for "new things." With the reinforcement of Pius X's *Pascendi Dominici Gregis* in 1907, which condemned theological "modernism," the net effect of this papal attention to transoceanic matters was the effective end of Ireland and his colleagues as a dominant force in American Catholicism for the immediate future. (Ireland was never made a cardinal.) The early and middle decades of American Catholic life in the twentieth century were therefore to be characterized not by intellectual and social experimentation but rather by a consolidation and expansion of a massive institutional presence, the groundwork of which had already been laid. It was only in midcentury that Catholic intellectuals would begin to vindicate Ireland with their charges that their fellow American Catholics had developed a "ghetto" mentality that was insulating them from the good that contemporary society had to offer. The ultimate results of this new, critical attitude became manifest only after the upheavals of Vatican II.

CHAPTER 37

Eastern Christianity in America

The floodtide of the "new immigration" that swelled the American population during the decades between the Civil War and World War I brought with it millions of new Americans who did not speak English and whose religion was none of the myriad varieties of Protestantism. The large majority of these culturally distinct new-comers were Jews and Roman Catholics. A significant minority, however, came from Greece, the Balkans, Turkey, Russia, Ukraine, and other parts of eastern Europe, and were Christian but neither Protestant nor Roman Catholic. Like other immigrants, they tended to form ethnic enclaves in the burgeoning cities of the East and Midwest, and to mark their neighborhoods with churches. These latter were conspicuous for their rounded or onion-shaped domes, which lent an exotic note to the architectural mixture that was then arising. Although the least familiar of the major European religious traditions of America, the various types of Eastern Christianity that have taken root on these shores have added a distinctive and permanent ingredient to American religious pluralism.

Although a short-lived Greek colony was founded in New Smyrna, Florida, in 1768, the real beginnings of the Orthodox presence on the North American continent were the work of Russian explorers, military personnel, and especially missionaries in the eighteenth century. A diocese was established at New Archangel (Sitka) in Alaska in 1840, and the Russian Imperial Missionary Society, founded in 1870, helped support missions in Alaska and the adjoining islands until the 1917 revolution. Notable among the Alaskan missionaries in this period was Ivan Veniaminov (1797–1879), who later became Bishop Innocent. Veniaminov translated biblical and liturgical texts into native languages, designed churches, and collected valuable ethnographic information on the native Alaskan peoples. His respect for local traditions and cultures was emblematic of the broader Russian missionary enterprise in the region. Orthodoxy continues to be significant in Alaska, and after the sale of Alaska to the United States, native peoples became even more devoted to this tradition that had become their own, and served as a means of preserving native traditions against pressures of Americanization.

In 1874 the diocese, which had undergone various jurisdictional reorganizations and had few Russians to serve after the acquisition of "Seward's Icebox" by the United States in 1867, was relocated to San Francisco. This small Russian presence on the West Coast was rapidly overshadowed by the massive arrivals of Russian and other Orthodox on the East Coast, and in 1905 the *see* (bishop's residence) was moved across the continent to New York City. Eastern Orthodoxy is thus the only major religious tradition of European origin in the United States to experience a movement of its center of gravity from west to east.

During the years following the Civil War, Eastern Orthodox immigrants from a variety of backgrounds began to settle in America, and generally worshiped at Russian-founded parishes whether they themselves were of Greek, Syrian, or other ethnic extraction. The Russian leadership welcomed this expression of "pan-Orthodoxy" and was willing to appoint priests of other backgrounds to positions of responsibility—for example, the Syrian Raphael Hawaweeny became vicar-bishop of Brooklyn in 1904. However, Greeks and others preferred to worship in their own familiar languages and traditions, and the Orthodox community rapidly acquired the diversity—and with it, a measure of contention and confusion—that characterizes it to the present day.

The large-scale emigration of Eastern Christians to America was part of the broader movement of peoples that collectively constituted the "new immigration" of the post–Civil War era. Many of the Orthodox who came to America seeking a better life were young single males who possessed little in the way of education or occupational skills. However, the rapid industrialization of the nation had ample need of unskilled labor, and these central Europeans found ready, if ill-paid, employment in the anthracite fields of Pennsylvania and the industrial cities emerging into economic prominence around the lower Great Lakes. Greeks were less likely to perform heavy labor, and many found success as restaurateurs, confectioners, and stationers in Detroit, Chicago, and other "Greektowns" that sprang up in turn-of-the-century cities. Arabs, many of whom were Eastern-rite Christians, often began as itinerant peddlers on the Jewish model. Small churches bearing the traditional Russian onion domes or Byzantine-Greek rounded domes are still good markers, whether in mining towns or ethnic neighborhoods, of this early Eastern Christian presence.

One religious anomaly that this massive immigration brought to a head was the arrival and rapid defection to Orthodoxy of thousands of Eastern-rite Catholics known as *Uniates*. The "Unia" are a group of communities following rituals and customs more similar to Eastern than Western practice, who at various times entered into union with the Roman church in exchange for a guarantee that their traditions would be respected. When arriving in America, however, these Uniates usually found that the American hierarchy, many of whom were hostile to the continuation of old-world customs, were unwilling to acknowledge the legitimacy of their clergy who, unlike Latin-rite Western Catholic priests, were not required to be celibate and often had wives. After much delay, the Vatican backed the American hierarchy and declared that, though Eastern-rite liturgies and a certain measure of juridical independence might be maintained, Uniate clergy in America must be celibate. Even before this long-delayed resolution had come about, thousands of Carpatho-Russians (or Rusyns), Galicians, Ukrainians, and other Uniates renounced their Roman allegiance and were welcomed into the Russian and, later, the Greek Orthodox folds.

Despite major organizational advances by the able Bishop Tikhon Bellavin (1865–1925) in the early years of the century, the impact of World War I and the subsequent upheavals that beset Russia and southeastern Europe had dramatic repercussions on Eastern-rite Christians in America, who as much as any ethnic and religious groups maintained close ties with their lands of origin. The Russian Revolution threw the status of Russian Orthodoxy in America into great confusion, and bitter and prolonged jurisdictional disputes plagued it and other Orthodox communities for decades. Financial support from the mother country now vanished, and Orthodox churches abroad were left to support themselves on the American denominational model. Among the Russians, the pressing question was whether continuing allegiance to Moscow was possible in a situation where an antireligious Communist regime now controlled the patriarchate. As a result, three distinct factions eventually emerged in the American scene:

1. The *Orthodox Church in America* (OCA), which had a membership of slightly over a million in 2004, is without question the dominant force in Orthodoxy of Russian heritage in America. Though second to the Greek Orthodox in size, it is arguably the most important Eastern Christian community in the New World in terms of cultural and theological influence, in part because it has become the cradle of an American Orthodoxy increasingly independent of traditional ethnic identity. Although the Metropolia, as it was previously known, was at odds with Moscow for decades over questions of jurisdiction, these issues were finally resolved in 1970 when the Russian Orthodox Church recognized the OCA as autocephalous—that is, a fully self-governing member of the Orthodox "family" of churches (literally, "self-headed"). The OCA has headquarters in Syosset, New York, and is divided into nine dioceses in America. It sponsors Saint Vladimir's Orthodox Theological Seminary in Crestwood, New York, which in the years after World War II became an academic home for such distinguished Orthodox theologians as Georges Florovsky, Alexander Schmemann, and John Meyendorff.

2. The *Patriarchal Parishes of the Russian Orthodox Church in the United States and Canada* are a group of Orthodox in the United States (and others in Canada) who chose to maintain direct ties with Moscow even after the OCA had been recognized as autocephalous. This group has never been

particularly numerous or influential, and membership is in the low five figures.

3. The *Russian Orthodox Church outside of Russia* represents the wing of Russian Orthodoxy that has refused in any way to acknowledge the legitimacy of the postrevolutionary Moscow leadership. Unlike the OCA, which has aimed to become an Orthodox church for Americans, ROCOR has worked to maintain its Russian identity. Its intellectual center is the Holy Trinity Seminary in Jordanville, New York. In recent years its dialogue with the Patriarchate in Moscow has made steady progress towards a reestablishment of communion between the two bodies. Membership of ROCOR was about a half-million in 2006.

All three of these churches maintain national headquarters in metropolitan New York.

The largest of the Eastern churches in America is the *Greek Orthodox Archdiocese of America,* with headquarters in New York City. Although Greek Orthodoxy in America was bitterly divided over the contest between monarchist and democratic factions that split the Greek homeland after World War I, unity was finally achieved under the leadership of Archbishop Athenagoras, who later was named ecumenical patriarch. Greek Orthodox in the United States are led by an archbishop who represents the ecumenical patriarch in Istanbul (as Constantinople has been known for some time). It maintains the Hellenic College–Holy Cross School of Theology in Brookline, Massachusetts, and in 2006 claimed approximately 1.5 million members. As with most of the Orthodox churches other than the OCA, membership is almost exclusively drawn from the Greek American community, which is concentrated in major urban centers with an especially large population in Chicago.

In addition to these churches of Russian and Greek background, American Orthodoxy is also represented by Albanian, Antiochian (Syrian-Lebanese), Bulgarian, Romanian, Ruthenian (Carpatho-Russian), Serbian, and Ukranian branches, some of which are further split by the sorts of issues that the Russians and Greeks had experienced, and some of which are under the jurisdiction of the OCA or the Ecumenical Patriarchate. Although some misunderstandings and hostilities still persist—for example, over the autocephaly of the OCA—all of these churches share an allegiance to what is known as "Chalcedonian" Orthodoxy, which affirms the validity of the first seven ecumenical councils and rejects Roman claims to primacy. These churches first entered into a cooperative relationship in their effort to gain recognition for Orthodox military chaplains during World War II, and have subsequently represented their collective tradition as America's "Fourth Faith" along with Judaism, Protestantism, and Roman Catholicism. Further recognition of "pan-Orthodoxy" has been manifest in the formation of the Standing Conference of Canonical Orthodox Bishops in the Americas in 1960, as has a broader ecumenical stance in the participation of several of the Orthodox churches in the originally Protestant National Council of Churches.

Eastern-rite Christianity in America, however, is not confined solely to the "Chalcedonian" church bodies. The Uniate traditions continue to be maintained under the jurisdiction of the Roman Catholic Church, despite their severe numerical losses at the turn of the century. In the late 1990s they numbered about 650,000–700,000 adherents divided into eleven constituencies, including the Melkite (Syrian), Maronite (Lebanese), Armenian, Ruthenian (Russian), and Ukranian. These five enjoy their own ordinaries (that is, bishops, known as "exarchs" or "eparchs"), whereas the remainder are under the jurisdiction of Latin-rite bishops. Eastern-rite Catholics are heavily concentrated in the areas of original settlement, especially Michigan, Ohio, New York, and Pennsylvania. A tour of the industrial and mining communities of these states will often reveal a whole panorama of small churches, many with Eastern-style onion domes, representing their various Orthodox and Uniate constituencies.

Finally, those Eastern Christians who early on rejected the Christological definition of Chalcedon as to the nature of Jesus have found representation in contemporary America as well. The largest of these "Non-Chalcedonian" or "Oriental Orthodox" is the Armenian Apostolic Church, which listed a membership of about 360,000 in 2006. In the same family can be placed the Coptic Church and other small groups of Middle Eastern, North African, and Indian provenance for which membership figures are not too reliable.

During the decades since World War II, Eastern Christians in North America have been pulled in a variety of sometimes contradictory directions as they have adapted to both the domestic and the international situation. Intellectually, a major challenge was presented by Florovsky, Meyendorff, and other postwar émigrés who abandoned the traditional route of exile in Paris or other European capitals and instead found a congenial home in the New World. These men were theologians of the first order who sought to transcend what they perceived as the political and ethnic captivities into which many Orthodox had fallen and desired instead to rediscover a purer Christianity that was faithful to early traditions. This thrust was consonant with similar currents in Protestant Neo-Orthodoxy as well as the theological ferment generated by the Roman Catholic theologians who were laying the intellectual groundwork for Vatican II.

This intellectual reappropriation of Orthodoxy attracted a considerable number of converts from a wide variety of traditions, both liturgical and evangelical, who found satisfaction in the richness of worship as well as the motif of return to Christian origins. Recent academic luminaries who have taken this path include Yale's Jaroslav Pelikan, a Lutheran, and Princeton's Albert Raboteau, a Roman Catholic, known respectively for their studies of the histories of Christian doctrine and of African American religion. Although these conversions have enriched the Orthodox churches—especially the Russian and Antiochian—both numerically and intellectually, they have also created tensions between those who have been raised in traditions whose distinctive practices they have always regarded as normative and newcomers whose sometimes romantic expectations do not square with everyday ethnic reality. In 1987, for example, a group of Protestant evangelicals who had earlier organized themselves as the Evangelical Orthodox Church (EOC) were received into the Antiochian Orthodox Christian Archdiocese of North America, a community of primarily Syrian origins. Conflict between some of the EOC's leaders and Antiochian bishops over issues such as authority and liturgy came to a head in 1998, with many of the recent converts switching allegiance to the Patriarchate of Jerusalem, which seemed to them more authentically (that is, traditionally) Orthodox than what they perceived as more Americanized Antiochians.

Other forces have also been at work within the Orthodox communities that have periodically resulted in similar tensions between tradition and Americanization. Orthodox ranks have been enhanced not only by theologically motivated conversions but also by intermarriage and immigration. Intermarriage, now virtually the rule among Americans of "new immigrant" descent, has resulted in many suburban parishes especially where the number of members of non-Orthodox background approaches a majority. These same parishes are also subject to the same forces and evidences of modernization parallel to those that have characterized Jewish and Roman Catholic communities—English-language liturgies, open icon screens, and pews (as opposed to the traditional absence of seating except for the elderly).

One example of tensions between tradition and accommodation is the case of Michael Dukakis, governor of Massachusetts and a second-generation Greek American. When Dukakis received the Democratic nomination for the presidency in 1988, reporters were puzzled by his curious status within his own church. Because Dukakis had married outside the faith—his wife, Kitty, is Jewish—he was automatically excommunicated and has not been able to receive Communion since his marriage. His identification with the Greek American community nevertheless remained strong, and even the archbishop helped bring him together with wealthy potential contributors to his unsuccessful campaign.

Recent immigration, renewed by more welcoming congressional policies since 1965, has had an impact on American Orthodoxy largely opposite to that of intermarriage. Accustomed to conditions where Orthodoxy is a given part of a broader culture, where local customs have been taken for granted as normative and unalterable, and where the authority of the clergy in religious matters is not shared with a theologically sophisticated laity, many recent immigrants have not been comfortable with the cosmopolitanism and ethnic pluralism that have become common in the American scene. Near Milwaukee, for example, the Greek Orthodox Church of the Assumption in the suburb of Wauwatosa was designed by Frank Lloyd Wright in his characteristically nontraditional style and dedicated in 1961. In the late 1990s, controversy broke out over plans by the incumbent priest to make the church's interior more traditional by replacing the highly stylized paintings commissioned by Wright with Byzantine icons. Interestingly, older parish members who had been present at its creation were among those most vehemently opposed to the proposed traditionalization.

Another dramatic example of these tensions emerged during the brief reign of Archbishop Spyridon, who in 1996 had been appointed by the ecumenical patriarch as the spiritual leader of the Greek Orthodox Archdiocese of America. Although American-born, Spyridon had been raised in an old-world environment that had emphasized episcopal authority, and he rapidly alienated many of his new-world flock through behavior they considered autocratic. When Spyridon dismissed several faculty members and administrators at the Holy Cross School of Theology near Boston in the wake of a sexual harassment scandal, many parishes withheld financial contributions to the archdiocese and otherwise registered in vocal American fashion their protest against this perceived high-handedness. To the relief of many, Spyridon resigned in 1999 and was replaced by Archbishop Demetrios, who holds a doctorate from Harvard and taught for several years at the Boston seminary.

The world of Eastern Orthodoxy in North America is thus a veritable laboratory of religious transformation. Its ethnic division and particularism, emphasis on church tradition, relatively small numbers, and reinvigoration through continuing immigration has served to inhibit its rapid accommodation to the broader American scene. On the other hand, an infusion of theological cosmopolitanism, intellectually motivated conversions, continuing intermarriage, and financial prosperity have all militated in the direction of assimilation. What seems clear is that, although the Eastern Orthodox churches in the United States will continue to experience controversy and change, their characteristic combination of ethnic pride and theological identity makes it unlikely that they will soon lose the distinctive character that has always made them appear somewhat exotic to Americans of other European backgrounds.

CHAPTER 38

Ethnic Diversity and Denominationalism in American Judaism

From the later colonial period to the 1830s, Ashkenazic Jews from northwestern Europe had begun to arrive in small numbers and intermingle with their Sephardic predecessors. In the early decades of the nineteenth century, they had founded synagogues of their own in New York and Philadelphia. This gradual shift in ethnic background took a sudden dramatic turn in a new direction during the 1830s, when thousands and soon tens of thousands of German-speaking Ashkenazim began, with their Christian compatriots, to leave Bavaria and other German states for the New World.

These new immigrants lacked both the elite cultural background and the financial skills and resources of the Sephardim, and were forced to seek a new place for themselves in the rapidly expanding new nation. Frequently they set themselves up as peddlers, on foot or with horse-drawn wagons, and made the circuit of frontier settlements selling household items. Those who were particularly successful in this line often settled in small towns and established dry goods stores, some of which evolved into the major department stores of the twentieth century (Macy's, for example). In many cases these merchants and their families constituted the only Jewish presence in large portions of the South and West. Although many stayed on for generations, others who were able liquidated their holdings and took up residence in more established Jewish communities such as those of New York and Cincinnati.

Communities of successful Ashkenazim had arisen in American cities from Atlanta to San Francisco by the Civil War era, establishing synagogues (now with rabbis), schools, mutual benefit and charitable societies, hospitals, cemeteries, and the other voluntary institutions that Americans of all sorts loved so well. When the Civil War arrived, Jews like other Americans tended to follow sectional allegiances, and Judah P. Benjamin of Louisiana held several cabinet posts in the Confederacy. It was during the Civil War, however, that one of the first public signs of anti-Semitism began to appear. Responding to accusations of war profiteering, in 1862 General Grant issued an executive order expelling all Jews from the military district of Tennessee. Although Jewish protests led to a reversal of this decree by President Lincoln, ancient motifs of Jewish disloyalty and covetousness had now played a distinct role in American public policy.

American Jewry in the years immediately following the Civil War tended to be urban, German descended, English speaking, public-school educated, commercially oriented, quite prosperous, and generously supportive of philanthropic causes, Jewish and otherwise. Their status on the American scene, however, was soon to be affected radically from two different directions: the vast influx of eastern European Jews beginning in the 1880s, and the quiet but effective raising of barriers to Jewish participation in the higher reaches of gentile society.

Just as a combination of social and economic upheavals earlier in the century had touched off the massive immigration of German speakers of all sorts, including Jews, to the New World, so did a similar array of forces precipitate the even vaster rush of eastern and southern European peoples, most of them non–English speaking and non-Protestant, to America from about 1880 until the World War I era. For Jews especially, economic distress was reinforced by violent persecution in the form of pogroms on Jewish settlements by Czarist Cossacks. In consequence, hundreds of thousands of Yiddish-speaking Jews from Russia, Lithuania, Poland (or, rather, what once had been Poland), Ukraine, Hungary, and Romania began to arrive in the "promised land" of America—usually New York City, to which most immigration was channeled after the creation of a federal processing center at Ellis Island in 1892. It was from here that hundreds of thousands of Jewish newcomers—"greenhorns"—found themselves thrust into the turmoil of Manhattan's Lower East Side, where Hester Street and other crowded tenement-lined avenues resonated with the Yiddish cries of pushcart vendors.

To keep these greenhorns from falling victim to exploiters, the already established and now largely English-speaking New York Jewish community began to organize efforts to help the newcomers orient themselves. Even though both groups were technically Ashkenazim, however, the prosperous second- and third-generation merchants, who had frequently adopted the new Reform as their religious expression, were generally dismayed by their newly arrived remote kinspeople. The German American Jews looked askance at the prevalence of Yiddish, the abysmal poverty, and the traditional, "oriental" Orthodoxy or new socialist ideologies of these creatures of the "new immigration." Although large numbers of the newcomers found employment in the garment workshops maintained by the older Jewish community, and welcomed the chance for Sabbath observance that working for fellow Jews usually made possible, the workplaces were frequently no better than sweatshops, the hours long, the work tedious, and the pay wretched.

It was therefore in the context of one class of Jews protesting conditions imposed by another that much of America's first labor organization took place, with the Jewish immigrant cigar roller Samuel Gompers playing a leading role in that struggle. Although the traditionally religious newcomers were less susceptible to such movements, the considerable numbers who had abandoned religion entirely proved enthusiastic converts to such new social causes. *Landsmanchaften,* or societies of immigrants from the same European city or province, played a major role in the social, political, and economic life of this dynamic Yiddish-speaking outburst of American Jewish life, which was destined to last for scarcely more than a generation.

The socioeconomic and cultural diversity that had come to characterize American Jewry by the late nineteenth century had religious implications as well. The division of American Jews into a number of organized, formally separate communities or "traditions" is an instance of the tendency of American religious groups to form into denominations, or independent organizations representing variations on a common theme. In their European experience, Jews had lived together in ghettoes or *shtetls,* existed as isolated itinerants, formed movements, such as the Hasidic disciples of the Baal Shem Tov or the followers of the "messiah" Sabbatai Zevi, or assimilated into gentile society. In none of these cases, however, had it been desirable or even legally possible to organize into discrete religious "camps," each with its own interpretations of Jewish thought, life, and worship, and each with its own formal organizational structure. In the broad sweep of the European experience, Jews were characterized by law as one separate people, and their communal life was defined by the implications of such laws. In America, however, constitutional separation of church and state on the one hand and the voluntary, denominational model provided by American Protestantism on the other were to shape the course that Judaism would take on these shores.

For the first two and a half centuries of its existence, Judaism in America did not know formal division. The synagogue was the fundamental unit of Jewish life from the beginning, and the half-dozen or so in the colonies were Sephardic in membership and ritual. These colonial-era synagogues were lay dominated, with an occasional *hazzan* the only professional in the universal absence of rabbis. By the end of the eighteenth century, sufficient Ashkenazim had arrived so that splits began to occur in Sephardic-dominated congregations (for example, B'nai Jeshurun separating from New York's Shearith Israel in 1825) or new Ashkenazic congregations were founded (Rodeph Shalom in Philadelphia, 1795).

Ethnicity alone, however, was not to be the principle that prompted the division of American Judaism into clearly delineated "denominations." The influx of German-speaking Ashkenazim during the middle decades of the nineteenth century brought with it many Jews, including a number of rabbis, who had become imbued with the principles of Reform that had their origins in the Enlightened ideas of Moses Mendelssohn. The American Reform movement, led by Bohemian-born Isaac Mayer Wise (1819–1900), took the lead in developing an institutional infrastructure for Jewish life in America, including Hebrew Union College, America's first lasting Jewish seminary, which Wise founded in Cincinnati in 1875.

It was at the banquet held for Hebrew Union's first graduating class in 1883 that tensions between "traditional" and "progressive" American Jews reached a breaking point. As waiters began to serve the successive courses, observant Jews were shocked to see that much of the food was *trayf:* shrimp, crab meat, and frogs' legs. Although this unfortunate choice of provender was possibly a caterer's mistake rather than a deliberate affront, Wise refused to apologize for the offense against *kashrut.* From that time it became clear that Hebrew Union would not be a satisfactory school for other than Reform rabbis, and that the elements of the American Jewish community not comfortable with Reform's rejection of tradition would have to provide their own organizational structures.

Reform was the first of America's Jewish traditions to adapt itself to the American denominational pattern. It was, in fact, Reform that defined the issues that would precipitate the eventual institutionalization of Orthodoxy and the subsequent emergence of Conservatism as an alternative to both. Reform had its early origins in the thought and work of Moses Mendelssohn in eighteenth-century Germany, and began to express itself more concretely in the modernization of worship that took place in a number of early nineteenth-century German synagogues.

The emphasis among these Westernized Jews was on "decorum" in worship, as opposed to what they saw as the "Orientalism" and confusion of Orthodox services conducted in Hebrew, with the often illiterate congregation talking and milling about as they pleased. (These complaints would be echoed in America later in the century as assimilated German American Jews contemplated the conduct of their eastern European brethren with bemusement or contempt.) These reformers generally sought models in contemporary Protestant practice, and adapted such innovations as the seating of families together in pews rather than segregating the sexes, utilizing organs and choirs, and discontinuing the wearing of such traditional marks of male piety as the *yarmulke* (skull-cap) and prayer shawl. In addition, Hebrew was displaced as the language of worship by the vernacular—German or, later in America, English— which was also used in the delivery of another borrowing, the sermon.

It was such German-speaking Jews who began to carry the program of Reform with them as they settled in America in the early and middle decades of the nineteenth century, but its systematic implementation and the development of a philosophical rationale awaited the advent of German rabbis. Although early experiments with the reform of worship were introduced beginning in Charleston in the 1820s, it was the coming of first Max Lilienthal and then Isaac Mayer Wise to Cincinnati in the 1850s that provided the movement with its first organized leadership. It was Wise especially who used his base at Cincinnati's Bene Yeshurun systematically to create a denominational infrastructure for American Reform. His accomplishments included the founding of an English-language Jewish newspaper, *The American Israelite,* in 1853; the drafting of an early Reform prayerbook, the *Minhag America,* in 1856; the founding of the first real Jewish denominational vehicle, the Union of American Hebrew Congregations, in 1873; and, perhaps his crowning achievement, the establishment of Hebrew Union College in 1875 (which later merged with the Jewish Institute of Religion).

After all of this apparatus was in place, Reform in America moved into its next phase, the creation of a systematic program of ideas that would give it more coherent identity than simply a modernization of worship. These ideas had their roots in nineteenth-century German "scientific" approaches to Judaism, and found their first significant American expression in the "Pittsburgh Platform" promulgated by nineteen rabbis in 1885. Although the by-now-venerable Wise presided over this gathering, its moving spirit was Kaufmann Kohler (1843–1926), the son-in-law and disciple of Wise's more radical East Coast rival, David Einhorn. This brief statement was dramatic in the starkness with which it presented the central tenets of Reform as an ideology. These included the definition of Judaism as a "progressive religion, ever striving to be in accord with the postulates of reason" and not inextricably bound by the "primitive ideas" of biblical language and thought patterns; a rejection both of the laws of *kashrut* and of Zionism; an empathetic identification of its own ideals with those of Christians and Muslims in a common quest for "the reign of truth and righteousness among men"; and a reaffirmation of the primarily ethical character of the Jewish mission.

The Reform commitment, then, was to design a program for a Judaism to be practiced normatively in diaspora—and, most particularly, in America. Though all three of the national Jewish denominational organizations accepted America and the English language, Reform was by far the most aggressive in promoting Americanization positively and, as a negative corollary, rejecting virtually all of the cultural, linguistic, and cultic apparatus of Jewish tradition. Emphasis throughout was on the reasonableness of Judaism, as reflected in the *Union Prayer Book* adopted in 1894, which was based on Einhorn's earlier version. Worship was in many ways hard to distinguish from that of liberal Protestants, which harmonized with the Reform program of emphasizing continuities with rather than differences from other religions. Similarly, the role of the rabbi changed from that of the traditional scholar of Torah and Talmud to something much more like that of the typical Protestant minister—preacher, counselor, and administrator.

Orthodoxy as a distinct branch of Judaism began to take shape in America with a meeting of twenty-six congregations in 1879, who attempted unsuccessfully to invite a distinguished European Talmudist to become their chief rabbi. The heavily eastern European and localistic character of Orthodox communities in America worked against the process of organization, but success was eventually attained in 1898 with the formation of the Union of Orthodox Jewish Congregations of America. This group, though dedicated to a traditionalist emphasis on Torah and Talmud, alienated other Orthodox through their use of English rather than the Yiddish spoken by most recent immigrants. Their primary accomplishment was the regularization of kosher food preparation; their "U" symbol on food is still a reliable indication that the product conforms to the standards of *kashrut*.

Although Orthodox Jews have never been as uniformly committed to national organizational structures as their coreligionists, the beginnings represented in the UOJCA, together with the Union of Orthodox Rabbis, provided the groundwork for the generation of many of the structures that characterize most branches of American religious life. The first elementary *yeshiva*, or Hebrew school, was established in New York in 1886, followed by the Rabbi Isaac Elchanan Theological Seminary on the Lower East Side eleven years later. The two institutions merged in 1915 into the Rabbinical College of America. To this rabbinical foundation, Yeshiva College (later University) was added in 1928 to combine secular studies with traditional Jewish education. The founding of the Chicago Hebrew Theological College in 1922 provided a major midwestern alternative for the training of Orthodox rabbis, and a considerable number of small schools of advanced Talmudic study exist as well. A network of Hebrew schools at all levels has proven the major source of supply for Orthodox rabbinical students during the twentieth century.

Orthodox Judaism, then, despite its lack of unity, is generally united around the

precepts that traditional Jewish law remains binding on Jews even today in its multiplicity of prescriptions and prohibitions. The Torah, revealed by God to Moses, is
the ultimate religious authority, and attempts to subject it to contemporary critical
scrutiny meet with a chilly reception. Although it served at first primarily as a refuge
for the most traditional, Yiddish-speaking members of the "new immigration," its
character has changed as that generation has died off, and its resurgence of popularity
especially among younger Jews in the later twentieth century has been a remarkable
development.

Conservative Judaism is the most distinctly American Jewish tradition and originated in an attempt to provide an alternative to the polarization the Hebrew Union
trayf banquet helped to bring about. Some have traced the movement's origins to the
policies of various American rabbis in the earlier nineteenth century, such as Isaac
Leeser and Sabato Morais at Philadelphia's Mikveh Israel. The founding of Jewish
Theological Seminary in New York in 1886 by Morais helped to lay the infrastructure
for this emergent "tradition," although the original intent was to provide a more
Orthodox alternative to Wise's Hebrew Union. When the Union of Orthodox Rabbis
excommunicated the new seminary in 1904 on the grounds of excessive flirtation
with contemporary biblical criticism, however, it became clear that a tertium quid,
or "middle way," between extreme liberalism and traditionalism was in the making
almost in spite of itself.

Solomon Schecter (1847–1915), the president of JTS at the time of its censure by
Orthodoxy, was the guiding spirit who gave form to Conservatism as a positive force
within American Judaism. Formal status for the movement came with the founding
of the United Synagogue of America in 1913. The Rabbinical Association of America
provided another institutional vehicle and still supervises the publication of a Conservative prayerbook and the journal *Conservative Judaism*. A distinctive development within the Conservative movement was the *synagogue-center,* a combination
of house of worship with facilities for education, recreation, and other community
activities (sometimes known irreverently as a "*shul* with a pool"). The first of these
was founded in New York in 1916 by Mordecai Kaplan, founder of Reconstructionism, for the purpose of emphasizing the unity of Jewish life as a culture and tradition
and not simply a "religion" in the narrow sense of the term.

This emphasis on Jewish life seen holistically in the context of a living, ongoing
tradition is a major key to understanding the character of Conservative Judaism.
Schecter himself expressed this idea in his phrase "Catholic Israel." By this he meant
that the life of Judaism existed in the present as much as in the past. The current
generation of Jews ought to help shape the character of Jewish life in the light of, but
without being rigidly bound by, the precedents of Torah and Talmud. ("Positive historical Judaism" is another phrase used by early Conservatives to express this idea.)

A sense of historical perspective was also introduced by Schechter, whose German academic training in Jewish history imbued him with a sense of perspective

not frequently found in rabbinical schools. Revelation, from this vantage point, was divinely inspired, but need not be taken literally—an approach that various Christian groups were also moving toward around the turn of the century. On the other hand, Conservatism recognized that being Jewish was more than simply a matter of proper belief and observance. A sense of participation in a millennia-old tradition, whose legacy could not simply be reduced to propositional form, was a major part of the Conservative outlook that emphasized Jewish culture and peoplehood as well as ethics and ritual.

In terms of worship and ritual observance, Conservatism can best be seen as a flexible middle way between the paths of Reform and Orthodoxy. The prayerbook is in Hebrew, but sermons and other communication have always been in English. The maintenance of tradition in worship varies in detail from synagogue to synagogue, but in general the innovations of Reform have tended to prevail. In addition to synagogue worship, Conservatism has also emphasized home-centered rituals and stresses the role of the family as a primary preserver and transmitter of Jewish tradition. Daily attendance at Hebrew school has also been part of the Conservative program.

Conservative Jews tend to keep kosher, but even this is by no means universal. Jewish law—*halacha*—is taken seriously but not literally, and innovation is possible to accommodate traditional dictates with contemporary exigencies. The decision in the 1980s by Conservative Jews to ordain women to the rabbinate is a good example of this flexibility which, needless to say, does not sit well with the Orthodox.

By the time of World War I, American Judaism was well on its way in adjusting institutionally to its American circumstances by adopting the American pattern of denominationalism. One result of this was to give concrete expression to the real differences, both religious and cultural, that divided America's Jewry. Like many Roman Catholic, Eastern Orthodox, and Lutheran Christians, Orthodox Jews wanted to enjoy the political and economic benefits of life in the New World without surrendering their distinctive cultural heritage. Isaac Mayer Wise, like Samuel Simon Schmucker and Archbishop Ireland, enthusiastically led his Reform following into a wholesale adoption of American ways. The tension between the two approaches was mediated for many by the Conservative movement, an indigenous approach to a compromise between the two extremes. In the twentieth century, the emergence of Reconstructionism and the settlement of large numbers of Hasidic Jews in the New York City area would further enrich and complicate this pluralism.

Denominationalism, however, did more than simply express these emergent differences in attitudes toward tradition and modernity. The very process of institutionalization inexorably led American Jews into an encounter with modernity through being forced to differentiate themselves formally from one another. Further, the very process of establishing organizational structures, periodicals, seminaries, and the like was a further venture into Americanization. Some Orthodox Jews managed to resist this process through continuing a very decentralized, traditional style of worship and education, but many of their compatriots succumbed willy-nilly. America may have given them freedom to live as they liked, but it was also subtly prodding them to become something they had never imagined.

C. Old and New Frontiers

CHAPTER 39

Native American New Religions

In earlier chapters, we have discussed the indigenous traditions of the Native American peoples and a variety of attempts by European Americans to convert them to various interpretations of Christianity. In neither case have we been dealing with absolutes. Native traditions were fluid rather than fixed, a fluidity abetted by intercultural contacts and by the nature of orally transmitted culture itself. Although many missionaries, both Catholic and Protestant, were unbending in their determination that their prospective converts give up their traditional beliefs and life patterns completely, others, such as the Jesuits and Quakers, were considerably more accommodating in their willingness to adapt Christian teaching to a non-Western cultural matrix. It should not be entirely surprising, then, to discover that during the past two centuries a number of movements have risen among Native Americans that have combined elements of both old and new religious cultures in their content.

One major category of new religious movements in North America has been what the anthropologist Anthony F. C. Wallace has called *revitalization movements.* The theme of revitalization—literally, of bringing back to life again, usually through a return to an older, purer state of being—is hardly confined to American Indians. The Protestant Reformation, for instance, was not originally conceived by Luther and Calvin as a radically new act but rather as a return to the pure beginnings of the New Testament church after centuries of decline and corruption during the Middle Ages. Similarly, in Roman Catholicism, a whole series of monastic reform movements as well as ecumenical councils—for example, Trent and Vatican II—have been interpreted by their advocates not as something new but rather as the restoration of something very old. "Secular" movements as diverse as Romanticism and Naziism similarly have components of renewal through restoration, as do nineteenth-century movements in American Christianity such as the Latter-day Saints and the Disciples of Christ. Revitalization or restoration, in short, are variants on the basic religious theme that Eliade has called "the Eternal Return."

Among Native Americans, revitalization movements usually embodied the related themes of the rejection of European American religion and culture and the restoration of traditional Indian ways. Some early examples that also involved active resistance to white ways were the "conspiracy" of Pontiac in 1763 and the uprising orchestrated by Tecumseh at the time of the War of 1812. In each case, an armed campaign against Anglo-Americans was waged by a military leader abetted by a visionary advisor—the "Delaware Prophet" in Pontiac's case, and Tecumseh's brother Tenskwatawa. The visions of these seers added a supernatural legitimation and rationale to what might otherwise be interpreted as purely secular uprisings. However, as we have already noted repeatedly, natural and supernatural were never rigidly separated in the Native American worldview, especially at crucial times in the life of an individual or a people.

Another feature characteristic of many such movements appeared for the first time in Tecumseh's case. Instead of the movement's being confined to one particular tribe or people, Tecumseh attempted the first pan-Indian alliance against the whites. Native Americans had previously not identified themselves as sharing a common identity with other native peoples. Now a new sense was arising from prolonged contact and conflict with European Americans that the native peoples were more similar than different in their character and interests, and that it was to their advantage to pursue their common interests in coordination.

It was on the West Coast, toward which the Indians had been pushed continually during the course of the nineteenth century, that the most dramatic examples of this sort of movement took shape. One of the earlier versions resulted from the visions of the Wanapum shaman Smohalla ("the Dreamer") in the state of Washington beginning in the 1850s. Smohalla, who had been educated by Catholic missionaries, learned from his visionary experiences that the Indians had been the first humans to be created, and that Mother Earth, which the whites were now wounding with their metal ploughs, rightfully belonged to its original inhabitants who lived on the natural bounty of fish from the sea instead. Although Smohalla's movement was pacifistic, it was adopted by the neighboring Nez Percé led by Chief Joseph, who used its teachings as a rationale for armed, and ultimately unsuccessful, resistance against the whites who were pressuring the Nez Percé and others onto reservations. The movement continued well into the twentieth century after Smohalla's death, but only a handful of faithful outlasted its initial failure to produce any tangible positive results.

Similar to Smohalla's movement was the first Ghost Dance, which originated among the Paviotsos of Nevada and California in 1870. The moving spirit in this case was the prophet Wodziwub (or Wodziwob), who had a vision that was at once more far-reaching and more revealing of white influences than had been those of his predecessors. Whereas Smohalla's vision had taken the form of a reaction against white practices and a summons to return to traditional ways, Wodziwub saw his version of a restoration taking place in images explicitly supplied by Anglo-American culture. In this vision, the departed ancestors of the Indians of the day would return to life on a train. After this restoration, the earth would open up and swallow all of humanity; however, the followers of the Ghost Dance would then be resurrected and would take over the property that had formerly been owned by the now-vanished whites. The sources of this vision are not clear, and some of its elements may have been derived from a stock of images circulating among the western tribes, which had also been incorporated into Smohalla's movement. However, it is clear that Western technology was now an element that had to be reckoned with, even in visions. Also, the motifs of the return of the dead, the restoration of the faithful in a land of peace and prosperity, and the obliteration of the wicked all parallel elements of traditional Christian eschatology (that is, teachings about the end of the world), even though no direct connection may be at work here.

The early Ghost Dance spread among the western peoples and took a variety of forms. Even Mormons became interested, since the message contained elements similar to some of Joseph Smith's prophecies. However, the movement was not militant, and began to dissipate when Wodziwub's visions were not fulfilled. Some of the major themes of the movement, however, were revived in 1889 through the prophecies of the Paiute Wovoka (or Jack Wilson), who was the son of an assistant of Wodziwub. In a visionary trip similar to his predecessor's, Wovoka visited a land that was filled with game and inhabited by all of the dead Indians of the past. While in this visionary land, he received instructions that the living Indians were to refrain from warfare and to perform the dance revealed to him. Those who kept these conditions would be reunited with the dead and would live forever in health and prosperity in a world free of the whites.

Wovoka's movement spread rapidly among channels of intertribal communication that were now well established. Black Elk, for example, recounts how the Lakota Sioux dispatched envoys to learn of this new ritual once word of it had reached them. As the movement spread, it underwent local variations. The Sioux, who were among the most militant in their resistance to white encroachments and for whom the victory at Little Big Horn was still fresh, adopted the use of a "Ghost Shirt," which was supposed to provide its wearers with invulnerability against the whites. White opposition to the dance and the general level of tensions among the Sioux culminated at Wounded Knee, South Dakota, in December of 1890, when a series of misunderstandings led to an outright massacre of some two hundred Sioux by federal troops. From that time on, the Ghost Dance and similar movements fell into decline as their ineffectuality in bringing about a literal restoration of a happier past became manifest.

All of the movements discussed so far have demonstrated both the ability of Native American religious patterns to incorporate motifs from Anglo-American culture into visions promising a restoration of the old ways and the elimination of the hostile newcomers from the earth. Other movements have exhibited a similar *hybridity*—the emergence of a new religion from the interplay of two older traditions—while advocating a new way of life based on an accommodation of the old ways to the new. One of the most interesting and successful of such *accommodationist movements* was that founded by the Seneca, Handsome Lake, around 1800. At this time, the Seneca of upstate New York had been profoundly demoralized by the effects of decades of military defeat, famine, disease, and exploitation by land speculators, all in consequence of prolonged contact with the whites. Alcoholism and witchcraft accusations, two common signs of social disintegration among Indians, were rife, and the Seneca were living in hovels, which Wallace has described as "slums in the wilderness."

In the midst of this squalor and confusion, Handsome Lake, who himself had fallen prey to poor health and drunkenness, began to experience a series of remarkable visions. Their way had been prepared by a number of sources: the Delaware Prophet, the role of visions in Seneca culture, and the presence of Quaker missionaries, who had provided a low-keyed witness through the establishment of a school and model farm. In his first vision, Handsome Lake encountered three angelic visitors, who called for the revival of the old Seneca customs and abstention from such destructive practices as alcohol abuse, witchcraft, magic, and abortion. In a subsequent vision, a fourth angel appeared, who took Handsome Lake on a tour of heaven and hell, where he could see, as had Dante, how the faithful were rewarded and the wicked punished. While in heaven, he met and conversed with both George Washington and Jesus Christ, and learned how the latter had also been betrayed by the white man.

These visions are clearly indicative of how much of the Christian worldview and symbolic vocabulary had been absorbed by the Seneca at the time, in part through the quiet presence of the Quakers. The supernatural world that Handsome Lake had toured was clearly that of Christianity in its structure and general landscape, and it bore little resemblance to the traditional native view of the world beyond. The message that Handsome Lake brought back to his fellow Seneca as well as the other members of the Hodenosaunee (Iroquois) confederacy, which they rapidly adopted, was similarly hybrid. The *Gaiw'iio* (guy-WITZ-zee-oh or guy-WICK'yo), as this message was called, was originally apocalyptic in character, and predicted the end of the present world within three generations. However, the spread of the message among the Seneca and the ups and downs of the reputation of Handsome Lake himself brought about a gradual change in emphasis from the cataclysmic to the ethical. The virtues and lifestyle it stressed were basically those of Anglo-American Protestant Christianity, with perhaps a trace of Quaker influence: temperance, peace, settled agriculture, social unity, domestic harmony, the primacy of the nuclear family, and prohibitions on gambling, dancing, and alcohol.

The rapid adoption of the *Gaiw'iio* and its continuation after Handsome Lake's death in 1815 to the present day are indicative of its appeal as a much-needed force for stabilization in a society that was disintegrating rapidly but was not ready to give up. Handsome Lake's message made sense out of a permanently divided world by providing a system of symbols that incorporated aspects of both sides of the division. On the one hand, traditional native patterns of seminomadic existence were no longer viable and had to be abandoned for a more sedentary lifestyle. Many of the virtues of Protestant Christianity similarly had to be substituted for the older, more individualistic ways. On the other hand, traditional elements such as the coming of new revelation through a shamanic vision persisted. The Seneca thus accommodated themselves to the new temporal dispensation, but still kept a certain physical, social and religious distance from it. That they can still be found in and around Tonawanda, New York, is potent evidence of the power of the *Gaiw'iio*.

The other accommodationist movement that has proven to be enduring and has also attracted more public attention than any other form of Native American religious expression, is the peyote religion or "cult." (*Cult* in this sense is used to refer to a ritual system rather than to contemporary movements focused on a strong, charismatic leader with a novel and demanding message.) The ritual use of peyote (*Lophophora williamsii*) has deep roots among many of the peoples of the Southwest and Mexico, but emerged in its modern form among the Mescalero Apache around 1870. From them it spread regionally among the Kiowa, Comanche, and Caddo, and ultimately among a wide variety of Native peoples as far away as Wisconsin and British Columbia. The specific context of its spread as a *pan-Indian movement* was the failure of the Ghost Dance. The chain of events that culminated in Wounded Knee had simultaneously helped to create a climate of pan-Indian sentiment and a network of communication and cultural borrowing among a number of widely dispersed peoples, and had also demonstrated the lack of realism of movements based on a hope of violent cataclysmic upheaval. The Indians of the West were thus now prepared to accommodate themselves to the necessity of long-term nonviolent coexistence with the whites, and a new religion based on the ritual use of peyote provided an appropriate symbolic vehicle.

The focus of Peyotism is the ritual ingestion of a dried cactus resembling a button, which contains nine alkaloids, of which mescaline is the most potent. The immediate reaction in the user is usually nausea, but eventually the bitterness recedes and a sense of euphoria accompanied by an altered state of consciousness and perception ensues. The result is a sense of personal relationship with the universe as a whole, which establishes a mood that can be developed and explored in the ritual context. This ritual is usually conducted in a tipi (teepee) around a fire and a crescent-shaped mound of earth. It begins on Saturday evening and runs until the following morning. A fixed part of the rite is set in English, but more spontaneous participation tends to be in native languages. The basic act is the eating of the peyote and subsequent meditation on the visions that are thereby produced. The goal of this contemplation is a contact of the individual with the power that permeates the cosmos—a diffuse sense of spiritual force characteristic of Native American tradition—and the use of this power to achieve an altered and more positive perspective on the problems of everyday life. A balance is thus maintained between individual and social observance, much like traditional Catholics saying the rosary during Mass. In this case, however, there is no priest to officiate, and each participant enters into a private journey while surrounded by others engaged in the same pursuit.

Although the basic ceremony remains fairly standard among Peyotists, the context in which it is performed varies from group to group. Among the more assimilated, Christian symbols are identified with various aspects of the Peyote rite; among other groups, the experience itself is stressed in unmediated form, with little interest in a hybridized blending of native and European approaches. The more assimilated branches of the religion also stress, as did Handsome Lake, a distinctive path of ethical conduct called the "Peyote Road." Like the *Gaiw'iio,* this is an adaptation of Christian teachings to the Indian context, and stresses similar virtues such as care of family and avoidance of alcohol. Although organizational forms are as alien to the Peyote religion as to native religious practice in general, followers have had to enter into formal groups to attain exemption from state and federal laws that prohibit the use of drugs. John Collier was instrumental in helping achieve this organization while serving as commissioner of Indian Affairs, and the present structure, the Native American Church, was organized in 1944. This institutional superstructure exists almost entirely to represent the group to the external world and has virtually no impact on the actual character of Peyotism's beliefs and rituals.

The Peyote religion is the most enduring example of accommodation between the Christianity of Anglo-America and the traditions of the Native American peoples. While adapting some of the symbols, ethical values, and organizational forms of Western religion, it still maintains the flexibility, the individualism, and the sense of a cosmos filled with diffuse spiritual power that has always characterized Native religious attitudes. In its appeal to Indians of a wide variety of cultural backgrounds and geographical locales, it is an excellent example of the emergence of a pan-Indian consciousness that recognizes and builds on the similarities that unite all native peoples in collective contrast with the dominant society of European Americans. Finally, it provides a nonviolent means of perpetuating what has emerged as viable in the Native tradition in the context of the necessity of coexisting realistically with that dominant society, adapting from it that which has value, and rejecting the rest with reasonable freedom from external harassment. It is, in short, a paradigm of cultural accommodation—the ability to live in two conflicting worlds simultaneously and to find the spiritual power to make that division endurable and, perhaps ultimately, to create a new whole.

The political ferment of the 1960s resulted in a new interest and appreciation of native cultures, and a series of publications ranging from Carlos Castaneda's accounts of encounters with the Yaqui visionary, Don Juan, to Vine Deloria Jr.'s *God Is Red* (1973), which advocated a rejection of Christianity and a return to the traditional religious ways. Whether Castaneda's accounts, beginning with *The Teachings of Don Juan* (1968), were actual records of his experience or clever, ethnologically plausible inventions has been the subject of considerable scholarly debate. Their continual source of popular appeal lies in their sympathetic presentation of a drug-induced alternative to the linear world of mundane reality, which persists wherever the "countercultural" impulse of the 1960s endures. The political and social radicalism of Deloria and his contemporary, Dee Brown (*Bury My Heart at Wounded Knee,* 1971), has gone the way of most of the protest movements of the era, although many tribal peoples have continued, with mixed success, to pursue legal paths to securing their traditional rights. A strong interest in Native American practices is also diffused throughout the New Age movement, although some Indians are thoroughly unamused by what they regard as the desecration of traditional places and practices by "New Agers" attempting to re-create rituals with little regard to cultural context.

Another Native American literary work, reissued in 1959, has attained what seems likely to be a permanent place in both popular and critical esteem. *Black Elk Speaks,* a hauntingly evocative autobiographical account of an Oglala Sioux shaman's life, has now achieved the wide readership it had been denied when first edited and published by the poet John Neihardt in 1932. Black Elk's narrative, as rendered by Neihardt, interweaves the linear history characteristic of the *Wasichus*—the Anglo-Americans—with his own visionary account of his life and the events surrounding it. Black Elk personally participated in Buffalo Bill's traveling Wild West show, including a trip to Europe and a meeting with Queen Victoria; the last stand of General George Armstrong Custer and his men in 1876 at Little Bighorn; the Ghost Dance of Wovoka and its spread eastward to the Lakotas; and the subsequent massacre of the Sioux at Wounded Knee in 1890. (Although it is not mentioned anywhere either in Black Elk's own words or Neihardt's commentary, Black Elk also served as a Roman Catholic catechist in his later years.) Black Elk does not see these events so much as items in a chronicle, but rather he relates them in the context of the visions of the supernatural world he experienced from early boyhood. In one of his most memorable images, he laments at the end of his life that his "nation's hoop is broken and scattered. There is no center any longer, and the sacred tree is dead." Although parts of the narrative may owe as much to Neihardt as to Black Elk, their book nevertheless opens a door into a powerful alternative view of both cosmos and history.

Whether the vital source of Native American life is dead is debatable, but the patterns of that life have unquestionably changed dramatically since Wounded Knee, the last significant episode in Native resistance to *Wasichu* encroachment. Alcoholism is still a major scourge, and endemic poverty has been offset only selectively by the proliferation of casino gambling, a form of entertainment that legal decisions have made possible for Indians to sponsor even when it is prohibited to others. (The Pequots in Connecticut, for example, have used their gains to sponsor a state-of-the-art museum of Native American history, whereas other peoples regard commercialized gambling as antithetical to their traditional values.) One thing that is readily apparent about contemporary Native American religious life, though, is its hybrid or "creolized" character. At Taos Pueblo in New Mexico, for example, an active Catholic church is situated within the wall that marks the settlement's sacred precincts, and within which no electricity or running water is permitted. On their reservation in eastern Nebraska, a number of Catholic Omaha also participate in peyote ceremonies and build sweat lodges of plastic in their back yards. The neighboring Winnebago conduct ritual gift exchanges in which the gifts exchanged are commercial goods that might have come from the local Walmart. Traditions do live, but often in ways in which old forms contain a thoroughly modern material content, and coexist with other traditions, such as those of Christianity, with little apparent sense of incongruity or cognitive discomfort—a sort of third way, or tertium quid, between two very different traditional religious worlds.

CHAPTER 40

Black Nationalism and New Urban Religions

The revolutionary rhetoric of the Black Panthers in the late 1960s and early 1970s was by no means the first attempt by American blacks to call for an overthrow of American society or to abandon it entirely. The recovery of African American history that the movements of the 1960s prompted focused new attention on a series of slave rebellions that had taken place in the early nineteenth century. Most notable of these was that led by Nat Turner in 1831 in Southampton County, Virginia. Turner's rebelliousness was nurtured by his sense of a divine calling. Although Turner and a number of his followers were killed in the course of the rebellion or hanged after their subsequent capture, sixty whites also died in the uprising, and the South was more than ever alert to the possibility that blacks could not be expected to remain docile.

The notion of black separatism also found expression in the nineteenth century. Most black clergy opposed the American Colonization Society's program of relocating free blacks and later manumitted slaves in Africa—especially in Liberia, the African state founded in 1821 as a result of the society's work. This approach to ending slavery was widely perceived by blacks as racist, and the clergy joined instead in the work of William Lloyd Garrison, Frederick Douglass, and other abolitionists. However, they generally supported those blacks who chose to return to Africa voluntarily to serve as Christian missionaries. Similarly, after the Civil War, the African Methodist Episcopal bishop Henry McNeal Turner (1834–1915) remained within the camp of Christianity but urged blacks to arm for self-protection and later to abandon the United States and emigrate to Africa. Turner also called on blacks to imagine God as black, a theme that would resurface in both Christian and other black religious movements of the twentieth century. Not a great deal came of these and other attempts to establish a black Christian civilization in Africa, but a critique of American society and a rhetoric of separatism were clearly being forged.

It was not until the mass migrations of southern blacks to northern cities beginning early in the twentieth century that a new series of social and religious movements began to arise based on either a distinctively black Christianity or, more usually, a repudiation of Christianity altogether. The most influential of these nationalistic movements was led by a Jamaican named Marcus Garvey (1887–1940), who arrived in Harlem in 1916 and there introduced his Universal Negro Improvement Association (UNIA) into the United States. The UNIA had as its ultimate aim the creation of an entirely black society and culture that would eventually abandon the New World and restore American blacks to their ancestral home in Africa.

To accomplish this, Garvey and his followers created a broad network of symbols and organizations intended to unite American blacks into a unified social whole. This network included a motto, "One God! One Aim! One Destiny!"; a newspaper, *The Black World;* an African Legion and a corps of Black Cross Nurses, with appropriate uniforms; and meetings, rituals, and a national anthem, "Ethiopia, Thou Land of Our Fathers." A religious dimension was provided in the African Orthodox Church headed by George Alexander McGuire, an Anglican priest from the West Indies who helped promote a new interpretation of Christianity with a black Jesus and Madonna and other Christian religious figures re-presented as literally black.

Garvey's movement also had an economic dimension, which proved its undoing. Central to this program was the founding of a Black Star steamship line, which was intended ultimately to provide a means for Garvey's followers to return to the African homeland. Infighting, ineptness, and governmental hostility doomed the venture, and resulted in Garvey's conviction and imprisonment for mail fraud and his eventual deportation during the 1920s. Like its radical precursors of the nineteenth century, the UNIA was not successful in its own terms, but it helped establish ideas and images that would continue to resurface in later contexts.

The conditions of life in the urban ghettoes of the 1920s and especially the Depression era also led to new religious movements centered on charismatic figures who went beyond traditional Christianity by claiming divine inspiration or even divinity itself. Most notable among these was Father Divine (1877?-1965), who may (or may not) have been born George Baker in Georgia or South Carolina. Like other black urban "cult" founders, Baker/Divine maintained a certain aura of mystery about himself, shrouding his origins in obscurity and changing his name and residence a number of times as his persona evolved. He can best be seen as a sort of protean or "trickster" figure, deliberately twitting his opponents and attracting followers through claims such as having been "combusted one day in 1900 on the corner of Seventh Avenue and 134th Street in Harlem."

After undergoing various metamorphoses, Divine actually claimed to be God in an equivocal sort of way, and his followers coalesced into the Father Divine Peace Mission Movement. He first established a headquarters at Sayville, Long Island, where he and a number of followers were arrested in 1931 on charges of disturbing the peace. Three days after Divine was sentenced to jail, the judge who had pronounced sentence suddenly and unexpectedly died. Divine, whose conviction was later reversed on appeal, remarked, "I hated to do it."

From bases first on Long Island and later in Harlem and Philadelphia, the Peace Mission Movement attracted large numbers of both black and white followers with the abundant banquets and semicommunal lifestyle that it offered in the midst of widespread scarcity and want. Controversy surrounded almost every aspect of the movement, from the sources of its extensive income to the female "angels" who surrounded Divine as his secretaries. A large majority of his followers were female, many of them "seekers" who had experimented with a number of religious movements, including the "New Thought" that Divine himself found attractive, before finding their needs fulfilled in Divine's charisma. A major teaching of Divine was the nonexistence of racial differences, and white and black followers coexisted harmoniously.

The Peace Mission Movement had little theology but rather was based on a lifestyle and allegiance to a unique individual's claims to divinity. The exact number of Divine's followers during the movement's heyday is hard to reckon, but it has been estimated at fifty thousand distributed among 160 centers in various cities. Although the movement has continued to exist in Philadelphia since Divine's death, focusing on the second "Mother Divine," it has recruited few new members without the founder's charismatic presence and seems destined to eventual extinction since celibacy is the norm.

One of Father Divine's rivals for the allegiance of Depression-era urbanites was Charles Emmanuel Grace (1881–1960), the founder of the United House of Prayer for All People in 1921 in New Bedford and Wareham, Massachusetts. Like Divine, he was a consummate showman and relished an abundance of life in a Los Angeles mansion and a New Jersey estate. As "Sweet Daddy" Grace, he attracted followers primarily from the black "sanctified" (holiness and pentecostal) churches. Though he was even more cautious than Father Divine in claiming divinity, his followers showed less hesitation. In addition to participating in worship services on the "sanctified" pattern, they found relief from their sufferings in the curative powers of special

Grace products, including magazines, soaps, cold cream, toothpaste, and cookies. After Grace's death, the House of Prayer was reorganized as a holiness church that claims (probably unrealistically) three million followers in sixty cities.

Still another approach to the question of black religious identity outside of the mainstream of black Christianity lay in an identification with non-Christian traditions that were seen as more authentically linked to the historic black experience. As illustrated in the Garveyite movement, Ethiopia held a particular fascination as a meeting place of Africa and the Middle East, and news about the dark-skinned Falasha Jews of that country aroused great interest in the 1920s. Garvey's choirmaster, Arnold Josiah Ford, was one of several founders of black Jewish groups that arose among American urban blacks in the early decades of the twentieth century. These movements have had various relations to the mainstream of American Judaism, and some have claimed that only blacks can be authentic Jews. In addition, occasional blacks such as the entertainer Sammy Davis Jr. have converted to historic Judaism, although their numbers have never been great.

More significant in the African American religious experience has been the identification of American blacks with Islam. Although a significant but indeterminate number of black slaves may have been Muslims, the story of the "Black Muslims" as an American phenomenon begins with the career of Timothy Drew (1886–1927), the founder of the Moorish-American Science Temple (among its several names) in Newark, New Jersey, in 1913. Under the name of Noble Drew Ali, the Prophet, he taught that blacks were really Asians and therefore Moors or Muslims. His teachings bore only a tenuous resemblance to traditional Islam, and acknowledged besides Muhammad the spiritual authority of the Buddha, Confucius, and Jesus, who was black. The movement, which had its own *Holy Koran,* which bore no relation to the Qur'an of Islam, survived Drew, who died under controversial circumstances in 1927. Reliable data on its present state is scarce, but temples exist in a number of cities in the north and upper South.

Another urban prophet whose life is shrouded in mystery was W. D. Fard (one of various names he used), who appeared in the black ghettoes of Detroit around 1930 as an itinerant silk peddler. Fard simply disappeared in 1934, but not before he had established in Detroit a temple and a set of teachings, activities, and institutions that also linked Islam with antiwhite sentiment. His place as leader of this nascent movement was taken by Elijah Poole (1897–1975), who as Elijah Muhammad led this Nation of Islam into national prominence as a militant challenge both to white dominance and African American Christianity during the 1960s.

Until his fall from grace in 1964, the most effective spokesman for these "Black Muslims" in the national forum was Malcolm Little (1925–65). In his posthumous *The Autobiography of Malcolm X* (1965), he set forth his own pilgrimage through the worlds of the black ghettoes of the North as well as the message and sources of appeal of the Nation of Islam. Central to the movement was the story of Mr. Yakub, a rebellious scientist among what had originally been a superior black race that had dominated the earth. Through a series of experiments, Yakub created the white race as an inferior but evil enemy of the blacks, who became enslaved through this act of trickery. The future, however, offered a millennial hope in the prediction that this inverted order of things would end soon, the "white devil" would be exterminated, and the black people would return to their original position of authority.

Like many other Black Muslims, Malcolm Little first received this message while serving time in prison. He converted and, after being released, rose rapidly in the Nation's ranks, becoming minister of the #7 Temple in Harlem. The Nation can best be understood as systematically attempting to raise American blacks out of the social and personal disorganization of ghetto life, and to instill instead a collective sense of pride and achievement through a puritanically disciplined lifestyle. This was implemented through a rejection of traditional "soul food" and all stimulants and intoxicants in favor of a nutritious regimen, marital fidelity, collective ownership of a variety of small businesses and farming enterprises, and as thoroughgoing a rejection and avoidance of white society as was possible. The "Fruit of Islam" formed a militant guard for the movement, and Muslims aggressively hawked the newspaper *Muhammad Speaks* on urban street corners during the 1960s. As was the case in many black movements, names were important carriers of meaning: when Malcolm Little joined the Nation, he repudiated his surname, which was seen as a heritage of slavery, and instead adopted an *X,* signifying the traditional identity that had been lost when his ancestors had been forcibly alienated from their African past.

Clearly, the teachings of the Nation of Islam had as little to do with those of the original Muhammad as had those of Noble Drew Ali. A series of events led to a parting of the ways in 1964 between Malcolm X and his former mentor Elijah Muhammad. Malcolm, after a pilgrimage to Mecca, became convinced that traditional Sunni Islam offered a superior religious path based on racial inclusiveness rather than antagonism, and became a convert. In 1965 he was assassinated while speaking in New York City.

The Nation of Islam, however, did not continue indefinitely in the direction of racial separation. When Elijah Muhammad died in 1975, he was succeeded by his son Wallace Deen Muhammad, who rapidly espoused traditional Islam and changed the movement's name to the American Muslim Mission. Now welcoming members of other races, it was recognized by the World Muslim Council and dissociated itself from the nonorthodox teachings and more extreme behavior of Elijah Muhammad's group. The old ways lived on, however, in the splinter movement led by Louis Farrakhan, who as Louis X had succeeded Malcolm X as minister of the Harlem temple in the older Nation. Farrakhan's group, also known as the Nation of Islam, attracted considerable attention during the 1984 presidential campaign through the anti-Semitic pronouncements of its leader, who also endorsed Jesse Jackson's presidential bid.

Farrakhan gained considerable media coverage in 1997 with his "Million Man March" to Washington, D.C., as an affirmation of African American manhood. Farrakhan and Muhammad became reconciled publicly early in 2000, though their movements remained separate. Precise figures are hard to come by but it has been estimated that some two million African Americans had become Muslims of one sort or another by the late 1990s, with the American Muslim Mission accounting for by far the greatest share.

A final group worthy of mention brings this account full circle, with a return both to the West Indies and to Ethiopia as its sources. The Rastafarians attracted considerable attention on the broader American scene during the 1970s and 1980s for their association with a popular West Indian musical form called *reggae* and their ritual use of marijuana. This loosely organized movement originated in Jamaica in the wake of a prophecy of Marcus Garvey that a black king would be crowned in Africa in the near future, which would inaugurate a new era of liberation for blacks. When in 1930 Ras Tafari Makonnen was crowned emperor of Ethiopia and took the name Haile Selassie ("Power of the Holy Trinity"), several Jamaican ministers believed that Garvey's prophecy had been fulfilled, and began spreading the message through the island.

The Rastafarian movement that began to take shape through this preaching saw Selassie as a messiah for black people and a descendant of King Solomon and the queen of Sheba. The movement is thus a variant on Black Judaism; its founders believe that the Hebrews of old were, in fact, black. Although the movement is pacifist, young Jamaicans in America who have selectively adopted aspects of its lifestyle—the wearing of "dreadlocks" (tightly braided hair), the smoking of *ganga* (marijuana), and the reggae music of Bob Marley—have not always kept to the older path, and have brought the group a reputation for violence. In the United States, the Rastafarians have little organization or ideology and exist more as a counterculture than as a religious movement.

Black nationalist movements in twentieth-century America have exhibited a protean character, absorbing and transforming elements from a number of religious, political, and cultural traditions, while adding their own novel myths and symbols to the mix. Like the "invisible institution" of slave religion and later organized forms of black Christianity, they have not been bound by European American traditions; rather, like black musicians, they have improvised themes according to the needs of the hour. Although many have proved ephemeral and some have taken surprisingly traditional new forms, their persistence illustrates the perennially problematic character of the experience of blacks in American society and their attempts to forge religious responses to that experience.

American Judaism

Dr. Isaac Mayer Wise, leader of the Reform Movement in American Judaism (ca. 1890). Photo courtesy of the Jacob Rader Marcus Center of the American Jewish Archives.

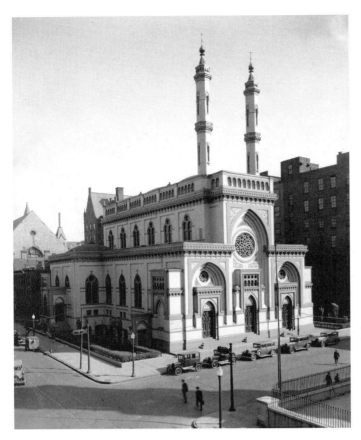

Cincinnati's Plum Street Temple (B'nai Yeshurun), a center for Isaac Mayer Wise's Reform Judaism movement and a fine example of Victorian eclectic synagogue design (1865). Photo courtesy of the Jacob Rader Marcus Center of the American Jewish Archives.

Reading the Torah scroll, circa 1894, at the Eldridge Street Synagogue in New York's Lower East Side, one of dozens in that neighborhood at the flood tide of Jewish immigration. Image courtesy of the Eldridge Street Project, New York City.

Mordecai M. Kaplan, founder of the Reconstructionist movement in American Judaism. Photograph courtesy of The Eisenstein Reconstructionist Archives, Reconstructionist Rabbinical College.

African American Religion

Richard Allen, first bishop of the African Methodist Episcopal Church (ca. 1800).
Print reproduced courtesy of the Mother Bethel AME Church, Philadelphia.

Slave preaching on a cotton plantation near Port Royal, South Carolina. *The Illustrated London News,* 5 December, 1863.

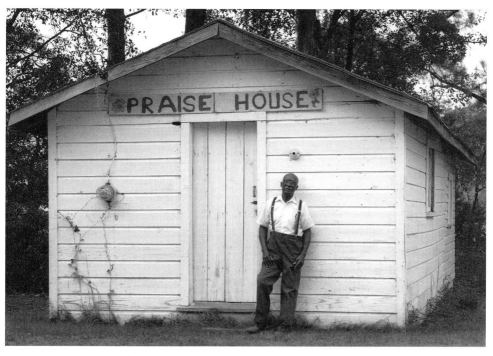

A Gullah "praise house," St. Helena, South Carolina, 1995. Photo by Julia Cart, reproduced with the permission of Julia Cart.

Reverend Major J. Divine was known as Father Divine by his Depression-era followers (ca. 1935). Courtesy of Mrs. M. J. Divine, used with her permission.

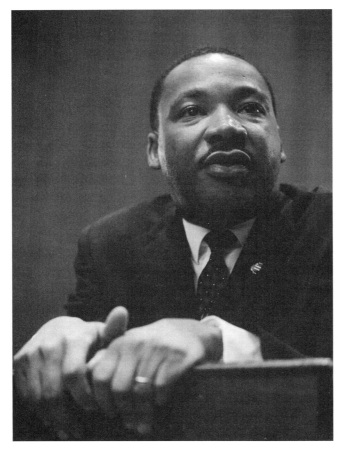

Martin Luther King Jr. combined the rhetoric of African American Christianity with the American "civil religion" to rally Americans of all backgrounds to the Civil Rights Movement (early 1960s). Photo courtesy of the Library of Congress, LC-U9- 11696-9A.

Malcolm X and the Nation of Islam presented a radical counterpoint to Martin Luther King's call to reform (ca. 1960). Photo courtesy of the Library of Congress, LC-USZ62-111167.

Religious Diversity in Contemporary America

The World's Parliament of Religions held in Chicago in 1893 brought together for the first time in the United States representatives of the Hindu, Buddhist, Muslim, and a wide variety of other traditions and introduced them to the American public. Photo courtesy of the Chicago History Museum.

Mother Mosque of America in Cedar Rapids, Iowa, indicates the modest beginnings of American Muslims in the early twentieth century (1934). Photo courtesy of Imam Taha Tawil, Islamic Cultural and Heritage Center, Cedar Rapids.

The Byodo-In Buddhist Temple near Honolulu is modeled on a prototype in Kyoto, Japan. It is situated in the Buddhist section of a cemetery that accommodates Christians and Jews as well (1968). Photo courtesy of John Fischer—About.com Hawaii/South Pacific for Visitors.

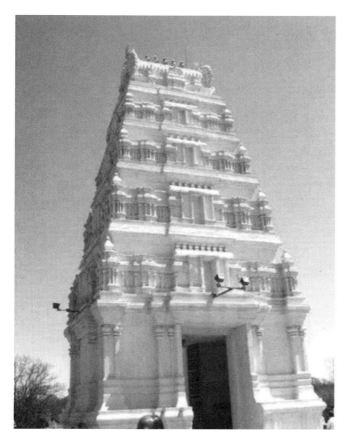

Gate to Hindu Temple of Dayton, Ohio. Hindu temples in contemporary America include shrines to a variety of deities that are worshipped in separate temples across the Indian subcontinent. Photo courtesy of Pandit Ashwani Kumar.

The Mormon Temple and Tabernacle, Temple Square, Salt Lake City, Utah (ca. 1927). The Latter-day Saints devised an entirely new style of architecture to accommodate their distinctive rituals. Photo courtesy of the Denver Public Library.

Health, Wealth, and Metaphysics

One American character trait frequently noted by Alexis de Tocqueville and other observers from abroad has been a propensity to organize into voluntary groups. The prototype for this incessant organization has been as much religious as political. The panoply of denominations that took on a formal, legal structure after the coming of independence pressed religious life into organized form, as did the "Benevolent Empire," that loosely affiliated collection of voluntary societies devoted to advancing the cause of evangelicalism in a country in which religion could not be legally established. Benevolent, fraternal, and reform societies have proliferated ever since. Some, such as the Knights of Columbus, are explicitly religious. Others, such as the Christian Coalition and a variety of antiabortion groups, have strong religious roots, though ostensibly aimed at nonsectarian goals. Still others, such as ecological and animal rights movements, have no specific religious content but are nevertheless based on deeply held moral convictions.

Religious and moral life, in short, do not begin and end with denominational boundaries. Many aspects of religious expression, such as revivalism, cut across organizational lines and emerge as forces of their own, alternately challenging and reinvigorating formal church life. Although a sizeable majority of Americans belong to specific, mutually exclusive denominations, most nevertheless participate in one way or another in religious activities beyond the scope and control of those denominations. This may involve watching "televangelists," reading popular devotional books, or contributing to interdenominational causes. Even Roman Catholics, who prior to Vatican II stood firmly aloof from any religious participation not explicitly authorized by their leadership, now sometimes join with fundamentalists in picketing abortion clinics or films offensive to their sensibilities.

Since the colonial era, however, there have been a number of Americans who have never been comfortable with membership in any formally organized religious body. For them, the religious life is an ongoing quest, and they have often been called "seekers" after the as-yet-undiscovered truth to which this quest will hopefully lead. Much of this questing takes place in their own minds and hearts, through reading and reflection. When the quest goes beyond this to the public forum, such seekers are usually reluctant to enter into any permanent commitments, and are content instead to ally themselves on an ad hoc basis with fellow questers in the continuing pursuit of an elusive answer that lies beyond the boundaries of the visible and tangible. Such seekers also tend, in Robert Ellwood's phrase, to suffer from "status inconsistency"—alienated from or at least not well integrated into the society in which they find themselves forced to function due, for example, to a lack of formal education commensurate with their intellectual abilities. Such people are often *autodidacts*—self-educated—and steer away from the conventional channels of learning and religious expression. By the standards of the dominant society, their philosophical and religious expression often seems highly eccentric. Institutions that arise in the course of their collective pursuit of truth, not surprisingly, are often evanescent, here one day and gone the next.

The organization, beliefs, and symbolism of Judaism and Christianity—the "classic" religions of the West—all express a rootedness in the social and material orders of this world. Belonging to a church or a synagogue usually entails a commitment to a community and an acceptance of the necessity of seeking one's ultimate destiny in the context of a network of social relations and institutions. For Judaism, the family has been an especially potent locus of religious life, and blessedness in the Hebrew scriptures is often expressed in the begetting of an ample posterity. For Christians, the doctrine of the Incarnation is a powerful symbol of the rootedness of humanity in the realm of creation—this world—in which "the Word was made flesh and dwelt among us" (John 1:14). The realms of matter and spirit, in short, are not radically alien from one another but rather intersect.

Although most Americans have been at least informally aligned with some aspect of Christianity or Judaism, there has nevertheless existed from colonial times an alternate tradition that is fundamentally different from these distinctively Western religions. This tradition has manifested itself not usually in formal structures but in a bewildering variety of ever-changing forms at the edges of the mainstream of American religious life, sometimes aligning itself with that mainstream but frequently going its own unobtrusive way at the sidelines.

Several terms can be used to describe aspects of this alternative tradition evocatively. One, popularized by the English novelist Aldous Huxley, is the *philosophia perennis*—the "perennial philosophy" found in the mystical traditions of both East and West. In Asia, Buddhism and Hinduism have been its dominant forms, whereas the Platonic, and especially Neoplatonic, philosophy has been its major Western expression. What these highly diverse traditions share is a repudiation of the Judeo-Christian affirmation that ultimate truth has broken through into the realm of earthly history and can be personally experienced through participation in that history. As its name implies, the "perennial philosophy" rejects the historical realm as transient and illusory, devoid of enduring or ultimately significant reality.

The historian Sydney Ahlstrom coined another term, *harmonialism,* to describe this tradition from a slightly different angle. (Catherine Albanese has more recently employed the phrase "metaphysical religion" to describe a similar range of phenomena.) Harmonialism in its myriad shifting forms is based on the premise that this-worldly phenomena are in correspondence with higher truths in other realms of being, which are the ultimate objects of our ongoing quest. The achievement of this truth is primarily intellectual, though it may be accompanied by the ecstasy of a mystical vision or by very this-worldly benefits, such as physical healing, psychological comfort, or even business success. What is sought after, fundamentally, is a state of harmony with the ultimate principles that underlie the universe. These principles themselves are impersonal but when humans come into contact with them they can activate faculties that have profoundly personal repercussions.

A final relevant term for aspects of this tradition is *occultism.* The term *occult* has not been in favor in recent years, in part because of its similarity to *cult,* and possibly as well because of its somewhat dated flavor. ("New Age" is a good-sounding phrase for much that once passed as occultism.) *Occult* suggests something that is hidden from the common view and needs to be encountered through special investigations if its potential benefits are to be reaped. Any number of activities and movements have been lumped under "occultism"—from dowsing for water to astrology to theosophy to "pyramid power" and healing crystals. Though far removed from Buddhism and Neoplatonism, their role in American religious life nevertheless shares some interesting features with these stately traditions of antiquity.

The America of the Second Great Awakening—roughly the period of 1790 to 1830—was one of extraordinary social and religious effervescence. This was the time of rapid westward movement, and with it a panoply of new religious movements: the Cane Ridge camp meeting, Finney's revivals in upstate New York, the rapid growth of the Shakers and of the Baptist and Methodist movements. In the midst of this ferment, the young Joseph Smith emerged in Palmyra, New York, as a prophet of a new, distinctively American religion. Part of Mormonism's roots lay in the folk magic that Michael Quinn has shown to have been a pervasive part of Joseph Smith's cultural background: divining rods, buried treasure digging, seer stones, and other practices employed for generations by humble people to connect with literal hidden treasures that lay below the earth and which could be enriching when discovered. It was in this context that the angel Moroni's revealing to Smith the location of buried golden tablets and a stone for translating them makes cultural sense.

In addition to this popular tradition of folk magic, however, Smith began to align himself with another source of occult knowledge. Smith founded a Masonic lodge at the Mormon settlement he established at Nauvoo, Illinois, and much of the esoteric symbolism he bestowed on the Nauvoo temple had Masonic origins. Although its social status lapsed considerably in the later twentieth century, Freemasonry was an elite movement in the early days of the Republic and boasted Washington and Franklin among its devotees. (The sun/eye atop the pyramid on the reverse of the dollar bill resonates with Masonic imagery and reflects the ambience out of which the nation's iconography emerged.) American Masonry, which began as early as 1730, traces its origins to the London Grand Lodge, founded in 1717. Early Masonry was a complex mixture of Renaissance occultism, Enlightenment rationalism, and, eventually, American fraternalism, which claimed a direct continuity with the esoteric wisdom of the stonemasons who had built Solomon's temple. In America, it served as a means of creating bonds among the aspiring professional classes dispersed across the country, and only later became associated with processions of miniature dune buggies driven by balding men wearing odd hats.

In addition to the "Burned-Over District" of upstate New York, northern New England, the source of many of these transplanted "Yorkers," also continued to be hospitable to a variety of popular movements with religious implications during this fertile era. Some, like the Free Will Baptists and Universalists, provided liberal alternatives to traditional Calvinism and were explicitly both religious and Christian. Other movements, however, occupied the ill-defined "liminal" (transitional) territory between the sacred and the secular. Though not embodying themselves in any church or theology, they nevertheless offered the promise of a personal wholeness that transcended the body, frequently by promising the attainment of harmony with forces hidden from the ordinary senses.

One current of "harmonialism" during this era that took explicitly religious form came with the popularization in America of the *Arcana Coelestia* and other writings of the Swedish scientist and mystic Emanuel Swedenborg (1688–1772). Swedenborg was a latter-day exponent of the Neoplatonist tradition, which had enjoyed a new popularity during the Renaissance era. At the core of this tradition was the belief that earthly phenomena were not ends in themselves but rather corresponded to higher levels of truth in realms of reality that lay beyond the visible. His ideas were popularized at different levels by Ralph Waldo Emerson, who selected Swedenborg as one of his "representative men," and by Jonathan Chapman ("Johnny Appleseed"), who distributed both fruit trees and esoteric religion as he wandered the frontier. A Swedenborgian Society in America was organized in Baltimore in 1792, and today two different groups sharing the name "Church of the New Jerusalem" maintain the tradition in denominational form.

Another movement that claimed contact with the unseen realms that surround the everyday world was *Spiritualism,* whose chief publicist, Andrew Jackson Davis, was clearly influenced by Swedenborg. The craze for séances and communication with the departed that swept America in the 1840s was precipitated by the Fox sisters, three young women near Rochester, New York, who claimed in 1848 that they had established contact with the ghost of a murdered man who had previously lived in their house. Communication from the beyond took place through clicking noises, which the sisters eventually confessed were created by the cracking of their toe joints. Nevertheless, the will to believe that some people had the power of acting as *mediums*—intermediaries between the living and the dead—easily survived the Fox phenomenon and flourished especially during the Victorian era in many a genteel parlor. Although much Spiritualism today, such as that utilizing the ubiquitous Ouija board, is rather lighthearted in character, dedicated groups such as those loosely allied in the National Spiritualist Association (founded 1893) take the phenomenon very seriously in a religious context.

A related though much less clearly religious popular movement of the day was Mesmerism, named for its originator and popularizer, the Viennese physician Franz Anton Mesmer (1734?-1813). Through the use of magnets and other physical apparatus, Mesmer attempted to cure people of a variety of ailments that had proven insusceptible to more conventional remedies. From his empirical work, Mesmer generalized to a philosophical position that all disease was essentially the same and resulted from the lack of equilibrium of "animal magnetism" in a person's body. His methods aimed at a restoration of this equilibrium through natural means, and achieved a crazelike popularity throughout much of Europe for some time. His followers began to emphasize the trancelike state that was induced as part of this curing process, and "Mesmerism" thus became synonymous with a kind of hypnotism. From France the enthusiasm for this new kind of psychological manipulation spread to America, where it enjoyed a wide popularity beginning in the 1830s. As Robert C. Fuller has argued, this essentially secular cure for human ills laid much of the groundwork for both popular and academic psychology, as well as for any number of later movements based on psychological adjustment.

Following the Civil War, the rapid transformation of America from an agricultural to an urban-industrial society began to take its toll on city- and country-dwellers alike. Those who found themselves falling through the cracks of this nascent new social order often expressed their malaise in psychological and psychosomatic form. A representative work of the era was the pioneering neurologist George Beard's *American Nervousness* of 1881, which popularized the concepts of "neurasthenia" and "nervous exhaustion." Although the seeds of the science and profession of clinical psychology lay in this sort of approach, the decades before World War I were still a time of protean exploration of the implications of these insights.

William James, the Harvard scholar who gained a lasting reputation for his pioneering *Principles of Psychology* (1890), also continued in Emerson's footsteps as a sort of popular sage, and drew from his explorations in both religion and psychology to offer easily accessible wisdom on applying both to everyday life. His *Varieties of Religious Experience* (1902) remains a classic work in the psychology of religion, but it is also eminently readable and down-to-earth in its concern with human needs and suffering. Similarly, a title such as *Talks to Teachers on Psychology: And to Students on Some of Life's Ideals* (1899) indicates James's sense of his role as a moral as well as intellectual guide for his unsettled contemporaries. It is noteworthy that his father, Henry James Sr. was an active Swedenborgian, and his brother Henry attained classic status as the author of psychologically profound fiction.

At another social level, the notion that a profound mental or spiritual reality lay concealed behind the facade of external appearances began to take root in the small towns of northern New England in the practice of one Phineas P. Quimby (1802–66). Quimby, a Maine clockmaker, became impressed with mesmerism and soon took up the practice himself. From here he moved in both theory and practice to a preoccupation with the mental causes of physical disorders and acquired a considerable reputation regionally as a healer. In his manuscripts, which were not published until after his death, Quimby worked on providing his healing practice with a philosophical rationale, namely, that physical disease was caused by mental error—a fundamental misapprehension as to the nature of reality. These ideas finally saw print after being edited by Quimby's disciple and successor, Warren Felt Evans, a Methodist minister turned Swedenborgian.

Phineas Pankhurst Quimby would probably be little more than a footnote in American social history were it not for his influence on one of the most remarkable figures in American religious history, Mary Baker Eddy. Eddy (1821–1910), the founder of Christian Science, has probably evoked more scholarly controversy as to the character and meaning of her career than any American religious figure other than Joseph Smith. The literature on her is extensive, including Mark Twain's satirical *Christian Science* of 1907 (Twain had also ridiculed the Mormons), and Edwin F. Dakin's hostile, muck-raking *Mrs. Eddy: The Biography of a Virginal Mind* (1929), as well as Robert Peel's scholarly and appreciative three-volume study of her life. The divergence that continues in contemporary interpretation can be profitably noted in a comparison of Sydney Ahlstrom's biographical sketch in *Notable American Women* (1971) and Stephen Gottschalk's essay on "Christian Science and Harmonialism" in the *Encyclopedia of the American Religious Experience* (1988). A particularly vexing, ongoing object of dispute is the role Quimby himself played in the development of Eddy's ideas: had Quimby moved beyond pragmatic healing techniques to a religious or at least metaphysical position, or did Eddy build so far beyond Quimby that they taught entirely different systems in their mature phases?

Mary Baker Eddy was raised on a farm near Bow, New Hampshire, in the very heart of the area where popular religious and healing movements had for many years been thriving. Her chronic poor health and nervous disposition were exacerbated by two marital disappointments—one to George Washington Glover, a building contractor who died shortly after their union and was buried with Masonic ceremonies. Her next alliance was with Daniel Patterson, an itinerant and not very reliable dentist who eventually abandoned her and from whom she was ultimately divorced. Physical and mental suffering, emotional disappointment, financial insecurity, and a disorienting series of changes of residence all conspired to make Eddy—the name she acquired upon her third marriage—an archetypal seeker after the relief and sense of personal wholeness that her native Congregationalism did not provide for her.

The rural and small-town culture of Eddy's New England exposed her over the years to the whole panoply of popular movements to which the region played host: Spiritualism, mesmerism, hydropathy (the "water cure"), and the like. None of these provided her with any significant relief until her path crossed that of the itinerant Quimby, now resident in Portland, Maine, in 1862. Quimby's "science of health" provided her with just what she needed in both theory and practice, and her own health and spirits improved rapidly and markedly. It was not until shortly after Quimby's death early in 1866, though, that Eddy underwent her ultimately decisive experience. After being immobilized for several days following a fall on the ice, and possibly in danger of death, she was suddenly cured after reading Matthew 9:2—in which Jesus heals a paralytic—and, "on the third day," arose from her bed.

This combination of physical healing and religious conversion galvanized this woman who had been approaching a condition of helpless invalidism into a veritable dynamo of activity. Success, however, did not come easily. The next decade she spent peripatetically changing residences, drifting through what Sydney Ahlstrom has described as a nearly irrecoverable subculture of New England boardinghouses where popular movements proliferated and where the spiritually displaced continually and, with uncertain success, desperately sought relief. It was among and for just such a clientele that Mary Baker Eddy appeared as the prophet of a new, uniquely urban religion, which paradoxically had its roots in the religious culture of a vanishing hinterland. Like her New England–born contemporary, Dwight L. Moody, she "discovered"—in her own word—a new approach to the spiritual life that met the needs of countless like-minded among the spiritually and socially dislocated.

Christian Science, which continues to this day in substantially the same form Eddy gave to it, consists of an idea—or set of ideas, a method, and an organization. The core idea is expounded in Eddy's central work, *Science and Health with Key to the Scriptures* (1875, and many subsequent, revised editions). Her basic idea is central to all monistic systems of metaphysics: that physical matter is illusory and unreal. All that is real is Spirit, and salvation—or healing—lies in the realization of this truth and the working out of its full range of implications and applications. Disease, sin, and death are ultimately illusory, and will vanish once the individual has assimilated this truth completely.

Eddy and her followers have always insisted on the *Christian* character of Christian Science, although she would have been the first to admit, even insist, that only she has been able to provide Christian revelation with an authoritative interpretation. She thus enjoys a status in some ways similar to that of Joseph Smith among Mormons, as an inspired vehicle through which the fullness of revelation is now made accessible to all. Christian Science is of divine origin, and Eddy declared it to be a dimension of the Second Coming of Jesus. The *Key to the Scriptures,* included in later editions of *Science and Health,* offers an exegesis of Genesis and Revelation along Swedenborgian lines, and is based on the premise that the Bible cannot be understood without a specially revealed key to its interpretation according to its "spiritual" sense.

The last portion of *Science and Health,* titled "Fruitage," consists entirely of a distinctive aspect of Christian Science practice: testimonials to physical and psychological healings. Christian Science has always focused on healing as central to its message and has rigorously forbidden its followers to employ conventional medical techniques in seeking healing. (This has over the years led to many lawsuits, especially concerning medical emergencies involving children. On the other hand, Sydney Ahlstrom, not the most sympathetic of Eddy's interpreters, has observed that her greatest service was keeping people away from the many grotesquely incompetent doctors of her day.) Early in the movement's development, the title "pastor" was dropped in favor of "practitioner," emphasizing the practical focus of the church. In addition to practitioners, who devote their full time to healing ministries, the church licenses teachers and readers. A pair of the latter, usually a man and a woman, are assigned to each church and read alternatively at Sunday services from the Bible and *Science and Health.* On Wednesdays, testimonial meetings on healings effected by Christian Science are also held.

The thought and practice of Christian Science are supported by an organization—the Church of Christ, Scientist—which was given definitive shape by Eddy herself, the movement's "Discoverer and Founder." After various attempts at teaching her ideas in Lynn, Massachusetts, she began to give the movement formal structure, and the Church of Christ, Scientist, was chartered by the state in 1879. Two years later, while still in Lynn, she also obtained a charter for the Massachusetts Metaphysical College. Following a series of bitter controversies with her disciples, which characterized much of her later career, she moved her establishment to Boston, which has remained the world headquarters of the Christian Science movement.

The mature Eddy unquestionably exerted a charismatic influence on her followers, but one which in the longer run could produce both intense loyalty and equally intense revulsion. She became convinced that her third husband, Asa Eddy, with whom she had enjoyed a happy relationship, had died not of the heart ailment attested to in an autopsy but rather as the result of "mental assassination" brought about by her jealous former disciples exerting "Malicious Animal Magnetism" on him. "M.A.M.," a term drawing on the vocabulary of mesmerism, later became an integral part of Christian Science teaching. Quarrels and even lawsuits involving former disciples were frequent in her later days, most of which were spent withdrawn from the public, and many branches of the "New Thought" movement had their origins in these rifts.

Despite continual leakage to incipient rival movements, Christian Science grew rapidly under Eddy's autocratic but compelling leadership, with twenty churches, ninety societies, 250 practitioners, and thirty-three teaching centers around the country by 1890, and a membership of about 85,000 in 1906. (The church does not release membership statistics, but U.S. membership in the early twenty-first century appears to be in the low six figures.) In 1886 the National Christian Science Association was founded, and then reorganized in 1889 to provide even firmer centralized control. The Church of Christ, Scientist, as it is now known, is governed by a self-perpetuating board of directors originally appointed by Eddy herself, which took charge of the church's affairs after her death. The Mother Church, which forms the core of a headquarters complex near Copley Square in Boston, consists of two parts:

an older, rather intimate Romanesque church (1895) and the grand neoclassical "Extension" (1906), which takes its place with such nearby public structures as Trinity and New Old South churches and McKim, Mead and White's grand public library. A more recent high-rise office structure and reflecting pool by I. M. Pei (1968–73) extend the monumentality into a later twentieth-century idiom and provide a physical plant for a cluster of church-sponsored activities, such as the publication of the well-regarded *Christian Science Monitor,* a genuinely national newspaper.

The impressive scope of the appeal of both Christian Science and its New Thought competitors—many of them also led by women—on first a local and then a national scale was hardly accidental. Christian Science to this day remains among the foremost of America's religious communities in terms of per capita wealth, as well as in the female and urban character of its constituency. A unique Christian Science institution is the "Reading Room," usually found in downtown shopping districts or suburban malls. Clean and well-lighted if somewhat austere, it offers passersby an opportunity to sit down and examine a variety of the church's literature. The interaction here is impersonal, between the drop-in patron and the printed word.

Christian Science from the beginning shared the urban propriety and impersonality that these reading rooms perpetuate. The reverse side of Eddy's intense and problematic relationship with many of her early disciples was her later withdrawal into seclusion, regulating the church from a distance but avoiding personal interaction with its adherents. Although Christian Science churches today—many of them designed on the monumental scale of the Mother Church—resemble other Christian denominations in holding regular worship services, they differ from most in their lack of communal activity, except for education programs. Christian Science as a group has been largely apolitical, has little involvement in philanthropic work, and lacks a sense of community, even at the local level. The emphasis is very much on the well-being of individuals, who are left to seek social life and community involvement on their own if they care to.

This individualistic emphasis has from the beginning marked both the breadth and the limitations of the appeal of the movement. Eddy's message had its greatest impact especially on Victorian women who were of or at the margins of the middle classes and were unsure of their role in a rapidly urbanizing society. As Donald Meyer has argued, Christian Science, as exemplified in the career of Eddy herself, represented a way for women to come to terms with the sense of powerlessness and futility many of them experienced, and frequently to set themselves up as allies, or rivals, of Eddy in spreading this new message of personal wholeness. This emphasis on female empowerment is especially well illustrated in Eddy's use of the term "Our Father-Mother God, all harmonious," in her paraphrase of the Lord's Prayer in *Science and Health,* and in the near-divine status accorded her by her followers. Her own prodigious success as a religious founder and organizer indicates that she especially was a woman of enormous talent that could not find profitable outlet in conventional Victorian channels. This is not to detract from what may have been the authentic healing power of Christian Science, especially on the "neurasthenics" diagnosed by Dr. Beard as the typical American invalids of their day, but rather to set the appeal of a radically new religious movement in the context of its time.

Christian Science remains unique in the American "harmonial" tradition in its strict and effective organization, its exclusive claims to truth, and its insistence on its explicitly Christian character. The impulses its founder drew together clearly came from a variety of sources and, in turn, almost immediately began to diffuse in many new directions. Religious healing took a number of forms, ranging from pentecostalism, which grew out of a very different strain of popular religion, to the Emmanuel movement, which emerged at the turn of the century in Boston among Episcopal clergy who collaborated with local physicians in their therapeutic and counseling endeavors. By the 1920s, courses in pastoral counseling with strong psychological components began to be added to the curricula of many seminaries as well.

A very different current in American religious life also found itself at home in the Victorian parlor and lecture hall, as did early Christian Science, and similarly drew on imagery of the attunement of the individual to impersonal metaphysical currents that lay behind the veil of the everyday world. The archetypal representative of Victorian occultism was Helena Petrovna Blavatsky (1831–91), a Russian émigrée and spiritualist who formed a liaison with her longtime collaborator, Henry S. Olcott, in New York in the 1870s. Theosophy (that is, divine wisdom), as explicated in such writings of Blavatsky as *Isis Unveiled* (1877) and *The Secret Doctrine* (1888), began as an exposition of the Western *philosophia perennis,* but began to look increasingly to Asia as Blavatsky traveled extensively in India, seeking contact with Hindu and Buddhist teachers. In its later versions, Blavatsky's teaching was based on the premise that all reality is ultimately one and grounded in Consciousness, and that individual souls must be successively reincarnated through long cosmic cycles to approach their ultimate source. She claimed to have received her teachings through mysteriously appearing letters from "masters" or "mahatmas" who had attained high stages of enlightenment, which not surprisingly gave rise to charges of fraud and plagiarism.

After Blavatsky's death in 1891, the Theosophical Society split into rival fragments under the leadership of Annie Besant, Blavatsky's chosen successor, who established a headquarters in India, and William Q. Judge, who founded a separate group. The movement continues to have a few thousand adherents in America, but the loose organization of theosophy has never conduced to precise record keeping. A wide variety of other groups are also part of the American scene. Perhaps the best known are the Rosicrucians, who advertise widely in the popular press under the initials AMORC (Ancient and Mystical Order of the Rosae Crucis ["rosy cross"]). This group, founded in 1915, maintains a complex that occupies an entire block in a residential neighborhood of San Jose, California. Its exotic and impressive Egyptian museum points up its claims to continue the ancient esoteric wisdom of that tradition. All such groups appeal more to a sense of individual study and development than to any group participation, and their sense of community tends to be rather abstract.

If charismatic faith healing and occultism represent two dimensions of harmonialism taken to their extremes, New Thought is much more clearly related to Christian Science and what one might identify as the "center" of the tradition. *New Thought* is a generic term that emerged in the 1890s for a series of loosely related groups and movements that developed in the wake of the success of Christian Science, often as split-offs from the latter following quarrels between Eddy and such disciples as Augusta Stetson, Emma Curtiss Hopkins, and Ursula Gestefeld. Unlike Eddy, these and a seeming myriad of other New Thought leaders have seldom been preoccupied with power and structure, but have attracted a fluid constituency that is not often interested in long-term institutional commitments, and instead finds nurture within a whole continuum of teachings. Like Christian Science, most branches of New Thought teach that ultimate reality is singular, impersonal, and spiritual, and that human ills can be eliminated by a proper alignment of the individual consciousness with the vaster metaphysical reality of which it partakes. However, most followers of New Thought do not argue very strenuously for the Christian character of their movement; if they do, it is to claim that Christian symbols can be interpreted in a way compatible with broader cosmic truth.

One of the most successful manifestations of New Thought, and one that is also most explicitly Christian in its self-description, is the Unity School of Christianity. "Unity," as it is usually known, was founded by Charles and Myrtle Fillmore in 1889 in Kansas City. The Fillmores were typical Victorian-era "seekers," who experimented with Christian Science, theosophy, Rosicrucianism, Spiritualism, and Eastern religions before lighting on a metaphysical mixture that cured them of their various ills, including financial. Unity, which combines an emphasis on Jesus as the Christ with a belief in reincarnation, maintains some three hundred centers across the country. Although Unity sponsors such traditional religious activity as preaching and baptism, its central work is conducted at long distance from Unity Village in Missouri, which receives hundreds of thousands of phone calls and letters annually requesting counsel and spiritual aid. Its message is also disseminated widely through books and radio and television programs.

In addition to Unity, New Thought is today represented by a probably uncountable number of groups that share the sorts of principles that resulted in the founding of the International New Thought Alliance in 1915. New Thought groups are widely distributed over the entire United States and beyond, having spread originally from New England to Chicago and other parts of the Midwest and rapidly to California, whose protean and optimistic culture continues to encourage nontraditional religious and philosophical movements. Some of these, like Annie Rix Militz's "Home of Truth," counted numerous branches in their heyday but eventually declined as their offshoots took on an independent character. Much of the ongoing New Thought impulse today has been incorporated into the similarly named "New Age" movement (discussed at greater length in chapter 55), which incorporates in the loosest possible fashion enthusiasts for, for example: channeling (long-dead individuals using those alive today as "channels" for communication), astrology, healing crystals, tarot cards and palmistry, meditation, near-death experiences, reincarnation, ecological mysticism, radical feminism, acupuncture, yoga, UFO cults, and so on ad infinitum. Instead of the church or even the parlor or lecture hall, however, the shopping mall chain book outlet has become the principal link of distribution for New Age matter, which includes cassettes and videotapes as well as paperbound books.

A final offshoot of the harmonial impulse worth noting is the cult of self-help, which has taken both secular and religious forms in its distinctive twentieth-century career. Related to such other American enthusiasms as "do-it-yourself"—a motto appropriate for New Age phenomena as well—self-help emerged as a very this-worldly, individualistic strain of New Thought preoccupations in its belief that individuals can overcome their difficulties and achieve material success and physical and emotional health simply by thinking correctly. Emile Coué attracted wide audiences in the 1920s with his verbal formula, "Day by day, in every way, I am getting better and better," and Dale Carnegie's best-selling *How to Win Friends and Influence People* (1936) gave the notion that success was the direct result of positive thinking and self-projection, one of its classic expressions.

"Positive thinking" began to be expressed in more religious terms as well, beginning in the success-oriented climate of the 1920s when postwar "normalcy," a bustling economy, and the influx of country folk to the grand cities of speakeasies and Art Deco skyscrapers promised fulfillment and gratification beyond one's wildest imaginings. Bruce Barton, a partner in the Batten, Barton, Durstine and Osborne advertising agency, brought the spirit of that brand-new marketing enterprise to bear on Christianity. His widely circulated *The Man Nobody Knows* (1925) presented Jesus as the ultimate go-getter, putting together a highly effective team of promoters of his message from a selection of rather ordinary locals.

The ultimate correlation of religious belief and personal confidence leading to this-worldly success, of course, is that formulated by Norman Vincent Peale in his best-selling *The Power of Positive Thinking* (1952) and other, similar works. Peale had been a Methodist before becoming associated with the Reformed Church of America, the more liberal branch of the Dutch Reformed tradition in this country, through his call to Manhattan's Marble Collegiate Church in 1932—a position he held until his retirement in 1984. Peale's message, which has been widely disseminated first through the printed word in various forms and more recently through audio/video materials, involves a kind of autosuggestion verging on self-hypnosis, whereby the subject acquires increasing self-confidence through repetition of affirming messages. As in Christian Science, testimonials also play a major part in Peale's literature; here, however, they are more likely to attest to business success than to physical healing.

Although Peale's career continued past his formal retirement, his clear successor in the field was another Dutch Reformed pastor, Robert Schuller of Garden Grove, California. (Schuller retired in favor of his son, Robert A. Schuller, in 2006.) Schuller early demonstrated his adaptability to changing social circumstances by preaching from the top of a drive-in theater's refreshment stand to a congregation who remained in the parking lot in their cars. The rapid success of his message, which is based on the idea of "possibility thinking," is manifest in his colossal "Crystal Cathedral," an ultramodern church on a gigantic scale designed by the prominent architect Philip Johnson. Completed in 1980 at a cost of $16,500,000, it stands on the site of the original drive-in complex—a mile or so from Disneyland in Anaheim—and transmits services to those in their cars as well. The cathedral's plant also includes a bookstore, which features success-inspiring materials in a variety of genres and media, as well as a thirteen-story Tower of Hope office building. Schuller has been best known to most Americans, though, through televised services as exuberant as those of his fundamentalist "televangelist" counterparts though far more decorous in style. Although Schuller has remained within the Reformed tradition, he has been criticized by fellow evangelicals for downplaying a traditional concern with sin and forgiveness in favor of a very this-worldly optimism—a trend on the rise within the early twenty-first-century megachurch movement more broadly.

Clearly, the differences that separate Christian Science, New Thought, the loose cluster of "New Age" enthusiasms, and Schuller's "possibility thinking" are significant. However, all of these movements share certain themes. None places a great deal of emphasis either on formal worship or on a sense of religious community. Each focuses instead on realizing the possibilities inherent in each individual, which have thus far been repressed through inadequate knowledge and negative thoughts. That individual realization, moreover, tends to manifest itself in very this-worldly forms, sometimes stressing physical health, at other times psychological integration or material success. Donald Meyer has argued that underlying these emphases and attitudes is a strategy for adapting to the exigencies of twentieth-century American life, in which success is achieved through acceptance of and conformity with the dominant social and economic system. Once one has aligned with this system correctly, the system then promises a never-ending supply of material and emotional abundance. Although it is dangerous to affirm too uncritically any explanation that reduces religious experience to something else, the propensity of these movements toward either an apolitical or a conservative stance toward the social and economic orders lends plausibility to Meyer's observation—as do a few moments spent in one's living room in the company of the Reverends Schuller or Peale.

PART V

THE TWENTIETH CENTURY AND BEYOND: FURTHER ENCOUNTERS WITH MODERNITY AND PLURALISM

It is tempting to characterize every era of American history as one of rapid social and cultural change, but the decades following World War I seem particularly worthy of this description. With the 1920 census, demographers declared that the United States had become a nation with an urban majority. The dislocations brought about by World War I and the disillusionment with internationalist idealism that followed brought about a new sophistication and skepticism among some, and a strong reaction among others who feared the worst. The polarization within the Protestant community between modernist and fundamentalist had become unbridgeable, and the Scopes "Monkey" Trial of 1925 seemed to vindicate the former. A Protestant "mainline," theologically moderate and socially cautious, enjoyed an ascendancy that would remain unchallenged until the turmoil of the 1960s and 1970s.

The Depression and World War II brought with them further shocks to middle-class complacency. Franklin Roosevelt's New Deal not only challenged the economic assumptions to which nineteenth-century evangelicalism had given divine legitimation but also worked to include Catholics and Jews in its inner councils. World War II also brought with it a knowledge of radical evil that took the faces of Auschwitz, Dresden, and Hiroshima. "After such knowledge," T. S. Eliot asked, "what forgiveness?"

The trauma of the war rapidly receded in the face of postwar economic recovery, accompanied by a flight of returned GIs to both the suburbs and college. Roman Catholics especially enjoyed new access to the delights of middle-class life, and the election of one of their number to the American presidency in 1960 confirmed this acceptance. "Religion in general," as it was sometimes called, spread like wildfire during the 1950s, and Billy Graham and Bishop Sheen both demonstrated the expanded variety of forms it could take in polite company. Both of these media celebrities were united as well in their militant opposition to Communism, which served as a symbol of cosmic evil for that generation.

The 1960s began on an upbeat note with the style of the Kennedys and the music of the Beatles promising a more lively cultural mixture in an era where youth seemed destined to dominate. Instead came violent death—for John and Robert Kennedy, Martin Luther King Jr., John Lennon, and tens of thousands of young Americans who found themselves entrapped in a hopeless war whose misery was relieved only by "dope." Before his death, though, King helped mobilize the anger and determination of millions of black Americans and their white allies to bring about an irreversible upheaval in the nation's social arrangements regarding race.

The promise of the Civil Rights Movement triggered other drives toward liberation—among women, Hispanics, and gays. Their militancy soon generated a reaction among many who feared that the newly "permissive" attitudes the nation seemed to be taking toward sexual behavior and sex roles especially would rapidly undermine the moral fabric of the Republic. Jimmy Carter, America's first self-described "born again" president, symbolized the enfranchisement of evangelicals; his subsequent defeat by Ronald Reagan, however, indicated that their religiosity came freighted with conservative social values. The nation seemingly remained polarized between an increasingly secular and pluralist professional culture and an emergent middle class that yearned to return to what it remembered as the old ways. By the early twenty-first century, neither seemed to have won a decisive victory.

The last third of the twentieth century was also characterized by massive demographic changes. The suburbs had displaced the city as the preferred and actual place of residence for most middle-class Americans, with a new polarization of residence patterns brought about no longer by law but by ability to pay. The inner cities now were inhabited mainly by minority communities, including many descendants of African Americans who had earlier abandoned the Deep South for the lure of formal freedom and often illusive opportunity, as well as more recently arrived Mexicans and other Hispanics and refugees from southeast Asia. More prosperous immigrants, such as professionals from south Asia, headed directly for the suburbs, where Hindu temples and Islamic centers conspicuously began to alter the symbolic landscape. America, as always, was still in process, and its religious configuration in process with it.

The beginnings of the twenty-first century saw a simultaneous continuation of this process of expanding pluralism balanced by a trend towards retrenchment into tribalism. The Religious Right, which had begun to coalesce in the 1970s, continued to be a potent force in an ongoing set of "culture wars" for control of American opinion and public policy, as well as a potent force instrumental in the election of George W. Bush as president in 2000 and his reelection four years later. The impact of the September 2001 attacks on the Twin Towers of the World Trade Center and on the Pentagon resulted in a heightened sense of American vulnerability to militancy from developing nations, and a suspicion of anything Middle Eastern was an immediate result. The American incursion into Iraq in 2003 was justified in the traditional language of "American exceptionalism," the idea that the United States is providentially destined and guided in an ongoing campaign, in Woodrow Wilson's phrase, "to make the world safe for democracy." To what degree these ideological forces would succeed in reshaping the nation according to the programs of early Puritan and evangelical campaigns for social hegemony remained unresolved towards the end of the first decade of the new century.

CHAPTER 42

Neo-Orthodoxy and Ecumenism: The Foundations of "Mainline" Protestantism

The trauma of the fundamentalist reaction to the rapidly entrenching liberal movement in Protestantism in the early twentieth century put an end to what remained of the "Evangelical United Front" of nineteenth-century America. The Scopes "Monkey" Trial of 1925, though hardly resolving the legal questions raised by state laws constricting the teaching of contemporary science in public classrooms, dramatically illustrated the social and cultural rift that divided "cosmopolitan" from "provincial" America and that often was characterized by religious issues as its symbolic currency. Until the subsequent cultural trauma of the 1970s, American Protestants divided into a dominant cluster of denominations, united by shared premises about religion and culture and by a recognized social status, and an opposition forced into the status of a resistance movement by its defeat on the battlegrounds both of the mass media and of the denominations themselves.

The "princes of the pulpit" of Victorian America—Henry Ward Beecher, Phillips Brooks, and their contemporaries—had laid the foundations for a "mainline" Protestantism that emerged triumphant in the fundamentalist-modernist controversy of the 1920s and persisted in its essentials for the next four decades as the arbiter of American religious life. Its constituency came primarily from native-born Protestants of northwestern European descent, who tended to be middle to upper middle class in social status. Its organizational expression subsisted in seven denominations, or denominational clusters, which were more united than divided in their interpretations of a common Reformation heritage.

Of these groupings, Congregationalists, Episcopalians, and Presbyterians—the colonial "establishment"—were the most prestigious and influential. (This prestige they shared regionally with the theologically unorthodox Unitarians in the Boston area and the Friends in Philadelphia, although defections from both to the Episcopal Church were not uncommon.) Outside the Northeast, mainline status was also characteristic of four other denominations of humbler origins, whose constituents had frequently acquired middle-class or even higher status in the smaller cities and towns of the South, the Midwest, and the Far West: Methodists, Baptists (Northern or American), Lutherans, and Disciples of Christ.

Establishment Protestantism defined itself against several other clusters of socioreligious groups. Closest to them in religious and ethnic background were the conservative Protestants who controlled individual churches in the urban North but who were achieving far greater cultural influence in the South. Presbyterians and Methodists, together with a remnant of Episcopalians, still provided much southern leadership, but their affiliation was with the more conservative southern branches of those denominations. Southern Baptists were slowly gaining strength, together with the Churches of Christ and a variety of holiness and pentecostal groups. In many cases, though, the latter cluster still could be characterized as "churches of the disinherited." (It is not accidental that H. Richard Niebuhr's influential *Social Sources of Denominationalism*, which popularized the latter phrase, was first published in 1929.)

Sharing a common theological heritage with the southern white Protestants but sharply differentiated by the "color line" were the black churches—Baptist, Methodist, and "sanctified"—which exercised little influence outside their own constituencies. Black preachers, like Catholic priests, did serve as mediators with the external community, and the prestige of secular black cultural forms—especially jazz—was clearly on the rise by the 1920s. It would be several more decades, however, before blacks began slowly to gain entrance into the "establishment"—which, by the 1970s, had itself changed significantly in its character.

The third "out group" against which establishment Protestantism could be defined consisted of Catholics, Jews, and other non-Protestants. The ranks of these "outsiders" had swollen to what many felt were alarming proportions through the "new immigration" of the decades that bracketed the turn of the century. These ethnic groups were a much more serious challenge to the "East Coast Establishment"—as it would come to be known in later years—in a variety of ways. Catholics, especially those of Irish descent, were quick to develop their legendary political skills, and by the 1880s had begun to control political machines in a number of cities. Catholic episcopal and clerical leadership was also eager to influence public policy, especially in the realm of morals, and often attempted to regulate film content, the sale of contraceptives, and the like, though frequently in collaboration with more conservative mainline Protestants.

Jews were too few in number to attain much political influence except locally, as in parts of New York City and environs. However, the eagerness with which Jewish immigrants and their offspring pursued higher education began to put some stress on what for the older stock had become a comfortable system. As Jews gained the financial and educational credentials that would seemingly qualify them for entrée into a strictly meritocratic social order, they began to discover that the American system was not based so strictly on the merit of achievement. Beginning in the late nineteenth century, Jews began to be turned away from country clubs, resort hotels, and other institutions that—as women in the later twentieth century have discovered—serve covert economic as well as overt social and recreational functions. In particular, Ivy League and similarly prestigious colleges began to enforce unannounced quotas on admission of otherwise qualified applicants to preserve a high percentage of WASP enrollment. (An acronym for white Anglo-Saxon protestant, WASP has of late become something of an ethnic slur, much like its coarser counterpart, "redneck.")

Genteelly in the North and more overtly and even violently in the South, Protestants moved to ensure their traditional role as molders and protectors of society. Covert anti-Semitism and anti-Catholicism in the Northeast was counterpointed by the rise of the Ku Klux Klan in the 1920s, led now by the lower fringes of the southern middle classes. In addition to its traditional role, fashioned after the Civil War, of keeping blacks "in their place," the resurgent Klan turned its attention to harassing both native-born and immigrant Catholics and Jews as well as "damyankees" interfering in regional affairs. The Klan's influence also extended well into the North, especially southern-oriented Indiana, where it was a dominant force in state politics during much of the decade. The drastic restriction of immigration by Congress during the 1920s was a legislative manifestation of the same nativist impulse that seized much of the country and contributed substantially to the defeat of Irish Catholic Al Smith in the 1928 presidential election.

It would be a mistake, however, to equate mainline Protestantism, even during these turbulent decades, with political reaction and social bigotry. The Social Gospel had its origins within this same social and religious milieu, and exerted a powerful progressive influence in the decades prior to World War I and after its "decline and revival" in the 1920s and 1930s described by historian Paul Carter. Franklin Delano Roosevelt, for example, was the quintessential patrician of Dutch descent and Episcopal affiliation. Roosevelt came into power in the midst of a profound economic crisis that called the conventional wisdom of the "establishment" into radical question, and with the support of a coalition of Catholic, Jewish, black, and other minority voters. His New Deal, which in many ways applied Social Gospel principles to the secular realm, was supported by many Catholic and Jewish intellectuals as harmonious with their own social ethics.

It was in part the crisis of the Depression that brought about a major shift in the theological underpinnings of establishment Protestantism during the 1930s. Both liberalism and its close relative, the Social Gospel, could not weather the challenges of World War I and then the Depression without some serious adjustments to their optimistic appraisal of the human condition and the possibilities of indefinite social progress. In addition, the very accommodation with the secular culture that had been a leading characteristic of the liberal movement was now working against its success, as the 1920s witnessed a flourishing of mass-media entertainments and diversions that no longer needed the legitimation that the clergy had been willing to provide it. Babe Ruth, Charles Lindbergh, and Rudolph Valentino drove the likes of both Harry Emerson Fosdick and Billy Sunday from center stage; it took a media spectacle as grand as the Scopes "Monkey" Trial to recapture for religion the spotlight even momentarily—and under the most doubtful of circumstances. In Robert Handy's words, the era from 1925 to 1935 underwent a "religious depression" from which Americans were jarred loose only by a social crisis of the first magnitude.

By 1935 even Harry Emerson Fosdick, who had championed the liberal cause against the fundamentalist challenge so eloquently a decade before, was now moved to ask in a widely distributed sermon whether it was not now necessary for Protestants to move "Beyond Modernism." What lay beyond modernism was a powerful new theological movement whose name, Neo-Orthodoxy, suggested its content and its method—a tension between the traditional and the modern held together in a dialectical interaction.

Neo-Orthodoxy, which might equally well have been called "neo-liberalism" and which was never so much a formal school as it was a climate of theological opinion, had its most immediate origins in continental Europe in the wake of the devastation of World War I. Its first major spokesman was the Swiss Reformed thinker Karl Barth (1886–1968), whose multivolume *Church Dogmatics* has provided countless seminary students with a challenge comparable to that posed by one of Barth's major sources, John Calvin's *Institutes*. Barth first captured the attention of his contemporaries with his *Römerbrief* of 1918—published in English in 1932 as *The Epistle to the Romans*. In this and subsequent works, Barth rejected the conclusions to which German-language New Testament scholarship had been pointing. This tendency continually to refashion Jesus according to the wants and needs of the present day was extensively described by Albert Schweitzer in his classic *The Quest of the Historical Jesus* (1906). Sydney Ahlstrom, echoing the English modernist George Tyrrell, characterized Schweitzer as having "found the scholars peering down the 2,000–year-long shaft of history and seeing their own bourgeois faces reflected from the bottom of the well." For Barth and his followers, the task instead was to rediscover "the strange world of the Bible," where the earliest Christians saw the world through eschatological categories far different from the optimistic assumptions of modern science and liberal theology.

The orthodoxy that was now being cast into new forms consisted for the most part of the ideas and writings of several of the classic figures of the Protestant traditions and their antecedents. Prominent among these were Augustine, Luther, Calvin, and the nineteenth-century Danish theologian Søren Kierkegaard (1813–55). Kierkegaard's copious writings, such as *Fear and Trembling* (1843), began to be available through the English translations of Walter Lowrie beginning in 1939. His "dialectical" thought was intended to transcend metaphysics, doctrine, and the cultural captivity of much of European church life, and to focus instead on the immediacy of the encounter of the individual with God—in a state of "fear and trembling." This existentialist motif became widely influential in Christian, Jewish, and secular philosophy in the twentieth century, and many of Kierkegaard's themes were taken up in Paul Tillich's (1886–1965) influential *The Courage to Be* (1952), *Dynamics of Faith* (1957), and other widely read works.

Unlike Tillich, though, Barth drew very directly on the Reformed (Calvinist) tradition for his most direct inspiration. Central to his thought were two complementary emphases developed first by Augustine and then again by Luther and Calvin: the potency of original sin and the absolute sovereignty of God. For Barth, the realms of the human and the divine were utterly incommensurable, and came together only at the "tangent point" of the Incarnation, which made salvation possible. Despite Barth's heavy stress on human sinfulness and its consequences, however, he departed from his austere mentors in his rejection of predestination and his optimism about the ultimate salvation of all of humanity.

The forbidding character of much of Barth's writing precluded the widespread readership that his sometimes-friend, sometimes-antagonist Paul Tillich was to receive. (*Time* magazine's promotion of Tillich and other theologians helped make his work known, if not always understood, among a broader audience than most religious thinkers have enjoyed in recent times.) Many of Barth's ideas became influential in America as they resonated in the work of a remarkable pair of brothers, Reinhold (1892–1971) and H. Richard Niebuhr (1894–1962). The two were sons of a German Evangelical pastor in St. Louis, where they attended Eden Theological Seminary—now under the aegis of the United Church of Christ—after which they proceeded to earn doctorates at Yale. Reinhold began his career as a pastor—in what was then the Evangelical and Reformed Church—in 1920s Detroit, where he had a chance to observe firsthand the inequities of the social order as manifested especially in race and labor relations. His early *Leaves from the Notebook of a Tamed Cynic* (1929) consists primarily of very personal theological reflections on these experiences, and reflects a combination of Barthian "theology of crisis" with a political critique of the American social and economic order that bordered on the radical.

After thirteen years in the parish, Reinhold followed the academic path already chosen by his brother and began a long professorship in social ethics at the inter-denominational Union Theological Seminary in New York City (where Paul Tillich also taught for a number of years before leaving for the University of Chicago and then Harvard). With Union as a base, Niebuhr rapidly gained national prominence as an "applied ethicist," leveling a profound criticism of American institutions in particular from his theological roots in the American Social Gospel and Euro-pean Neo-Orthodoxy. Two of the most influential of his extensive works are the two-volume *The Nature and Destiny of Man* (1941–43), a systematic exposition of his theological position, and *Moral Man and Immoral Society* (1932), in which he explored the premise that human groups, such as nations, pursue an ethic based primarily on self-preservation, with little of the altruism found in at least occasional doses in individual consciences. Niebuhr was also instrumental in the founding of the magazine *Christianity and Crisis* (1941–93), which brought to bear a somewhat sterner theological perspective on world events than in the long-established, more liberal, and at the time pacifist *Christian Century*. (The latter, still widely influential journal dates its present existence from its purchase in 1908 by Charles Clayton Mor-rison, a Disciples of Christ minister in Chicago. Its title is reflective of the optimism about the possibilities of Christian influence in the world that prevailed in liberal circles of the time.)

H. Richard Niebuhr spent over thirty years of his career teaching ethics, theology, and church history at Yale Divinity School. Sometimes characterized as a "theologian's theologian," H. Richard received less public attention than his more prolific brother but arguably had an even greater long-range impact in academic circles. His earli-est work, *The Social Sources of Denominationalism* (1929), has already been cited as a pathbreaking analysis of American religious groupings in terms not of theology but rather such sociological categories as social class, race, region, and ethnicity. Al-though taken largely for granted by later generations of scholars, Niebuhr's perspec-tive was at the time radical, and drew on the thought of such German sociologists of religion as Max Weber and Ernst Troeltsch as well as that of Karl Marx. *The Social Sources* was hardly a bloodless social-scientific exercise; instead, Niebuhr went well beyond the academic to level a scathing attack on American Christianity for what he bluntly called in his first chapter "the ethical failure of the divided church."

In his later work, Niebuhr refined his perspective into one more appreciative of the richness of the American theological tradition, as in *The Kingdom of God in America* (1937). In this work, Niebuhr attuned himself with the movement underway among Harvard's literary historians, especially Perry Miller, to rehabilitate the reputation of the New England Puritans. The latter worthies, especially the more conspicuous Cotton Mather and Jonathan Edwards, had received rough going in the 1920s from the likes of journalist H. L. Mencken and the historian Vernon Louis Parrington, who had caricatured them as antidemocratic bigots more like repressive spokesmen for Victorian evangelicalism than their true selves. (Puritan studies flourished so abundantly during the next several decades that by 1970 one historian had observed that we then knew more about seventeenth-century Massachusetts than any sane person would want to.) Niebuhr's later works, such as *Radical Monotheism and Western Culture* (1960) and *The Responsible Self* (1963), were intended primarily for academic audiences and helped shape the "contextual ethics" later developed by, for example, James Gustafson. No other Neo-Orthodox thinkers became nearly as widely known or influential as the Niebuhrs, but the primary emphases of the loosely constituted movement remained highly influential in many seminaries and pulpits until at least the 1960s.

Neo-Orthodoxy even became popular for a time in political circles, with prominent Kennedy-era figures such as George Kennan and Arthur M. Schlesinger Jr. declaring their indebtedness to Reinhold Niebuhr's thought. The association of Presidents Nixon, Carter, Reagan, and the Bushes with various aspects of evangelicalism, however, displaced what influence Neo-Orthodoxy might have exerted in these quarters. In the seminaries, the "liberation theologies" of blacks, feminists, and third-world advocates, as well as newly influential work of Roman Catholic and evangelical thinkers, displaced the prominence of the older line of thought.

Still, the impact of Neo-Orthodoxy is hardly finished. Its staying power, if only in residual form, has subsisted in part in its refusal to reject the methods and findings of contemporary biblical criticism, as did its fundamentalist contemporaries, but rather to rescue those findings from what both groups concurred were the excessive conclusions drawn from them by earlier liberals. Another major strength of the movement has been its sense of critical relativism. The doctrine of the sovereignty of God set limits on human possibilities, both moral and intellectual, thereby precluding an overly easy identification of any creed, theology, or political position with the divine will. Reinhold Niebuhr expressed this stance memorably in *The Irony of American History* (1952), in which he argued that America's grand designs to lead the world have been repeatedly undermined by its inability to foresee the often ironically destructive consequences of its prideful actions. (A flurry on renewed interest in this aspect of Niebuhr's thought was occasioned by the seeming repetition of the errors of Vietnam in the 2003 American invasion of Iraq.) On the one hand, this caution restricted the movement's influence; on the other, it shielded it from the faddish impermanence that befell the "Death of God" and "Situation Ethics" movements of the 1960s.

The theological basis of much of mainline Protestantism from the 1920s through the 1960s consisted of a mixture of themes from liberalism, the Social Gospel, and the variations and critiques of these movements that Neo-Orthodoxy embodied. Many clergy were trained and much theological scholarship produced during these years not only in denominational seminaries but in interdenominational divinity schools such as Harvard, Yale, Union (New York), and the University of Chicago. By the 1960s, consortia of theological schools began to develop in major academic centers such as Boston, New York, Atlanta, Chicago, and Berkeley, in which the seminaries of several traditions, including Roman Catholic, combined—often around the nucleus of a major university or interdenominational theological school—to share academic resources. In these ventures is manifest another major aspect of mainline religious life: ecumenism.

Ecumenism is derived from the Greek *oikoumene,* that is, the whole inhabited world. The term *ecumenical* received widespread circulation during the 1960s, when the "ecumenical council" meeting at Rome—Vatican II—gave rise to "ecumenical discussions" between Roman Catholics and representatives of other religious traditions. The council also fostered a broader "spirit of ecumenism" aimed at promoting interfaith understanding, cooperation, and even possible reunion among the "separated brethren." In the sense of common action or merger between similar Christian groups, though, ecumenism has been a particularly potent force in twentieth-century mainline Protestant life and thought.

The need for an ecumenical movement within the Protestant community can ultimately be traced to the fragmentation of the churches during the Reformation era, but is rooted more particularly in the distinctively American phenomenon of *denominationalism.* Again, as H. Richard Niebuhr demonstrated so memorably, the divisions within American Protestantism have had as much to do with social factors such as race, region, ethnicity, and social class as with ostensible differences over belief, worship, and polity. Polity, however, has played a role in that churches without a strong, centralized governance structure—Baptists, Campbellites, Lutherans—have been particularly subject to schism over various issues.

Although the frontier era was a time of fierce competition for the allegiance of the unchurched, it also promoted cooperation, as in the interrelated agencies of the "Benevolent Empire." The Plan of Union of 1801, in which Congregationalists and Presbyterians agreed to avoid duplication of effort in newly settled territory, was another major indication of the bonds that held the evangelical denominations together. Issues of race and region, however, brought about long-lasting rents within the Presbyterian, Methodist, and Baptist communities—which, in the latter case, have not and are not likely to heal. Immigration patterns also worked against unity among the Lutherans, who created a bewildering plethora of synods based on various combinations of doctrine, ethnicity, and geography. Among Congregationalists, issues of doctrine combined with cultural and social issues to produce the Unitarian controversy and the split-off of the latter community in 1825. Only the Episcopalians emerged from the century relatively unscathed, with a brief regional division during the Civil War and a small-scale schism in 1873, which gave rise to the Reformed Episcopal Church.

If the nineteenth century was characterized by division, the twentieth has witnessed much healing. At the most liberal end of the spectrum, the Unitarians and

Universalists overcame a diversity of origins based primarily on social class to form the Unitarian-Universalist Association in 1961. The Unitarians' onetime conservative adversaries, the Congregationalists, had also grown considerably more liberal over the years. In 1931, they united with the Christian Churches, a restorationist group related to the Campbell-Stone movement, to form the Congregational Christian Churches. Parallel to this union of English-speaking churches was the uniting of the (German) Reformed Church with the German Evangelical Synod of North America—itself the product of earlier mergers—into the Evangelical and Reformed Church (1934). Finally, these two church unions combined in 1957 to form today's United Church of Christ. (A smaller number of Congregational churches rejected the merger and remain independent.)

Methodists and Presbyterians both moved to repair the breaches that had involved other issues but were precipitated by the issue of the morality of slaveholding. In 1939, the Methodist Episcopal Church, the Methodist Episcopal Church, South, and the Methodist Protestant Church, the heir of an 1830 division over the role of laity, combined to form the Methodist Church. In 1968, this amalgamated body joined with the Evangelical United Brethren, which itself was the result of two earlier mergers (1922 and 1946) of several pietist groups of German background. Until eclipsed in recent decades by the Southern Baptists, the resultant United Methodist Church was for a time America's largest single Protestant denomination. Similarly, the northern and southern branches of the Presbyterian Church merged in 1984 to form the Presbyterian Church in the United States of America (PCUSA). Like the Methodists, the northern branch (UPCUSA) has been the result of several earlier mergers, which included the absorption of the Welsh Calvinistic Methodists in 1920.

The final series of mergers worth mentioning in this connection is that which led to the creation of the Evangelical Lutheran Church in America (ELCA) in 1988. Nineteenth-century Lutherans had been divided into dozens of distinct groupings based primarily on the arrival at various times and in various parts of the country—primarily Pennsylvania, Ohio, and the upper Midwest—of separate migrations of Germans and Scandinavians. By the early 1960s, two principal mergers had taken place to form the American Lutheran Church (ALC, primarily midwestern) and the Lutheran Church in America (LCA, more eastern). In 1976, a liberal spin-off from the very conservative Missouri Synod gave rise to the Association of Evangelical Lutheran Churches (AELC), which considered itself a holding operation, maintaining a temporarily distinct identity while awaiting, and helping to precipitate, a merger with the two larger merged groups. As the names of these more recent groups indicate—the ALC and LCA, for instance, could scarcely be differentiated simply by name—the older sources of disunity had vanished in the wake of Americanization, and ecumenicity finally triumphed over residual particularism.

A final aspect of the ecumenical movement that deserves mention is the emergence of cooperative associations that have worked to transcend denominational differences in the interests of enhanced mutual understanding and cooperative endeavors. The "Benevolent Empire," the Plan of Union, and the broader-based American Evangelical Alliance of the nineteenth century all provided precedents for these endeavors. The immediate stimulus to a genuinely national association of churches came from the Social Gospel movement, and resulted in the creation of the Federal Council of Churches of Christ in America (FCC) in 1908. This new alliance, which included thirty-three denominations as members, immediately turned its attention to such contemporary social issues as the Bethlehem steel strike of 1910, on which it issued a caustic report. The FCC was absorbed in 1950 into the newly created National Council of Churches of Christ in the U.S.A. (NCC), with offices at 475 Riverside Drive (the "God Box") in New York City. The NCC includes as members the mainline Protestant denominations, the major black Baptist and Methodist churches, most of the Eastern Orthodox churches, and a few smaller groups such as the Church of the Brethren. Its work focuses on areas of interdenominational cooperation such as evangelism, education, and ecumenism; because of its frequent championing of controversial political movements as well as its liberal theological foundations, its work has frequently come under fire from conservatives within and outside its member churches, with the Eastern Orthodox particularly unhappy participants.

Another source of interfaith cooperation at a still broader level was the missionary movement, which from the days of the Benevolent Empire had been a major concern of American Protestants. The Student Volunteer Movement for Foreign Missions had been organized in 1886 by America's most distinguished organizer of mission work, John R. Mott, at a conference convened by Dwight L. Moody. Together with representatives of the Young Men's Christian Association (YMCA)—another evangelical vehicle whose constituency transcended denominational lines—and of several northern European countries, Mott helped organize the World Student Christian Federation (WSCF) in 1895 at a meeting in Sweden. This new group took as its goal and slogan "the evangelization of the world in our generation," reflecting an optimism still possible among evangelicals and liberals alike in the calm before World War I. Mott was also involved in the first world missionary conference held at Edinburgh, Scotland—an impetus that gave rise eleven years later to the International Missionary Council (IMC).

The IMC was one of the component organizations that would eventually combine to form the most global expression of Christian unity yet devised: the World Council of Churches (WCC), which was formally established in 1948 in Amsterdam. The WCC's other major sources were two international Christian movements that had both originated in the early twentieth century for parallel reasons. The Life and Work movement focused on applied social ethics in a turbulent world, and had its first conference at Stockholm in 1925. Similarly, Faith and Order—concerned with the theological and political grounds of Christian cooperation—first met in 1927 in Lausanne, Switzerland, with representatives of 108 churches in attendance. Both of these movements continued to sponsor international conferences after they had become absorbed into what was in considerable part their own creation, the WCC.

The World Council of Churches in the early twenty-first century consisted of some 350 participating churches from one hundred different countries. The members span the Protestant spectrum and also include many of the Eastern Orthodox communions. Prior to Vatican II, the Roman Catholic Church refused to take part in the activities of the WCC and its constituents. Though it has never formally joined, it now sends observers to WCC events and has created a permanent structure for dialogue. In addition, bilateral ecumenical dialogues between Roman Catholic theologians and representatives of many other major Christian traditions—especially Anglican and Eastern Orthodox—have become ongoing affairs, with a considerable degree of agreement already attained on key matters of belief (though not polity). In recent years, the issue of the ordination of women has put a particular strain on Anglican-Roman dialogue.

Interfaith dialogue among the Eastern Orthodox, Roman Catholic, and mainline Protestant groups now is a commonplace of American religious life. (Fundamentalists and some evangelicals, however, keep their distance.) Similarly, a considerable degree of reunion has taken place within the major denominational clusters with the exception of the Baptists, who remain divided among the conservative Southern Baptist Convention, the mainline American Baptist Churches, the black National Baptist groups, and a plethora of smaller churches. On the other hand, even liberal and mainline Protestants have balked at the prospect of actual organic union with groups outside their own "families" whenever such proposals seem to become actual possibilities. This ambivalence was dramatically illustrated in the 1997 vote by ELCA Lutherans to approve full communion with three denominations of Reformed origin: PCUSA Presbyterians, the United Church of Christ, and the [Dutch] Reformed Church in America. Simultaneously, the same assembly narrowly defeated a "Concordat of Agreement" that would have opened the way for a full recognition and exchange of ministries with the Episcopal Church. This motion, which had already been overwhelmingly adopted by Episcopalians and would later be approved in 1999 by the ELCA after minor revision, was opposed particularly by Lutherans of Scandinavian descent in the upper Midwest, who were suspicious of the implications of the concordat's recognition of the apostolic succession of bishops inherent in the Anglican tradition, and the need for subsequent Lutheran bishops to receive episcopal consecration.

The most ambitious ecumenical scheme of recent times has been the Churches Uniting in Christ—formerly the Consultation on Church Union (COCU)—launched by Presbyterian leader Eugene Carson Blake in 1960, though it has largely remained in the realm of good wishes. Conceived as a plan for the close association, if not actual merger, of the principal mainline and black Methodist denominations, it continues to hold periodic meetings, but does not give promise of very concrete results in the foreseeable future. At the core of each major tradition seems to lie a conservatism that balks at its uniqueness becoming submerged in a broader synthesis. Perhaps Andrew Greeley was right in his hypothesis that denominational allegiance has replaced ethnic identity for many Americans, and that the need for some such particularistic identification remains unshakable—at least for those for whom mainline Protestantism has become a way of life.

CHAPTER 43

"Mainline" Protestantism in the Later Twentieth Century

Although the term *mainline* as applied to Protestantism is hardly a technical term, the phrase still evokes a constellation of religious ideas, institutions, and movements specific enough to be very useful as an informal description. The following are some of the more important constituents of that constellation:

1. The seven denominational clusters: American Baptist, Congregational (UCC), Disciples, Episcopal, Lutheran, Methodist, Presbyterian
2. Social status of membership based in the middle and upper classes, implying a relatively high degree of income, education, prestige, and influence in the community
3. Membership primarily of northwestern European ancestry, especially British, Dutch, German, and Scandinavian
4. National or at least interregional geographical distribution
5. Worship varying in its degree of formality but conducted in English, decorous in its avoidance of public displays of emotion, and sharing a common heritage of music and hymnody as well as architectural styles
6. Use of a variety of biblical translations, such as the *Revised* and *New Revised Standard Version* (1946, 1952, 1989), reflecting ecumenical scholarship
7. Theology, reflected in preaching, strongly influenced by the liberal, Social Gospel, and Neo-Orthodox movements
8. Inclusivity with regard to theological, social, and political opinions among clergy and membership, with the balance differing somewhat from group to group (for example, there is considerable evangelical sentiment among Presbyterians, Methodists, and Baptists, but little within the UCC)
9. Employment of an often-complex denominational structure for the coordination of periodical and book publishing, the production and distribu-

tion of Christian education curricula and materials, missionary work and evangelism, political lobbying, and other activities

10. Patronage, especially by the clergy, of nondenominational journals such as the *Christian Century* and the now-defunct *Christianity and Crisis*

11. Frequent reliance on interdenominational divinity schools as well as denominational seminaries for clerical education

12. Receptiveness to ecumenical activity, ranging from community worship services on special occasions to participation in the National Council of Churches to organic mergers within the same tradition

13. A relatively low sense of denominational commitment among many constituents, who are willing to change affiliations according to local circumstances

14. Involvement in social issues regarded as having moral dimensions, ranging historically from Prohibition to gay rights

15. Reliance primarily on public or secular private education, with religious instruction provided through active Sunday school programs

16. More broadly, an acceptance of and support for the American government and social order until the multiple crises of the 1960s

17. Growing out of this, a participation in the cluster of patriotic activities and attitudes sometimes known as the "Civil Religion"—again, prior to its challenge by the Vietnam War and subsequent crises

18. Eventual receptiveness to the inclusion of minority groups and the ordintion of women

19. Openness, if sometimes cautious, to new ideas in the scientific, social, and ethical realms

20. A tension between a tendency to accept American society and culture as given and good—to be "at ease in Zion"—with a prophetic mandate for active engagement in social change and reform

The 1960s were a major turning point for the fortunes of these churches. At the seminaries and among the denominational bureaucracies and leadership, strong support emerged for the social movements of the era—civil rights, protest against the war in Vietnam, and acceptance of and access by women, gays, and other minorities to full opportunity in church and secular life. The ordination of women and, still more controversially, of gays became divisive in some denominations. As the nation grew weary of turmoil and a more conservative mood began to prevail in the 1970s, however, discontent among the rank-and-file occupiers of local pews began to manifest itself in a variety of ways. Pressure from the grassroots to slow down or halt the rapid changes of the previous decade began to be felt at higher levels of governance. More dramatically, membership began to decline conspicuously.

As Wade Clark Roof and William McKinney point out in their important sociological study, *American Mainline Religion* (1987), this decline had a number of facets besides a widespread and growing social conservatism represented most conspicuously at the national level in the persona of Ronald Reagan. One important demographic factor was the declining birthrate among mainline members, with a resultant increase in the average age of their membership, which by the first decade of the twenty-first century was approaching sixty in many denominations. This decline in family size correlates with high levels of income and education, and has affected Jews even more dramatically than mainline Protestants.

The other major external sources of attrition lie in the two broad religious constellations flanking the mainline on either side of the ideological spectrum. On the one side, evangelical, pentecostal, and other conservative churches began to experience extremely high growth rates, drawing in part on alienated mainliners for recruits as well as enjoying a high birth rate among their membership. Whereas the mainline had once benefited from the appeal of its churches as badges of upward mobility, the new respectability of the conservative Protestant spectrum, as well as reduced social pressure for religious belonging as a prerequisite for community (though not necessarily political) acceptability, now undercut this (perhaps doubtful) advantage. On the other side, mainline socialization of the young had not proven strong enough to resist the pull of secularity, or the attraction of a "do-it-yourself" spiritual life offered by "New Age" religiosity. Although the pattern of the return to church life by youthful dropouts once they themselves had become parents continued, it was not strong enough to counteract the corrosive effects of these other trends. Table 1 demonstrates this pattern concretely.

All this is not to say that any of these denominations were in danger of dying out. With the exception of the Disciples of Christ, which by the early twenty-first century had sunk below seven hundred thousand members, each still maintained a membership ranging from one to eight and a half million, which are hardly paltry figures. However, all remain concerned both with their losses in numbers as well as with the diminished influence on national social issues that this decline portended.

So far we have been speaking of the mainline churches in collective terms. Un-

Table 1. Mainline denominational membership, 1960 versus 2005–6 (in descending order, rounded off to the nearest thousand)

	1960	2005 or 2006
United Methodist	10,641,000	7,995,000
ELCA Lutheran	N/A	4,774,000
Presbyterian USA	4,161,000*	3,026,000
Episcopal	3,269,000	2,155,000
American Baptist	1,521,000	1,371,000
United Church of Christ	2,241,000	1,218,000
Disciples of Christ	1,801,000	698,000

*Northern and southern branches combined, prior to 1984 reunion.

derneath these useful generalizations, however, are a collection of highly particular religious communities, each with its own history, character, polity, membership, and characteristic emphases. Rather than write their collective obituary, it seems more appropriate to provide some sense of their still-vital individual stories. There are a number of plausible ways of grouping them—Roof and McKinney, for example, divide them into "liberal" (Episcopal, Presbyterian, UCC) and "moderate" (American Baptist, Disciples, Lutheran, Methodist). The following sequence is based instead on liturgy and polity, beginning with the "liturgical churches"—Lutheran and Episcopal—which have as much in common in many ways with Roman Catholics as with fellow Protestants; continuing with the Methodists and Presbyterians, which have rather complex polities but less elaborate liturgies; and ending with those with the least complicated structures—Congregationalists, American Baptists, and Disciples.

Where nineteenth-century Lutheranism in America had been characterized by fragmentation, the twentieth century was marked by movement toward a unity eased by the ongoing process of Americanization. The first major intra-Lutheran union was the creation of the United Lutheran Church in America through the 1918 merger of the two major "Eastern" groups, the General Synod and the General Council, with the United Synod of the South, which had split from the General Synod in 1862 over sectional issues. This new denomination was among the most eastern-based and liberally inclined of the Lutheran denominations. It entered into a further merger in 1962 with the Augustana Lutheran Church (Swedish, 1860), the Suomi Synod (Finnish, 1890), and the American Evangelical Lutheran Church (Danish, various origins) to form the Lutheran Church in America (LCA), which later became one of the major components of the still more comprehensive union of the late 1980s.

The second major coalescence of Lutheran synods took place in the formation of the American Lutheran Church (ALC) in 1960. This merger consisted primarily of midwestern synods of a variety of ethnic backgrounds: an earlier (1930) group of the same name, that had united the Buffalo, Ohio, and Iowa synods, all primarily German; the Evangelical Lutheran Church (Norwegian, 1917); the United Evangelical Lutheran Church (Danish, 1896); and, in 1963, the Lutheran Free Church (Danish, 1897). Most of these participating groups were the results of earlier mergers as well. The ALC traditionally had a primarily midwestern constituency, with only a limited geographical overlap with the somewhat more liberal LCA.

Whereas the LCA and ALC stood for comprehensiveness, the third major Lutheran "family" of the twentieth century represented an unyielding firmness. The Missouri Synod had always stood for an uncompromising position on doctrine and practice, and some hints at a softening were dissipated with the ascendancy of J. A. O. Preus to its presidency in 1969. The Missouri Synod had never officially followed other Lutheran groups, especially the ULC/LCA, in accepting modern approaches to biblical interpretation, and this long-standing issue came to a head in the early 1970s at Concordia Seminary in St. Louis. Concordia was the premier seminary of the synod, and its faculty were considerably more open in their approach to theology and biblical studies than the denominational leadership—a situation not without parallel in other traditions. When the two parties were unable to agree on a solution, a large majority of the faculty left to found Christ Seminary, or "Seminex" ("Seminary in Exile"), which found a temporary home at nearby Jesuit-run St. Louis University. This move precipitated the formation of a temporary denomination, the Association of Evangelical Lutheran Churches, in 1976. The AELC drew its support primarily from dissidents on both coasts and from the synod's nongeographical but largely midwestern English District.

The AELC was never intended as a permanent denominational structure, and it rapidly took the initiative in bringing about discussions with the two other comprehensive and moderate American Lutheran groups. To the surprise of many, these discussions proved successful: they resulted in the formation of a new church including all three of these parties, known as the Evangelical Lutheran Church in America (ELCA). Final ratification of the merger took place at simultaneous meetings of the three groups in Chicago, Milwaukee, and Minneapolis—an indication of the geographical focus of their constituents—and went into effect on 1 January 1988. The extraordinary organizational complexity of American Lutheran denominational history thus was reduced to a remarkable simplicity by the late twentieth century, with the ELCA, the Missouri Synod, and the smaller and very conservative Wisconsin Evangelical Lutheran Synod accounting for all but about one hundred thousand Lutherans in America—that is, roughly 99 percent.

The increasing comprehensiveness and ecumenicity of the groups that now constitute the ELCA is indicative of a broader change in attitudes among many American Lutherans, especially their clergy. Historically, the close relationship between church and state in the German princedoms and Scandinavian countries where the Lutheran Church had been established militated against extensive or critical involvement in the social order, and Luther himself supported the German princes strenuously against challenges to their legitimacy. In America, linguistic and geographical factors, together with the task of ministering to a large immigrant population, reinforced a predisposition among many of the later immigrants in particular to distance themselves from political and social affairs. (No Lutheran has ever been elected president of the United States.) The movement toward social involvement had its earlier leadership in the eastern wing, where the evangelical drive toward social reform found a friendly audience among Schmucker and his followers. It was in this camp that first abolitionism and then temperance found Lutheran support, and also where Lutheran women first took an active role in social causes.

During the twentieth century, Lutherans divided over Prohibition, which ran against their traditional folkways in its inclusion of beer and wine among forbidden beverages. The impact of the world wars and the Civil Rights Movement, however, combined with the growing acculturation of all Lutheran groups, led to a greater receptivity to involvement in social causes, although by no means all AELC Lutherans could be classified as liberal or activist in their stance toward society. A major sign of change was the decision of both the ALC and the LCA in 1970 to ordain women, a constituency that still lacked even a vote in Missouri Synod congregational affairs until about the same time. The differences between the AELC and the Missouri Synod, in short, reflected broader divisions in American Protestantism in the later twentieth century. Despite some measure of inter-Lutheran cooperation, as in the development of a common *Book of Worship* in 1978, that division gave no signs of ending.

In worship, Lutherans have in recent years tended to identify themselves strongly with the other "liturgical churches" in their adherence to an elaborate, formal, traditional liturgy. Many congregations, accustomed for long to a simpler, more Protestant style of worship, have been reluctant to carry out the liturgy of the *Book of Worship* in its fullness. Hymnody and music more broadly are a strong component of worship, reflecting the heritage of Bach and Handel. With Episcopalians and Roman Catholics, Lutherans—even the tradition-minded Missouri Synod—have been in the forefront of architectural innovation. Here a major influence has been the work of the outstanding Minnesota-based architect and writer E. A. Sövik, who has advocated a discarding of the traditional longitudinal church shape in favor of an arrangement in which the altar table is located centrally among the congregation.

Lutheran verbal culture has been dominated by religious writing; it is difficult to identify an American Lutheran literary tradition other than that represented in regional writings of the upper Midwest from Ole Rölvaag's *Giants in the Earth* to Garrison Keillor's *Lake Woebegon Days*. (The latter author, who eventually became a Lutheran himself for a time, acquired a considerable following beginning in the 1980s through his humorously sympathetic depiction of Lutheran and Catholic church life in an imaginary small town in Minnesota on his PBS radio program, *A Prairie Home Companion*.) Although the Lutheran theological tradition in Europe has produced some of the intellectual giants of modern Christianity, including Søren Kierkegaard, Albrecht Ritschl, Adolf Harnack, and Dietrich Bonhoeffer, American Lutheran thought has been concentrated more on historical work, as manifest in the studies of Arthur Carl Piepkorn, Martin E. Marty, and Jaroslav Pelikan (who in retirement converted to Russian Orthodoxy). Lutheran theologians such as Yale's George Lindbeck, however, have made major contributions to the ecumenical movement.

In demographic terms, Lutheran population continued to grow following the diminution of immigration after World War I, but primarily now through natural increase. Lutherans remain primarily of German or Scandinavian descent, and membership is predominantly by birth or marriage rather than conversion. The upper Midwest remains a Lutheran stronghold, with other pockets of influence stemming from colonial roots in New York and Pennsylvania, the Carolina Piedmont, and later settlements in the Pacific Northwest and parts of Texas and southern California. Lutherans have traditionally been weakest in the Deep South and the Rocky Mountains. A sociological study conducted by Carl Reuss in 1980 indicated that Lutherans tended to be neither rich nor poor, to live in small cities or rural areas in the Midwest, and not to be involved in community activities other than those involving church, school, or service groups. Although their educational and income levels tend to be higher than average, their influence is predominantly local, and disproportionately few live near centers of financial and political power.

By the time of the merger of three major Lutheran groups in the late 1980s, the membership of the respective constituencies was approximately the following: ALC, 2,330,000; AELC, 110,000; and LCA, 2,900,000; for a total of about 5,340,000. In addition, the Missouri Synod claimed approximately 2,630,000 members; the Wisconsin Evangelical Synod, another conservative group, had about 410,000; and several small groups continued to exist autonomously. By the late 1980s, then, combined Lutheran membership was in the vicinity of eight and a half million; by the end of the twentieth century, this figure had dropped by about three hundred thousand.

The twentieth century was largely a quiet one for the Episcopal Church until the controversies of the 1960s and 1970s rendered it a major storm center. Denominational stances on public issues during the first half of the twentieth century were generally moderate, reflecting a constituency that was Anglophiliac (for example, firmly committed to the British cause in World War I) and moderately Republican in its social and political outlook. (Franklin and Eleanor Roosevelt, however, provided an alternative model of the Episcopalian in public life during the 1930s and beyond.) Rapid growth, similar to that of the other mainline denominations, prevailed after World War II, but by the 1960s the denomination's association with upper-middle-class gentility began to undergo some major shocks. The church had already begun to take antisegregation measures during the 1950s, including moving the 1957 General Convention from Houston to Honolulu when the former city could not provide interracial accommodations. The most controversial action, however, was the 1967 General Convention's voting of three million dollars for minority "empowerment," which in the context of antiwar and other liberal denominational positions led to considerable discontent and at times abrupt and dramatic declines in diocesan financial support. The falling-off of membership that subsequently began to afflict the Episcopal Church, like other mainline denominations, almost certainly reflected the distance between the political and social stances of the denominational leadership and the sentiments of the grass roots.

The issues that were most troubling to Episcopalians in the later twentieth century, however, were internal questions about the ministry and the liturgy. With respect to gender as a qualification, pressures from the rapidly developing feminist movement militated toward a thorough reconsideration of the role of women in the church. The 1967 General Convention first authorized women to serve as deputies in succeeding conventions. The real turning point came in 1974 and 1975, when several groups of women were irregularly ordained, in some cases by retired bishops. Although these actions incurred the censure of the House of Bishops, the momentum for women's ordination had reached a point of irresistibility, and it was approved finally by the 1976 General Convention assembled in Minneapolis. However, an "escape clause" was included that recognized the rights of individual bishops to refuse to ordain women on grounds of conscience—a right to dissent exercised by, among others, Presiding Bishop John M. Allin of Mississippi. Although women have since entered the priesthood in considerable numbers, they have frequently encountered the usual problems faced by female clergy of most denominations: reluctance of congregations to call them as rectors and subsequent relegation to functioning as institutional chaplains and other roles lacking in full clerical authority. In 2005, there were 4607 women ordained to the Episcopal priesthood, though a considerable number were not engaged in full-time parish work. About 29 percent of Episcopal parish clergy were female in the first decade of the twenty-first century.

The General Convention meeting in Detroit in 1988 anticipated that a woman would almost certainly be elected a bishop in the near future, and again provided an "escape clause" whereby congregations unwilling to accept the episcopal authority of a woman could import a male bishop on occasions such as confirmation when a bishop was required. The situation of women as clergy and bishops was further complicated by the reluctance—overcome in 1992—of the Church of England to take similar steps, in part out of fear of endangering ecumenical conversations with Rome, and also in response to resistance in other parts of the Anglican Communion, especially in developing nations, to women clergy on cultural grounds. Despite these various sources of opposition, however, the Diocese of Massachusetts elected Barbara C. Harris, a black woman priest from Philadelphia, as suffragan (assistant) bishop on 24 September 1988, and she was subsequently consecrated on 11 February 1989. Her election touched off rumbles throughout not only the Episcopal Church but the entire Anglican world over the question of women and the apostolic succession. By 2005 there were twelve female bishops.

One other blistering question echoed throughout the 1970s and 1980s, and together with the ordination of women led to vocal dissent, desertion from the ranks of the faithful, and even schism. Anglicans have periodically followed a variety of quests for spiritual fulfillment, including the "Renewal," or charismatic, movement of the 1960s. More dramatic were the bizarre ventures into spiritualism that led to the death in the Israeli desert of former Los Angeles bishop James A. Pike (1913–69), who had earlier been censured by his fellow bishops for his radical theological views. The traditional focus of Anglican piety, however, has been the public liturgy according to the rituals of the *Book of Common Prayer*. In 1967 the General Convention in Seattle authorized a reappraisal of the 1928 edition, which had preserved much of the language of versions dating back to the time of Cranmer. Various trial services were utilized during the 1970s, and a thoroughly revised version was adopted by convention in 1979. Traditionalists, who saw the older *Prayer Book*'s sixteenth-century language as a great source of comfort and beauty, were outraged, and a society for a return to the older ways was organized to carry on a campaign to allow at least alternative use of the 1928 version, which can no longer be used officially in its entirety except with special episcopal permission.

In addition to protest, disgruntlement, and estrangement leading to withdrawal from active participation in church life, the twin innovations of women's ordination and *Prayer Book* revision helped precipitate what had previously been a rarity in the Episcopal Church, schism. The brief life of the Protestant Episcopal Church in the Confederate States of America during the Civil War years had no permanent institutional impact, and the only overt break in church ranks that had taken place prior to the 1960s had been the formation of the Reformed Episcopal Church by discontented evangelicals in 1873. (This group continues to exist with a rather small constituency of about eleven thousand members and 142 congregations in 2003.) The fallout of the "hot" issues of the 1960s and 1970s, however, led to the proliferation of a whole new set of traditionalist groups, including the Anglican Orthodox Church (1963), the American Episcopal Church (1968), the Old Episcopal Church (1972), the Anglican Episcopal Church of North America (1972), and the Anglican Church in North America (1977), which later became the Anglican Catholic Church. The relationships among these, which include schisms within schisms, are too complex to describe, but are typical of dissident movements without strong centralized control. Sewanee historian Don S. Armentrout, the leading student of these movements, estimated in 1986 that the groups formed after 1976 (the year in which the General Convention authorized women's ordination and gave preliminary approval to the revised *Prayer Book*) had a combined membership of about fifteen thousand, while those formed earlier had roughly the same number of adherents. The most severe losses to the Episcopal Church, though, have almost certainly come through a quiet dropping out into the realm of secularity rather than through losses to schismatic groups or other denominations.

More recently, one of the thorniest problems for many denominations, including Episcopalians, has been the ordination of homosexuals. New York bishop Paul Moore Jr.—whose own bisexuality came to light posthumously in 2008—created a stir when he ordained an overt lesbian in 1977, but a subsequent motion of censure in the House of Bishops failed. In reaction, the General Convention of 1979 went on record against the ordination of practicing homosexuals and any others whose sexual relationships were carried out beyond traditional marital bonds, although it did allow for the ordination of celibate homosexuals. Subsequently, a number of bishops, including New Jersey's controversial John Spong, ordained openly gay candidates; one bishop, in fact, was formally charged with heresy but was acquitted.

The issue of gay clergy reached flashpoint in 2003 when Gene Robinson, who was openly living with a male partner, was elected the ninth bishop of the diocese of New Hampshire. Since his election had taken place within 120 days of the Episcopal

Church's General Convention, meeting that summer in Minneapolis, it came before the House of Bishops and, after considerable controversy, was ratified by a 62–45 vote of that body.

Opposition to Robinson's consecration was led by groups such as the American Anglican Council, founded in 1996, and by the Network of Anglican Communion Dioceses and Parishes, led by Pittsburgh bishop Robert Duncan, which pursued strategies for remaining within the Worldwide Anglican Communion while distancing themselves institutionally from the Episcopal Church. In 2008 the diocese of San Joaquin voted to leave the Episcopal church, and others, including Duncan's, seemed poised to follow suit. This American movement allied itself with Anglicans in developing nations, such as Nigerian Archbishop Peter Akinola. The issues raised by this protest, national and international, are complex. At one level there are fundamental issues of biblical authority and interpretation, such as what to make of those biblical passages that have been construed as explicit or oblique condemnations of homosexual behavior. There are also questions of moral theology as to what kinds of sexual expression can be construed as normative or "natural." Complicating these issues are the respective claims of majority and minority, in a national church at once democratic and hierarchical, within a communion of churches based more on mutual recognition and respect rather than on centralized authority. A further set of issues involves the legacy of colonialism, in which churches in regions once part of the British Empire have taken roles as prophetic voices against what they see as heterodoxy and immorality on the parts of those that once posed as their cultural superiors. The liberal, prophetic majority in the Anglo-American context thus becomes the heretical and immoral minority in the world context. To say the least, the issues here are convoluted.

Several Anglican churches in developing countries, who numerically outnumber the more liberal Western churches (e.g., in United States, Canada, and England) in both individual membership and number of national bodies, began to threaten to divide the Worldwide Anglican Communion or eject the Episcopal Church from it if the American and Canadian churches continued their policy of ordaining those who openly practiced homosexual relationships or proceeded, as seemed possible, to authorize rites for the union of gay couples. As a result, late in 2003, Archbishop of Canterbury Rowan Williams appointed a commission headed by Irish Archbishop Robin Eames to make recommendations on how to deal with the growing conflict. Their recommendations, issued the following year as the Windsor Report, included a call for a moratorium on the consecration as bishops of those living in same-sex relationships until the underlying issues could be sorted out further, as well as consultation among members of the Communion prior to any church's taking actions that others might consider provocative. The report may have bought some time through a "cooling-off" period, but tensions remained high as neither side in the controversy appeared willing to back down from what each regarded as principled but incompatible commitments. Whether the Anglican Communion—which had since the dissolution of the British Empire following World War II served as a loose fellowship of religious communities of common origin and liturgical practice rather than as a church bound by legal authority—and the Episcopal Church would survive intact remained very much an open question in the midst of the twenty-first century's first decade.

In demographic terms, the Episcopal Church has always been national in scope but never vast in membership. Its traditional centers of geographical strength have been primarily in urban areas, especially in the Northeast, the Great Lakes, and the Tidewater South, all of them concentrations of wealth and influence. There are many Episcopal parishes or missions (congregations unable to support themselves and receiving diocesan assistance) in smaller towns throughout the country; however, there are also many counties in the rural South, Midwest, and Far West with no Episcopal presence at all. In a few areas of the West, however, there is a numerical plurality or even majority of Episcopalians originating in nineteenth-century missionary work on Indian reservations. Episcopalians have the highest percentage of African American members among the mainline denominations, in part because of immigration from the West Indies, in many parts of which the Church of England had been established in colonial times. In many larger cities are parishes that historically have been primarily African American in membership, often preferring a "high" church—that is, elaborately liturgical—style of worship.

According to virtually all sociological surveys, Episcopalians rank near or, usually, at the very top of American Christian denominations in income, educational level, occupational prestige, and other measures of social standing. However, a considerable number of traditionally Episcopal families of wealth and influence are not active church members, and the church actively maintains and supports missions for poorer congregations. Although the image of the Episcopal Church as an "elite" or "establishment" denomination remains and in many ways continues to be based on social reality, the liberal social attitudes of the denomination as a whole stand in tension with some of the traditional associations of that image.

Statistically, Episcopal Church affiliation remained very small until about 1840; increased continually and rapidly until the mid-1960s, when its overall strength stood at over 3,400,000 million; then began to experience the attrition that overtook other mainline denominations during the 1970s and 1980s. Statistics for 2006 indicate approximately 2,154,000 baptized members, a slight decline over the previous decade. Other statistics for 2006 indicate a total of 7,095 churches and 15,051 clergy, 5534 serving parishes. The prospect of an aging clergy and the lack of a large cohort of younger candidates for the priesthood—a result in part of an earlier retreat from denominational support of campus ministries—had begun to worry the church's leadership, which was beginning again to redirect funds toward college work.

Methodism, which originated as a devotional movement with a strong missionary

outreach to the socially marginalized, had by the twentieth century acquired a reputation as the most typically American of the mainline denominations. A Gallup poll
taken in 1967–68 revealed that the Methodist church was the religious group "most
liked" by members of other denominations. It was also the largest single American
religious group other than the Roman Catholic Church until its curve of declining
membership intersected with the growth curve of the Southern Baptists in the late
1960s. At one time there were more Methodist churches in America than post offices;
they can in fact still be found at assorted unlikely hamlets and crossroads in many
parts of the country. Throughout most of its history, it has worked as a consensus
church, exhibiting a moderation and a pragmatism that have been major factors in
its large and widely disseminated membership.

Today's United Methodist Church is the result of a series of mergers that reflect
several variants on the pietist-Wesleyan theme. The 1968 merger that created the
UMC brought together the Methodist Church with the Evangelical United Brethren.
The first group had been constituted through an earlier church union in 1939. This
union brought together the Methodist Episcopal Church and MEC South, which
had split in 1845 over the permissibility of slaveholding by Methodist clergy, as well
as the Methodist Protestant Church, which had split from the parent group in 1830
over demands for a more democratic polity. The Evangelical United Brethren were
similarly the product of a merger, this one dating from 1946. The uniting groups here
both represented the German-speaking pietist tradition in America. The Church of
the United Brethren in Christ had been founded in Maryland in 1800 by followers
of two German immigrant preachers, Philip William Otterbein and Martin Boehm.
(The movement had begun when Otterbein first met Boehm some years earlier and,
on hearing him preach, exclaimed "Wir sind Brüder" [We are brothers]!) A similar movement grew around the Pennsylvania German, Jacob Albright. "Albright's
people," as his followers were originally known, banded together in 1816 to form
Die Evangelische Gemeinschaft—later anglicized to the Evangelical Association. All
shared the style of piety for which Wesley was noted, and subsequent Americanization eventually rendered the original divisions among these groups superfluous.

From its beginnings both in Britain and America, Methodism navigated between a
nurture in the Anglican tradition and a willingness to adapt to new situations. Its distinctive polity illustrates this interplay between old and new. John Wesley's "classes"
and the frontier circuit riders were early examples of this adaptability. Today's United
Methodist Church, like most denominations, is organized at the national, regional,
and local levels. (Organization aimed at practical results is a very Methodist characteristic.) *Conference* is the term used at each level:

1. The *General Conference* meets every four years, and makes policy for the
   denomination as a whole. It consists of about eight hundred delegates, including some from overseas churches belonging to the UMC, divided equally

between clergy and laity. An extensive bureaucratic structure is organized into commissions and boards, which report to the General Conference. The denomination also operates an active publishing house and assists a considerable number of colleges and other educational facilities. (The proliferation of colleges with "Wesleyan" as part of their name is testimony to the scope of Methodist involvement in higher education.) Missions, also a traditional area of Methodist emphasis, are directed at the national level as well. The *Discipline,* which dates back in its original form to John Wesley and contains the denomination's rules and standards, is revised periodically by the General Conference.

2. Five *Jurisdictional Conferences* operate on a regional basis and are primarily charged with the election of bishops. A nongeographical "Central Jurisdiction" for blacks was abolished in the course of the formation of the UMC in the 1960s. Although many African Americans participate in the Methodist tradition, the large majority belong to one of the three major black Methodist denominations (African Methodist Episcopal [AME], AME Zion, and Christian Methodist Church).

3. *Annual Conferences* are the rough equivalent of dioceses, but are defined in terms of constituent churches rather than geographical area as such. They are presided over by *bishops.* A bishop presides over an *area,* which may include more than one annual conference. In Methodist usage, bishops are not considered part of an apostolic succession. They receive life tenure in office, but usually can only remain for a maximum of eight years in any one area. In 1980 Marjorie Swank Matthews was elected United Methodism's first female bishop, for the Wisconsin area. There were about sixty-six active bishops in the UMC in the United States at the end of the twentieth century.

4. *District Conferences* are subdivisions of Annual Conferences and are presided over by a distinctively Methodist officer, the *District Superintendent.* He or she is especially responsible for advising the bishop on the appointment of clergy and supervising their relationships with their churches.

5. The *Charge Conference* is organized around each local minister, who may serve more than one church in rural areas. The ministry is divided into two orders: *deacons* and *elders.* Ordination to the latter rank, which usually takes place at Annual Conference, is a prerequisite for full conference membership, which carries with it a guarantee of a ministerial assignment. Female clergy, now quite numerous, did not receive full recognition as Annual Conference members until 1956, although they had been licensed to preach as early as 1866. Clergy couples, in which both mates have been ordained and share a ministry, had become quite common by the 1980s. By the turn of the twenty-first century, controversy over the ordination of openly gay people had led to heated controversy and, in the minds of some, the possibility of schism.

Methodist worship derives from the Anglican *Book of Common Prayer,* but its exact form varies considerably from church to church. Communion is most frequently celebrated quarterly, and a service for it similar to the Anglican observance is included in the hymnal for other Sundays, though many congregations prefer a more free-form style of worship. Methodist hymnody is eclectic, but at its core is the corpus of work of the incomparable Charles Wesley. Periodic attempts at purging the hymnal of "old-time" favorites, including both sentimental gospel hymns and militant Victorian works such as "Onward, Christian Soldiers" have usually not been very successful—an experience common to other denominations whose leadership may not realize the deep conservatism of ordinary churchgoers in matters of song. In the realm of architecture, the "Akron Plan," which featured an interior arrangement in which large worship spaces could be quickly divided into smaller areas for Sunday school classes, was briefly popular around the turn of the twentieth century. No one style has ever prevailed, but the Gothic Revival, advocated tirelessly by Elbert M. Conover, the director of the MEC's Bureau of Architecture in the 1920s, was extremely popular for many decades. More recently, Methodist churches have generally been designed in stylized, simplified versions of traditional forms.

Demographically, United Methodism is preeminently a national denomination. It is by far the largest of the mainline groups, with a membership of about eight and a quarter million in 2002. Its traditional constituency has been solidly middle class, although a church of such size and scope—like the Roman Catholic—almost necessarily includes many representatives of virtually every region, social class, and ethnic group as well. Geographically, its center of strength has been described as the "south of the North and the north of the South." In the South, it has for well over a century constituted, with the Presbyterians and Baptists, one of the three dominant religious groups. Further statistics for 2002 include approximately 35,100 churches and 24,269 clergy, a decline in both categories from previous decades. Like the Episcopal and other mainline churches, the United Methodist Church was torn internally by disputes over the recognition of homosexual relationships during the first decade of the new century.

For the Presbyterians, as for the Methodists and Lutherans, the twentieth century was a time of overcoming long-standing separations. Presbyterian divisions, as recounted earlier, lay in part in long-forgotten disputes in Scotland as well as in more pertinent arguments about theology (Old Side/New Side, frontier revivalism, Old School/New School, fundamentalism) and slavery. The fundamentalist controversy of the 1920s took its toll as heavily on Presbyterianism as on any denomination. J. Gresham Machen's Orthodox Presbyterian Church and the Bible Presbyterian Church remain today as small reminders of that dispute.

The largest division for many decades, however, was that which had resulted from the denomination's sundering by the Civil War. In the South, the Presbyterian Church in the United States (PCUS) was the primary institutional embodiment of an ongoing determination to maintain a militantly conservative stance on both theological and social issues. (The latter thrust was codified in theologian James Henley Thornwell's phrase, "the spirituality of the church.") In the North, the United Presbyterian Church in the United States of America (UPCUSA) was formed in 1958 through the merger of the erstwhile "Northern Presbyterians" (PCUSA) with the United Presbyterian Church in North America, a group mainly of Scottish origin. (The PCUSA had already absorbed most of the Cumberland Presbyterians and the Welsh Calvinistic Methodists in earlier unions.) In a joint meeting in Atlanta in 1983, North and South managed to overcome traditional differences to form the Presbyterian Church (U.S.A.) (PCUSA), which is today by far the dominant denominational expression of the Presbyterian/Reformed tradition in the United States.

Presbyterianism has traditionally distinguished itself most conspicuously from other members of the Reformed tradition (except the Dutch) through its polity—to which its very name calls attention. This polity is spelled out in the PCUSA's *Book of Order,* which with the accompanying *Book of Confessions* makes up the denomination's constitution. (The *Book of Confessions* includes a number of historic documents such as the "Westminster Confession," but its concluding "Confession of 1967" has little Calvinism left in it.) On the other hand, contemporary Presbyterian polity does not differ radically in practice from other denominations of national scope, such as the Methodists and Episcopalians, in its succession of increasingly more comprehensive units of governance. Specifically, these include the following in descending order.

At the national level, the *General Assembly* meets annually to legislate on matters of national significance. It consists of equal numbers of clerical and lay delegates elected by each presbytery and is presided over by a moderator, assisted by a stated clerk. As with most major denominations, a panoply of boards, agencies, and councils supervise national programs. Following a broader trend toward relocation in the "heartland," Presbyterian national headquarters was moved from New York City to Louisville, Kentucky, in 1988.

After the General Assembly come *synods,* regional bodies of somewhat less significance than in earlier days when travel and communication were less rapid. More important is the *presbytery,* roughly the equivalent of a diocese or annual conference in scope but not headed by a bishop. Rather, like all other Presbyterian governing bodies, the presbytery consists of equal number of lay and clerical delegates from each of its constituent churches—or, more properly, the *sessions* which govern each local church. The presbytery functions rather like a collective bishop, ordaining clergy, settling disputes, and otherwise providing central authority and governance for its region.

In the local churches, clergy are known officially as "pastors" or "associate pastors." Although their functions are similar to those in other denominations, the Reformed tradition stresses preaching as a central concern, and "preaching tabs,"

which project from a clerical collar, are still at times worn with a robe while performing this task. In addition to the pastors, lay people are regularly elected to the
offices of elders and deacons; it is from the ranks of the elders, who are technically
ordained to their posts, that delegates to the presbytery are chosen. Governance of
the individual church is primarily the responsibility of the session, which consists
of pastors and elders together.

Presbyterian worship closely resembles that of other heirs of the Reformed tradition, such as Congregationalists and Baptists. It is liturgical in the sense that it usually
follows an accustomed order, but that order is not as elaborate as in the Episcopal
or Lutheran churches—and, according to the *Book of Order,* "public worship need
not follow prescribed forms." Usual components include congregational and choral
singing, the offertory, the Doxology ("Praise God from Whom all blessings flow . . ."),
the Gloria Patri ("Glory be to God the Father . . ."), the prayer of confession, other
prayers from the service book or composed for the occasion, and, of course, the
sermon. Communion ("the Lord's Supper") can be celebrated at varying intervals,
from weekly to quarterly, with monthly observance—usually with grape juice taken
from individual cups passed among the aisles—being most common. (This description of Sunday morning worship is applicable to many Methodist churches as well
as the other three denominations described next: the United Church of Christ, the
Disciples of Christ, and the American Baptist Churches.) Several hymnals are employed, including the UCC's worship book, since none is mandated. Hymnody is
for the most part similar to that of other mainline churches; a few hymns, such as
several adaptations of the Psalms and later works such as Henry van Dyke's "Joyful,
Joyful, We Adore Thee," are of specifically Presbyterian origin. Architectural styles
vary, with neo-Georgian a clear favorite especially in the South.

Historically, the Presbyterian Church has been national in scope (though for
over a century divided regionally) and usually "elite" in clientele, with a membership not surprisingly heavy in British and especially Scottish descent. Though the
membership, and especially the clergy, are sufficiently to the left of the political and
theological spectrum for the denomination to be classified by some as "liberal," the
Presbyterian Church, like the Episcopal, has usually been regarded as one of the
"status" churches in the many communities in which it is represented. A traditional
Presbyterian emphasis has been on divine law and good order. In the past this emphasis has often been associated with a moral rigidity that has certainly diminished
(if not entirely vanished) in more recent times. The membership of PCUSA at the
time of the 1983 merger stood at about 3,200,000 (of which roughly three-quarters
came from the old UPCUSA) in twelve thousand churches, placing it third after the
UMC and the ELCA among the mainline churches. In 2006 it had fallen to about
two million.

The close New England cousin of the PCUSA is the United Church of Christ
(UCC), the result of the 1957 merger of the Congregational Christian churches and

the Evangelical and Reformed Church. Each of these branches was itself the result of an earlier union. In the first case, the dominant partner was clearly the Congregational Churches, the lineal descendants (together with the even more liberal Unitarians) of the Puritan churches of colonial New England. In the latter case, the merger had taken place between two formerly German-speaking groups who, like their Catholic and Lutheran counterparts, had gradually become Americanized and desired union with their fellow heirs of the Reformed tradition. Two small split-off denominations were also formed at the time of 1957 merger by dissident Congregationalists.

The Congregational churches of the earlier nineteenth century were divided in sympathy among the new evangelicalism represented by Lyman Beecher, the "New Divinity" of Jonathan Edwards's followers, or still more traditional Calvinism. The open breach in 1825 with liberal Unitarians, who preferred to stay in fellowship with the more traditional clergy, was precipitated by pressure from militant conservatives such as Jedidiah Morse. Connecticut theologians Horace Bushnell and Lyman Beecher's confidante, Nathaniel William Taylor, began to provide an intellectual opening to the left, and by the Victorian era liberalism and the Social Gospel found widespread support and leadership. The 1957 Statement of Faith adopted at the time of the union—as a "testimony rather than a test of faith"—is clearly Christian in content but just as clearly nondogmatic and even loosely poetic in form.

Today, the UCC is probably the most consistently liberal of the mainline groups on issues both of theology and of individual and social ethics. Stances by the General Synod on public policy issues such as abortion, euthanasia, nuclear warfare, and gay rights are usually much to the liberal end of the spectrum. The UCC is consciously inclusive in its self-conception, and any number of caucuses of recognized interest groups, ranging from Hispanics to charismatics, are recognized by the denomination. Although policies on ordination are made locally, the ordination of homosexuals has not usually been controversial. Women have been ordained by Congregational churches since Antoinette Brown became the first woman formally to enter the ranks of the clergy of a major denomination in 1853.

In polity, the UCC is, not surprisingly, highly faithful to the congregationalism that was first represented in this country by the Puritan churches, who had broken from the Church of England in part over this very issue. Final authority over all local governance questions, from finance to the engagement of clergy, resides firmly in the local congregation. Beyond the congregational level, however, the governance structure more closely resembles that of Presbyterianism, with local *associations,* regional *conferences,* and a national *general synod* that meets biennially. This larger structure, however, has no authority over local churches, but formulates policy and coordinates activity for the denomination as a whole. In addition, a considerable network of boards, commissions, and other "instrumentalities" carries on the usual variety of denominational activities, including an active program of foreign missions.

Geographically, the UCC is not surprisingly strongest in those parts of the country where its constituent parts are most firmly rooted. On the Congregationalist side, this points to New England as the major point of origin (with the footnote that many formerly Puritan churches in the Boston area are now part of the Unitarian-Universalist Association). From New England, Congregationalists participated in the "Yankee Exodus" of the early nineteenth century, bringing New England religion and culture with them as they settled upstate New York, the lower Great Lakes area (for example, northeastern Ohio), and across the continent to the Pacific Northwest and the San Francisco Bay. The other area of concentration of membership lies in areas of heavy German immigration where the Evangelical and Reformed Church once found its constituency, such as Pennsylvania, Ohio, and Missouri. Lancaster Theological Seminary, in the heart of "Pennsylvania Dutch" country, now houses the denomination's archives, and Eden Seminary in St. Louis is honored in part as the site of the Niebuhr brothers' theological education. Denominational membership in 2006 stood at about 1,200,000, spread among some 5,452 churches and served by some 4,076 parochial clergy—statistics that, like most other mainline denominations, reflected a continuing gradual decline in membership. Just as the Presbyterians moved their headquarters to Louisville, so did the UCC join in this movement to the "heartland" by relocating to Cleveland in 1989.

The very name of the UCC indicates its receptivity to ecumenical discussion and merger. One of the denominations with which it has pursued such discussions most closely in recent years has been the Christian Churches (Disciples of Christ), the branch of the Restoration Movement that has become most fully part of the mainline. From the beginning, Alexander Campbell and other leaders of the movement were committed to an ecumenical policy, and they saw their efforts as a way to transcend the differences dividing Christian communions by a return to scripture as the sole guide for Christian belief and practice. This did not work out so well in practice, because the movement has since then experienced two major schisms. In 1906, a large group of more conservative and rural churches split from their more urbanized counterparts—ostensibly over the permissibility of instrumental music in worship—to form the Churches of Christ. By 1952, another split had separated what are now known as the "Disciples" from a loose aggregate of more conservative congregations that refer to themselves as "Christian Churches and Churches of Christ." This latter group continues an early Campbellite theme by resisting formal denominationalization, and exists more as a loose fellowship of some 5,500 like-minded independent congregations.

The second split in the Restoration Movement ranks was occasioned by the Disciples's "restructuring" that culminated in 1968 and was made final in 1977. Though still firmly congregational, the Disciples now participate in a national denominational structure similar to that of the UCC, with a General Assembly and General Secretary providing coordination. The relationship of this leadership, based in Indianapolis, with the numerous denominational agencies, which are mostly in St. Louis, is sometimes described as "covenantal," without the formal hierarchical structure characteristic of, for example, the Methodists and Presbyterians. This noncoercive decentralization within the structures providing a broader unity is again very much in the Campbellite tradition. Periodicals also help bind the denomination together, as they do even more prominently in its more conservative counterpart, the Churches of Christ.

The Disciples have been particularly active in seeking ecumenical unity, and continue to pursue active conversations with the UCC without necessarily taking organic union as an ultimate goal. Disciples share a joint commission on the ministry with the UCC in New York state, and most clergy there hold joint standing in both groups. Cooperation between the two has also been achieved in such areas as foreign missions and church school curriculum. Conversations with other like-minded churches such as the American Baptists and participation in broader ecumenical endeavors such as COCU have been favorite Disciples's pursuits as well.

Although the Disciples stress their commonality with other Christians, their particular set of emphases and practices makes them distinctive. Worship services are in the Reformed pattern, and vary in elaborateness and formality with the character of the individual congregation. Little distinction is made between clergy and laity, and the latter can administer communion, which is celebrated weekly. Women have been recognized in the ministry since the nineteenth century. Like the Baptists, Disciples practice believer's (that is, adult) baptism, but do not insist on it as a prerequisite for members transferring from other traditions.

Demographically, the Disciples are primarily a middle-class denomination; this emergent status was most likely a significant but covert reason for the split-off of the Churches of Christ early in the century. Their geographic concentration lies in the middle vertical third of the nation: Texas, Oklahoma, Arkansas, Tennessee, Kentucky, Indiana, Ohio, and Missouri are all Disciples strongholds, as evidenced further by their administrative centers in Indianapolis and St. Louis. Conversely, Disciples congregations are less abundant in the Deep South, and very scarce in the Northeast, where the UCC and American Baptists provide regional alternatives. Membership in 2006 had fallen to less than seven hundred thousand, distributed among about 3,800 churches and served by approximately 4,000 clergy in parishes—the most significant decline in membership of all the mainline denominations.

The American Baptist Churches in the U.S.A. (ABC) were held together during the nineteenth century by the missionary and publication societies maintained collectively by a loose alliance of Baptist churches in the North. (Prior to the formation of the Southern Baptist Convention in 1845, Baptists from all regions had been involved in this alliance. The Baptists were the first major tradition to split definitively over the slavery issue.) In 1907 they coalesced into more strictly denominational form under the name of the Northern Baptist Convention, which later underwent two further name changes. (The shift from "Northern" to "American" in 1950 indicated a change in consciousness from regional to national status.)

It is noteworthy that the present name is plural in form, underscoring the traditional Baptist emphasis on decentralization and congregational autonomy, and the belief that the essence of the church resides in the local congregation. Paul M. Harrison, a sociologist of religion and an American Baptist, has pointed out the implicit and unacknowledged tensions between the Baptist insistence on local independence and the de facto power exerted by the national bureaucratic structures the denomination has created to coordinate the use of its collective resources. Delegates—several thousand in number—from potentially each of the 6,300 local churches converge every two years for a national Biennial Convention, at which they are presented with requests for action by the various missionary and other agencies supported by the denomination as a whole. Local, state, and regional associations also provide means for coordinated activity, as does a national board, which formulates policy between national meetings.

American Baptist churches consciously strive to play a mediating role between the liberal and conservative wings of the Protestant heritage, which results in comprehensiveness and, in the minds of some, identity confusion. Their theological heritage has been molded by both wings, as represented in the evangelical Augustus Hopkins Strong (1836–1921) at Rochester Seminary; Walter Rauschenbusch (1861–1918), the theorist of the Social Gospel, who taught at the same institution for part of his career; the liberal Harry Emerson Fosdick (1878–1969) at New York City's Riverside Church; and Fosdick's fundamentalist antagonist, William Bell Riley (1861–1947) of Minneapolis. Baptist ecumenism has been strong, but no organic mergers have yet resulted from negotiations with such kindred groups as the Disciples and the Brethren. Worship is very similar to that in other heirs of the Reformed tradition, with "old-time" gospel hymns playing a larger role than they would, perhaps, in most UCC churches. American Baptists recognize two "ordinances," baptism and communion. Baptism is, of course, of adults—"believers"—and by immersion, in a tradition dating back to the Radical Reformation.

American Baptist churches are predominantly middle class. As their original name indicates, they are concentrated in the northern part of the country, as well as in the Far West; however, the possibility of dual identification with other Baptist bodies has drawn a number of black congregations into joint affiliation, such as Martin Luther King's Ebenezer Baptist Church in Atlanta. Baptist diversity is also enhanced by its ethnic mix. This has benefited from both the "new immigration" of the turn of the century, which brought in a number of Swedes, Italians, and other Europeans of diverse religious backgrounds, and the more recent Hispanic and Asian influx into the United States. Membership in 2006 was in the 1,400,000 range, with roughly 5,700 churches and 3,400 parochial clergy—a modest decline over the preceding decade.

Such is the panorama of the mainline, whose fortunes have tended to wax and wane together. In the late twentieth century, their major institutional concern continued to be the leveling off, if not any longer the absolute, even precipitous decline, in membership that had befallen most of them in the previous decades. For many, the causes of this decline lay not only in the competition offered by evangelical churches on the one hand and secularism on the other but also in what was perceived as a lack of spiritual vitality. The effervescence of individual spiritual experience and of community achieved in worship seemed to have yielded to the proliferation of bureaucratic structures and the special-purpose organizations, which sociologist Robert Wuthnow has identified as one of the most important characteristics of what he has called the "restructuring" of American religion since World War II.

Another facet of this decline was a continuing unrest among the grass roots of the appropriateness of the identification at the national level of several of these denominations with liberal positions on public issues. By the late 1980s, most of the mainline churches had tempered their positions on abortion and the ordination of homosexuals, while continuing to advocate somewhat bolder stances on nuclear warfare and economic justice. In theory, issues of racial and sexual equality had been resolved, and conscious discrimination against women or racial minorities had become unthinkable. In practice, however, the sparse number of blacks in these denominations and the difficulty women clergy have encountered in being called to larger churches indicate that the figurative millennium has hardly yet been ushered in. The issue of the ordination of practicing homosexuals that emerged in the 1990s has continued to be the most visible fault line within most of these groups, and the possibility of schism has been actively raised within the Episcopal, Methodist, and Presbyterian folds.

Despite controversy and numerical decline, mainline religious life has by no means been static. During the same era that the Roman Catholic and Episcopal churches were moving toward a modernization of their somewhat archaic liturgies, many "mainstream" Protestants were converging with them in a renewed interest in more formal and traditional worship. The Gothic Revival spread widely among Methodists, Baptists, and Presbyterians in the early part of the century—until the Depression put a halt to most new construction—and arguably abetted this new inclination. The common body of hymnody of highly diverse origin—medieval, Lutheran, Reformed, Wesleyan, Victorian—shared by all of these groups is another sign of convergence. More recently, most of these churches share a common lectionary, so that identical passages from scripture are read in thousands of churches of very different background on any given Sunday. Revision of liturgy, hymns, and even the Bible itself to omit gender-specific references, both to believers and to God, is another ongoing process that often generates heated controversy. Though it is still not difficult to tell the difference between Baptist and Episcopal worship, the convergence in between is dramatic evidence of the continuing ecumenical thrust of the life of the Protestant mainline.

In addition to public worship, many mainline Protestants in the early twenty-first century had begun to acquire an interest in *spirituality,* a theme that had affinities both with traditional Christian devotional practices and with aspects of the New

Age movement. Labyrinths, for example, which were used in medieval Catholicism as an aid in focusing one's consciousness, now appear in Presbyterian churches and Episcopal cathedrals. Kathleen Norris, a Presbyterian laywoman who is also an oblate (affiliate) of a local Benedictine monastery, popularized monastic meditative practices in her *The Cloister Walk* (1997) and reflected on the spiritual dimensions of her adopted prairie homeland in *Dakota* (1993). Another lay Presbyterian, Anne Lamott, draws spiritual lessons in highly uninhibited fashion from her daily life as a single mother in works such as *Traveling Mercies* (1999) and *Grace (Eventually)* (2007).

Finally, the 2008 presidential campaign demonstrated the ongoing vitality and diversity of the mainline as a source of ethical formation, especially for its Democratic protagonists. Whereas Republican nominee John McCain, a nominal Episcopalian, let it be known that he was more comfortable attending a Baptist church, both Hilary Clinton and Barack Obama, the Democratic hopefuls, demonstrated a new openness within their party in acknowledging their mainline nurture. Obama—rumored, with malice aforethought, to be a Muslim—is a member of Trinity United Church of Christ in Chicago, whose pastor, Jermiah Wright Jr., created considerable controversy with public remarks critical of white racism and American support for Israel. (Trinity is atypical of its denomination in its remarkable size—some eight thousand members— as well as its "black values" orientation.) Clinton was raised in the Chicago suburb of Park Ridge and was profoundly influenced as an adolescent by one of the First United Methodist Church ministers there, Don Jones, who instilled in her and her contemporaries a sense of social commitment. Both candidates demonstrated in their campaign rhetoric the ongoing impact of the Social Gospel tradition, which had become muted during the ascendancy of the Religious Right in earlier decades but reemerged in widespread concern about access to health care and other issues of social justice after Democratic victories in the 2006 congressional election.

CHAPTER 44

Conservative Protestantism: Culture and Politics

From the onset of the Depression through the years of World War II, conservative Protestantism fell into a period of cultural eclipse. Liberalism and Neo-Ortho-doxy were clearly the theologies that dominated the seminaries and pulpits of the "mainline" denominations, and aggressive conservatism was viewed in these circles as a mark of ignorance and poor taste. At their most respectable, fundamentalism and conservative evangelicalism were represented in the career of J. Gresham Machen (1881–1937), a professor of New Testament at Princeton Theological Seminary who abandoned that institution in 1929 in frustration over its repudiation of the fundamentalist interpretation of orthodoxy and went to teach at the newly founded Westminster Theological Seminary in Philadelphia. He was soon thereafter expelled from the northern Presbyterian Church for his role in a controversy over foreign missions, and in 1936 he helped found a schismatic denomination, the Presbyterian Church of America, which three years later took on the name of the Orthodox Presbyterian Church after another schism involving millennialism. It survives today with a membership of some three hundred thousand. The General Association of Regular Baptists (1932) and the Conservative Baptist Association of America (1947) were similar split-offs within the northern Baptist community.

For most Americans outside its cultural orbit, the term *fundamentalist* was likely to evoke an image not of Machen-style doctrinal conservatism but rather the Bible-thumping tent evangelism associated with Billy Sunday, whose "sawdust trail" had relegated him to the smaller cities and towns of the South in the declining years of his tempestuous career. Faith healers, some of doubtful authenticity, similarly worked the circuit of the sleepy towns of Oklahoma, Arkansas, and Tennessee, claiming miracles that enthralled their audiences but met with skepticism and derision in the wider world. Sinclair Lewis's *Elmer Gantry,* a genial fraud probably based on Sunday, joined *Babbitt* and *Main Street* in the collection of images the 1920s had provided "sophisticated" Americans for dismissing small-town life and the right wing of Protestantism as shallow and contemptible.

Whereas the holiness and pentecostal denominations withdrew almost completely from the broader arena of American religious life to form self-contained, largely regional subcultures of their own, much of the fundamentalist community continued to define itself negatively in terms of mainline Protestantism and American culture more broadly. The National Association of Evangelicals, founded in 1942, represented a more ecumenical attempt to bring together conservatives of various stripes, but constituted a clear alternative to the Federal (later National) Council of Churches. On the right, it was flanked by Carl McIntire's more radically separatist American Council of Christian Churches (1941), which insisted on members' keeping a strict distance from denominations tolerating liberalism.

By the 1940s conservatives were beginning to align along issues of this sort; during the next decade, the journal *Christianity Today,* edited by accommodative evangelicals such as Carl F. H. Henry, emerged as a rallying point for "neo-evangelicals" who repudiated the aggressive intransigence of more militant fundamentalists such as McIntire. Since conservative Protestantism crossed and often repudiated denominational boundaries, it has from its beginnings lacked clarity of institutional definition, as witnessed in its constituents' ongoing experimentation with nomenclature. (There is no clear line separating "evangelicals" and "fundamentalists"; the latter, however, tend to be more aggressive in their postures—of late, in the political as well as the religious realm—and to emphasize biblical literalism and premillennialism.) Another consequence of its lack of firm institutionalization has been its lack of ability to settle doctrinal disputes definitively; instead, they have frequently led to internecine warfare between contending leaders and their factions, which has often resulted in lasting and unresolvable bitterness. (George Marsden's account of the history of Fuller Theological Seminary provides an interesting case study and analysis of this phenomenon.)

During these years of internal reassessment, conservative Protestantism rapidly emerged into the national spotlight through the career of William Franklin "Billy" Graham. Born in North Carolina in 1918 into an extremely conservative Presbyterian family, Graham was shaped by what William G. McLoughlin has identified as the Bible-centered subculture of between-the-wars fundamentalism nurtured in summer camps and Bible schools and colleges. Graham prepared for what would be a stunning career as an evangelist in such hard-core fundamentalist institutions as Bob Jones College (now University)—then located in that latter-day "burned-over" hotbed, Cleveland, Tennessee—as well as at Wheaton College in Illinois, a more moderate evangelical institution and today the home of the Billy Graham Center for research on evangelicalism. Ordained as a Baptist minister, Graham began his career as a worker for the Youth for Christ movement, and from that base moved into revival preaching. His entrance into the national spotlight came through the widespread media coverage his Los Angeles "crusade" of 1949 attracted—possibly through William Randolph Hearst's legendary telegram that commanded his editors to "Puff Graham." From that time on, Graham's crusades, first in tents and later in giant coliseums, became regular features of the American landscape, and the "decision for Christ" indicated by hitting what had once been a literal sawdust trail and shaking Graham's hand took its place in the vocabulary of the popular evangelical tradition.

Graham's subsequent career is representative of many of the profound changes that took place within the conservative Protestant camp from World War II to the 1980s. His early preaching was heatedly animated in tone and premillennial in content. Graham capitalized on American fears in the postwar years that the world was headed for nuclear annihilation, and the impending threat of "the Bomb" gave his apocalyptic message a new resonance. Handsome, clean-cut, and earnest, Graham soon acquired national celebrity status through his crusades and a radio program, "The Hour of Decision," in much the same way that his Roman Catholic contemporary Bishop Fulton J. Sheen became a national figure. Graham and Sheen both demonstrated how a skillful spokesman for a minority tradition could exploit the mass media to help bring his religious community into the mainstream of American life, gaining sympathy and acceptance if not massive conversions.

Like Sheen, Graham was also associated during the 1950s with militant anti-Communism, a cause that further enhanced the "American" image of each. (Other fundamentalist anti-Communists such as Carl McIntire and Billy James Hargis were less successful in reaching a mass audience, most likely through their obsessive and harsh preoccupation with a single issue.) By the end of the decade Graham had become the head of a virtual empire of communications, publishing, and preaching in his Minneapolis-based Billy Graham Evangelistic Association (established in 1950). His public prominence made his friendship highly desired by national politicians, and Dwight Eisenhower and his successors were all pleased to receive Graham's patronage. As a sort of informal national chaplain, Graham was perceived to be "friends" with presidents Kennedy and Johnson, but was clearly more comfortable with the conservative Richard Nixon.

The Watergate debacle of the 1970s, however, taught Graham a potent lesson about the dangers to his credibility in becoming too closely associated with politicians whose careers might take unexpectedly disastrous turnings. (Graham expressed shock especially at Nixon's revealed penchant for foul language.) Since that time, Graham has emerged as an elder statesman of conservative Protestantism, expanding his sphere of influence while simultaneously moderating his message. In the 1970s and '80s he began to hold crusades in previously unthinkable locales such as the Notre Dame campus, Moscow, and various then-Soviet-bloc countries. He was regularly rated in opinion polls as the most influential figure in American Protestantism, and his message can be best described as a moderate, ecumenical evangelicalism rather than the red-hot fundamentalism with which he began his career. At the turn of the twenty-first century, his son Franklin was beginning to assume many of the elder Graham's responsibilities, including a role in the inauguration of George W. Bush in 2001.

The turmoil of the 1960s had a great impact on conservative Protestantism as well as on the broader society. The crisis in the South over segregation brought about by the Civil Rights Movement generated considerable resistance, which took religious form in the establishment of numerous "Christian academies" as white-only alternatives to the integrating public schools. Bob Jones University, a bastion of aggressive fundamentalism since 1926 and presided over by Bob Jones III since 1971, took an aggressive stance in maintaining racial segregation and was denied tax-exempt status by the federal government for its defiance of public policy. Its explicit anti-Catholicism (later toned down) was the occasion of considerable controversy when Republican politicians made appearances there during the 2000 presidential campaign.

On the other hand, many neo-evangelicals, especially of the younger generation, began to argue that liberal ideas of social justice were compatible with a traditionalist theology. More radically, "Jesus People," such as the Living Word Fellowship (1970) in the San Francisco bay area, adopted the communitarian lifestyle of the nearby hippies of Haight-Ashbury as a means of adapting evangelical teachings and values to the culture of the time. Still another path for younger people was taken by such militantly evangelistic groups as Bill Bright's Campus Crusade for Christ, which aggressively seeks out converts on college campuses. (InterVarsity Christian Fellowship, a more academically oriented evangelical campus group of British origin, had already been on the American scene since 1941.)

Accommodation to a more conventionally middle-class lifestyle also began to emerge in such 1970s phenomena as a "Christian Yellow Pages," which promoted evangelical patronage of businesses owned by the like-minded, and Christian book stores, which specialized in Bibles, paperbacks, and audiovisual materials promoting conservative Christianity. (The term *Christian* in these contexts became equated solely with its evangelical form.) Marabel Morgan's best-selling *The Total Woman* (1973) was a good example of this new drive to reconcile evangelicalism with mainstream culture in its simultaneous espousal of a traditionalist role for women with such sexually provocative techniques as greeting one's husband at the door wearing only "black mesh stockings, high heels and an apron." (One unsuspecting spouse's reaction was to exclaim "Praise the Lord!")

On a different tack, one of the best-selling nonfiction works of all time other than the Bible itself has been Hal Lindsey's *The Late Great Planet Earth* (1970; several subsequent editions). Lindsey here added a flair for drama to the tradition of dispensational premillennialism, and produced a scenario in which the events supposedly foretold in the Book of Revelation are acted out in the contemporary Middle East, with the United States and the Soviet Union as principal contenders. Lindsey's association of fundamentalist theology with the political realm helped pave the way conceptually for the dramatic turn conservative Protestantism was to take during the 1970s in its relation to the political order. Shifts in global politics, such as the collapse of the Soviet Union, necessitated some rather abrupt changes in the specifics of the book's scenario, but did not seem to discourage the apocalyptically minded from finding in this and many similar works a guide to the unfolding of the divine plan in the present. The phenomenally successful *Left Behind* series, written by Tim LaHaye and Jerry Jenkins between 1995 and 2007, enjoyed a similar success. Although it was hardly the first attempt to dramatize the premillennialist scenario from the Rapture to the defeat of the Antichrist, the series, which had sold over sixty million copies by the first decade of the twenty-first century, found a broad audience beyond the usual consumers of evangelical literature through its entertaining, fast-paced format. (Similarly popular enthusiasm for Dan Brown's 2003 best-seller, *The Da Vinci Code,* which cast doubts on traditional accounts of Jesus' identity, indicated the eclectic religious enthusiasms of American readers.)

The entry of conservatives into politics on a large scale was symbolized by the victory of Jimmy Carter in the presidential election of 1976—a year celebrated by *Time* and *Newsweek* as "the year of the evangelical." Carter, a moderate Democrat and Southern Baptist who had previously served as governor of Georgia, was a self-proclaimed "born-again Christian," and the ensuing publicity about his religious convictions helped push conservative Protestantism into the public spotlight in a generally positive fashion. (The antics of Carter's brother Billy also nurtured a sort of "redneck chic" manifested as well in the growing popularity of country music, television programs such as *The Dukes of Hazzard,* comedy routines such as Jeff Foxworthy's "you might be a redneck" jokes, and country-cooking restaurant chains such as Cracker Barrel. Carter's sister, Ruth Carter Stapleton, was also well known as a faith healer.) In response, Carter's opponent Gerald Ford, an Episcopalian, felt prompted to declare himself to have been "born again" as well, as would countless presidential candidates in years to come. In any case, evangelicalism had now become respectable and even fashionable.

Carter's subsequent defeat four years later at the hands of Ronald Reagan was a tangible indication that a major transformation had taken place in the realm of American religion and politics in the latter years of the 1970s. Reagan, whose religious background lay in the Disciples tradition but whose actual church affiliations were rather dim, had first acquired prominence as governor of California during the 1960s at a time when political conservatism was making a new impact on the American scene. Although fundamentalist leaders such as Carl McIntire had for years been involved in militant anti-Communist activities, the candidacy of Arizona senator Barry Goldwater, an Episcopalian with Jewish antecedents, in the 1964 presidential election marked the entrance of secular conservatism into the national scene. Although Goldwater was soundly defeated, his ally Reagan was simultaneously launching himself on a political career that would involve a new alliance between social and economic conservatives and evangelicals now willing to abandon their traditional aloofness from compromising alliances. Goldwater's and Reagan's bases in the "Sun Belt" also betokened a geopolitical shift in the nation, in which the South, the traditional seat of religious conservatism, was enjoying a prosperity and demographic resurgence in conjunction with its neighbors in the Southwest.

The Religious Right that emerged in the later 1970s and promoted Reagan's candidacy drew on a variety of ideas and tactics to lead conservative Protestants into a vigorously engaged style of political involvement. First, the tradition of church/ state separation, which had prevailed in the Baptist tradition since the days of Roger Williams, was quietly abandoned in favor of an activist stance by these churches on social and political issues. Second, conservative Christians demonstrated an eagerness and aptitude for taking advantage of the technological and logistical mechanisms of contemporary politics such as direct-mail solicitation, computerized data banks, and, especially, television. Fund-raising and legislative lobbying through mail campaigns rapidly became major components of the Religious Right's repertoire of tactics. Their alienation from modernity was thus objectively at an end, at least in regard to their appropriation of "high tech" media for their purposes. Third, an ideology that transcended denominational lines rapidly developed to explain what many conservatives perceived as the decadence of contemporary society and to provide a "social agenda" in the political realm to reverse these tendencies. Here again, their accustomed position as outsiders railing against modern society began to yield to a new and activist role in the political order, even as they maintained a continual barrage of criticism toward that order.

The ideology thereafter promoted by Jerry Falwell's Moral Majority, Inc. (later changed to the Freedom Foundation), and other Religious Right vehicles such as the Religious Roundtable, the Christian Voice, Focus on the Family, and, later, the Christian Coalition, resembled very closely that advocated by Roman Catholic spokesmen during the Cold War years. In the international realm, anti-Communism took on mythical dimensions, as exemplified in Ronald Reagan's characterization of the Soviet Union as an "evil empire." (This phrase was reminiscent of Stephen Spielberg's popular *Star Wars* film trilogy, which had self-consciously incorporated many mythical themes.) Domestic "witch-hunting" of suspected subversives, though, never reached the dimensions of Senator McCarthy's crusade of the 1950s, and only ultra–far right politicians such as North Carolina senator Jesse Helms rattled this particular cage very frequently until the collapse of the Soviet Union effectively defused the issue. International items such as opposition to American ratification of the treaty returning the Panama Canal to Panama, however, periodically emerged as items on the Religious Right's agenda.

Usually more pressing were domestic issues, in which "secular humanism" emerged for a period as a bugbear comparable in symbolic portentiousness to the "International Communist Conspiracy." "Secular humanism," personified in Religious Right rhetoric as an organized movement, was in reality more of a general trend in the society toward edging the supernatural out of the realm of public discourse. Crucial here was the role of the public schools, which conservatives feared were being corrupted by the Supreme Court ban (*Engel v. Vitale,* 1962) on school prayer. A prominent item on the "social agenda" of the 1980s, which received support from the Reagan administration and subsequent Republican activists but has never been successful legislatively, was a "School Prayer Amendment" to the Constitution that would supersede the High Court's interpretation of the First Amendment in this case. Other conservatives, following the Roman Catholic example, opted for a parallel system of private religiously oriented "Christian" schools, and have lobbied—again, largely unsuccessfully—for direct federal aid for such enterprises.

Closely related to the school prayer question was that perennial bone of contention, the teaching of evolution in the public school biology curriculum. During the 1970s, a number of state legislatures, primarily in the South, passed various laws not outlawing the teaching of evolution but rather mandating that an alternative, conservative Christian interpretation of human origins known as "creationism" or "creation science" be taught as well. The issue came to a head in 1982, when an Arkansas law requiring the teaching of creationism was overturned by a federal court judge on the grounds that it violated First Amendment guarantees of church/state separation. This decision in what became popularly known as "Scopes II" was reinforced by a 1987

Supreme Court ruling that struck down a similar Louisiana statute. The continuing vitality of the issue was demonstrated again when, in 1999, the Kansas Board of Education voted to omit evolution from state standards for high school curricula, a move that was only the beginning of a series of policy debates and reversals on the issue in Kansas and other states, including Ohio. The attempt to introduce the idea of "Intelligent Design" as an alternative to creationism, in which the identity of the designer of the universe was never specifically equated with God, ran into a major reversal in the 2005 decision of Federal Judge John E. Jones in a case brought against the school board in Dover, Pennsylvania. Jones, a Republican appointee, ruled that "ID" was simply a repackaging of creationism and was not appropriate for inclusion in a public school science curriculum.

Still other issues continue to play out in the realm of public education, a particularly sensitive area of American life in which the socialization of the young in manners and morals cannot be easily separated from the inculcation of skills such as reading and writing. (Even the latter areas are hardly neutral, and the battle between "progressives" and "traditionalists" parallels the issue of secularism versus conservative Christianity.) With the exception of some "Christian academies" in the South, founded originally in the 1960s in part to avoid court-mandated racial integration, and the growing home-schooling movement, conservative evangelicals have generally chosen to contest the curriculum of the public schools rather than follow the Catholic model of setting up an independent, parallel, tuition-supported educational system. Politically, control of local school boards has been one area in which slates loyal to the values of the Religious Right have been able to achieve victories, although they are not always lasting victories once more centrist opposition becomes mobilized. Issues that generate controversy include the celebration of holidays, including Halloween, which some evangelicals view as demonic. Which texts and other books are to be included in the curriculum or otherwise utilized in the schools is another touchy area; beginning in the late 1990s, for example, the English author J. K. Rowling's *Harry Potter* series has been extremely popular among schoolchildren, but has also been opposed by conservatives on the grounds that it deals too positively with magic and the supernatural. (Similar charges were raised in 2005 against the film adaptation of evangelical hero C. S. Lewis's Narnia story, *The Lion, the Witch, and the Wardrobe.*)

In addition to the schools, the "social agenda" also focused extensively on the realm of sexual morality and its public regulation. Earlier raised frequently by Roman Catholics, this theme now drew many conservative Catholics into political alliances which three decades earlier would have been unthinkable. A key issue here was the Supreme Court's *Roe v. Wade* decision of 1973, which legalized abortion, and which social conservatives now worked to overturn. Picketing or disruption of abortion clinics, opposition to Planned Parenthood on the grounds that it promoted abortion, and other protest activities attracted support from conservatives from a wide variety of religious backgrounds, and occasionally resulted in a violence condemned by all but the most extreme factions. *Roe v. Wade* also became a major rallying-point in a conservative attack on the Federal judiciary as overly "activist" in its interpretations of the Constitution, a document now raised to almost biblical status.

Opposition to gay rights, which had become an open and usually controversial cause since the 1970s, was another aspect of conservative reaction to what was often portrayed as a nationwide cult of permissiveness and consequent collapse of moral fiber. A frequently invoked source of this disorder was the dislocations of the counterculture of the 1960s and the Watergate debacle of the 1970s. "Secular humanism" here again became a focus for opprobrium in allegations that it had penetrated the prayerless public school curricula and substituted "values clarification" for instruction in moral absolutes. Finally, rapid cultural changes in the realm of sex roles as well as sexuality manifested themselves in the quest for an Equal Rights Amendment to the Constitution, which in the 1970s passed both houses of Congress but failed to secure the requisite approval of three-quarters of the state legislatures. The maintenance of traditional male-female relationships and patriarchal nuclear family patterns was dear to the conservative cause, which had lobbied heavily against ERA passage. During the 1990s, legislation at various levels protecting gay rights, including both freedom from discrimination and the ability of gay partners to receive the same benefits as heterosexual spouses met with varying fates in different locales, often after extensive lobbying on both sides. The question of gay marriage—legalized in Massachusetts in 2004—or at least the legal recognition of gay partnerships, emerged as an especially compelling symbolic issue, with many states passing bans on such actions, but with no general resolution on the horizon.

By the end of the Reagan administration, it appeared that the "social agenda" had been more successful in its negative than its positive goals. The defeat of the ERA was quite possibly the Religious Right's most conspicuous achievement. The Reagan administration had continually espoused most of its other causes, but had not been successful—or very energetic—in promoting them in Congress. Simultaneously, organizations such as the Moral Majority began to lose popular support, due in part to the harsh character of their rhetoric as well as the disrepute into which "televangelism" more generally was falling at the time. (Jerry Falwell and Pat Robertson later came in for particular criticism in their 2001 characterization of the 9/11 attacks on New York and Washington as divine retribution for national tolerance of homosexuality.) Reagan had appointed one vocal premillennialist, James Watt, to be his secretary of the interior, but Watt was eventually forced to resign in the face of widespread protest against his environmental policies. Despite this lack of legislative success and the president's own ambiguous religious and family life, Ronald Reagan has continued to be an icon of conservative values, religious and otherwise.

Reagan's successor, Episcopalian George H. W. Bush, was widely endorsed by conservative religious groups and engaged in campaign activities such as attacking the American Civil Liberties Union (ACLU) for its "permissiveness." The Religious Right played little visible role in the 1988 presidential campaign and, in irritation over Bush's failure to "get" their concerns, did not actively support his reelection effort in 1992. Bush's successor, Southern Baptist and Democrat Bill Clinton, steered a moderate to liberal course on social issues and became himself the object of the moral outrage of the Religious Right when word of his sexual involvement with White House intern Monica Lewinsky became the object of the zealous attention of special prosecutor Kenneth Starr, and resulted in an unsuccessful impeachment trial. The loss of longtime Democratic dominance of Congress in 1994 under the leadership of Georgia Republican Newt Gingrich ushered in an era of conservative rhetoric but little decisive legislation. The division of the Republican Party among moderates, more secular and pragmatic conservatives such as Gingrich, and hard-core conservatives such as House Whip Tom DeLay of Texas, worked against the passage of controversial legislation, especially after the Republican near-loss of control of the House in 1998 and Gingrich's subsequent resignation. A widely reported speech of DeLay in June of 1999, in which he denounced evolution, family planning, day care, abortion, "liberal relativism," and a host of other perceived contemporary social ills, made clear the continuing appeal of this mind-set to an important Republican constituency, but did not seem to translate readily into a passable legislative agenda. DeLay's resignation from the House in 2006 after his indictment on charges of corruption was a further setback for Right-backed causes.

This frustration with the legislative process had led by the end of the 1990s to suggestions by such leaders as Paul Weyrich that evangelicals drop out of the political arena altogether. This sentiment was reflected in the rapid growth of the home-schooling movement as an attempt by families to insulate children from the corruptions of the public arena altogether. The controversies during the 2000 Republican primaries over George W. Bush's campaign appearance at ultraconservative Bob Jones University in South Carolina and Bush's rival John McCain's attack on Religious Right leaders Jerry Falwell and Pat Robertson as "forces of evil" further demonstrated the ambiguous role that the Religious Right's drive for a major role in shaping public policy had reached by the millennial year.

That same year, however, saw the election of George W. Bush over former Vice President Al Gore by the narrowest victory in the Electoral College after confusion over vote counting in Florida had dragged on for weeks and was finally settled by a Supreme Court decision split on a 5–4 vote. Bush, the son of the forty-first president, was raised primarily as an Episcopalian in Texas but later joined his wife in the United Methodist Church. A product of Andover and Yale, the younger Bush led something of a prodigal life in his early Texas adulthood until his classically evangelical conversion led to a dramatic change in lifestyle, especially with regard to his once-prodigious alcohol consumption. Bush had served as a liaison to the evangelical community during his father's successful 1988 campaign, and subsequently set out on his own political career to become governor of Texas. After his election to the presidency in 2000, Bush rapidly made it clear that his evangelical religious identity was firmly linked with the goals of the Religious Right as well as the more secular neo-Conservative movement that informed his foreign policy, especially the American invasion of Iraq in 2003. Although his administration clearly reflected many of the ideals of the Religious Right in its policies, Bush's loss of political capital by the middle of his second term made the achievement of major social policy goals more difficult. His main accomplishment in this area was most likely the successful appointment of two conservative Catholic Supreme Court justices, John Roberts and Samuel Alito; whether their joining the high court would result in success in, for example, overturning *Roe v. Wade* as the basis of national abortion policy, would only be revealed in the future.

Midway through the first decade of the twenty-first century, there were indications that the Religious Right's ability to align evangelicals uniformly behind their programs was beginning to wane. The 2006 congressional elections swept Democrats into the majority in both houses in response to public disillusionment with an ongoing war in Iraq as well as a sense that social issues such as medical care had been neglected by the Republican administration. One area in which evangelicals began to express a dissenting voice was that of the environment. Although the National Association for Evangelicals (NAE) had been issuing statements on the issue since the 1970s, it was only with the widespread conviction that global warming and climate change were serious threats to human welfare that stronger responses began to issue from the NAE and newer, specialized initiatives such as the Evangelical Environmental Network and the Au Sable Institute. Although Richard Cizik, NAE's chief lobbyist, drew heavy fire from the Right for his claim to have undergone a conversion to the cause of environmentalism and ultimately did not sign the document, the Evangelical Climate Initiative of 2006 was endorsed by more than eighty evangelical leaders, who used Cizik's concept of "Creation Care" to steer a middle a course between a fundamentalist "Dominion Theology" that asserted absolute human priority over the rest of creation and what many evangelicals regarded as "nature worship" on the part of more radical environmentalists.

Beside the political arena, there were other dimensions to the evangelical resurgence of the late twentieth century. The series of scandals in the mid-1980s—labeled by the media as "Preachergate" or "Pearly Gate"—highlighted the role that the skillful use of modern media technology had played in that resurgence. Media ministries of one sort or another had appeared in America since the introduction of radio in the 1920s, although Roman Catholic Father Charles Coughlin and Bishop Fulton J. Sheen had been the most successful clerical exploiters of radio and television in the earlier days of those media. The major prototype for latter-day "televangelism" was Charles E. Fuller's "The Old Fashioned Revival Hour," which was broadcast nationwide from Long Beach, California, on the Mutual radio network beginning in 1937.

(Fuller was later instrumental in the establishment of Fuller Theological Seminary in California, to which he gave his name as well as substantial financial backing.)

Whereas earlier radio and television preachers had generally been scorned by larger audiences for the crudity of their appeal—as encapsulated in their catch-phrase, "keep those cards and letters coming in"—the television preachers of the new "Electronic Church" were far more sophisticated in their tactics. By the late 1970s, Independent Baptist Jerry Falwell (1933–2007), Assemblies of God ministers Jimmy Swaggart (b. 1955) and Jim Bakker (b. 1939), charismatic Southern Baptist Pat Robertson (b. 1930), and the Reformed Church of America's Robert Schuller (b. 1926), had all emerged as national celebrities who attracted vast audiences through their smoothly produced television offerings. Their styles varied considerably. Swaggart—first cousin to rock-and-roller Jerry Lee Lewis—was an "old-time religion" preacher who sang and screamed and wept and moved about antically on the stage in a manner reminiscent of Billy Sunday. Jim Bakker (BAY-ker) and his wife Tammy Faye conducted *The PTL Club* ("PTL" was an acronym for "Praise the Lord" or "People that Love") as a sort of evangelical talk and variety show, a format also employed by Pat Robertson in *The 700 Club*. Schuller was the furthest of the group from the evangelical norm, and emphasized a message of worldly success from his Crystal Cathedral; his doctrine of "possibility thinking" was more in the lineage of Norman Vincent Peale than Billy Sunday.

By 1987, however, the "Electronic Church" seemed about to come apart at the seams. Robertson had resigned from the ministry and *The 700 Club* to pursue, unsuccessfully, the 1988 Republican presidential nomination, and had attracted negative attention through such extravagant claims as having diverted a hurricane from the path of his Christian Broadcasting Network headquarters in Virginia Beach. Jim Bakker was forced to resign as head of PTL in the wake of sexual peccadilloes in his past as well as serious irregularities in PTL's finances. The extravagant lifestyle led by Bakker and his wife (who had promoted, among other things, a line of cosmetics on their show) aroused considerable criticism for their worldliness as well as satire in the form of the country music single, "Would Jesus Wear a Rolex on His Television Show?" Bakker subsequently served time in prison for various financial irregularities, and his enterprises passed into other hands. These enterprises included an evangelically oriented resort complex in North Carolina, which was sold off and ultimately abandoned. Jimmy Swaggart was suspended by the Assemblies of God after revelations became public about his association with a Louisiana prostitute; Robert Schuller and that perennial media personage, Oral Roberts, both received unfavorable publicity over financial questions. Scandal among celebrity clergy was nothing new, as the adultery trial of Henry Ward Beecher and the escapades of Aimee Semple McPherson had indicated decades earlier. To the televangelists' followers, however, the shock was considerable.

The media ministries of Swaggart, Bakker, and company involved vast sums of money, raised by continual solicitations on their television programs as well as through the mail. In addition to the programs themselves, many of these evangelists also developed large-scale auxiliary enterprises, which in turn demanded large-scale support. Oral Roberts, for example, began his career in the demimonde of itinerant faith healing, while his older contemporary A. A. Allen was casting out demons and William Branham allegedly raised the dead (including a defunct fish). After a successful career as a faith healer, Roberts left behind his tent and the Pentecostal Holiness Church, affiliated with the United Methodists, and embarked on an "upscale" career as the host of a religiously oriented variety program on television. He went on to found the pentecostally oriented Oral Roberts University in Tulsa, together with the adjoining City of Faith medical center. Financial problems with the latter led Roberts to declare that God might "call him home" if his supporters did not produce sufficient funds to rescue the operation. (They did, and God didn't.) Other examples of the entrepreneurial inclinations of successful televangelists include Falwell's Liberty University near his Liberty Baptist Church in Lynchburg, Virginia; Robertson's Christian Broadcasting Network, CBN University, Freedom Council, and other allied organizations; and the Bakker's Heritage Village, the Disneyland-like vacation resort in North Carolina that now lies abandoned.

Another enterpreneurial strain of television ministry with pentecostal roots can be found in the Word of Faith movement (also known, less complimentarily, as "Health and Wealth" or "Name It and Claim It.") This movement arose with the teachings of E. W. Kenyon in New England in the early part of the twentieth century, and was popularized by Oklahoma Pentecostal Kenneth Hagin (1917–2003), although strains of its teachings can also be found in such widely varied sources as Henry Ward Beecher, Mary Baker Eddy, and Norman Vincent Peale. Central to this movement, which relocated these strains within a pentecostal context, is the practice of "Positive Confession." By verbally "claiming" a promise in Scripture, the believer becomes thereby entitled to the fulfillment of that promise, which might involve physical healing or material prosperity. The best known exponents of this doctrine are the televangelists Jan and Paul Crouch, who preside over the far-flung Trinity Broadcasting Network (TBN), one of the largest broadcasting operations both in the United States and in the world. The Crouches combine the Word of Faith message with the traditional broadcast evangelist's exhortation to contribute generously, linking the size of the contribution to that of the expected reward.

An expansive scale of operation can also be seen in the emergence of the "megachurch" phenomenon, especially in the extended South (including, for example, Oklahoma and Indiana). Churches of a vast scale, whose memberships may each exceed fifteen thousand, run the range of conservative affiliation from Southern and Independent Baptist to pentecostal (especially Assemblies of God) to unaffiliated evangelical congregations, such as Willow Creek Church in the Chicago suburb of South Barrington. (Only a few belong to mainline denominations.) Churches of this sort are frequently sited near the exit ramps of interstate highways and feature vast parking lots as well as extensive physical plants that include auditoriums for worship (Willow Creek's main auditorium seats 4,650 and employs television monitors for those in its farthest reaches). Many also feature Christian education facilities; meeting rooms for various interest groups (divided by age, gender, or other characteristics); dining facilities (including, in Willow Creek's case, an actual food court); as well as bookstores, information booths, and other facilities that invite the total involvement of their members, not simply attendance at Sunday morning worship, on the model of the turn-of-the-century urban "institutional church."

Megachurches did not just happen, but emerged through marketing research, based on secular business practices, and modeled and aimed at the continually expanding exurban population of newly moved, upwardly mobile, and religiously unrooted Americans who now constituted a major new demographic category. Externally, these buildings often avoid the traditional trappings of Christian houses of worship, such as steeples and crosses, and more closely resemble secular structures such as conference hotels or shopping malls. Names, such as "Christian Life Center," are also frequently nontraditional, reflecting the Reformed tradition's rejection of the notion of sacred space while simultaneously appealing to the sensibilities of the secularized suburbanite. The worship spaces themselves echo the "auditorium churches" of the late nineteenth century in their focus on preaching and music rather than elaborate liturgy. Arrays of musical instruments are often found on the stages, together with state-of-the-art technological systems of amplification and projection. The old-time gospel songs have in many cases yielded to new-style "praise songs," musically uncomplicated pieces influenced by contemporary secular styles; similarly, the organ has given place to the electronic keyboard or electric guitar.

Megachurches are often linked with another recent phenomenon, the emergence of what Donald E. Miller has called "new paradigm" churches. These loosely connected networks of churches can best be described as postdenominational, because they are held together more by common origins and mutual affinities than any central, authoritative organization. An early source of this trend was the "Jesus Movement" of the 1960s, in which young people influenced by the counterculture of the era were attracted to new ministries that were free of the traditional institutional trappings of Christianity. These innovative ministries spoke to a generation that found traditional evangelical and mainline culture unappealing. The prototypes for these networks, such as Saddleback and Vineyard churches, originated mainly in California in the 1970s and '80s, although Willow Creek in Illinois is sometimes included in their number. Central to the movement is "church planting," in which new congregations are founded not through denominational channels but by committed laity with an entrepreneurial spirit. The theology is evangelical but ethos and liturgy are contemporary. The proliferation of different lay-led ministries and activities in such a congregation make them especially attractive to young individuals and families.

Related to the "new paradigm" church movement is the "emerging (or emergent) church," which has built on many of the leads established by the new paradigm churches, but which also emphasizes a selective appropriation of tradition, sometimes within the context of already established denominational churches. A figure who has been influential in both movements, as well as in the broader culture, is Rick Warren and his Purpose Driven Network. Warren, the founder of Saddleback Church in Lake Forest, California, became a best-selling author in 2002 with *The Purpose Driven Life,* which had sold some twenty-five million copies by mid-decade. Warren's book is a sequence of inspirational readings with a New Age flavor based on biblical texts and aimed at a practical transformation of one's daily life. His Saddleback movement has been called a franchising operation, with a variety of methods and materials available to local churches from the central operation. It has been criticized by more traditional evangelicals for being too seeker-friendly and insufficiently demanding in not insisting on personal conversion as a primary goal.

The Baptist wing of the Reformed tradition especially has for many years been a nursery of the megachurch phenomenon. Churches such as the late W. A. Criswell's (1909–2002) First Baptist in Dallas often have memberships in the ten- to twenty-thousand range, with a vast array of sponsored activities, including the radio programs that fundamentalists such as William Bell Riley first began to sponsor in the 1920s. Independent Baptist churches such as Falwell's Liberty Baptist in Lynchburg were especially a "growth phenomenon" of the 1970s and 1980s. The two groups differ mainly in polity—Independent Baptists have no formal ties with any other churches, whereas Southern Baptists participate in annual conventions which maintain, among other commonly sponsored enterprises, theological seminaries. In addition to rapid growth—membership in the Southern Baptist Convention (SBC) exceeded 16,200,000 in 2006—the two communities have emerged as institutional bulwarks of aggressive fundamentalism and conservative political causes.

The SBC, however, has been torn between a fundamentalist majority that gained ascendancy in the mid-1980s and a large moderate minority that has resisted, for example, the largely successful drive to impose fundamentalist orthodoxy on the denomination's seminary faculties. In a number of cases the latter group has, at state and local levels, either severed its SBC ties outright or worked to promote alternative and more moderate seminary options outside the denominational structure. Former president Jimmy Carter's renouncing his SBC membership in 2000 further underlined the rift in that denomination. The Cooperative Baptist Fellowship, organized in 1991 as an alternative quasi-denominational vehicle for such moderates. Among the alternative models for Baptist theological education that emerged from this movement is the Wake Forest University Divinity School, founded in 1999 and defining itself as "Christian by tradition, ecumenical in outlook, and Baptist in heritage."

Though Independent and Southern Baptists have enjoyed rapid growth and exerted considerable leadership within resurgent fundamentalism, the spectrum of conservative Protestantism by no means ends with them. Pentecostalism has also seen rapid growth, as evidenced in the dramatic membership increases enjoyed by such denominations as the Assemblies of God and the Church of God in Christ. The continuing existence and success of the latter, which is predominantly black, also emphasizes the fact that conservatives still remain institutionally and culturally divided along racial lines. Fundamentalism, with its theological roots in the Reformed tradition, also differs doctrinally and experientially from the Wesleyan-descended holiness and pentecostal communities, though cooperation in politically oriented endeavors such as the Moral Majority and the "bridge" role of charismatic-oriented Southern Baptist Pat Robertson have diminished some of these historic differences in recent years.

In addition to politically oriented groups such as the Christian Coalition, extra-ecclesiastical agencies such as Demos Shakarian's Full Gospel Business Men's Fellowship International and Women Aglow have also been instrumental in promoting these religious movements—pentecostalism, in the case of the latter two. Very different conservative traditions are also maintained by sizeable groups such as the Lutheran Church, Missouri Synod, and the Churches of Christ, which separated in 1906 from the more urban and liberal Disciples of Christ. (Respective membership figures in the early 2000s for the latter two groups were roughly 2,600,000 and 770,000.) In addition, many Mormons, Roman Catholics, and even Orthodox Jews share some of the cultural emphases that characterize conservative Protestants, and have cooperated with them in political lobbying activities.

Internal diversity within the evangelical community is considerable, and cannot be catalogued in all its detail. Note, however, should be made on the emergence in recent years of an intellectually oriented academic cadre among conservative Protestants, which has some of its origins in the group—including Harold Lindsell and Carl F. H. Henry—that launched *Christianity Today* as an intellectually respectable conservative alternative to the *Christian Century* in 1956. (Billy Graham, interestingly, played a major role in the journal's founding and hoped that it would serve as a moderate evangelical alternative to the militant anti-intellectualism of radical separatists such as Carl McIntire.) Institutions such as Fuller Theological Seminary in California (now the largest independent theological seminary in the world), Calvin College in Michigan, and Wheaton College in Illinois have also attained in recent years a level of academic maturity comparable with that of their older Roman Catholic counterparts such as Notre Dame and Georgetown (not, however, without provoking attacks from the separatist right wing of fundamentalism). Further, a number of younger scholars, identifying themselves as evangelicals and based at major research institutions such as Duke, Yale, and even Notre Dame, have begun to produce a scholarship on the histories of their own movements of the highest quality. As their counterparts in the churches continue to create conservative history, these scholars are poised to interpret it.

Two examples of contrasting evangelical views of the role of religion in the political realm can be seen in the movements known as Christian Reconstructionism and the Sojourners community. The former is one of the most influential manifestations of a broader movement known as Dominion Theology, formulated primarily by R. J. Rushdoony (1916–2001). A principal concept in this movement is "theonomy," that is, the idea that divine law, a la Calvin's Geneva and Puritan New England, ought to be the explicit basis of civil government. The major implications of this notion for public policy would involve strict government regulation of sexual conduct and public religious expression, accompanied by a radical cut-back in other government functions, such as taxation or regulation of the economy. Although small in numbers of formal adherents, the movement has exerted a significant influence on the thought of the broader Religious Right in framing the possibilities of the role of conservative Protestant values in the American social and political context.

In dramatic opposition to Rushdoony and his followers is Jim Wallis (b. 1948), the founder of the *Sojourners Journal* and movement. Sojourners began among a group of students at Trinity Evangelical Divinity School in Deerfield, Illinois, in the early 1970s; the journal began in 1971, and it and the community that generated it relocated in Washington, D.C., in 1975. The movement, originally an "intentional community" on the 1960s countercultural model, underwent a variety of changes in form and generated a number of neighborhood ministries before morphing into its present status as a loosely connected national network of the like-minded centered on the Washington-based journal and the Call to Renewal organization. Wallis has spent his career as an evangelically rooted advocate for peace and social justice issues, and spends much of his time on the national speakers' circuit. Unlike the Religious Right, he is critical of both political parties, as expressed in his influential 2004 work, *God's Politics: Why the Right Gets It Wrong and the Left Doesn't Get It.*

The conservative upsurge that began in the 1970s has had a number of implications for American religious life. At one level, it reflects the swing of the pendulum away from a period of extreme social stress and cultural confusion, namely, the era of the Civil Rights Movement, the Vietnam War, the counterculture, and Watergate. Another dimension lies in the relationship of religion to social mobility. As Frances Fitzgerald reported in her account of Jerry Falwell's Liberty Baptist Church in her *Cities on a Hill,* Falwell's constituency lay not with the "disinherited"—the stereotypical fundamentalists and pentecostals of the Depression era—but in young people in the process of ascending into the lower and middle reaches of the middle class. The appeal of conservative religion for this upwardly mobile group lies in its sense of assurance that absolutes exist in a world in dizzying transition—in Grant Wacker's phrase, a social cohort "searching for Norman Rockwell." Parallels with the American Catholic community, which underwent a similar transition in status from working class to middle and upper middle class a generation earlier, are again instructive.

Finally, no look at contemporary American evangelicalism would be complete without noting how it pervades modern society in any number of tangible ways. In addition to the megachurches that can often be found at the nodes of interstate highways, countless smaller structures, often resembling ranch houses with small spires on top and perhaps a facade of columns at the front, have filled in the suburban and rural landscape not only in the South but in much of the rest of the country as well. (The Northeast and Pacific Northwest are probably least affected.) "Christian bookstores" are widespread, and can be found in mini-malls almost anywhere, stocking not only books but CDs, DVDs, and any number of artifacts with evangelical messages and themes. Many *Christian*—the unmodified word has been given a distinct meaning in evangelical usage—radio stations not only carry sermons and lectures but also feature "contemporary Christian music," a distinctive genre recognized as such by the industry and featuring such "crossover" performers as Amy Grant, Bob Carlisle, Michael W. Smith, and Jars of Clay, recording on labels such as Word, Myrrh, Brentwood, and Sparrow, mostly now owned by conglomerates such as Gaylord Entertainment. In 1998 such music was fifth in popularity by genre, ahead of jazz, classical, and New Age. An annual televised Dove Awards program bestows public recognition on the most popular artists and recordings of the genre. Although independently produced evangelical films seldom reach the mainstream market at shopping mall multiplexes, an occasional crossover such as 1999's *The Omega Code* attracts a wider audience.

The rapid rise of a complex religious culture that combines a conservative theological and social outlook with financial power and political activism will certainly continue to influence the shape of American society into the indefinite future. As already noted in passing, however, the enthusiastic appropriation by religious conservatives of modern techniques of communication—including the Internet—and political lobbying are indicative of their ability to embrace many aspects of contemporary American society even as they denounce others. In addition, the emergence of complex bureaucratic structures within the megachurches and the conservative denominations may result before long in the same problems of impersonality and alienation that brought about serious membership loss from the mainline churches into the conservative ranks. (In 2008 megachurch leaders expressed public dismay over polls revealing a perception that personal spiritual growth in these institutions was insufficient for the needs of many.) How distinct this subculture will remain from mainline Protestantism as its constituents continue to become more sophisticated and acculturated—"at ease in Zion"—thus remains to be seen.

Mormons and the "Mainstream"

The history of the Latter-day Saints in Utah underwent an abrupt and decisive shift in 1890, with President Wilford Woodruff's *Manifesto* bringing to an end the distinctive practice of polygamy. Heretofore, the Mormons had lived apart, distancing themselves from the larger American society by physical separation, doctrinal peculiarity, economic semicommunitarianism, theocratic leadership, and—most notoriously for "Gentiles"—the practice of plural marriage. This distinctiveness had proved invaluable in rallying the morale, determination, and willingness to subordinate the will of the individual to the good of the group necessary to make the western deserts into veritable gardens. Its main function was to remind all that the Mormons were not like the Gentiles: they had an identity, a mission, and a destiny all their own.

The price this distinctiveness exacted in a continual tightening of the screws by the federal government eventually proved too costly. A series of congressional acts, with escalating enforcement by federal marshals, proved impossible to resist in the long run, and the 1890 *Manifesto* was a signal that the Saints were now willing to adjust their self-interpretation to bring it sufficiently into conformity with that of the dominant society to ensure survival. Not all Mormons accepted President Woodruff's revelation as binding, though, and splinter groups of polygamists still survive in remote towns of Utah, other parts of the Southwest, in Mexico, and even, discreetly, in the vicinity of Salt Lake City, to the present day. Some of these polygamous families are affluent, with the "sister wives" pursuing professional careers and employing architects to design houses adapted to their distinctive lifestyles; others subsist near the poverty level, and the Utah state government began to scrutinize them carefully in the late 1990s because of their reliance on welfare for support as well as reported coercion and abuse. One estimate had it that there were about fifty thousand practicing polygamists in Utah in the year 2000.

The ending of polygamy was both a symbol and a precondition of a new age in which Mormons would become much more thoroughly integrated into national life, although in a highly distinctive fashion. Mormons have remained a dominant force in the political and social life of Utah, where they still constitute roughly 80 percent of the population, and in parts of contiguous states; however, they have also diffused throughout the nation—as witnessed in their spectacular temple near Washington, D.C.—and, through vigorous evangelism, in many developing nations as well. Whereas religion and government had once been inextricably intertwined, the Church of Jesus Christ of Latter-day Saints now became a denomination—albeit a highly demanding one—and the government of Utah now follows the broader

American pattern, but with Mormons prominent in its affairs. Instead of participating in a semicollective economy, Mormons now are among the most vocal advocates of individualistic capitalism in the nation, and the LDS Church continues to have extensive investments in the private sector and provides relief for Mormons down on their luck.

Mormonism has thus adapted to its incorporation into American society not by abandoning its earlier practices and values (except in extreme cases such as polygamy) but by creating a network of beliefs, values, and structures capable of maintaining their identity as a distinctive people in the face of the pressures of religious competition as well as secularization. They have done so in part by abandoning their earlier critical posture toward America at large, and instead embracing certain aspects of American culture as religiously normative. The anthropologist Mark Leone probably overstated his case when he argued that Mormons have done such a turnabout on capitalism that they have changed from a "counter-culture" to a "colonial" people without a clear identity of their own. However, he is certainly perceptive in noting that, whatever continuities may exist in the underlying social reality, the overt Mormon posture toward American society has executed a highly dramatic about-face in the course of the past century or so.

Like other branches of Christianity, with which Mormons identify despite the distinctiveness of their attitude toward revelation, the Latter-day Saints have developed a distinctive theology, a pattern of worship, and an organizational structure. For many, in practice, the latter is the most important of the three, since Mormon life is organized around a pattern of seemingly ceaseless activity. This activity, generated and sustained in large part by the group's structures, further contributes to a pattern of life that is intense and distinctive enough to be called a *culture*—or, perhaps, more accurately, a subculture, partaking of and yet curiously distinct from the patterns of life of other middle-class white Americans. Some Mormons, though not religiously active, nevertheless continue to participate in this culture, which has become a major part of the way in which they live their lives and find their indentity. To understand the reality of twentieth-century Mormonism, it is useful to examine belief, worship, structure, and, finally, culture.

The Mormon belief system is inextricably tied to the unique revelation that its founder and prophet, Joseph Smith, claimed to have derived through his encounter with the angel Moroni. The authenticity of the *Book of Mormon* and of Joseph Smith's prophetic role are cardinal points of faith, which also serve to distinguish Mormon from Gentile in a clear-cut fashion. Out of this revelation and subsequent interpretations of it, however, has arisen a distinctive body of religious beliefs at once closely related to that of Christians who believe revelation to have been closed with the New Testament, but possessing some features virtually unknown elsewhere.

The most important general feature of the Mormon belief system is its lack of a sense of transcendence. There is no sharp line drawn between the realms of the natural and the supernatural, but rather a difference in quality (and visibility). The elements of the universe are uncreated, eternal, and material. There is certainly a personal God, but one who lacks the distinctively transcendent character of the traditional Christian God. The God of the Mormons, though invisible, is part of the world of time and space, and is continually engaged in a process of development and self-creation. Jesus Christ, who plays a role in the dispensation of salvation in many ways similar to that of traditional Christians, is the first-born of this God; Adam, one of God's earliest "spirit children," assisted Jesus in the creation of the world.

Humans, the offspring of Adam, are not really that different from God. Like him, they are uncreated and eternal. Like him, they are capable of change and development, both in this world and the world yet to come. Further, in the Mormon interpretation, human nature is not flawed by original sin; sin is real, but it is the direct responsibility of each individual who commits it. Humanity thus enjoys extraordinary freedom to fashion itself into something quite literally divine. Humans are like what God once was, and from which God made himself into what he now is. To pursue this path of becoming godlike, however, humans are in need of the redemption made possible by the saving act of Jesus Christ who, on his future coming to earth, will enlist his "latter-day saints" into the task of re-creating the world.

Life in this world, however, is neither the beginning nor the ultimate end of human existence. All humans enjoyed a preexistence in the supernatural world, which they voluntarily left to come to earth to grow further in knowledge. Depending on their choices and progress in this life, they will continue to progress after physical death. Although a few will be damned, the majority of humanity will enjoy a future existence at one of three levels of increasing felicity: the Telestial, the Terrestrial, and the Celestial. Life here will be an exalted version of that experienced in this world, with pain and suffering gone; for the particularly worthy, it will involve reunion with one's earthly family. Mormons, of course, will have the advantage in the pursuit of bliss in the afterlife because they alone have been privy to the fullness of truth in this existence; similarly, they are also in greater jeopardy of damnation because of this privileged status.

The elaborate structure of the Church of Jesus Christ of Latter-day Saints is designed to assist the Saints in the pursuit of salvation through a lifelong involvement in the Mormon community. First, it should be noted that the paths followed by men and women are substantially different from one another. Patriarchal imagery from the Hebrew scriptures informed Joseph Smith's vision from the beginning. Mormons have never aspired as a group to a vision of identical status for the sexes, maintaining rather that men and women have separate but equal roles. Women participate actively in public worship and in the Women's Relief Society, but cannot aspire to the priestly roles that are reserved exclusively for their fathers, brothers, husbands, and sons.

The priesthoods established by Joseph Smith—or, as he would have it, *re*-established—are two: the *Aaronic* and the *Melchizedek*. The first consists of a series of three levels—deacon, teacher, and priest—which boys begin at age twelve and progress through until reaching eighteen or nineteen. At the latter age, they are recognized as adults through initiation into the status of elder, the first of the two stages of the Melchizedek order that function at the local level. As elders, at nineteen years of age, they spend two years, supported by themselves, as missionaries in the United States or abroad. (The spectacle of pairs of neatly groomed, conservatively dressed young men ringing doorbells and testifying to their faith is a familiar one for many Americans.) The final rank of high priest is that to which bishops and other holders of higher office are ordained on the basis of performing a particular role, and not simply age.

The basic unit of Mormon organization is the *ward,* roughly the equivalent of a parish, and typically including about seven hundred members. The ward is presided over by a bishop—like all priests, a layman engaged in a secular occupation as well—and provides the structure for weekly worship, Sunday school classes for all ages, meetings of the various priesthoods, and various other social, educational, and charitable activities. The basic unit of worship is the sacrament meeting, which is held weekly at the ward chapel, usually a rather ordinary building with appropriate facilities for assemblies and classes. Worship typically consists of informal talks by members of the congregation, hymn singing, and the administration of the sacrament in the form of bread and water. On the first Sunday of each month a Fast and Testimony Sunday is observed, before which worshipers maintain a complete abstinence from food for twenty-four hours and then offer personal testimonies at the sacrament meeting.

Besides supervising worship and other aspects of ward life, bishops also exercise the important gate-keeping function of certifying whether their congregants are worthy of admission to temple ordinances. The temple, which as an institution dates back to the early days at Kirtland and Nauvoo, is a distinctive Mormon institution where equally distinctive rituals are regularly carried out. As the Mormon population has dispersed so widely from its center in Utah, new temples are in an almost continual process of construction, and exist not only throughout the United States but much of the rest of the world as well. Unlike ward chapels, they are architecturally elaborate and frequently visually striking, evoking Gothic cathedrals, fantastic palaces, or Aztec temples in their eclectic, monumental designs—though, with their proliferation in recent years, their size, elaborateness, and cost have been scaled down.

The rituals performed at Mormon temples are known as *ordinances,* participation in which is restricted exclusively to worthy believers, and the details of which are carefully guarded from outsiders. The ordinances, which seem to derive in form (though not in meaning) from those of the Freemasonry in which Joseph Smith and other early Mormons participated, are said to have been revealed directly to Smith, and do not have direct analogues in Judaism or Christianity. Prominent among them is the baptism for the dead, which is performed vicariously in the immersion of a living person. Such baptism permits the enjoyment of the company of a large family extended through the generations in the afterlife, which is central to the Mormon vision of blessedness. In part to further this process, the Latter-day Saints maintain a vast genealogical library in Salt Lake City, and older people especially are encouraged to spend their time in tracing their ancestors for retroactive initiation into the fold. These holdings, now available on the Internet, are the result of an extensive international microcopying of demographic records, and are a treasure trove for secular researchers as well.

Two other important ordinances are carried out in Mormon temples as well. *Endowment* ceremonies are rites of initiation undergone by young adults before setting off on missionary work or marriage, as well as by converts of any age. Those participating wear special garments and engage in ritual bathing, during which their significant organs are anointed with oil. They witness a dramatic reenactment of cosmic history, are instructed in the Plan of Salvation, and are given secret biblical names. *Sealing* ceremonies bind a man and woman together for "time and eternity," and children may be sealed into this everlasting relationship as well. (Divorce is frowned on by Mormons, but Utah's divorce rate is fairly high nevertheless.)

At the higher levels of governance, *stakes* are administrative units that typically include eight to twelve wards, for a total of about five thousand people. (Their full name, which indicates their significance and their Old Testament derivation, is "Stake of Zion.") Stakes are presided over by a stake presidency of three and a high council of twelve or fifteen. The highest leadership of the Church resides with the *General Authorities,* who are based in Salt Lake City. Prominent among these are the Council of Twelve Apostles and the First Presidency, which consists of the president and two counselors. The first president is more than a powerful bureaucrat; as the successor of Joseph Smith, he inherits the latter's titles of "Prophet, Seer and Revelator," and may become the vehicle for communicating ongoing revelation on important matters (such as, in 1890, the cessation of polygamy).

The eldest of the Twelve Apostles automatically assumes the office of first president upon its vacancy, so that the highest leadership may take on the aspect of a gerontocracy, or government by the elderly, at times. Like all members of the priesthoods, the General Authorities are not specially trained for their roles, and are usually successful businessmen. (Ezra Taft Benson, secretary of agriculture under Dwight Eisenhower, served as first president beginning in 1985.) Because all males are expected to play leadership roles and belong to the several ranks of the priesthoods, there are no seminaries, and theology is largely the product of each individual's reflections on revelation and experience. Religious instruction for children, youth, and adults is offered each Sunday, however, as part of the ward's activities.

In addition to these formal structures of belief, worship, and authority, Mormons participate in a culture closely linked to but still transcending all of these formal components. Like the Hebrews, on which much of their collective identity is modeled, Mormons may be viewed not simply as a religious denomination, however distinctive its identity, but also as a *people*. Central to this notion of "peoplehood" is the Mormon notion of the *gathering*—the sorting-out of the followers of Joseph Smith from the Gentiles, which entailed, in the nineteenth century, the physical relocation of the Saints into gathered centers. Mormon teenagers are given a "Patriarchal Blessing," which lets them know from which part of the House of Israel they are descended. In short, the Mormons in the present age represent in a very real way a reconstitution of the nation of Israel, in a spiritual if not a literally genetic sense. (The recruitment of the early Mormons primarily from Americans of northwestern European descent, and Europeans of similar provenance, has in fact given many Mormons a common gene pool, reinforced by generations of intermarriage. Continual evangelization, especially in developing nations, has diluted this homogeneity in recent years, however.)

Although Mormons are now dispersed throughout the nation and the world, the original land of settlement in the Great Salt Basin retains a powerful significance. Salt Lake City is not only the administrative but also in many ways the symbolic and spiritual center for Latter-day Saints as well. Temple Square, where Brigham Young's great temple and other structures are located, serves as a sort of *axis mundi*—a "center of the world"—much as Jerusalem and, more broadly, Israel function for the Jewish people. Particularly interesting is the seagull monument in Salt Lake City, commemorating the deliverance of the earliest Utah settlers from famine when crickets devouring the crops were unexpectedly consumed by a flock of seagulls. (The parallel with the children of Israel feeding on heaven-sent manna during their years in the wilderness is striking, as are other features of the nineteenth-century Mormon "Exodus.") Other shrines commemorating major events in the life of Joseph Smith, such as the site of his birthplace in Vermont, are also maintained by the LDS Church as shrines, and a colorful historical pageant is enacted each summer in Palmyra, New York, at the site where Smith unearthed the gold plates he would translate into the *Book of Mormon*.

The life of the Mormon people is thus rooted in a shared history that even recent converts share vicariously and adopt as their own. Other parallels with the Hebrew people are instructive in understanding the Mormon way of life and self-understanding as a people, and are by no means accidental. A parallel to the Hebrew *kashrut* laws on clean and unclean foods is derived from the "Word of Wisdom," section 89 of the *Doctrine and Covenants* (which is composed of further revelations to Joseph Smith). Mormons are thereby enjoined from using tobacco, alcohol, and "hot drinks" (usually interpreted as caffeinated beverages including, today, many soft drinks), and to be moderate in the consumption of meat. These probably reflect the evangelical ethos of Smith's day—John Wesley gave his Methodist followers very similar dietary advice—as well as the exigencies of frontier life. The Mormon custom of keeping a year's supply of food always at hand—which is no longer universally honored in its literal sense—reflects a similar prudence in dealing with frontier hardships, and may take on eschatological overtones for some as a preparation for the "last days." (Mormons had few worries as "Y2K" approached.)

Other aspects of Mormon culture also reflect the stresses and isolation of the frontier years. Many towns in Utah were built along patterns prescribed by Brigham Young, and the older houses constitute a distinctive vernacular style. Much of Utah today is still shaped by a distinctive Mormon landscape, reflected in the arrangement of houses, lots, and streets, plantings of Lombardy poplars, fences, and other patterns of material culture. A body of folk songs, many dealing with the hardships endured during the trek to Utah and later adversities, persists, as does a distinctive Mormon hymnody. (The Mormon Tabernacle Choir is an ongoing source of national publicity and goodwill, and performs from a wide musical repertory.) The frontier years also generated a folklore, in which stories of providential deliverances (such as that commemorated in the seagull monument) and legends about Smith and Young join with versions of standard folklore motifs such as the story of the three Nephites. In these stories, from one to three strangers mysteriously appear to aid Mormons in distress and then vanish. It later turns out that these strangers were Nephites, the good people of pre-Columbian days whose story is told in the *Book of Mormon.* In other forms, the story still makes its anonymous rounds—most recently in modern America as the urban legend of "the phantom hitchhiker."

As the prohibitions on intoxicants and stimulants indicate, cleanliness and health are primary components of the Mormon value system—part of what has sometimes been called their "Work, Health, Education, Recreation" complex. Hard work, usually now in white-collar and professional occupations; a general emphasis on "clean living"; education, such as that provided at Brigham Young University and other Mormon-sponsored institutions; and a stress on the recreational value of sports—all are characteristic Mormon virtues, echoing the earlier American religious cultures of Puritanism and nineteenth-century evangelicalism.

Combined with these virtues is a social and political conservatism that continues to make Mormonism controversial among other Americans. Mormons tend to vote Republican, and Utah's delegates to Congress are usually firmly within the conservative wing of the Republican Party. Until 1978 black males were barred from the priesthoods, until a revelation similar to that which had ended polygamy brought about a change in policy. (The pressures generated by the Civil Rights Movement, as well as the difficulties of evangelism in Latin American countries with much more interracial mixture than is common in the United States, may both have played a role in this reversal.) Mormon attitudes toward the role of women remain very conservative. Large families are encouraged, and Mormon evangelism stresses heavily the attractiveness of a stable, traditional family. Although a feminist movement has been making itself felt in recent years within the more liberal wing of the Mormon community, considerable media attention focused in 1979 on Sonia Johnson, who was excommunicated for overly vocal public support of the Equal Rights Amendment.

Two events of the 1980s that received widespread media coverage are indicative of tensions within the Mormon community. In 1987 Mark W. Hofmann, a rare book dealer, pleaded guilty to two counts of murder that he had committed in the course of negotiating the sale of a series of forged documents on Mormon origins to prominent members of the LDS community. Apart from the gory details of the bombings involved, the central issue at stake here is the emphasis Mormons place on the precise authenticity of the community's origins in the events narrated by Joseph Smith. In particular, Mormon leaders were concerned with documents providing alternate accounts of Smith's discovery of the golden plates, which emphasized the folk-magical character of these events as well as the possible unreliability of Smith's narrative. Fortunately for traditionalist Mormons, the documents, which spoke among other things of a "white salamander," proved to be skillful forgeries by Hofmann. More recently, threats provoked by the publication of revisionist Mormon historian D. Michael Quinn's 1996 book, *Same-Sex Dynamics among Nineteenth-Century Americans: A Mormon Example,* led to the author's going into hiding. (This latter occurrence is indicative of the negative attitude toward homosexuality in Mormon culture, but highly atypical in the extremity of the reaction.)

Illustrative not of history but rather of the Mormon role in contemporary politics was the controversy over the administration and subsequent impeachment and removal from office of Arizona governor Evan Mecham, a Mormon, in 1988. Mecham aroused considerable opposition over a number of remarks on racial and sexual subjects (including a militant aversion to homosexuality), as well as his repeal of the state's observance of the birthday of Martin Luther King Jr. (a stance by no means shared by many of his coreligionists). Although his impeachment took place as the result of alleged financial irregularities on his part, some of his Mormon defenders were firmly convinced that he had been divinely chosen to be governor and that attacks on him were attacks on the LDS community as well.

Strains within the LDS community are clearly real, as is continuing opposition from without. The principal external foes of the Mormons had at one time been mainly evangelical Protestants exercised both about polygamy and about the deviance of Mormon belief from what they held to be the Christian norm. More recently, however, conservative Protestants and Mormons have converged on their traditionalist attitudes on social and political issues, and political and religious liberals have become increasingly critical about Mormon conservatism. This shift in alliances forms an interesting parallel to the cooperation of conservative Catholics with fundamentalists on the abortion issue.

Conflict within the Mormon ranks—real but muted today—is hardly something new. The persistence of a "fundamentalist," polygamous minority demonstrates the schismatic potential of such a radical change in direction as that which occurred in 1890. Though these groups are small and decentralized, and for obvious reasons prefer to avoid publicity, their continuing existence demonstrates the pluralism that has characterized the Mormon tradition since the time of Joseph Smith. The largest rift in the tradition in fact dates back to Smith's death and the temporary vacuum in leadership in which it resulted. The majority of Smith's followers quickly accepted Brigham Young as their leader, and followed him across the plains to Utah. A number of small splinter groups also emerged, such as that led by James Jesse Strang, who briefly headed a theocratic community of Mormon dissidents on Beaver Island, Michigan, from 1845 until his murder in 1856.

Although the "Strangites" still survive vestigially, most of his followers after his death left to join what today is still the principal organized alternative to the "Utah Mormons." The "Missouri Mormons," as they are sometimes known, constitute the Reorganized Church of Jesus Christ of Latter-Day [sic] Saints (RLDS), with a national headquarters in Independence, Missouri. This group was organized by several early Mormons who rejected Young's leadership and eventually persuaded the Prophet's son, Joseph Smith III, to assume the group's presidency—which he did in 1859. One of its principal differences from "Utah Mormonism" is its principle of leadership, through which until recently the presidency automatically devolved upon Smith's descendants. Although it affirms the authenticity of Smith's revelations, the RLDS have never accepted more distinctive later Mormon practices such as polygamy, "blood atonement" (the killing of murderers, which sometimes took place in Young's day), and the various temple ordinances. The RLDS church is much more liberal in social attitudes than its larger counterpart: it ordains women to the priesthood, has never drawn lines based on race, and is open to ecumenical relations with other Christian groups. Its membership in the middle of the first decade of the twenty-first century stood at about 130,000, compared with the much larger (3,800,000) numbers of its Utah-based counterpart. (At least as many Mormons lived outside the United States at that time, and officials anticipate a total membership of thirty-five million by the year 2020.) In 2001 the RLDS renamed themselves the Community of Christ, emphasizing their affinity with other mainline Protestant denominations.

These controversies over Mormon identity and inclusiveness have been carried out in the broader context of what historian Philip Barlow sees as a far-reaching transformation of the identity and character of the entire Mormon community. As we have seen, the Latter-day Saints have undergone a series of such transformations in the past: with the passage of leadership from Smith to Young and the subsequent creation of a semiautonomous "kingdom" in Utah, and with the later acknowledgment of the power of the United States government and the acceptance of a measure of social conformity as the price of freedom from federal interference.

More recently, an internally generated transformation has arisen from the LDS adoption of a policy known as *Correlation*. This is essentially a policy of administrative rationalization in which control of the church's teachings and activities remain firmly in the hands of centralized authorities. This has resulted in an increasing uniformity of LDS practice in areas ranging from architectural design of church buildings to the scheduling of communal activities to the format and content of periodicals and educational materials, with a concomitant decrease of influence by groups such as the Women's Relief Society. Prompted by fears of decreased central control in the face of rapid numerical growth and geographical expansion, this policy has been criticized by some as a covert adoption of the values of corporate America in a religious community where such values were already powerfully evident. The issue of LDS identity came to a head in the 2008 campaign for the Republican presidential nomination when Mitt Romney, the former governor of Massachusetts and a Mormon, attempted to persuade his party's conservative base that his religion was not an obstacle. In doing so, he stressed the commonalities of Mormonism with more traditional Christianity, but his argument was received with skepticism by many evangelicals who regarded the LDS as theologically aberrant. Romney, in any case, failed to receive the nomination.

Mormonism has been called the most American of religions, and has at times been treated as subversively un-American. It is clearly a community of apparent paradoxes: although its teachings strike most traditional Christians as extremely deviant, its social attitudes have brought it into increasing visibility as the American cultural and religious mood drifted rightwards since the 1970s. Although appearing to compromise on issues such as polygamy and, later, racial segregation, it has nevertheless continued on a conservative course that both aligns and estranges it from major sectors of American society. Its growing "normality" has led to higher levels of acceptability, and its aggressive evangelism and high birth rate have resulted in continuing dramatic growth. Whether its cultural "success" will lead to further erosion of its distinctiveness, and the relegation of its distinctive beliefs to vestigially symbolic status, remains to be seen.

CHAPTER 46

Traditions and Structures in the American Jewish Community

By the end of World War I, the institutional foundations had been thoroughly established for an American Judaism that was definitively divided into denominations, sharing a common tradition but irreparably split over differences on how to interpret and implement the dictates of that tradition. As the presence of a radically secular socialist element among New York's immigrant Jewish proletariat at the turn of the century illustrates, by no means all American Jews were religious. But for the many who remained so, a choice was necessary—first among the three major "denominations" or "traditions," and later among still other choices that the twentieth century presented.

The fourth and by far the smallest of the Jewish denominations is Reconstructionism, an outgrowth of the Conservative movement and inextricably bound up with the thought and work of Mordecai Kaplan (1881–1983). Kaplan, a professor at the Jewish Theological Seminary, was active throughout his long career in a variety of causes aimed at promoting the ideal expressed in the title of his most influential work, *Judaism as a Civilization* (1935). Kaplan's ideas combined several important concepts: that God is not personal, that the Jews are not a chosen people, and that Judaism is best understood as a complex of culture and tradition. The Reconstructionist emphasis on Jewish culture was a logical extension of some of the basic premises of Conservatism, but the de-emphasis on a personal god was a radical break with tradition.

The Reconstructionist movement was not originally intended to form the basis of a new denomination but rather to promote an emphasis within the Conservative community. The original synagogue-center that Kaplan helped found in New York in 1915 was the first institutional expression of this emphasis and provided a means of promoting Jewish culture in a nonsupernaturalist context. In 1940 the Jewish Reconstructionist Foundation was established, which published the journal *The Reconstructionist* and promoted the *havurot* movement, that is, small fellowships within synagogue congregations for focused pursuits of Jewish studies and causes. A Reconstructionist press was established in 1945 and published a controversial prayer book that same year. The Reconstructionist Rabbinic Fellowship was organized in 1950, followed by the Reconstructionist Federation of Congregations in 1955, which in 1961 added the words "and Fellowships" to indicate the inclusion of this particular vehicle for disseminating the movement's ideas. Finally, in 1968 the Reconstructionist Rabbinical College opened in Philadelphia.

Reconstructionism had thus traveled the road from a movement into a full-fledged denomination, though by far the smallest of America's Jewish traditions—about fifty to sixty thousand members in the late 1980s to the early 1990s. By the latter time, however, the tradition was beginning to modify its early de-emphasis on the supernatural by including references to biblical miracles and the Messianic age in its newly revised prayer book. Most Reconstructionist Jews, however, understand these previously omitted themes as symbolic or mythical rather than factual in character. In addition, the inclusion of the Matriarchs with the Patriarchs in the new prayer book was an indication that movement was not entirely in a traditionalist direction.

Although they do not constitute a formal denomination, the *(C)Hasidim* concentrated in metropolitan New York represent one of the most picturesque and also controversial aspects of Jewish life. The Hasidic movement began in eighteenth-century Poland among the followers of Israel ben Eliezer, the Baal Shem Tov ("Master of the Good Name") or, for short, *Besht*. The Besht's message was shaped in a mysticism expressed in ecstatic singing and dance and a life of down-to-earth, extremely traditional Jewish piety. The Hasidic movement spread rapidly through the Jewish communities of central Europe, and then, following World War II, to the United States. Of the approximately one-quarter of a million Hasidim in the world today, roughly 80 percent live in America, and about half of those in Brooklyn.

The Hasidic communities of Crown Heights, Williamsburg, Rockland County, and other enclaves in greater New York practice a "total immersion" style of Orthodox (that is, traditional) Judaism in which all other considerations are subordinated to the imperative of leading as pure a religious life as possible. One keynote of Hasidic practice is the sanctification of everyday life, even in its minutest details. Hasidic neighborhoods possess all of the material needs for strict observance: synagogues, religious schools, Hebrew bookstores, kosher restaurants and butcher shops, and at least one *mikva,* or ritual bathhouse where Jewish women cleanse themselves before marriage and after menstruation and childbirth. Women, whose marriages are arranged, play traditional family roles, are encouraged to have many children, and are strictly segregated from men during services. Hasidim of both sexes, however, eschew the life of the secular world as much as possible, and are easily recognizable by their distinct style of dress. Men wear beards (though not necessarily sidelocks), fur-rimmed hats, and long black coats, all characteristic of shtetl life in the Old World. Women shave their natural hair and wear wigs instead, on the grounds that their sexual provocativeness is thereby diminished.

The Hasidim in America are divided into a number of separate, sometimes violently antagonistic communities reflecting old-world divisions as well as contrasting attitudes to contemporary issues such as Zionism. The Lubavicher are probably the best known, in part because of their greater openness to outsiders and their zeal in evangelizing young Jews on secular college campuses. (Group names are derived from Hasidic "courts" in Europe or occasionally America where *rebbes,* or charismatic leaders, first attracted the community's core.) Their bitter enemies are the anti-Zionist Satmar, who in 1976 moved from Williamsburg to Monroe, New York, where they established a suburban complex of houses and apartments geared to Hasidic needs (for example, twin sinks and stoves for ultra-kosher cooking). Hasidic groups periodically clash not only with one another but also with their neighbors over such issues as Hasidic boys refusing to ride school buses driven by women.

Hasidism is the least centralized of the branches of Judaism, because each community, or court, looks to its *rebbe* (a variant of rabbi) for personal direction. Education at all levels is separate from that provided by other Jews as well as by secular society. Some groups maintain small rabbinical seminaries, and the Skvirer of Rockland County, New York, help support a significant number of their young men while they engage in full-time Talmudic study.

Reconstructionism and Hasidism represent almost polar alternatives, each illustrating the diversity of interpretations possible within the broader Jewish tradition.

Neither, however, has ever attained great numerical strength. The large majority of American Jews who express their heritage in religious terms have continued to divide themselves among the three major denominations or traditions—Orthodox, Reform, and Conservative. The National Jewish Population Survey for 2000–01 elicited the following self-identification: Orthodox, 10 percent; Reform, 35 percent; Conservative, 26 percent; "Just Jewish," 20 percent; and other, 9 percent. During the twentieth century, however, each of these traditions saw some significant changes.

Although Reform enjoyed great popularity in its early years, its appeal to American Jewry, and even to many of its own followers, began to come into serious question as the events of the twentieth century cast doubts on the optimistic rationalism of its early proponents. The Depression, the Holocaust, and the reestablishment of the State of Israel all raised new questions about the agenda expressed in the Pittsburgh Platform. Demography also had its impact, as the ranks of the latter generations of Reform rabbis arose from Jews of East European rather than German stock.

As a result of these pressures, post–World War II Reform began to exhibit some significant differences from its earlier character. Like most other American Jews, Reform Jews became enthusiastic supporters of Israel, and some, like Rabbis Stephen S. Wise of New York and Abba Hillel Silver of Cleveland, became prominent advocates of the Zionist cause. Hebrew began to find its way back into the liturgy, as did the voluntary practice of other Jewish traditions and observances. As early as 1937 the Central Conference of American Rabbis, the Reform counterpart of similar groups formed by the other Jewish denominations, drafted a new set of "Guiding Principles" that superseded the Pittsburgh document. This "Columbus Platform," as it came to be called, stressed Jewish particularity, as opposed to the universal aspects of Judaism emphasized by earlier reform, and the importance of Sabbath and holiday observation, including the use of Hebrew. A later statement adopted in 1976 in San Francisco made clear the impact that the Holocaust and Israel had on Reform consciousness; in 1999, another meeting of the rabbinical Central Conference in Pittsburgh gave its blessing to the wearing of yarmulkes, following the kosher laws, and other observances of traditional Judaism, although none of these was declared mandatory. Despite these shifts in priorities in a more traditional direction, all of these successive platforms have reaffirmed the Reform commitment to social justice and ethics—Prophetic Judaism—as manifested most recently in a receptivity to homosexuals. (Gay rabbinical ordination was approved in 1990, and in 1996 the Reform rabbinical association went on record as opposing a legal ban on same-sex unions.

Conservative Judaism has continued to serve as a mediating force in the Jewish community, preferring to follow tradition but not averse to even dramatic breaches of long-standing custom when such a breach appears warranted by contemporary needs. One of the most striking examples of this is the Conservative decision to follow the example of Reform Jews in ordaining women to the rabbinate, of which Amy Eilberg became the first in 1985—following the example of Sally Preisand, ordained in the Reform tradition in 1972. Women rabbis of whatever tradition, however, have faced the same obstacles to full employment as those ordained in the various Christian traditions, and they frequently are called to chaplaincies rather than synagogues. In 2006, the Conservative movement's Committee on Jewish Law and Standards declared that several contradictory positions on the issue of gay rabbinical ordination were all permissible options, leaving the decision to individual rabbis and rabbinical schools.

Although Conservatism, which modified the strict literalism of Orthodoxy in scriptural interpretation and ritual observance in a variety of ways, achieved numerical predominance in the twentieth century, the questions about Jewish identity raised by the Holocaust, together with an influx of European Jews following World War II, have given Orthodoxy a new vitality in America during the past few decades. Many highly Americanized business, professional, and academic people have lately been drawn back to the traditional observance of their ancestors, and the "Modern Orthodox" movement has been receptive to contemporary scientific and philosophical thought while remaining firmly rooted in religious tradition. One example of the adaptability of the Modern Orthodox movement has been the appearance in recent years of kosher Chinese restaurants in New York, Washington, and other cities with significant numbers of young Jewish professionals for whom religious tradition remains important but for whom the calorie-laden cuisine of the Old Country is no longer appealing. (This also illustrates that the kosher laws provide general guidelines as to what may be eaten, and do not prescribe any specific content or method of preparation.)

In addition to the denominations, American Jewish life has taken institutional form in a wide variety of other ways. One of the first groups to take as its goal the service of the American Jewish community as a whole was *B'nai B'rth* (b'-NAY brith, "Sons of the Covenant"), which began in 1845 as an Ashkenazic fraternal organization but soon branched out into broader endeavors. Two of its best-known activities are its Anti-Defamation League, which investigates and publicizes instances of anti-Semitism, and its Hillel Foundations on secular college campuses for the promotion of Jewish religion and culture. Similar work in civil and human rights is carried out by the American Jewish Committee (1906) and the American Jewish Congress (1918), which also publishes the journal *Judaism. Hadassah* ("myrtle") was founded in 1912 by Henrietta Szold as a women's Zionist organization concerned particularly with the promotion of health in Palestine/Israel. The United Jewish Appeal (1934) has also been a major force in raising funds for the support of Israel. The UJA merged in 1999 with the Council of Jewish Federations and the United Israel Appeal to form the United Jewish Communities (UJC), which in 2007 raised over 2.4 billion dollars in support of Jewish causes. For many secular Jews, support of the UJC is a primary means of identification with the broader Jewish community and tradition.

This list could be extended almost indefinitely to include any number of other

Jewish activities and organizations, including such marginal ones as the Hineni Ministries, or "Jews for Jesus," founded in 1973 by aggressively evangelistic Jewish converts to Christianity. This panoply of institutions is indicative of the appeal of the American style of voluntary organization to the needs and temperaments of American Jewry, as well as the multiplicity and complexity of answers to the question of what it means to be a Jew in America. Religious options range from various forms of Hasidism on the right to Reconstructionism at the other extreme. Even then, membership in one of the four "denominations" can entail a great deal more than worship, as the panoply of educational, cultural, and recreational activities sponsored by many synagogues indicates. And, though the synagogue has from the beginning served as the focus of American Jewish life, the emergence of such causes and organizations as those coordinated by the UJC is indicative of possibilities for identification and participation for those unwilling to make a particular affirmation.

CHAPTER 47

Jewish Identity and Jewish Culture in Twentieth-Century America

To be Jewish in twenty-first-century America involves making choices—more so, perhaps, than for any other major religious group. Even among religious Jews, to live as a Jew is to participate to a greater or lesser degree in a subtle network of social and cultural patterns that are rooted in part in the long historical experience of the Jewish people and in part among particularly American circumstances. To understand more fully the complexity involved in making such choices, we need first to review the social transformation of the American Jewish community after the end of the great influx of eastern European Ashkenazim during the "new immigration.".

While the assimilated and established earlier wave of Ashkenazim was engaged in coming to terms on one hand with these Yiddish-speaking newcomers, they were also experiencing similar pressures in reverse from their gentile counterparts. The era of the new immigration was also that of the emergence of a new "upper crust" of American urban society precipitated by the amassing of vast new fortunes by the "robber barons." This elite was symbolized in the famous list of "The 400" New York families who constituted a closed social clique in which Jews, no matter how wealthy or cultivated, were unwelcome. During succeeding decades, social institutions such as urban and country clubs, resort hotels, and the more prestigious eastern colleges began either to bar Jews entirely or, as in the case of the "Ivy

League" schools, to impose tacit but very definite quotas on the number of Jewish applicants who could be admitted.

These policies, which did not begin to come under serious public scrutiny until the close of World War II (for example, in the 1947 film *Gentleman's Agreement*), precipitated the creation of a parallel set of institutions catering primarily to Jews. American Jews had from early in the nineteenth century banded together for a combination of religious, fraternal, and philanthropic purposes, and external pressures now advanced the process still further. (Stephen Birmingham has amusingly chronicled the emergence of a "Jewish 400" in his popular *Our Crowd* and similar, later developments among Jews of Eastern European descent in *The Rest of Us.*) The ultimate result was a network of institutions such as Grossinger's and other resorts in the Catskills's "Borscht Belt," country clubs catering respectively to German and eastern European Jews, Jewish debutante parties, lavish bar and bas mitzvah celebrations, and the like.

In the economic sphere, a similar process was at work through which Jews, together with others not of British descent and Protestant affiliation, found entry into the higher reaches of the larger corporations and law firms difficult or impossible. Jewish fortunes were rather made in firms founded and maintained by Jews themselves, such as the clothiers Hart Schaffner and Marx or the brokerage house of Lehman Brothers, Kuhn, Loeb. Entry into academic and professional life was facilitated by traditionally free tuition at New York's City College, which emerged for thousands of immigrants and their children as a symbol of secular salvation in this new "promised land," supported by a strong work ethic and the prestige that Talmudic learning had enjoyed in the Old World. Medicine, dentistry, and psychiatry attracted many young Jews, and the numerous universities of the New York area provided opportunities in teaching and scholarship.

American Jews, especially those born in America of old-world parents, thus found themselves in a problematic situation. On the one hand, they were still perceived by many Gentiles as the perennial outsiders, simultaneously strange and familiar. Like other ethnic groups especially of eastern Mediterranean origin, they were superbly adapted by temperament and experience for success in a commercially oriented culture where education, enterprise, and adaptability all conduced toward material reward. However, they were often barred from access to the highest levels of acceptance—into business and law firms, prestigious colleges, and resorts and social clubs. In a few brand new areas of American life, such as motion pictures, they were able to enter at the proverbial ground floor and give that industry a distinctive culture of its own. Whether creating or reacting, however, American Jews of the early to middle twentieth century took part in shaping a distinctive social and cultural realm of their own, drawing in part on tradition and in part on contemporary experience for its ingredients. To seek the roots of this distinctively Jewish American culture, we have to retrace our steps many centuries to reconsider the historical experience of the Jewish people after the final downfall of ancient Israel.

Jewish culture is a rich and complicated subject, reflecting the long and intricate history of the Jewish people. Its ultimate roots are in the Hebrew Bible and the Talmud, which are obviously religious in character but which also reflect the intertwining of religious motifs and regulations in the minutest details of everyday life. From the beginnings, Jewish culture was not primarily a matter of detached theological speculation but one that permeated the lives of ordinary Jews and gave shape to the very stuff of their existence.

With the onset of the long process of Diaspora, a separation began to take place in this wholeness that had been possible when the Hebrew people had lived with one another in their own land and under their own governance. The Septuagint, for instance, reflects the Hellenization of Jewish culture in the translation of scripture from Hebrew into the previously alien Greek. The Sephardim and the Ashkenazim had to come to terms with the dominance of Muslims and Christians respectively, and the cultures they developed reflected an accommodation of Hebrew tradition with gentile ways. Again, language reflects this process of accommodation. The Sephardim in Iberia developed a speech called *Ladino,* based on Castilian Spanish but with an admixture of words from Hebrew and other Mediterranean languages. More important for the American Jewish experience, the Ashkenazim gradually came to speak *Yiddish,* a Germanic language, like Ladino modified with additions from Hebrew but drawing from the various Slavic languages of the host cultures—Polish, Russian, Czech—as well. In both cases, these distinctively Jewish languages served as a vernacular tongue for everyday affairs, while Hebrew, pronounced somewhat differently in each case, continued to be the language of worship and learning.

The role of Yiddish is a useful way of posing the question of the meaning of Jewish culture in America. Sephardic Jews were quick to adapt to American ways, and the Portuguese spoken by most of them did not survive long in the new-world environment. Although some of the early Ashkenazim in America spoke Yiddish, the later, larger contingents from the German states were among the most assimilated of American Jews; they spoke German, and soon learned English as well. It was not until the influx of hundreds of thousands of eastern European Jews in the later nineteenth century that the question of language became seriously problematic in the Jewish community. German American Jews looked down their noses at the newcomers' Yiddish, which could not claim, like Hebrew, a religious justification. Yiddish was clearly a mark of ethnic, or cultural, identity, rather than of religion. Even the organized Orthodox community shared with Reform a desire to Americanize these newcomers by teaching them English as rapidly as possible. The use of Hebrew in ritual may have been debatable, but the vernacular was not.

As Irving Howe has demonstrated in his popular *World of Our Fathers,* the Yiddish language was the core of the Jewish American culture that flourished briefly but ardently in Manhattan's Lower East Side during the decades around the turn of the century. Yiddish was the language of coffeehouse debates, poems, popular drama, innumerable newspapers, the *Landsmanschaften* (benevolent societies), and the everyday conversations in the home and on the street. It was spoken by learned rabbis and labor organizers alike. It expressed, in short, the identity of the eastern European Jews as a people and a culture rather than as a religion. The separability of these concepts—people, culture, religion—has been a perennial topic of debate among religious and secular Jews alike.

As the Jewish immigrants and their offspring in New York and elsewhere began rapidly to assimilate into American society, Yiddish started to disappear as a living language. By the latter part of the century, only the *Jewish Daily Forward* survived as a Yiddish-language newspaper, and it was mostly among the elderly that the language continued to be a means of casual communication. (The *Daily Forward*'s building continues to tower over today's Lower East Side, but with Chinese characters emblazoned on it.) YIVO, the American Yiddish archives, has had to campaign vigorously for the preservation of Yiddish-language publications in recent years, because little is now published in Yiddish and much of the output of the past has met the fate of ephemera regarded by later generations as of doubtful value. Except for the elderly and for recent immigrants, the language of American Jews has thus universally become American English. Yiddish has become, in Jeffrey Shandler's phrase, a "postvernacular language," used today not for everyday speech but rather as a means of identifying with a heritage. For Shandler, its use is more important than it's ostensible content.

American English, however—like the English language more generally—is a complex amalgam of elements from the widest variety of sources—including Yiddish. Leo Rosten, the author of the delightful *The Joys of Yiddish,* identifies a distinct variety of speech known as "Yinglish," that is, a variety of English vernacular in which Yiddish words, phrases, constructions, and intonations play a prominent role. Yinglish is spoken not only by some Jewish Americans, particularly those nurtured in predominantly Jewish neighborhoods, but by others as well, for example, those participating in the "show biz" cultures of New York City and Hollywood. Yiddish words that have entered the American vocabulary are especially those that characterize distinctive personality types or social roles: the *gonif,* or crook; the *yenta,* or gossip; the *kibitzer,* who offers unsolicited comments; the *schnorrer,* or beggar; the *schlemiel,* or clumsy unfortunate. Although these are character types that were once familiar in the now-vanished shtetl, their universality has rendered Yiddish a happy medium with which to render them in Yinglish. In addition to words, phrases such as "alright already," "so I lied," and "fancy-schmancy" use English words in Yiddish constructions or rhythms to indicate exasperation, sarcasm, or other desired special emphases.

In addition to language, food is another fundamental component of everyday life that has given Jewish American culture a special flavor. Dishes such as corned beef and pastrami, matzoh balls, gefilte fish, and latkes (potato pancakes) have multiple origins: in the laws of *kashrut,* in the special holiday foods such as those used in the

Seder, and in borrowings from the host cultures of central Europe. Restaurants and delicatessens in Jewish neighborhoods feature these and similar dishes, and many supermarkets have special sections of kosher foods. In addition to products that carry the U sign indicating approval as kosher, there is another label—"kosher style"— that indicates only that the item is prepared in a traditional way, not that it carries rabbinical approval. Jewish American cuisine, then, has both religious and secular origins and may be consumed in conformity with traditional dietary prescriptions or simply as an exercise in secular enjoyment. The emergence of kosher Chinese restaurants in East Coast cities in recent years as an accommodation to the tastes of younger Jewish professionals is an interesting marker of the distinction between "kosher" as a ritual designation and "kosher-style" as an ethnic foodway.

The emergence of a distinctive Jewish American culture in the twentieth century has also generated an expression and reaction in what we might call "high culture," that is, literature and the arts that aim at more than simple entertainment. The moral and emotional ambiguities of the immigrant drive for material success were evoked in the now-classic novel *The Rise of David Levinsky* (1917). The author of this poignant work was Abraham Cahan, an immigrant labor organizer who later edited the *Jewish Daily Forward.* The plays of Clifford Odets and Elmer Rice reflected the social concerns implicit in Cahan's work. Henry Roth's *Call It Sleep* (1934) and Michael Gold's *Jews without Money* (1930) also drew on the immigrant experience for their subject matter, as did some of Bernard Malamud's earlier works such as *The Assistant* (1957) and *The Magic Barrel* (1958). The postwar transition of much of the Jewish community from immigrant slum to prosperous suburb received scathing attention in Philip Roth's *Goodbye, Columbus* (1959) and *Portnoy's Complaint* (1969), which dealt satirically and even scatologically with such stereotypes of American Jewish culture as the "Jewish American Princess" and the "Jewish Mother." At a somewhat lower level of literary aspiration, popular novels such as Leon Uris's *Exodus* (1958) and Herman Wouk's *Marjorie Morningstar* (1955) dealt respectively with the independence of Israel as well as the ambiguities of assimilation and the quest of success among American Jews.

As already noted, film, a medium in which "high" and "low" are confusingly intertwined, has been a realm in which a uniquely Jewish American presence was established from its beginnings. Because the film industry had no establishment, it offered a level playing field in which Jewish immigrants such as Samuel Goldwin (né Goldfish) of Metro-Goldwin-Mayer could simultaneously make their fortunes and profoundly influence a major new segment of American popular entertainment. Themes of tradition versus assimilation were explored in some early films, such as *The Jazz Singer* of 1927, in which a cantor's son, played by Al Jolson, leaves the world of Jewish liturgy for success as a secular entertainer. Growing distrust of the medium's blatant sexuality, coupled with a concern for distribution in a Europe rapidly coming under Nazi domination, resulted in a suppression of Jewish themes and identifiable actors during the 1930s, a process that transmuted John Garfinkel into John Garfield. Following World War II, growing awareness of and revulsion against the Holocaust created an atmosphere in which Jewish issues could be explored openly on the screen. Some examples included *Exodus* (1960), an epic story of the creation of Israel as an independent nation; *The Pawnbroker* (1965), the story of a Holocaust survivor's subsequent experience in the United States; and *The Fixer* (1968), a screen adaptation of novelist Bernard Malamud's story of anti-Semitism in czarist Russia. The Jewish vaudeville tradition, originally brought to the screen by the Marx Brothers, was now revived in the films of Mel Brooks (né Kaminsky), in which identifiably Jewish actors such as Madeline Kahn, Marty Feldman, and Gene Wilder made good-humored fun of a succession of film genres, beginning with *Young Frankenstein* in 1974. Woody Allen's neurotic personae similarly wrought variations on contemporary Jewish social and cultural themes, as in the 1986 *Hannah and Her Sisters*.

One interesting way in which traditional Judaism and contemporary American popular culture have converged during the past decade is through an interest in *Kabbalah* (one of a wide variety of spellings for the term), a tradition of esoteric Torah interpretations with medieval roots. Kabbalah was popularized by the twentieth century Jewish scholars Martin Buber and Gershom Sholem, but its contemporary American appropriation is rather different from what those gentlemen had in mind. The Kabbalah Centre in Los Angeles, led by Rabbi Yehuda Berg, came to public attention through the efforts of the performer Madonna, who subsequently recruited celebrities such as Britney Spears, Demi Moore, and David and Victoria (aka Posh Spice) Beckham to the cause. This version of Kabbalah involves wearing a "Red String" on the left wrist (available through the Centre for twenty-six dollars), which is billed as useful in warding off the Evil Eye; reading Berg's *The 72 Names of God;* and reciting meditations several times daily. In the wake of the anxieties generated by 9/11, some fifty thousand students each week at one time are said to frequent the Centre's fifty branches worldwide, presumably in search of the same easing of tensions accorded others by yoga, Zen, meditation, transcendental meditation (TM), and other techniques associated with New Age spirituality.

The works of three Jewish American winners of the Nobel Prize also illustrate aspects of what has sometimes been called a Jewish American literary renaissance, displacing the role the South had previously enjoyed as a cultural source of powerful fiction. Elie Wiesel, born in Romania in 1928, is a survivor of Nazi concentration camps who later emigrated to America and has written some of the most significant fictional interpretations of the experience of the Holocaust. Whereas Wiesel composes in French, Isaac Bashevis Singer's writings were first written in Yiddish—like those of his predecessor, Sholem Aleichem—and then translated into English and frequently printed in such literary outlets as the *New Yorker*. Singer (1902–91), who was born in Poland, takes as his world the pre-Holocaust culture of central Europe's ghettoes and shtetls. His themes are drawn from everyday experience; the mystical world of the Hasidim and the Kabbalah's system of esoteric and occult interpretation of scripture; and the realm of Jewish folklore, populated with strange and wonderful figures like the *dybbuk,* or evil spirit, and the *golem,* or artificial human. (The golem is though by some to be the prototype of the comic book hero Superman, created by Jewish American artists Jerry Siegel and Joe Shuster in 1932.)

In contrast with those of both Wiesel and Singer, the novels of the third Jewish Nobelist, Saul Bellow (1915–2005), are set very much in twentieth-century America, especially Bellow's *Chicago.* (Bellow was born in Canada in 1915.) His characters, from the protagonists of *The Adventures of Augie March* (1953) to *Henderson the Rain King* (1958) to *Herzog* (1964), are usually Jewish, but the religious dimension of their lives, if any, is not a primary concern. Beginning with the situation of the Jew in America, Bellow expands into more universal questions of human meaning in the twentieth-century urban context. As such, he represents a transition into the realm of a number of other distinguished contemporary American writers who, though of Jewish origin, do not deal explicitly for the most part with distinctively Jewish subject matter—for example, Norman Mailer, J. D. Salinger, Arthur Miller, and E. L. Doctorow. Rather, their work reflects a Jewish perspective in a broader sense, namely, that of the "marginal man" seeking meaning in modern secular life and developing—or failing to develop—personal or political responses in a postreligious world where the traditional rootless, alienated situation of the Jew has become normative for humanity in general.

On the latter theme, American Jews have reacted to their society with ambivalence. On the one hand, America has provided a refuge for millions of Jewish as well as other immigrants, offering economic opportunity in addition to freedom from overt persecution. On the other hand, the disparities between the land where the streets were allegedly paved with gold and the actualities of American life have prompted two typically Jewish responses: satirical critique and political protest. Early in the twentieth century many second- and third-generation Jews, like other minority-group members, found the emergent world of popular and mass entertainment an area in which institutional practices were too fluid for them to be automatically excluded. Although Jews more typically became sports commentators than sports heroes, the possibilities of show business seemed ready-made for their talents. First in the "Borscht Belt" of the Jewish resorts in the Catskills and in the vaudeville houses of New York, then in radio, film, and television, Americans Jews became intimately involved in entertainment, and especially in comedy.

Comic styles have ranged greatly, including the long-suffering, penny-pinching persona of Jack Benny; the antic vulgarity of Milton Berle; the sophisticated monologues of Shelley Berman; and the bitter, iconoclastic social commentary of Mort Sahl. The films of the Marx Brothers, in which the irrepressible Groucho, Chico, and Harpo wrought havoc with the conventions and pretensions of proper gentile society, perhaps best encapsulate the possibilities of this kind of social critique. On the other side, reflecting a corresponding Jewish American strain of ironic self-criticism, is Woody Allen's self-description of being "Jewish, with an explanation."

The line separating theater and politics is a fine one, and is also illustrative of some of the ambiguities of Jewish American identity. A number of Jews representing states with large Jewish constituencies have achieved distinction in Congress—for example, New York's senator Jacob Javits—and in 2000 the number of Jewish senators had reached eleven, including California's Diane Feinstein and Barbara Boxer. Also in 2000, the nomination of Connecticut senator Joseph Lieberman, a Modern Orthodox Jew, as the Democratic Party's candidate for vice president was a major breakthrough for Jewish visibility on the national political scene. Although lobbying efforts by Jewish groups have been instrumental in securing American support for Israel, American Jews have more generally been supportive of political and social movements rooted in the ancient prophetic tradition of advocacy of social justice. Jews, for example, have been disproportionately influential not only in the B'nai B'rth Anti-Defamation League but in secular organizations such as the National Association for the Advancement of Colored People (NAACP) and the American Civil Liberties Union (ACLU)—as well as, traditionally, the Democratic Party.

Jews in both Europe and America have also played a leading role in more radical causes, beginning with Karl Marx himself. Jewish immigrants such as Samuel Gompers and Abraham Cahan were active as leaders in the early days of the American labor movement, and many Jews involved themselves in socialist causes. More controversial was the heavily Jewish membership in the American Communist Party in its heyday, before revelations about Stalin's purges and the anti-Semitic character of Soviet Communism induced serious afterthoughts in many. The trial and 1953 execution of Julius and Ethel Rosenberg underscored this association and alarmed many American Jews about its implications concerning anti-Semitism in their own country. In a less political vein, the "Beat" culture of the 1950s found expression in the poems of Allen Ginsberg, including his "Kaddish." Later, during the "counterculture" era of the 1960s, the Jewish American Abbie Hoffman and Jerry Rubin played central roles in the formation of the "Yippie" Party, and were arraigned as part of the "Chicago Seven" following the militant protests against the Democratic National Convention in Chicago in 1968. Many other young Jews were active in various phases of the antiwar movement and such radical organizations as Students for a Democratic Society (SDS). More recently, a number of "New York Jewish intellectuals" such as Norman Podhoretz and Irving and William Kristol have aligned themselves with the neoconservative political movement, and secular Jewish journals of opinion such as *Commentary* have reflected this drift.

Kurt Lewin's explanation for the prominence of Jews in a wide variety of contemporary secular movements is based on the hypothesis of a simultaneous need by many Jews to divorce themselves from traditional Jewish particularism while continuing to maintain the tradition of prophetic witness. According to this theory,

Marxian Communism, Freudian psychoanalysis, and a variety of other political and ideological movements are seen as an attempt to resolve the illusions and injustices of society by resorting not to religion but rather to some other, nontheistic but nevertheless ultimate explanatory principle. To embrace such a cause is thus a means of being simultaneously Jewish and non-Jewish—an escape from the burden of a problematic religious heritage and ethnic identity while nevertheless carrying out the prophetic mission of Judaism. Although such an approach inevitably oversimplifies, it does present some interesting insight into certain aspects of the secular dimension of contemporary Jewish culture.

In the realm of education, Jews again have excelled in academic pursuits far out of proportion to statistical expectations. The roots of this may lie in part in a "success ethic" and also in the prestige that religious learning was accorded in the Old World. In America, that kind of learning has been displaced by the secular, and many American Jews have utilized nonreligious educational institutions extensively. The public school system and the tuition-free City College of New York both became vehicles for the "melting pot" and the process of upward social and economic mobility that characterized the second generation of the eastern European immigrants. Although most American religious groups vied with one another during the nineteenth and earlier twentieth centuries in the establishment of colleges, Jews generally held back and preferred public and nondenominational private schools instead. One exception is the network of institutions maintained by the Hasidim and to a lesser extent by the Orthodox, of which Yeshiva University is the focus for the latter. The other exception is Brandeis University, established as a secular Jewish institution in 1948, and one of the few major private American universities to be founded since World War II.

For most American Jews, the pursuit of Jewish learning takes place in addition to rather than in place of secular schooling. All of the Jewish denominations have sponsored educational programs for younger people, though with different strategies. Reform Jews have generally utilized instruction on weekends, whereas Conservative and Orthodox congregations have also sponsored day schools. Jewish community centers and synagogue-centers have also included extensive adult education in their programs. Only the Hasidim and some of the Orthodox, however, have attempted to erect an entire educational system parallel to and apart from the American social mainstream.

In the realm of theological education, the leading Jewish seminaries—Hebrew Union College, Jewish Theological Seminary, and Yeshiva—have provided the bases not only for rabbinical education but also for research in Jewish studies in America. As with other American religious groups, most theology as well as other religious scholarship has emerged from the seminary context, augmented by the work of Jewish academics on secular university faculties. Prior to World War II, Jewish theology was mainly conducted in the context of the emergent denominational communities. Orthodox generally pursued traditional Talmudic studies. Early Reform spokesmen such as Isaac Mayer Wise, David Einhorn, and Kaufman Kohler expressed themselves in that movement's early manifestos and other writings. They advocated in particular the notion that Judaism's mission was universal, and that America rather than Palestine was the place to promote the call to spread monotheism in cooperation with liberal Christians. Conservatives such as Solomon Schecter began to articulate a more distinctive and particularistic path for Jews rooted in the preservation of Jewish traditions. Mordecai Kaplan, the founder of the Reconstructionist movement, began with the matrix of Conservatism but went on to substitute for the traditionally personal God of Judaism the phrase "God-idea," thus transforming God into a force arising out of the collective social experience of the Jewish people.

The experience of the Holocaust and the reemergence of Israel, however, led to a distinctive shift in emphasis in Jewish thought in America and elsewhere. The most urgent question was now that of *theodicy*: if there is a God, how and why does that God permit evil in the world? At one extreme, Richard Rubenstein denied in his work *After Auschwitz* (1968) that there was a God, thus joining ranks with the "Death of God" movement then popular in radical Christian theological circles. Rubenstein did not call for an end to Judaism, however, but rather argued that solidarity among the Jewish people, even without a theistic basis, was now more necessary than ever.

The more dominant note in contemporary Jewish thought, however, was not so radical, but emerged out of the broader intellectual movement known as *existentialism*. This approach was clear in the title of what has probably been the most broadly influential work of modern Jewish writing, Martin Buber's *I and Thou*, which takes as its starting point the personal encounter between God and the individual. Whereas Buber's popularity has been even greater among Christians than Jews, given the universality of his message, his German contemporary Franz Rosenzweig rooted a similar approach more directly in traditional Jewish categories of God, Torah, and Israel. Variations on the theme of individual response to divine commandment in the context of Jewish tradition and community can be found in the work of twentieth-century American Jewish thinkers such as Eugene Borowitz, Emil Fackenheim, Will Herberg, and Abraham Joshua Heschel as well. Heschel (1907–72), a professor first at Hebrew Union College and then at Jewish Theological Seminary, gained special influence through his active participation in the Civil Rights Movement and other social causes.

Creativity in the American Jewish experience has manifested itself primarily in the realm of verbal expression, but has not been entirely lacking in the other arts. That it has not always taken primarily religious form, however, is clear from the preeminence of Jews as violin virtuosi, but in the context of secular performance. The religious arts have focused on worship, where there has not been a strong distinctively Jewish tradition. Jewish American liturgical music, for example, has been derived from a combination of Jewish and gentile sources, and has not been aesthetically notable. Its main distinction has been in liturgical pieces specially commissioned from secular

Jewish composers such as Leonard Bernstein, Ernst Bloch, Arnold Schoenberg, and Kurt Weill. Folk music derived from both European and Middle Eastern sources, such as that popularized by recently revived *klezmer* bands, has gained a wide audience, and folk or folklike songs such as "Hava Nagila" are now well known among Jews and Gentiles alike. Folk elements have also been incorporated into the paintings of Marc Chagall and the stories of Isaac Bashevis Singer.

As a consequence of the Diaspora, a distinctive style of Jewish religious architecture never developed in the Old World, and synagogues were usually designed in the styles of Christian or Muslim host cultures. America's first Jewish house of worship was the Touro Synagogue in Newport, Rhode Island (1763), designed by the prominent architect Peter Harrison in the neoclassical style. Nineteenth-century synagogues similarly utilized contemporary modes such as the Greek Revival, the Romanesque, and the Gothic. The desire for a more distinctively Jewish expression in the era of Romantic revivalism led to such structures as Cincinnati's B'nai Yeshurun (1866), which incorporated the intricate design elements of the Venetian Gothic with minaretlike towers evoking the Islamic tradition. This, interestingly, was the setting for Reform worship led by Isaac Mayer Wise. Even more exotic were the bulbous domes that graced the towers of New York's Central Synagogue (1872) and other "Jewish-Victorian" structures. The later twentieth century saw dramatic experiments in new architectural idioms, such as Norman Brunelli's tentlike B'nai Jehudah in Kansas City (1958 and 1969). Modern synagogues sometimes feature striking sculptural renditions of biblical motifs as well.

A commentary on the character of Jewish culture in contemporary America should finally include a few words on the demographic and geographical patterns of the distribution of the American Jewish community. The approximately six and a half million Jewish Americans of the first decade of the twenty-first century constituted the largest Jewish population of any nation in the world, equaling the combined total of its two nearest competitors, Israel and Russia. The New York City metropolitan area represented by far the largest concentration, with an estimated Jewish population of roughly 1,400,000 in 2002. Chicago, Los Angeles, Miami, Philadelphia, and Washington, D.C., together with northern New Jersey, are other areas of heavy Jewish residence, though almost every major metropolitan area in America has a significant Jewish population.

Although Jews continue to be overwhelmingly urban or suburban in their residential preferences, their original concentrations in the cities of the Northeast and Great Lakes area have been modified by dispersion throughout the Sunbelt states of the South and West, following the broader national trend. At the turn of the twenty-first century, roughly 43 percent lived in the Northeast; 13 percent in the Midwest; 22 percent in the South, and 22 percent in the West. (Movement in recent decades, as with Americans more generally, has been from the northeastern quadrant into the "Sun Belt.") Patterns of residential segregation, partially through self-selection and partly as a result of discrimination, persist in many areas, and "Jewish neighbor-hoods" can be identified not only in older urban areas but in newer suburbs as well. A distinctive instance of special settlement is Miami Beach, to which Jewish retirees from New York City began to flock in the 1930s and where the Art Deco hotel district represents a unique ethnic and architectural enclave in American society.

This brief survey of Jewish American culture should make clear the complexity of the issue. Its sources are multiple, from folklife as well as the heights of contemporary thought, from Europe and the Middle East, all blended in the American crucible. One can attempt to differentiate "high" and "low" (or everyday) culture, religious and secular culture, or the amalgamation of various strata in such movements as Reconstructionism. For analytic as well as ideological purposes, it is possible to speak of the religion of Judaism, of Jewish culture(s), and of Jewish nationality or peoplehood, rooted in history and genetics—all as separate and separable categories, which in actuality are often inextricably entangled. Much of American Jewish dialogue has focused on the relationship of these aspects of the Jewish experience, and the plurality of answers to the question of American Jewish identity indicates that this dialogue is likely to continue with vigor into the indefinite future.

CHAPTER 48

Vatican II and the End of the Catholic "Ghetto"

The decades that followed Leo XIII's encyclical *Testem Benevolentiae* were a period of physical expansion and intellectual retrenchment in the American Catholic Church, in which the attitudes of Irish-descended, English-speaking conservatives were to dominate. Hopes for the perpetuation of foreign-language ethnic parishes were dashed by episcopal policy, which frequently resulted in the assignment of English-speaking pastors to German or other ethnic parishes. Further, the onslaught of World War I brought about a sometimes hysterical public revulsion against all things German. The war itself and the restrictive legislation passed by Congress during the 1920s slowed Catholic immigration considerably, and the passage of the years also promoted the process of Americanization as new generations were brought up speaking English as their first language and having it reinforced in parochial as well as public schools. The expansion of Catholic education at the secondary as well as the primary level by the 1920s also had the indirect result of promoting further standardization by bringing into being centralized high schools, diocesan school boards, and certification programs for teaching sisters.

This drive toward centralization and standardization was typical of institutional American Catholicism as a whole during the decades between World War I and Vatican II. This was the era of the "builder bishop," exemplified in such figures as Cardinals George Mundelein of Chicago and Francis Spellman of New York. These princely figures reigned over their sees with unchallenged authority, presided over ambitious building programs of churches, schools, and hospitals, and served as nationally recognized spokesmen on the "Catholic position" on public issues. Among these positions were calls for American intervention or a pro-Catholic neutrality abroad where Catholic interests were threatened, such as the Mexican Revolution and the Spanish Civil War; government aid to parochial schools, which were still promoted as an alternative to the secularism of the public system; opposition to Prohibition, which was interpreted as implicitly anti-Catholic in its incompatibility with European folkways and sacramental use of wine; censorship of films, many of which were said to promote immorality; and vigorous opposition to artificial contraception. After World War II, both Pope Pius XII and Cardinal Spellman emerged as incarnations of militant anti-Communism as much of eastern and central Europe fell under Soviet dominance, with a corresponding persecution of Catholic leaders such as Hungary's Cardinal Jozsef Mindszenty. American Catholic opinion on the wisdom of Joseph McCarthy's anti-Communist tactics during the 1950s varied considerably, though Cardinal Spellman's endorsement of the Catholic junior senator from Wisconsin created the impression of a more monolithic support from his own church than was really the case.

Throughout this era the public stance of the institutional Catholic Church was remarkably uniform—only a few lay-edited journals such as *Commonweal* and *The Catholic Worker* publicly dissented on the issue of American neutrality in the Spanish Civil War, which would aid the pro-Catholic cause of Francisco Franco and which became a touchstone of loyalty within the Catholic leadership. On political issues that primarily involved economics, however, Catholic sentiment was considerably less conservative than that suggested by these other positions on matters of public morals and international affairs. Leo XIII's encyclical *Rerum Novarum*, which promulgated the idea of the "just wage" and took a generally progressive stance on other issues involving the rights of working people, provided the groundwork for an influential movement in the American church exemplified in the career of Monsignor John A. Ryan (1869–1945), the "Bishops' Program of Social Reconstruction" of 1919, and the National Catholic Welfare Conference. Ryan and other Catholic clergy were also employed in labor mediation and other social programs during the administration of Franklin Roosevelt. Roosevelt, an Episcopalian of an old and wealthy family, had come to power in part through the support of Catholic working people, and in turn appointed unprecedented numbers of Catholics to the cabinet, the judiciary, and other branches of the federal government.

Other, more extreme political options also began to be promulgated by articulate Catholics during the 1930s and beyond. Father Charles Coughlin (1891–1979) gained national attention as the "radio priest," broadcasting from his Shrine of the Little Flower in Royal Oak, Michigan, and publishing his views in his periodical, *Social Justice*. Coughlin began during the Depression era as a supporter of the New Deal, but soon turned against Roosevelt and toward a not-too-covertly anti-Semitic populist program similar to that of Louisiana's Huey Long. Coughlin helped form a new Union Party to oppose Roosevelt in 1936, but its complete failure and subsequent pressure from his bishop forced him into political retirement by the end of the decade.

At the other end of the political spectrum was the Catholic Worker Movement, formed by the ex-Communist Catholic convert Dorothy Day (1897–1980) and her French anarchist friend, Peter Maurin. Inspired by a philosophy of Christian personalism, which made the integrity of each human being the central object of religious concern, Day and her compatriots set about the propagation of a critique of the American capitalist economic order in their tabloid, *The Catholic Worker*. Another major feature of the workers' program was the "houses of hospitality" they established in many large cities, where volunteers provided food and shelter for the down-and-out. The Catholic Worker Movement, which has survived its founders, taught that the American system erred in its dehumanization of the poor and tried to provide positive Christian alternatives to the facelessness of the contemporary social order. Although Day's ideas were in many ways radical, her doctrinal orthodoxy and care not to offend ecclesiastical leadership saved the movement from episcopal interference or censure. Her life was the subject of the 1996 feature film *Entertaining Angels,* starring Moira Kelly and Martin Sheen.

This strain of Catholic radicalism received a new lease on life during the 1960s, when the Civil Rights Movement and the Vietnam War engaged many Catholics in new forms of political activism. Particularly prominent in this era were the brothers Daniel and Philip Berrigan, respectively a Jesuit and Josephite priest. Both were imprisoned for their roles in a variety of antiwar protests, including the destruction of draft files at Baltimore and Catonsville, Maryland. Catholic opinion on Vietnam was by no means homogeneous, however, as Cardinal Spellman continued his public anti-Communist stance in support of American involvement in southeast Asia.

Catholic support for World War II had been much less controversial, and the "last good war" helped to promote the integration of many "ethnic" Catholics into the mainstream of American life through the inevitable mixing of peoples brought about by military service and the emphasis of wartime propaganda on the "melting pot" motif. Following the war, thousands upon thousands of Catholic veterans benefited from the provisions of the "G.I. Bill" of 1944, which made higher education a reality for unparalleled numbers of young men and which also promoted the expansion of educational facilities, including those sponsored by the Catholic Church, on a vast scale. This opening up of educational and career possibilities may also, in the long run, have made the celibate priesthood a less attractive path to professional status for young Catholic men. The effects of the postwar exodus to the suburbs, where previously separate ethnic groups now mingled easily in parishes with no history of national or linguistic particularity, also furthered the process of assimilation and homogenization. Television also contributed to the progress of these latter social forces. During the 1950s the Catholic Church's public image was especially enhanced by the *Life Is Worth Living* series, the video vehicle for the extraordinarily mediagenic Bishop Fulton J. Sheen.

The early 1960s were dominated in American Catholic public life by the "two men named John": John F. Kennedy and Pope John XXIII. Previously, only one Catholic had ever received the nomination of a major party for the American presidency. Al Smith, the Irish American governor of New York who ran unsuccessfully as a Democrat against Herbert Hoover in 1928, was defeated in part through organized anti-Catholic efforts, but also because of his urban and ethnic image, his anti-Prohibition stance, and the futility of any Democrat's trying to oppose the high tide of Republican prosperity prior to the Great Crash of 1929. Kennedy was also an Irish American with ties to a big-city ethnic political machine—his grandfather "Honeyfitz" Fitzgerald had been mayor of Boston during the 1920s—but his Harvard pedigree and personal charm helped him overcome prejudice and eke out a narrow victory over Richard Nixon in 1960 despite a modest attempt by anti-Catholics to use the religious issue against him. Kennedy's assassination in 1963 elevated him to the status of virtual popular sainthood; since his breakthrough, the Catholic affiliation of political figures such as his brothers Robert and Edward, as well as Edmund Muskie, Alexander Haig, Sargent Shriver, Mario Cuomo, and Thomas P. "Tip" O'Neill, has seldom been problematic. (Early in the 1990s the *New York Times* noted that two Catholics in a row—Edmund Muskie and Alexander Haig—had occupied the sensitive position of secretary of state with virtually no notice of their religious affiliation, an occurrence that a generation earlier would have prompted considerable public alarm in some quarters.)

During the 1984 presidential election, however, Democratic vice-presidential candidate Geraldine Ferraro, an Italian American Catholic congresswoman from New York's borough of Queens, became engaged in a public controversy with New York archbishop John O'Connor over her refusal to oppose government funding for abortions. The same issues came to a fore during the 2004 presidential election, when Democratic nominee John Kerry came under fire from several members of the hierarchy for his stands on abortion. Many conservative Catholics had by this time abandoned their traditional association with the Democratic Party. Instead, they supported the "social agenda" of Ronald Reagan, which called for a strong public stand against abortion, pornography, and other sexually related issues. This alliance of Catholics with militant Protestant evangelicals such as Jerry Falwell and Pat Robertson represented a dramatic change from the hostility between the two camps that had characterized American religious politics in the past. Since then, the drift of Catholics into the Republican camp has been steady though not overwhelming or irreversible, arising both from ideological affinity and the ascent of large numbers of non-Hispanic Catholics into middle- or upper-middle-class status. By 2006 George W. Bush's successful nominations of Samuel Alito and John G. Roberts Jr. to the United States Supreme Court resulted in that body's having, for the first time, a majority of Roman Catholic members, including Roberts as chief justice. (Anthony Kennedy, Antonin Scalia, and Clarence Thomas were the others.) The impact of Vatican II—"Pope John's Revolution"—on the American Catholic community was even more profound. Its thoroughgoing program of reappraising traditional thought and practice created a mood of great hope and expectation among many Americans, as well as a profound sense of disorientation for others—at times the same people. The abandonment of the Latin Mass and experimentation with new liturgical forms, including the use of folk music, was the most visible change. It contributed to the loss of a sense of certainty that was exacerbated by the widespread disregard of Paul VI's condemnation of artificial contraception. On the right, the Catholic Traditionalist Movement led in the United States by Father Gommar A. De Pauw led a number of parishes into near-schism in their rejection of the vernacular liturgy. At the other end of the political spectrum, both lay and religious women became more and more vocal in their protest against the exclusion of their sex from positions of authority and participation in the life of the church. Controversies on this subject ranged from the use of "altar girls" at Mass to the ultimate question of the ordination of women to the priesthood, which Pope John Paul II in the mid-1990s declared not to be an open subject for discussion by Catholics.

Still another manifestation of ferment in the postconciliar church was less easily classified on a scale of "left" to "right." This was the charismatic movement that affected the Catholic community as well as many "mainline" Protestant denominations beginning in the 1960s. This "Catholic pentecostalism" was based on the premise that ordinary believers could receive such "gifts" of the Holy Spirit as speaking in tongues (*glossolalia*) and spiritual healing. Beginning on college campuses—Duquesne, Notre Dame, the University of Michigan—it spread throughout many parishes and frequently resulted in stresses between its proponents and skeptics. On the other hand, such practices were not contrary to official church teaching and were never condemned. By the 1980s the charismatic movement had subsided somewhat, though it continued as a minor current in church life.

Ethnic pluralism had also been a continuing source of change and challenge in twentieth-century American Catholicism, though the cast of characters changed almost completely from that of the era of "new immigration." Immigration from Europe was delayed substantially by the outbreak of World War I and was curbed drastically afterwards during the nativistic 1920s by a series of laws passed by Congress placing severe limits on the numbers of immigrants allowed yearly from regions other than predominantly non-Catholic northwestern Europe. Other regions of the world were rather to provide much of the new American stock of the present century, whether in response to periodic changes in immigration policy or in spite of federal laws. The influx of significant numbers of Spanish-speaking Catholics into the United States did not commence until the end of the nineteenth century, when Mexican *braceros,* or migrant laborers, began to seek work in American agriculture. The acquisition of Puerto Rico as an American territory in the aftermath of the war with Spain in 1898 added another potential source of Hispanic population, one which resulted in massive immigration to the mainland, especially New York City, following World War II. Then, following Fidel Castro's overthrow of the Batista regime in 1959, a new exodus of middle-class Cuban Catholics began, this time settling mainly in Miami and South Florida. French-speaking Haitians, again mainly Catholic, followed in the 1980s, as did refugees from the strife-torn countries of Central America. In both of the latter cases, controversial immigration policies made easy settlement in the United States difficult, and Catholic and other church groups began to devise such counterstrategies as the "sanctuary" movement—the sheltering of illegal refugees by church groups—to deal with the newcomers' needs. The religious cultures of the Spanish-speaking immigrants will be dealt with more thoroughly in chapter 50.

In addition to Spanish-speaking and Haitian immigrants, new groups of Catholics arrived as a result of various worldwide political upheavals later in the twentieth century, particularly after the modification of the quota system by Congress in 1965. In many cities, Catholic communities arose: Hungarian refugees following the abortive 1956 uprising against the Communist government, Cubans fleeing Castro's socialist regime in 1959 and afterwards, and many from southeast Asia, Central America, and the Middle East seeking refuge from the chronic political instability of those regions. In a number of cases, there were conflicts between Anglicized bishops and clergy and newcomer Catholics from very different cultures, resulting in the same sorts of misunderstandings and bad feeling that had taken place repeatedly between the Irish and Germans, Poles, French Canadians, and other non-English-speaking immigrants in previous generations.

To round out this portrait of ethnic diversity, conflict, and comprehension, a final word needs to be said about the Catholic presence among two other significant minority communities in America. Although the vast majority of churchgoing blacks are affiliated with the Baptist, Methodist, and holiness-pentecostal traditions, a successful Catholic outreach to African Americans did take place in two areas where a Catholic presence had existed since colonial days, that is, Maryland and southern Louisiana. Other significant work was carried on by Katherine Drexel (1858–1955; canonized 2000), the wealthy Philadelphian (and now a saint) who founded the Sisters of the Blessed Sacrament to promote home missionary work among blacks and Native Americans, as well as a few predominantly black religious orders such as the Oblate Sisters of Providence. Most dioceses and religious orders were unenthusiastic about black candidates for the priesthood until fairly recently; however, James Augustine Healy, one of three brothers of African and Irish origin who entered the priesthood, served as bishop of Portland, Maine, from 1875 to 1900.

In recent years, African Americans have been attracted to the Catholic Church as much for social and cultural as for religious reasons. As Catholics abandoned their old urban parishes in the onrush of suburbanization, upward mobility, and new educational opportunities following World War II, the churches and educational plants in the old neighborhoods faced a crisis. Some were sold to other groups, others were torn down, and a few were saved through massive lobbying and fund-raising efforts by the remnants of the old parish in alliance with historic preservationists. In a number of cases, though, new demographic configurations emerged to allow a kind of institutional recycling. In the case of St. Stanislaus Kostka in the heart of Chicago's old Polish section, for example, the influx of Catholic Mexicans compensated for the loss of Polish Americans; today one finds shrines to the Virgins both of Czestochowa and Guadalupe within. In other cases, teaching sisters rethought the missions of the parochial schools they served, turning now to the needs of non-Catholic inner city children whose parents saw these schools as attractive because of their high academic and disciplinary standards. In one dramatic case, Clarence Thomas, the Supreme Court justice, came from an African American Baptist family in South Carolina that sent him to Catholic schools as a preferable educational alternative to the public schools. After attending an Episcopal church in the Washington, D.C., suburbs for several years—a denomination often favored by successful African Americans such as Thomas's more liberal predecessor, Thurgood Marshall—Thomas had by the late 1990s formally become a Roman Catholic.

Liturgical and theological experimentation, new forms of charismatic religious experience, and ethnic diversity all converged from the 1960s onward to promote a spirit of pluralism and effervescence within the American Catholic community, which included approximately one of every four Americans by this time. Other forces, however, worked in the direction of consolidation and retrenchment. The pontificate of John Paul II (1978–2005) resulted in the same tensions in the American church as in western Europe and Latin America, as the new pope attempted to reassert an authority that had been relaxed, deliberately or otherwise, by his predecessors.

In America, signs of this new attitude were reflected in the character of episcopal appointments, for example, of the conservative John O'Connor and Bernard Law to the crucial sees of New York and Boston. In addition, the Vatican in 1986 intervened directly into the life of the American church by suspending the teaching privileges of Charles Curran, a controversial professor of ethics at the Catholic University of America. Curran's stances on a number of issues, including abortion, euthanasia, and homosexuality, were regarded as moderate by many American Catholics, but seemed to Rome to deviate too far and too publicly from traditional Catholic teachings. During the same year the Vatican also deprived Archbishop Raymond Hunthausen of Seattle of some of his authority and delegated supervision of such sensitive matters as marriage annulments and the employment of ex-priests to an auxiliary bishop. Further examples of a "crackdown" in the 1980s were a whole series of attempts to discipline religious women who were involved in a variety of ways in activities that seemed to compromise the unbending opposition to abortion that had emerged in this decade as a test of Catholic rigor on matters of private and public morality. By the late 1990s, few bishops who could be classified as "liberal" remained within the American hierarchy. The election of German Cardinal Joseph Ratzinger as Pope Benedict XVI in 2005 did little to signal a change in basic policies during the pontificate of John Paul II's successor.

The major event affecting the course of American Catholicism during the early years of the twenty-first century was the national scandal that arose in the late 1990s when the *Boston Globe* began a series of articles reporting that the leadership of the Boston Archdiocese had engaged for many years in the practice of transferring priests accused of sexually abusing children from one parish to another with little attempt at treatment or discipline. Soon similar reports began appearing across the country, with accompanying legal investigations and lawsuits by those claiming to have been victims of clerical abuse. Another response was the formation of organizations of laity, such as the Boston-based Voice of the Faithful, determined to seek an accounting from the bishops involved. Some Catholics stopped supporting the Church financially, and others left to join other churches.

In 2002 the Catholic bishops issued a "Charter for the Protection of Children and Young People." The Charter created a review board that drew up a comprehensive report on the situation, and a zero-tolerance policy for keeping pedophiliac priests in assignments where they might have access to children was adopted by the bishops for the national church. Nevertheless, legal settlements running into eight figures were reached in many dioceses, and some, including Tucson, Arizona, and Portland, Oregon, filed for bankruptcy. The other most visible fallout was the resignation of Cardinal John Law as Archbishop of Boston in the face of his unwillingness to cooperate in the ongoing investigations. (Law was subsequently appointed to a post in the Vatican.)

The large majority of the cases of abuse uncovered in the course of these investigations appear to have taken place not in recent years, but rather during the period stretching from the 1960s to the 1980s. Although there was little disagreement within the American Catholic community as to the repulsiveness of such revelations of sexual exploitation, opinion did differ as to cause, responsibility, and remedies. For some, the primary responsibility lay on the shoulders of those bishops who had put the public reputation of the Church ahead of obligation to the faithful in keeping accusations of clerical misconduct quiet, whereas others defended the hierarchy as doing the best they could within the limited knowledge of the nature of pedophilia professionally available at the time. Still others focused on the culture of seminaries. Many of the priests involved in the scandal had entered minor (high school level) seminaries at the beginnings of adolescence, and had not been given the opportunity to attain a mature psychosexual identity in an institutional atmosphere that worked against such development. Others maintained that the problem lay with an insufficiently rigorous process of seminary admission, which should have discovered and excluded those of homosexual orientation to begin with. To these latter, some responded that this approach confused pedophilia or ephebephilia—a pathological sexual attraction to children or adolescents—with homosexuality, an adult sexual orientation that is not a pathology. In any case, issues that had seldom been aired before in public now demanded attention and reform—although the nature of that reform remained in dispute.

The situation of the Catholic Church in America in the early twenty-first century was one of considerable ferment and uncertainty. Liberal Catholics were firmly at odds with the Vatican and a significant portion of the American hierarchy in their use of artificial contraception, their rejection of traditional stances on sexual morality, and their advocacy of a fuller role for women in the life of the institutional church. ("Cafeteria Catholicism" is a popular phrase describing the Catholicism of those who are selective about which teachings they follow.) Conservatives found themselves more comfortable in many ways with their Protestant counterparts who shared their concerns with the maintenance of traditional authority and their firm stands on such matters of public morality as abortion, homosexuality, and pornography. Complicating the picture even further was a shortage of clergy and religious, which had begun in the wake of the council as many left the religious life. Many seminaries, which had been filled to overflowing with candidates for the priesthood during the 1950s, now stood nearly empty, and a number of the smaller ones had to be closed because of underutilization. Those that enjoyed reasonable enrollments were the beneficiaries of the lay women who now sought theological education, some out of a desire for ordination not available to them. Most dioceses were formulating contingency plans for the continuing life of parishes for which priests would not be available. New models of staffing involving the sharing of the time of priests and the increased active participation of the laity and religious women in parish governance and various forms of ministry were accentuated in these plans. This greater participation came about in part out of sheer necessity, but also from an enhanced sense of the responsibilities of the laity in the church that Vatican II had articulated.

Whether seemingly radical solutions to the problems of the day—such as the ordination of married men or, more daringly, of women—will come to pass still remains to be seen. As one tongue-in-cheek scenario has it, at the Third Vatican Council, the bishops will bring their wives; at the Fourth, they will bring their husbands. The lengthy reign of Pope John Paul II and his pattern of conservative appointments to the episcopate over more than two decades made the realization of at least the second part of this scenario seem remote, and the policies of his successor give little reason to expect dramatic change.

The policies of the Vatican and the American hierarchy, however, do not always reflect the attitudes of many American Catholics. According to a *National Catholic*

Reporter survey of 2005 conducted by sociologist William V. D'Antonio and associates, three-quarters of American Catholics believed that it was possible to be a good Catholic while disregarding their church's teaching on birth control; 67 percent had the same attitude towards divorce, and 58 percent towards abortion. Similarly, 75 percent approved married priests, and 61 percent were favorable towards the ordination of celibate women. (Approval of ordination for married women was 54 percent, still a majority.) Helping the poor was rated an important Catholic value by 84 percent, whereas only 34 percent deemed Catholic teachings against the death penalty as weighty. Not surprisingly, younger Catholics tended to be more liberal on controversial issues than their elders, and were also less likely to be regular church-goers. Clearly, "Cafeteria Catholicism" is in the ascendancy in the United States: many Catholics remain loyal to the tradition—which they regard as "family"—while their commitment to the offical values and practices of the institution are considerably more qualified.

The American Catholic Church in the early twenty-first century remains numerically strong—23.9 percent of the population, according to the Pew Forum survey released in 2008—but that undigested percentage conceals a number of tensions. Although nearly one out of three Americans (31 percent) were raised as Catholics, only about one in four (24 percent) now describe themselves that way. This high rate of leakage among native-born American Catholics is offset by the large proportion of Catholics among immigrants: fully 46 percent of foreign-born Americans are Catholic affiliated. Many of these latter are Mexicans and other Latin Americans who themselves manifest a high percentage of loss to pentecostal and other evangelical groups. Although the history of American Catholicism is intimately bound up with the themes of immigration and assimilation, the future impact of this particualr demographic shift will be especially challenging as the institutional church struggles to find resources among a diminishing, largely English-speaking clergy to minister to those from a very different culture.

CHAPTER 49

Roman Catholic Education, Thought, and Culture

The history of the Roman Catholic community in the United States of America as it has emerged in preceding chapters can be divided into a number of distinct phases. The colonial period saw only scattered English-speaking settlements, characterized by a high degree of sophistication but very small numbers. The influence

of these early English and French Catholics was soon diluted by the massive immigration from Ireland, Germany, and central and eastern Europe, which flooded
the church with logistical problems and demands on its resources. As these began to
succumb to organization, the conflicts over the question of Americanization came
to a head and were resolved in favor of a cautious middle road between the extremes
of ethnic nationalism and complete assimilation. This pattern dominated American
Catholic life until the era of Vatican II, which brought to a head movements for
change that had been slowly emerging for some time. The liberalization that Vatican
II launched, however, soon ran into resistance from more conservative papal leadership, and precipitated a struggle over issues of authority, especially among American
Catholics, that remain unresolved to this day.

   The development of a distinctively Catholic culture in the United States follows the
contours of this broader history. On the one hand, American Catholics, especially
those speaking English, have participated in the dominant culture shaped primarily
by its British roots. Many other Catholics of a wide variety of ethnic and linguistic
backgrounds have attempted to maintain alternative patterns, usually of continental
European or Latin American origin, with greater or lesser success. Although some
interesting beginnings of a distinctively American Catholic school of thought took
shape in the mid-nineteenth century, it was not until the mid-twentieth that the
American Catholic community had achieved sufficient maturity and independence to
take on a significant identity of its own—after the Catholic community as a whole was
well on the way to thorough acceptance and assimilation. Throughout this process
of cultural development, a systematic and thoroughgoing drive toward providing
education at all levels created an institutional infrastructure through which cultural
life could find nurture and expression.

   During the colonial period, Catholic efforts in education, thought, and the arts
were severely restricted by low numbers, especially in the English-speaking Mary-
land-Pennsylvania area. The mission complexes built under the direction of the
Spanish friars in the Southwest aimed at providing the Indians with some rudi-
mentary secular and religious education, and also featured striking architectural
design and artistic achievement. In the chain of California missions built under
the direction of Junípero Serra and Fermin Lasuén especially, native materials and
workmanship fused with imperfectly remembered Iberian patterns to produce
forceful if rough mission chapels and accompanying decorative arts. The stark,
thick-walled mission churches of New Mexico and their more European Baroque
counterparts in Texas (for example, the Alamo in San Antonio) provide an indication of the variety within this range of vernacular frontier building. In Maryland,
on the contrary, Catholic life was entirely the province of the English settlers, with
no serious attempts at Indian evangelization. The first Catholic school was opened
in 1640, but all overt Catholic activity had to be conducted in private from the establishment of Anglicanism in 1692 until independence. Some German-speaking

Jesuit schools were founded in Pennsylvania during the eighteenth century, but these efforts were small and scattered.

John Carroll, the first Roman Catholic bishop in the United States, was also the first significant English-speaking American Catholic figure on a variety of fronts besides the organizational dimensions of his career. It was under Carroll's aegis that the first comprehensive set of Catholic educational institutions was begun in the new nation. In 1791 the French Sulpicians began the first seminary, Mt. St. Mary's, and Georgetown Academy also opened its doors. In addition, Elizabeth Bayley Seton's newly founded Sisters of Charity established a school in Emmitsburg, Maryland, in 1810. Carroll also manifested in his numerous writings the influence of many currents of the same Enlightenment that had molded the shape of American institutions, and he vigorously defended the spirit of American democracy in the ecclesiastical as well as the civil order.

This same spirit manifested itself when the prominent architect Benjamin Henry Latrobe presented Carroll with two alternate designs for the new cathedral at Baltimore. Instead of choosing the Gothic, whose historical resonances were those of the medieval Catholic tradition, Carroll opted for a domed Roman Revival plan that seemed to him more in harmony with the classically inspired ideals of the New Republic. The resultant Basilica of the Assumption (its present name), erected in Baltimore in 1804, remains as one of the architectural gems of the early national period, though it is no longer used as a cathedral. As Jay Dolan has noted, Carroll also fostered a "plain style" in Catholic piety that focused on Sunday liturgy and private, individual piety, a style reflected in the stark character of Catholic church design and ornament in the antebellum era.

The middle decades of the nineteenth century were dominated by the need for rapid expansion to accommodate the floodtide of Catholic immigration, and creative "high" cultural expression did not generally flourish. Education was undertaken on a rather ad hoc basis, with religious orders such as the Jesuits and Ursulines taking a good deal of the initiative for the founding and staffing of schools at all levels. The impetus for a more systematic approach to Catholic education came in large measure from the external pressures of nativism. In 1834, for example, the first Catholic school in the Boston area, which had been established by the Ursuline Sisters in 1820 and which educated many non-Catholic young women, was burned by a mob enraged by anti-Catholic propaganda that claimed that the Catholic Church was inimical to American democracy. At a subtler level, the "common" or public schools in most American cities were supervised by boards dominated by evangelical Protestants who thought that a necessary component of education was the inculcation of a nondenominational but still Protestant version of Christianity, as disseminated in *McGuffey's Readers* and symbolized by the use of the King James rather than the Catholic Douay version of the Bible.

A series of court cases during the middle decades of the nineteenth century succeeded in removing many of these overt manifestations of Protestantism from the public classroom, but the secularized alternative was scarcely more acceptable from the Catholic viewpoint. The edict of the Third Plenary Council of Baltimore in 1884, which mandated parochial elementary schools for all parishes, marked the beginning of the American Catholic movement to create systematically a set of educational institutions parallel to those provided by secular society. This centralized program of educational development gradually displaced the previous pattern of schools—frequently called "academies"—maintained by religious orders, which often charged tuition and were thus out of reach of most immigrant and working-class Catholics.

The drive toward centralization and standardization within education and the professions in the culture as a whole also promoted this tendency. The first diocesan school board was created in New York in 1886, and the Catholic Educational Association came into being in 1904. Teaching sisters were required in the twentieth century to conform to state norms for certification, which again promoted both higher standards and standardization. These trends also tended to subordinate the autonomy of religious orders, especially those of women, to episcopal control.

Nineteenth-century Catholic thought and culture did not have a very conducive matrix for development in the flood of practical concerns that dominated the church's attention. Two notable exceptions, Orestes A. Brownson (1803–76) and Isaac Hecker (1819–88), proved this rule through their entrance into the church as converts. Both had been involved in the ferment of Jacksonian politics and transcendentalist religious thought and social experimentation, but neither found the wide variety of options he explored satisfying until conversion to Catholicism brought relative peace. Brownson was a prolific journalistic editor and writer, and made the *Boston*—later *Brownson's*—*Quarterly Review* the vehicle for his voluminous polemics on virtually every topic imaginable. Brownson sought in the thought of contemporary European writers such as Victor Cousin, Pierre Leroux, and Vincenzo Gioberti the basis for a philosophy in which the problem of the isolation of the individual was overcome by involvement in a broader social context. The ultimate version of this context for him was the Catholic Church, which overcame the perennial Protestant (and transcendentalist) dilemma of excessive individualism.

Hecker, who became the founder of the Paulist order, took as his mission the positive presentation of the Catholic faith to other Americans, and argued that the genius of American institutions and character was more compatible with Catholicism than with any other religious system. Neither was very influential within the Catholic community or overly successful in making other converts, but each attained an originality of thought which, perhaps because of its novelty, was uncharacteristic of the Catholic intellectual life of the era. It was Hecker's Paulists especially who, through their emphasis on the Holy Spirit, provided an alternative to the emphasis on authority and devotion that came to dominate American Catholic culture by the early twentieth century.

More characteristic of Catholic writing during the later nineteenth and earlier twentieth centuries was a massive outpouring of various genres intended for widespread consumption and edification, including diocesan newspapers, devotional manuals, prayer books, popular novels, and children's literature. These efforts were based on an expanding Catholic reading public and the emergence of a number of Catholic publishers, among which P. J. Kenedy, Bruce, Benziger, and Sheed & Ward became the best known. Journalism was generally of the episcopal house-organ sort, although an important exception was the *Boston Pilot* while under the editorship of John Boyle O'Reilly from 1870 to 1890.

As Ann Taves has pointed out, a convergence of technological, economic, and sociological factors brought about something resembling mass-market publishing within the Catholic community by the 1840s. The staples of this new printed culture reflected the "devotional revolution" that had transformed both European—especially Irish—and then American Catholicism in the middle decades of the nineteenth century. Frequent collective observance at the parish level of public exercises such as *novenas* (nine successive days of prayer) and the exposition of the Blessed Sacrament began to rival and even displace the celebration of the Mass as the focal point of Catholic religious life. Organizations known as *confraternities* and *sodalities* began to multiply in response to popular demand for these devotions, and clergy—especially itinerant "mission" preachers from the religious orders—and bishops were enthusiastic in encouraging their proliferation. Fostered by popular literature, the Catholic school curriculum, household religious objects, and the ornate interior decoration of churches built during these years, devotionalism molded a cosmos for Catholics in which the supernatural, as manifested in Jesus, Mary, and the company of saints, took on a vivid reality in the midst of mundane life.

The locus for this paraliturgical activity was the *parish* which, as Jay Dolan has pointed out, by the late nineteenth century had assumed a new importance in American Catholic life. One stimulus to this change was the "new immigration," which brought to the nation's emergent cities a flood of physically and cognitively displaced persons who sought a firm point of reference in the social chaos that confronted them. Public devotions were only one of a host of parochial activities that rapidly generated networks of local organizations for carrying out social, charitable, educational, literary, athletic, and any number of other collective enterprises that simultaneously served the needs of parishioners and reinforced the role of the church as the focus of its members' lives. In the decades around the turn of the century, many parishes were dominated by particular ethnic groups, so that their activities were often re-creations of the religious cultures of Polish, Italian, or Mexican villages. As ethnicity began to fade, both through assimilation and through episcopal policy, the parish organizational networks continued, together with the Catholic educational system, to be potent vehicles for socialization and the maintenance of group loyalty. It was not until the 1960s that a convergence of new social and theological forces began to erode, or at least significantly transform, this powerful role of the parish in American Catholic life.

The transformation of the character of the parish from ethnic particularism to the social expression of a common American Catholic culture took place at different rates, but the 1920s represented something of a watershed. In the days of heavy immigration, many urban parishes especially were dominated by non-English-speaking immigrants for whom the parish and its staff were significant agents in mediating between an older world that had grown economically untenable, and therefore irrecoverable, and a new world filled with apparent promise but that in its initial appearance was hostile and forbidding. Together with the saloon, the urban political machine, and other less respectable agencies, the Catholic parish provided a milieu where the old celebrations of saints' days could be conducted in the familiar language and where pressing material problems could be alleviated through kinship networks, fraternal societies, and in many cases the intervention of priests and sisters in helping cope with any number of unfamiliar and often desperate situations.

Life for the second and third generations of American Catholics, though not always easy, was usually less desperate. Parochial culture in the years following World War I, which had helped put a damper on all things foreign, was shaped by American-born bishops and clergy, usually of Irish descent, more than by the panoply of foreign-born priests and nuns and their immigrant clientele who had molded an earlier era of Catholic life. The emphasis on devotional piety and ecclesiastical authority developed in the nineteenth century was now continued in a more extensive and centralized institutional network in which Catholic schools played a rapidly growing role. Emphasizing the dangers of Protestant and secular society, this new, English-speaking "ghetto" culture provided an insular but reassuring environment as Catholics tentatively moved into the middle-class mainstream. Garry Wills, the historian and columnist, evoked its distinctive ethos in his bittersweet memoir of "growing up Catholic," *Bare Ruined Choirs*, in 1972:

> We grew up different. There were some places we went, and others did not—into the confessional box, for instance. There were other places we never went, though others could—we were told, from youth, to stay out of non-Catholic churches.
>
> The habits of childhood are tenacious, and Catholicism was first experienced by us as a vast set of intermeshed childhood habits—prayers offered, heads ducked in unison, crossings, chants, christenings, grace at meals; beads, altar, incense, candles; nuns in the classroom alternately too sweet and too severe, priests garbed black on the street and brilliant at the altar; churches lit and darkened, clothed and stripped, to the rhythm of liturgical recurrences; the crib in winter, purple Februaries, and lilies in the spring; confession as intimidation and comfort (comfort, if nothing else, that the intimidation was survived), communion as revery and discomfort; faith as a creed, and the creed as catechism, Latin responses, salvation by rote, all things going to a rhythm, memorized, old things always returning, eternal in that sense, no matter how transitory. (15–16)

One cost of this sense of changelessness—what Wills goes on to call the "dirty little secret" of pre–Vatican II Catholicism—was an imposed uniformity of thought and practice. The quashing of the impact of contemporary European thought signaled by the papal encyclicals *Testem Benevolentiae* in 1899 and *Pascendi Dominici Gregis* in 1907 put an end to some mildly venturesome intellectual activity at the Catholic University of America, the seminary at Dunwoodie, New York, and the University of Notre Dame. At the latter, which like most Catholic colleges remained basically a secondary-level boarding institution until well into the twentieth century, Father John Zahm's 1896 work *Evolution and Dogma* was suppressed by Rome in 1898 when he tried to incorporate evolutionary thought into a Catholic framework. (Later popes, including John Paul II, would assert the compatibility of biological evolution and Catholic belief.)

The intellectual and cultural life of American Catholics during the first half of the twentieth century has frequently been characterized by Catholic critics as that of a religious "ghetto," shielded by internal and external pressure from active contact with the broader world. This criticism is not without some substance, since the emergence of a strong centralized domestic hierarchy and the defensive stance of Rome did not promote intellectual adventuresomeness. Seminaries flourished at a variety of levels: minor seminaries for high-school age prospects for the priesthood, major seminaries for more direct preparation for ordination at the collegiate level, and others maintained by religious orders as an alternative to seminaries under diocesan sponsorship. Most, however, offered a curriculum that stressed character and spiritual formation, physical exercise, and a theology derived from textbooks expounding derivative versions of the system of St. Thomas Aquinas, whose thought was made normative by papal decree in 1913.

Curriculum at the primary and secondary levels of Catholic education was similar to that offered in the public schools, but with systematic instruction in religion and texts reflecting a distinctive Catholic outlook in controversial areas. Bishop Richard Gilmour of Cleveland, for example, created a popular series of readers in the late nineteenth century that were Catholic versions of those of the Presbyterian William Holmes McGuffey. During the 1940s, the Faith and Freedom series originating from Catholic University stressed much the same values, especially patriotism, character-istic of the nation at large, but emphasized Catholic themes and achievements where appropriate. Catholic book clubs and radio programs arose to present alternatives in the various media, as did a wide variety of periodicals, such as *Our Sunday Visitor,* that paralleled the dominant popular culture.

It was in the realm of film especially that the American Catholic Church exerted a significant impact not only on its own communicants but on the culture at large. Widely acknowledged excesses of sex and violence in the films of the 1920s and early 1930s led to public pressure for reform, and the Catholic hierarchy was one of the most effective voices of protest. The creation of a production code by the film industry in 1930 did not result in significant reform until the institution in 1934 of the Legion of Decency, a Catholic organization whose pledge was more or less imposed on lay Catholics by the hierarchy until the 1960s. In some cases, such as in Philadelphia, pressure on the film industry was escalated through effective boycotts of all Hollywood films. After the Legion's creation, a revitalized production code was overseen by Catholic layman Joseph Breen, and a strict set of standards now governed the production of virtually all American cinema.

In addition to the banishment of overt sexual activity and unpunished crime from the silver screen, a side effect of increased Catholic militancy in this arena resulted in the emergence of a new film genre, that of the "hero priest." Beginning with Pat O'Brien in *Angels with Dirty Faces* (1938) and continuing through Spencer Tracy in *Boys Town* (1938) and Bing Crosby in *Going My Way* (1944), Catholic priests were now depicted uniformly not only as morally flawless but as handsome, affable, muscular, and even, in Crosby's case, musical. In addition, they were often able to accomplish seeming miracles, ranging from saving financially strapped parishes to providing a nurturing environment for abandoned children. Both Code and Legion endured until the 1960s, when changes both in Catholic and secular cultural climates brought about a seemingly wide-open approach to filmic themes, including films critical of institutional Catholicism such as *The Verdict* (1982) and *Priest* (1994). The sensational 1973 film *The Exorcist,* although not overtly critical, introduced clerical characters into situations so bizarre that the genteel piety of the films of earlier decades seemed to have come from a different planet.

In other realms of cultural and intellectual life, exceptions to the general rule of uniformity did gradually appear throughout the decades between *Testem Benevolentiae* and Vatican II. The Jesuit order began publication of the weekly *America,* a journal of religion, culture, and politics, in 1909, and a group of laymen led by Michael Williams founded the similar but more liberal and independent *Commonweal* in 1924. Most significant authors of Catholic background during this period, such as Eugene O'Neill, F. Scott Fitzgerald, and Theodore Dreiser, no longer practiced their familial faith, and the depth of the Catholic religious identity of the converts Ernest Hemingway and Robert Lowell was questionable. The Catholic presence in literature was more evident in American appreciation of the work of English and continental Catholic authors such as Evelyn Waugh, Graham Greene, François Mauriac, and Sigrid Undset, and occasionally in the sensitive depiction of Catholic themes by non-Roman Catholics such as T. S. Eliot, Henry Adams, and Willa Cather.

It was not until the 1950s and 1960s that genuinely distinguished Catholic fiction began to appear in such work as that of the southern writers Flannery O'Connor and Walker Percy and the midwestern satirist J. F. Powers. The cultural impact of Vatican II was ambiguous. After its impact began to be felt, any number of writers of American, and especially Irish American, Catholic background reflected on their experiences in their fiction. Although it has not always been clear how committed they have remained to institutional Catholicism, the impact of Catholic culture on their work has been unmistakable.

In the more strictly intellectual sphere, American Jesuits, already prominent in their educational enterprises and their journal *America,* began to distinguish themselves especially in aspects of theology and ethics impinging on the public and political spheres. Gustav Weigel (1906–64), for example, helped pave the way for serious ecumenical outreach to other Christians. His *An American Dialogue,* written in collaboration with Presbyterian theologian Robert McAfee Brown in 1960, was a pioneering work of serious interfaith conversation. John La Farge (1880–1963) promoted papal social teaching in his work at *America* and anticipated later civil rights involvements through the Catholic Interracial Council of New York (founded in 1934).

Perhaps the most eminent of these Jesuits, for whom *America* and the seminary in Woodstock, Maryland, provided intellectual foci, was John Courtney Murray (1904–67). In *We Hold These Truths* (1960), Murray argued that American principles of religious liberty were consistent with traditional Catholic teachings. Although his earlier writings had encountered some suspicion in official circles, his work as Cardinal Spellman's *peritus* (expert theological advisor) at Vatican II was instrumental in the tradition-breaking "Declaration of Religious Liberty" promulgated by the council in 1963.

Ferment was at work in other ways in Catholic circles during the 1950s and 1960s. Through the work of Notre Dame's Theodore Hesburgh, C.S.C., and other educational leaders, a small group of Catholic institutions—Notre Dame, Georgetown, Boston College, Holy Cross, Fordham, and a few others—began to modify their traditional emphasis on orthodoxy and sports with a new emphasis on intellectual inquiry and scholarly research—the goals for which Catholic University had been founded several decades before but which had never been very fully realized in that context.

A major rallying point in this movement was John Tracy Ellis's "American Catholics and the Intellectual Life," published in *Thought* in 1955. Ellis, a priest and one of America's leading Catholic historians, took his coreligionists to task for the anti-intellectualism of the Catholic "ghetto" culture that had developed in America and called for a new ethos in which active intellectual inquiry would be nurtured. This summons to a new maturity became fulfilled in considerable measure in the decades to come, due in large part to the change in atmosphere brought about by Vatican II. The reassertion of papal authority in the 1980s by John Paul II, however, began to put some of these gains at risk as controversial thinkers such as Charles Curran, the Catholic University ethicist, began to come under fire for nonconformity with official teaching.

At the primary and secondary levels, Catholic education also began to undergo some major transformations beginning in the 1960s. Under the impetus of the Third Plenary Council of Baltimore's decree, the infrastructure of parochial education had expanded rapidly for several decades. Catholic school attendance increased from about 400,000 in 1880 to 1,700,000 in 1920, and tripled again by the early 1960s. By the time of Vatican II, however, and perhaps even a few years before, this long-term trend began to shift. The entrance of more and more Catholics into the middle classes brought about a drop in birth rate, and the increasing acceptance by Catholics of American social mores made the public schools a more attractive and less expensive alternative. The rapid drop in the availability of low-paid teaching sisters in the later 1960s necessitated a rethinking of the most effective use of diminished resources.

Still another factor was the abandonment of many inner-city parishes in the relentless movement during that era toward the suburbs; the announcement of the closing of dozens of such parishes by Archbishop Szoka in Detroit in 1988 touched off widespread controversy, especially among the black Catholics who comprised their major constituency. Many parochial schools now lacked their traditional demographic base as a result; on the other hand, however, many upwardly mobile black families, only a few of whom were Catholic, saw the discipline and generally high standards of the Catholic schools as a preferable alternative to the public system for their children. Desegregation had come slowly but steadily within the American church since the end of World War II—at times in the face of massive resistance, as in traditionally Catholic southern Louisiana—but it had come, and a new social mission thus presented itself for Catholic education.

One way to provide a retrospective on the development of American Catholic thought and culture is to examine some ways in which Catholics viewed the Christian past. Much of the nineteenth century was conspicuous in the absence of much systematic speculation of this sort. The church's personnel were absorbed in the exigencies of the present, and too little of a scholarly community existed to pay much attention to earlier ages. Churches for the most part were designed in the common styles of the day, which were derived from the work of the Anglican Christopher Wren. The first attempts at monumental Catholic architecture were often the work of Protestant architects, such as Latrobe's Baltimore Cathedral and St. Patrick's Cathedral (1858–79) in New York City, which was designed by the Episcopalian James Renwick Jr.

An enhanced historical consciousness began to emerge toward the end of the nineteenth century as Catholic resources increased substantially. The Irish-born Patrick Keely executed Boston's Holy Cross Cathedral in the popular Gothic style in 1875, and all told he probably designed over six hundred Catholic churches, most of them in similar modes, throughout the entire eastern United States. This focus on the Middle Ages as the "strong time" of Catholic history was reflected in the more sophisticated Gothic Revival architecture of Maginnis & Walsh and Allen & Collens in the early twentieth century, as well as in the often-reprinted *The Thirteenth, Greatest of Centuries* by James J. Walsh (1907). On an international level, the revival of Gregorian chant, the papal declaration making the theology of Thomas Aquinas normative, the creation of the Pontifical Institute of Mediaeval Studies, and the emergence of a strong school of neo-Thomist thinkers such as Etienne Gilson and

Jacques Maritain as the twentieth century progressed also betokened a preoccupation with the Middle Ages as a source of contemporary inspiration. A historiography of American Catholicism of professional caliber also began to emerge in the work of John Gilmary Shea (1824–92) and Peter Guilday (1884–1947). In both cases, however, their solid documentary work seldom transcended the level of informed chronicle—a marked contrast with the sophisticated interpretive viewpoints of Notre Dame historians Jay Dolan and Philip Gleason in the 1970s and 1980s. Catholic historians of a still later generation, such as Yale-trained Paula Kane of the University of Pittsburgh and Robert Orsi, successively at Indiana University, Harvard, and Northwestern, incorporated new interdisciplinary techniques of analyzing issues such as ethnicity and devotionalism.

A new historical point of reference began to emerge in 1937 with the founding of the Catholic Biblical Association of America, which two years later commenced publication of the *Catholic Biblical Quarterly*. (The *Catholic Historical Review* had already come into being in 1915.) Catholic scholarship was by this time beginning to emerge from the damper put on contemporary biblical scholarship by earlier papal condemnations of modernism, and a new wind blowing from Rome was signaled by the encyclical Divino Afflante Spiritu, issued by Pius XII in 1943 and encouraging modern "scientific" approaches to biblical research. By the 1960s American Catholic biblical scholars began to exert leadership within their professional circles, and men such as Roland Murphy, O. Carm., Joseph Fitzmeyer, S.J., and Raymond Brown, S.S., came to be regarded as among the leading lights in their fields.

More critical attitudes toward the Catholic past and its relationship to the American heritage were also emerging in the work of John Tracy Ellis and John Courtney Murray mentioned earlier. The combination of these new intellectual currents, together with the work of the liturgical movement and new forces in theology, helped to provide the intellectual undergirdings for Vatican II, whose "constitutions" reflected a much more thorough grounding in scripture, viewed historically, than had ever been the case in modern times. This shift of point of reference from the medieval to the biblical period, together with a newly critical sense of the institutional past and present as a whole, helped shape the entire course of reforms brought about by the council. Conspicuous among these was the abandonment of medieval revival styles in architecture in favor of new geometrical shapes, especially rounded forms, that enhanced the sense of congregational participation in the celebration of the sacraments, as well as a new emphasis on scripture and vernacular worship. The medievalism of earlier American Catholicism thus yielded on a variety of fronts to an enhanced appreciation of the age of Christian origins on the one hand and a new receptivity to the culture of the present—and the future—on the other.

The Religions of Spanish-Speaking Peoples

At the back of a vacant lot in downtown Tucson is a niche that contains a statue surrounded by racks containing votive candles. A sign nearby announces that this National Historic Landmark is "the only shrine in the United States dedicated to the soul of a sinner buried in unconsecrated ground." This improbable locale is the shrine of El Tiradito—"the little cast-away one"—who, as ethnologist James F. Griffith tells us, was a young sheepherder who became involved in an affair with his mother-in-law and, when taken *in flagrante,* was killed by that lady's husband with an axe. (This, at least, is one of many versions of the story.) Over the years, a cult somehow grew up around the burial site of the hapless young adulterer, which became an unofficial but well-preserved shrine. This fusion of Roman Catholic devotional form with a very un-Catholic content is a dramatic example of the kind of folk religion brought to and further developed in the American Southwest by the vast numbers of Spanish-speaking immigrants to this country during the twentieth century.

The 2000 census indicated that some 35,300,000 Americans were of Hispanic background—roughly 13 percent of the United States population, and about as many as those of African descent. Although a few Hispanics can be found in many parts of the country, their concentration in some areas is striking. In Texas, for example, they make up nearly 20 percent of the population; in San Antonio they number 56 percent, and in El Paso nearly 70 percent. Two-thirds of the population of Miami is of Hispanic background, mostly Cuban, and a half-million New Yorkers are of Puerto Rican origin. Over 10 per cent of the recent population of El Salvador may now be living, mostly illegally, in the United States. High birth and immigration rates have led demographers to conclude that by 2010 Hispanics will outnumber African Americans, and by 2050 will constitute one-quarter of the population of the United States. From a small and only regionally conspicuous minority at the end of World War II, people who trace their ancestry to Latin America are on their way to becoming the most numerous distinctive group in the nation.

These Americans, however, cannot be called an ethnic group; in fact, what to call them collectively is problematic. What unites them is a common ancestral language—Spanish—and a general geographical origin, that is, the several dozen nations of Latin America, the Caribbean, and regions of the current United States that were at one time part of the Spanish Empire. Each of these countries possesses its own culture, or, as in the case of Mexico, a number of different regional cultures with corresponding differences in dialect, customs, values, and interpretation of a (mostly) common religion, Roman Catholicism. Even here, generalization is dangerous. Although the Catholic Church was part of the imperial apparatus throughout most of Latin America, and has been the official religion until recently of most of the former colonies of Spain (as well as in those of France and Portugal), the Latino interpretation of Catholicism has often reflected distinctive folk traditions, especially in rural areas where the institutional presence of the church has not been strong. In addition, aggressive evangelization in recent years by conservative Protestant groups, especially pentecostals, has eroded the hegemony that Catholicism had long enjoyed through force of both law and custom.

As a result, "Hispanic"—or "Latino/Latina," as members of the group are frequently called—functions in the United States more as a general demographic category rather than as the name of a coherent ethnic group. (What collective designation to use has been the subject of ongoing controversy, with "Spanish speakers" the most neutral.) Although language and Catholic religion are commonalities for Spanish speakers, for the most part, an understanding of their religious experience can only come about through a consideration of the particular circumstances of each of the groups represented in significant numbers in the United States, namely, Mexicans, Cubans, and Puerto Ricans, who are located primarily in three distinct regions of the United States—the Southwest, peninsular Florida, and greater New York City.

In the colonial era, what is now Mexico and the southwestern region of the United States constituted the better part of the viceroyalty of Nueva España, or New Spain, with its capital in Mexico City. The northern fringe that was ceded to the United States by the recently independent Mexico in the 1840s was border country, never extensively settled by the Spanish because of the paucity of mineral resources that were a principal spur to colonization. Although parts of New Mexico are still populated by a people of mixed ancestry who have lived there since the colonial period, and the Catholic religion is still practiced among many Pueblo, Navajo, and other native peoples of the region as a result of Spanish missionary efforts, the large current Spanish-speaking population of the United States is mainly the result of massive immigration that has taken place in the twentieth century.

The cultural, social, and religious experience that Mexican immigrants have brought with them to the United States has been very different from that of their Catholic coreligionists who came to American shores directly from Europe and established a powerful, widespread, and, by the mid-twentieth century, predominantly English-speaking church. The evangelization of Mexico during the colonial era has already been described in an earlier chapter. It was part of what has been called the "Constantinization" of the New World—that is, the wholesale adoption of a new religion as the result of political change from the top down, in the manner in which Constantine imposed Christianity on the Roman Empire early in the fourth century. The overall result of the colonization process was a complex colonial society the structure of which had profound implications for religious life. At the top of the heap were the *gachupines,* or Spanish-born, who provided the highest levels of civil and ecclesiastical leadership. Next were the *criollos,* or creoles, who were born in Mexico but whose parentage was entirely European. This was the class from which most of the clergy would originate. Below them were a variety of socioracial categories that were based on various combinations of Spanish, native, and African descent, as well as those of purely indigenous or African origin. In time, the largest numbers of Mexicans were *mestizos,* that is, people of mixed European and Indian descent. It was from this cohort that leadership of the eventual movement for independence from Spain would come: Miguel de Hidalgo, whose *grito de Dolores*—"shout from Dolores," the name of Hidalgo's parish—began the struggle that overthrew Spanish rule, was a priest of mestizo background.

One of the major weaknesses of the colonial system was the failure in both church and state to nurture an indigenous leadership, so that resentments based on race and class continued to disturb Mexican society after independence had been achieved in 1821. Likewise, the ambitious *criollo* class, which depended on Indian labor, had often clashed with the regular clergy's efforts to oppose inhumane treatment of natives. The Constitution of 1857, adopted during the presidency of Benito Juárez, the first Indian to hold the office, was a profoundly anticlerical document, restricting severely the traditional exemptions of the Catholic Church from legal controls. Even more devastating was the Constitution of 1917, which culminated the revolutionary epoch of the 1910s during which folk heroes such as Pancho Villa and Emiliano Zapata vied for power in the aftermath of the long regime of the autocratic president Porfirio Díaz. Among other things, this new constitution expelled all clergy who were not Mexican-born, forbade religious processions and the wearing of clerical attire in public, and, most devastatingly, nationalized all church-held property and all education. Propagandists for the new regime such as mural painter Diego Rivera depicted the church as having been hand in glove with the repressive colonial and nineteenth-century regimes, and glorified the Indian and mestizo heritage as the authentic expression of the national cultural genius. An armed Catholic resistance movement during the 1920s, originating in the provincial middle classes, made little headway in regaining power for the church, and official anticlericalism dominated national policy until the post–World War II era. Since then, successive governments either ignored many of the 1917 constitution's restrictive provisions or, more recently, began to repeal them.

The result of this long and divisive heritage was a profound national ambivalence about organized Catholicism. On the one hand, it remained a part of the fabric of national life, despite opposition from the government and intelligentsia; on the other hand, many ordinary practitioners found themselves unable to identify completely with what remained in some ways a simultaneously native and alien institution. One compromise was the emergence of a folk religion that coexisted with the formal structures and teachings of the church, in some ways complementarily, in others uneasily. The most dramatic and pervasive example of complementarity is in the image of the Virgin of Guadalupe, which can be found almost universally in homes, stores, cars, and buses wherever those of Mexican origin live. According to legend, *la Virgen Morena*—"the Dark Virgin"—first appeared to the Indian Juan Diego in 1531 on a hill north of Mexico City associated with the Aztec goddess Tonantzín, and instructed him to go to the bishop and ask him to build on the place of her appearance a church where the native people could readily behold her image. Rebuffed by the bishop, Juan Diego returned to the site of the first appearance, where the Virgin now gave him out-of-season flowers to take to the bishop in the Indian's cloak. When opened at the episcopal residence, the cloak was imprinted with the image of the Virgin, arrayed with symbols from the book of Revelation, that eventually became a symbol of a Mexican people whose own dark coloring was reflected in that of the Mother of God.

The popular religion that can be found in one form or another throughout most of Latin America has part of its roots in the traditional folk piety of peninsular Spain that antedated the centralizing reforms of the Council of Trent and that was brought to the New World with the earliest Spanish settlers. Other folk practices originated in various parts of Mexico and elsewhere as a consequence of the scarcity of religious personnel and the ease with which Catholic beliefs and practices could be assimilated with those of folk tradition to produce a hybrid or *creolized,* popular religion. For example, as with Native American peoples in the United States, disease was often regarded not in the terms of scientific medicine but rather from a perspective in which human maladies could result from malicious intentionality, such as witchcraft, performed by *brujos,* or the *mal de ojo,* evil eye. Other ailments not recognized by the medical profession include *empacho,* a somewhat vague disorder of the stomach; *susto,* or fright; and *el mal puesto,* a curse resulting from envy. These and similar problems could be cured not by antibiotics, even if they had been available, but rather by the work of *curanderos* and *curanderas,* folk-healers whose powers had a spiritual dimension and who were opposed by the organized church. Some of these, such as El Niño Fidencio and don Pedro Garamillo, are popularly revered on both sides of *la frontera* (that is, the border between Mexico and the United States). More conventionally, those who had come to shrines, official or otherwise, in quest of successful cures often left behind *milagros*—metal miniatures of body parts for which healing was desired—or *ex votos,* that is, images depicting and narrating a miraculous cure, as thank-offerings. Crutches, eye-patches, and other medical apparatus now no longer needed may also be seen at such shrines in the Southwest, although they are also familiar objects at similar sites in French Canada such as Ste. Anne du Beaupre near Quebec and St. Joseph's Oratory in Montreal and even in shrines in the northeastern United States. The *Santuario de Chimayo* on the "high road to Taos" in New Mexico is a good example of a Catholic church in good standing to which pilgrims come from afar seeking healing through the good offices of *Nuestro Señor* (Our Lord) of Esquípulas—also known as *El Cristo Negro,* or "the black Christ"—an image that originated in Guatemala. Holy dirt from the chapel here is said to have miraculous effects.

Folk practices may reflect a number of situations that are thought to require ritual mediation in the absence either of appropriate sacraments or those to administer them, whereas others are officially sanctioned extensions of official church practice. *Compadrazgo,* for example, is the widespread fictive kinship practice in Latin America of godparents—*compadres*—becoming an integral part of the extended family unit, far more than the usually nominal role played by such baptismal witnesses in "Anglo" (English-speaking American) Catholicism. *Rezadores* are unofficial lay ministers who may lead prayers in the absence of a priest or sing the *decenario de difuntos,* or rosary for the dead, at a *velorio,* or wake. The *quinceañera* is a celebration—in middle-class circles, often highly elaborate and expensive—of a girl's fifteenth birthday, in which she takes a vow of chastity until marriage. *Promesas* or *mandas* are vows made to God to carry out some act in thanksgiving for a healing or other favor. The transmission of religious lore was often the role of women, and their particular take on it has come to be known as *abuelita*—grandmother—theology. Many of these practices are looked on benignly and even participated in by members of the clergy, especially in urban areas. Whether favored, tolerated, or actively opposed by the official hierarchy and clergy, however, this complex of folk practices is an integral part of a distinctively Latino Catholicism.

In the United States, a gulf between the traditional practices of Mexican Catholics and the attitudes and policies of the official church hierarchy existed from early on. In New Mexico, for example, a lay confraternity known as *los hermanos penitentes*—"the penitent brotherhood"—arose during the nineteenth century in the absence of a formal church structure and gained a reputation for its bloody reenactments of the scenes of Holy Week. Although the Penitentes still exist today, their suppression was part of the agenda of Jean Baptiste Lamy, a Frenchman appointed archbishop of Santa Fe, New Mexico, in 1875 and memorialized in Willa Cather's novel, *Death Comes for the Archbishop* (1927). Lamy saw little of value in the old Spanish religious culture over which he now presided, expelled the old clergy, and proceeded to erect a new cathedral in the French Romanesque mode. In general, the policy of most American bishops—mainly of Irish extraction—in the Southwest was to promote the use of the English language and policies designed to favor an English-speaking local elite.

The Mexican population in the United States began to increase significantly early in the twentieth century, when irrigation made possible a commercial agriculture in need of labor. Mexicans were exempted in the restrictive immigration laws of the period, and by 1930 nearly a million and a half persons of Mexican birth or descent lived in this country. World War II brought both service in the military and a movement to work in urban war industries, experiences that worked against an easy acceptance of political, economic, and religious disenfranchisement and the fatalism of their traditional religious culture. Los Angeles in particular developed populous *barrios,* or Mexican neighborhoods, and the "Zoot Suit" riots in that city in 1943 ignited a latent tension between "Anglos" and newcomers. *Braceros*—workers with their *brazos,* or arms—whether legal or otherwise, swelled the agricultural work force by the millions. Even from the time of World War I, Mexicans had also begun to migrate into the nation's interior as agricultural and industrial workers, creating sizeable communities in inland cities such as Kansas City, Detroit, and Chicago.

The appointment of Robert E. Lucey as archbishop of San Antonio in 1941 was a turning point for the ever-increasing Mexican American community. Although Lucey himself was not particularly sympathetic to Mexican culture or comfortable with Mexicans, he nevertheless realized that their treatment by both church and civil society was a violation of the norms of social justice that had been promulgated in the encyclicals of Pope Leo XIII. In 1945 he helped bring about the Bishops' Commission for the Spanish Speaking, the first national Catholic organization aimed at the concerns of Hispanics in general and of Mexican Americans, then and now by far the largest Spanish-speaking community in the nation, in particular. In 1970 PADRES, an organization of parish priests engaged in ministry to Mexican Americans, arose in the wake of support for César Chávez (1927–73), whose United Farm Workers led a series of strikes in the mid-1960s against the growers of grapes, lettuce, and other produce in which braceros worked at low pay and under poor conditions. Chávez, an active lay Catholic, and his followers marched for *La Causa*—"the Cause"—under the banner of the Virgin of Guadalupe, and gained support both from "mainline" Protestant and Catholic groups. Chávez's visibility and the sympathy generated for La Causa were instrumental in bringing the issues facing Latinos into national prominence and especially to the attention of Catholic church leaders.

Although Mexican Americans are the largest—nearly two-thirds—of the Spanish-speaking peoples in the United States, they are by no means the only such group, and their culture and experience are not identical with those of, for example, Puerto Ricans and Cubans. Puerto Rico is distinct from all other sources of Hispanic immigration to the United States in the fact that it is actually part of the United States, and its residents are citizens who can move between their island and the mainland freely and, with the advent of affordable air transport, easily. This practice of frequent change of residence in response to economic need and opportunity has been described as "revolving door immigration" as well as the establishment of a new ethnic designation, the "Niurican" or "New Yorican."

Although a Catholic diocese was first established in Puerto Rico in 1511—the first in the New World—the development of religion on the island has been anomalous. The aboriginal inhabitants, the *Tainos,* rapidly disappeared as a distinct people after the coming of the Spanish, and the ethnic mix that subsequently became characteristic was Afro-European. *Mulataje*—the Spanish word for this particular racial mixture— rather than *mestizaje,* the Euro-Indian blend characteristic of Mexico and other Latin American countries, is the source of one sort of distinctiveness. During most of the colonial period, Puerto Rico was largely isolated from the rest of the Spanish

Empire, and an infusion of largely anticlerical Spanish settlers during the nineteenth century did little to enhance the presence of an already weak church. Annexation by the United States in 1898 after a brief period of home rule granted by Spain led to various programs of Americanization by the government, Protestant missions, and a new English-speaking Catholic church leadership whose goals were focused on the urban middle classes. Although Catholics are an overwhelming majority of the island's population, a tradition of folk religion, an alienation from American church leadership, and a highly independent and secular political culture have all worked against any strong official church influence.

Puerto Rican entrée to the mainland and the development of a unique political identity was facilitated by Congress's granting of citizenship to the territory's population by the Jones Law of 1917 and of commonwealth status in 1972. Periodic attempts to attain either statehood or independence have been occasionally violent but never very successful. Serious migration to the American mainland, primarily the greater New York City area, began following World War II, but has always had the character of frequent reversibility. As a result, many Puerto Ricans see themselves as carriers of a distinctive culture and identity, legally American but Spanish-speaking, racially unclassifiable, and generally loyal to a noninstitutional brand of folk Catholicism resembling that of Mexican Americans in many ways. By the 1950s, the New York Catholic hierarchy began to respond to the social and religious issues raised by the growing Puerto Rican presence, and programs both for social action and the cultural sensitizing of clergy resulted. On the whole, such ministries have had mixed success, in part because of Puerto Rican indifference to the mixing of religion and politics as well as their loyalty to an indigenous and highly particular religious culture.

The situation of the Catholic Church in prerevolutionary Cuba resembled that in Puerto Rico in a number of ways. During the period of Spanish rule prior to 1898, the institutional church was weak and tended to ally with the Spanish elite. The strong African presence represented among enslaved sugar workers engendered Santería, a syncretic Afro-Christian religion akin to Haitian Vodun (Voodoo). During the nineteenth century, the Cuban presence on the American mainland consisted primarily of political exiles in New York and cigar makers in Tampa, Florida, neither of whom were particularly receptive to religion for the most part.

The formation of a significant Cuban American community began abruptly in the wake of the overthrow of the dictatorial regime of Fulgencio Batista by Fidel Castro in 1959. Castro's hostility toward the island's wealthier classes led to some two hundred thousand "Golden Exiles," primarily from the business and professional classes, fleeing Cuba for southern Florida until the 1962 missile crisis made further immigration difficult. Movement from island to mainland resumed in the mid-1960s, however, and several hundred thousand more refugees, less affluent than the first wave, began to arrive and settle in Miami's emergent "Little Havana" and surrounding areas. The anti-Communist motivation for this immigration endeared these newcomers to the American government and the Catholic Church in a way not experienced by the economically motivated Mexican and Puerto Rican immigrants, and the Cuban newcomers received considerable aid for relocation from both church and government. The result has been the creation of a politically and economically powerful enclave in Dade County, which exerts considerable influence on American foreign policy toward Cuba and also is the base for a great deal of Latin American financial life. Middle-class, politically conservative, and supportive of institutional Catholicism, the Cubans of south Florida share little with their fellow Latinos other than the Spanish language and a formal attachment to the Catholic Church.

One powerful symbol of the Cuban Catholic presence is *La Ermita,* a shrine on the Miami waterfront erected in 1973. Conical in form, flanked by palm trees, and oriented toward the island of Cuba, it houses an image of *La Virgen de la Caridad del Cobre*—Our Lady of Charity of Cobre, the place in the mother country where the original statue resides. The subject of a variety of miraculous origin stories, this manifestation of the Virgin became associated with the nineteenth-century struggle for independence from Spain, and is also know as *La Virgen Mambisa,* the creole Virgin, which has subsequently become a symbol of resistance to the Castro regime and the desire of the Miami exile community for a return to their homeland. Similar to the Virgin of Guadalupe as a symbol of national identity, Our Lady of Charity and her shrine have become a symbol of what Thomas Tweed calls *diasporic religion:* the distinctive rituals fashioned by a people in exile, whether voluntary or enforced, which provide a focus for their collective identity and aspirations.

During the 1960s, the spirit of racial and ethnic self-discovery and political assertion helped bring about a sense of collective identity and solidarity among Spanish-speaking Americans, regardless of their differences. The publication of Rodolfo "Corky" Gonzales's poem "Yo Soy Joaquín"; the founding of the journals *El Grito* and *Aztlán;* and the strikes led by César Chávez in the name of *La Causa* were manifestations of a new spirit especially among *Chicanos*—Mexican Americans—but among *Latinos* in the United States more broadly. This resurgence had a religious dimension as well, made up of initiatives from both the Latino community and from the "Anglo" institutional Catholic Church. (A certain irony resides in such a designation for a traditionally Irish-dominated organization.) One important development within the Spanish-speaking Catholic community was the introduction of the *cursillo* ("little course") movement which was brought to the United States from Spain in the late 1950s. *Cursillos,* which are now sponsored by non-Hispanic Catholics and various Protestants as well, are lay-led retreats in which personal spirituality is nurtured in small groups. The grass-roots character of the movement was a means through which lay leadership in both religious and civic causes was developing among Hispanic Catholics, and it played an important role in Chávez's movement.

Beginning in the 1970s, a variety of Catholic Church–sponsored efforts have emerged with the goal of Latino empowerment. In addition to PADRES, the alliance for clergy mentioned earlier, a similar group, *Las Hermanas*—"Sisters"—was organized for religious women. Virgilio Elizondo, one of the most influential Hispanic theologians in the United States, established the Mexican American Cultural Center (MACC) in San Antonio, where *mariachi* (traditional Mexican street musicians) masses are regularly celebrated at the cathedral. Orbis Books, edited by Moises Sandoval of the Maryknoll order of missionaries, has emerged as a major publisher of work on liberation theology, despite the bad repute that that teaching has enjoyed during the regime of John Paul II. In general, the official policy of the institutional Catholic Church, as carried out through agencies such as the Secretariat for Hispanic Affairs of the United States Catholic Council, has been the promotion of multiculturalism, especially the use of Spanish language and Latino customs, in Catholic life and worship in dioceses and parishes where Spanish speakers abound—a major shift from the policy of ethnic homogenization begun early in the twentieth century and still vigorous through the 1950s.

Despite these efforts, however, the role of the Catholic Church among Spanish-speaking Americans remains somewhat precarious. The paucity of indigenous clerical leadership that was the heritage of centuries of colonialism has never been compensated for sufficiently, and it is only recently that Catholic leadership in the United States has become seriously aware of the problem. The casual attitude of many Latinos, especially men, to formal religious life has also contributed to a culture in which the role of the institutional church has been marginal. Aggressive evangelization by Protestants, especially pentecostals, has also been effective, since the minimal educational requirements for clergy and the grass-roots character of local church organization enable its rapid spread in the *barrios* of American cities: in 1990, about 25 percent of the Latino population in the United States was Protestant-affiliated. Without doubt, the task of mobilizing sufficient personnel with the requisite linguistic skills and cultural sensitivities to develop ministries within the Hispanic community is one of the most daunting challenges that faces the American Catholic Church in the twenty-first century.

CHAPTER 51

African American Christianity: "Eyes on the Prize"

Whether in slavery or relative freedom, black life in America has mainly been lived at the edge of society, restricted in its development by enslavement, discrimination, and poverty. The religious experience of many African Americans has thus been highly adaptive, combining elements of traditional African culture, American Christianity, and a free-form imagination that has resulted in a wide variety of expressions, ranging from the ring-shouts of the slave community to the miracle working of Father Divine to the militancy of Malcolm X. The overwhelming majority of black Americans who have acquired formal religious affiliation, however, have been Protestant Christian, especially within the Baptist, Methodist, and "sanctified" (holiness and pentecostal) traditions. To bring the story of African American religion up to the present requires a focus on black Christianity, which began to take on institutionalized form around the beginnings of the nineteenth century among the free blacks of the cities of the Northeast.

Although the lot of free blacks in nineteenth-century America was considerably more favorable than that of their enslaved counterparts, they were far from being universally regarded as the equals of whites in North or South. The churches were no exception. One of the classic stories illustrating this situation was the reception of Richard Allen (1760–1831) and his black colleagues when they attempted to participate fully in worship at St. George's Methodist Church in Philadelphia in November 1787. (This, at least, is the date traditionally given; these events may in fact have taken place in the early 1790s.) Although Allen, a Methodist preacher, and other members of the free black community had contributed extensively to the church's remodeling, they were barred by white ushers from assuming the places they had chosen, and physically removed when they demurred. Perhaps not surprisingly, they collectively withdrew from the church, and Allen was launched on a path that would soon lead to the formation of a network of black churches that paralleled the white denominations in which they could not find acceptance.

Allen founded the Bethel African Methodist Episcopal Church in Philadelphia in 1794, the lengthy name indicating both its Methodist identity ("Methodist Episcopal" was the name of the parent body at the time) and its conscious affirmation of the African origins of its congregation. (The current "Mother Bethel" church is both a Philadelphia landmark and museum as well as an active African Methodist Episcopal congregation.) A convention of black Methodists in 1816, tired of fighting white trustees for control of their church property, organized an independent denomination, the African Methodist Episcopal (AME) Church, and elected Allen their first bishop. An affiliation developed with a group of black Methodists in New York led by James Varick (1750?–1827), but tensions between the leaders resulted in the New York group's founding a separate though very similar denomination in 1821 that eventually adopted the name African Methodist Episcopal Zion (AMEZ) Church. The two groups attracted considerable membership in both North and South, and engaged in many of the same sorts of denominational activities that characterized their white counterparts, such as publishing and education. Wilberforce University (1856) and the adjoining Payne Theological Seminary in Ohio were two of the more enduring results of the AME educational effort.

Various other black Methodist bodies also arose, the largest of which is the Christian (previously Colored) Methodist Episcopal Church. This was founded in 1870 by southern blacks who no longer chose to belong to the Methodist Episcopal Church, South, which had earlier split from its northern counterpart over the slavery issue. A considerable number of blacks also belonged to the latter, usually in segregated annual conferences (the Methodist equivalent of a diocese), which at the time of the reunion of the northern and southern branches (1939) were consolidated into a Central Jurisdiction. (This and other segregated branches of Methodism were dissolved, beginning in 1964, in the context of the coming together of the United Methodist Church.) Table 2 gives comparative statistics for the three major independent groups.

The other major Protestant tradition to attract large numbers of free blacks was the Baptist. Like the Methodists, they stressed self-discipline, the need for an emotional personal conversion, and highly expressive worship. Unlike the Methodists, who benefited from a tight organization, Baptists of both races enjoyed the advantage of congregational independence and maximal flexibility. Throughout the nineteenth century, this independence stood in the way of any extensive denominational organization. Regional groupings began to emerge by the 1830s, with the Providence Baptist Association in Ohio the first in 1836. It was finally in 1895 that the National Baptist Convention was founded in Atlanta as a coalescence of several related earlier groups that had arisen to deal with education, missions, and other traditional denominational needs. As Baptists are wont to do, however, the convention split in 1915 over internal political issues into the National Baptist Convention of America and the National Baptist Convention of the U.S.A., Inc. A further schism in the latter group in 1961 gave rise to the Progressive National Baptist Convention, Inc. The most recent statistics available for these three groups are given in Table 3.

The third major family of black Christian churches is made up of those groups with origins in the holiness and pentecostal ferment of the late nineteenth century. The holiness movement arose from Methodism and emphasized the experience of "entire sanctification," through which the believer becomes free from voluntary sin.

Table 2. Membership Statistics for African American Methodist Denominations

African Methodist Episcopal Church (1999)	2,500,000
African Methodist Episcopal Zion Church (2006)	1,443,795
Christian Methodist Episcopal Church (2006)	850,000

Table 3. Membership Statistics of African American Baptist Denominations

National Baptist Convention of America, Inc. (2000)	3,500,000
National Baptist Convention, USA, Inc. (2004)	5,000,000
Progressive National Baptist Convention, Inc. (1995)	2,500,000

Note: These figures are approximations.

Pentecostalism built on the foundations of holiness but stresses the reception of the "gifts of the Holy Spirit," of which speaking in tongues and healing through faith are among the most conspicuous. In the early days of pentecostalism especially, the boundaries between the races counted for little in the effervescence created by the sense of having the Holy Spirit in the midst of the believers. The most important early center of black pentecostalism was the Azusa Street Mission in Los Angeles, where in 1906 William J. Seymour, a black Baptist preacher, became the focus of a powerful interracial pentecostal revival that lasted for three years. Little else is known about Seymour, and even the dates of his birth and death are obscure.

After these heady beginnings, the usual forces of schism, routinization, and segregation overtook what became known as the "sanctified" black churches, and a number of denominations began to take on organizational form. Notable among these was the Church of God in Christ, which was organized as a holiness church in Memphis by Charles Harrison Mason and Charles Price Jones Sr. in 1897. After Mason and other leaders of the movement converted to the pentecostal way on a visit to Azusa Street, the two founders parted company over the issue: Mason and the original denomination followed the pentecostal path, whereas Jones and his holiness group withdrew in 1907 and soon established the Church of Christ (Holiness) U.S.A. Other schisms plagued the latter group, which still exists but has dwindled to a very small membership. On the other hand, the Church of God in Christ remains based in Memphis, has been extremely active in overseas evangelism, and in 1996 claimed some five and a half million members. There are a considerable number of other holiness and pentecostal denominations, most rather small in size, and innumerable independent churches, many of which meet in storefronts in urban neighborhoods.

Worship in black churches shares many of the theological and liturgical premises of the broader Methodist, Baptist, holiness, and pentecostal traditions in which they participate, but few black services are exactly like their white counterparts. Social class plays some role here, with middle-class black churches tending toward more restraint and decorum in their style. Much of the distinctiveness of black Christian worship has roots in patterns developed in the era of slavery, some of them most likely echoing earlier African sources. These include preaching, which is often based on a narrative held together by formulaic phrases that make it possible virtually to chant a biblical story by inserting set verbal units that maintain cadences and provide brief respites when memory temporarily falters. Narrative and moral exhortation are much more common in black preaching than doctrinal instruction, which has never been emphasized. In addition, the congregation interacts enthusiastically with the preacher, responding with *amen* and other interjections in keeping with the rhythms of the sermon. Open emotional expression is a common feature, especially in "sanctified" worship.

A direct derivative of the slave tradition of "spirituals" is the gospel music of the late nineteenth and twentieth centuries. This style was originally made popular with black and white audiences alike by the Jubilee Singers of Fisk University in Nashville, beginning in the 1870s. Although their versions of black spirituals were heavily modified to conform with middle-class Victorian taste, they greatly aided the cause of black education and helped to legitimate a distinctively black musical tradition.

The more immediate origins of the modern black gospel tradition lie in the 1920s, when jazz and the blues were attracting wide attention as highly sophisticated and somewhat daring secular musical styles with distinctly black origins. Thomas A. Dorsey, who gave the movement its first coherent shape, was born in 1899 in rural Georgia, the son of a Baptist preacher. Dorsey joined in the exodus of southern blacks moving to the cities of the North, which was already under way, and settled in Chicago. He first made a name as a blues musician, then joined a Baptist church, experienced a conversion, and turned his attention to religious music. Dorsey's compositions, such as "Precious Lord, Take My Hand" and "Peace in the Valley," found an enthusiastic audience among whites as well, but their emphasis on the distinctively black experience of hope amidst suffering made it clear that here was a music significantly different from the gospel songs of white evangelicals such as Fanny Crosby and Ira D. Sankey.

Black gospel had its origins at a time when popular music in the modern sense was being made possible by the expansion of the recording industry and radio, and its distinctive rhythms spread rapidly through the record companies that served primarily black audiences, who were known as the "race market." Black gospel music thus had a double character, incorporated as part of the worship of black congregations but also enjoyed as popular music via records and radio. (Interestingly, recorded "sermons with singing," such as J. M. Gates's "Black Diamond Express to Hell" and A. W. Nix's "Death's Black Train Is Coming," were best-sellers in the 1920s, outselling Bessie Smith by quite a bit.) Some gospel singers such as Mahalia Jackson attained star status, and gospel groups such as the Drinkard Sisters and the Soul Stirrers provided the early musical experience for popular secular artists such as Dionne Warwick and Sam Cooke, respectively. Much of the "Motown Sound" of the 1960s and after, as exemplified in popular groups such as the Temptations and the Four Tops, was firmly rooted in the gospel tradition. Aretha Franklin, the "Queen of Soul," is the daughter of the prominent Detroit Baptist minister C. L. Franklin, and began her career at age fourteen with Checker Records, which had recorderd her father's sermons and gospel vocals. The relationship between secular and sacred in African American culture is often a problematic one: sometimes the two are starkly opposed, as in the case of 1920s blues and gospel; at other times, the lines separating them are so fine as to be nearly invisible.

The development of gospel music is very closely tied to broader events that deeply affected the black community in America and its religious expression. Fisk University, which gave black music its first national exposure, was one of a number of colleges founded in the post–Civil War era by the American Missionary Association. Many of these have continued to provide higher education for black professionals and clergy to the present day. (Others among the many black colleges founded during the Reconstruction era through collaboration of the Freedmen's Bureau with the AME or denominational bodies include Howard University in Washington, D.C., Morehouse College in Atlanta, Talladega in Alabama, and Tougaloo in Mississippi.) Jim Crow laws enforcing new patterns of segregation, economic hard times, and the reduction of many southern blacks to virtual serfdom through the sharecropping system combined with new economic opportunities stimulated by the war economy of the 1910s to lead thousands of blacks into the great cities of the North—an exodus that had already begun late in the nineteenth century. Harlem, Chicago, and Detroit joined New Orleans, Atlanta, and Memphis as centers of black cultural life, which expressed itself most vividly in music and religion. The traditional woes of African Americans were then compounded by the Depression of the 1930s, which hit both rural and urban blacks particularly hard, given the precarious situation in which most lived.

One of the few centers of stability within this constant state of social marginality and economic insecurity was the church. Among more prosperous congregations, large-scale urban structures were built in the Victorian eclectic (primarily Romanesque) style of the late nineteenth and early twentieth centuries. Frequently older churches outgrown by white congregations moving to more fashionable quarters were taken over by black Methodists and Baptists, and the poorer "sanctified" groups often made do with storefronts or small rural wooden churches. The interior arrangements were usually similar to those of other Baptist and Methodist churches of the period, with curved rows of "opera-style" seats and a large frontal platform with room for a preacher and a colorfully robed choir.

The preacher occupied an especially prominent role in the black community, because he was one of its few members who, if not formally educated, at least had extensive experience in public speaking, organization, and other social and political skills useful not only in mediating differences within the black community but in representing that community in the broader society as well. Large urban churches provided a ready-made political base for those who sought to cross the "color line" into national politics, as exemplified in the congressional career of Adam Clayton Powell Jr., pastor of Harlem's Abyssinian Baptist Church. Martin Luther King Jr. (1929–68) was similarly descended from a family of black Baptist ministers and utilized his position first in Montgomery and then Atlanta as a platform for his leadership in the Civil Rights Movement. More recently, Jesse Jackson of Chicago has gained attention as the founder of the "Rainbow Coalition" for interracial social justice and as a candidate for the Democratic nomination for the American presidency, the only black to mount a serious campaign for America's highest office in a major political party prior to Barack Obama's in 2008.

The Civil Rights Movement that began with the Montgomery, Alabama, bus boy-

cott of 1955–56 was the culmination of many themes in the African American experience. Black clergy had long played a leading role in early civil rights organizations
such as the National Association for the Advancement of Colored People (NAACP,
founded in 1910), and had often made their churches available as meeting places for
such groups. The Southern Christian Leadership Conference (SCLC), founded in
Atlanta in 1957 with King as the first president, was a new organization consisting
primarily of southern black clergy dedicated to pursuing the traditional interests of
the black community in the political realm under clerical leadership.

Another source of continuity lay in the motif of liberation, which had been a
staple of black preaching and religious thought since slavery days. This quest for
freedom found particularly memorable expression in the rolling cadences of Martin
Luther King's "I Have a Dream" address delivered from the Lincoln Memorial on 28
August 1963, during the "March on Washington for Jobs and Freedom," one of the
culminating events of the movement. King's rhetoric had an Old Testament quality
to it. Following in the tradition of the Hebrew prophets, he made it clear that the
black Christian quest for deliverance was not simply confined to longings for a better
world in the hereafter but was based on a demand for social justice in the here and
now. "We Shall Overcome," which became the universal anthem of the movement,
further echoed the traditional rhythms of the black spiritual.

Even before the movement had achieved some important victories in a series of
laws passed by Congress, especially the Civil Rights Act of 1964, it was becoming
clear that the influence of Christianity on the black movement was problematic.
King, who held a doctorate in theology from Boston University, was very much
committed to the black Baptist tradition but was also deeply influenced by such
non-Christian thinkers as Henry David Thoreau and Mohandas Gandhi. These ideas
combined with a traditional emphasis on love for one's enemies in the philosophy
of nonviolent resistance that was exhibited in the campaign on sit-ins and peaceful
demonstrations that dominated the early Civil Rights Movement. More traditional
groups such as the NAACP and SCLC, however, were soon augmented and to some
degree rivaled by militant secular organizations such as the Student Nonviolent Coordinating Committee (SNCC) and the older Congress of Racial Equality (CORE),
which organized "freedom rides" from the northern states to help mobilize change
in the South. Among the leaders of the former group was Stokely Carmichael, one of
a new breed of black militants who found the pace of actual social change too slow
and who were ready to challenge the older leadership to espouse more aggressive
tactics to secure their goals.

Until his assassination in 1968 in Memphis, where he had gone to support a municipal workers' strike, King himself had broadened his critique of American institutions to include an attack on American involvement in the war in Vietnam. It
soon became clear that the implications of what had begun as a reform movement
were becoming radical, leading to an indictment of American institutions on the

one hand and a transformation of consciousness on the other. A new vocabulary was coming into being, indicative of the inadequacy of earlier language to deal with the issues involved. *Negro,* which had long been the socially acceptable term for "colored" Americans, now yielded to *Black, Afro-American,* and, eventually, *African American,* as preferred designations. *Soul,* a traditional religious term, now acquired a new significance as expressive of the deeply felt longings, experience, and spiritual character of American blacks, and appeared in such forms as "soul food," "soul music," and "soul brother."

A related new phrase that indicated a dramatic change in the aspirations of many African Americans was "Black Power." The title of a 1967 book by Stokely Carmichael and Charles V. Hamilton, it became the focus for a new emphasis among many black leaders on the need to take aggressive measures to ensure that blacks enjoyed not only abstract legal rights but also the specific political and economic power that could alone guarantee their genuine equality with other Americans. One strategy to this end was the "selective patronage" campaign led by an alliance of black Philadelphia ministers, who helped achieve greater black employment by urging their congregations to boycott those businesses that did not cooperate with their aims. A more startling manifestation of this new militancy was the proclamation of the "Black Manifesto" by James Forman in the midst of a service in progress at Manhattan's liberal Riverside Church in 1969. The manifesto was an indictment of American society and especially its white religious groups for their obliviousness to injustices done to the black community, and it demanded of them extensive financial "reparations" to begin to rectify the economic imbalance between the races. Although the effects were not clearly those that Forman and other militants had hoped for, the message delivered was one of impatience with gradual change and a reliance on directly confrontational tactics.

The impact of this militancy also made itself felt in the realm of black religious thought. One of the more radical expressions of the desire to reconcile Christianity with the new black consciousness was the Detroit minister Albert Cleage's *The Black Messiah* of 1969, which argued that Jesus had quite literally been black in physical appearance. A more systematic articulator of this sort of emphasis was Union Theological Seminary's James Cone, whose *Black Theology and Black Power* of 1969 set forth the argument that the goal of the Christian Gospel was the liberation of the poor and powerless. Although Cone relied heavily on European theologians in his early work, he later shifted his emphasis to exploring more fully the resources of the African American tradition, as in *The Spirituals and the Blues* (1972) and *Martin and Malcolm and America* (1992).

Still more militant factions of the black community identified both with the Marxism that had informed some of Forman's rhetoric and the new consciousness that was emerging throughout many nonwhite developing nations. Radical secular ideologies were espoused by the Black Panthers as well as the erratic Symbionese Liberation

Army, which came to a violent end in California in 1974. After the dust had settled from the wake of these movements and the unsystematic violence that had erupted in many urban black ghetto neighborhoods in the late 1960s and early 1970s, however, the national mood began to turn in different directions. The force of the radical movements dissipated, and such moderate colleagues of King as Fred Shuttlesworth and Ralph Abernathy were unable to sustain the momentum of the earlier movement. Much of black religious life, especially in the "sanctified" churches, went on more or less as usual. Nevertheless, a new level of consciousness and expectation had been introduced into the black community, religious and secular, that could never be reversed. Black caucuses had formed in such primarily white denominations as the Roman Catholic and Episcopal churches that continued to articulate black needs and perspectives to the broader Christian community, though most blacks retained their traditional denominational affiliations. Jesse Jackson continued in the 1980s and 1990s the role of the black minister as political leader; declaring himself a candidate for the Democratic presidential nomination in both 1984 and 1988, he made an impressive though ultimately unsuccessful showing in the latter race against Michael Dukakis.

By the early decades of the twenty-first century, the impact of several decades of social, political, and cultural change had made itself felt within the realm of African American religion. Radicalism had retreated dramatically, if it had not died entirely. Many African Americans had entered the middle and upper-middle classes, and a number of these were attracted to churches in which Euro-Americans predominated. African American Baptist and Methodist churches and their clergy continued to enjoy prestige, but their role as bases for political activity, especially on behalf of tbe Democratic Party, were coming under growing scrutiny, even as some of their clergy began to be attracted to Republican candidates for their conservative stands on social issues such as gay marriage. The impact of the civil rights revolution had been successful in breaking down old barriers to black assimilation, but the price of that liberation has been a lessening of the social bonds, forged in discrimination, that had previously promoted solidarity.

CHAPTER 52

Islam in the United States

Of all the major religious traditions represented in the United States, Islam is probably the one that many Americans have the greatest difficulty understanding. This is not so much because of its complexity—its essential teachings are really quite brief and lucid—but because of the cultural baggage with which it has been laden by non-Muslim observers. In addition, Americans have long been accustomed to think about religion (along with race and gender) in binary terms. Most Americans historically have been Christian, a category readily divisible into "Protestant" and "Catholic." (Apparent exceptions, such as Anglicans and Eastern Orthodox, could be tacitly if not very accurately lumped with the first and second categories respectively.) A further dichotomy of "Christians" and "Jews" could later be postulated, with the second category again constituting the "other" for the culturally dominant majority. Will Herberg's "Triple Melting Pot" image for describing 1950s Americans suggests that, by that time, Catholicism and Judaism had shed a considerable amount of their "otherness," a void perhaps filled by the African Americans that Herberg has frequently been criticized for omitting.

By the 1970s, however, whatever lack of domestic otherness that existed was becoming filled by the new waves of non-European immigration made possible by the liberalized immigration rules of 1965. During the World War II era Japanese Americans, many of them Buddhist, had been classified as potentially dangerous "others" and locked away in detention camps for the duration of the conflict. In the latter decades of the century, however, neither Buddhism nor Hinduism seemed to pose a threat to the dominant culture, even as numerous practitioners arrived from Asia. Rather, the swelling number of Muslim immigrants brought with them what many Americans perceived as both ancient cultural associations and contemporary political resonances, not all of them positive. Islam, therefore, has often played the role of "other" in the American imagination in an ongoing process in which scapegoats are identified as responsible for perceived or genuine national ills.

This view of Muslims and Islam as "the other" is a manifestation of what the literary scholar Edward Said has identified as "Orientalism"—that is, the propensity in the Euro-American West to regard Asia in general and the Middle East in particular as an exotic cultural construct that at once complements and defines the "West" (a rather arbitrary notion in itself, when one thinks about it). Said cites a series of phrases formed by prefixing various words with "Oriental"—despotism, splendor, cruelty, sensuality—to suggest what the term *Orient* evokes for "Westerners" (or "Occidentals") at some level of consciousness. These negative, or at best ambiguous, associations with the Orient have been reinforced in recent decades by various hostile acts committed by Middle Eastern extremists against Europeans and North Americans, including disruption of an Olympics, air hijackings, and the taking of ninety embassy staff as hostages in Tehran by Iranian militants in 1979—an event that contributed to the defeat of Jimmy Carter in his subsequent bid for reelection as president. The attack on monumental buildings in New York and Washington, D.C., in the 2001 events now universally known as "9/11," raised American suspicion of and hostility towards all things Islamic to a level not even imaginable previously. Middle Eastern oil-producing countries had earlier soured many Americans on the region and its associated religious culture, and the 9/11 events ensured that anyone in the United States who seemed classifiable as an "Arab," whatever their political or religious beliefs, was in danger of public scorn and hostility if not actual violence.

A related point worth making here is that, even though many (though by no means all) Arabs are Muslims, the majority of Muslims worldwide are not Arabs. Only about one in eight American Muslims, for example, is of Arab (that is, Arabic-speaking) background (compared with one in five worldwide). More than twice that number have roots in the Indian subcontinent (India, Pakistan, Bangladesh), and more than two in five are African Americans, almost entirely recent converts.

The "otherness" of Islam is very different from that evoked by the Hindu or Buddhist traditions in its very familiarity. Islam is, first of all, a "Western" religion, arising in the same general part of world as did Judaism and Christianity before it—that is, what we now call the "Middle East." Islam further recognizes elements of authenticity in these other "religions of the Book," although it claims a revelation that supersedes what Christians call the Bible. Its monotheistic concept of God is also very familiar to "Westerners." Its relationship to the traditions more firmly embedded in European American culture might be characterized by Sigmund Freud's phrase, "the narcissism of minor differences": those with whom you share a great deal sometimes seem more threatening than those who are completely unfamiliar.

Historically, the relationship between Muslims and Christians has also been similarly close, if not exactly friendly. Within a century of the death of the prophet Muhammad in A.D. 632, the Islamic religion had spread by conquest and conversion through much of the Middle East and northern Africa into the Iberian peninsula in the west and as far as what is now Pakistan in the east. The Crusades, which began in 1095, were a series of seven not very successful "holy wars" summoned by the pope to "liberate" the Holy Land from the rule of the "infidel" Muslims. Later, the more successful Spanish *reconquista* of Iberia in 1492, through the defeat and expulsion of the Muslims who had long occupied its southern portion, had monumental consequences for both the Sephardic Jews and the Muslims who had long dwelt there together in relative peace. (It was here in Iberia that Europeans had access to a long history of Islamic contributions to science, mathematics, philosophy, and religion, which had a profound effect on medieval Christian and Jewish learning and which is still evident in our use of Arabic numbers and such words and concepts as algebra and chemistry.) Despite this and other reverses, such as the Turkish defeat at the Battle of Lepanto in 1571, a Muslim presence has persisted into the present in Balkan regions such as Albania and war-torn Bosnia and Kosovo.

Islam—the correct term for the religion practiced by Muslims—is an Arabic word that means "submission"—in this case to the will of *Allah* (God.) Most generally, Muslims regard their faith as both a natural and a revealed religion. The fundamental truths of Islam are embedded in the order of things and are accessible through human reason, although the latter faculty is often obscured and needs prophetic assistance. Human nature, similarly, is not fundamentally corrupt; rather, it is good but weak, and needs guidance in achieving its true aims.

The religious essentials of the Islamic religion can easily be summarized in two brief lists: the six elements of faith and the Five Pillars of Islam, which summarize the religious duties of believers. The elements of faith—the essential points of belief—which vary somewhat in number and in the order in which they are listed, are as follows:

1. There is no god (*Allah*) but God (*Allah*). Like Judaism and Christianity, Islam is *monotheistic,* affirming the existence of one God and only one God.

2. *Angels,* which are God's messengers, exist. This belief is also common to Christianity and Judaism, and has in fact enjoyed considerable currency in American popular religious culture since the 1990s.

3. God's message to humanity is contained in the writings known as the *Qur'an* (less accurately also known as the "Koran"). The Qur'an (kuh-RAHN), which is authoritative only in its original Arabic version, contains the fullness of divine revelation, and supersedes the Jewish and Christian scriptures that preceded it. Believers come into a relationship with the Qur'an not so much through reading as through reciting it in Arabic during prayer.

4. The *prophet Muhammad* (570–632), although not divine himself, was the final and definitive member of a *prophetic line* that also includes Jesus, Abraham, Moses, and a variety of other figures found in Hebrew scripture.

5. At the end of time will come a *resurrection* of all human bodies and a time of *judgment* at which all will be consigned to eternal rewards or punishments according to how they have fulfilled God's commandments on earth.

6. All human events are shaped by *destiny* or, more literally, a "measuring out" of human affairs according to the providential will of God. Nothing, in short, can take place in the realm of human affairs without divine acquiescence. (Whether this teaching is the equivalent of predestination has long been a matter of debate in Muslim circles.)

The *Five Pillars of Islam* are an important part of the *Shari'a* (shah-REE-ya), or Muslim religious law. They are a more formal statement of the rules that govern "living Islamically" by which one may be considered a part of the *umma* (OOM-mah)—Muslim community. They include:

1. The *shahada,* which states that there is no God but God and that Muhammad is his messenger (or, less accurately, prophet). Like the Jewish Shema, this is a brief statement of the core of Islamic belief.

2. Ritual *prayer (salat)*, which all believers are to perform five times daily while facing Mecca. During this prayer, the faithful prostrate themselves, recite verses of the Qur'an in Arabaic, and also offer personal prayers. Although this can be done anywhere individually, communal prayer—especially the one time required for men, Friday afternoon—particularly in Muslim countries, takes place in a mosque (*masjid*). In countries where Islam is the dominant

religion, the call to prayer is sounded publicly by a *muzzein* from a *minaret* (tower), much as the church bells tolled the time of worship in Catholic regions. In the United States, such calls for prayer are generally confined to the interior of the mosque, and public disputes have sometimes ensued when they have been broadcast publicly.

3. *Almgiving* (*zakat*), for the support of the needy as well as the broader Islamic enterprise, such as the building of mosques. This latter cause is more important in non-Islamic countries, where such giving (usually about 2.5 percent of net worth) is voluntary. In countries in which Islam is the established religion, a tax renders this duty automatic and provides for religious infrastructure such as houses of prayer. In recent times in the United States, money has often been directed toward places around the world where Muslims have experienced distress, such as Bosnia, Kosovo, Chechnya, and Kashmir.

4. *Fasting* (*sawn*) during the month of *Ramadan,* the month during which the Qur'an was revealed. (Islamic months are calculated on a lunar calendar of 354 days, and Ramadan thus begins approximately eleven days earlier each year.) During this period, abstinence from food, drink, and sexual relations is observed during the daylight hours—dawn until sunset. Evenings are marked by enhanced family activities such as communal meals. Unlike the Christian Lent, the emphasis in Ramadan is not on penance for transgressions but rather on learning increased reliance on God and compassion for the poor. Ramadan ends with a festival—*'id al fitr*—that is a major event in the Muslim liturgical calendar.

5. At least once during their lifetimes, Muslims who are financially able are obliged to undertake a pilgrimage (*Hajj*) to Mecca, the original home of Muhammad and the site of the *Ka'ba.* (Also spelled *Kaabah;* the transliteration of Arabic, like Hebrew, into English sometimes varies.) The Ka'ba is a cubic building associated with the prophet Abraham, and Muslims believe it to be the first temple devoted to the worship of the one true god. It is thus Islam's most sacred place. Mecca, more broadly, is Islam's holy city, and non-Muslims are banned from entering.

In addition to the five pillars, some Muslims add a sixth: *jihad,* or "exertion" in the Islamic cause. Although most Muslims regard this as an injunction to living Islamically and to nonviolent moral persuasion of others, its more radical interpretation as "holy war" has been utilized by extremists as a rationale for militancy. Like much about Islam, however, the nuances of this concept have often been misrepresented by Western media.

Like Jewish and Catholic immigrants before them, many Muslims emigrating to the United States have found it easy enough to bring their religion with them but considerably more difficult to transplant the way of life entailed by that religion, having previously lived in a society where that lifestyle was taken for granted and socially and legally supported. Alcohol, for example, is forbidden, and is not much of an issue in countries like Saudi Arabia where it is not legally available. A more significant example would be finding time for evening prayer or the Ramadan fast in the American calendar and broader social context. A concern shared by Muslims and Jews is in the realm of diet; as in Judaism, pork is forbidden, and other meats must be slaughtered in a *halal* (lawful) manner. Halal meat markets can now be found in larger North American cities with significant Muslim communities; otherwise, kosher meat is an acceptable substitute. The borrowing and lending of money at interest is also forbidden in Islamic law, and mutual aid societies that provide no-interest loans have been another adaptation to American circumstances.

Another realm of adjustment for Muslims to the ways of a pluralistic and largely secular society is that of sexuality and gender roles. In Muslim societies, men and women tend to operate in separate spheres that many Americans would not regard as equal. Men, for example, can marry any woman as long as the children are brought up as Muslims; women can only marry Muslim men. In the United States and other non-Muslim countries, teenagers may be discouraged from dating, and marriages may be arranged, sometimes today with help from the Internet. Worship at mosques is segregated by sex (as in traditional Judaism), with men and women either occupying different sides of the worship area or women relegated to the rear or the balcony. Another issue is the public demeanor of women, who in traditional Muslim cultures do not appear in public without a *hijab* (head scarf). (The imposition of the *chador,* a garment that covers the head and body, on Iranian women after the Islamic revolution in that country remains a major source of controversy.) Although American Muslim women generally agree on the desirability of refraining from the extremes of bodily exposure that are not uncommon today, their degree of adaptation to secular norms, such as the exposure of their hair, varies considerably.

Another public realm of adaptation is the site of prayer itself, which is central to Muslim life. In Muslim countries, the periodic public call to prayer from the minaret is a regular feature of the urban scene. In North America, however, such behavior can be seen as politically provocative and is therefore not usually practiced. Mosques, however, are now proliferating in cities and suburbs in the United States and Canada, and the buildings vary considerably in size and elaborateness. A mosque is in its essence a space in which public prayer can be conducted; although there are architectural traditions that may be drawn on if resources permit, there are few requirements. Converted houses or storefronts are frequently used for the purpose in lower-income communities. A more elaborate mosque will often have a dome and minarets as identifying external features. Although, as in Judaism, the representation of human or divine figures is prohibited, geometrical patterns and verses from the Qur'an may be inscribed on the interior walls. A place for ablutions (ritual purification through washing of various body parts) and the storage of shoes is usually located outside of the area for prayer. Inside is an open space, sometimes covered by a carpet, on which worshipers can prostrate themselves during prayer. At one end, oriented toward Mecca, are a *minbar* (pulpit) and *mihrab,* or *qiblah* (KIB-lah) niche, indicating the direction of Mecca. Although worship (similar to the traditional Jewish pattern) does not require a formal leader, prayers at a mosque are usually presided over by an *imam* (ee-MOM or ee-MAAM), who may also assume other religious duties in the American context. (In praying groups of three or more, one is chosen to function as imam when a professional is not available.) In theory, however, there is no such thing as a "clergy" in Islam.

Mosques are traditional houses of worship and can be found—many of great splendor—throughout the Islamic world. A North American innovation is the *Islamic community center,* examples of which can be found in most good-sized cities. (The first and still one of the most notable of these was that which opened on Embassy Row in Washington, D.C., in 1957 to serve the multinational diplomatic community.) These centers are similar in origin and function to the Catholic parishes, Jewish synagogue-centers, and Protestant institutional churches and megachurches that developed at various times to provide a range of services beyond that of worship itself. In Muslim countries, there is no need for these services, since religion, society, and culture are coextensive. In North America, however, Muslims need a variety of institutional supports, such as educational and recreational facilities, if they are to create a sense of community as a minority religious group intent on preserving its values and traditions. This process is further complicated by the fact that North American Muslims are united by religion but not always by ethnicity—that is, the possession of a shared culture distinct from that of the majority. The dozens of flags that fly outside the Islamic Center of Greater Cincinnati, for example, indicate that its members come from all parts of the Muslim world, which includes not only the Middle East but also North Africa and southern and southeastern Asia. Coming together for the first time in North American cities, these Muslims presumably share English as their principal common tongue, and have to adjust to the fact that their previous experience of Islam may have been considerably different in detail if not in essence. Their desire not only for worship facilities but for a social life in religiously supportive circumstances as well as the socialization of their children into the Islamic tradition makes necessary facilities more elaborate than a mosque itself, which may still be the architecturally dominant element of such a complex. The imam, in his role as director of the activities of such a center, may take on the gamut of duties long familiar to Christian and Jewish clergy as well. (Imams are always male, and almost all in North America have received training abroad.) At the turn of the millennium, there were over 1300 mosques and/or Islamic centers in the United States, with the largest numbers in New York and California.

Although it is impossible to obtain an accurate count of Muslims in the United

States today, the more generous estimates place their number at roughly equal to or possibly even in excess of that of American Jews—that is, in the six to seven million range in 2000. If Christians are regarded as one religious community—a problematic assumption—Muslims may now be the second largest in the United States. This Islamic burgeoning, as visually exemplified in the appearance of the domes and minarets of mosques on interstate highways near many major cities, is very recent. (In 1960, for example, the number was about one hundred thousand, and 1970 in the half-million range.) Prior to the late nineteenth century, Muslims were a presence in North America only as isolated individuals or small communities, including an indeterminate number of slaves from sub-Saharan Africa. These early American Muslims existed without any community support, however, and made no impact on the broader religious scene. Many of their descendants, however, became respected professionals and positive examples of Muslim Americans in their communities.

The foundations of the American Muslim community were first laid around 1875, when emigrants from Syria/Lebanon (then one political unit) fled the declining Ottoman Empire seeking economic relief in the New World. Like their Italian contemporaries in particular, these early emigrants were mainly single males who had little interest in settling permanently. A scattering of mosques began to spring up—both Ross, North Dakota, and Cedar Rapids, Iowa, claim priority. The first significant Muslim community arose in response to the economic opportunities offered by the thriving automobile industry in greater Detroit in the 1920s; Dearborn, Michigan, where Henry Ford's Greenfield Village is now located, soon became a major center of Muslim settlement and activity.

The combination of liberalized immigration laws, especially the changes of 1965; overseas political upheavals such as the 1979 revolution in Iran; and the continuing allure of America as an economic promised land catalyzed the transformation, beginning in the 1960s, of Muslims from a small and somewhat scattered minority to the status of America's "second faith"—numerically, if not culturally. Whereas earlier emigrants were primarily unskilled workers, more recent newcomers have been business or professional people, including a number who had earlier come to the United States as students. Patterns of settlement have correlated partially with national origins, with many Yemenis and Iranis, for example, attracted to California. Not too surprisingly, major metropolitan areas such as New York City, Chicago, and Los Angeles have become centers of settlement for Muslims throughout the world. (Some 140 mosques served the approximately six hundred thousand Muslims in New York City in the first decade of the twenty-first century.)

North American Muslims differ from one another in a variety of ways: ethnically, racially, socially, and religiously. Conversion to Islam by European Americans has not been widespread—perhaps some fifty thousand at most—and often come about through intermarriage. African Americans have been much more likely to convert, both to the more traditional American Muslim Mission of Wallace Deen Muhammad and Louis Farrakhan's smaller and more controversial Nation of Islam. (African American Islam is discussed more fully in chapter 40.) A considerable majority of Muslims in North America today, however, are immigrants from Islamic areas and their offspring.

American Muslims, like their old-world counterparts, are also divided religiously. The major religious division within Islam—that between the majority *Sunni* (SOO-nee) and minority *Shiite* (SHEE-ite) Muslims—arose early over the issue of the succession of leadership after the death of the founder, Muhammad. Sunni Muslims believe that Muhammad made no specific provision for such a succession, and that his followers selected Abu Bakr from among their own number for this role. Abu Bakr, according to this theory, was the first caliph (KAY-liff), or leader of the entire Muslim community (*umma*). Shiite Muslims, on the other hand, believe that Muhammad designated his cousin and son-in-law, Ali, as his successor, and that this succession was to continue indefinitely through the line of Ali's son and descendants. Another Shiite emphasis is on the martyrdom of Muhammad's grandson, Husayn, who is regarded as a prototype of resistance to oppression. Shiites subsequently split into various factions—Twelvers, Fivers, and Seveners—who have conflicting interpretations of the implications of this succession. The *Druze* are a small sect from Syria-Lebanon whose beliefs differ greatly from traditional Islam; its American adherents, however, have been reasserting their Muslim identity.

Although most Muslims define themselves as Sunni or Shiite, they may also follow a devotional path known as *Sufism* as well. Sufism is the name given to various movements, at first individual and later organized into brotherhoods, of Muslims who sought mystical contact with the divine through asceticism and contemplation as well as ecstatic ritual, music, and dance. Its literary expression—for example, in the writings of the thirteenth-century Persian-Turkish poet Rumi—has been particularly attractive to non-Muslim intellectuals and has accounted for a fair number of recent conversions. More recent authors and teachers, such as the Indian father and son, Hazrat Inayat Khan and Pir Vilayat Khan, and the Afghan Idries Shah (1924–96), helped publicize and establish Sufism in the West as a path of orthodox Islam; in the United States, for example, Sufi masters from India to Bosnia lead groups of believers. In addition, New Age enthusiasts have appropriated its teachings more selectively, though few have actually converted to Islam. (Deepak Chopra, the popular promoter of health reform, has produced a CD of music inspired by Rumi's poems rendered by such unlikely performers as Madonna and Demi Moore.)

Organizationally, the Federation of Islamic Associations in the United States and Canada became in 1952 the first group to try to coordinate Muslim activity on the continent. It later yielded its influence to other groups, such as the Muslim Student Association (1963) and the Islamic Society of North America (1981), the latter of which now plays the role of a national coordinating body but does not speak for all Muslim groups. The latter's large annual meeting is a major event in promoting

American Muslim discourse. The American Muslim Council and the Council on American-Islamic Relations promote political causes of Islamic concern, ranging from the recognition of Islamic holidays in the public schools to the rights of prisoners to live Islamically to the appointment of Muslim chaplains in the armed services, which was first achieved in 1993. Local Islamic councils deal with issues such as the organization of mosques and community centers. After they are founded, such centers are directed by boards in which women sometimes participate.

Although the Muslim community in North America has been expanding rapidly and has become increasingly prosperous, it is only now beginning to jell into a distinctive cultural presence. The formation of the latter is a complicated business, since many American Muslims have to balance three centers of cultural gravity: their native culture, the English-speaking mass culture of the United States, and, for the majority of Muslims whose native language is not Arabic, a religious culture in which that language is normative. (Most Muslims know and use at least a few traditional Arabic phrases of greeting.) Since a majority of Muslims in North America are immigrants or the children thereof, they have not yet had enough collective experience in the New World to have developed distinctive "takes" on being American Muslims. Therefore, a literature reflective of adaptation and its stresses, the process of negotiating between old and new worlds, as well as "making it" economically—the traditional preoccupations of newcomers—has not yet emerged.

A culture that is at once Islamic and American is also being influenced by new technologies, especially the Internet. Jane Smith, for example, describes the array of Muslim-related products now available in the United States, many of them specifically developed to resolve the dilemmas of living according to Islamic law and custom in a secularized culture. These include a variety of videos, CDs, and software; package pilgrimage tours to Mecca; watches and clocks indicating the times for daily prayer; women's fashions; and advice services, in which a *fatwa* (FAHT-wah), or legal opinion, on contemporary issue can be obtained by dialing 1-800-95-FATWA.

The events of 9/11 and its aftermath have had a pronounced effect on the American Muslim community. The immediate reaction of many Americans was one of suspicion and hostility not only towards Muslims as an undifferentiated group but towards anyone resembling an Arab or South Asian. A heightened attention to security, especially at airports, resulted in many Muslims being singled out for particular, and oftentimes annoying, attention. The Muslim community itself has reacted as have earlier minority groups, such as Catholics and Jews, who were suspected of harboring un-American attitudes, by an enhanced attention to its public image through community education and outreach. American Muslims have in the process entered a process of collective self-definition, addressing consciously the issues of how they are perceived not only by outsiders but by themselves. The result is an on-going process of interpretation and communication enhanced and accelerated by distinctive circumstances. In the longer run, though, this process is characteristic of those through which minority religious communities have learned how to maintain their integrity and identity within the broader context of the perennial tension in the United States between an appreciation of pluralism and pressures towards conformity.

CHAPTER 53

Asian Traditions and American Transformations

Late in the 1960s, many middle-class Americans were startled to see numbers of young people—some of them their own children—dancing in the streets, clad in saffron robes, repetitively chanting "Hare Krishna, Hare Rama." A few years later, these same folk might be driving down a major boulevard in their suburb of residence and behold a mountainlike Hindu temple built by the south Asian doctors and engineers who were now their neighbors. Still other of their European American professional counterparts, who a decade or two earlier might have worshiped at a nearby Episcopal church or Reform temple, might now be found sitting cross-legged in meditation at a local Zen center. Obviously, something important changed in the American religious landscape during the last few decades of the twentieth century.

The Hart-Celler Immigration Law of 1965 had one of the most profound impacts on the religious makeup of the United States of any federal legislation in the twentieth century. Immigration from Europe had been brought to new lows by a series of restrictive acts passed by Congress during the 1920s and aimed at the "new immigration" that had stemmed primarily from southern and eastern Europe. Periodic but fairly small influxes of European and Cuban refugees from Communist regimes diversified American demographics somewhat during the Cold War period, but the nation's basic ethnic mix was only lightly affected by these new arrivals. One major source of newcomers that had effectively been shut out of the country in previous years, however, was Asia. The immigration act of 1917 had created an "Asiatic Barred Zone," and the Supreme Court ruled in 1923 that immigrants arriving from the Indian subcontinent were not "free white persons" within the meaning of the Constitution and therefore not eligible for American citizenship. During the intervening decades, during which Japanese aggression further inflamed anti-"Oriental" sentiment, emigration from Asia came to a virtual standstill, and may even have reversed itself to a small extent. During the entire span of national history prior to 1960, for example, fewer than fifteen thousand Asian Indians entered the United States.

Since 1965, however, this situation has abruptly reversed itself. In 1990, for example, there were approximately 1,650,000 Americans of Chinese origin; 850,000 from Japan; 815,000 from India; and 300,000 from Korea. As with Spanish speakers, though, this population is distributed unevenly throughout the nation. Hawaii, California, and Washington State, for example, have historically hosted emigrants from east Asia in greater proportions than most other states. New York City has continued in its role as "cosmopolis," and its Chinatown continues to be a haven for an ongoing stream of newcomers, legal and otherwise. The highly traditional Hmong people from Laos have settled heavily in the Minneapolis area, whereas professionals from south Asia have scattered across the nation's urban centers. It is a rare population area beyond the smallest of towns that does not have a Chinese restaurant (often staffed by Cambodians or other southeast Asians), a motel operated by Indians from the state of Gujarat, or perhaps a physician from Pakistan. Some of these Asian immigrants are Christian—Koreans, for example, have embraced Presbyterianism in impressive numbers—whereas many from the subcontinent are Muslims. Many other Asian immigrants, though, have brought with them other religions that not long ago were seldom represented in the United States and Canada, and thus were considered exotic. Today, the sight of a massive Hindu temple on suburban Nashville's Old Hickory Boulevard or a variety of Vietnamese Buddhist temples in California's conservative Orange County is an occasion for comment only by visitors from small towns or right-wing political commentators seeking a scapegoat for endemic social problems.

This proliferation of religions of Asian origin is a formidably complex topic, given the variety and complex intersection of nations, cultures, and religions within Asia itself. India, China, Japan, and the several smaller nations that have sent emigrants to the United States have had different but interacting national histories, and the religions that have dominated their cultures have not been respecters of national borders (themselves a complex and often recent phenomenon). The religious cultures of Asia—and of Asian Americans—are complex, and include the practice of Jainism and Sikhism in south Asia and of Confucianism and Taoism among traditional Chinese. Other Asians practice varieties of Christianity, Judaism, and Islam. However, it makes sense to focus here on two major Asian religious traditions—*Hinduism* and *Buddhism*—that are closely related historically and geographically and that have taken root in the United States in significant numbers in three general forms:

1. *Ethnic* religions are those, like Pure Land Buddhism, which have been brought to the New World by Asian immigrants or refugees and practiced primarily within their own communities.* They first reached American shores with immigrants from China and Japan attracted by economic opportunities generated by the 1849 Gold Rush; after a lengthy period of dormancy brought

---

*The term *ethnic* here is problematic in a variety of ways, but is frequently used in this context to describe a kind of religious culture that is thoroughly bound up in its practice with the broader cultural practices of an immigrant community.

about by anti-Asian sentiment from the late nineteenth century through World War II, they were revived in a dramatic way by the influx of newcomers triggered by the 1965 changes in immigration law. Some would make a further distinction between those religions, such as Pure Land Buddhism, that have been practiced in this country for several generations and have thus become significantly Americanized, and others, like various forms of southeast Asian Buddhism, that are practiced by recent immigrants in a substantially Asian form.

2. *Export* religions usually have their origins in one of Asia's ancient traditions, but during the past century or two have emerged in new, aggressive forms like Japan's Soka Gakkai. Brought to North America by missionary-minded adherents, they have sought converts not so much among ethnic Asians as among European Americans. During the 1970s, some, such as ISKCON ("Hare Krishnas"), came in for bad publicity as "cults." Export religions generally have their origins in situations of cultural ferment in their countries of origin, and reached their apex in the United States during the flourishing of the youth counterculture of the 1960s and 1970s.

3. *Elite*—or, perhaps, *import*—religions are those strains of Buddhism and Hinduism that have attracted considerable followings among well-educated Americans seeking alternatives to Christianity and Judaism. Vedanta, Zen, and Tibetan Buddhism are good examples of these Asian movements, which generally have strong metaphysical dimensions and/or stress meditation as a central practice.

These three designations are rough-hewn and not entirely accurate, since particular movements, such as Zen and Tibetan Buddhism, may appeal to more than one clientele and be practiced in a variety of interpretations. However, they are useful in emphasizing that Asian religions are not monolithic, either in this country or their lands of origin, and that their appeal in an American setting may be to different constituencies in different times and ways.

The "deep background" of Asian traditions in the United States lies in the realm of "elite religion," and can be traced to the availability of Hindu and Buddhist texts in English translation in the 1830s that inspired "transcendentalist" authors such as Ralph Waldo Emerson, Henry David Thoreau, and Walt Whitman to draw on Asian metaphysical themes in a serious if eclectic way. Later, in the 1870s, Henry Steel Olcott and Mme. Helena Petrovna Blavatsky, the founders of the Theosophical Society, became what were probably the first American converts to Buddhism; Olcott, in fact, gained a considerable following in what is now Sri Lanka through his successful efforts at encouraging Asian Buddhists to band together to resist the incursions of Christian missionaries. Later, in 1893, the World's Parliament of Religions, held in Chicago in conjunction with the Columbian Exposition, provided for the first time an American forum for learned and eloquent representatives of Asian traditions such as the Hindu Swami Vivekananda and the Buddhist Shaku Soyen. An important offshoot of the parliament was the founding of Open Court Publishing by Paul Carus, who collaborated with Japanese Buddhist D. T. Suzuki to provide the first native source of Buddhist texts in accessible form. From this time, an Asian missionary presence has continued to work in America, though its clientele in early years were predominantly among receptive intellectuals.

It was on the West Coast, however, that ethnic Asian religions found their first major opening. The need for inexpensive labor as the railroad network linking the East and West Coasts was coming to fruition brought over three hundred thousand Chinese, mainly unskilled workers, to this country as part of a larger number of emigrants who were fleeing political and economic change at home. Other Chinese labor was invested in agriculture, mining, and manufacturing, especially throughout the rapidly developing state of California. A series of Chinese exclusion acts passed by Congress beginning in 1882 resulted in a rapid reduction of the Chinese community in America, which declined from 107,000 in 1890 to a low of 61,000 in 1920. A similar pattern characterized Japanese immigration, primarily to the West Coast, with a decline in immigration from over 100,000 during the years 1901–7 to slightly more than 6,000 from 1925 to 1940.

Among the earliest Chinese settlers, religious life was sponsored mainly by merchant groups, who allocated space in the upper floors of their headquarters in San Francisco's Chinatown for worship. Eight such makeshift temples were present in that city by 1875, and several hundred—mostly small, makeshift, and short-lived—dotted the West Coast by 1900. Worship in these "joss houses"—a term derived from a corruption of the Portuguese *deos,* "god"—followed the patterns of Chinese folk religion and was a mixture of elements derived from Taoism, Confucianism, and Pure Land Buddhism. The T'ien Hou temple in San Francisco's Chinatown is still standing and is one of the oldest examples of this kind of facility. Worshipers enter by ascending several flights of stairs within a typical Chinatown structure, essentially a tenement house with some external Chinese-style ornament. Within are arrayed a statue of the Taoist deity T'ien Hou, Queen of the Heavens and Goddess of the Seven Seas, as well as shrines to the Buddha, Confucius, and an eclectic array of other celestial figures, as well as a number of family shrines to which offerings are periodically brought. Worship is completely individualistic, with no priests or regular congregation.

Of the several components that make up the folk religion practiced at T'ien Hou temple and its counterparts, *Taoism* (also, and more phonetically, spelled "Daoism") is a following of the *Way*—the meaning of *Tao*—in which the universe is moving, as expressed in the tradition's classic text, the *Tao Te Ching* (dow day JING). Its symbol is the circle divided by a symmetrically curved line into light and dark halves, which represent the complementary principles of *yin* and *yang*—female and male energies, respectively. *Confucianism,* on the other hand, is based on a similar notion of a correct following of the *Way* as taught by the sage Confucius. Whereas Taoism stresses the sources of the Tao in nature, including the human unconscious, the Confucian path is essentially social and stresses the proper alignment of the individual personality with the orders of society and the particular importance of filial piety, that is, reverence for one's ancestors. These two traditions themselves are implicitly regarded by Chinese as complementary opposites, and their simultaneous presence in folk religion is less problematic than it may seem at first glance.

The Pure Land Buddhism that is the other major component of this popular devotion is the oldest example of ethnic Asian religions in this country. Before discussing it further, however, a few words should be said by way of introduction to the Buddhist tradition more broadly.* Unlike Hinduism, which will be discussed in some detail later in this chapter, Buddhism began as a founded movement at a particular point in history within the broader context of south Asian religion. The historical Buddha—an honorific title meaning "enlightened one"—was a young man of princely family named Siddhartha Gautama, who lived in what is now Nepal; although precise details as to his life and career are the subject of considerable debate, a commonly accepted set of dates for him is 624–544 B.C.

According to tradition, Gautama had been raised in a luxurious, protected royal environment, married, and had a child; then, however, he had a series of life-changing encounters: with an old man, a sick man, a corpse, and an ascetic. As a result of these experiences, which made him realize how sheltered he had thus far been from the human experience, he renounced his worldly life and took up a career as a wandering ascetic himself. After an initial period of excessive self-denial, he arrived at a "Middle Path," the aim of which was detachment from both pleasure and pain. Then one day, while seated under the "Bodhi tree," he attained enlightenment in the form of the realization that he was now free from earthly temptations. He was thus now the Buddha—that is, the Enlightened One—and the historical prototype for the many who would subsequently seek through his example to acquire a similar state of consciousness in which they were set free from the dual bondages of pleasure seeking and pain avoidance.

In the two and a half millennia since the time of Gautama, Buddhism spread throughout much of Asia and, in more recent times, beyond, to acquire the status of a world religion. As such, it has developed many branches—Mahayana ("Great Vehicle"), which includes Pure Land, Zen, and Nichiren; Theravada in southeast Asia; and Vajrayana, or Tibetan—which have evolved in the contexts of a variety of

---

*Perhaps needless to say, such a summary can only skim the surface of such ancient and complex traditions as the Hindu and Buddhist. For more detailed accounts, please consult entries in the bibliography (section X) by Seager, Prebish, and Williams. Brief treatments of both traditions can be found in Fenton and colleagues' *Religions of Asia,* and Jacob Neusner, ed., *World Religions in America* (Louisville, 1994). This narrative draws extensively on several of these sources.

Asian regional and national cultures and which now are firmly established in North America in a very different social and cultural context. Some of their differences will become clear soon. However, it is worth stating very briefly at this point some of their more important shared assumptions beyond their taking as normative the example of the historical Buddha.

One fundamental assumption about the human condition and the broader nature of things that Buddhism acquired from its Hindu matrix is the belief in *reincarnation.* Without enlightenment, human souls are trapped in an endless cycle of birth and rebirth known as *samsara* (SAHM-sah-rah). One's actions during a particular incarnation—*karma*—determine one's fate the next time around, as a higher or lower form of being. Whether high or low, though, one is still trapped in this endless cycle of repetition and suffering. The one way out is through following the *dharma* (DAAR-mah), that is, the teachings of the Buddha, which are symbolized by a wheel and summarized in the Buddha's first sermon as the "Four Noble Truths." The first of these is that "all is suffering." This suffering is fundamental, given the propensities of human nature to seek pleasure and avoid pain and thus remain trapped in samsara. The second noble truth teaches that this suffering is rooted in chronic human ignorance as to the fundamental unreality of the state of consciousness that we experience as a sense of selfhood that manifests itself as a ceaseless craving or grasping. The truth, on the contrary, is found in the teaching of "no-self," that is, that selfhood is fundamentally illusory. The third truth is that cessation of suffering becomes possible when one throws off illusion and achieves a state of *nirvana* (nur-VAH-nah), that is, the wisdom and serenity that come from the existential realization that selfhood is illusory. Finally, the fourth noble truth outlines the "noble eightfold path" that leads to liberation. This involves correct, ethical living, including abstinence from killing, stealing, lying, improper sexual relations (a subject of current debate), and the use of intoxicants. Beyond this, a proper state of consciousness needs to be cultivated through *meditation,* one of the most fundamental of Buddhist practices and a major source of its current attraction for non-Asians. Buddhist teaching has traditionally been carried out in the context of the *sangha* (SAHNG-hah), or community of followers. In the Asian context, this usually involves a division between monks, who meditate and provide religious leadership, and lay disciples who support the monks and carry out devotional practices. These communal arrangements have often been modified in the American context where lay people often both meditate and provide leadership.

A final note on Buddhist fundamentals that is worth stressing is that Buddhism, though sometimes called "atheistic," is perhaps better described as "transtheistic," that is, asserting the existence of gods and goddesses but subordinating them in importance to the Buddha's teachings. For Buddhists, the many divine beings that populate the cosmos have little relevance to the individual's pursuit of salvation. There is, however, ultimate meaning that can be attained not only intellectually but experientially by human beings through proper understanding and practice. Buddhism, therefore, is not simply a philosophy, or set of abstractions for knowing and living, but rather a *religion* that aims at the transformation of the entire person. In its actual historical manifestations, however, Buddhism has taken on a wide variety of incarnations, some of which bear considerable resemblance to the theistic religions in their personalization of cosmic principles and their stress on ritual rather than meditation.

Pure Land Buddhism, where we began our historical and cultural survey of Buddhism in the United States, is the oldest form of institutionalized Buddhism in North America and a prime example of ethnic religion brought to this country by immigrants and perpetuated by their descendants and subsequent newcomers of similar origin. Although we first encountered it as one of the elements in the eclectic mix represented in the T'ien Hou temple, the Pure Land tradition was introduced in more traditional form into the United States by Japanese immigrants who first arrived in Hawaii in 1868 as contract laborers; it was first practiced in Hawaii in 1889 and in California ten years later. Its subsequent fortunes have been affected both by the more general process of Americanization over several generations and by the unique history of the Japanese American community during the twentieth century.

Japanese, like other Asians, were the object of particularly early and rigorous exclusion, in large part because their differences from European Americans were broadly perceived as not only cultural but racial. Anti-Japanese sentiment early in the twentieth century brought about the "Gentlemen's Agreement" between the American and Japanese governments, in which immigration was restricted to the wives of men already resident in this country. In 1924 the Oriental Exclusion Act was one of a series of pieces of legislation that brought Asian immigration to a virtual standstill, and that also complicated the question of property ownership, including houses of worship, for Japanese residents along the West Coast. More dramatically, the forced resettlement by Executive Order 9066 of over 111,000 Japanese Americans, of whom nearly two-thirds were American citizens, in "relocation" camps during World War II marked the culmination of anti-Asian sentiment, which attained a virulence unmatched in American treatment of any other people identified as an enemy. (War-era propaganda against Germany lacked the racist dimensions of that directed against the "Japs.") Japan's postwar prosperity and democratization have led to an abatement of this attitude, although American resentment of Asian economic success occasionally results in unpleasant incidents. Although emigration from Japan has not reached the degree of that from other, less prosperous Asian nations, Americans of Japanese descent remain a major and enduring presence especially in Hawaii and along the West Coast.

Pure Land Buddhism was founded in Japan by an ex-monk, Shinran (1173–1263), as Jodo Shinshu, the "True Sect of the Pure Land." It is a devotional rather than meditation-centered interpretation of the Buddhist tradition and focuses on Amida Buddha, the Buddha of Eternal Life and Infinite Light. (It is worth noting here that

Gautama, the historical Buddha, is supplemented in later Mahayana traditions by an infinite range of nonhistorical "cosmic" Buddhas with different attributes.) In this case, Amida Buddha has created a heavenlike Pure Land into which anyone may enter by having faith and reciting the name of Amida Buddha with gratitude. Although Jodo Shinshu in Japan developed an elaborate hierarchical structure, it is oriented not toward monks but rather toward lay people, who do not need to renounce the world and undergo elaborate training and renunciation to receive spiritual benefits. Its parallels with the Christianity that developed in medieval Europe during the same period are worth noting.

In the United States, fully institutionalized Pure Land Buddhism began in 1898 as the Buddhist Mission to North America (BMNA), a name indicative of the intentionality with which Japanese Buddhists supervised its transmission rather than allowing it to be brought over haphazardly. The Gentlemen's Agreement mentioned earlier had the positive effect of stabilizing Japanese American family units and creating a social atmosphere in which an American-style religious community with Asian content could develop. The small and isolated Japanese American community turned to the BMNA, which had twenty-five branches by 1914, not only for religious functions but also as a social and cultural center that sponsored scout troops and sports teams. The internment experience of World War II led to a change of name to Buddhist Churches of America (BCA) in an attempt to demonstrate even more dramatically the group's Americanization. (The appropriateness of this Americanized name has recently been the subject of new discussion in BCA circles.)

The BCA has in fact been one of the most dramatic examples of how a group of Asian provenance has adapted to the circumstances of a dramatically different and not very friendly culture. The interior layout of the Buddhist Church of San Francisco on Pine Street, for example, is that of a Christian church, with pews, hymnals, organ, and the like. The exterior is also churchlike except for the presence of a *stupa*—a shrine containing a relic of the historical Buddha—at the top. Conspicuously different, however, are the sanctuary and altar, which are ornately decorated in traditional Buddhist fashion. The BCA more generally has adopted a strategy of combining Buddhist content with Western form in its sponsorship of Sunday ("dharma") schools and use of language such as "church," "hymn," "bishop," and "minister." It has also been ritual centered, and the participation of many members primarily in life-cycle events has led to its being called "funeral Buddhism" by some. Its conservatism and ethnocentric character have led to a decline in membership in recent decades.(Accurate recent membership statistics are difficult to come by; one 2004 estimate puts membership at about 17,000.)

Before moving along to discuss other strains of Japanese Buddhism, it is worth noting that for many Japanese Americans as well as Japanese Buddhists, it is possible, and in fact quite common, to follow both Buddhism in one of its various forms and *Shinto*. Like many aspects of Chinese popular and "civil" religion, Shinto is the collective name for the myths, symbols, and rituals with which the Japanese endow everyday life with sacred meaning. Its dimensions range from the cult of the emperor, who is thought to rule in direct succession from Amaterasu-O-Mikami, the sun goddess, to household and village shrines where seasonal and life-cycle festivals are observed. In the United States, "Imperial Shinto" came in for hard times through its association with Japanese militarism during World War II. Although a small number of Japanese Americans in Hawaii and the mainland are affiliated with various sectarian forms of Shinto, such as *Tenrikyo* ("Religion of Heavenly Wisdom"), the religious impulse that Shinto embodies is manifested more typically in seasonal festivals, the cultivation of gardens, and the maintenance in the home of alcoves of *kami*—the sacred power that Shinto shrines delineate.

Undoubtedly the best-known form of Japanese Buddhism in this country is *Zen* (in China, Ch'an), which was introduced into the United States at the 1893 World's Parliament of Religions and subsequently spread by the work of D. T. Suzuki and other missionaries. Unlike Pure Land Buddhism, Zen emphasizes the attainment of enlightenment through structured meditation, a much more individualistic and interiorized form of religious life even when practiced traditionally in monasteries. Two major strains of Japanese Zen have been introduced into the United States. *Soto Zen* is known for the practice of *zazen,* that is, sitting in a cross-legged (lotus) posture while trying to become detachedly aware of the "busyness" of the ordinary stream of consciousness that makes up most of our mental life. *Rinzai Zen* is a less ritualistic form that in addition to zazen utilizes *koans*—riddles or paradoxes, such as "What is the sound of one hand clapping?"—as aids to breaking through the ordinary constraints of language and logic to an awareness of a deeper layer of meaning. In American Zen practice, elements of both of these traditions are often drawn upon freely.

Zen in America has a much more complicated history than, for example, Jodo Shinshu, since its followers more often than not have been European Americans who have appropriated elements of Zen in a variety of ways. The "Zen boom" of the 1950s, for example, saw a burgeoning of interest in Zen, if not that much serious practice of Zen itself, through the writings of the "Beats" (for example, Jack Kerouac's *The Dharma Bums* of 1958) and popularizations such as those by Episcopal priest Alan Watts. The 1960s counterculture further promoted an interest in Zen, but not often in the context of traditional spiritual discipline. By this time, however, a serious literature on Zen by D. T. Suzuki as well as native converts such as Philip Kapleau (*Three Pillars of Zen,* 1965) provided the intellectual basis for its serious practice. Also, a coming together of Japanese and American Zen masters now made possible the emergence of an American Zen as an institutional reality rather than a free-floating climate of opinion of which philosophical dilettantes might occasionally partake.

The founding of the San Francisco Zen Center in 1962 by Shunryu Suzuki was a major turning point for the history of Zen in the United States. Suzuki had a few years earlier come to San Francisco to serve the Soto Zen Temple in Japantown, where

Zen was practiced as an ethnic religion. Soon, however, European Americans began to come in sizeable numbers seeking instruction in Zen meditation techniques, and a whole complex of institutions began to arise that constituted the first major institutional center for Zen in this country. Before long the center had acquired a rural retreat at Tassajara Hot Springs, Green Gulch Farm in Marin County, and a variety of properties in the city itself. Activities included publications such as Edward Espe Brown's *Tassajara Cooking* (1973). This and other Tassajara titles are part of a lineage of writing demonstrating the applicability of a Zen outlook to any number of everyday activities such as Eugen Herrigel's popular exposition, *Zen and the Art of Archery* (1953), and Robert Pirsig's *Zen and the Art of Motorcycle Maintenance* (1974).

Suzuki died in 1971 and was succeeded as leader of the center by Richard Baker, one of a number of European American disciples whom Suzuki had previously ordained. Although Baker was forced to resign a few years later in the midst of what came to be called the ZCM ("Zen Center Mess"), the accession to a major leadership role by a non-Asian nevertheless marked the coming of age of a distinctly American Zen, with both institutions and a lay-oriented practice now independent of traditional Asian norms and oversight.

Zen in America as it has developed since World War II is certainly a very different phenomenon from that which had prevailed in Asia. One way of visualizing it is a series of concentric circles. At the center is the monastic regimen, consisting of those who have received ordination into a lineage of Zen priests and whose entire lives are dedicated to meditative practice and instruction. In American Zen, however, even this core is no longer exclusively Asian or male, and many women have ascended to positions of leadership at prominent Zen centers. In the next layers are those who practice Zen seriously but who hold "day jobs" in the world, usually within the academic and professional sector. ("Anglo" Zen practitioners tend to be well-educated and disproportionately of Jewish background.) At the periphery are those who dabble in what has been called *bujizen,* or "night-stand Buddhism"—that is, an often dilettantish interest in Zen ideas and literature that is not accompanied by any systematic disciplined practice. To this array might be added those Asian Americans who frequent ethnic-oriented Zen centers as part of a cultural observance but who do not practice meditation, a traditional approach to the role of the laity.

If Pure Land Buddhism can be called "ethnic" and Zen "elite," *Sokka Gakkai* is a good example of "export" Buddhism. Sokka Gakkai, or "Value Creation Society," is one of the "new religions" that arose in Japan during the past century, having been founded by Tsunesaburo Makiguchi in 1937. It is an offshoot of a much older strain of Buddhism, *Nichiren Shoshu* ("true teaching of Nichiren"), which in turn was founded in the thirteenth century by Nichiren Daishonin. Nichiren taught that the sole path to salvation was the *Lotus Sutra,* a first-century Buddhist scripture that depicted the Buddha as an eternally existing being manifested historically as Gautama; his followers (*sangha*) regard Nichiren himself as the Buddha of their own age. Nichiren Shoshu was a popular movement that emphasized the chanting of the *daimoku*—"Hail to the wonderful dharma Lotus Sutra"—rather than meditation, but developed a priesthood that still controls the movement in Japan from its temple at Taisekiji. The priesthood controls distribution of the *Gohonzon,* a scroll modeled on that originally inscribed by Nichiren, which embodies the dharma, or Buddhist teaching.

Makiguchi's conversion to Nichiren Shoshu brought about an alliance between that Buddhist sect and his own society, which was oriented toward humanistic education, and provided a vehicle for the transformation of Nichiren Shoshu into a missionary movement. The message of Soka Gakkai International (SGI), as it is now known, was spread originally in this country by the Japanese wives of American servicemen on their return from the Korean War. Recruitment came about through *shakubuku,* an aggressive form of street evangelization that had considerable appeal to counter-cultural youth and that led to fears by some that the movement might be a coercive cult. After the Jonestown episode of 1979, the leadership declared that SGI was now moving into phase 2, and shakubuku was scaled back considerably.

SGI attracted a considerable European American as well as an African American and Hispanic American following because of its low-demand character and its growing compatibility with American cultural values. (In 1976 it claimed a half-million American members, reduced to perhaps three hundred thousand by 1997, including pop singer Tina Turner.) Its devotional practices were said to promote internal change to make the individual more confident, energetic, and goal oriented, whereas its external message was one of social harmony and world peace. The increasingly democratic character that SGI was taking on in its American context, however, led to a rift with Nichiren Shoshu's Japanese priestly leadership, with the latter excommunicating all SGI members in 1991. The movement, however, seems to be surviving well enough, and has turned to former Nichiren priests for its ritual needs.

One of the most conspicuous strains of Buddhism in the United States during the 1990s was *Vajrayana,* also known as Tantric or Tibetan Buddhism. Until the influx of Tibetan refugees into India and western countries in recent years, Tibetan Buddhism was regarded as rather exotic, known primarily though the *Book of the Dead* and a collection of *tantras,* or sacred texts, which at times utilized vivid sexual imagery. It is akin in some important ways to the Mahayana tradition, emphasizing the role of *bodhisattvas,* that is, practitioners who have forsworn final enlightenment until the task of achieving it for all of humanity has been completed—a manifestation of the Buddhist virtue of compassion. Tibetan Buddhism further stresses the process of visualization of Buddhas and bodhisattvas as an aid to meditation, accompanied by the use of *mudras* (MOO-drahs), or ritual gestures; *mantras* (MAHN-trahs), chanted syllables or phrases; and *mandalas* (MAHN-dah-lahs), intricate geometric designs depicting the human person as a microcosm of the greater cosmic scheme.

Another feature of Tibetan Buddhism is social organization. After their devastating takeover of Tibet in 1950, the Chinese began systematically to dismantle an archaic society that had heretofore resisted modernization and had been governed as a theocracy in which monks, or *lamas,* played a role in governance; at the time of the Chinese invasion, 20 percent of the nation's population were monks or nuns. Many of these went into exile in India, including the Dalai Lama, the nation's spiritual leader, who is regarded as an embodiment of the compassion of all Buddhas, past, present, and future, and is also a reincarnation of his predecessors. The current Dalai Lama, Tenzin Gyatso, is the fourteenth in this succession, and has won widespread goodwill in the West—including the 1989 Nobel Peace Prize—through his extensive speaking and consulting, especially on behalf of Tibetan independence. His presence has, in fact, inspired a sort of "Tibetan chic" in the United States, as expressed in a series of films (*Little Buddha,* 1993; *Seven Years in Tibet* and *Kundun,* both 1997; *The Cup,* 2000) and the Friends of Tibet, a network of groups concerned with alleviating the nation's suffering under Chinese rule.

The transplantation of the four orders of Tibetan Buddhism to the United States took place within the last three decades of the twentieth century and, as in the case of Zen, has resulted in the establishment of an indigenous European American leadership working in cooperation with Tibetan exiles. Although there is a small component of Tibetan immigrant followers as well, much of the movement's North American constituency has come about through the conversion of Westerners, and has much of Zen's elite flavor. Two important spokesmen are the academics Robert Thurman and Jeffrey Hopkins, who teach, respectively, at Columbia University and the University of Virginia. Leading publishers of Tibetan texts and scholarship are Snow Lion Publications and Shambala International. *Tricycle: The Buddhist Review,* is a leading journal of convert Buddhist opinion as well. Institutionally, Shambala maintains a retreat center in Colorado, which is the site of the Great Stupa of Dharmakaya, one of the monumental Buddhist structures of North America. The Naropa Institute, also based in Colorado, is an accredited college that, in addition to philosophical and meditative practices, offers advanced training in transactional psychology.

Buddhism also exists in a variety of other forms in the United States, primarily focused on ethnic communities from east and southeast Asia who have arrived either as immigrants seeking economic opportunity or, in the case particularly of Vietnamese, Cambodians, and Laotians, as refugees from war and political turmoil. Not all Asians, it should be noted, are Buddhist; many Vietnamese, for example, are Roman Catholics—a heritage of decades of French dominance—and many Koreans are Presbyterians. (There are more members of that tradition in Korea than in the United States.) Most ethnic Asian Buddhists practice sometimes eclectic and regionally tinged versions of the tradition, and practice is usually of the devotional rather than the meditative sort. This may include prostrating one's self before a temple image of the Buddha, chanting, the offering of *puja*—gifts of food, incense, or flowers—to sacred images, or the provision of necessities for the monks who maintain temples. These latter often begin as rooms in suburban homes, but gain new form as elaborate public structures when a local ethnic community has become sufficiently wealthy to erect them.

The experience of American Buddhists has been both similar to and significantly different from that of earlier European religious communities such as Catholics, Eastern Orthodox, and Jews. Immigrants and refugees have faced the same challenges of assimilation and adaptation as did their Western counterparts, adopting both an English vocabulary as succeeding generations take over the tradition and democratic forms in the absence of old-world hierarchies. The decentralized and many-faceted character of Buddhism makes it more analogous to Eastern Orthodoxy or Judaism than to Catholicism, even though the prestige of visiting or resident Asian-born teachers helps ensure a continuity of tradition. On the other hand, none of the European immigrant-borne religions ever generated the enthusiasm for conversion that some of Buddhism's meditation-based strains have inspired, and have never faced the challenges of absorbing a numerous and independent-minded native elite into its ranks. Although the early years of "foundation" were occasionally characterized by discord and even scandal, American Buddhists seem to be developing an indigenous version of the *dharma* that has already claimed a significant role in American cultural and intellectual as well as religious life.

Buddhism arose originally as a reform movement within the religious matrix that would evolve into *Hinduism,* which has for millennia been the dominant religious tradition of the Indian subcontinent. Buddhism is a nearly pan-Asian phenomenon, with one or more branches represented in most of the continent's regions, the result of the movement of ideas (from India to China, for example, and from China to Japan) resulting in complex transformations and variations in widely different linguistic and cultural matrices. Hinduism is also a highly complex tradition, but one that until recently has flourished primarily within what is now a single nation-state, namely, India. Whereas Buddhism arose from a single cluster of teachings attributed to one historical, if highly mythologized, individual, Hinduism has no datable beginnings. It is an *unfounded* tradition with roots in a prehistoric past, and has developed in a variety of directions, affected by numerous political and cultural changes on the one hand and by the highly regional character of Indian life, where today over eight hundred million people speak some 325 different languages, nineteen of which carry official status. Even though India is today an officially secular democracy, the Hindu religion and the Indian nation are closely identified with one another, though neither is by any means a very simple entity.

Unlike Christianity, which has a fairly compact set of scriptures and creeds, Hinduism is rooted in a long lineage of sacred texts, all of which are revered but not all of which are actually read or utilized very widely. The most central of these is the *Bhagavad Gita* (BAHG-a-vahd GEE-tah), an insertion in the long epic poem, the *Mahabharata.* The Gita tells the story of the hero Arjuna, caught in a highly conflicted situation, and his conversations with his charioteer Krishna, who turns out to be an incarnation of the god Vishnu. Here Krishna teaches Arjuna the three disciplines, or *yogas,* that bring liberation from the same *karma* that is a central teaching of Buddhism. These are *karma yoga,* or detachment and selfless action; *jnana yoga,* knowledge of one's true self; and *bhakti yoga,* or devotion to deities such as Krishna. These disciplines constitute complementary paths to the attainment of liberation, and still represent the core of Hindu practice. (More broadly, yoga refers to the various disciplines that lead to self-realization; *hatha yoga* is the practice of physical control and accompanying meditation that many non-Hindu Americans associate with the term and practice in pursuit of a general sense of focus and well-being.)

Hinduism as practiced in India is similar in some ways to Judaism; there is no *orthodoxy,* or written creed, but rather a stress on *orthopraxis,* or living in conformity with tradition. Just as American Reform Jews were the first to attempt to express their beliefs in summary form (the Pittsburgh Statement of 1885), so American Hindus, responding to the absence of an all-pervasive sense of tradition in a new land, have begun a similar expression. One such attempt lists the following beliefs and duties as central to Hinduism: the existence of one supreme being; an endless cycle of creations, preservation, and dissolution; the seeking of *moksha,* or liberation, from this cycle by all souls; *karma,* the law of cause and effect; reincarnation; providing worship to divine beings at the temple and in the home (*puja*); following a spiritual master (*sat guru*); the pursuit of *ahimsa* (nonviolence) on the premise that all life is sacred; and a recognition that spiritual truth is found in all religions, not only Hinduism.

Although this summary, provided by the Himalaya Institute, is useful in understanding the fundamentals of the tradition, Hinduism does not exist in the abstract and is not surprisingly turning out to be somewhat different in its American practice from the ways in which it has been carried on for centuries in the Indian subcontinent. Part of this particularity lies in the distinct sociology of the Indian community in the United States, which differs from that found in other nations of the "Indian Diaspora," most of which were formerly parts of the British Empire. As noted earlier, Indian immigration to the United States was severely restricted by law and was practically nonexistent prior to 1965. The new law of that year was not only much more welcoming but included a hierarchy of categories, affording preference particularly to highly trained professionals whose skills were needed in the American economy. As a result, Indian (and Pakistani) emigrants have generally come from the highly educated classes and, for the most part, have settled not in inner-city ethnic ghettoes but rather in affluent suburbs. They also differ geographically from most Buddhist immigrants in their scattering into urban centers throughout the entire nation, rather than clustering in those areas, such as Hawaii, California, and the Pacific Northwest, that are closest to Asia. Many are young and single, and molded by the influence of the secularism that has accompanied the formation of a modern independent Indian state. Although most eventually settle into the middle-class routine of family raising, the intellectual sophistication of much of this population has made them less wedded to village tradition and, together with the press of circumstances, more open to new ways of interpreting the ancient faith.

As noted in the above outline of fundamental Hindu beliefs and practices, worship is conducted both at home and in the temple. In the process of resettlement, home, often in single-family suburban form, has generally come first. As with many Buddhist immigrants, Hindus coming to America often began to reconstitute their religious lives by getting together with others in the area for home worship in the absence of a temple. These gatherings, no longer necessary in most larger communities, laid the groundwork for a distinctively American *ecumenical Hinduism,* in which Indians from very different regional and linguistic traditions came together to devise a common worship out of necessity rather than theological impulse. English (an official language of India, reflecting its imperial heritage) functions here as the language of communication, with Sanskrit as the sacred language of ritual. The parallels with the earlier transplantations of Judaism and Catholicism to American shores should be fairly obvious here.

The defining act in the emergence of an American Hinduism has most likely been that of temple building. In India, temples are part of the landscape, both in a superficially descriptive sense and in the deeper sense of being structures that give religious depth and being to a community. In India, however, the constitutive inter-relationships of building, land, nation, people, and gods is so basic as to be taken for granted. In foreign parts, especially the polyglot United States, though, the whole relationship has to be reexamined, much as Jews had to reassess their situation once forced into their archetypal diaspora. Therefore, building a temple is not simply the erection of a house for worship but an act of reestablishing a relationship of people with tradition, an establishment of new roots now that the old ones have been voluntarily forsaken but not abandoned. As Joanne Punzo Waghorne has observed in her study of the Sri Siva-Vishnu temple in the Washington, D.C., suburbs, "the 'space' of the . . . Temple exists somewhere amid the concreteness of the traditional temple, the ethereal space of 'traditional' India, the newer creation of an ideological motherland, and the shifting space of the everywhere/nowhere / everybody's/ nobody's split-level world of the migrating international middle class."*

Another complication in the building of Hindu temples in the American context is the complexity of Indian society and the Hindu religion. Even in India, the process had already begun, since the families of many of the city dwellers who would subsequently emigrate to the United States had previously made the move from village to city. Since each locality in India has its own distinctive *cultus*—that is, style of worship—the act of transplantation carries with it religious consequences. Already accustomed to dislocation, the Indians now living in the American suburbs found themselves worshiping with Indians from many regions of the subcontinent, speak-

---

*"The Hindu Gods in a Split-Level World," in Orsi, *Gods of the City,* 110–11.

ing different languages and accustomed to different "takes" on the protean tradition that constitutes Hinduism. The Washington, D.C., temple studied by Waghorne illustrates this pluralism in its very name. S(h)iva and Vishnu are two distinct gods in the Hindu pantheon, one associated with preservation and the other with destruction. (A third, Brahma, the creator, completes this "trinity.") Where in India *Shaivas* and *Vaishnavas*—followers of Shiva and Vishnu—are distinct religious groupings following regional lines, the circumstances of the Indian diaspora in America have brought about their cooperation. (In other cities, such as Pittsburgh, northern and southern Indians have erected two different major temples.)

The architecture of American Hindu temples, of which there were over fifty major examples at the end of the twentieth century, is also illustrative of the adaptations and compromises that settlement in a new land has brought about. Bricks and mortar instead of stone are now the usual building materials. Instead of the usual one story, American temples often have two, the upper for worship, the lower with facilities for the multitude of activities associated with American churches and synagogues: education, cultural activities, sociability, dining, and even waste elimination. (Restrooms are not found in Indian temples.) In addition, where temples in the motherland are dedicated to the worship of one deity, American "ecumenical" temples frequently house many—for example, Shiva and Vishnu—in recognition of the various regional traditions of their mixed clienteles. Roles also reflect American adaptations. Women, for example, are barred from food preparation in Indian temples but perform this typically American "women's role" here; even though they cannot conduct worship, they engage in such nontraditional women's activities as temple decoration and fund-raising.

Like American Jews, Hindus in the United States have rapidly implemented a reconfiguration of identity, since they have had to come to terms with compatriots from very different local religious cultures and have needed to arrive rapidly at workable compromises. Unlike the Jews of the "new immigration," however, most Hindu immigrants of the "new new immigration" come with a considerable degree of professional capital as well as a cosmopolitan outlook engendered by the modernization and urbanization of postwar India. The everyday religious life of most Indian Americans is also similar to that of Jews since it is bipolar, with foci both in the home and in the temple. Home worship—*puja*—takes place at an often elaborate shrine, and may include both meditation and the offering of food to the gods prior to its consumption by the family. Temple worship, now available to considerable numbers of Indians, is presided over by *Brahmins,* that is, members of the highest, priestly caste of Indian society, who may serve as full-time ritualists or hold day jobs when a local temple cannot provide full employment. (Even though the caste system, which dictates patterns of occupation and marriage, has been the object of modernizing campaigns in India and has not been widely transplanted to this country, it still dictates who may follow a priestly vocation.) The provision of these religious specialists for an American clientele is one major link between Hindus in the homeland and the diaspora; similarly, Indians in the United States often make pilgrimages to India, or send their children there for extended visits.

The ceremonies conducted by Brahmins in the temple are of several sorts, with both similarities to and differences from Christian and Jewish patterns. Except for holiday festivals, which are mainly associated with various deities, worship is not communal but family based; a family will typically employ a priest for rituals marking life-cycle passages—the full repertory, not often observed in this country, numbers sixteen—as well as auspicious events such as a new business undertaking. Families may also employ freelance Brahmins on home visits for the conduct of rituals. In general, the relationship of an Indian American to a temple has distinct parallels with that of many ethnic Buddhists (not to say Christians and Jews), who may not give a great deal of thought to the practice of personal piety or meditation but nevertheless regard family- and community-centered rituals as important reaffirmations of their own identity, especially in a secular society where they are a minority without the support of a traditional culture.

In terms of "elite" religion, the first major impact of Hinduism in its more philosophical dimensions among Americans began in the 1830s, when Emerson, Thoreau, and other New England transcendentalists began to familiarize themselves with the Hindu scriptures, which were slowly becoming available in English translations. In his poem "Brahma," Emerson articulated an interpretation of the cosmos and human destiny very distinct from that of his Unitarian and Calvinist contemporaries, and one which implied a severe criticism of the materialistic civilization that those creeds fostered. ("If the red slayer thinks he slays / Or if the slain thinks he is slain, / They know not well the subtle ways / I keep, and pass, and turn again.") Some decades later, Henry Adams would express an even harsher judgment on Western religious attitudes in his longer "Buddha and Brahma."

As was the case for Buddhism and Islam as well, the turning point for Hinduism in America came with the World's Parliament of Religions. This latter gathering, which met in conjunction with the World's Columbian Exposition in Chicago, was convened by the Unitarian Jenkin Lloyd Jones in 1893 to promote understanding among the world's religious faiths. The parliament thus provided an opportunity for representatives from a wide variety of traditions scarcely known to most Americans to represent themselves publicly. It was here that Swami Vivekananda found a base for acquainting Americans with the Hindu tradition and subsequently for founding the Vedanta Society, which today has twelve locations in major cities such as New York and San Francisco.

Vedanta, as interpreted by Vivekananda, struck a minor but real chord among Victorian Americans who were simultaneously intrigued by the claims of Christian Science, New Thought, Theosophy, Spiritualism, and other manifestations of "harmonialism" that were enjoying a wide popularity in the parlors and lecture halls of the period. It was rooted in the Upanishads and presented the traditional Hindu teaching that the task of the individual is to free the *atman*—one's individual manifestation of the *Brahman,* or ultimate reality—from the web of illusion in which it is caught. Vedanta stresses meditation and exercises an intellectual, individual appeal very different from the popular "ethnic" versions of the Hindu tradition. Vivekananda also added a syncretistic dimension to the gospel he preached to Americans by recognizing such figures as Jesus and the Buddha as *avatars*—earthly manifestations or incarnations—of perfect realization of the Brahman. The English writers Aldous Huxley and Christopher Isherwood were associated with the Vedanta Society, which enjoyed a considerable cultural cachet. Other early versions of "export" Hinduism at the elite level were promoted by Swami Paramahansa Yogananda and his Self-Realization Fellowship (1925) and Jeddu Krishnamurti, who was promoted by the American occult community in the 1920s as a world savior until he became an independent teacher of hatha yoga and author and lecturer on a variety of topics.

Another "elite" movement of Hindu provenance is Transcendental Meditation, or TM, introduced in this country in 1959 by the Maharishi Mahesh Yogi (1911–2008) and publicized by the patronage of the Beatles, among others. Transcendental Meditation does not claim to be a religious movement; rather, it calls itself "the science of creative intelligence." As such, TM is an adaptation of yogic meditation techniques, especially the repetition of a personalized *mantra,* to the more secular "harmonial" goals of stress reduction and the achievement of personal composure. Although it has taken on some of the trappings of an institution, with a colorful guru as founder and the campus of failed Parsons College in Iowa as the headquarters of Maharishi University, it bears more affinity to the less intensive side of the "Human Potential Movement" of the New Age than to various "cultic" groups. In the 1990s it also sponsored a new political movement, the Natural Law Party, that has not enjoyed a great deal of electoral appeal.

India has also contributed its share of *export religions* to the American scene, some of which figured prominently in the public brouhaha about "cults" during the 1970s. These groups stress various forms of bhakti (devotional) yoga rather than meditation, and their communal dimensions at one time attracted a considerable following of young middle-class European Americans while alarming their parents, some of whom engaged "deprogrammers" to bring them back from their new lifestyle commitments. The Divine Light Mission, for example, was introduced to America in 1971 by the erratic young Guru Maharaj Ji (mah-hah-RAHJ-ji), who claimed to be a *satguru* or "perfect master" of this age just as his father had earlier been. Physical techniques for inducing a very sensuous religious experience, such as pressing on the eyeballs until flashes of light appear, were a major part of the mission's practice. Maharaj Ji's public prank playing, and subsequent abandonment of such early essential teachings as a vegetarian diet, led to a power struggle within his family and his mother's withdrawing support in favor of his brother. The movement's communitarian lifestyle, supported by restaurants and other enterprises as well as the surrender of worldly goods by converts, seemed to many outsiders to be very like that of a cult. An active membership of ten thousand in 1977 had diminished substantially even by the end of that decade.

A better-known version of devotional Hinduism given a new guise is presented in the International Society for Krishna Consciousness (ISKCON), whose followers are better known as "Hare Krishnas" after their continuous chanting (which was also incorporated into the popular mock-countercultural musical *Hair*). Brought to America by the late A. C. Bhaktivedanta Swami Prabhupada in 1965, ISKCON is derived from the *bhakti yoga* movement founded by the sixteenth-century Bengali Caitanya. Central to this movement, which has much in common with various "ethnic" versions of Hinduism, is devotion to the god Krishna, who is here presented as the supreme personality of the godhead. In addition to the continual chant that invokes Krishna and his consort, food offerings (*prasada*) and other features of *puja*, including the use of fire, are part of the routine of the movement's devotees. The latter live communally in many American cities as well as in rural retreats such as the elaborate compound known as New Vrindaban, billed as "America's Taj Mahal" and located at the end of a narrow mountain road a few miles off Interstate 70 near Wheeling, West Virginia. (New Vrindaban is visited as an authentic Hindu temple by many ethnic Indians as well as group members.)

The saffron robes, shaved heads, and continual chanting of devotees as they solicited donations and converts at airport terminals, shopping malls, and other public places made the "Hare Krishnas" widely known as well as disliked by those put off by exotic evangelists. Their communal lifestyle also alienated many relatives of devotees, who charged that their children had been alienated from their families by isolation and "brainwashing." Although the movement had begun to fade from view by the late 1980s, the 1986 drug-related murder conviction of one of the New Vrindaban commune's members did not enhance the group's public image.

The Divine Light Mission and ISKCON reached their heyday in the late 1970s, when public alarm over "cults" was at its peak, and they were only two among many movements vying for youthful converts and raising public alarm over the safety of the nation's vulnerable adolescents and young adults. In the 1980s, after the initial hue and cry had subsided, yet another movement of Hindu origins came into the public view in a spectacular trajectory of well-reported rise and subsequent meteoric decline and demise. Its leader, known as the Bhagwan Shree Rajneesh, denied that his movement was a religion; actually, it combined elements of the Hindu tradition with a heavy dose of Human Potential Movement practices, some of which bore a superficial resemblance to the "harmonial" aspects of Hinduism.

As such, the bhagwan, first at his *ashram* (Hindu meditational community) in India and then at his self-styled "commune" (a deliberately chosen Westernism) in Oregon, attracted a clientele that can only be described as "Yuppie" (young urban professional) in sociological composition. Rajneesh openly embraced a playful and sexually permissive approach to communal life, and he and his followers enjoyed a hard-working but affluent lifestyle based on an explicit teaching that financial insecurity and enlightenment did not go well together. Most conspicuous was the bhagwan's fleet of Rolls Royces, which numbered about eighty-five in their heyday. Frances Fitzgerald's account of the community in her *Cities on a Hill* (1986) captures vividly the mixture of exoticism with very familiar American elements that characterized life at Rajneeshpuram.

The bhagwan's commune seemed at first only mildly eccentric to many Americans who had been accustomed to their own domestic "rush hour of the gods" of the 1960s and 1970s. It began to attract first local and then national attention, however, when it became overtly aggressive and even hostile in its attempts to take over the nearby town of Antelope, Oregon. Antelope had been a small ranching community in a remote part of the state, and the presence of an exotic commune was in itself rather upsetting to the traditionally minded local residents. After tensions with the government at all levels from the local to the federal increased, the entire experiment suddenly disbanded in a flurry of revelations of the bhagwan's arrest and deportation for immigration fraud—he had arranged numerous false marriages to allow followers to enter the country illegally—as well as the conviction of his sometime-lieutenant, Ma Anand Sheela, on charges of having poisoned Rajneesh and various other of her "enemies," together with a variety of other crimes including the dynamiting of municipal offices.

Obviously some religious groups of Asian provenance, such as the bhagwan's, have been short-lived (not to say trivial) and have had little impact on the broader American religious scene other than as illustrations of the ease with which such groups may arise and even prosper in the continuing turmoil of American social and cultural change. Other groups, however, seem destined for a continuing and even prosperous career on North American soil. The Buddhist Churches of America, which are surviving if not exactly thriving, are a case study of the process of adaptation over generations and invite comparisons especially with Orthodox Judaism and Eastern Orthodoxy. The recent transplantation of Hinduism is perhaps more comparable with the rise of Reform Judaism in the nineteenth century, with an already modernized clientele showing considerable adaptability to new circumstances even during the first generation of residence (while harboring concerns for subsequent, more thoroughly Americanized generations). Among "missionary" or "export" movements, those of a communitarian or "cultic" character have not generally done well, either waning rapidly or dropping their more extreme claims and practices. Most dramatic has been the success of Zen and other forms of meditative Buddhism, with less dramatic analogues in the Hindu-inspired Vedanta and TM movements. The appeal of disciplined meditation to an American upper middle class fraught with the stresses engendered by a fast-moving social and economic order in which family and professional goals seem to be in continual tension has been phenomenal, especially in those forms that do not demand a full-blown religious commitment or lifestyle alteration. In any case, both Asian Americans and their teachings are here to stay.

CHAPTER 54

Liberalism, Radicalism, and Secularism

Religious liberalism in the twentieth century, as in the past, has acted more as a moving spirit than as an organizing principle. With the exception of a few extremely conservative denominations, such as the Southern Baptist Convention, it has influenced almost every major religious group in America, from Mormons to Methodists. Its fortunes have varied: forced underground by papal encyclicals at the turn of the century, the liberal spirit in American Catholicism did not receive widespread legitimation until the upheavals of Vatican II in the 1960s. On the other hand, the pervasive influence of liberal theology and its descendant, Neo-Orthodoxy, on "mainstream" Protestantism remained strong until the 1970s, when a new, national wave of cultural conservatism called into question its premises and led to a significant decline in the strength and influence of those denominations in which it had previously flourished.

Liberal religion in nineteenth-century America had found its firmest institutional base in Unitarianism. As Unitarians emerged into the present century, though, they found their leadership challenged from a number of directions. Agnosticism had become socially acceptable, at least among the educated classes, and distinguished figures from prominent Unitarian families such as Henry Adams and Charles Eliot Norton made no pretense of keeping up any formal religious affiliation or espousing any belief system. At the same time, many of the ideas that Unitarians had developed decades earlier, such as a stress on the benevolence of God, the potential for human happiness through moral growth, and the compatibility of religious faith with contemporary science and philosophy were now disseminated widely through other Christian denominations under the generic name of "liberal Protestantism" or "modernism." A humanist movement began to assume organized form, resulting in the publication of such provocative documents as the "Humanist Manifesto" of 1933. Finally, the Depression and uncertain leadership impaired the denomination's ability to mount an effective witness for its principles—assuming that its members could agree on what the latter might be.

The revival of Unitarianism in the middle decades of the twentieth century was based on administrative reorganization, a renewed commitment to inclusiveness, a reassertion of traditional social concerns, a willingness to experiment with new forms of local structure, and ultimately a consummation of a long-term interest in merging with like-minded groups. One tactic for recruitment of new members was the Lay Fellowship Plan launched in 1948. Traditionally, most Unitarians were either natives of New England or else residents of cities or academic communities where churches had been founded by emigrant Yankees and attracted others who were sympathetic with liberal principles. The fellowship movement was based on the idea that, where potential recruits were scattered and few, they might be better attracted by a small, informal group meeting in private homes or rented quarters without having to make a commitment to build a church and support a minister. The movement was advertised in newspapers throughout the nation. It resulted in the founding of a considerable number of fellowship groups, some of which eventually grew into churches, others of which remained small and informal. In contrast to the more traditional worship patterns that continued to be popular in New England and in urban churches, fellowships tended to resemble discussion groups more than church services, sometimes with recorded classical music used to establish an atmosphere conducive to ethical reflection and debate. Unitarian churches until recently followed the styles of their eras; more recently, though, many are avant garde in their symbolism, such as Louis Kahn's design in Rochester, which was meant to suggest a question mark.

In 1961 the American Unitarian Association merged with the Universalist Church of America to form a new denomination, the Unitarian Universalist Association. This merger followed decades of discussions and brought together into one body the two oldest and most successful institutional embodiments of the liberal religious impulse in America. The new denomination exhibits the New England origins of both traditions in maintaining its headquarters at 25 Beacon Street in Boston, in the shadow of the State House. It publishes a monthly journal, *UU World,* and also supports Beacon Press, which has for several decades taken the lead in publishing books with a liberal, sometimes highly controversial, perspective. Since "UUs," as they refer to themselves, have always disliked rigid boundaries, their publications are not restricted to denominational authors or issues but reflect a broad range of contemporary religious, social, and intellectual perspectives.

As appropriate to their tradition, Unitarian Universalists in recent decades have typically been involved in the social issues of the day. Many nineteenth-century feminist leaders, such as Elizabeth Cady Stanton, Susan B. Anthony, and Lucy Stone, had been Unitarians, and both Unitarians and Universalists had been among the first denominations to ordain women to the ministry. Although Unitarian involvement in the antislavery movement had been ambivalent, twentieth-century UUs were notably active in the civil rights movement of the 1960s, although only a handful of the membership and clergy are black. UUs were especially vocal in the 1980s in championing gay rights, including the ordination of gay men and lesbian women, as well as other liberal causes of the day such as the protection of the environment. The UUA's statement of "Principles and Purposes," expressed as a covenant affirmation, includes the following:

> The inherent worth and dignity of every person.
> Justice, equity, and compassion in human relations.
> The goal of world community with peace, liberty, and justice for all.
> Respect for the interdependent web of existence of which we are a part.

The statement goes on to list sources of the UU tradition, which include "direct experience of . . . transcending mystery and wonder," "words and deeds of prophetic women and men," "wisdom from the world's religions," "Jewish and Christian teachings," and "Humanist teachings" (from 1984–85 bylaws).

Today's UUA is a small denomination, with an adult membership of approximately 150,000 distributed among some 1,050 churches and fellowships in 2000. Approximately 80 percent of the membership have come to the association through voluntary affiliation rather than birth; the latter is most important in New England. Membership is concentrated in the northeastern quadrant of the nation, with churches and fellowships elsewhere usually found in urban and suburban areas, college and university communities, as well as "high tech" centers such as Oak Ridge, Tennessee. Education and income levels of members are high. Polity is congregational, continuing the tradition of its New England roots. Like the Quakers, Unitarian Universalists do not seriously contemplate becoming a major denomination in size. Rather, they constitute a small elite who see themselves as evangelists not for their group itself but rather for the causes it espouses. Advancement of social and spiritual ends, not the triumph of organizational means, is the ultimate goal.

The liberal spirit has also found itself institutionalized—in so far as that may be possible—in other forms. The Ethical Culture Society, discussed more fully below, goes even beyond Unitarian Universalism in its rejection of traditional theism, but has never gained a widespread following. Quakers (Friends), especially the Philadelphia Yearly Meeting, have historically allied themselves with liberal or even radical social stances, but their distinctive theology has distanced them from the more rationalistic approaches of Unitarian Universalism and Ethical Culture. Among the "mainline" Protestant denominations, the United Church of Christ stands out as the most clearly liberal in both theology and social and political positions. Ironically, its historical roots are in large part in the conservative Congregationalist churches from which the early Unitarians were forced to separate in 1825. The Episcopal and Presbyterian (PCUSA) churches are also identified by some as liberal, but the range of outlook found among their memberships makes the accuracy of such a label seem more doubtful.

Liberal religionists have often been perceived by their more conservative compatriots as not only unsound in belief but scarcely distinguishable from nonbelievers. As Martin Marty has pointed out, the role of the "unbeliever" or "infidel" has often been a construct, a straw man, devised by conservative believers as a way of arousing alarm and renewed zeal among the faithful. As such, it is analogous to the phenomenon that David Brion Davis has called "countersubversion" in American history. By this, Davis means those crusades that flourished especially in the early nineteenth century against a number of groups that were labeled as deviant and therefore dangerous to the Republic. Among these were Roman Catholics, Masons, Mormons, and southern slaveholders, all of whom were accused at one time or another of a combination of sexual immorality and political subversion—charges that were spread through lurid, inflammatory literature that might be called the moral equivalent of pornography. Identifying deviants, even if their deviance has to be invented from the whole cloth, is a way of establishing or reinforcing one's own identity when the latter is called into doubt by rapid social change.

This is not to say, however, that there have not been self-proclaimed "infidels" in American history. During the revolutionary era, Tom Paine and Ethan Allen, both with substantial reputations as patriots, published tracts that repudiated traditional Christianity. Allen, known as the leader of the "Green Mountain Boys," mounted a rather amateurish attack in his *Reason the Only Oracle of Man* (1785). Paine had been an especially effective propagandist for the American cause through his pamphlets "Common Sense" and "The American Crisis"; later, his *Age of Reason* (1794–96) presented an equally eloquent but less effectual argument for Deism, combined with an attack on the effects of institutional religion. Although Paine tried his hand at organizing a "Theophilanthropist" society, he attracted few followers.

The early Republic, which Alice Felt Tyler identified as the great era of "freedom's ferment" in the realm of religious and social experimentation, was characterized simultaneously by the rapid growth of evangelical Protestantism in the "Second Great Awakening" and by a bewildering diversity of alternatives such as the Mormons, Shakers, and other sectarian groups. Unbelief provided a convenient target for militant evangelicals such as Timothy Dwight, the president of Yale, and Lyman Beecher, one of evangelicalism's leading orators, propagandists, and organizers. Dwight, for example, helped launch a phase of the Second Awakening at Yale through his cry of alarm over undergraduates calling one another "Voltaire," "Rousseau," and other names of French Enlightenment leaders. Deist Thomas Jefferson became for the New England Federalist-Congregationalist establishment a symbol of the evils of unbridled democracy. More sophisticated attacks on traditional religion than the affectations of young Yalies came from such utopian socialist thinkers as Robert Dale Owen and Fanny Wright. Their experiments were generally short lived; however, the dozens of communitarian societies that were founded in the early nineteenth century attracted an inordinate amount of attention, especially from the never-ending stream of bemused foreign visitors to American shores.

Meanwhile, the majority of Americans never joined any religious group in a formal way. This did not mean that they were hostile or skeptical; it indicated rather that, in a fluid society with free religious choice, there was not enough tradition or other pressure to make church membership an urgent matter, except perhaps during flurries of revivalism. During the earlier nineteenth century, such widespread lack of affiliation was characteristic of ordinary people, who seldom articulated their preferences publicly.

After the Civil War, attacks on traditional religion played a small but important role in the public realm of debate. Colonel Robert Ingersoll drew fame on the lecture circuits with such attacks, while simultaneously playing a leading role in Republican Party politics. Mark Twain, probably the best-loved author of the era, satirized not only "deviant" religious groups such as Mormons and Christian Scientists but also questioned traditional religion itself in such brooding later works as *The Mysterious Stranger* (1916). Moreover, a subtle change began to pervade the more articulate strata of society. The cumulative impact first of Enlightenment rationalism and skepticism and then of Darwinian naturalism certainly played a role in this process, as did the erosion of dogma in much of Christian thought.

Although many Protestants expressed this change in religious sensibility by espousing one or another variety of liberalism, others quietly dropped out of the ranks of believers altogether. *Agnosticism,* a term coined by the English Victorian skeptic Thomas Henry Huxley, now entered the American vocabulary to describe those who did not deny the existence of a personal god but rather did not think that the question could be resolved by human minds. The "cult" of science as a virtual alternative to religion became widespread in many academic and professional circles. Another poignant example of this process of "dropping out" is narrated in *The Education of Henry Adams* (1907), the autobiographical account of the personal and intellectual odyssey of a scion of New England's leading family.

The clash between fundamentalism and modernism in the 1920s evoked further "elitist" attacks on religion, such as the journalist H. L. Mencken's ridicule of the Bible Belt and its unenlightened denizens. (Mencken covered the Scopes "Monkey" Trial for the *Baltimore Sun* in 1925.) Such stridency, however, was less common than the gradual shift of mood among many of the leaders of thought and culture away from religious questions altogether. For many academics, professional writers, and other shapers of opinion, a more or less conscious secularism became the norm.

As society itself grew more pluralistic, court decisions began to constrict the expression of religious themes in public arenas. This judicial caution combined with a fear by politicians and advertisers of offending popular opinion to lead to the banishment of religion from much of the public sphere: the schools, the political arena, and the mass media. By the 1970s, a backlash against this gradual development took shape in the form of aggressive fundamentalist attacks on "secular humanism," the generic term that gained popularity as a label for these accumulated social forces.

"Humanism" in the sense of a conscious rejection of a personal god and a corresponding exaltation of human moral capacities has remote roots in the Renaissance, clearer sources in the Enlightenment, and a genuine though modest history of institutional expression in America. The Free Religious Association, founded in 1866 by dissident Unitarians who objected to their denomination's explicitly Christian identity, was an early though short-lived attempt in this direction. More enduring has been its offshoot, Ethical Culture, which in 1983 had about four thousand members spread among twenty-two churches. Ethical Culture came into being in 1876 through the work of Felix Adler (1851–1933), a Reform rabbi who had served as the second president of the Free Religious Association. Similar in spirit to humanistic Unitarianism, Ethical Culture stresses human moral responsibility and potential, and provides an organized forum for discussion and education for families who are not comfortable with traditional religion.

The term *humanism* gained currency through the "Humanist Manifesto," first issued in 1933 and signed by the philosopher John Dewey and other intellectual and liberal religious leaders (including several Unitarians), and reissued in 1973 as the "Humanist Manifesto II." An American Humanist Association was organized in 1941; with headquarters at Yellow Springs, Ohio (home of Antioch College), it continues to publish *The Humanist,* and maintains a small membership. Allied with organized humanism in a very limited way are a number of groups that are vocal defenders of civil liberties and are continually alert to what they regard as violations of the proper boundaries separating church and state. These include the American Civil Liberties Union (ACLU); Norman Lear's People for the American Way, which was founded specifically to counteract the "Social Agenda" of the Moral Majority and other Religious Right groups; and various Jewish organizations sensitive to claims that America is basically a "Christian nation." In addition, a few very small groups of organized atheists, such as the late Madalyn Murray O'Hair's "American Atheists, Inc.," periodically attract publicity through their combination of philosophical unbelief and legal challenges in church-state separation cases.

It is difficult to assess the impact on American life of this combination of organized movements that might be collectively identified as "secularist"—that is, working against the involvement of organized religion in the political and social realms. The ACLU and kindred groups have the most documentable force, and have made a genuine impact in their advocacy in courts and legislatures on behalf of church-state separation. The claim of fundamentalists that "secular humanism" as an organized, conscious force has been successful in eroding the fabric of American society, however, is much harder to demonstrate, because it is difficult to find very many people who identify themselves as "secular humanists," organized or otherwise. What seems to be happening here is a resurfacing of the theme of "countersubversion": an attempt to blame long-term undesirable social forces such as pluralism and secularism on concrete, personalized forces that behave conspiratorially to achieve their wicked ends. (The phrases "atheistic Communism" and "international Communist conspiracy" that were current in the 1950s McCarthyite stir are indicative of the same preoccupations.)

If secular humanism is primarily a bugbear of the political and religious right, this is not to say that secularism and secularity are illusory as well. What distinguishes such secularists from the very small number of organized "secular humanists" is the former's passive rather than active rejection of traditional, theistic religion. Such secularists are not united in any campaign to combat or destroy religion; they simply are not very interested in the whole issue, and they express this disinterest simply by distancing themselves from any organized religious activity. This is particularly pronounced in the "None Zone"—the Pacific Northwest, the part of the nation in which those listing their religious affiliations as "none" particularly abound.

Intellectually, the 1960s provided a rationale for a distancing from traditional, organized religion significantly different in kind from earlier skepticism and "infidelity." A classic text of that era was Harvey Cox's *The Secular City* (1965), which argued that authentic biblical Christianity was not to be found so much in the churches but rather in the midst of social change and conflict in contemporary urban America. Part of the theological underpinnings for Cox and other like-minded writers of the period came from Dietrich Bonhoeffer's *Letters and Papers from Prison* (published 1953). Bonhoeffer, who had been executed in 1945 for resistance to the Third Reich, argued in this last and posthumous work for what he called a "religionless Christianity" in which God's will for humanity should be interpreted in secular rather than supernaturalistic terms. Various interpretations of this line of argument also helped shape the short-lived "Death of God" movement popularized by theologians such as Thomas J. J. Altizer and Gabriel Vahanian. Although the recipient of much media attention, the "Death of God" did not enjoy a long life span nor exert a great deal of influence on subsequent speculation. A further variation on the theme of "radical theology" was embodied in Richard Rubenstein's *After Auschwitz* (1966), a Jewish reflection on the significance of the Holocaust that concluded with serious doubts about the existence of a God who could permit such atrocities.

At least as disturbing to readers who were most likely to encounter such ideas through the cover story in *Time* or in one-minute segments on network evening news was the "radical turn" in ethical thought that was occurring simultaneously. The civil rights movement, which by the mid-1960s had achieved many of its initial goals, held a broad appeal outside the South because of its deep roots in earlier American thought and experience and the biblical themes and cadences brought to bear on its behalf by Martin Luther King. Not so the protest movement against the Vietnam War. Its more extreme adherents' burning of draft cards and desecration of flags evoked for the historically minded the more radical tradition of Garrisonian abolitionism and raised considerable alarm and anger among the newly self-conscious "Hardhats" and other conservative segments of society. (William Lloyd Garrison had denounced the Constitution in biblical terms as "a covenant with Death and an agreement with Hell.")

These challenges to racism and war helped generate for many young people a broader challenge to the structures and values of American middle-class culture. Theodore Roszak fixed a label on this loosely organized but culturally powerful impulse in his popular *The Making of a Counter Culture* (1969), significantly subtitled "Reflections on the Technocratic Society and Its Youthful Opposition." For Roszak, the components of this new movement of opposition to prevailing norms and lifestyles included neo-Marxist and post-Freudian cultural criticism (as exemplified in the thought of Herbert Marcuse and Norman O. Brown); a fascination with Asian religions, especially Zen and Tibetan Buddhism; and the pervasive use of drugs, particularly LSD, as a way to escape the trammels of everyday consciousness. The popularity of Carlos Castaneda's *The Teachings of Don Juan* (1969) among young people also reflected a simultaneous fascination with alternative worlds of consciousness, drugs, and unmodernized cultures.

In the more private sphere, the conservatively minded also found cause for distress in the "New Morality" advocated in such works as Joseph Fletcher's *Situation Ethics* (1966). The core of this new approach to personal, and especially sexual, responsibility lay in the rejection of traditional arguments that both divine and natural law laid down certain inflexible rules with regard to human conduct. According to the "New Morality"—which tended to lose any nuances it may have originally possessed as it became dispersed through the media—the only guide for personal decision making was the question of whether one's actions were likely to foster love. Traditional cautions about premarital sex were the most conspicuous victim of this new attitude, and the impact on campus mores was especially striking. Buttressed by a more general revolt of the young against traditional authority, as expressed in the fascination of the youthful "counterculture" for consciousness-altering drugs, the "sexual revolution" was launched on its inexorable course.

Themes raised both by the Civil Rights Movement and the "New Morality" combined in another set of causes. Feminism was hardly a newcomer to the American scene, but the impulse toward the equality of women had become submerged in the quest for suburban "normalcy" that had dominated the 1950s. Sparked by Betty Friedan's *The Feminine Mystique* (1963), many women began to question—sometimes radically—the assumptions about their proper social, economic, and sexual roles that seemed implicit in the American society of the day. This new women's movement rapidly became embroiled in questions about philosophy and tactics: whether its aim should focus on correcting traditional economic equalities and other concerns of women who were working in the marketplace by choice or necessity, or whether it should challenge more basic societal assumptions about sexuality and sex roles. At the beginning of the current century, the question is far from resolved, although institutions for its debate, such as women's studies programs on many college campuses, caucuses in many religious denominations, and groups such as the National Organization for Women (NOW), have become permanent features of the public forum.

Other "liberation" movements, many accompanied by theological and ethical re-flections in the seminaries and among denominational leaders, followed in the wake of the black power and women's movements. Gay men and lesbian women rapidly began to "come out of the closet," avow their sexual identities publicly, and protest against the opprobrium and discrimination that had traditionally been their lot. Chicanos (Mexican Americans) and Native Americans also began to find articulate advocates for their grievances. On the other hand, something of a backlash began to take shape among *ethnics,* a term at the time reserved for Americans, often of the second to the fourth generation in this country, descended from the stock of the "new immigration" of the turn of the twentieth century. Often of the lower middle classes, these Italian-, Polish-, and other "hyphenated" Americans found a voice for their conservative concerns in Michael Novak's *The Rise of the Unmeltable Ethics* (1972). Novak, who had begun his academic career as a liberal lay Roman Catholic voice, executed an abrupt turn to the right in his sociopolitical outlook, and eventually helped form the cadre of "neo-conservatives" who would later articulate the intel-lectual groundwork of Reagan-style Republicanism. Many working-class Catholics, formerly reliable Democrats, were now as likely to vote for conservative Republicans especially because of the latter party's opposition to legalized abortion.

Many younger people who were influenced by some combination of these move-ments in the 1960s and early 1970s began as a result to question the need for tradi-tional religious practice and institutions. Though not necessarily irreligious, these baby boomers tended to drop out of their parents' churches and synagogues, and did not automatically reenter as they matured. This trend away from organized religion that reemerged among a significant segment of the population at this time has his-torical roots both in the particular nature of the American republic and in broader, macro-social forces pervasive in the Western world during the past century and a half. Changes from a predominantly localistic, village-oriented, agricultural society to an impersonal, specialized, urban industrial order have inevitably undermined the bonds that held people together and promoted participation in churches inclusive of entire communities by definition within their membership. The "Ozzie and Har-riet" cult of neighborhood, family, and domesticity promulgated in the Cold War atmosphere of the 1950s also intensified, and most likely exaggerated, the cleavage between the religious cultures of previous and subsequent decades.

In the United States, cultural and religious pluralism received legal validation through the First Amendment. Social pressures in many more traditional communi-ties often made church membership prudent for those desiring acceptance and success, but no legal means could henceforward be brought to compel participation. Sociologist Philip Hammond has identified the 1970s as one of the turning points in the process of what he identifies as a series of "disestablishments," that is, the elimina-tion or erosion of organized religion's role as a component in an individual's public identity. The First Amendment, of course, was the first. The second, which undercut

Protestantism's normative status, began with the repeal of Prohibition in 1933 and reached public consciousness in Will Herberg's *Protestant, Catholic, Jew* (1955), which argued that the United States had become a "triple melting pot" in which it was equally legitimate for an individual to espouse *any* of these three religious identities as a sign of good Americanism. By the 1970s, however, Hammond argued that it was no longer necessary for an American to profess any formal religious affiliation in order to achieve public respect and acceptance. Although this generalization may need some modification—many politicians, for example, have to put on at least a pretense of religious conviction to win votes—it is probably valid for much of urban and suburban American professional life today.

By the late twentieth century, then, what we might call "passive secularism" had emerged as a major, though invisible, force in American religious life. As Wade Clark Roof and William McKinney demonstrated in their influential *American Mainline Religion* (1988), a major source of attrition from the mainline (liberal and moderate) Protestant denominations has not been loss to other churches but rather the widespread practice of simply "dropping out." Closely related is the phenomenon described by Robert Bellah and his associates in their *Habits of the Heart* (1985). In one of the interviews on which this study of contemporary American social values was based, they encountered a young woman named Sheila who described her own religious position as "Sheilaism." By this she meant that she had no need of traditional, organized religious groups; rather, she was content to fashion her own, eclectic, individualistic system of beliefs for herself. In short, "Sheilaism" is a vividly specific example of religion in the modern world not disappearing but rather become so highly personalized that it has entirely detached itself from the sense of community that has traditionally characterized the religious life. These findings are underscored by the Pew Forum U.S. Religious Landscape Survey of 2008, which found that 16 percent of Americans had no religious affiliation, a percentage that rose to 25 percent when limited to those between the ages of eighteen and twenty-nine. The same survey also found that 28 percent of Americans no longer belonged to the faith in which they had been raised, and that those identifying as Protestant had fallen to 51 percent of the population.

At the end of this investigation, there remains a paradox: that American society has simultaneously grown both more secular and more religious. A significant majority of Americans in the early twenty-first century belong to organized religious groups and attend worship at least occasionally. When those who are not affiliated with any religious group but who claim to believe in God are added to this already large number, the total is overwhelmingly large. (A 1988 Gallup Poll found that some 85 percent of respondents claimed to believe in the divinity of Jesus Christ.) The percentages of affiliation are much higher than in the early nineteenth century during the heyday of revivalism. On the other hand, the reality of religious pluralism, the impact of the marketplace and the mass media, and the dilemmas of dealing with beliefs and values in the context of universal public education have all led to the banishment of specific religious symbols and discourse from the public arena. "America" as a sentimental idea may involve the notion of divine sanction, but the "United States" as a functioning society has become pervasively secular. How to resolve the emotional and practical tensions that result from this contrast remains an unsolved issue on the public agenda.

CHAPTER 55

Popular Religion in New Keys

Popular religion is a somewhat undigested but still evocative term that describes a multitude of phenomena, past and present, that contribute to the ever-shifting American religious spectrum. On the one hand, it may refer to religious motifs in what at first glance seems the relentlessly secular popular culture that has grown up along with the mass media of the twentieth century. When Obi-Wan Kenobi tells Luke Skywalker to use the Force, he invokes not only high-tech laser weaponry but also a fictionalized version of the harmonial religion that has long been a mainstay of popular religiosity. On the other, "popular religion" encompasses a variety of movements that have arisen outside of or alongside the multitude of institutionalized forms of religion in this country in which many people partake eclectically, attending, say, a Methodist church while simultaneously shopping at a New Age bookstore and watching evangelical videos with their children. The loss of confidence in institutions that has characterized American society since the 1960s has had a profound impact on popular religiosity, nurturing some forms while effectively discouraging others. Among these forms have been the *American civil religion,* which by most accounts has declined significantly in appeal; the New Age movement, a transmutation of earlier strains of harmonialism that has been thriving now for several decades; the brief flourishing of *cults,* or new religious movements, at the fringes of Asian religions, the New Age, and popular evangelicalism; and the reemergence of *millennialism* as a major theme, spurred for a time particularly by the approach of Y2K.

Civil Religion

The American "civil religion," which has been discussed in passing in a variety of places earlier in this work, first came into focus as a distinctive concept at the very time when it was most under attack and about to fall into what seems like a permanent decline. The sociologist Robert Bellah gave the notion its distinctive name and definition in a 1967 article at the same time that the phenomenon itself was under attack from a number of quarters in the midst of widespread controversy and civic stress precipitated by escalating American involvement in Vietnam. Although the term itself is imprecise, *civil religion* (also known as "civic religion" and "public religion") has been used to designate a tendency of Americans to attribute a religious significance to the life of the nation itself, and especially to the idea that the American people and nation are uniquely guided by divine providence as an example to the rest of the world. This kind of devotion manifested itself in the singing of national hymns, such as "The Star-Spangled Banner," "America the Beautiful," and "The Battle Hymn of the Republic"; the maintenance of national shrines, concentrated on the Mall in Washington, D.C., but supplemented by national parks and historic sites throughout the nation; and the veneration of national scriptures, such as the Declaration of Independence and the Gettysburg Address. Rituals involving these symbols took place particularly on national holidays such as Memorial Day, the Fourth of July, and what has now become conflated into Presidents' Day (formerly separate observances of Washington's and Lincoln's birthdays). Votaries of this civil religion included government officials and politicians who invoked such images and themes during public addresses; schoolteachers who began the day's activities with the Pledge of Allegiance (into which the phrase "under God" had been inserted in 1954); and clergy who displayed the American flag in church sanctuaries and helped officiate on public holidays. These are some of the more conspicuous examples of an unofficial national cultus, never established by law as mandatory but nevertheless recognized, observed, and practiced by most Americans to some degree.

Because the civil religion had never been formally established, it could not be repealed. However, the events of the 1960s and 1970s brought about a reversal of fortune from which it has never recovered. One feature of the way in which the civil religion had traditionally been observed that became acutely problematic during this period was its association with war. Much of its imagery—"the rockets' red glare," for example—arose out of armed conflict in which American victory had been read as confirming the providential guidance and ultimate rightness of the national cause. World War II particularly had been an experience that had been at once costly and unifying, much as the Civil War had earlier been, at least for the North. The conflict between the Allies and the Axis—Germany, Italy, and Japan—had for most Americans seemed a clear-cut struggle between good and evil that was confirmed by the liberation of the Nazi concentration camps and that had justified the use of atomic weapons on Japan to bring a speedy end to the conflict. The Korean conflict—never officially recognized as a war—of the early 1950s, however, was much less conclusive; even though many Americans saw there a confrontation starkly drawn in cold war terms of a virtuous American-led United Nations coalition arrayed against the godless forces of Communism, the inability of the former to gain an unambiguous victory over the latter left a residue of discontent among a people accustomed to victory. The gradual escalation of American involvement in southeast Asia during the 1960s, according to the "domino theory" that the loss of any territory in that area would lead inevitably to the Communist takeover of the entire continent, was launched in an atmosphere of subdued skepticism and generated open and vocal opposition as American victory proved elusive, brutal tactics against civilians aroused moral revulsion, and young Americans of draft age registered resistance in a variety of forms, from public demonstrations to draft-card burning to expatriation. (Canada's welcoming of many of them irked American authorities considerably.)

The United States' ultimate withdrawal from Vietnam and recognition that the Communists were there to stay was in many ways the death knell for the civil religion as it had been practiced during the 1950s and 1960s as an expression of consensus on national goals and destiny. This is not to say that the Pledge of Allegiance disappeared suddenly from Kiwanis Club meetings, or that high school seniors no longer made spring break trips to Washington to visit the Washington Monument and Lincoln Memorial, or that "In God We Trust" disappeared from the coinage. In fact, a new national holiday, in honor of Martin Luther King Jr. was added to the official roster of civil religion commemorations in most states. What did change was the sense of communal solidarity behind such observances in many places. In part, this was the result of the secularization—or, perhaps, rationalization—exhibited in the metamorphosis of the observance of the two great February-born presidents into one bureaucratically convenient long weekend. The aging of veterans from the two world wars was another factor, and attempts at enthusiasm for the commemoration of the two inconclusive conflicts fought on the Asian mainland never elicited a great deal of positive response. Although Ronald Reagan's rhetoric during his two administrations during the 1980s revived some of the patriotic fervor of the cold war, the abrupt disintegration of the Soviet Union in the early 1990s soon put an end to "evil empire" rhetoric. Domestically, wars on both poverty and drugs proved frustrating, and distrust of government by both left and right rendered its status as the object of religious affirmation questionable. Finally, the Supreme Court's outlawing of prayer in the public schools undercut that institution as a vehicle for the perpetuation of the civic cultus.

What did result was not so much a disappearance of civil religion but rather its appropriation by the Religious Right at the same time that it was falling into desuetude among the more cosmopolitan sectors of society. The South in particular, with its heritage of affirmation of sports, the military, patriotism, and evangelical religion, proved especially receptive to its continuance, and most challenges in the courts to the blending of religious symbolism with secular institutions originated in that region. Throughout most of the country, however, public observances such as Memorial Day parades quietly faded into the background.

The New Age

Just as the events of the 1960s undercut the American civil religion, they simultaneously infused new energy into another sort of diffuse religiosity that had long been
a part of the American scene—namely, what religious historian Sydney Ahlstrom
dubbed "harmonialism," and Catherine Albanese more recently has called "metaphysical religion." In earlier phases of American life, this belief that the resolution of
the conflicts that beset the individual could be found in the recovery of knowledge
that contained the key to harmony between the material and spiritual worlds had
taken a variety of forms, including Christian Science, New Thought, and Theosophy—movements very different from one another in important ways but nevertheless
based on some similar themes. Where the antiwar and anti-institutional threads of
1960s culture worked against the civil religion, the age's countercultural dimensions
abetted the emergence of new forms of metaphysical thought and practice. The image
of the "Age of Aquarius"—the title of a song in the popular musical *Hair*—as a nascent
epoch of universal love and good feeling brought about by a fortunate convergence of
the planets, was one that embodied well a new set of "spiritual" pursuits that loosely
converged into what would come to be called the *New Age*. This term, now part of
the national vocabulary, emerged through intensive media coverage in the late 1970s
and has become the adopted self-designation of millions who selectively participate
in some or many of its manifold aspects. The notion that history had reached a major
turning point with regard to human consciousness was further promoted in James
Redfield's best-selling 1993 novel, *The Celestine Prophecy,* which deals with the quest
for an ancient Peruvian manuscript containing the nine insights that humanity needs
to understand in order to enter into this new era.

The first important characteristic of the New Age movement is that it has no center. In many ways, it resembles the Religious Right (or, more broadly, contemporary
conservative evangelicalism) in that it lacks any central institutionalized authority;
rather, its tenets are circulated through a variety of publications, bookstores, musical
recordings, and prominent individuals to whom many look for, if not leadership, at
least inspiration. Unlike the Religious Right, though, it maintains few alliances with
institutions, whether religious, educational, or political, of any size, and makes even
less effort to promote a "party line." Rather, like the World Wide Web, it consists
of a series of continually shifting and expanding cognitive options from which an
individual can devise a satisfying combination, or ally, however fleetingly, with other
like-minded spirits in quest of personal fulfillment.

The clientele of the New Age is similarly hard to pin down, since participation is
not linked to institutional affiliation, no rolls are kept, and many of the movement's
adherents see no difficulty in being simultaneously affiliated with a formal religious
denomination. Many who find its teachings attractive, though, are members of the
post–World War II baby boomer generation that came of age accustomed to the

suburban middle-class prerogatives of education and security while at the same time distanced from the social, political, and religious institutions that had helped define their parents' identities. Central to the New Age movement is the idea of personal choice: for them, identity is not defined *ascriptively*—that is, by the social circumstances into which one is born and the expectations and restrictions which they subsequently generate; rather, what we are is what we choose to be, an assumption born of affluence and sophistication in a society where mobility in its various senses is taken as a given. Identity is thus *elective*—a matter of personal choice. One term frequently used to characterize "New Agers" is *seekers*—those who are not content with any religious identity handed them by their family but rather are in continual quest of new spiritual experiences in an ongoing process of growth and redefinition. What is central is a preoccupation with self-realization; unlike the Religious Right, New Agers see the attainment of truth as coming not with the imposition of a divinely given and immutable morality on the social order through political means but rather in the continuing transformation of the self in a never-ending quest for experience and authenticity.

Two other concepts central to the New Age movement are "holistic" and "healing." Healing, of course, is hardly a new concept in religion, as is evidenced in the miracles worked by Jesus. American religious communities have frequently stressed the possibility of physical regeneration through spiritual means, from pentecostal invocations of the gifts of the Holy Spirit to Roman Catholic shrines to various saints, which the infirm visit and at which they leave behind their no-longer-needed crutches. In both of these explicitly Christian examples, the underlying theology postulates the seeking and receiving of healing power from a divine source outside the individual. The New Age movement, however, has a lineage that instead includes earlier American movements such as mesmerism, Christian Science, and New Thought that have stood at the edge of or outside traditional Christianity. In all of these cases, the premise is that healing comes through the correct alignment of the individual with the spiritual forces that permeate the universe and are already potentially immanent with us all. Philosophically, one might call this perspective *monistic:* body and spirit, mind and matter, the human and the divine are no longer seen as separate or even opposed, but rather as part of a single continuum of being and power that simply needs to be discovered and properly realized to bring about wholeness and harmony within the individual and, potentially, in society as a whole. (Although the diffuseness of the movement does not lend itself to the sorts of organized political effort that has been characteristic of the Religious Right, many individual participants have been active in causes such as environmentalism that mesh with New Age concerns.)

Potential sources of such healing are manifold and eclectic. Native American and Asian traditions, for example, have both been drawn on as providing monistic metaphysical systems in which bodily health is a corollary of a broader correct spiritual alignment. The Holistic Health Movement of the 1960s, which is especially associated with California, gave rise to manifestations such as the Esalen Institute and the practice of rolfing, which promoted various techniques for bringing body, mind, and spirit into harmony, and the works of popular psychologists such as Robert Bly, Sam Keen, Abraham Maslow, and Fritz Perls have helped to publicize the movement widely. (*Body Mind Spirit,* in fact, is the name of a major New Age journal.) The use of bioenergetics, crystals, aromatherapy, acupuncture, massage, visualization, and other techniques for access to healing cosmic energy are all part of the New Age repertoire as well. The use of consciousness-expanding or psychedelic drugs, which was central to much of the 1960s counterculture and promoted by "gurus" such as Carlos Castaneda and Timothy Leary, has remained as a part of New Age practice for some; most, however, remain content with strictly legal means of access to enlightenment.

The quest for health and healing is not usually the end of the New Age adventure. Rather, it is one outcome of a broader search for cosmic meaning of a sort not readily available in traditional, institutional forms of religion or philosophy. The sources of such meaning are not confined to any one system, although New Age followers tend to be drawn especially to the unconventional and exotic. In addition to Native American and Asian traditions mentioned earlier, the pre-Christian religions of Europe, such as those of the ancient Celts and Druids, are frequently seen as a source of spiritual wisdom. *Wicca,* or modern witchcraft, is a particularly popular form of this broader "Neo-Pagan" movement, which originated in its modern form in England and was transplanted to the United States in the 1960s. A major theme of Wicca and an American offshoot, the Goddess movement, is the imbalance in contemporary life between the complementary masculine and feminine sexual principles that infuse the cosmos, and a concern for restoring the feminine to a place of equality if not dominance. Needless to say, these movements are also very much part of contemporary feminism as well. New Age resource lists, however, do frequently include Christian sources, such as the metaphysical fiction of C. S. Lewis and Madeleine L'Engle, and Christian churches at times re-adopt New Age forms of spirituality such as walking through labyrinths. The whole notion of "spirituality," in fact, as opposed to traditional organized religion, is a realm in which the New Age movement and individual Christian and Jewish believers intersect.

One of the most controversial and widely publicized aspects of the New Age movement has been its fascination with *channeling*—the belief that contemporary individuals with the proper gift can become "channels" through which beings who have lived in past ages can now communicate with those living today. Some channelers and their sources such as Jane Roberts and "Seth" and J. Z. Knight and "Ramtha" have become nationally known, and the actress Shirley MacLaine has been particularly influential in popularizing this phenomenon. Channeling can be read in part as a latter-day manifestation of Spiritualism, the nineteenth-century quest for contact with the spirits of the departed. In both cases, women have been particularly active as earthly contacts or channels for supernatural beings; both, in addition, exemplify the quest of many, usually middle-class, Americans, for knowledge, assurance, and healing that they have not readily found through the more traditional offerings of organized religion. This fascination with sources of knowledge that transcend the empiricism of modern science emphasizes again the themes of openness and eclecticism in the quest for personal growth and wholeness that characterize the movement in general.

The New Age movement might in summary be described as bearing a sort of yin/yang relationship, one of complementary opposition, to the Religious Right, and adherents of each often wind up as political opponents. Whereas "New Agers" are frequently comfortably settled into middle-class status and able to take much of the security (and, possibly, monotony) of suburban life as a given, many conservative evangelicals are new to such a lifestyle and not secure either in its economic or cognitive implications. Whereas the New Age is optimistic about human possibilities, the Christian Right retains a considerable dose of Calvinistic pessimism. Whereas New Age adherents reject tradition, authority, and structure in their quest for religious truth, conservative evangelicals emphasize the need for all of those qualities as an antidote to fallen human nature. Whereas New Age followers tend to embrace liberal political and social causes such as environmentalism and feminism, the Christian Right is firmly allied with conservative Republican politics and advocates a traditional role for women. Whereas the New Age is open to spiritual enlightenment from virtually any potential source, evangelicals stress the absolute, unique, exclusive, and necessary truth of Christian revelation. In many ways, these dichotomies can be traced back, or at least paralleled, in American religious life to the internecine quarrels between liberal and orthodox Congregationalists in the 1830s—transcendentalism, in fact, is one clear New Age precursor—or the split between fundamentalists and modernists in the northern Protestant denominations at the turn of the previous century. What is different here is the much more diffuse character of both New Age and New Right. Each has a distinctive, even pervasive, culture, purveyed through literature, film, music, periodicals, Web sites, bookstores, and the like, but neither is easily confined within any given set of institutions, old or new. Both, in fact, help shape the "spirituality" that has supplemented and rivaled, though by no means replaced, denominational religion in contemporary America. In the twenty-first century, the megachurch trend in the direction of personal fulfillment—as exemplified in the teachings of Rick Warren—may signify that the New Age and popular evangelicalism may in fact be converging.

"Cults" or New Religions

Another phenomenon of the 1960s that momentarily attracted considerable media attention and generated public alarm was the rapid rise (and, a decade or so later, decline) of *cults*—or, more neutrally, new religious movements. This loose aggregation includes groups that demonstrate affinities for a variety of other popular currents, including the New Age, evangelical Christianity, Asian religiosity, and apocalypticism. The term, which derives from the Latin *cultus* ("worship") and ultimately from the same root as "cultivation" and "agriculture," is used neutrally in religious studies as a term for devotion to special object of reverence, for example, the cult of the Virgin Mary. In popular usage, however, the term *cult* usually designates a sectarian group that deviates significantly, and perhaps ominously, from the "mainstream" of accepted Christian belief and practice. In the fairly recent past, such indigenous groups as Unitarians, Christian Scientists, Seventh-day Adventists, Jehovah's Witnesses, and Mormons have been singled out as "cults," especially in fundamentalist literature. In more recent usage, charismatic leadership, a communal and highly regimented lifestyle, isolation from the rest of the world, and teachings that deviate radically from the mainstream are usually part of most people's intuitive definition of the term. Some of these groups, such as Krishna Consciousness and the Divine Light Mission discussed in chapter 53, as well as the "Moonies" (Unification Church) treated below, aroused sufficient alarm in their time that a number of parents engaged the services of "deprogrammers" such as Ted Patrick to abduct their adult children and subject them to an intensive program of resocialization to break their newly found religious allegiances and communal lifestyles. Deprogramming met with legal obstacles—Patrick was jailed a number of times—and the rapid passing of such groups from the scene, at least in their more aggressive forms, soon rendered such concerns moot.

The countercultural ferment of the late 1960s and early 1970s led to a whole new ethos among America's middle-class young people. This ethos proved highly conducive to the formation of new religious groups that seemed, at least to concerned parents and clergy, to deviate even more alarmingly from accepted norms. Some of these groups were combinations of conservative Protestant theology with countercultural lifestyles, often involving communitarianism. Such groups of "Jesus People" as David Berg's "Children of God" occasionally took on some of the characteristics of cults that had been coalescing through these years into a typology of alarm. On the whole, however, most groups that were within the Christian tradition tended to meld themselves into the broader conservative upsurge that was gaining strength through the 1970s, though even here the single-minded conversion of college-age young people to aggressive fundamentalist movements such as the Navigators and the Campus Crusade for Christ prompted dismayed "mainline" parents to wonder whether something insidious might not be afoot. (Usually, in fact, there wasn't; these groups are now accepted parts of the religious landscape of most college campuses.)

Bordering on the New Age movement and the humanistic psychology closely allied with it is *Scientology*, founded by science-fiction writer L. Ron Hubbard in 1954, which is nontheistic and combines elements of depth psychology with a belief in reincarnation. Its primary activity, called "auditing" with the aid of devices known as

"E-meters," is aimed at helping individuals attain a state known as "clear." The expensive and intimate character of this process, together with questionable intelligence-gathering tactics employed by the group's leadership, led to extensive difficulties with governments at various levels in the United States and abroad in the 1970s. Hubbard died in 1986, having spent much of his controversial later years in isolation at sea or in southern California. Since then the organization, which has been endorsed by popular culture figures such as John Travolta, has gained a reputation for litigiousness and has been suppressed in a number of European countries with less rigorous policies of church-state separation than is the case in the United States.

The Unification Church, which is of Asian origin but Christian in theology, is another classic instance of the continuing controversy that cults can arouse. If founding and leadership by a charismatic leader is a cult characteristic, the role of Sun Myung Moon, a Korean businessman who organized the movement in Korea in 1954, certainly qualifies the Unification Church for this designation. In the movement's theology, which is expounded in the *Divine Principle* (1977), Moon outlined a reinterpretation of Christianity, reminiscent in some ways of early Christian Gnosticism as well as of Mormonism, which introduced ideas extremely alien to most "mainstream" Christians. In the beginning, God had intended that Adam and Eve would beget a perfect family. Eve's seduction by "Lucifer" ruined this hope, and successive divinely chosen figures have been appointed to restore the pure family relationship originally intended. One of these, Jesus, was spiritually successful in this program but died before he could go on to restore physically the perfect family.

It is only in the present day that this long-frustrated fulfillment is now taking place. Sun Myung Moon and his wife are referred to by Moon's followers as "Our True Parents," and the entire movement is viewed as constituting the beginnings of the newly restored perfect family. One characteristic of Unification lifestyle that has aroused the ire of more conventional Americans has been the practice of arranged group marriages presided over by Moon, in which unmarried followers are united with mates, often of different cultural backgrounds and whom they have not previously known, in mass ceremonies. Together with charges of alienation of converts from their biological families, in some cases through alleged "brainwashing," this sort of practice was central to the designation of the Unification Church as a cult and to the widespread hostility and suspicion it has aroused.

Although the Unification Church is much more unconventional than the Mormons by today's standards, accusations against the two groups at different eras are instructive. During the nineteenth century, Mormons were widely accused not only of radical religious innovation (hardly a crime) but also of sexual irregularity (polygamy), separation from the mainstream of society, and of hostile, even violent actions directed against dissenters as well as external enemies. Today, Mormons are disliked by liberals especially because of their church's extensive economic holdings and the tendency of the group to vote heavily for extremely conservative political candidates. Similarly, the Unification Church has considerable wealth, obtained in part in its early years through the sale of artificial flowers at airport terminals and other public places by neophyte converts. These proceeds were often used lavishly in public-relations ventures to influence skeptical clergy and religion scholars to think better of them. The church also has heavy investments in a wide variety of secular enterprises, ranging from fishing fleets to the very conservative *Washington Times,* which were the occasion of Moon's conviction in 1982 and subsequent imprisonment for tax fraud. The conservative tenor of the movement's politics is based in part on a messianic interpretation of American destiny as a bulwark against Communism, a teaching interestingly comparable to early Mormon views of this country's divinely guided historical mission.

The Unification Church, which in its heyday probably numbered between five and ten thousand American members (out of a considerably larger worldwide total), may thus be viewed as a nonlethal cult par excellence, which has managed to survive and even thrive on the hostility, culminating in Moon's imprisonment, that it has experienced. By the 1990s, it had largely fallen into the background of the American scene, experiencing little publicity and presumably little growth as well. What will happen after Moon's death, and after the children of the original adherents reach maturity, will be an interesting test of its staying power: whether it can withstand the process of "routinization of charisma" that must invariably be faced by a new religion's second generation.

Perhaps the last gasp of the "cult scare" took place in the 1980s, after the varied alarms over groups such as the "Moonies" had died down. Across the country, a number of arrests were made of adults, especially those working in day-care centers, on the charges of the ritual abuse of children. These allegations and subsequent convictions, most of them eventually dismissed or reversed, were part of a broader pattern of suspicions and accusations centered on satanic rituals and physical and sexual abuse, especially of children, growing out of them. Although there have been various organizations in the United States that have claimed to worship Satan, their numbers have been few, their activities mostly innocuous, and their influence vastly exaggerated. In some cases, teenagers did in fact commit mischief, even violence, in the context of such rituals, but these were locally improvised activities rather than part of any larger network. More serious mischief arose on the side of those intent on combating such activity, a campaign that turned into a new kind of "countersubversion" similar to that of nativist anti-Catholic crusades in the antebellum years. This arose from a convergence of anticult sentiment still in the air, a growing conservative evangelical movement intent on taking demonic rhetoric and symbolism (such as that of Halloween) literally, and a short-lived psychological movement that claimed to be able to resuscitate memories of abuse from those who had endured and repressed it. The discrediting of the latter in a variety of court cases came only after a number of innocent persons had been imprisoned or otherwise harassed, and the campaign soon dissipated. It is instructive, however, as an example of the power of rumor and the ongoing need in society to find scapegoats when anxiety is in the air.

Apocalypticism and Millennialism

The turn of the millennial century—"Y2K"—became the occasion of alarms and excursions focused on the possibility that computer networks throughout the world would fail and plunge a humanity that had become alienated from its ultimate sources of meaning into chaos. Jerry Falwell, the early prophet of the Religious Right, advised his followers to lay in supplies not only of food and water but also of guns and ammunition to protect themselves against the less provident. Other American religious leaders took a less militant tack, seeing the occasion as a time for spiritual stock-taking, even though the relationship of the date to the first advent of Jesus or even to the turn of a thousand-year calendrical cycle was highly problematic. Other than a considerable number of hangovers, not much happened on 1 January 2000, but the probability that Americans would lose their preoccupation with the meaning of time and change remained low.

Perhaps the most dramatic and alarming examples of "cultic" movements during the latter decades of the twentieth century were those whose teachings prominently invoked the themes of *apocalypticism* or *millennialism*. These included the "Peoples Temple" at Jonestown, Guyana, and David Koresh's compound in Waco, Texas, which will be discussed at some length later in this section. On the other hand, much of the excitement at the turn of the new millennium was rooted in imagery and motifs deeply embedded in the American evangelical Protestant tradition and had little direct institutional impact. This is a theme that has been discussed periodically in earlier chapters, in the contexts, for example, of the Millerites, Jehovah's Witnesses, and dispensational premillennialism. The latter theology, which has been promulgated for decades through the *Scofield Reference Bible* as a mainstay of fundamentalism and conservative evangelicalism, has continued to inspire attempts to interpret the coded narrative of the biblical books of Daniel and Revelation in terms of contemporary events. In such works as Hal Lindsey's *The Late, Great Planet Earth* (frequently revised to take account of rapidly changing world political developments), Pat Robertson's *The New World Order* (1991), and Tim LaHaye and Jerry Jenkins's *Left Behind* and other novels, apocalyptic symbols such as the Rapture, the Mark of the Beast, and the Antichrist become part of dramatic scenarios in which, for example, the Council on Foreign Relations and the United Nations use computer technology to bring about a world government in which a New Age "religion of humanity" becomes the official creed. The now nearly ubiquitous bar codes through which supermarket and Wal-Mart cashiers scan the prices on purchased products take on a sinister meaning as part of the devices through which the Antichrist seizes control of a technologically unified society. The faithful are at some point "raptured" into the supernatural realm, whereas the rest of humanity must suffer through the horrendous events that must run their course before Jesus returns to defeat the forces of evil once and for all. The inevitability of this scenario varies according to the teller; in many contemporary versions, for example, these predictions take on the character more of a warning of what might happen than an absolute prediction of future events. The dangers of making overly detailed predictions, in the fashion of William Miller in the 1840s, which are subject to instant disconfirmation, have presumably been taken to heart by at least some of these latter-day prophets.

As Paul Boyer and Robert Fuller have argued, this kind of reading of scripture represents a kind of religious populism that has over the past two centuries reflected many of the themes, and especially the fears, of American life in coded form. One premise is that the Bible—including its more cryptic components, such as Daniel and Revelation—is accessible to the average believer with no specialized training in scriptural interpretation other than nurture in the Christian faith, properly understood. (This is sometimes called the doctrine of the *perspicuity of Scripture*.) This populist approach to biblical interpretation, however, is modified in practice by recourse to the extensive annotation of the Scofield Reference Bible (which assumes the King James Version as a particularly, if not uniquely, authoritative text), as well as the gifts of such latter-day interpreters as Hal Lindsey. Mainline seminary and university scholars who resort to historical and critical assumptions for their analysis of such texts are generally dismissed as betrayers of the texts' literal meaning. This populist distrust of "experts" is historically linked to a fear, dating back at least to the late nineteenth century, of small farmers and artisans losing control of their livelihoods to large, impersonal corporations employing experts and technology, as well as bankers and financiers whose arcane manipulations could affect the well-being of many less powerful Americans, such as midwestern and southern farmers, far removed from them. In recent times, the role that high technology such as computers plays in these dramas is another indication of a widespread distrust of knowledge and power that is not readily available to those without specialized expertise. The attribution over the decades of a variety of identities to the Antichrist—from the pope to Saddam Hussein—as a major player in a contemporary unfolding of the Revelation scenario is revealing of the anxieties of each age.

The large majority of the many Americans (25 percent of Christians, in one late 1990s poll) who believe that Jesus will return during their lifetimes go about much of their lives with little apparent external difference from those who interpret such beliefs more figuratively or pay no heed to them. In a few dramatic cases, however, cults have formed around charismatic leaders who have made the interruption of history in the near future either by the Second Coming of Jesus or some other dramatic force a central tenet of their belief system and have organized all aspects of their lives around such expectations—sometimes with disastrous results. The first major American confrontation with this sort of phenomenon occurred on 18 November 1978, when 912 members of the Peoples Temple, including their leader Jim Jones, drank soft drinks laced with cyanide and died in Jonestown, Guyana. Jones did claim to be a divinely inspired prophet; however, his movement was not technically millennialist, since the ideology that informed the commune had drifted far from Jones's pentecostal origins and much toward Marxism. Jones had earlier established himself in the San Francisco Bay area as a social activist and had gathered an extensive group of followers, many of them minority group members, who later accompanied him to South America when they grew impatient with the American political system. When Congressman Leo Ryan led a delegation to investigate reports that some Jonestown residents were being abused, he was ambushed and killed by some of Jones's disciples, although it has never been clear whether Jones himself gave the order. When it became apparent that the commune's future was no longer safe from external interference, Jones did command his followers to follow him in an act of self-destruction, ostensibly as a dramatic protest against the political injustice that had promoted the commune's departure from the United States. As a result, all but a handful perished, and Jonestown became a byword for dangerous apocalyptic cults.

Closer to home and more clearly in the mainstream of Christian apocalyptic speculation was the rise and fall of the Branch Davidian compound, Mount Carmel, near Waco, Texas, led by David Koresh. The Branch Davidians were an offshoot of the Seventh-day Adventists, which is today very much a "mainstream" denomination but whose distinctive teachings had their origins in the prophecies of Ellen White in the wake of the "great disappointment" that followed William Miller's failed attempt at predicting the Second Coming of Jesus in the 1840s. The Davidians arose in 1934 when their leader, a Bulgarian named Victor Houteff, was expelled by the Adventists when he began to produce his own prophecies about the coming of the Davidic kingdom. Houteff's followers remained at the Mount Carmel commune he had founded in Texas after his death in 1955, and the movement underwent several changes in prophetic leadership until the ascendancy in 1990 of one of their number, Vernon Howell (1959–93), who took the name of David Koresh. (*Koresh* is a Hebrew version of Cyrus, the Persian king who allowed the Israelites to return to their homeland after the first diaspora.)

Howell became David Koresh after a mystical experience in Israel, which convinced him that he had the power to interpret scripture, especially the Book of Revelation. For Koresh, Jesus had fulfilled the prophecies of Hebrew scripture only spiritually; Koresh was now divinely called to do so literally. The commune at Mount Carmel began to take on "cultic" characteristics reminiscent of some of the radical sects, like that in Münster in Germany, which had broken out in the heyday of the Radical Reformation in the early sixteenth century. Koresh married a number of teenaged girls and fathered several children by them, and the group began to aim at complete economic self-sufficiency, isolating itself from the outside world and stockpiling guns and ammunition. Koresh, who had an extremely detailed knowledge of scripture, maintained that the prophecies concerning the seven seals in Revelation 6–8 were now being acted out in the world and that only he possessed the key to the true meaning of these prophecies and their unfolding.

As word of activities in the compound began to spread, the FBI began to take an interest. Reports that children were being abused led to an escalation of concern, and a siege by heavily armed agents resulted after several agents were killed when they attempted to enter the compound to search for illegal firearms in February of 1993. Negotiations with Koresh, who maintained that he needed more time to complete his prophetic exegesis of Revelation, took place for several weeks while the government forces intensified psychological pressure on his followers. Finally, an assault approved by Attorney General Janet Reno was launched on 19 April, which resulted in eighty-six deaths, including that of Koresh.

Four years later, shortly before Easter in 1997, media reports of a similar incident began to reach the American people. This time, however, the thirty-nine deaths reported at Rancho Santa Fe, California, were self-inflicted; not only was the government uninvolved but scarcely anyone outside the Heaven's Gate community had known anything about the group whose mass suicide now attracted national attention. The leader of Heaven's Gate was Marshall Herff Applewhite, a former choir director who, with his deceased partner Bonnie Lu Trusdale Nettles, had been received by their followers as teachers like Jesus who would die and soon be resurrected. Applewhite and Nettles, also known as "Bo" and "Peep," identified themselves as the two lamp stands mentioned in the eleventh chapter of the Book of Revelation. Even though the movement had a specific reference to Christian apocalypticism, its theology also drew, in New Age fashion, on a variety of other sources, including Asian religions, spiritualism, astrology, and science fiction.

Beginning in 1975, when the pair had begun to gather recruits in Oregon, the movement eventually settled into communal life in a rented house in Rancho Santa Fe where, after Nettles's death, Applewhite and his followers supported themselves by designing Web sites and lived an idiosyncratic lifestyle featuring communal property ownership, androgynous clothing, celibacy and, in some cases, self-castration. In 1992 Applewhite issued a "Last Call," predicting the imminent end of the world. In 1997 the Heaven's Gate group became convinced that a spaceship was waiting for them in the wake of the Hale-Bopp comet then illuminating the sky. With packed flight bags by their sides, all those in residence hastened their departure into the next realm of being by ingesting a lethal mixture of food and drugs.

Jonestown, Waco, and Heaven's Gate shared some dramatic similarities and attracted a great deal of media coverage and public attention. It is difficult, however, to generalize about three events separated in time and space and sharing little ideologically except an often tangential concern with prophecies based on Christian apocalyptic. Roots of such movements can be found in the nineteenth-century wave of communitarian enthusiasm of antebellum days, as well as more proximately in the similar outburst of "Hippie" experiments with communal living during the heyday of the 1960s counterculture. The flourishing of various religious cults in the 1970s provided another analogue, although many of those were based in Asian religious traditions. The ideologies of these three groups differed greatly, drawing variously on Marxist social thought, Adventist theology, and eclectic bits of religious and popular cultural fragments in the New Age manner, respectively. Collectively, they perhaps demonstrate that the last quarter of the twentieth century was a time of social and religious unsettlement, when a vast variety of theological and ideological options were readily available, à la the Internet, to most Americans, and social controls were sufficiently weakened to allow the formation of new communities based on teaching and practice that most Americans would regard as radical and alien. They certainly demonstrate the perennial fascination with the theme of the interruption of history by a dramatic intrusion into the temporal order, whatever the origins of that intrusion, and the accompanying hope that we are not trapped by the present order of things.

On the other hand, these three episodes, however dramatic and unsettling, were brief, self-contained, and involved only a relative handful of people. To read too much into them would probably be a mistake. What is clear, though, is that the currents of popular religion, whether evangelical, New Age, or even the broader media-disseminated popular culture, remain strong in the American imagination. To be sure, institutionalized religion has always been strong in American life, from the colonial establishments to today's denominations. In counterpoint with it, though, has been a continual effervescent process in which the social diversity and legal freedoms of American life have permitted a continual free-market competition between the traditional options and any number of new movements, whether imported from abroad or arisen full-blown on American soil. Mormonism, Christian Science, pentecostalism, and Adventism have been notable as domestic movements that have been successful enough to routinize into denominations. Others, such as the Oneida and Shaker communities and the Father Divine Peace Mission Movement, eventually ran out of steam, and sooner or later lapsed into nonexistence or a radically transformed character. Evangelicalism and harmonialism, though, have both been protean, broad-based, loosely defined presences in the American scene since the colonial era, and have over the centuries continued to provide the cultural rudiments through which new movements have been fashioned and refashioned over and over again. The two together may be seen as constituting an often opposed and contradictory but perhaps more fundamentally complementary seedbed of American popular religious culture.

Conclusion:
Culture Wars and Great Awakenings

Writing in the early 1970s, the late Sydney Ahlstrom concluded his monumental *A Religious History of the American People* with the assertion that an era—"The Puritan Epoch"—was coming to an end amidst the ferment of the civil rights revolution, the "counter culture," the turmoil generated by American participation in a costly and unpopular war, and other signs that the confidence and idealism that had heretofore characterized the American people were coming to an end. More broadly, Ahlstrom believed that this era, which had begun with Calvinistic religious ferment in Elizabethan England, had come to a symbolic end with the election of John F. Kennedy in 1960 as the nation's first Roman Catholic president.

In many ways Ahlstrom was correct in sensing that the 1960s were a major turning point in American life, religious and otherwise. Kennedy's election did indeed put an end to anti-Catholicism as a factor in politics; ironically John Kerry, the next Catholic to be nominated for the presidency, was attacked by leaders of his own church as not being sufficiently Catholic. The vice presidential candidacy of Senator Joseph Lieberman in 2000, though unsuccessful, was singularly marked by an absence of public anti-Semitic expression. At this writing in 2008, an African American is a leading candidate for the Democratic presidential nomination, and two have served as Secretary of State. How long it will take before a Buddhist, Hindu, or Muslim—religious affiliations with scant representation in the nation at the time Ahlstrom wrote—becomes such a contender remains to be seen.

The most important thing that Ahlstrom was unable to foresee from his own vantage point in our history—a point that this writer shared as his teaching assistant during the troubled year, 1969–70—was the resilience of the Puritan strain in American religion and culture. Major newsmagazines declared 1976 the "Year of the Evangelical," a phenomenon that no sane person would have dared predict only a few years earlier. That this resurgence of conservative Protestantism would continue for three decades, affecting not only the religious but also the political, social, and cultural aspects of American life in profound ways, remains in many ways astounding.

The benefit of historical hindsight may help to diminish that astonishment. The evangelical resurgence of recent decades was, quite literally, unpredictable, but it is certainly not inexplicable, for reasons that Ahlstrom would rapidly acknowledge. In the remainder of this concluding essay, I would like to argue that the components that have contributed to this resurgence should be, for the most part, very familiar to anyone acquainted with the broader patterns of American religious and cultural development. What have been novel, and therefore unpredictable, are the particular historical circumstances in which they have been so successfully resurrected and reassembled in our own day. In particular, I want to focus not on evangelical Protestantism as a specifically religious tradition, but rather on the alliance of parts of that community—especially its fundamentalist wing—with advocacy groups such as the Moral Majority, the Christian Coalition, and Focus on the Family, as well as with the leadership of the Republican Party, to form the Religious Right. It is this religio-political phenomenon's remarkable success that exemplifies the enduring continuity of a distinctively American interaction of religion, politics, and culture traceable back to our earliest beginnings as a New World society. In what follows, I will use the terms *militant evangelicalism* when referring to nineteenth-century and early twentieth-century Protestant social militancy; *fundamentalism* for the period from the 1920s to the 1950s; and *Religious Right* when discussing similar, more recent blendings of conservative religion and politics. In doing so, however, I am not referring to the significant numbers of Christians who today identify with the term *evangelical* but reject or are indifferent to the political agenda of the Right.

Sydney Ahlstrom saw the origins of a distinctively American religious culture in the Puritan colonies of seventeenth-century New England. Although he has been criticized for neglecting other sources, such as the Enlightenment, his fundamental insight seems in retrospect to have been sound. First, the New England Puritan leadership took its cues from Calvin's Geneva in their premise that earthly society is founded on divine law—more specifically, the Law entrusted by Yahweh to Moses and the Hebrew people in the form of a divine covenant as expressed, in one enduring form, in the Decalogue, or Ten Commandments. The persistence of a movement to enshrine the Decalogue in monumental form in public places has led to a number of episodes in the latter-day "culture wars"; its adherents have not been deterred by a series of adverse court decisions, such as the Supreme Court's 2003 removal of Alabama's Chief Justice Roy Moore when he defied the higher court's order to desist.

A similar example of the pervasive role that religion played in the public sphere in Puritan times was in the realm of education. Beginning at least with the Massachusetts Bay Colony's "Old Deluder Satan" law of 1647, public policy required that all towns of a certain size maintain schools for the inculcation on literacy, in this case to make Scripture accessible and thereby counteract the Devil's ability to exploit ignorance. Although the rationale for public education changed periodically in later centuries, the notion that such education is necessary for the public moral good, as well as good order, has persisted over the centuries as well.

Another relevant aspect of the early New England Puritan regimes was the influential role clergy played in their society. Though Christian ministers were barred from holding civic office, they nevertheless participated actively in shaping public opinion through their pulpits. One particularly important example of this role was one of their number's being called on to address the assembled electorate in Boston each spring, when colonial officials were chosen by the public. The resultant genre of sermons, dubbed "jeremiads" by historian Perry Miller, established a potent and enduring vehicle through which clergy and morally-minded laity alike might rehearse the terms of the covenant, the recent grievous offenses by the populace against it, and the well-deserved punishments visited upon them by an offended God, together with a call to repentance and action. The jeremiad is based on the nearly universal mythic theme that the time of origin is the time of greatest purity, and that inevitable declension from this purity over time must be periodically acknowledged and purity restored. Numerous public addresses by clergy such as Jerry Falwell and Pat Robertson as well as their political allies, such as sometime House Majority Leader Tom Delay, are classic examples of the jeremiad form in only mildly modernized dress.

The Great Awakening revivals of the 1740s constituted another step in the development of a distinctively American style of religious and civic interaction. At one level, the sermons of George Whitefield and his imitators were spiritual in content, aimed at bringing about individual conversions rather than social change. At a deeper level, however, these revivals, conducted often against the opposition of the local "settled" clergy of a variety of denominations, were subversive, calling into question the criteria that for centuries had conferred legitimacy on the clergy. Formal education and church and civil law now were challenged in the name of the direct calling of the Holy Spirit. By this standard, "settled" parish clergy had to demonstrate anew their worthiness to hold office, and the centuries-old alliance between Church and civil society manifested in the "parish"—simultaneously a religious and political entity—was now threatened by "itinerants" (preachers on the move) who refused to recognize the understandings that the parish system embodied. What was being played out here was an illustration of the perennial religious theme of *communitas*: the disruption of established social structure by new, effervescent forces creating a new experience of community in the midst of an old order that was no longer sufficiently backed by charismatic power to command universal acknowledgement of its legitimacy.

Thus simultaneously arose two closely related forces in American Christianity—evangelical Protestantism and, to coin a phrase with the same initials, entrepreneurial prophecy. Protestant clergy from now on would have to depend on personal charisma rather than institutional legitimacy if they were to keep a hold on their increasingly independent-minded followers.

The Revolutionary era that followed the Great Awakening aroused the support of many clergy, especially those of Reformed lineage, who revived the engines of historical interpretation that had cast the Puritan enterprise in a providential light. King George became the new Pharaoh, whereas George Washington was cast as a latter-day Moses by many preachers. Following the revolution, and especially after his death, Washington ascended to cult status in the "civil religion" that began to develop around the New Republic. "Parson" Mason Weems, an Episcopal clergyman turned author and itinerant bookseller, published in 1800 the first edition of his *Life of Washington,* which would enjoy enormous popularity over the ensuing decades in its various versions. Weems embroidered freely on the basic narrative facts of the first president's life. Among these was the notorious "cherry tree" story, in which young George declared himself incapable of prevarication, as well as ill-documented legends of Washington's piety later in his career. The cult of Washington continued in numerous other forms, as illustrated in the depiction of his apotheosis—his triumphant ascent into heaven—in the dome of the Rotunda of the nation's Capitol in Washington, D.C. Here again appears the exaltation of the time of origins, with Cotton Mather's depiction of John Winthrop as an American Nehemiah replayed with Washington as the founder chosen by the gods.

Washington, in fact, appears to have been a rather conventional Episcopalian, sharing the Deist sentiments of his fellow "Founding Fathers" and rarely if ever taking Communion. Franklin and Jefferson, of course, went much further, openly expressing skepticism as to the claims of Christianity to any significant truth beyond those it shared with other religions, which were knowable to reason unaided by revelation. Though appreciative of the social benefits of organized religion—Franklin contributed to the support of a wide range of Philadelphia churches, although seldom attending any—these men qualified that endorsement with the caveat that the political power of such religion had to be kept within bounds to avoid such catastrophes as the Catholic-Bourbon alliance in France. These highly constricted expressions of religiosity, however, have been frequently represented—in the discourse of the Religious Right, most recently—as manifestations of evangelical piety and affirmations of religious expression in the public sphere.

The practice of circulating apocryphal stories—*exempla*—that made moral points but were based on little, if any, reliable sources has a long history. In a time when critical historiography insists on the distinction between historical narrative and moral fable, however, the practice becomes more questionable. Although virtually all recent American presidents can be faulted for the telling of what Mark Twain might have called "stretchers," Ronald Reagan was particularly fond of such exemplary stories, such as that of the "Chicago welfare queen" with eighty names, thirty addresses, and twelve Social Security cards, who had allegedly collected over $150,000 from the government. Although the prototype for this story had actually used two aliases and collected $8000, Reagan continued to retell it even after being repeatedly corrected. Similarly, Reagan liked to claim that if a criminal carried a gun in England, he would be tried for first-degree murder and hung if found guilty, even if he had never used it. Reagan's spokesman Larry Speakes commented that "It's a good story, though. It made the point, didn't it?" The point here is not to cast aspersions on Reagan's veracity, but rather to underline his reliance on a fabulistic, morally-laden story-telling mode with a long American lineage.

The foundational documents of the new republic—not surprisingly, given the cast of mind of their authors—brought new challenges to traditional practices of religious establishment, beyond those raised earlier by the Great Awakening. Most dramatic of these was the First Amendment to the Constitution of the new nation in 1791, which definitively put to an end any possibility of an established church in America, and simultaneously forbade any interference with freedom of religious belief and, to a considerable extent, religious action. The implications of this profound piece of fundamental legislation for organized religious forces were enormous, especially for those still dependent psychologically as well as financially on the state support that had characterized many colonial arrangements.

This new and revolutionary turn in church-state relations was based both on ideological grounds, such as Enlightened distrust of religious establishments, but also on the growing importance of pluralism as a fundamental fact in an emergent and distinctively American way of life. Whereas many of the colonies were fairly homogenous in ethnic stock, others, like Pennsylvania, were not. Even in those that were, religious diversity existed, born partly in immigration and also in the fissiparous nature of Protestant Christianity itself. Like it or not, diversity—ethnic, religious, cultural—was there for the long haul.

Not everyone did like it. The Second Great Awakening, especially in its northeastern manifestations, and its institutional offspring, the "Benevolent Empire" of the 1820s, were attempts by the contemporary religious establishment to counteract the effects both of de facto and de jure pluralism on their desires for cultural and religious hegemony. In the course of these campaigns, a rhetoric began to emerge from the pulpits of evangelical leaders such as Ezra Stiles and Lyman Beecher, which aimed at the creation of a sense of "culture war" between their followers and their opponents, real and imagined. The French Revolution and the Catholic Church were among their major putative antagonists and a distinct sense of the virtuous "we" versus the corrupt and menacing "they" became a fixture of the now militantly evangelical rhetoric of the day. These rhetorical strategies are vividly exemplified in a sermon by Ezra Stiles, the president of Yale, delivered in New Haven in 1801. After thoroughly denouncing the French Revolution and its American admirers for its role in promoting infidelity, Stiles goes on to appeal to the sensibilities of his own constituency:

> There can be no halting between two opinions. You must marshal yourselves, finally, in your own defense, and in the defense of all that is dear to you. You must meet face to

face the bands of disorder, of falsehood, and of sin. Will you teach your children that death is an eternal sleep? That the end sanctifies the means? That moral obligation is a dream? Religion a farce? And your Saviour the spurious offspring of pollution? Will you send your daughters abroad in the attire of a female Greek? . . . Will you make marriage the mockery of a registers' office?

You are endeared by a thousand ties. Your common country is a land of milk and honey; in it a thousand churches are vocal with the praise of your Creator; and four thousand schools receive your children to their bosom, and nurse them to wisdom and piety. In this country you all sprang from one stock, speak one language, have one system of manners, profess one religion, and wear one character. Your laws, your institutions, your interests, are one. No mixture weakens, no strangers divide, you. You have fought and bled, your fathers have fought and died, together.

Let me at the same time warn you, that your enemies are numerous, industrious, and daring, full of subtlety and full of zeal. Were it a war of arms, you would have little to dread. It is a war of arts; of temptations; of enchantments; a war against the magicians of Egypt, in which no weapons will avail, but "the rod of God."

The work of the "Benevolent Empire" that grew out of this campaign to preserve the youth of Connecticut, and the American people more broadly, was based on many of the premises contained in Stiles' address. Not only was it imperative to spread the Christian message in regions such as the American West, which lacked churches and clergy, but it was also necessary to defend it against the legion of enemies that seemed to lurk around every corner, whether in the form of a Jefferson or a Jesuit. Christians were not engaged only in a campaign of expansion, but in a warlike crusade—a Christian jihad—against foes of different sorts. The goal was the creation of what historian Robert Handy has called "a Christian America," with religion nominally disestablished but with militant evangelicals taking advantage of the new competitive ethos to ensure that Christian beliefs and practices would become so pervasive as to constitute an informal hegemony.

The campaign launched by the two dozen or so national agencies of the "Empire" included the distribution of Bibles and religious tracts; ministries to marginalized populations, such as sailors, prostitutes, and native peoples; moral reform, such as the promotion of temperance and the abolition of dueling; and lobbying against offensive governmental practices, such as delivery of mail on the Sabbath. The latter is a particularly good instance of the incipient notion that the implications of church-state separation needed to be tested, especially in liminal situations where the line between secular public goods and religious purposes was murky.

Both the rhetoric and the strategy of these militant evangelical reformers developed into further forms, still easily recognizable today. An attack began to mount against a variety of putative opponents of "Christian America." These foes included Roman Catholics, a perennial favorite of evangelicals; Southern slaveholders; and the newly minted and quintessentially American movement, the Latter-day Saints, or

Mormons. The historian David Brion Davis, in his classic 1960 essay, "Some Themes of Countersubversion," argued that all three of these communities were attacked both as subversive of "traditional American values" in their antidemocratic practices and also in the sexual immorality—exploitation of slaves, nuns, and plural wives—that accompanied them. The uncritical nationalism, the circulation of undocumented atrocity stories, and the formation of undemocratic "countersubversive" secret societies that characterized these movements have, of course, carried over into the twentieth century and beyond in campaigns against domestic Communism and in the various crusades of the later Religious Right.

Another tactic with great staying power was the effort of the abolitionists led by Theodore Dwight Weld in the 1830s to lobby Congress to take up debate over the "peculiar institution" to the end, of course, of abolishing it. Although many militant evangelical reformers found this particular cause too radical for their tastes, the strategy of arousing public opinion at the grass roots and galvanizing local, church-based support into a national campaign to influence legislation was successfully employed in many subsequent campaigns for moral reform. Coupled with the direct-mail tactics employed by the Religious Right since the 1970s (and imitated by other causes across the political spectrum as well), it has been a potent means of raising funds and shaping political agendas.

The dominant crusade for moral reform in the decades following the Civil War was waged in the name of temperance, which by that time had morphed from an emphasis on voluntary abstinence from alcohol into a campaign for governmental prohibition of the manufacture and sale of intoxicants. Prohibition was by no means the exclusive preserve of militant evangelicals, but was also backed by many secular Progressives who saw it as a valuable means of combating poverty, corruption, and other social ills that had resulted from rapid urbanization and large-scale immigration. The rhetoric of the Women's Christian Temperance Union (WCTU), however, included an emphasis on moral purity that went beyond public-minded social reform. One of the main perceived (and, most likely, genuine) threats of the corner saloon was the hardship it brought to women and children whose husbands' and fathers' health and earning capacities were endangered by alcoholism. The presentation of the home as the morally pure realm of women and children vulnerable to the onslaughts of the corrupt world of business and politics—coupled with the phenomenon of activist women such as Carrie Nation and Frances Willard—introduced a set of themes into the militant evangelical repertoire that would be revived in the reaction against feminism exemplified in the rhetoric of (Roman Catholic) Phyllis Schlafly and her Eagle Forum (1972), a major component of the latter-day Religious Right's alliance. The paradox here, of course, is that the women leading these campaigns were thrusting themselves into the same external world from which they were arguing that women needed to be sequestered.

The emergence of fundamentalism as a distinct movement in the late nineteenth and early twentieth centuries laid much of the explicitly religious groundwork for later activist religious conservatism. Dwight L. Moody's evangelism was not overtly political, although the enthusiastic support by contemporary business magnates indicated his potential value as a bulwark of the status quo. Billy Sunday's more strident revivalism in the early decades of the twentieth century was more openly partisan, including nativist denunciations of Germany as the source of beer and biblical criticism, support for laissez-faire capitalism, and a ringing jeremiad-like call for a newly invigorated old-stock Protestant American populace to regain their rightful control over their lives and their nation through moral purity and physical toughness.

In the public sphere, however, it was the Scopes "Monkey" Trial of 1925 that most clearly illustrated the issues confronting traditional evangelicalism in its struggle to maintain hegemonic control over a rapidly changing nation. Since the Civil War, the South, though forced to abandon slavery, had nevertheless maintained traditional racial barriers and the myth of a pure white race through its system of Jim Crow laws. This arrangement was complemented by an emphasis on moral purity advocated by the militantly evangelical churches that exercised dominance over the middle and working classes of most of the region. Not surprisingly, it was the Southern states that were most likely to resist actively such inroads of modernism as Darwinian evolution. An equally activist American Civil Liberties Union (ACLU), based in New York City, challenged the Tennessee law that forbade the teaching of Darwinian evolution in its public schools, and fought to a legal draw that reinforced the position of each side in its respective region of cultural dominance.

The entrance of William Jennings Bryan into the Scopes proceedings was a major event in the definition of "culture war" issues that has had a lasting impact in this realm. Bryan was a three-time presidential nominee of both the Democratic and the short-lived Populist Party, campaigning on behalf of the farmers and small-town dwellers of the Midwest and South who felt themselves victimized by the impersonal and exploitative manipulation of the financial powers of the Northeast. That Bryan identified himself both with Populism and fundamentalism is an important development in the story of the affinities between the two movements. *Populism* may be defined as an ideology that exalts the moral superiority of the average, productive citizen and the consequent claim of that citizen to political dominance. The average citizen—who later morphs into the "middle American," part of the "silent" or "moral" majority—stands in contrast with the parasitic upper and lower classes, who derive their livings from unearned wealth or exploitation on the one hand or from servile work or welfare on the other. During the nineteenth century the populist impulse—manifested transiently at century's end in the short-lived Peoples' Party— was primarily political and economic in character, gaining force as an emergent nationally integrated market economy, based on finance capitalism, was seen to be marginalizing the social standing of the industrious "middling classes" whose heroes were Jackson, Lincoln, and, ultimately, Bryan.

Bryan's populism was at first economic—exemplified in his enormously popular "Cross of Gold" speech of 1896—and mixed with a Progressivist support of Prohibition. In his later years however, he became strongly identified with the fundamentalist wing of the northern Presbyterian Church, which was struggling with liberals for denominational control. His ill-advised volunteering as an expert witness on the Bible for the prosecution of the Scopes Trial was not simply based on strictly religious issues, however. In his many speeches on the issues surrounding Scopes, he stressed two in particular: the relationship of moral authority represented by Scripture to the maintenance of social order, and the right of the majority to determine matters of cultural policy. He was thus giving expression to a popular resentment, especially strong in the rural South and Midwest, against the rights of alleged "experts"—who would later become the "pointy-headed intellectuals" of George Wallace and the "nattering nabobs" of Spiro Agnew—to determine what should be taught to children in the public schools in areas where the religiously informed "common sense" of the "average person" carried greater moral weight than the theories of cosmopolitan, secular professionals.

The "culture wars" of the 1920s were resolved regionally rather than nationally, and were soon overshadowed by the more urgent questions of national policy raised by the Depression and World War II. During the 1950s, however, a new set of symbolic issues linking religion with the social and political orders began to emerge. Communism, of course, was the most potent symbol of both internal and external menace to the republic, and was frequently portrayed—in language Ezra Stiles would have recognized, and might have crafted—as subtle, insidious, deceptively attractive, and morally corrosive. And, in good countersubversive manner, fears of Soviet aggression were augmented by widespread suspicions that the "godless Communists" of Russia were being abetted by their domestic American allies, such as Julius and Ethel Rosenberg and their many, frequently more elusive comrades.

Two of the most visible religious personalities of the era utilized this symbolism in skillful combination with the enhanced means of mass communication that television now offered. Fulton Sheen, the Roman Catholic auxiliary bishop of New York, often focused on the "Communist menace," contrasting its atheistic ideology unfavorably with that of Catholicism, and pointing out the apocalyptic possibilities that nuclear weapons now presented. Billy Graham used his fundamentalist platform to aim more pointed jeremiads at the American public, and drew on the doctrine of Dispensational Premillennialism, in parallel with Sheen's Marian piety, to give a theological twist to popular fears of a nuclear apocalypse. Neither was overtly political in his public stances at the time, but the rhetoric of both fostered a Manichean we-they division of the world into good and evil spheres and an association between American nationalism and Christian morality lacking the nuance of their contemporary, Reinhold Niebuhr. In addition, the visibility of American Catholic leaders in the realm of public and political morality foreshadowed the not-too-distant day when evangelicals and Catholics would become once-unthinkable allies in the context of the Religious Right.

The momentum of the Civil Rights Movement and the charisma of the liberal and Catholic president John F. Kennedy lent to the early 1960s an aura of progressive momentum. As the decade progressed, however, a number of forces converged that soon led to cultural polarization and backlash. The growing unpopularity of the war in Southeast Asia, fuelled by a military draft that affected affluent and vocal youth as well as their poorer, less articulate counterparts; Southern resentment against the Civil Rights acts of mid-decade, abetted by working-class urban fears in the North of the dismantling of racial boundaries; a "counterculture" that flaunted traditional middle-class fears involving consciousness-altering drugs (other than alcohol), exotic religions, sexual expressiveness, the work ethic, and a general sense of cultural decorum; all combined to create a growing gulf between complex constituencies divided by region, religion, class, and culture. The accumulated resentments of working-class Christian white voters in both North and South were addressed first by Alabama governor and presidential candidate George Wallace, with modest results. Soon, however, Richard Nixon and a Republican Party struggling to escape from the ideological and political disaster of the 1964 defeat of Barry Goldwater by Lyndon Johnson, as well as Nixon's own political humiliations during his turbulent career, were to employ this same neo-Populist rhetoric with much greater success.

The 1970s was a decade when it became possible for a Religious Right to take shape that could combine the opportunities of the present with a centuries-old vocabulary of theological and moral rhetoric and a panoply of organizational and communication skills. Jimmy Carter's successful candidacy in 1976 was in part a reaction against the squalor of the Watergate scandals, as well as Carter's own cultivated image as a "squeaky-clean" Southern evangelical who was also politically moderate. Carter's own political failings and misfortunes, however, left him vulnerable to a growing movement that at first welcomed his thrusting of evangelicalism—albeit his own moderate version—into the national scene in a positive light.

The emergence of Ronald Reagan as a national political force coincided with the eclipse of President Carter's own fortunes. The mid-seventies also were ripe for the blossoming of regional fundamentalist leaders such as Jerry Falwell and Pat Robertson, both of Virginia, into national prominence. Falwell, Robertson, and others helped fashion the network of organizations, beginning with Falwell's Moral Majority of 1979, that would coalesce into the movement known as the (New) Religious Right.

The New Religious Right was the collective heir to the entire panoply of issues and strategies we have traced from Puritan New England through the Great Awakenings to the present. Among these are the following:

> Entrepreneurial evangelical or fundamentalist clergy, largely independent of
>   denominational supervision, who set out not only to found new and often
>   very large congregations—today's giant exurban "megachurches"—but to

establish themselves as public interpreters of morality and promoters of political action.

The revival of the jeremiad sermonic form to denounce collective moral transgressions, link them with putative signs of social decay, and call for a revival of "traditional" Christian values and beliefs as an antidote. These sermons differ from their Hebrew prototypes, however, in primarily denouncing sins against moral purity—modern analogues to the holiness codes of Leviticus—rather than the ethical offenses on which the original Jeremiah focused.

An idealization of various eras and aspects of earlier American culture—including the "Founding Fathers," McGuffey's *Readers,* and the decade of the 1950s—as morally normative markers against which we can measure latter-day declension.

A proclivity for defining and demonizing enemies, such as "Communists" and "secular humanists," as potentially subversive of a morally pure American Christian civilization.

The polarization of the American population into mutually exclusive camps based on their religious and cultural identifications.

A similar bifurcation of the world into "good" or "bad" based on their affinities for American-style religiously infused democratic values and practices.

A rejection of "exotic" religions such as Islam, but a new willingness to collaborate with like-minded American allies such as conservative Catholics and secular Neo-Conservatives, sometimes of Jewish or African American background.

A moral endorsement of the free market and laissez-faire capitalism as social corollaries of religiously validated individualism and self-reliance.

A preoccupation with issues of sexual morality, focusing on abortion and gay marriage, while skirting the more prevalent issue of divorce.

Reaffirmation of traditional gender roles, exemplified in policy statements by the Southern Baptist Convention, as well as the primacy of the nuclear family in determining the nurture of children.

A focus on education as an area in which "traditional values" are particularly endangered, with a resultant

Militancy in influencing local public educational policies, especially regarding issues such as sex education and evolution, and

The promotion of alternatives to public education, especially "Christian" schools and homeschooling.

A harsh and punitive attitude towards crime, especially drug- and sexually related offenses, and strong support for capital punishment.

Continued espousal of Dispensational Premillennialism, but in a form open to the forestalling of an apocalyptic consummation through the rechristianization of America.

Skillful and extensive use of television, radio, the Internet, and direct mailing
   to attract a public following and raise funds.
An activist role in local and national politics, including the endorsement of
   sympathetic candidates, dissemination of informational materials on candidates and issues, and the mounting of organized efforts to bring likely voters
   to the polls at election time.

All of these themes, in one form or another, have appeared in early phases of
American history. The most important novelty that today's Religious Right represents is its explicit alliance with a particular political party, the Republican Party.
The presidency of George W. Bush (2001–9) especially illustrates—both in successful electoral strategies and in subsequent presidential rhetoric—the success
the movement has had in shaping American public life. What remains unsettled,
as of this writing, is whether such key policy concerns as the prohibition of gay
marriage, the repeal of *Roe v. Wade,* and the displacement of evolution's centrality
in the school curriculum by alternatives such as Creationism or Intelligent Design
will ultimately prevail. (The latter seems the most doubtful of these in light of recent
court decisions.)

From this survey of the development of a distinctively American alliance of militant evangelical religion and cultural politics, it should be apparent that the major
themes of American history, broadly defined and identified in this work's introduction, all become apparent in this selective but highly representative swatch of the
nation's religious composition.

The reality of both geographical and social mobility from the beginnings of the
Euro-American presence in the colonies and the new nation, combined with the
ideologies of the Reformed strain of Protestant Christianity, destabilized the possibilities of recreating the more stratified social orders of Europe, about which the
new arrivals generally demonstrated considerable ambivalence. The result was the
undermining of the parochial principle—the notion that an educated and settled
clergy ought to preside over discrete areas of settlement in a church that demanded
compulsory membership. The erosion of the hegemony of the established churches
ensued as entrepreneurial "free-agent" clergy such as George Whitefield challenged
their rights to deference on spiritual grounds. The continuing mobility of Americans
from older areas of settlement into twenty-first century "exurbs" in pursuit of the
suburban dream today provides a ready clientele for freelance clergy, untrammeled
by requirements of advanced education or denominational endorsement, willing to
undertake new "plantings" that may grow into megachurches.

From the *Arbella* to the Hart-Cellar Act, the immigration that has been the main
engine of population growth has continually resulted not only in increase but in
conflict and a resultant nativism and xenophobia that has persisted from the Revolutionary era to the present in various guises. (The "freedom fries" served in the

national Capitol in protest against France's refusal to join in the American invasion of Iraq in 2003 recalled Ezra Stiles's hostility to the French revolution during the Second Great Awakening.) Ironically, many contemporary Americans whose ancestors experienced discrimination upon their arrival now share in an ideology that suspects the foreign-born as alien "others" rather than as potential productive citizens.

The temporal and political priority of *British culture* in the pattern of Euro-American settlement has, as demonstrated in Ezra Stiles' rhetoric, fed into a myth of Anglo-Saxon superiority, manifested today in the "English only" movement. Although the Religious Right today is far less ethnocentric than some of its ideological forebears, the privileging of an evangelicalism of Anglo-American lineage has obvious affinities with the practice of identifying "we" with English language and culture.

Although slavery and its offspring, "Jim Crow" laws, have disappeared as legally sanctioned institutions, *race* has nevertheless played a significant factor in the development of the Religious Right. To be sure, some African Americans such as Supreme Court justice Clarence Thomas have associated themselves with that movement, and few leaders of the Right continue to espouse overtly racist attitudes, regardless of their earlier histories. Nevertheless, the primary geographical source and contemporary locus of the contemporary Religious Right is the South, which underwent a startling transformation following the Civil Rights Movement and the ensuing federal legislation that resulted in the rapid dismantling of institutionalized segregation. For generations Southern culture had been characterized by an evangelical hegemony in the realm of religion and racial segregation as distinctive features of its social arrangements. The former had for decades directly or indirectly reinforced the latter, arguing either that the church should concern itself with personal morality rather than social reform, or that racial segregation could be justified on biblical grounds. The rapid formation of "Christian academies" throughout much of the South after the end of public school segregation in the mid-1960s was motivated in part by an evangelical revulsion against the secular ethos of those schools, but the timing suggests a correlation with contemporary racial rearrangements. Although there is an overlap in attitudes between black and white evangelicals today in the realm of issues such as homosexuality, the two religious communities are characterized more by their separation than their political and social commonalities.

Earlier historians have argued that one of the most important characteristics of a distinctively American form of religion, Protestant or otherwise, has been the impact of a *democratic ideology* and practice that have their origins as much in Puritan congregationalism as in Enlightenment ideals. To be sure, Jews and Catholics have, together with Lutherans, Anglicans, and other Protestant denominations with more hierarchical lineages, embraced the notion of congregational responsibility and influence, if not autonomy, in practice if not in theory. Nevertheless, it has been evangelical Protestants who have been particularly enabled by their congregational forms of polity to respond vigorously to the challenges of a religiously destabilized society, and to develop tactics, from George Whitefield through Charles Finney to Rick Warren, that have made possible new "plantings" in entrepreneurial fashion.

Although *populism* is in many ways an offshoot of democratic ideology, it goes against the grain of democracy in some important ways. Although populism exalts "the people," its definition of that entity is rather restrictive, limiting its scope frequently, in practice, to middle-class white Christians. And, although populism is ostensibly the enemy of elitism, it frequently generates its own elite in the form of religious and/or political leaders who invite their followers to entrust them with the formulation of rhetoric and policies that the followers are expected to endorse and promote uncritically. This has certainly been the case with the contemporary Religious Right, where leaders of megachurches are often regarded by their congregations with adulation.

Although the First Amendment and its state-level adaptations have made *pluralism* the law of the land from the beginnings of the Republic, the Religious Right and its antecedents have never been fully comfortable with its implications. Phases of the Second Great Awakening were aimed at achieving a de facto establishment of militant evangelicalism. That aim has continued intermittently in the campaigns for Prohibition and, more recently, in crusades against abortion and gay marriage on the one hand and for the reintroduction of prayer and other religious themes into the public sphere, especially the schools. The result has been a continuing public dialogue on the respective roles of a religious and cultural majority (or at least plurality) versus the rights and interests of dissenters, including "mainline" Christians, religious minority groups, and secularists. The Supreme Court, the final arbiter of these disputes, has to date attempted to steer a careful course in which a certain zone for generic religious expression in the public sphere—military chaplains, prayers in Congress, display of religious symbols in public places when appropriately contextualized—is permitted, whereas anything constituting government endorsement of or support for particular religious groups is prohibited.

One of the main transformations of the populist sensibility in the United States from its heyday in the age of Bryan to the present has been the displacement of a critique of *capitalism* by symbolic issues. Bryan's cause grew out of a perceived gulf that had arisen within the American economy and society between those who produced wealth and those who reaped its rewards, that is, between workers and capitalists. This sense of injustice, however, was usually tempered in the American context by an ideology of individual self-sufficiency, fortified by the "Protestant ethic," which taught that hard work—an expression of moral rightness—would inevitably lead to worldly success. That it was becoming increasingly difficult for the unaided individual to succeed in a world dominated by massive corporations in both the public and private spheres tended to produce a sense of cognitive dissonance resulting in denial, and helps to account for the continuing lack of receptivity of Americans to socialist approaches to economic organization. The success of the leadership of both the Religious Right and the Republican Party in displacing economic self-interest with symbolic and religious issues has been one of the most dramatic changes in the history of both Populism and militant evangelicalism in American history.

The affinities between militant evangelicalism and *nationalism* in the form of "American Exceptionalism" date back to Puritan New England, in which the entire legitimacy of the political and social order was based on providential election. During the nineteenth century, the notion of a similar providential guidance of the Republic in the form of "manifest destiny" was highly congenial to a postmillennial evangelical agenda, in which the nation was the primary locus of God's progressive victories over the forces of evil. Both world wars evoked broad support from most the nation's religious communities, but were not the particular cause of fundamentalists.

The alliance between patriotic nationalism and the Religious Right was most definitively forged during the early Cold War years, when Communism emerged as a symbolic enemy of apocalyptic proportions. The interpretive engines of Dispensational Premillennialism were singularly suited for this new crusade, and they were reinforced, at a safe distance, by Catholic Marian apocalypticism and McCarthyite zeal. The Vietnam War reinforced this alliance, with many Catholic ethnics joining conservative Protestants in their alienation from "hippies" and burners of flags, draft cards and, at least in legend, brassieres. With the collapse of the Soviet Union and its alliances, the euphoria generated by the ideological victory of America and its allies gave way to the dilemma of how the moral and metaphysical opposition—"the other"—was to be represented by the Religious Right. Earlier attempts at casting domestic "secular humanism" as the villain had met with mixed success. The horror and fear engendered by the melancholy events now known universally as "9/11" filled the vacuum with the specter of militant Islam, which was easily extended in the popular imagination to the entire Muslim population and its religion, as well as to other Asians and their completely unrelated traditions. This anger and insecurity, coupled with continued insistence on the priority of "moral values," helped ensure George W. Bush's defeat in 2004 of a liberal Catholic Democrat less skilled in the manipulation of symbols.

In one sense, the militant evangelical/Religious Right strain in American religious and political life can be interpreted as a vehicle for the *Americanization* of newcomers. When it has not opposed the further inclusion of immigrants of other than Western European Protestant origin, it has been a force urging their conformity to the norms of the dominant culture it has sought to fashion. Whereas German-speaking beer drinkers were once the "other," Protestants—and, eventually, Catholics—of German descent and Americanized demeanor eventually became perfectly acceptable American citizens.

On the other hand, it can be argued that militant evangelicalism is itself a product of distinctively American circumstances, and thus can be understood as a distinctive, even unique, form of religious organization and expression. It has been remarkably adept at accepting the reverses it has periodically experienced—from its disestablishment in New England in the early republic to the failure of Prohibition in the 1920s to later Supreme Court decisions legalizing abortion and prohibiting school prayer—and to turn them into opportunities for reorganizing and crafting a new rhetoric of moral victory and restoration. Its disestablished and entrepreneurial character has proven a continuing source of vigor, and possible reversals in the future should not be readily interpreted as signs of ultimate defeat or irrelevance.

———————

Sydney Ahlstrom concluded his 1973 magnum opus on two distinct notes, each intentionally in tension with the other. On the one hand, he cautioned against using the past to gain a clear reading of the future, since historically-generated expectations have a way of becoming rapidly confounded. Given that possibility—indeed, the probability—of the unexpected's occurring, he expressed a hope that "future interpreters will see increasing evidence that the American people, in their moral and religious history, were drawing on the profounder elements of their traditions, finding new sources of strength and confidence, and thus vindicating the idealism which has been so fundamental in the country's past." Though this optimistic note was the one on which he chose to end, he prefaced it with the more lugubrious observation that "[a]s the American people moved towards the bicentennial of the nation's independence, they could see few living signs of the self-confidence and optimism that had marked the centennial observations of 1876, and even less of the revolutionary generation's bold assurance. Still more attenuated was the Puritan's firm conviction that America had a divine commission in the world. The nation's organic connections with the sources of its idealism and hope were withered."

A third of a century of additional historical experience does not make it easy to think that Ahlstrom's assessment of the ethos of our own time would differ greatly from the cold eye he cast on his own. The notion of a republic based on divine law, protected by divine providence, and dedicated to the execution of the divine will, lives on in politically potent form, but at the cost of the exclusion and alienation of the larger portion of the American people. Crusades to roll back public policy on abortion and school prayer have met with limited success and face uncertain futures, although the polarization they generate is unlikely to subside in the near future. American attempts to intervene in unsettled and threatening foreign situations have proven fruitless in Vietnam and parts of Africa, and the possibilities of future successes in nation building in the Middle East seem equally doubtful. Even dramatic social transformations, such as those brought about by the civil rights and women's movements, have led to vexing contemporary questions—how to end systemic poverty in urban ghettoes? how to stabilize families unsettled by divorce? how to combine a demanding career with a demanding family?—that do not invite easy solutions.

America, and the world, have entered into a new century in which neither apocalyptic cataclysm nor irrepressible social progress seems likely. The collapse of the Soviet Union and its potential for nuclear confrontation has, to be sure, brought about dramatic transformations in parts of Europe. On the other hand, the monolithic and hostile Soviet presence has given way to a much more complicated and intractable challenge in the emergence of an anarchic, diffuse, and militant Islamism that has successfully "othered" America as its "Great Satan." The globalization of a "high-tech" economy based on services rather than labor-intensive manufacturing has benefited many in this country and elsewhere, but has also destabilized a considerable part of a national economy unable to respond quickly and effectively to rapidly changing circumstances.

The Religious Right appeals to many who are caught in this confusion of broad, dimly understood forces whose import for the future of most Americans is ambiguous. We are unlikely, collectively, to experience again the traumas of worldwide war or economic depression. On the other hand, we are equally unlikely to achieve the millennial kingdom within any foreseeable future. Neither triumph nor disaster is within our realm of reasonable expectation. What are we—given that there is an actual, as opposed to a merely imagined, American "we"—to do?

America's past does offer some resources for hope. Our nation can best be understood not as an essence, but as a process. That process involves a dialectic between the vision of one people united by a common self-understanding and sense of purpose, and a competing vision of a noisy, colorful, creative congeries of peoples of all sorts and conditions united by a common democratic polity. Neither vision is wholly accurate, but both have been essential components in the nation's ability not only to survive but to thrive. Inclusion into the national body as full members of this diversity of newcomers and moral consensus on vexing issues such as race have emerged, but at a high cost, including that of civil war.

It is difficult now to imagine an America in which blacks were held as property and women barred from voting. What now seems like common sense, a shared moral vision, was, a century or two ago, anything but that. It is equally possible to imagine that, several generations from now, the legal prohibition of gay marriage may seem as antiquated as laws forbidding miscegenation do today. Or not. The question is, how do we get to whatever that future moral consensus may be?

One way not to arrive at a moral consensus is through the persistence of mythical thinking about national issues, at the expense of a pragmatic confrontation with actual social, economic, and historical realities. The United States has had a remarkable and in some ways a unique history among modern nations, but it has certainly not been an example of unalloyed success either domestically or abroad. Internationally, our nation set a noble example of self-sacrifice in rallying to defeat a genuine Axis of Evil during World War II, and similarly exerted far-reaching wisdom in helping rebuild Europe through the Marshall Plan. Since then, however, as political reality has become more and more confusing and intractable, efforts to intervene on the side of the angels have had ironic consequences similar to those resulting from our intervention in an earlier world war. We seem to be recapitulating the career of John Barth's fictional Ebenezer Cooke who, in *The Sot-Weed Factor,* wrought havoc throughout colonial Maryland by intervening in situations he only dimly understood and generally made matters worse than they had been beforehand. The doctrine of American Exceptionalism, rooted in Puritan notions of Providence, has all too often given rise to the temptations of prideful self-interest, resulting in far more disasters than successes in the realm of foreign policy.

Similarly, in the domestic realm, many Americans have been captivated by a self-interpretation in which the illusion of self-determination and moral purity has taken the place of a level-eyed pursuit both of enlightened self-interest and altruistic justice. In following the will-o'-the-wisp of countersubversion narratives, we have too often been led to overlook the actual evils growing out of a social and economic system that do not automatically lead to the best of possible worlds. Since the emergence of a market-based economy, Americans have especially been susceptible to the tendency to attribute individual failure not to imbalances of power inherent in an underregulated economic system, but rather in conspiracies to undermine the national moral fiber.

The American tradition does offer resources for addressing the propensities of Americans to see themselves as an on-going third testament of Scripture, recapitulating or reinventing the narratives of ancient Israel and the apostolic church as they careen through contemporary history. Abraham Lincoln, in his second inaugural address, wisely refused to read the Civil War as a simple struggle of Northern good versus Southern evil. He instead confronted the seeming paradox that both sides read the same Bible and prayed to the same God, and yet the war had come. Instead, he saw that God's purposes are not the same as those of his human creation, and that humans seek to equate their wills and understandings of historical responsibility with God's only at their own peril. On the other hand, Lincoln did not conclude that the only possibility lay in blind submission to an inexorably ordained fate. Rather, the national task was to proceed "with firmness in the right, as God gives us to see the right," and to forgo retribution in favor of reconciliation.

In a later century, Reinhold Niebuhr spoke to the crises of his own time in similar language. In his 1952 classic, *The Irony of American History,* Niebuhr inserted a note of sanity into the often extravagant rhetoric of the Cold War by reminding Americans that, as bad as many of the ideologically prompted actions of the Soviet Union had been, Americans continued to make their own mistakes by pridefully equating their own motivations with God's. The result was irony in the classical Greek sense: unintended consequences arising from a lack of awareness of underlying self-interested motives as well as from willful ignorance of the complexities of a given situation. On the whole, wrote Niebuhr, American values were far better than those of our opponents, and deserved to prevail. If they did not prevail, though, the fault would more probably be due to American willfulness than the wiles of the enemy. As Lincoln knew, action is always necessary, but must always be taken with humility, lest we overreach and learn painfully the limits of our own power, wisdom, and goodness.

Bibliography

The following is a comprehensive but hardly exhaustive selection from the vast scholarship in the study of American religion, which has proliferated especially during the past two decades. Instead of corresponding directly to each chapter in the text, it is organized according to clusters of topics, paralleling in many cases the scheme outlined in the "Topical Guide to Chapters." Most sections include references to Charles H. Lippy and Peter W. Williams, eds., *Encyclopedia of the American Religious Experience,* 3 vols. (New York: Scribner, 1988) (hereafter *EARE*); the pages cited pertain to specific chapters, each of which includes lengthy bibliographical sections in which readers will find more extensive references to work of the mid-1980s. CQ Press is scheduled to publish a new *Encyclopedia of American Religion,* with the same editors, in 2010.

What follows is a combination of selected works—mostly books—of the following sorts: classic studies of particular topics; recent scholarship of high quality; bibliographies, anthologies, and reference works; scholarly works alluded to in the narrative and/or works on which portions of the narrative are based; and works on special topics such as music (including a few recordings), architecture, and popular culture. Except in a few cases I have tried to avoid multiple listings of titles, and have generally listed books only under the tradition to which they are most directly related: for example, a book on Catholic women would appear under Roman Catholicism. Works not focused on a specific tradition are generally found under Categories A–D. Many subtitles have been omitted in the interest of brevity and are included only when necessary to identify a work's contents. Primary works cited in the narrative are not usually included; data on current editions can best be located in a Web-based listing such as Amazon.com.

Since this bibliography is very long as it is, I have decided not to even attempt to include periodical literature except for a small number of important articles. The best print sources for current information on religion in the United States are the *New York Times* and the *Christian Century*. For scholarly articles, the best general periodical sources are *Church History* (comprehensive for the history of Christianity); *Material Religion*; *Religion and American*

Culture (historical and topical articles on religion in the United States); and the *William and Mary Quarterly* (colonial period, including religion). Many denominations also publish historical journals, including *American Presbyterians, Anglican and Episcopal History, Catholic Historical Review,* and *Methodist History.*

The bibliography is organized as follows:

A. American Religion: Surveys and Overviews
B. American Religion: Reference Works and Collections
C. Church, State, Society, and Civil Religion
D. Religion and American Culture
    1. Aesthetics
    2. Architecture and Sacred Space
    3. Death and Burial
    4. Economics
    5. Education
    6. Film, Sports, and Popular Culture
    7. Food and Drink
    8. Fraternal and Youth Movements
    9. Holidays
    10. Literature, Journalism, and the Printed Word
    11. Material Culture
    12. Medicine and Healing
    13. Music
    14. Nature and Science
    15. Painting and the Visual Arts
    16. Regionalism
    17. Sexuality and Gender
    18. Spirituality and Religious Experience
    19. Theology and Intellectual History
E. Religion in Early America
F. Native American Religions (including Christian Missions)
G. African, Afro-Caribbean, and African American Religions
H. Judaism
I. Eastern Christianity
J. Roman Catholicism
K. Protestantism and the Reformation Era
L. Luther and the Lutheran Tradition
M. Anglicanism and the Episcopal Church
N. The Reformed Tradition
    1. Calvin and Calvinism
    2. The Reformed Faith in Britain
    3. Britain and America: General
    4. New England Puritanism
    5. Presbyterianism

In some cases, most notably concerning women and American religion, I have chosen to integrate titles into the whole rather than to establish a separate category. For example, works dealing with religion and race are included in G. (African American Religions) or other appropriate categories.

A. American Religion: Surveys and Overviews

Ahlstrom, Sydney E., with David D. Hall. *A Religious History of the American People*. 1972. New Haven, Conn.: Yale University Press, 2004.

Albanese, Catherine L. *America: Religions and Religion*. Belmont, Calif.: Wadsworth, 1981, 1992.

Allitt, Patrick. *Religion in America since 1945: A History*. New York: Columbia University Press, 2003.

Becker, Penny Edgell, and Nancy L. Eiesland, eds. *Contemporary American Religion: An Ethnographic Reader*. Walnut Creek, Calif.: AltaMira, 1997.

Brekus, Catherine A., ed. *The Religious History of American Women*. Chapel Hill: University of North Carolina Press, 2007.

Butler, Jon, Grant Wacker, and Randall Balmer. *Religion in American Life: A Short History*. New York: Oxford University Press, 2003.

Butler, Jon, and Harry S. Stout, eds. *Religion in American History: A Reader*. New York: Oxford University Press, 1998.

Dolan, Jay P., and James P. Wind, eds. *New Dimensions in American Religious History*. Grand Rapids, Mich.: Eerdmans, 1993.

Fox, Richard Wightman. *Jesus in America*. San Francisco: HarperSanFrancisco, 2004.

Gaustad, Edwin S., and Leigh E. Schmidt. *A Religious History of America*. Rev. ed. San Francisco: HarperSanFrancisco, 2002.

Hall, David D., ed. *Lived Religion in America*. Princeton, N.J.: Princeton University Press, 1997.

Handy, Robert T. *A History of the Churches in the United States and Canada*. New York: Oxford University Press, c. 1976.

Holifield, E. Brooks. *God's Ambassadors: A History of the Christian Clergy in America*. Grand Rapids, Mich.: Eerdmans, 2007.

———. *Theology in America: Christian Thought from the Age of the Puritans to the Civil War*. New Haven: Yale University Press, 2003.

Hudson, Winthrop S., and John Corrigan. *Religion in America*. 6th ed. New York: Pearson, 1999.

Hutchison, William R. *Religious Pluralism in America*. New Haven: Yale University Press, 2003.

Juster, Susan, and Lisa MacFarlane, eds. *A Mighty Baptism: Race, Gender, and the Creation of American Protestantism*. Ithaca, N.Y.: Cornell University Press, 1996.

Krabbendam, Hans, and Derek Rubin, eds. *Religion in America: European and American Perspectives*. Amsterdam: VU University Press, 2004.

Lindley, Susan Hill. *"You Have Stept Out of Your Place:" A History of Women and Religion in America*. Louisville, Ky.: Westminster John Knox, 1996.

Lippy, Charles H. *Being Religious, American Style*. Westport, Conn.: Greenwood, 1994.

Maffly-Kipp, Laurie F., Leigh E. Schmidt, and Mark Valeri, eds. *Practicing Protestants: Histories of Christian Life in America, 1630–1965*. Baltimore, Md.: Johns Hopkins University Press, 2006.

Marty, Martin E., ed. *Modern American Protestantism and Its World: Historical Articles on*

Protestantism and American Life. 14 vols. Munich: K. G. Sauer, 1992–93. Each volume is a collection of articles on a specific topic, such as "Women and Women's Issues" or "Protestantism and Social Christianity."

———. *Pilgrims in Their Own Land: 500 Years of Religion in America.* Boston: Little Brown, 1984.

McDannell, Colleen, ed. *Religions of the United States in Practice.* Princeton, N.J.: Princeton University Press, 2001.

Mead, Sidney E. *The Lively Experiment.* New York: Harper and Row, 1963.

Moore, R. Laurence. *Religious Outsiders and the Making of Americans.* New York: Oxford University Press, 1986.

Orsi, Robert A., ed. *Gods of the City: Religion and the American Urban Landscape.* Bloomington: Indiana University Press, 1999.

Noll, Mark A. *A History of Christianity in the United States and Canada.* Grand Rapids, Mich.: Eerdmans, 1992.

———. *The Old Religion in a New World: The History of North American Christianity.* Grand Rapids, Mich.: Eerdmans, 2002.

Stout, Harry S., and D. G. Hart, eds. *New Directions in American Religious History.* New York: Oxford University Press, 1997.

Tweed, Thomas A., ed. *Retelling U.S. Religious History.* Berkeley: University of California Press, 1997.

Williams, Peter W., ed. *Perspectives on American Religion and Culture.* Oxford: Blackwell, 1999.

———. *Popular Religion in America.* 2d ed. Urbana: University of Illinois Press, 1989.

Wilson, John F. *Religion and the American Nation: Historiography and History.* Athens: University of Georgia Press, 2003.

Wind, James P., and James W. Lewis, eds. *American Congregations.* 2 vols. Chicago: University of Chicago Press, 1994.

B. American Religion: Reference Works and Collections

Albanese, Catherine L., ed. *American Spiritualities: A Reader.* Bloomington: Indiana University Press, 2001.

Bass, Dorothy C., and Sandra Hughes Boyd, eds. *Women in American Religious History: An Annotated Bibliography and Guide to the Sources.* Boston: G. K. Hall, 1987.

Bowden, Henry Warner. *Church History in an Age of Uncertainty: Historiographical Patterns in the United States, 1906–1990.* Carbondale: Southern Illinois University Press, 1991.

———. *Dictionary of American Religious Biography.* 2d ed. Westport, Conn.: Greenwood, 1993.

———. "The Historiography of American Religion." *EARE* 1:3–16.

Burr, Nelson R. *A Critical Bibliography of Religion in America.* 2 vols. Princeton, N.J.: Princeton University Press, 1961. Annotated bibliography.

Carroll, Bret E. *The Routledge Historical Atlas of Religion in America.* New York: Routledge, 2000.

Cayton, Mary Kupiec, and Peter W. Williams, eds. *Encyclopedia of American Cultural and Intellectual History.* New York: Scribners, 2001.

Fackler, P. Mark, and Charles H. Lippy, eds. *Popular Religious Magazines of the United States.* Westport, Conn.: Greenwood, 1995.

Gaustad, Edwin Scott. *A Documentary History of Religion in America.* 2 vols. Grand Rapids, Mich.: Eerdmans, 1982, 1983.

———. "Geography and Demography of American Religion." *EARE* 1:71–84.

———. *Historical Atlas of Religion in America.* Rev. ed. New York: Harper and Row, 1976.

Gaustad, Edwin Scott, and Philip L. Barlow. *New Historical Atlas of Religion in America.* New York: Oxford University Press, 2000.

Goff, Philip, and Paul Harvey, eds. *Themes in Religion and American Culture.* Chapel Hill: University of North Carolina Press, 2004.

Griffith, R. Marie, ed. *American Religions: A Documentary History.* New York: Oxford University Press, 2007.

Halvorson, Peter L., and William M. Newman. *Atlas of Religious Change in America.* Washington, D.C.: Glenmary, 1978.

Harvey, Paul, and Philip Goff, eds. *The Columbia Documentary History of Religion in America Since 1945.* New York: Columbia University Press, 2005.

Keller, Rosemary Skinner, and Rosemary Radford Ruether, eds. *Encyclopedia of Women and Religion in North America.* Bloomington: Indiana University Press, 2006.

Kosmin, Barry A., and Seymour P. Lachman. *One Nation under God: Religion in Contemporary American Society.* New York: Harmony Books, 1993. Statistics.

Laderman, Gary, and Luis Leon, eds. *Religion and American Cultures: An Encyclopedia of Traditions, Diversity, and Popular Expressions.* 2 vols. Santa Barbara: ABC-CLIO, 2003.

Lippy, Charles H. *Modern American Popular Religion: A Critical Assessment and Annotated Bibliography.* Westport, Conn.: Greenwood, 1996.

———, ed. *Religious Periodicals of the United States: Academic and Scholarly Journals.* New York: Greenwood, 1986.

———, ed. *Twentieth-Century Shapers of American Popular Religion.* New York: Greenwood, 1989.

Lippy, Charles H., and Peter W. Williams, eds. *Encyclopedia of the American Religious Experience.* 3 vols. New York: Scribners, 1988.

Mathisen, Robert R. *Critical Issues in American Religious History: A Reader.* Waco, Tex.: Baylor University Press, 2001.

Mead, Frank S. *Handbook of Denominations in the United States.* Nashville. Published every fifth year.

Melton, J. Gordon. The *Encyclopedia of American Religions.* 3d ed. Detroit: Wayne State University Press, 1989, and supplements.

National Council of Churches. *Yearbook of the American and Canadian Churches.* Nashville. Annual.

Newman, William M., and Peter L. Halvorson. *Atlas of American Religion: The Denominational Era, 1776–1990.* Walnut Creek, Calif.: AltaMira, 1999.

Piepkorn, Arthur C. *The Religious Bodies of the United States and Canada.* 4 vols. New York: Harper and Row, 1977, 1978, 1979.

Routledge. *The Religion Resource*. Collection of 29 reference works related to religion. New York: Routledge. www.reference.routledge.com. Restricted access.

Ruether, Rosemary Radford, and Rosemary Skinner Keller, eds. *In Our Own Voices: Four Centuries of American Women's Religious Writing*. San Francisco: Harper, 1995.

———. *Women and Religion in America*. 3 vols. San Francisco: Harper, 1981, 1983, 1986.

Shriver, George H., ed. *Dictionary of Heresy Trials in American Christianity*. Westport, Conn.: Greenwood, 1997.

Shriver, George H., and Bill J. Leonard, eds. *Encyclopedia of Religious Controversies in the United States*. Westport, Conn.: Greenwood, 1997.

Smith, H. Shelton, Robert T. Handy, Lefferts A. Loetscher, eds. *American Christianity: An Historical Interpretation with Representative Documents*. 2 vols. New York: Scribners, 1960.

Toulouse, Mark G., and James O. Duke, eds. *Sources of Christian Theology in America*. Nashville: Abingdon, 1999.

Turley, David, ed. *American Religion: Literary Sources and Documents*. 3 vols. New York: Routledge, 1997.

Williams, Peter W., ed. *Perspectives on American Religion and Culture*. Oxford: Blackwell, 1999.

Young, Arthur P., and E. Jens Holley, eds. *Religion and the American Experience, the Twentieth Century: A Bibliography of Doctoral Dissertations*. Westport, Conn.: Greenwood, 1994.

C. Church, State, Society, and Civil Religion
(*SEE ALSO* E. Religion in Early America and S.5. Reform, Antislavery, the Civil War, and Reconstruction)

Adams, David K., and Cornelis A. van Minnen, eds. *Religious and Secular Reform in America*. New York: New York University Press, 1999.

Ammerman, Nancy Tatom, and Wade Clark Roof, eds. *Work, Family, and Religion in Contemporary Society*. New York: Routledge, 1995.

Baker, James T., ed. *Religion in America: Primary Sources in U.S. History*. 2 vols. Belmont, Calif.: Wadsworth, 2006.

Bellah, Robert. *American Civil Religion in Time of Trial*. 2d ed. Chicago: University of Chicago Press, 1992.

Bellah, Robert, et al. *Habits of the Heart*. Berkeley: University of California Press, 1985.

Beneke, Chris. *Beyond Toleration: The Religious Origins of American Pluralism*. New York: Oxford University Press, 2006.

Blumhofer, Edith L., ed. *Religion, Politics, and the American Experience*. Tuscaloosa: University of Alabama Press, 2002.

Browning, Don S., and David A. Clairmont, eds. *American Religions and the Family*. New York: Columbia University Press, 2006.

Budd, Richard. *Serving Two Masters: the Development of the American Military Chaplaincy 1860–1920*. Lincoln: University of Nebraska Press, 2002.

Carter, Stephen L. *The Culture of Disbelief*. New York: Basic Books, 1993.

———. *God's Name in Vain: The Wrongs and Rights of Religion in Politics*. New York: Basic Books, 2000.

Chaves, Mark. *Congregations in America*. Cambridge, Mass.: Harvard University Press, 2004.

Cherry, Conrad, ed. *God's New Israel.* Rev. ed. Chapel Hill: University of North Carolina Press, 1998.

Cookson, Catharine. *Regulating Religion: The Courts and the Free Exercise Clause.* New York: Oxford University Press, 2001.

Crawford, Sue E. S., and Laura R. Olson, eds. *Christian Clergy in American Politics.* Baltimore: Johns Hopkins University Press, 2001.

Davis, Derek H., and Barry Hankins. *New Religious Movements and Religious Liberty in America.* Waco, Tex.: J. M. Dawson Institute of Church-State Studies/Baylor University Press, 2002.

Delfattore, Joan. *The Fourth R: Conflicts over Religion in America's Public Schools.* New Haven: Yale University Press, 2004.

Demerath, N. J., III, Peter Dobkin Hall, Terry Schmitt, and Rhys H. Williams, eds. *Sacred Companies: Organizational Aspects of Religion and Religious Aspects of Organizations.* New York: Oxford University Press, 1998.

Diamond, Etan. *Souls of the City: Religion and the Search for Community in Postwar America.* Bloomington: Indiana University Press, 2003.

Engeman, Thomas S., and Michael P. Zuckert, eds. *Protestantism and the American Founding.* Notre Dame, Ind.: University of Notre Dame Press, 2004.

Evans, Bette Novit. *Interpreting the Free Exercise of Religion: The Constitution and American Pluralism.* Chapel Hill: University of North Carolina Press, 1997.

Fransley, Arthur E. II, et al. *Sacred Circles, Public Squares: The Multicentering of American Religion.* Bloomington: Indiana University Press, 2004.

Fessenden, Tracy, "The Nineteenth-Century Bible Wars and the Separation of Church and State." *Church History* 74, no. 4 (Dec. 2005): 784–811.

Flowers, Ronald B. *To Defend the Constitution: Religion, Conscientious Objection, Naturalization, and the Supreme Court.* Lanham, Md.: Scarecrow, 2003.

Fuechtmann, Thomas G. *Steeples and Stacks: Religion and Steel Crisis in Youngstown.* Cambridge: Cambridge University Press, 1989.

Fuller, Robert. *Naming the Antichrist.* New York: Oxford University Press, 1995.

Garber, Marjorie, and Rebecca L. Walkowitz, eds. *One Nation under God?: Religion and American Culture.* New York: Routledge, 1999.

Greenawalt, Kent. *Does God Belong in Public Schools?* Princeton, N.J.: Princeton University Press, 2007.

———. Religion and the Constitution. 2 vols. Princeton, N.J.: Princeton University Press, 2006, 2008.

Haddad, Yvonne Yazbeck, Jane I. Smith, John L. Espisito, eds. *Religion and Immigration: Christian, Jewish, and Muslim Experiences in the United States.* Walnut Creek, Cal.: AltaMira, 2003.

Hamburger, Philip. *Separation of Church and State.* Cambridge, Mass.: Harvard University Press, 2002.

Hammond, Phillip E. *Religion and Personal Autonomy: The Third Disestablishment in America.* Columbia: University of South Carolina Press, 1992.

———. *With Liberty for All: Freedom of Religion in the United States.* Louisville, Ky.: Westminster/John Knox, 1998.

Handy, Robert T. *Undermined Establishment: Church-State Relations in America.* Princeton, N.J.: Princeton University Press, 1991.

Hanson, Charles P. *Necessary Virtue: The Pragmatic Origins of Religious Liberty in New England.* Charlottesville: University Press of Virginia, 1998.

Hatch, Nathan O., and George M. Marsden. *The Search for Christian America.* Westchester, Ill.: Helmers and Howard, 1983.

Herberg, Will. *Protestant, Catholic, Jew.* Garden City, N.Y.: Doubleday, 1955.

Hollinger, David A., "The 'Secularization' Question in the United States in the Twentieth Century." *Church History* 70, no. 1 (Mar. 2001): 132–43.

Hughes, Richard T. *Myths America Lives By.* Urbana: University of Illinois Press, 2004.

Hulsether, Mark. *Religion, Culture, and Politics in the Twentieth-Century United States.* New York: Columbia University Press, 2007.

Hutchison, William R. *Religious Pluralism in America.* New Haven: Yale University Press, 2003.

Jones, Donald G. "Civil and Public Religion." *EARE* 3:1393–1408.

Kessler, Sanford. *Tocqueville's Civil Religion: American Christianity and the Prospects for Freedom.* Albany: State University Press of New York, 1994.

Kirby, Dianne, ed. *Religion and the Cold War.* New York: Palgrave Macmillan, 2003.

Kniss, Fred, and Paul D. Numrich. *Sacred Assemblies and Civic Engagement: How Religion Matters for America's Newest Immigrants.* New Brunswick, N.J.: Rutgers University Press, 2007.

Lambert, Frank. *Religion in American Politics.* Princeton, N.J.: Princeton University Press, 2008.

Layman, Geoffrey. *The Great Divide: Religious and Cultural Conflict in American Party Politics.* New York: Columbia University Press, 2001.

Lee, Francis Graham. *Church-State Relations.* Westport, Conn.: Greenwood, 2002.

Lenski, Gerhard E. *The Religious Factor: A Sociological Study of Religion's Impact on Politics, Economics, and Family Life.* Garden City, N.Y.: Doubleday, 1961.

Lieven, Anatol. *America Right or Wrong: An Anatomy of American Nationalism.* New York: Oxford University Press, 2004.

Livezey, Lowell W., ed. *Public Religion and Urban Transformation.* New York: New York University Press, 2000.

Marty, Martin E. *The One and the Many: America's Struggle for the Common Good.* Cambridge, Mass.: Harvard University Press, 1997.

———. *Politics, Religion, and the Common Good.* San Francisco: Jossey-Bass Publishers, 2000.

———. *Religion and Republic.* Boston: Beacon, 1987.

McCloud, Sean. *Divine Hierarchies: Class in American Religion and Religious Studies.* Chapel Hill: University of North Carolina Press, 2007.

McGarvie, Mark Douglas. *One Nation Under Law: America's Early National Struggles to Separate Church and State.* DeKalb: Northern Illinois University Press, 2005.

McGraw, Barbara A., and Jo Renee Formicola, eds. *Taking Religious Pluralism Seriously: Spiritual Politics on America's Sacred Ground.* Waco, Tex.: Baylor University Press, 2005.

Maxwell, Carol. *Pro-life Activists in America.* New York: Cambridge University Press, 2002.

Mazur, Eric Michael. *The Americanization of Religious Minorities: Confronting the Constitutional Order.* Baltimore: Johns Hopkins University Press, 1999.

Meyer, Jeffrey. *Myths in Stone: Religious Dimensions of Washington, D.C.* Berkeley: University of California Press, 2001.

Miller, Glenn. "Church and State." *EARE* 3:1369–93.

Miller, Robert T., and Ronald B. Flowers. *Toward Benevolent Neutrality: Church, State, and the Supreme Court.* Waco, Tex.: Baylor University Press, 1987.

Morone, James A. *Hellfire Nation: The Politics of Sin in American History.* New Haven: Yale University Press, 2003.

Niebuhr, H. Richard. *The Social Sources of Denominationalism.* 1929. Reprint, New York: Meridian Books, 1957.

Noll, Mark A. *Religion and American Politics.* New York: Oxford University Press, 1990.

Noonan, John T., Jr., *The Lustre of Our Country: The American Experience of Religious Freedom.* Berkeley: University of California Press, 1998.

Nord, Warren A. *Religion and American Education: Rethinking a National Dilemma.* Chapel Hill: University of North Carolina Press, 1995.

Pelikan, Jaroslav. *Interpreting the Bible and the Constitution.* New Haven: Yale University Press, 2004.

Perlmutter, Philip. *Legacy of Hate: A Short History of Ethnic, Religious, and Racial Prejudice in America.* Armonk, N.Y.: M. E. Sharpe, 1999.

Peters, Shawn Francis. *The Yoder Case: Religious Freedom, Education, and Parental Rights.* Lawrence: University of Kansas, 2003.

Prothero, Stephen, ed. *A Nation of Religions: The Politics of Pluralism in Multireligious America.* Chapel Hill: University of North Carolina Press, 2006.

Richey, E. Russell, and Donald G. Jones, eds. *American Civil Religion.* New York: Mellen, 1974.

Rosenblum, Nancy R. *Obligations of Citizenship and Demands of Faith: Religious Accommodation in Pluralist Democracies.* Princeton, N.J.: Princeton University Press, 2000.

Ross, William G. *Forging New Freedoms: Nativism, Education, and the Constitution, 1917–1927.* Lincoln: University of Nebraska Press, 1994.

Rozell, Mark J., and Gleaves Whitney, eds. *Religion and the American Presidency.* New York: Palgrave Macmillan, 2007.

Sarna, Jonathan D., ed. *Minority Faiths and the American Protestant Mainstream.* Urbana: University of Illinois Press, 1998.

Schmidt, Frederick W., Jr. *A Still, Small Voice: Women, Ordination, and the Church.* Syracuse, N.Y.: Syracuse University Press, 1996.

Semonche, John E. *Keeping the Faith: A Cultural History of the U.S. Supreme Court.* Lanham, Md.: Rowman and Littlefield, 1998.

Sheffer, Martin S. *God versus Caesar: Belief, Worship, and Proselytizing under the First Amendment.* Albany: State University of New York Press, 1999.

Sittser, Gerald L. *A Cautious Patriotism: The American Churches and the Second World War.* Chapel Hill: University of North Carolina Press, 1997.

Smith, Christian, ed., *The Secular Revolution: Power, Interests, and Conflict in the Secularization of American Public Life.* Berkeley: University of California Press, 2003.

Stokes, Anson Phelps, and Leo Pfeffer. *Church and State in the United States.* New York: Harper and Row, 1964.

Sullivan, Winifred Fallers. *Paying the Words Extra: Religious Discourse in the Supreme Court of the United States.* Cambridge, Mass.: Harvard University Press, 1994.

Swanson, Wayne R. *The Christ Child Goes to Court.* Philadelphia: Temple University Press, 1990.

Swatos, William H., Jr., and James K. Wellman, Jr., eds. *The Power of Religious Publics: Staking Claims in American Society.* Westport, Conn.: Praeger, 1999.

Toulouse, Mark G. *God in Public: Four Ways American Christianity and Public Life Relate.* Louisville: Westminster John Knox, 2006.

Viteritti, Jospeh P. *The Last Freedom: Religion from the Public School to the Public Square.* Princeton, N.J.: Princeton University Press, 2007.

Wills, Garry. *Under God: Religion and American Politics.* New York: Simon and Schuster, 1990.

Wilson, John. *Religion in American Society.* Englewood Cliffs, N.J.: Prentice-Hall, 1978.

———. "Sociological Study of American Religion." *EARE* 1:17–30.

Wilson, John F., ed. *Church and State in America: A Bibliographical Guide: The Civil War to the Present Day.* New York: Greenwood, 1987.

———. *Public Religion in American Culture.* Philadelphia: Temple University Press, 1979.

Wilson, John F., and Donald L. Drakeman, eds. *Church and State in American History.* 2d ed. Boston: Beacon, 1987.

Wolfe, Alan. *The Transformation of American Religion.* New York: Free Press, 2003.

Wuthnow, Robert. *After the Baby Boomers: How Twenty- and Thirty-Somethings Are Shaping the Future of American Religion.* Princeton, N.J.: Princeton University Press, 2007.

———. *America and the Challenges of Religious Diversity.* Princeton, N.J.: Princeton University Press, 2007.

———. *The Restructuring of American Religion: Society and Faith since World War II.* Princeton, N.J.: Princeton University Press, 1988.

———. *The Struggle for America's Soul: Evangelicals, Liberals, and Secularism.* Grand Rapids, Mich.: Eerdmans, 1989.

D. Religion and American Culture

1. AESTHETICS

Brown, Frank Burch. *Good Taste, Bad Taste, and Christian Taste.* London: Oxford University Press, 2000.

Lapsansky, Emma Jones. *Quaker Aesthetics: Reflections on a Quaker Ethic in American Design and Consumption.* Philadelphia: University of Pennsylvania Press, 2003.

2. ARCHITECTURE AND SACRED SPACE (NOTE: OTHER RELEVANT TITLES ARE INCLUDED IN SECTIONS ON INDIVIDUAL TRADITIONS BELOW.)

Beal, Timothy K. *Roadside Religion.* Boston: Beacon, 2005.

Bruggink, Donald J., and Carl H. Droppers. *Christ and Architecture: Building Presbyterian/Reformed Churches.* Grand Rapids, Mich.: Eerdmans, 1965.

Buggeln, Gretchen T. *Temples of Grace: The Material Transformation of Connecticut's Churches, 1790–1840.* Hanover, Conn.: University Press of New England, 2003.

Chidester, David, and Edward T. Linenthal, eds. *American Sacred Space.* Bloomington: Indiana University Press, 1995.

Curran, Kathleen. *The Romanesque Revival.* University Park: Penn State University Press, 2003.

DeSanctis, Michael E. *Building from Belief: Advance, Retreat, and Compromise in the Remaking of Catholic Church Architecture.* Collegeville, Minn.: Liturgical Press, 2002.

Dodds, Jerrilyn D. *New York Masjid: The Mosques of New York City.* New York: PowerHouse Books, 2002.

Ivey, Paul Eli. *Prayers in Stone: Christian Science Architecture in the United States, 1894–1930.* Urbana: University of Illinois Press, 1999.

Kaufman, David. *Shul with a Pool: The Synagogue-Center in American Jewish History.* Hanover, N.H.: Brandeis University Press/University Press of New England, 1999.

Kieckhefer, Richard. *Theology in Stone: Church Architecture from Byzantium to Berkeley.* New York: Oxford University Press, 2004.

Kilde, Jeanne Halgren. *When Church Became Theatre: The Transformation of Evangelical Architecture and Worship in Nineteenth-Century America.* New York: Oxford University Press, 2002.

Lane, Belden. *Landscapes of the Sacred: Geography and Narrative in American Spirituality.* Baltimore: Johns Hopkins University Press, 2002.

Linenthal, Edward Tabor. *Sacred Ground: Americans and Their Battlefields.* Urbana: University of Illinois Press, 1991.

Loveland, Anne C., and Otis B. Wheeler. *From Meetinghouse to Megachurch.* Columbia: University of Missouri Press, 2003.

Nelson, Louis P., ed. *American Sanctuary: Understanding Sacred Spaces.* Bloomington: Indiana University Press, 2006.

———. *Beauty of Holiness: Anglicanism and Architecture in Colonial South Carolina.* Chapel Hill: University of North Carolina Press, 2009.

———. "The Rediscovery of American Sacred Spaces." Essay review. *Religious Studies Review* 30, no. 4 (Oct. 2004): 251–57.

Rankin, Tom. *Sacred Space: Photographs from the Mississippi Delta.* Jackson: University Press of Mississippi, 1993.

Sears, John F. *Sacred Places: American Tourist Attractions in the Nineteenth Century.* New York: Oxford University Press, 1989.

Smith, Ryan K. *Gothic Arches, Latin Crosses: Anti-Catholicism and American Church Designs in the Nineteenth Century.* Chapel Hill: University of North Carolina Press, 2006.

Vergara, Camilo José. *How the Other Half Worships.* New Brunswick, N.J.: Rutgers University Press, 2005.

White, James F. *Christian Worship in North America.* Collegeville, Minn.: Liturgical Press, 1997.

———. *Protestant Worship and Church Architecture.* New York: Oxford University Press, 1964.

Williams, Peter W. *Houses of God: Region, Religion, and Architecture in the United States.* Urbana: University of Illinois Press, 1997.

———. "Sacred Space in America." Essay review. *Journal of the American Academy of Religion* 70, no. 3 (Sept. 2002): 593–609.

3. DEATH AND BURIAL

Laderman, Gary. *Rest in Peace: A Cultural History of Death and the Funeral Home in Twentieth-Century America.* New York: Oxford University Press, 2003.

——. *The Sacred Remains: American Attitudes towards Death, 1799–1883.* New Haven: Yale University Press, 1996.

Prothero, Stephen. *Purified by Fire: A History of Cremation in America.* Berkeley: University of California Press, 2001.

4. ECONOMICS

Chaves, Mark, and Sharon L. Miller, eds. *Financing American Religion.* Walnut Creek, Calif.: AltaMira, 1998.

Eskridge, Larry, and Mark A. Noll, eds. *More Money, More Ministry: Money and Evangelicals in Recent American Culture.* Grand Rapids, Mich.: Eerdmans, 2000.

Giggie, John M., and Diane Winston, eds. *Faith in the Market: Religion and the Rise of Urban Commercial Culture.* New Brunswick, N.J.: Rutgers University Press, 2002.

Hudnut-Beumler, James. *In Pursuit of the Almighty's Dollar: A History of Money and American Protestantism.* Chapel Hill: University of North Carolina Press, 2007.

Lau, Kimberly J. *New Age Capitalism: Making Money East of Eden.* Philadelphia: University of Pennsylvania Press, 2000.

Moore, R. Laurence. *Selling God: American Religion in the Marketplace of Culture.* New York: Oxford University Press, 1994.

Noll, Mark. *God and Mammon: Protestants, Money, and the Market, 1790–1860.* Oxford: Oxford University Press, 2002.

Stoll, Mark. *Protestantism, Capitalism, and Nature in America.* Albuquerque: University of New Mexico Press, 1997.

Wuthnow, Robert, et al. *Faith and Philanthropy in America.* San Francisco: Jossey-Bass, 1990.

5. EDUCATION

Benne, Robert. *Quality with Soul: How Six Premier Colleges and Universities Keep Faith with their Religious Traditions.* Grand Rapids, Mich.: Eerdmans, 2001.

Blumhofer, Edith L., ed. *Religion, Education, and the American Experience.* Tuscaloosa: University of Alabama Press, 2002.

Cherry, Conrad. *Hurrying toward Zion: Universities, Divinity Schools, and American Protestantism.* Bloomington: Indiana University Press, 1995.

——, ed. *Religion on Campus.* Chapel Hill: University of North Carolina Press, 2001.

DelFattore, Joan. *The Fourth R: Conflicts over Religion in America's Public Schools.* New Haven, Conn.: Yale University Press, 2004.

Gaither, Milton. *Homeschool.* New York: Palgrave Macmillan, 2008.

Harrold, Philip. *A Place Somewhat Apart: The Private Worlds of a Late Nineteenth-Century Public University.* Eugene, Ore.: Pickwick, 2006.

Hart, D. G. *The University Gets Religion: Religious Studies in American Higher Education.* Baltimore: Johns Hopkins University Press, 1999.

Marsden, George M., and Bradley J. Longfield, eds. *The Secularization of the Academy.* New York: Oxford University Press, 1992.

Reuben, Julie A. *The Making of the Modern University: Intellectual Transformation and the Marginalization of Morality.* Chicago: University of Chicago Press, 1996.

Roberts, John H., and James Turner. *The Sacred and the Secular University.* Princeton: Princeton University Press, 2000.

Vásquez, Mark G. *Authority and Reform: Religious and Educational Discourses in Nineteenth-Century New England Literature.* Knoxville: University of Tennessee Press, 2003.

6. FILM, SPORTS, AND POPULAR CULTURE

(*SEE ALSO* S.13.)

Apostolidis, Paul. *Stations of the Cross: Adorno and Christian Right Radio.* Durham, N.C.: Duke University Press, 2000.

Anker, Roy M. *Self-Help and Popular Religion in Early American Culture.* Westport, Conn.: Greenwood Press, 1999

Bodner, Allen. *When Boxing Was a Jewish Sport.* Westport, Conn.: Praeger, 1997.

Burris, John P. *Exhibiting Religion: Colonialism and Spectacle at International Expositions, 1851–1893.* Charlottesville: University Press of Virginia, 2001.

Byrne, Julia. *O God of Players: The Story of the Immaculata Mighty Macs.* New York: Columbia University Press, 2003.

Chidester, David. *Authentic Fakes: Religion and American Popular Culture.* Berkeley: University of California Press, 2005.

DeChant, Dell. *The Sacred Santa: Religious Dimensions of Consumer Culture.* Cleveland: Pilgrim Press, 2002.

Forbes, Bruce David, and Jeffrey H. Mahan, eds. *Religion and Popular Culture in America.* Berkeley: University of California Press, 2000.

Forshey, Gerald E. *American Religious and Biblical Spectaculars.* Westport, Conn.: Praeger, 1992.

Goethals, Gregor T. *The Electronic Golden Calf: Images, Religion, and the Making of Meaning.* Cambridge, Mass.: Harvard University Press, 1990.

Hangen, Tona J. *Redeeming the Dial: Radio, Religion, & Popular Culture in America.* Chapel Hill: University of North Carolina Press, 2002.

Higgs, Robert J. *God in the Stadium: Sports and Religion in America.* Lexington, Ky.: University Press of Kentucky, 1995.

Hoberman, J., and Jeffrey Shandler. *Entertaining America: Jews, Movies, and Broadcasting.* Princeton, N.J.: Princeton University Press, 2003.

Kahn, Ava Fran, ed. *Jewish Voices of the California Gold Rush: A Documentary History, 1849–1880.* Detroit: Wayne State University Press, 2002.

Martin, Joel W., and Conrad E. Ostwalt, Jr., eds. *Screening the Sacred: Religion, Myth, and Ideology in American Popular Film.* Boulder, Colo.: Westview, 1995.

May, John R. *Image and Likeness: Religious Visions in American Film Classics.* New York: Paulist, 1992.

Mazur, Eric Michael, and Kate McCarthy, eds. *God Is in the Details: American Religion in Popular Culture.* New York: Routledge, 2001.

Miles, Margaret. *Seeing and Believing: Religion and Values in the Movies.* Boston: Beacon, 1996.

Mintz, Alan. *Popular Culture and the Shaping of Holocaust Memory in America.* Seattle: University of Washington Press, 2001.

Moore, L. Laurence. *Touchdown Jesus: The Mixing of Sacred and Secular in American History.* Louisville, Ky.: Westminster John Knox, 2003.

Ostwalt, Conrad Eugene. *Secular Steeples: Popular Culture and the Religious Imagination.* Harrisburg, Pa.: Trinity Press International, 2003.

Overdeck, Kathryn. *The Evangelist and the Impresario: Religion, Entertainment, and Cultural Politics in America, 1884–1914.* Baltimore: Johns Hopkins University Press, 1999.

Prothero, Stephen. *American Jesus: How the Son of God Became a National Icon.* New York: Farrar, Strauss, and Giroux, 2003.

Putney, Clifford. *Muscular Christianity: Manhood and Sports in Protestant America, 1880–1920.* Cambridge, Mass: Harvard University Press, 2000.

Reinhartz, Adele. *Scripture on the Silver Screen.* Louisville, Ky.: Westminster John Knox Press, 2003.

Remsberg, Rich. *Riders for God: The Story of a Christian Motorcycle Gang.* Urbana : University of Illinois Press, 2000.

Schultze, Quentin J. *Christianity and the Mass Media in America.* East Lansing: Michigan State University Press, 2003.

Scott, Bernard Brandon. *Hollywood Dreams and Biblical Stories.* Minneapolis: Fortress, 1994.

Stout, Daniel A., ed. *Religion and Popular Culture.* Ames, Iowa: Iowa State University Press, 2001

Walsh, Richard G. *Reading the Gospels in the Dark: Portrayals of Jesus in Film.* Harrisburg, Pa.: Trinity Press International, 2003.

Weisenfeld, Judith. *Hollywood Be Thy Name: African American Religion in American Film, 1929–1949.* Berkeley: University of California Press, 2007.

Williams, Peter W. "Essay Review: Religion Goes to the Movies." *Religion and American Culture* 10, no. 2 (Summer 2000): 225–39.

7. FOOD AND DRINK

Fuller, Robert C. *Religion and Wine: A Cultural History of Wine Drinking in the United States.* Knoxville: University of Tennessee Press, 1996.

Diner, Hasia. *Hungering for America: Italian, Irish, and Jewish Foodways in the Age of Migration.* Cambridge, Mass.: Harvard University Press, 2001

Gardella, Peter. *Domestic Religion: Work, Food, Sex, and Other Commitments.* Cleveland: Pilgrim, 1998.

Griffith, R. Marie. *Born Again Bodies: Flesh and Spirit in American Christianity.* Berkeley: University of California Press, 2004.

Lelwicka, Michelle Mary. *Starving for Salvation: The Spiritual Dimensions of Eating Problems among American Girls and Women.* New York: Oxford University Press, 1999.

Madden, Etta M., and Martha L. Finch, eds. *Eating in Eden: Food and American Utopias.* Lincoln: University of Nebraska Press, 2006.

Sack, Daniel. *Whitebread Protestants: Food and Religion in American Culture.* New York: St. Martin's Press, 2000.

8. FRATERNAL AND YOUTH MOVEMENTS

Bullock, Steven C. *Revolutionary Brotherhood: Freemasonry and the Transformation of the American Social Order, 1730–1840.* Chapel Hill: University of North Carolina Press, 1996.

Carnes, Mark C. *Secret Ritual and Manhood in Victorian America.* New Haven: Yale University Press, 1989.

Dumenil, Lynn. *Freemasonry and American Culture, 1880–1930.* Princeton, N.J.: Princeton University Press, 1984.

Kaufmann, Christopher J. *Patriotism and Fraternalism in the Knights of Columbus.* New York: Crossroad, 2001.

Mechling, Jay. *On My Honor: Boy Scouts and the Making of American Youth.* Chicago: University of Chicago Press, 2001.

9. HOLIDAYS.

Connelly, Mark. *Christmas: A Social History.* London: I. B. Tauris, 2001.

Forbes, Bruce David. *Christmas: A Candid History.* Berkeley: University of California Press, 2007.

Nissenbaum, Stephen. *The American Christmas.* New York: Knopf, 1996.

McCrossen, Alexis. *Holy Day, Holiday: The American Sunday.* Ithaca, N.Y.: Cornell University Press, 2000.

Schmidt, Leigh Eric. *Consumer Rites: The Buying and Selling of American Holidays.* Princeton, N.J.: Princeton University Press, 1995.

Thomas, Nancy Smith. *Moravian Christmas in the South.* Chapel Hill: University of North Carolina Press, 2007.

Wills, Anne Blue. "How Magazines Made Thanksgiving." *Church History* 72, no. 1 (Mar. 2003), 138–58.

10. LITERATURE, JOURNALISM, AND THE PRINTED WORD

Note: Given the vast literature on the subject of religion and American literature. I have chosen only to list some general works in this area. Readers interested in particular authors of drama, fiction, or poetry should consult other bibliographical guides for works on Dickinson, Faulkner, Melville, O'Connor, Percy, and any number of other American authors who have dealt directly or obliquely with religious themes.

Amory, Hugh, and David D. Hall, ed. *The Colonial Book in the Atlantic World.* New York: Cambridge University Press, 2000.

Detweiler, Robert. *Uncivil Rites: American Fiction, Religion, and the Public Sphere.* Urbana: University of Illinois Press, 1996

Fessenden, Tracy. *Culture and Redemption: Religion, the Secular, and American Literature.* Princeton, N.J.: Princeton University Press, 2006.

Gatta, John. *Making Nature Sacred: Literature, Religion and Environment in America from the Puritans to the Present.* New York: Oxford University Press, 2004.

Gutjahr, Paul C. *An American Bible: The History of the Good Book in the United States, 1777–1880.* Stanford, Calif.: Stanford University Press, 1999.

Hall, David D. *Cultures of Print.* Amherst: University of Massachusetts Press, 1996.

Lardas, John. *The Bop Apocalypse: The Religious Visions of Kerouac, Ginsburg, and Burroughs.* Urbana: University of Illinois Press, 2001.

Nord, David Paul. *Faith in Reading: Religious Publishing and the Birth of Mass Media in America*. Oxford, UK: Oxford University Press, 2004.

Silk, Mark. *Unsecular Media: Making News of Religion in America*. Urbana: University of Illinois Press, 1995.

Sweet, Leonard I., ed. *Communication and Change in American Religious History*. Grand Rapids, Mich.: Eerdmans, 1993.

Thuesen, Peter J. *In Discordance with the Scriptures: American Protestant Battles over Translating the Bible*. New York: Oxford University Press, 1999.

Versluis, Arthur. *The Esoteric Origins of the American Renaissance*. New York: Oxford University Press, 2001.

Wright, Melanie Jane. *Moses in America: The Cultural Uses of Biblical Narrative*. New York: Oxford University Press, 2003.

11. MATERIAL CULTURE

Gardella, Peter. *American Angels*. Lawrence: University Press of Kansas, 2007.

McDannell, Colleen. *Material Christianity: Religion and Popular Culture in America*. New Haven, Conn.: Yale University Press, 1995.

———. *Picturing Faith: Photography and the Great Depression*. New Haven, Conn.: Yale University Press, 2004.

12. MEDICINE AND HEALING

Barnes, Linda L., and Susan S. Sered, eds. *Religion and Healing in America*. New York: Oxford University Press, 2005.

Engs, Ruth Clifford. *Clean Living Movements: American Cycles of Health Reform*. Westport, Conn.: Praeger, 2000.

Fuller, Robert C. *Alternative Medicine and American Religious Life*. New York: Oxford University Press, 1989.

Ward, Jule Dejager. *La Leche League: At the Crossroads of Medicine, Feminism, and Religion*. Chapel Hill: University of North Carolina Press, 2000.

13. MUSIC

(SEE ALSO E., S.6., AND Y.6.)

Blumhofer, Edith L. *Her Heart Can See: The Life and Hymns of Fanny J. Crosby*. Grand Rapids, Mich.: Eerdmans, 2005.

Bohlman, Philip V., Edith L. Blumhofer, and Maria M. Chow, eds. *Music in American Religious Experience*. New York: Oxford University Press, 2005.

Gac, Scott. *Singing for Freedom: The Hutchinson Family Singers and the Nineteenth-Century Culture of Reform*. New Haven, Conn.: Yale University Press, 2007.

Goff, James R., Jr. *Close Harmony: A History of Southern Gospel*. Chapel Hill: University of North Carolina Press, 2002.

Howard, Jay R., and John M. Streck. *Apostles of Rock: The Splintered World of Contemporary Christian Music*. Lexington: University Press of Kentucky, 1999.

Jackson, Jerma A. *Singing in My Soul: Black Gospel Music in a Secular Age*. Chapel Hill: University of North Carolina Press, 2004.

Marini, Stephen A. *Sacred Song in America: Religion, Music, and Public Culture*. Urbana: University of Illinois Press, 2003.

Mouw, Richard J., and Mark A. Noll, eds. *Wonderful Words of Life: Hymns in American Protestant History and Theology.* Grand Rapids: Eerdmans, 2004.

Noll, Mary, and Edith Blumhofer, eds. *Sing Them Over Again to Me: Hymns and Hymnbooks in America.* Tuscaloosa: University of Alabama Press, 2006.

Powell, Mark Allen. *Encyclopedia of Contemporary Christian Music.* Peabody, Mass.: Hendrickson Publishers, 2002.

Sizer, Sandra S. *Gospel Hymns and Social Religion.* Philadelphia: Temple University Press, 1978.

Stowe, David W. *How Sweet the Sounds: Music in the Spiritual Lives of Americans.* Cambridge, Mass.: Harvard University Press, 2004.

Walker-Hill, Helen. *From Spirituals to Symphonies: African-American Women Composers and their Music.* Westport, Conn.: Greenwood Press, 2002.

14. NATURE AND SCIENCE

Albanese, Catherine. *Nature Religion in America.* Chicago: University of Chicago Press, 1990.

Gould, Rebecca Kneale. *At Home in Nature: Modern Homesteading and Spiritual Practice in America.* Berkeley: University of California Press, 2005.

Gilbert, James. *Redeeming Culture: American Religion in an Age of Science.* Chicago: University of Chicago Press, 1997.

Hazen, Craig James. *The Village Enlightenment in America: Popular Religion and Science in the Nineteenth Century.* Urbana: University of Illinois Press, 2000.

Holmes, Steven J. *The Young John Muir.* Madison: University of Wisconsin Press, 1999.

Numbers, Ronald. *Darwinism Comes to America.* Cambridge, Mass.: Harvard University Press, 1998.

Numbers, Ronald, and John Stenhouse, eds. *Disseminating Darwinism.* New York: Cambridge University Press, 1999.

Ostrander, Rick. *The Life of Prayer in a World of Science.* New York: Oxford University Press, 2000.

Roberts, Jon H. *Darwinism and the Divine in America: Protestant Intellectuals and Organic Evolution, 1859–1900.* Notre Dame, Ind.: University of Notre Dame Press, 2001.

Rosen, Christine. *Preaching Eugenics: Religious Leaders and the American Eugenics Movement.* New York: Oxford University Press, 2004.

Stephens, Lester D. *Science, Race, and Religion in the American South: John Bachman and the Charleston Circle of Naturalists, 1815–1895.* Chapel Hill: University of North Carolina Press, 2000.

Witham, Larry A. *When Darwin Meets the Bible: Creationists and Evolutionists in America.* New York: Oxford University Press, 2002.

15. PAINTING AND THE VISUAL ARTS

David, John. *The Landscape of Belief: The Holy Land in Nineteenth-Century American Art and Culture.* Princeton, N.J.: Princeton University Press, 1996.

Dyrness, William A. *Reformed Theology and Visual Culture: The Protestant Imagination from Calvin to Edwards.* Cambridge: Cambridge University Press, 2004.

Finney, Paul Corby, ed. *Seeing Beyond the Word: Visual Arts and the Calvinist Tradition.* Grand Rapids: Eerdmans, 1999.

Husch, Gail E. *Something Coming: Apocalyptic Expectation and Mid-Nineteenth-Century American Painting.* Hanover, N.H.: University Press of New England, 2000.

McDannell, Colleen. *Picturing Faith: Photography and the Great Depression.* New Haven, Conn.: Yale University Press, 2004.

Morgan, David. *Icons of American Protestantism: The Art of Warner Sallman.* New Haven, Conn.: Yale University Press, 1996.

———. *Protestants and Pictures: Religion, Visual Culture, and the Age of American Mass Production.* New York: Oxford University Press, 1999.

———. *The Sacred Gaze: Religious Visual Culture in Theory and Practice.* Berkeley: University of California Press, 2005.

Morgan, David, and Sally Promey, eds. *The Visual Culture of American Religions.* Berkeley: University of California Press, 2001.

Promey, Sally M. *Painting Religion in Public: John Singer Sargent's Triumph of Religion at the Boston Public Library.* Princeton, N.J.: Princeton University Press, 1999.

Schwain, Kristin. *Signs of Grace: Religion and American Art in the Gilded Age.* Ithaca: Cornell university Press, 2008.

16. REGIONALISM

(*SEE ALSO* N.4. NEW ENGLAND PURITANISM; S.6. THE SOUTH AND APPALACHIA; AND U. THE WEST AND THE PACIFIC RIM)

Balmer, Randall, and Mark Silk, eds. *Religion and Public Life in the Middle Atlantic Region.* Lanham, Md.: AltaMira Press, 2006.

Barlow, Philip, and Mark Silk, eds. *Religion and Public Life in the Midwest.* Walnut Creek, Calif.: AltaMira Press, 2004.

Conforti, Joseph A. *Imagining New England: Explorations of Regional Identity from the Pilgrims to the Mid-Twentieth Century.* Chapel Hill: University of North Carolina Press, 2001.

Jaffee, David. *People of the Wachusett: Greater New England in History and Memory, 1630–1860.* Ithaca, N.Y.: Cornell University Press, 1999.

Lindsey, William, and Mark Silk, eds. *Religion and Public Life in the Southern Crossroads.* Walnut Creek, Calif.: AltaMira Press, 2005.

O'Connell, Patricia, and Mark Silk, eds. *Religion and Public Life in the Pacific Northwest.* Walnut Creek, Calif.: AltaMira Press, 2004.

Roof, Wade Clark, and Mark Silk, eds. *Religion and Public Life in the Pacific Region.* Walnut Creek, Calif.: AltaMira Press, 2005.

Schantz, Mark S. *Piety in Providence: Class Dimensions of Religious Experience in Antebellum Rhode Island.* Ithaca, N.Y.: Cornell University Press, 2000.

Shipps, Jan, and Mark Silk, eds. *Religion and Public Life in the Mountain West.* Walnut Creek, Calif.: AltaMira Press, 2004.

Walsh, Andrew, and Mark Silk, eds. *Religion and Public Life in New England.* Walnut Creek, Calif.: AltaMira Press, 2004.

Wilson, Charles Reagan, and Mark Silk, eds. *Religion and Public Life in the South.* Walnut Creek, Calif.: AltaMira Press, 2005.

17. SEXUALITY AND GENDER

Brekus, Catherine A., ed. *The Religious History of American Women*. Chapel Hill: University of North Carolina Press, 2007.

DeRogatis, Amy. "What Would Jesus Do? Sexuality and Salvation in Protestant Evangelical Sex Manuals, 1950s to the Present." *Church History* 74, no. 1 (Mar. 2005): 97–137.

Erzen, Tanya. *Straight to Jesus: Sexual and Christian Conversion in the Ex-Gay Movement*. Berkeley: University of California Press, 2006.

Fessenden, Tracy, Nicholas Radel, and Magdalena Zaborowska, eds. *The Puritan Origins of American Sex: Religion, Sexuality, and National Identity in American Literature*. New York: Routledge, 2001

Gardella, Peter. *Innocent Ecstacy*. New York: Oxford University Press, 1985.

Juster, Susan, and Lisa MacFarlane, eds. *A Mighty Baptism: Race, Gender, and the Creation of American Protestantism*. Ithaca, N.Y.: Cornell University Press, 1996.

Lippy, Charles H. *Do Real Men Pray?: Images of the Christian Man and Male Spirituality in White Protestant America*. Knoxville: University of Tennessee Press, 2005.

Sands, Kathleen M., ed. *God Forbid: Religion and Sex in American Public Life*. New York: Oxford University Press, 2000.

Satter, Beryl. *Each Mind a Kingdom: American Women, Sexual Purity, and the New Thought Movement, 1875–1920*. Berkeley: University of California Press, 1999.

18. SPIRITUALITY AND RELIGIOUS EXPERIENCE

Taves, Ann. *Fits, Trances, and Visions: Experiencing Religion and Explaining Experience from Wesley to James*. Princeton, N.J.: Princeton University Press, 1999.

Wuthnow, Robert. *Creative Spirituality: The Way of the Artist*. Berkeley: University of California Press, 2001.

19. THEOLOGY AND INTELLECTUAL HISTORY

Bednarowski, Mary Farrell. *The Religious Imagination of American Women*. Bloomington: Indiana University Press, 1999.

Gilpin, W. Clark. *A Preface to Theology*. Chicago: University of Chicago Press, 1996.

Hamner, M. Gail. *American Pragmatism: A Religious Genealogy*. New York: Oxford University Press, 2003.

Hart, D. G. *The Lost Soul of American Protestantism*. Lanham, Md.: Rowman & Littlefield Publishers, 2002.

Hazen, Craig James. *The Village Enlightenment in America: Popular Religion and Science in the Nineteenth Century*. Urbana: University of Illinois Press, 2000.

Holifield, E. Brooks. *Theology in America: Christian Thought from the Age of the Puritans to the Civil War*. New Haven: Yale University Press, 2003.

McCarraher, Eugene. *Christian Critics: Religion and the Impasse in Modern American Social Thought*. Ithaca, N.Y.: Cornell University Press, 2000.

Noll, Mark A. *America's God: From Jonathan Edwards to Abraham Lincoln*. New York: Oxford University Press, 2002.

Roozen, David A., and James R. Nieman, eds. *Church, Identity, and Change: Theology and Denominational Structures in Unsettled Times*. Grand Rapids, Mich.: Eerdmans, 2005.

E. Religion in Early America
  (*SEE ALSO* N.4. New England Puritanism)

Albanese, Catherine L. *Sons of the Fathers: The Civil Religion of the American Revolution.* Philadelphia: Temple University Press, 1976.

Bonomi, Patricia U. *Under the Cope of Heaven: Religion, Society and Politics in Colonial America.* Rev. ed. 1986. New York: Oxford University Press, 2003.

Bremer, Francis J., and Lynn A. Botelho, eds. *The World of John Winthrop: Essays on England and New England, 1588–1649.* Charlottesville: University of Virginia Press, 2005.

Conforti, Joseph. *Saints and Strangers: New England in British North America.* Baltimore, Md.: Johns Hopkins University Press, 2006.

Davidson, James West. *The Logic of Millennial Thought: Eighteenth-Century New England.* New Haven, Conn.: Yale University Press, 1977.

Davis, Derek H. *Religion and the Continental Congress, 1774–1789.* New York: Oxford University Press, 2000.

Dreisbach, Daniel L. *Thomas Jefferson and the Wall of Separation between Church and State.* New York: New York University Press, 2002.

Egan, Jim. *Authorizing Experience: Refigurations of the Body Politic in Seventeenth-century New England Writing.* Princeton, N.J.: Princeton University Press, 1999.

Games, Allison. *Migration and the Origins of the English Atlantic World.* Cambridge, Mass.: Harvard University Press, 1999.

Gaustad, Edwin S. *Church and State in America.* New York: Oxford University Press, 1999.

———. *Faith of Our Fathers: Religion and the New Nation.* San Francisco: Harper and Row, 1987.

———. *Neither King nor Prelate: Religion and the New Nation, 1776–1826.* Grand Rapids, Mich.: Eerdmans, 1993.

Goldschmidt, Henry, and Elizabeth McAlister, eds. *Race, Nation, and Religion in the Americas.* New York: Oxford University Press, 2004.

Greer, Allan, and Jodi Bilinkoff, eds. *Colonial Saints: Discovering the Holy in America, 1500–1800.* New York: Routledge, 2003.

Griffin, Patrick. *The People with No Name: Ireland's Ulster Scots, America's Scots Irish, and the Creation of a British Atlantic World, 1689–1764.* Princeton, N.J.: Princeton University Press, 2001.

Gustafson, Sandra M. *Eloquence Is Power: Oratory & Performance in Early America.* Chapel Hill: University of North Carolina Press, 2000.

Hall, Timothy L. *Separating Church and State: Roger Williams and Religious Liberty.* Urbana: University of Illinois Press, 1998.

Hatch, Nathan O. *The Sacred Cause of Liberty: Republican Thought and the Millennium in Revolutionary New England.* New Haven, Conn.: Yale University Press, 1977.

Hoffman, Ronald, and Peter J. Albert, eds. *Religion in a Revolutionary Age.* Charlottesville: University Press of Virginia, 1994.

Holmes, David L. *The Faiths of the Founding Fathers.* New York: Oxford University Press, 2006.

Hutson, James R., ed. *The Founders on Religion: A Book of Quotations.* Princeton, N.J.: Princeton University Press, 2007.

———. *Religion and the New Republic.* Lanham, Md.: Rowman and Littlefield, 2000.

Juster, Susan. *Anglo-American Prophecy in the Age of Revolution.* Philadelphia: University of Pennsylvania Press, 2003.

Lambert, Frank. *The Founding Fathers and the Place of Religion in America.* Princeton, N.J.: Princeton University Press, 2003.

Lindenauer, Leslie J. *Piety and Power: Gender and Religious Culture in the American Colonies, 1630–1700.* New York: Routledge, 2002.

Main, Gloria L. *Peoples of a Spacious Land: Families and Cultures in Colonial New England.* Cambridge, Mass.: Harvard University Press, 2001

Morgan, Edmund S. "The Puritan Ethic and the American Revolution." *William and Mary Quarterly,* 3d ser., 24, no. 1 (Jan. 1967): 3–43.

Oberg, Barbara B., and Harry S. Stout, eds. *Benjamin Franklin, Jonathan Edwards, and the Representation of American Culture.* New York: Oxford University Press, 1993.

Pahl, Jon. *Paradox Lost: Free Will and Political Liberty in American Culture, 1630–1760.* Baltimore: Johns Hopkins University Press, 1992.

Pestana, Carla G. *Liberty of Conscience and the Growth of Religious Diversity in Early America, 1636–1786.* Providence, R.I.: J. C. Brown Library, 1986.

Round, Phillip H. *By Nature and Custom Cursed: Transatlantic Civil Discourse and New England Cultural Production, 1620–1660.* Hanover: University Press of New England, 1999.

Wilson, Lisa. *Ye Heart of a Man: The Domestic Life of Men in Colonial New England.* New Haven, Conn.: Yale University Press, 1999.

F. Native American Religions (Including Christian Missions)

Angel, Michael. *Preserving the Sacred: Historical Perspectives on the Ojibwa Midewiwin.* Winnipeg: University of Manitoba Press, 2002.

Basso, Keith H. *Wisdom Sits in Places: Landscape and Language among the Western Apache.* Albuquerque: University of New Mexico Press, 1996.

Berkhofer, Robert F., Jr. *Salvation and the Savage.* New York: Atheneum, 1976.

Blackburn, Carole. *Harvest of Souls: The Jesuit Missions and Colonialism in North America, 1632–1650.* Montréal: McGill-Queen's University Press, 2000.

Bourne, Russell. *Gods of War, Gods of Peace: How the Meeting of Native and Colonial Religions Shaped Early America.* New York: Harcourt, 2002.

Bowden, Henry Warner. *American Indians and Christian Missions.* Chicago: University of Chicago Press, 1981.

Browner, Tara. *Heartbeat of the People: Music and Dance of the Northern Pow-wow.* Urbana: University of Illinois Press, 2002.

Capps, Walter H., ed. *Seeing with a Native Eye.* New York: Harper and Row, 1976.

Cogley, Richard W. *John Eliot's Mission to the Indians before King Philip's War.* Cambridge, Mass.: Harvard University Press, 1999.

DeMallie, Raymond J., *The Sixth Grandfather: Black Elk's Teachings Given to John G. Neihardt.* Lincoln: University of Nebraska Press, 1984.

DeMallie, Raymond J., and Douglas R. Parks, eds. *Sioux Indian Religion.* Norman: University of Oklahoma Press, 1987.

Devens, Carol. *Countering Colonization: Native American Women and Great Lakes Missions, 1630–1900*. Berkeley: University of California Press, 1992.

Ellis, Clyde, Luke Eric Lassiter, and Ralph Kotay. *The Jesus Road: Kiowas, Christianity, and Indian Hymns*. Lincoln: University of Nebraska Press, 2002.

Elzey, Wayne. "Meso-American Religions." *EARE* 1:119–36.

Enochs, Ross Alexander. *The Jesuit Mission to the Lakota Sioux*. Kansas City, Mo.: Sheed and Ward, 1996.

Frisbie, Charlotte J., and David P. McAlester, eds. *Navajo Blessingway Singer: the Autobiography of Frank Mitchell, 1881–1967*. Albuquerque: University of New Mexico Press, 1978.

Galgano, Robert C. *Feast of Souls: Indians and Spaniards in the Seventeenth-Century Missions of Florida and New Mexico*. Albuquerque: University of New Mexico Press, 2005.

Geertz, Armin. *The Invention of Prophecy: Continuity and Meaning in Hopi Indian Religion*. Berkeley: University of California Press, 1994.

Gill, Sam D. *Native American Religions*. Belmont, Calif.: Wadsworth, 1982.

———. "Native American Religions." *EARE* 1:137–52.

Greer, Allan, ed. *The Jesuit Relations: Natives and Missionaries in Seventeenth-Century North America*. Boston : Bedford/St. Martin's, 2000.

Hackel, Steven W. *Children of Coyote, Missionaries of Saint Francis: Indian-Spanish Relations in Colonial California, 1769–1850*. Chapel Hill: University of North Carolina Press, 2005.

Hanke, Lewis. *Aristotle and the American Indians*. Bloomington: Indiana University Press, 1959.

Harrod, Howard L. *Becoming and Remaining a People: Native North American Religions on the Northern Plains*. Tucson: University of Arizona Press, 1995.

Hultkrantz, Ake. *Native Religions of North America*. Prospect Heights, Ill.: Waveland, 1998.

———. *The Religions of the American Indians*. Berkeley: University of California Press, 1979.

Kan, Sergei. *Memory Eternal: Tlingit Culture and Russian Orthodox Christianity through Two Centuries*. Seattle: University of Washington Press, 1999.

Kelley, Klara Bonsack, and Harris Francis. *Navajo Sacred Places*. Bloomington: Indiana University Press, 1994.

Koopman, LeRoy. *Taking the Jesus Road: The Ministry of the Reformed Church in America among Native Americans*. Grand Rapids, Mich.: Eerdmans, 2005.

LaBarre, Weston. *The Peyote Cult*. New York: Schocken, 1969.

Levy, Jerrold E. *In the Beginning: The Navajo Genesis*. Berkeley: University of California Press, 1998.

Lewis, Bonnie Sue. *Creating Christian Indians: Native Clergy in the Presbyterian Church*. Norham: University of Oklahoma Press, 2003.

Loftin, John D. *Religion and Hopi Life in the Twentieth Century*. Bloomington: Indiana University Press, 1991.

Martin, Joel W. *The Land Looks After Us: A History of Native American Religion*. New York: Oxford University Press, 2001.

———. *Sacred Revolt: The Muskogees' Struggle for a New World*. Boston: Beacon, 1991.

McLoughlin, William G., et al. *The Cherokee Ghost Dance*. Macon, Ga.: Mercer University Press, 1984.

———. *Cherokee Renascence in the New Republic.* Princeton, N.J.: Princeton University Press, 1986.

———. *The Cherokees and Christianity, 1794–1870.* Athens: University of Georgia Press, 1994.

———. *Cherokees and Missionaries, 1789–1839.* New Haven, Conn.: Yale University Press, 1984.

McNally, Michael D. *Ojibwe Singers: Hymns, Grief, and a Native Culture in Motion.* New York: Oxford University Press, 2000.

Muldoon, James, ed. *The Spiritual Conversion of the Americas.* Gainesville: University Presses of Florida, 2004.

Nabokov, Peter. *Where the Lightning Strikes: The Lives of American Indian Scared Places.* New York: Viking, 2006.

Nabokov, Peter, and Robert Easton. *Native American Architecture.* New York: Oxford University Press, 1988.

Niezen, Ronald. *Spirit Wars: Native North American Religions in the Age of Nation Building.* Berkeley: University of California Press, 2000.

Olmos, Margarite Fernandez, and Lisabeth Paravisini-Gebert. *Creole Religions of the Caribbean.* New York: New York University Press, 2003.

Ortiz, Alfonso. *The Tewa World.* Chicago: University of Chicago Press, 1969.

Radin, Paul. *The Trickster.* New York: Schocken, 1972.

Richter, Daniel K. *Facing East from Indian Country: A Native History of Early America.* Cambridge, Mass.: Harvard University Press, 2001.

Ridington, Robin, and Dennis Hastings (In'aska). *Blessings for a Long Time: The Sacred Pole of the Omaha Tribe.* Lincoln: University of Nebraska Press, 1997.

Rollings, Willard Hughes. *Unaffected by the Gospel: Osage Resistance to the Christian Invasion (1673–1906).* Albuquerque: University of New Mexico Press, 2004.

Roscoe, Will. *The Zuni Man-Woman.* Albuquerque: University of New Mexico Press, 1991.

Sandos, James A. *Converting California: Indians and Franciscans in the Missions.* New Haven: Yale University Press, 2004.

Schwarz, Maureen Trudelle. *Molded in the Image of Changing Woman: Navajo Views on the Human Body and Personhood.* Tucson: University of Arizona Press, 1997.

Smith, Theresa S. *The Island of the Anishnaabeg: Thunderers and Water Monsters in the Traditional Ojibwa Life-World.* Moscow: University of Idaho Press, 1995.

Smoak, Gregory E. *Ghost Dances and Identity.* Berkeley: University of California Press, 2005.

Stockel, H. Henrietta. *On the Bloody Road to Jesus: Christianity and the Chiricahua Apaches.* Albuquerque: University of New Mexico Press, 2004.

Sullivan, Lawrence E., ed. *Native American Religions: North American.* New York: Macmillan, 1987.

Szasz, Margaret Connell. *Indian Education in the American Colonies, 1607–1783.* Albuquerque: University of New Mexico Press, 1988.

Tooker, Elizabeth. *Native North American Spirituality of the Eastern Woodlands.* Mahwah, N.J.: Paulist, 1979.

Trigger, Bruce G., and Wilcombe W. Washburn, eds. *The Cambridge History of the Native Peoples of the Americas.* Vol. 1: North America. New York: Cambridge University Press, 1996.

Underhill, Ruth M. *Red Man's Religion.* Chicago: University of Chicago Press, 1965.

Vecsey, Christopher. *The Paths of Kateri's Kin*. Notre Dame, Ind.: University of Notre Dame Press, 1997.

Wallace, Anthony F. C. *The Death and Rebirth of the Seneca*. New York: Knopf, 1970.

Washburn, Wilcomb E. *The Indian in America*. New York: Harper and Row, 1975.

Waters, Frank. *Book of the Hopi*. New York: Viking, 1963.

———. *Masked Gods: Navaho and Pueblo Ceremonialism*. Athens, Ohio: Swallow Press, 1950.

Wilson, Bryan R. *Magic and the Millennium*. London: Heinemann, 1973.

Winiarski, Douglas. "Native American Popular Religion in New England's Old Colony, 1670–1770." *Religion and American Culture* 15, no. 2 (Summer 2005): 147–86.

Wyss, Hilary E. *Writing Indians: Literacy, Christianity, and Native Community in Early America*. Amherst: University of Massachusetts Press, 2000.

G. African, Afro-Caribbean, and African American Religions

Andrews, William L. *Sisters of the Spirit: Three Black Women's Autobiographies of the Nineteenth Century*. Bloomington: Indiana University Press, 1986.

Angell, Stephen Ward. *Bishop Henry McNeal Turner and African-American Religion in the South*. Knoxville: University of Tennessee Press, 1992.

Angell, Stephen Ward, and Anthony B. Pinn, eds. *Social Protest Thought in the African Methodist Episcopal Church, 1862–1939*. Knoxville: University of Tennessee Press, 2000.

Baer, Hans A., and Merrill Singer. *African-American Religion in the Twentieth Century*. Knoxville: University of Tennessee Press, 1992.

Bailey, Julius H. *Around the Family Altar: Domesticity in the African Methodist Episcopal Church, 1865–1900*. Gainesville: University Press of Florida, 2005.

Bass, S. Jonathan. *Blessed Are the Peacemakers: Martin Luther King, Jr., Eight White Religious Leaders, and the "Letter from Birmingham Jail."* Baton Rouge: Louisiana State University Press, 2001.

Beary, Michael J. *Black Bishop: Edward T. Demby and the Struggle for Racial Equality in the Episcopal Church*. Urbana: University of Illinois Press, 2001.

Battle, Michael. *The Black Church in America: African American Christian Spirituality*. Malden, Mass.: Blackwell, 2006.

Best, Wallace D. *Passionately Human, No Less Divine: Religion and Culture in Black Chicago, 1915–1952*. Princeton, N.J.: Princeton University Press, 2005.

Billingsley, Andrew. *Mighty like a River: The Black Church and Social Reform*. New York: Oxford University Press, 1999.

Branch, Taylor. *Parting the Waters: America in the King Years, 1954–63*. New York: Simon and Schuster, 1988.

Brandon, George, *Santeria from Africa to the New World*. Bloomington: Indiana University Press, 1993.

Brotz, Howard M. *The Black Jews of Harlem*. New York: Free Press, 1964.

Broughton, Viv. *Black Gospel*. Poole, Dorset, UK: Blanford Press, 1985.

Brown, Karen McCarthy. *Mama Lola: A Vodou Priestess in Brooklyn*. Berkeley: University of California Press, 1991.

Burkett, Randall K. *Garveyism as a Religious Movement*. Metuchen, N.J.: Scarecrow, 1978.

Butler, Anthea D. *Women in the Church of God in Christ.* Chapel Hill: University of North Carolina Press, 2007.

Callahan, Allen Dwight. *The Talking Book: African Americans and the Bible.* New Haven, Conn.: Yale University Press, 2006.

Campbell, James T. *Songs of Zion: The African Methodist Episcopal Church in the United States and South Africa.* New York: Oxford University Press, 1995.

Chappell, David L. *A Stone of Hope: Prophetic Religion and the Death of Jim Crow.* Chapel Hill: University of North Carolina Press, 2004.

Chireau, Yvonne Patricia. *Black Magic: Religion and the African American Conjuring Tradition.* Berkeley: University of California Press, 2003.

Chireau, Yvonne Patricia, and Nathaniel Deutsch, eds. *Black Zion: African American Religious Encounters with Judaism.* New York: Oxford University Press, 2000.

Click, Patricia C. *Time Full of Trial: The Roanoke Island Freedman's Colony, 1862–1867.* Chapel Hill: University of North Carolina Press, 2001.

Cone, James H. "Black Religious Thought." *EARE* 2:1173–88.

———. *Martin & Malcolm & America.* Maryknoll, N.Y.: Orbis, 1992.

Cornelius, Janet Duitsman. *Slave Missions and the Black Church in the Antebellum South.* Columbia: University of South Carolina Press, 1999.

Dannin, Robert. *Black Pilgrimage to Islam.* New York: Oxford University Press, 2002.

Davis, Cyprian, O.S.B. *The History of Black Catholics in the United States.* New York: Crossroad, 1990.

Davis, Davis Bryon. *In the Image of God: Religion, Moral Values, and Our Heritage of Slavery.* New Haven: Yale University Press, 2001.

Davis, Gerald L. *I Got the Word in Me and I Can Sing It, You Know: A Study of the Performed African-American Sermon.* Philadelphia: University of Pennsylvania Press, 1987.

De La Torre, Miguel A. *Santería.* Grand Rapids, Mich.: Eerdmans, 2004.

Dodson, Jualynne E. *Engendering Church: Women, Power, and the AME Church.* Lanham, Md.: Rowman & Littlefield, 2002.

DuPree, Sherry Sherrod. *African-American Holiness Pentecostal Movements: An Annotated Bibliography.* New York: Garland, 1996.

Dyson, Michael Eric. *Making Malcolm: The Myth and Meaning of Malcolm X.* New York: Oxford University Press, 1995.

Essien-Udom, E. E. *Black Nationalism.* Chicago: University of Chicago Press, 1962.

Evanzz, Karl. *The Messenger: The Rise and Fall of Elijah Muhammad.* New York: Pantheon, 1999.

Fauset, Arthur Huff. *Black Gods of the Metropolis.* 1944. Philadelphia: University of Pennsylvania Press, 2006.

Fett, Sharla M. *Working Cures: Healing, Health, and Power on Southern Slave Plantations.* Chapel Hill: University of North Carolina Press, 2002.

Fluer, Walter Earl, and Catherine Tumber, eds. *A Strange Freedom: The Best of Howard Thurman on Religious Experience and Public Life.* Boston: Beacon Press, 1998.

Franklin, Reverend C. L. *Give Me This Mountain: Life History and Selected Sermons.* Edited by Jeff Todd Titon. Urbana: University of Illinois Press, 1989.

Frazier, E. Franklin. *The Negro Church in America (1963), and C. Eric Lincoln, The Black Church since Frazier (1974).* Published as one volume. New York: Schocken, 1974.

Genovese, Eugene D. *Roll, Jordan, Roll.* New York: Pantheon, 1972.

Glaude, Eddie S., Jr. *Exodus! Religion, Race, and Nation in Early Nineteenth-Century Black America.* Chicago: University of Chicago Press, 2000.

Goff, James R., Jr. *Close Harmony: A History of Southern Gospel.* Chapel Hill: University of North Carolina Press, 2002.

Gregg, Robert. *Sparks from the Anvil of Oppression: Philadelphia's African Methodists and Southern Migrants, 1890–1940.* Philadelphia: Temple University Press, 1993.

Harding, Vincent. *Martin Luther King.* New York: Orbis, 1996.

Hardy, Clarence E., III. *James Baldwin's God: Sex, Hope and Crisis in Black Holiness Culture.* Knoxville: University of Tennessee Press, 2003.

Harris, Frederick C. *Something Within: Religion in African-American Political Activism.* New York: Oxford University Press, 1999.

Harris, Michael W. "African American Religious History in the 1980s: A Critical Review." *Religious Studies Review* 20, no. 4 (Oct. 1994): 263–75.

———. *The Rise of Gospel Blues: The Music of Thomas Andrew Dorsey in the Urban Church.* New York: Oxford University Press, 1992.

Herskovits, Melville J. *The Myth of the Negro Past.* Boston: Beacon, 1958.

Higginbotham, Evelyn Brooks. *Righteous Discontent: The Women's Movement in the Black Baptist Church, 1880–1920.* Cambridge, Mass.: Harvard University Press, 1993.

Hodges, Graham Russell, ed. *Black Itinerants of the Gospel.* Madison: University of Wisconsin Press, 1993.

———. *Root and Branch: African Americans in New York and East Jersey 1613–1863.* Chapel Hill: University of North Carolina Press, 1999.

Hopkins, Dwight N. *Down, Up, and Over: Slave Religion and Black Theology.* Minneapolis, Minn.: Fortress Press, 2000.

Israel, Adrienne M. *Amanda Berry Smith: From Washerwoman to Evangelist.* Lanham, Md.: Scarecrow, 1998.

Jackson, Jerma A. *Singing in My Soul: Black Gospel Music in a Secular Age.* Chapel Hill: University of North Carolina Press, 2004.

Jacobs, Charles F., and Andrew J. Kaslow. *The Spiritual Churches of New Orleans: Origins, Beliefs, and Rituals of an African-American Religion.* Knoxville: University of Tennessee Press, 1991.

Johnson, Alonzo, and Paul Jersild, eds. *Ain't Gonna Lay My 'Ligion Down: African American Religion in the South.* Columbia: University of South Carolina Press, 1996.

Johnson, Paul E., ed. *African-American Christianity.* Berkeley: University of California Press, 1994.

Johnson, Sylvester A. *The Myth of Ham in Nineteenth-Century American Christianity.* New York: Palgrave Macmillan, 2004.

Johnston, Clifton H. *God Struck Me Dead: Religious Conversion Experiences and Autobiographies of Ex-Slaves.* Philadelphia: Pilgrim, 1969.

Lawson, E. Thomas. *Religions of Africa.* San Francisco: Harper and Row, 1984.

Levine, Lawrence W. *Black Culture and Black Consciousness.* New York: Oxford University Press, 1977.

Lewis, Harold T. *Yet with a Steady Beat: The African American Struggle for Recognition in the Episcopal Church.* Valley Forge, Pa.: Trinity Press International, 1996.

Lewis, William F. *Soul Rebels: The Rastafari.* Prospect Heights, Ill.: Waveland, 1993.

Libby, Jean, ed. *From Slavery to Salvation: The Autobiography of Rev. Thomas W. Henry of the A.M.E. Church.* Jackson: University Press of Mississippi, 1994.

Lincoln, C. Eric. *The Black Muslims in America.* Boston: Beacon, 1961.

Lincoln, C. Eric, and Lawrence H. Mamiya. "Black Militant and Separatist Movements." *EARE* 2:755–74.

Lischer, Richard. *The Preacher King: Martin Luther King, Jr., and the Word That Moved America.* New York: Oxford University Press, 1995.

Little, Lawrence S. *Disciples of Liberty: The African Methodist Episcopal Church in the Age of Imperialism, 1884–1916.* Knoxville: University of Tennessee Press, 2000.

Luker, Ralph E. *Historical Dictionary of the Civil Rights Movement.* Lanham, Md.: Scarecrow, 1997.

———. *The Social Gospel in Black and White: American Racial Reform, 1885–1912.* Chapel Hill: University of North Carolina Press, 1991.

Martin, Sandy Dwayne. *For God and Race: The Religious and Political Leadership of AMEZ Bishop James Walker Hood.* Columbia: University of South Carolina Press, 1999.

McCloud, Aminah Beverly. *African American Islam.* New York: Routledge, 1995.

McRoberts, Omar. *Streets of Glory: Church and Community in a Black Urban Neighborhood.* Chicago: University of Chicago Press, 2003.

MacGregor, Morris J. *The Emergence of a Black Catholic Community: St. Augustine's in Washington.* Washington, D.C.: Catholic University of America Press, 1999.

Manis, Andrew M. *A Fire You Can't Put Out: The Civil Rights Life of Birmingham's Reverend Fred Shuttlesworth.* Tuscaloosa: University of Alabama Press, 1999.

Miller, Albert George. *Elevating the Race: Theophilus G. Steward, Black Theology, and the Making of an African American Civil Society, 1865–1924.* Knoxville: University of Tennessee Press, 2003.

Mitchell, Henry H. *Black Church Beginnings.* Grand Rapids, Mich.: Eerdmans, 2004.

Montgomery, William E. *Under Their Own Vine and Fig Tree: The African-American Church in the South, 1865–1900.* Baton Rouge: Louisiana State University Press, 1993.

Morgan, Philip D. *Slave Counterpoint: Black Culture in the Eighteenth-Century Chesapeake and Lowcountry.* Chapel Hill: University of North Carolina Press, 1998.

Morrow, Diane Batts. *Persons of Color and Religious at the Same Time: The Oblate Sisters of Providence, 1828–1860.* Chapel Hill: University of North Carolina Press, 2002.

Murphy, Joseph M. *Santería.* Boston: Beacon, 1988.

———. *Working the Spirit: Ceremonies of the African Diaspora.* Boston: Beacon, 1994.

Murphy, Larry G. *Down by the Riverside: Readings in African American Religion.* New York: New York University Press, 2000.

O'Brien, David M. *Animal Sacrifice and Religious Freedom: Church of the Lukumi Babalu Aye v. City of Hialeah.* Lawrence: University Press of Kansas, 2004.

Ochs, Stephen J. *A Black Patriot and a White Priest: André Cailloux and Claude Paschal Maister in the Civil War.* Baton Rouge: Louisiana State University Press, 2000.

O'Foran, Shelly. *Little Zion: A Church Baptized by Fire.* Chapel Hill: University of North Carolina Press, 2006.

Oliver, Paul. *Songsters and Saints: Vocal Traditions on Race Records.* New York: Cambridge University Press, 1984. Also 2–vol. record set with same title issued by Matchbox (Badminton, Glos., UK, 1984, distributed in United States by Down Home Music, El Cerrito, Calif.).

Olupona, Jacob K, and Regina Gemignani, eds. *African Immigrant Religion*. New York: New York University Press, 2007.

Overacker, Ingrid. *The African American Church Community in Rochester, New York, 1900–1940*. Rochester: University of Rochester Press, 1998.

Owens, Michael Leo. *God and Government in the Ghetto*. Chicago: University of Chicago Press, 2007.

Pierce, Yolanda. *Hell without Fires: Slavery, Christianity, and the Antebellum Spiritual Narrative*. Gainesville: University Press of Florida, 2005.

Pinn, Anner H., and Anthony Pinn. *Fortress Introduction to Black Church History*. Minneapolis: Fortress, 2002.

Pinn, Anthony B. *The Black Church in the Post–Civil Rights Era*. Maryknoll, N.Y.: Orbis, 2002.

———, ed. *Mortal Evil and Redemptive Suffering: A History of Theodicy in African American Religious Thought*. Gainesville: University of Florida Press, 2002.

———. *Varieties of African American Religious Experience*. Minneapolis, Minn.: Fortress Press, 1998.

Pinn, Anthony B., and Allen Dwight Callahan, eds. *African American Religious Life and the Story of Nimrod*. New York: Palgrave Macmillan, 2008.

Pitts, Walter F., Jr. *Old Ship of Zion: The Afro-Baptist Ritual in the African Diaspora*. New York: Oxford University Press, 1993.

Raboteau, Albert J. "Black Christianity." *EARE* 1:635–48.

———. *Canaan Land: A Religious History of African Americans*. New York: Oxford University Press, 2001. (Also published as *African American Religion*, 1999).

———. *A Fire in the Bones: Reflections on African-American Religious History*. Boston: Beacon, 1995.

———. *Slave Religion*. New York: Oxford University Press, 1978.

Raboteau, Albert J., and Timothy Fulop, eds. *African-American Religion*. New York: Routledge, 1997.

Rael, Patrick. *Black Identity and Black Protest in the Antebellum North*. Chapel Hill: University of North Carolina Press, 2002.

Rankin, Tom. *Sacred Space: Photographs from the Mississippi Delta*. Jackson: University Press of Mississippi, 1993.

Ransby, Barbara. *Ella Baker and the Black Freedom Movement*. Chapel Hill: University of North Carolina Press, 2003.

Ray, Benjamin C. *African Religion*. Englewood Cliffs, N.J.: Prentice-Hall, 1976.

Reagon, Bernice Johnson. *If You Don't Go, Don't Hinder Me: The African American Sacred Song Tradition*. Lincoln: University of Nebraska Press, 2001.

———, comp. *Wade in the Water: African American Sacred Music Traditions*. Washington, D.C.: Smithsonian, 1994. 4–vol. CD set issued by Smithsonian Folkways.

———, ed. *We'll Understand It Better By and By: Pioneering African American Gospel Composers*. Washington D.C.: Smithsonian, 1992.

Rivers, Larry, and Carter Brown, Jr. *Laborers in the Vineyard of the Lord: The Beginnings of the AME Church in Florida, 1865–1895*. Gainesville: University Press of Florida, 2001.

Roberson, Houston Bryan. *Fighting the Good Fight: The Story of the King Memorial Dexter Baptist Church, 1865–1977.* New York: Routledge, 2005.

Rosenberg, Bruce A. *The Art of the American Folk Preacher.* New York: Oxford University Press, 1970.

Ross, Rosetta E. *Witnessing and Testifying: Black Women, Religion, and Civil Rights.* Minneapolis: Fortress, 2003.

Saillant, John. *Black Puritan, Black Republican: The Life and Thought of Lemuel Haynes, 1753–1833.* New York: Oxford University Press, 2003.

Salvatore, Nick. *Singing in a Strange Land: C. L. Franklin, the Black Church, and the Transformation of America.* New York: Little, Brown, 2005.

Sanders, Cheryl J. *Saints in Exile: The Holiness-Pentecostal Experience in African American Religion and Culture.* New York: Oxford University Press, 1996.

Sensbach, Jon. *Rebecca's Revival: Creating Black Christianity in the Atlantic World.* Cambridge, Mass.: Harvard University Press, 2005.

Seralie, William. *Fire in His Heart: Bishop Benjamin Tucker Tanner and the A.M.E. Church.* Knoxville: University of Tennessee Press, 1998.

Sernett, Milton C. *African American Religious Studies.* Durham, N.C.: Duke University Press, 1989.

———. *Afro-American Religious History: A Documentary Witness.* 2d ed. Durham, N.C.: Duke University Press, 1999.

———. *Bound for the Promised Land: African American Religion and the Great Migration.* Durham, N.C.: Duke University Press, 1997.

Smith, R. Drew, ed. *New Day Begun: African American Churches and Civic Culture in Post–Civil Rights America.* Durham, N.C.: Duke University Press, 2003.

Smith, Theophus H. *Conjuring Culture: Biblical Formations of Black America.* New York: Oxford University Press, 1994.

Spencer, Jon Michael. *Protest and Praise: Sacred Music of Black Religion.* Minneapolis: Fortress, 1990.

Taylor, Clarence. *The Black Churches of Brooklyn.* New York: Columbia University Press, 1994.

———. *Black Religious Intellectuals: The Fight for Equality from Jim Crow to the Twenty-first Century.* New York: Routledge, 2002.

Townsend, Craig D. *Faith in Their Own Color: Black Episcopalians in Antebellum New York City.* New York: Columbia University Press, 2005.

Vergara, Camilo José. *How the Other Half Worships.* New Brunswick, N.J.: Rutgers University Press, 2005.

Walker-Hill, Helen. *From Spirituals to Symphonies: African-American Women Composers and their Music.* Westport, Conn.: Greenwood Press, 2002.

Watts, Jill. *God, Harlem U.S.A.: The Father Divine Story.* Berkeley: University of California Press, 1992.

Weisbrot, Robert. *Father Divine and the Struggle for Racial Equality.* Urbana: University of Illinois Press, 1983.

Weisenfeld, Judith. *African American Women and Christian Activism.* Cambridge, Mass.: Harvard University Press, 1997.

Weisenfeld, Judith, and Richard Newman, eds. *This Far by Faith: Readings in African-American Women's Autobiography.* New York: Routledge, 1996.

White, Marjorie L., and Andrew M. Manis, eds. *Birmingham Revolutionaries: The Reverend Fred Shuttlesworth and the Alabama Christian Movement for Human Rights.* Macon, Ga.: Mercer University Press, 2000.

Williams, Ethel L., and Clifton L. Brown, comps. *Afro-American Religious Studies: A Comprehensive Bibliography with Locations in American Libraries.* Metuchen, N.J.: Scarecrow, 1972.

Wimbush, Vincent L., ed. *African Americans and the Bible.* New York: Continuum, 2000.

Wolfe, Michael C. *The Abundant Life Prevails: Religious Traditions of Saint Helena Island.* Waco, Tex.: Baylor University Press, 2000.

H. Judaism

Alexander, Michael. *Jazz Age Jews.* Princeton, N.J.: Princeton University Press, 2001.

American Jewish Committee. *American Jewish Yearbook.* New York. Annual.

Ariel, Yaakov. *Evangelizing the Chosen People: Missions to the Jews in America, 1880–2000.* Chapel Hill: University of North Carolina Press, 2000.

Ashton, Dianne. *Rebecca Gratz: Women and Judaism in Antebellum America.* Detroit, Mich.: Wayne State University Press, 1997.

Aviv, Caryn S., and David Shneer. *New Jews: The End of the Jewish Diaspora.* New York: New York University Press, 2005.

Birmingham, Stephen. *Our Crowd: The Great Jewish Families of New York.* New York: Harper and Row, 1967.

Blau, Joseph L. *Judaism in America.* Chicago: University of Chicago Press, 1976.

Bodner, Allen. *When Boxing Was a Jewish Sport.* Westport, Conn.: Praeger, 1997.

Braunstein, Susan L., and Jenna Weissman Joselit, eds. *Getting Comfortable in New York: The American Jewish Home, 1880–1920.* New York: Jewish Museum, 1990. Museum exhibit catalog.

Chafets, Ze'ev. *Members of the Tribe: On the Road in Jewish America.* Toronto: Bantam, 1988.

Cohen, Jocelyn, and Daniel Soyer, eds. *My Future Is in America: Autobiographies of Eastern European Jewish Immigrants.* New York: New York University Press, 2005.

Davidman, Lynn. *Tradition in a Rootless World: Women Turn to Orthodox Judaism.* Berkeley: University of California Press, 1991.

Diamond, Etan. *And I Will Dwell in Their Midst: Orthodox Jews in Suburbia.* Chapel Hill: University of North Carolina Press, 2000.

———. *Jews and Violence: Images, Ideologies, Realities.* New York: Oxford University Press, 2002.

Diner, Hasia. *Jews in America.* New York: Oxford University Press, 1999.

Eisenstadt, Peter. *Affirming the Covenant: A History of Temple B'rith Kodesh, Rochester, New York, 1848–1998.* Syracuse, N.Y.: Syracuse University Press, 1999.

Encyclopaedia Judaica. 16 vols. New York: Macmillan, 1972.

Erens, Patricia. *The Jew in American Cinema.* Bloomington: Indiana University Press, 1984.

Feingold, Henry L., ed. *The Jewish People in America.* 5 vols. Baltimore: Johns Hopkins University Press, 1995.

Fishman, Sylvia Barack. *A Breath of Life: Feminism in the American Jewish Community.* New York: Free Press, 1993.

Friedman, Lester D. *Hollywood's Image of the Jew.* New York: Ungar, 1982.

Gamm, Gerald. *Urban Exodus: Why the Jews Left Boston and the Catholics Stayed.* Cambridge, Mass.: Harvard University Press, 1999.

Gerber, David A., ed. *Anti-Semitism in American History.* Urbana: University of Illinois Press, 1986.

Goldman, Karla. *Beyond the Synagogue Gallery: Finding a Place for Women in American Judaism.* Cambridge, Mass.: Harvard University Press, 2000.

Goldman, Shalom. *God's Sacred Tongue: Hebrew and the American Imagination.* Chapel Hill: University of North Carolina Press, 2004.

Goldy, Robert L. The *Emergence of Jewish Theology in America.* Bloomington: Indiana University Press, 1990.

Greene, Melissa Fay. *The Temple Bombing.* Reading, Mass.: Addison-Wesley, 1996.

Grossman, Susan. *Daughters of the King: Women and the Synagogue.* Philadelphia: Jewish Publication Society, 1992.

Gurock, Jeffrey S, ed. *American Jewish Life, 1920–1990.* New York: Routledge, 1998.

———. *Judaism's Encounter with American Sports.* Bloomington: Indiana University Press, 1999.

Harris, Lis. *Holy Days: The World of a Hasidic Family.* New York: Summit Books, 1985.

Hordes, Stanley. *To the End of the Earth: A History of the Crypto-Jews of New Mexico.* New York: Columbia University Press, 2008.

Howe, Irving. *World of Our Fathers.* New York: Harcourt Brace Jovanovich, 1976.

Hyman, Paula, and Deborah Dash Moore, eds. *Jewish Women in America: An Historical Encyclopedia.* 2 vols. New York: Routledge, 1997.

Jaher, Frederic Cople. *A Scapegoat in the New Wilderness: The Origins and Rise of Anti-Semitism in America.* Cambridge, Mass.: Harvard University Press, 1994.

The Jewish Experience in America: A Historical Bibliography. Santa Barbara: ABC-Clio, 1983.

Joselit, Jenna Weissman. *New York's Jewish Jews: The Orthodox Community in the Interwar Years.* Bloomington: Indiana University Press, 1990.

———. *The Wonders of America: Reinventing Jewish Culture, 1880–1950.* New York: Hill and Wang, 1994.

Kaplan, Edward K. *Spiritual Radical: Abraham Joshua Heschel in America, 1940–1972.* New Haven, Conn.: Yale University Press, 2007.

Karff, Samuel E. "Judaism." In *Religions of the World,* edited by Niels C. Nielsen, Jr., et al., part 6. New York: St. Martins, 1983.

Karp, Abraham J. "The Emergence of an American Judaism." *EARE* 1:273–90.

———, ed. *The Jewish Experience in America.* 5 vols. Waltham, Mass.: American Jewish Historical Society, 1969. Documents.

Karp, Deborah B., and Abraham J. Karp. "Jewish Thought and Literature." *EARE* 2:1015–38.

Kaufman, David. *Shul with a Pool: The Synagogue-Center in American Jewish History.* Hanover, N.H.: Brandeis University Press/University Press of New England, 1999.

Klapper, Melissa R. *Jewish Girls Coming of Age in America, 1860–1920.* New York: New York University Press, 2006.

Knox, Israel. *Rabbi in America: The Story of Isaac M. Wise.* Boston: Little, Brown, 1957.

Korros, Alexandra Shecket, and Jonathan D. Sarna. *American Synagogue History: A Bibliography and State-of-the-Field Survey.* New York: M. Wiener, 1988.

Kraut, Benny. *German-Jewish Orthodoxy in an Immigrant Synagogue*. New York: M. Wiener, 1988.

Levine, Hillel. *The Death of an American Jewish Community*. New York: Free Press, 1992.

Linzer, Norman, David J. Schnall, and Jerome A. Chanes, eds. *A Portrait of the American Jewish Community*. Westport, Conn.: Praeger, 1998.

Marcus, Jacob Rader. *The Colonial American Jew, 1492–1776*. 3 vols. Detroit: Wayne State University Press, 1970. Documents.

———. *United States Jewry, 1776–1985*. 4 vols. Detroit: Wayne State University Press, 1989–93.

Medding, Peter Y. *A New Jewry? America since the Second World War*. New York: Oxford University Press, 1992.

Mintz, Alan. *Popular Culture and the Shaping of Holocaust Memory in America*. Seattle: University of Washington Press, 2001.

Mintz, Jerome. *Hasidic People: A Place in the New World*. Cambridge, Mass.: Harvard University Press, 1992.

Moore, Deborah Dash. *GI Jews: How World War II Changed a Generation*. Cambridge, Mass.: Harvard University Press, 2004.

———. "Social History of American Judaism." *EARE* 1:291–310.

———. *To the Golden Cities: Pursuing the Jewish Dream in Miami and L.A.* New York: Free Press, 1994.

Moore, Deborsh Dash, and S. Ilan Troen, ed. *Divergent Jewish Cultures: Israel and America*. New Haven: Yale University Press, 2001.

Nadell, Pamela S, ed. *American Jewish Women's History: A Reader*. New York: New York University Press, 2006.

———. *Women Who Would Be Rabbis*. Boston: Beacon, 1998.

Neusner, Jacob. *American Judaism: Adventure in Modernity*. Englewood Cliffs, N.J.: Prentice-Hall, 1972.

———. "Judaism in Contemporary America." *EARE* 1:311–14.

———. *The Way of Torah: An Introduction to Judaism*. 4th ed. Belmont, Calif.: Wadsworth, 1988.

Omer-Sherman, Ranen. *Diaspora and Zionism in Jewish American Literature: Lazarus, Syrkin, Reznikoff, and Roth*. Hanover: University Press of New England, 2002.

Oren, Dan A. *Joining the Club: A History of Jews and Yale*. Rev. ed. New Haven: Yale University Press, 2001.

Papo, Joseph. *Sephardim in Twentieth-Century America*. San Jose, Calif.: Pele Yoetz Books, 1987.

Postal, Bernard, and Lionel Koppman. *American Jewish Landmarks*. 4 vols. New York: Fleet Press, 1977, 1979, 1984, 1986.

Raphael, Marc Lee. *The Columbia History of Jews and Judaism in America*. New York: Columbia University Press, 2008.

———. *Judaism in America*. New York: Columbia University Press, 2003.

———. *Profiles in American Judaism*. San Francisco: Harper and Row, 1984.

———, ed. *What Is American about American Jewish History?* Williamsburg, Va.: College of William and Mary Religion Department, 1993.

Riess, Steven A., ed. *Sports and the American Jew*. Syracuse, N.Y.: Syracuse University Press, 1998.

Rischin, Moses. *The Promised City: New York's Jews, 1870–1914*. Cambridge, Mass.: Harvard University Press, 1962.

———, ed. *The Jews of North America*. Detroit: Wayne State University Press, 1987.

Rosten, Leo. *The Joys of Yiddish*. New York: Pocket Books, 1968.

Roth, Cecil. *A History of the Jews*. Rev. ed. New York: Schocken, 1970.

Sarna, Jonathan. *American Judaism: A History*. New Haven: Yale University Press, 2005.

Sarna, Jonathan, et al., eds. *The Jews of Boston*. New Haven: Yale University Press, 2005.

Schappes, Morris U., ed. *A Documentary History of the Jews in the United States, 1654–1875*. New York: Schocken, 1971.

Schoener, Allon. *The American Jewish Album*. New York: Rizzoli, 1983.

Schultz, Debra L. *Going South: Civil Rights Movement*. New York: New York University Press, 2006.

Schwartz, Shuly Rubin. *The Rabbi's Wife: The Rebetzin in American Jewish Life*. New York: New York University Press, 2005.

Scult, Mel, ed. *Conjurings of the Spirit [Journals of Mordecai Kaplan]*. Detroit: Wayne State University Press, 2001.

Shandler, Jeffrey. *Adventures in Yiddishland: Postvernacular Language and Culture*. Berkeley: University of California Press, 2005.

Shapiro, Malkah. *The Rebbe's Daughter: Memoir of a Hasidic Childhood*. Philadelphia: Jewish Publication Society, 2002.

Silverstein, Alan. *Alternatives to Assimilation: The Response of Reform Judaism to American Culture, 1840–1930*. Hanover, N.H.: University Press of New England, 1994.

Sklare, Marshall. *Conservative Judaism*. New York: Free Press, 1955.

Slobin, Mark. *Chosen Voices: The Story of the American Cantorate*. Urbana: University of Illinois Press, 1989.

Sorin, Gerald. *Tradition Transformed: The Jewish Experience in America*. Baltimore: Johns Hopkins University Press, 1997.

Strassfeld, Michael. *The Jewish Holidays: A Guide and Commentary*. New York: Harper and Row, 1985.

Trepp, Leo. *Judaism: Development and Life*. 3d ed. Belmont, Calif.: Wadsworth, 1982.

Weissbach, Lee Shai. *Jewish Life in Small-Town America*. New Haven: Yale University Press, 2005.

Wenger, Beth. *New York Jews and the Great Depression*. New Haven, Conn.: Yale University Press, 1996.

Wertheimer, Jack. *A People Divided: Judaism in Contemporary America*. New York: Basic, 1993.

———, ed. *The American Synagogue: A Sanctuary Transformed*. Cambridge: Cambridge University Press, 1987.

Whitfield, Stephen J. *American Space, Jewish Time*. Hamden, Conn.: Archon, 1988.

Winston, Hella. *Unchosen: The Hidden Lives of Hasidic Rebels*. Boston: Beacon, 2005.

Wischnitzer, Rachel. *Synagogue Architecture in the United States*. Philadelphia: Jewish Publication Society of America, 1955.

Woocher, Jonathan S. *Sacred Survival: The Civil Religion of American Jews*. Bloomington: Indiana University Press, 1986.

Zborowski, Mark, and Elizabeth Herzog. *Life Is with People: Culture of the Shtetl*. New York: Schocken, 1962.

I. Eastern Christianity

Afonsky, Bishop Gregory. *A History of the Orthodox Church in America 1917–1934*. Kodiak, Alaska: St. Herman's Theological Seminary Press, 1994.

Benz, Ernst. *The Eastern Orthodox Church*. Garden City, N.Y.: Doubleday, 1963.

Black, Lydia. *Russians in Alaska 1732–1867*. Fairbanks: University of Alaska Press, 2004.

Bobango, Gerald J. *The Romanian Orthodox Episcopate in America: the First Half Century, 1929–1979*. Jackson, Mich.: Romanian-American Heritage Center, 1979.

Chadwick, Henry. *The Early Church*. Harmondsworth, Middlesex, UK: Penguin, 1967.

Dyrud, Keith P., Michael Novak, and Rudolph J. Vecoli, eds. *The Other Catholics*. New York: Arno Press, 1978.

Efthimious, Miltiades B., and George A. Christopoulos, eds. *History of the Greek Orthodox Church in America*. New York: Greek Orthodox Archdiocese of North and South America, 1984.

Erickson, John H. *Orthodox Christians in America*. New York: Oxford University Press, 1999.

Fitzgerald, Thomas E. The *Orthodox Church*. Westport, Conn.: Greenwood, 1995.

Galavaris, George. The *Icon in the Life of the Church*. Leiden: Brill, 1981.

Garrett, Paul D. "Eastern Christianity." *EARE* 1:325–44.

———. *St. Innocent: Apostle to America*. Crestwood, N.Y.: St. Vladimir's Press, 1979.

Gilquist, Peter E. *Becoming Orthodox*. Ben Lomond, Calif.: Conciliar Press, 1992.

Hardwick, Susan Wiley. *Russian Refuge: Religion, Migration, and Settlement on the North American Pacific Rim*. Chicago: University of Chicago Press, 1993.

Kan, Sergei. *Memory Eternal: Tlingit Culture and Russian Orthodox Christianity through Two Centuries*. Seattle: University of Washington Press, 1999.

———. "Russian Orthodox Missionaries at Home and Abroad: The Case of Siberian and Alaskan Indigenous Peoples." In *Of Religion and Empire*, edited by Robert P. Geraci and Michael Khodarkovsky, 201–28. Ithans, N.Y.: Cornell University Press, 2001.

Kopan, Andrew T. "Greek Survival in Chicago: The Role of Ethnic Education, 1890–1980." In *Ethnic Chicago*, edited by Melvin G. Holli and Peter D'A. Jones, pp. 80–139. Grand Rapids, Mich.: Eerdmans, 1981.

Mathewes-Green, Frederica. *At the Corner of East and Now: A Modern Life in Ancient Christian Orthodoxy*. New York: Jeremy P. Tarcher, 2000.

Meyendorff, John. *The Orthodox Church*. New York: Pantheon, 1962.

Netsvetov, Iakov. *The Journals of Iakov Netsvetov: The Yukon Years, 1845–1863*. Translated by Lydia Black. Fairbanks: University of Alaska Press, 1984.

Oleksa, Michael, ed. *Alaskan Missionary Spirituality*. New York: Paulist, 1987.

Parry, Ken, ed. *The Blackwell Companion to Eastern Christianity*. Malden, Mass.: Blackwell, 2006.

Parry, Ken, et al., eds. *The Blackwell Dictionary of Eastern Christianity*. Malden, Mass.: Blackwell, 2006.

Saloutos, Theodore. *The Greeks in the United States.* Cambridge, Mass.: Harvard University Press, 1964.

Tarasar, Constance J., ed. *Orthodox America, 1794–1976.* Syosset, N.Y.: Orthodox Church in America, 1975.

Ware, Timothy. *The Orthodox Church.* Baltimore: Penguin, 1964, 1993.

Znamenski, Andrei A., ed., *Through Orthodox Eyes: Russian Missionary Narratives of Travels to the Denai'ina Ahnta, 1850s-1930s.* Fairbanks: University of Alaska Press, 2003.

J. Roman Catholicism
(*SEE ALSO* V. "Latino Religion")

Abell, Aaron I. *American Catholicism and Social Action.* Notre Dame, Ind.: University of Notre Dame Press, 1960.

Abramson, Harold J. *Ethnic Diversity in Catholic America.* New York: Wiley, 1973.

Allitt, Patrick. *Catholic Converts: British and American Intellectuals Turn to Rome.* Ithaca, N.Y.: Cornell University Press, 1997.

———. *Catholic Intellectuals and Conservative Politics in America, 1950–1985.* Ithaca, N.Y.: Cornell University Press, 1993.

Appleby, R. Scott. *"Church and Age Unite!" The Modernist Impulse in American Catholicism.* Notre Dame, Ind.: University of Notre Dame Press, 1992.

Avella, Steven M. *This Confident Church: Catholic Leadership and Life in Chicago, 1940–1965.* Notre Dame, Ind.: University of Notre Dame Press, 1992.

Barry, Colman J., O.S.B. *The Catholic Church and German Americans.* Milwaukee: Bruce, 1953.

Billington, Ray Allen. *The Protestant Crusade, 1800–1860.* Chicago: Quadrangle, 1964.

Black, Gregory D. *The Catholic Crusade against the Movies, 1940–1975.* Cambridge: Cambridge University Press, 1998.

Brandewie, Ernest. *In the Light of the Word: Divine Word Missionaries of North America.* Maryknoll, N.Y.: Orbis, 2000.

Brown, Alden V. *The Grail Movement and American Catholicism, 1940–1975.* Notre Dame, Ind.: University of Notre Dame Press, 1989.

Brown, Dorothy M., and Elizabeth McKeown. *The Poor Belong to Us: Catholic Charities and American Welfare.* Cambridge, Mass.: Harvard University Press, 1997.

Burns, Jeffrey M., Ellen Skerrett, and Joseph M. White, eds. *Keeping Faith: European and Asian Catholic Immigrants.* Maryknoll, N.Y.: Orbis, 2000.

Butler, Anne M., Michael E. Engh, and Thomas W. Spalding, eds. *The Frontiers and Catholic Identities.* Maryknoll, N.Y.: Orbis, 1999.

Campbell, Debra. "Catholicism from Independence to World War I." *EARE* 1:357–74.

Carey, Patrick W., ed. *American Catholic Religious Thought.* New York: Paulist, 1987.

———. *Orestes A. Brownson.* Grand Rapids, Mich.: Eerdmans, 2004.

Catreine, Darryl V. *Conservative Catholicism and the Carmelites.* Bloomington: Indiana University Press, 2001.

Choquette, J. E. Robert. "French Catholicism in the New World." *EARE* 1:223–38.

Clark, Emily. *Masterless Mistresses: The New Orleans Ursulines and the Development of a New World Society, 1727–1834.* Chapel Hill: University of North Carolina Press, 2007.

Coburn, Carol K., and Martha Smith. *Spirited Lives: How Nuns Shaped Catholic Culture and American Life, 1836–1920*. Chapel Hill: University of North Carolina Press, 1999.

Cogley, John. *Catholic America*. Garden City, N.Y.: Doubleday, 1973.

Cort, John C. *Dreadful Conversions: The Making of a Catholic Socialist*. New York: Fordham University Press, 2003.

Crosby, Donald F., S.J. *God, Church, and Flag: Senator Joseph R. McCarthy and the Catholic Church, 1950–1957*. Chapel Hill: University of North Carolina Press, 1978.

Cross, Robert D. *The Emergence of Liberal Catholicism in America*. Cambridge, Mass.: Harvard University Press, 1967.

Cullen, Jim. *Restless in the Promised Land: Catholics and the American Dream*. Franklin, Wis.: Sheed & Ward, 2001.

Cunningham, Lawrence S. *Thomas Merton and the Monastic Vision*. Grand Rapids, Mich.: Eerdmans, 1999.

Curran, Charles E. *Catholic Social Teaching 1891–Present*. Washington, D.C.: Georgetown University Press, 2002.

Curran, Robert Emmett. "American Catholic Thought." *EARE* 2:997–1014.

D'Agostino, Peter R. *Rome in America: Transnational Catholic Ideology from the Risorgimento to Fascism*. Chapel Hill: University of North Carolina Press, 2004.

D'Antonio, William, James D. Davidson, Dean R. Hoge, and Katherine Meyer. *American Catholics: Gender, Generation, and Commitment*. Walnut Creek, Calif.: Altamira Press, 2001.

Davis, Cyprian, O.S.B. *The History of Black Catholics in the United States*. New York: Crossroad, 1990.

Deedy, John. *The Catholic Church in the Twentieth Century*. Collegeville, Minn.: Liturgical Press, 2000.

Deggs, Sister Mary Bernard. *No Cross, No Crown: Black Nuns in Nineteenth-Century New Orleans*. Bloomington: Indiana University Press, 2000.

DeSanctis, Michael E. *Building from Belief: Advance, Retreat, and Compromise in the Remaking of Catholic Church Architecture*. Collegeville, Minn.: Liturgical Press, 2002.

Dolan, Jay P. *The American Catholic Experience*. Garden City, N.Y.: Doubleday, 1985.

———, ed. *The American Catholic Parish*. 2 vols. New York: Paulist, 1987.

———. *Catholic Revivalism*. Notre Dame, Ind.: University of Notre Dame Press, 1978.

———. *The Immigrant Church*. Baltimore: Johns Hopkins University Press, 1975.

———. *In Search of an American Catholicism*. New York: Oxford University Press, 2002.

Dolan, Timothy Michael. *"Some Seed Fell on Good Ground": The Life of Edwin V. O'Hara*. Washington, D.C.: Catholic University of America Press, 1992.

Ebaugh, Helen Rose Fuchs. *Women in the Vanishing Cloister*. New Brunswick, N.J.: Rutgers University Press, 1993.

Ellis, John Tracy, ed. *Documents of American Catholic History*. 2 vols. Chicago: H. Regnery, 1967.

Ellis, John Tracy, and Robert Trisco. *A Guide to American Catholic History*. 2d ed. Santa Barbara, Calif.: ABC-Clio, 1982.

Fisher, James Terence. *The Catholic Counterculture in America, 1933–1962*. Chapel Hill: University of North Carolina Press, 1989.

———. *Catholics in America.* New York : Oxford University Press, 2000.

———. *Dr. America: The Lives of Thomas A. Dooley, 1927–1961.* Amherst: University of Massachusetts Press, 1997.

Fogarty, Gerald P., S.J., ed. *Patterns of Episcopal Leadership.* New York: Macmillan, 1989.

Franchot, Jenny. *Roads to Rome: The Antebellum Protestant Encounter with Catholicism.* Berkeley: University of California Press, 1994.

Froehle, Bryan T., and Mary L. Gautier, *Catholicism USA.* Maryknoll, N.Y.: Orbis, 2000.

Gamm, Gerald. *Urban Exodus: Why the Jews Left Boston and the Catholics Stayed.* Cambridge, Mass.: Harvard University Press, 1999.

Gillis, Chester. *Roman Catholicism in America.* New York: Columbia University Press, 1999.

Glazier, Michael, and Thomas J. Shelley, eds. *The Encyclopedia of American Catholic History.* Collegeville, Minn.: Liturgical Press, 1997.

Gleason, Philip. "A Browser's Guide to American Catholicism." *Theology Today* 38, no. 3 (Oct. 1981): 373–88.

———, ed. *Catholicism in America.* New York: Harper and Row, 1970.

———. *Contending with Modernity: Catholic Higher Education in the Twentieth Century.* New York: Oxford University Press, 1995.

———. *Keeping the Faith: American Catholicism, Past and Present.* Notre Dame, Ind.: University of Notre Dame Press, 1987.

Gray, Francine duPlessix. *Divine Disobedience: Profiles in Catholic Radicalism.* New York: Vintage, 1971.

Greeley, Andrew. *The American Catholic: A Social Portrait.* New York: Basic, 1977.

———. *That Most Distressful Nation: The Taming of the American Irish.* Chicago: Quadrangle, 1972.

Greeley, Andrew, and Peter H. Rossi. *The Education of Catholic Americans.* Chicago: Aldine, 1966.

Greene, Victor. *For God and Country: The Rise of Polish and Lithuanian Ethnic Consciousness in America.* Madison: State Historical Society of Wisconsin, 1975.

Halsey, William M. *The Survival of American Innocence.* Notre Dame, Ind.: University of Notre Dame Press, 1980.

Handlin, Oscar. *Boston's Immigrants.* Rev. ed. Cambridge, Mass.: Harvard University Press, 1991.

Hassan, Bernard. *The American Catholic Catalog.* San Francisco: Harper and Row, 1980.

Hedin, Raymond. *Married to the Church.* Bloomington: Indiana University Press, 1995.

Heineman, Kenneth J. *A Catholic New Deal: Religion and Reform in Depression Pittsburgh.* University Park: Penn State University Press, 1999.

Hennessey, Thomas C., S.J. *How the Jesuits Settled in New York: A Documentary Account.* New York: Fordham University Press, 2003.

Inchausti, Robert. *Thomas Merton's American Prophecy.* Albany: State University of New York Press, 1998.

Jenkins, Philip. *The New Anti-Catholicism.* New York: Oxford University Press, 2003.

———. *Pedophiles and Priests.* New York: Oxford University Press, 2001.

Kane, Paula M. *Separatism and Subculture: Boston Catholicism, 1900–1920.* Chapel Hill: University of North Carolina Press, 1994.

———. "'She Offered Herself Up': The Victim Soul and Victim Spirituality in Catholicism," *Church History* 71, no. 1 (Mar. 2002): 80–119.

Kantowicz, Edward T. *Corporation Sole: Cardinal Mundelein and Chicago Catholicism.* Notre Dame, Ind.: University of Notre Dame Press, 1983.

Kaufman, Christopher J. *Ministry and Meaning: A Religious History of Catholic Health Care in the United States.* New York: Crossroad, 1994.

———. *Patriotism and Fraternalism in the Knights of Columbus.* New York: Crossroad, 2001.

Kennelly, Karen, C.S.J., ed. *American Catholic Women.* New York: Macmillan, 1989.

Keyser, Les, and Barbara Keyser. *Hollywood and the Catholic Church.* Chicago: Loyola University Press, 1984.

Klejment, Anne, and Nancy L. Roberts. *American Catholic Pacifism: The Influence of Dorothy Day and the Catholic Worker Movement.* Westport, Conn.: Praeger, 1996.

Krugler, John D. *English and Catholic: The Lords Baltimore in the Seventeenth Century.* Baltimore: Johns Hopkins University Press, 2004.

Lewis, Helen M. and Monica Appleby. *Mountain Sisters: From Convent to Community in Appalachia.* Lexington, Ky.: University Press of Kentucky, 2004.

Light, Dale B. *Rome and the New Republic: Conflict and Community in Philadelphia Catholicism between the Revolution and the Civil War.* Notre Dame, Ind.: University of Notre Dame Press, 1996.

Lynch, Christopher Owen. *Selling Catholicism: Bishop Sheen and the Power of Television.* Lexington: University Press of Kentucky, 1998.

MacGregor, Morris J. *The Emergence of a Black Catholic Community: St. Augustine's in Washington.* Washington, D.C.: Catholic University of America Press, 1999.

———. *Steadfast in the Faith: The Life of Patrick Cardinal O'Boyle.* Washington, D.C.: Catholic University of America Press, 2006.

Mahoney, Kathleen A. *Catholic Higher Education in Protestant America: The Jesuits and Harvard in the Age of the University.* Baltimore: Johns Hopkins University Press, 2003.

Marlett, Jeffrey D. *Saving the Heartland: Catholic Missionaries in Rural America, 1920–1960.* DeKalb: Northern Illinois University Press, 2002.

Massa, Mark S. *Catholics and American Culture.* New York: Crossroad, 1999.

McDonough, Peter, and Eugene C. Bianchi. *Passionate Uncertainty: Inside the American Jesuits.* Berkeley: University of California Press, 2002.

McGreevy, John T. *Catholicism and American Freedom.* New York: Norton, 2003.

———. *Parish Boundaries: The Catholic Encounter with Race in the Twentieth-Century Urban North.* Chicago: University of Chicago Press, 1996.

McGuire, Meredith B. *Pentecostal Catholics.* Philadelphia: Temple University Press, 1982.

McKenzie, John L. *The Roman Catholic Church.* Garden City, N.Y.: Doubleday, 1971.

McNamara, Jo Ann Kay. *Sisters in Arms: Catholic Nuns through Two Millennia.* Cambridge, Mass.: Harvard University Press, 1996.

Miller, Randall, and Jon Wakelyn. *Catholics in the Old South.* Macon, Ga.: Mercer University Press, 1999.

Moloney, Deirdre M. *American Catholic Lay Groups and Transatlantic Social Reform in the Progressive Era.* Chapel Hill: University of North Carolina Press, 2002.

Morris, Charles R. *American Catholic*. New York: Times Books, 1997.

Morrow, Diane Batts. *Persons of Color and Religious at the Same Time: The Oblate Sisters of Providence, 1828–1860*. Chapel Hill: University of North Carolina Press, 2002.

Namorato, Michael V. *The Catholic Church in Mississippi, 1911–1984*. Westport, Conn.: Greenwood Press, 1998

Nelson, Sioban. *Say Little, Do Much. Nurses, Nuns, and Hospitals in the Nineteenth Century*. Philadelphia: University of Pennsylvania Press, 2001.

New Catholic Encyclopedia. 15 vols. 2nd ed. Detroit, Mich.: Thomson/Gale Group; Washington, D.C.: Catholic University of America, 2003.

Oates, Mary J. *The Catholic Philanthropic Tradition in America*. Bloomington: Indiana University Press, 1995.

O'Brien, David J. *Isaac Hecker*. New York: Paulist, 1992.

Ochs, Stephen J. *A Black Patriot and a White Priest: André Calloux and Claude Paschal Maister in the Civil War*. Baton Rouge: Louisiana State University Press, 2000.

———. *Desegregating the Altar: The Josephites and the Struggle for Black Priests, 1871–1960*. Baton Rouge: Louisiana State University Press, 1990.

O'Connell, Marvin R. *Critics on Trial: An Introduction to the Catholic Modernist Crisis*. Washington, D.C.: Catholic University of America Press, 1994.

———. *Edward Sorin*. Notre Dame: University of Notre Dame Press, 2000.

———. *John Ireland and the American Catholic Church*. St. Paul: Minnesota Historical Society Press, 1988.

O'Connor, Thomas H. *Boston Catholics*. Boston: Northeastern University Press, 1998.

Oetgen, Jerome. *Mission to America: A History of Saint Vincent Archabbey*. Washington, D.C.: Catholic University of America Press, 2000.

The Official Catholic Directory. New York. Annual.

Orsi, Robert Anthony. *The Madonna of 115th Street: Faith and Community in Italian Harlem, 1880–1950*. New Haven, Conn.: Yale University Press, 1985.

———. *Thank You, St. Jude: Women's Devotion to the Patron Saint of Hopeless Causes*. New Haven, Conn.: Yale University Press, 1996.

O'Toole, James M. *Militant and Triumphant: William Henry O'Connell and the Catholic Church in Boston, 1859–1944*. Notre Dame, Ind.: University of Notre Dame Press, 1992.

Piehl, Mel. *Breaking Bread: The Catholic Worker and the Origin of Catholic Radicalism in America*. Philadelphia: Temple University Press, 1982.

———, ed. *Habits of Devotion: Catholic Religious Practice in Twentieth Century America*. Ithaca, N.Y.: Cornell University Press, 2004.

Plante, Thomas G., ed. *Sins Against the Innocent: Sexual Abuse by Priests and the Role of the Catholic Church*. Westport, Conn.: Praeger, 2004.

Prendergast, William B. *The Catholic Voter in American Politics*. Notre Dame, Ind.: University of Notre Dame Press, 1999.

Reese, Thomas J., S.J. *Archbishop*. San Francisco: Harper and Row, 1989.

Schier, Tracy, and Cynthia Russet, eds. *Catholic Women's Colleges in America*. Baltimore: Johns Hopkins University Press, 2002.

Schultz, Nancy Lusignan. *Fire and Roses: The Burning of the Charlestown Convent*. Boston, Mass.: Northeastern University Press, 2002.

Shea, William M., and Daniel Van Slyke, eds. *Trying Times: Essays on Catholic Higher Education in the 20th Century.* Atlanta: Scholars Press, 1999.

Shelley, Thomas J. *Greenwich Village Catholics.* Washington, D.C.: Catholic University of America Press, 2003.

Sisters, Servants of the Immaculate Heart of Mary, Monroe, Michigan. *Building Sisterhood: A Feminist History of the Sisters, Servants of the Immaculate Heart of Mary.* Syracuse, N.Y.: Syracuse University Press, 1997.

Slawson, Douglas J. *The Department of Education Battle, 1918–1932: Public Schools, Catholic Schools, and the Social Order.* Notre Dame, Ind.: University of Notre Dame Press, 2005.

Southern, David W. *John LaFarge and the Limits of Catholic Interracialism, 1911–1963.* Baton Rouge: Louisiana State University Press, 1996.

Spalding, Thomas W. *The Premier See: A History of the Archdiocese of Baltimore, 1789–1994.* Baltimore: Johns Hopkins University Press, 1995.

Sparr, Arnold. *To Promote, Defend, and Redeem: The Catholic Literary Revival and the Cultural Transformation of American Catholicism, 1920–1960.* New York: Greenwood, 1990

Sterne, Evelyn Savidge. *Ballots and Bibles: Ethnic Politics and the Catholic Church in Providence.* Ithaca, N.Y.: Cornell University Press, 2003.

Taves, Ann. *The Household of Faith: Roman Catholic Devotions in Mid-Nineteenth Century America.* Notre Dame, Ind.: University of Notre Dame Press, 1986.

Tentler, Leslie Woodcock. *Catholics and Contraception: An American History.* Ithaca, N.Y.: Cornell University Press, 2004.

Thorn, William, et al., eds. *Dorothy Day and the Catholic Worker Movement: Centenary Essays.* Milwaukee: Marquette University Press, 2001.

Vinyard, JoEllen McNerney. *For Faith and Fortune: The Education of Catholic Immigrants in Detroit, 1805–1925.* Urbana: University of Illinois Press, 1998.

Walsh, Frank. *Sin and Censorship: The Catholic Church and the Motion Picture Industry.* New Haven, Conn.: Yale University Press, 1996.

Weaver, Mary Jo. *Cloister and Community: Life within a Carmelite Monastery.* Bloomington, Ind.: Indiana University Press, 2002.

———. *New Catholic Women.* San Francisco: Harper and Row, 1985.

———. "The Roman Catholic Heritage." *EARE* 1:153–70.

———, ed. *What's Left?: Liberal American Catholics.* Bloomington: Indiana University Press, 1999.

Weaver, Mary Jo, and R. Scott Appleby, eds. *Being Right: Conservative Catholics in America.* Bloomington: Indiana University Press, 1995.

White, James F. *Roman Catholic Worship.* New York: Paulist, 1995.

Wieczerzak, Joseph. *Bishop Francis Hodur.* New York: Columbia University Press, 1998.

Williams, Peter W. "Catholicism since World War I." *EARE* 1:375–90.

Wills, Garry. *Bare Ruined Choirs.* Garden City, N.Y.: Doubleday, 1972.

Woods. Thomas E. *The Church Confronts Modernity: Catholic Intellectuals and the Progressive Era.* New York: Columbia University Press, 2007.

Woolen, David B., and Richard G. Kurial, eds. *FDR, the Vatican, and the Roman Catholic Church in America, 1933–1945.* New York: Palgrave Macmillan, 2003.

Wrobel, Paul. *Our Way: Family, Parish, and Neighborhood in a Polish-American Community.* Notre Dame, Ind.: University of Notre Dame Press, 1979.

Zimdars-Swartz, Sandra L. *Encountering Mary: From La Salette to Medjugorje.* Princeton, N.J.: Princeton University Press, 1991.

Zöller, Michael. *Washington and Rome: Catholicism in American Culture.* Notre Dame, Ind.: University of Notre Dame Press, 1999.

K. Protestantism and the Reformation Era

Chadwick, Owen. *The Reformation.* Grand Rapids, Mich.: Eerdmans, 1965.

Dillenberger, John, and Claude Welch. *Protestant Christianity.* New York: Macmillan, 1988.

Hillerbrand, Hans J., ed. *The Protestant Reformation.* New York: Macmillan, 1968.

MacCulloch, Diarmid. *The Reformation.* New York: Penguin, 2003.

Ozment, Steven. *Protestants.* New York: Walker, 1992.

Spitz, Lewis W. *The Protestant Reformation, 1517–1559.* New York: Harper and Row, 1985.

L. Luther and the Lutheran Tradition

Bainton, Roland H. *Here I Stand: A Life of Martin Luther.* Nashville: Abingdon, 1950.

Bodensieck, Julius, ed. *The Encyclopedia of the Lutheran Church.* 3 vols. Minneapolis: Augsburg, 1965.

Cimino, Richard, ed. *Lutherans Today: American Lutheran Identity in the Twenty-first Century.* Grand Rapids, Mich.: Eerdmans, 2003.

Coburn, Carol K. *Life at Four Corners: Religion, Gender, and Education in a German-Lutheran Community, 1868–1945.* Lawrence: University Press of Kansas, 1992.

Dillenberger, John, ed. *Martin Luther: Selections from His Writings.* Garden City, N.Y.: Doubleday, 1961.

Erikson, Erik H. *Young Man Luther.* New York: Norton, 1958.

Groh, John E., and Robert H. Smith, eds. *The Lutheran Church in North American Life.* St. Louis: Clayton, 1979.

Klein, Christa R. "Lutheranism." *EARE* 1:431–50.

Kleiner, John W., ed. *Henry Melchior Muhlenberg.* Lewiston, N.Y.: E. Mellen, 1998.

Kuenning, Paul P. *The Rise and Fall of American Lutheran Pietism.* Macon, Ga.: Mercer University Press, 1988.

Lagerquist, L. DeAne. *In America the Men Milk the Cows: Factors of Gender, Ethnicity, and Religion in the Americanization of Norwegian-American Women.* Brooklyn: Carlson, 1991.

Nelson, E. Clifford, ed. *The Lutherans in North America.* Philadelphia: Fortress, 1975.

Nichol, Todd W. *All These Lutherans.* Minneapolis: Augsburg, 1986.

Oberman, Heiko. *Luther.* New Haven: Yale University Press, 2006.

Pelikan, Jaroslav J. *Bach among the Theologians.* Philadelphia: Fortress, 1986.

———. "The Lutheran Heritage." *EARE* 1:419–30.

Reuss, Carl F. *Profiles of Lutherans in the U.S.A.* Minneapolis: Augsburg, 1982.

Todd, Mary. *Authority Vested: A Story of Identity and Change in the Lutheran Church–Missouri Synod.* Grand Rapids, Mich.: Eerdmans, 2000.

M. Anglicanism and the Episcopal Church

Armentrout, Don S. "Episcopal Splinter Groups: Schisms in the Episcopal Church, 1963–1985." *Historical Magazine of the Protestant Episcopal Church* 55, no. 4 (Dec. 1986): 295–320.

Armentrout, Don S., and Robert B. Slocum, eds. *An Episcopal Dictionary of the Church.* New York: Church Pub., 1999.

Bates, Stephen. *A Church at War: Anglicans and Homosexuality.* New York: Palgrave Macmillan/I. B. Tauris, 2006.

Beary, Michael J. *Black Bishop: Edward T. Demby and the Struggle for Racial Equality in the Episcopal Church.* Urbana: University of Illinois Press, 2001.

Bernard, G. W. *The King's Reformation: Henry VIII and the Remaking of the English Church.* New Haven: Yale University Press, 2005.

Bond, Edward L. *Damned Souls in a Tobacco Colony: Religion in Seventeenth-Century Virginia.* Macon, Ga.: Mercer University Press, 2000.

Bourgeois, Michael. *All Things Human: Henry Codman Potter and the Social Gospel.* Urbana: University of Illinois Press, 2004.

Boyer, Peter J. "A Church Asunder." *New Yorker,* Apr. 17, 2006, 54–65.

Bridenbaugh, Carl. *Mitre and Sceptre.* London: Oxford University Press, 1967.

Butler, Diana Hochstedt. *Standing against the Whirlwind: Evangelical Episcopalians in Nineteenth-Century America.* New York: Oxford University Press, 1995.

Chapman, Mark. *Anglicanism: A Very Short Introduction.* Oxford, UK: Oxford University Press, 2006.

Chorley, E. Clowes. *Men and Movements in the American Episcopal Church.* New York: Scribners, 1946.

Davies, Horton. *Worship and Theology in England.* 5 vols. Princeton, N.J.: Princeton University Press, 1961–75.

DeMille, George E. *The Catholic Movement in the American Episcopal Church.* Philadelphia: Church Historical Society, 1950.

Doll, Peter M. *Revolution, Religion, and National Identity: Imperial Anglicanism in British North America, 1745–1795.* Cranbury, N.J.: Farleigh Dickinson University Press, 2000.

Donovan, Mary Sudman. *A Different Call: Women's Ministries in the Episcopal Church, 1850–1920.* Wilton, Conn.: Morehouse-Barlow, 1986.

Duffy, Eamon. *The Stripping of the Altars: Traditional Religion in England, 1400–1580.* New Haven: Yale University Press, 2005.

The Episcopal Church Annual. Wilton, Conn.: Morehouse-Barlow.

Evans, G. R., and J. Robert Wright, eds. *The Anglican Tradition: A Handbook of Sources.* Minneapolis: Fortress, 1991.

Griffiss, James E. *The Anglican Vision.* Cambridge, Mass.: Cowley, 1997.

Guelzo, Allen C. *For the Union of Evangelical Christendom: The Irony of the Reformed Episcopalians.* University Park: Pennsylvania State University Press, 1994.

Harp, Gillis J. *Brahmin Prophet: Phillips Brooks and the Path of Liberal Protestantism.* Lanham, Md.: Rowman & Littlefield, 2003.

Hassett, Miranda K. *Anglican Communion in Crisis: How Episcopal Dissidents and Their African Allies Are Reshaping Anglicanism.* Princeton, N.J.: Princeton University Press, 2007.

Hein, David. *Noble Powell and the Episcopal Establishment in the Twentieth Century.* Urbana: University of Illinois Press, 2001.

Hein, David, and Gardiner H. Shattuck, Jr. *The Episcopalians.* Westport, Conn: Praeger, 2004.

Holmes, David L. "The Anglican Tradition and the Episcopal Church." *EARE* 1:391–418.

———. *A Brief History of the Episcopal Church.* Valley Forge, Pa.: Trinity Press International, 1993.

Isaac, Rhys. *The Transformation of Virginia, 1740–1790.* Chapel Hill: University of North Carolina Press, 1982.

Jones, Tod E. *The Broad Church: A Biography of a Movement.* Lanham, Md.: Lexington Books, 2003.

Lewis, Harold T. *Yet with a Steady Beat: The African American Struggle for Recognition in the Episcopal Church.* Valley Forge, Pa.: Trinity Press International, 1996.

Loveland, Clara O. *The Critical Years: The Reconstruction of the Anglican Church in the United States of America, 1780–1789.* Greenwich, Conn.: Seabury Press, 1956.

Marshall, Paul V. *One, Catholic, and Apostolic: Samuel Seabury and the Early Episcopal Church.* New York: Church Publishing, 2004.

Mullin, Robert Bruce. *Episcopal Vision/American Reality.* New Haven, Conn.: Yale University Press, 1986.

Neill, Stephen. *Anglicanism.* 4th ed. New York: Oxford University Press, 1978.

Nelson, John K. *A Blessed Company: Parishes, Parsons and Parishioners in Anglican Virginia, 1690–1776.* Chapel Hill: University of North Carolina Press, 2002.

Prelinger, Catherine M. *Episcopal Women.* New York: Oxford University Press, 1994.

Prichard, Robert W. *A History of the Episcopal Church.* Harrisburg, Pa.: Morehouse, 1999.

———. *The Nature of Salvation: Theological Consensus in the Episcopal Church, 1801–73.* Urbana: University of Illinois Press, 1997.

Rankin, Richard. *Ambivalent Churchmen and Evangelical Churchwomen: The Religion of the Episcopal Elite in North Carolina, 1800–1860.* Columbia: University of South Carolina Press, 1993.

Rhoden, Nancy L. *Revolutionary Anglicanism: The Colonial Church of England Clergy during the American Revolution.* New York: New York University Press, 1999.

Rowthorn, Anne W. *Samuel Seabury.* New York: Seabury Press, 1983

Sachs, William L. *The Transformation of Anglicanism.* Cambridge: Cambridge University Press, 1993.

Sachs, William L., and Thomas Holland. *Restoring the Ties That Bind: The Grassroots Transformation of the Episcopal Church.* New York: Church Publishing, 2003.

Shattuck, Gardiner H. *Episcopalians and Race.* Lexington: University of Kentucky Press, 2000.

Steiner, Bruce. *Samuel Seabury.* Athens: Ohio State University Press, 1971.

Sumner, David E. *The Episcopal Church's History, 1945–1985.* Wilton, Conn.: Morehouse-Barlow, 1987.

Townsend, Craig D. *Faith in Their Own Color: Black Episcopalians in Antebellum New York City.* New York: Columbia University Press, 2005.

Upton, Dell. *Holy Things and Profane: Anglican Parish Churches in Colonial Virginia.* Cambridge, Mass.: Harvard University Press, 1986.

Vaudry, Richard W. *Anglicans and the Atlantic World: High Churchmen, Evangelicals, and the Quebec Connection.* Montreal: McGill-Queen's University Press, 2003.

Wall, John N., Jr. *A New Dictionary for Episcopalians.* Minneapolis: Winston Press, 1985.

Ward, Kevin. *A History of Global Anglicanism.* Cambridge, UK: Cambridge University Press, 2006.

Williams, Rowan. *Anglican Identities.* Cambridge, Mass.: Cowley, 2003.

Woolverton, John F. *Colonial Anglicanism in North America.* Detroit: Wayne State University Press, 1984.

———. *The Education of Phillips Brooks.* Urbana: University of Illinois Press, 1995.

———. *Robert H. Gardiner and the Reunification of Worldwide Christianity in the Progressive Era.* Columbia: University of Missouri Press, 2005.

———, ed., "Special Pre-General Convention 2006 Issue" *Anglican and Episcopal History* 75, no. 1 (Mar. 2006). Collection of articles providing background on debate over homosexuality.

Wright, J. Robert. *Saint Thomas Church Fifth Avenue.* Grand Rapids, Mich.: Eerdmans, 2001.

N. The Reformed Tradition

1. CALVIN AND CALVINISM

Benedict, Philip. *Christ's Churches Purely Reformed: A Social History of Calvinism.* New Haven: Yale University Press, 2002.

Bouwsma, William J. *John Calvin.* New York: Oxford University Press, 1988.

Dillenberger, John, ed. *John Calvin, Selections from His Writings.* Garden City, N.Y.: Doubleday, 1971.

Dyrness, William A. *Reformed Theology and Visual Culture: The Protestant Imagination from Calvin to Edwards.* Cambridge, England: Cambridge University Press, 2004.

Finney, Paul Corby, ed. *Seeing Beyond the Word: Visual Arts and the Calvinist Tradition.* Grand Rapids: Eerdmans, 1999.

McNeill, John T. *The History and Character of Calvinism.* New York: Oxford University Press, 1954.

———, ed. *Calvin: Institutes of the Christian Religion I and II.* Philadelphia: Westminster, 1977.

Stroup, George W., ed. *Reformed Reader: A Sourcebook in Christian Theology.* Louisville, Ky.: Westminster/John Knox, 1993.

Tipson, Baird. "The Calvinist Heritage." *EARE* 1:451–66.

Wendel, François. *Calvin.* London: Collins, 1963.

2. THE REFORMED FAITH IN BRITAIN

George, Charles H., and Katherine George. *The Protestant Mind of the English Reformation, 1570–1640.* Princeton, N.J.: Princeton University Press, 1961.

Haller, William. *The Rise of Puritanism.* New York: Harper, 1938.

Hill, Christopher. *Society and Puritanism in Pre-Revolutionary England.* New York: Schocken, c. 1964 and 1967.

Knappen, M. M. *Tudor Puritanism.* Chicago: University of Chicago Press, 1939.

Little, David. *Religion, Order and Law: A Study in Pre-Revolutionary England*. New York: Harper and Row, 1969.

New, John F. H. *Anglican and Puritan*. Stanford, Calif.: Stanford University Press, 1964.

Ridley, Jasper. *John Knox*. New York: Oxford University Press, 1968.

Simpson, Alan. *Puritanism in Old and New England*. Chicago: University of Chicago Press, 1955.

Walzer, Michael. *The Revolution of the Saints*. Cambridge, Mass.: Harvard University Press, 1965.

Wilson, John F. *Pulpit in Parliament: Puritanism during the English Civil War Years, 1640–1648*. Princeton, N.J.: Princeton University Press, 1969.

3. BRITAIN AND AMERICA: GENERAL

Cashdollar, Charles D. *A Spiritual Home: Life in British and American Reformed Congregations, 1830–1915*. University Park. Pa.: Pennsylvania State University Press, 2000.

Hart, D.G., ed. *Dictionary of the Presbyterian and Reformed Tradition in America*. Phillipsburg, N.J.: P&R, 2005

4. NEW ENGLAND PURITANISM

Anderson, Douglas. *William Bradford's Books: Of Plimmoth Plantation and the Printed Word*. Baltimore: Johns Hopkins University Press, 2003.

Benes, Peter, ed. *New England Meeting House and Church: 1630–1850*. Boston: Boston University, 1979.

Benes, Peter, and Philip D. Zimmerman, eds. *New England Meeting House and Church, 1630–1850*. Boston: Boston University, 1979.

Bercovitch, Sacvan. The *Puritan Origins of the American Self*. New Haven, Conn.: Yale University Press, 1975.

Boyer, Paul, and Stephen Nissenbaum. *Salem Possessed*. Cambridge, Mass.: Harvard University Press, 1974.

Bozeman, Theodore Dwight. *To Live Ancient Lives: The Primitivist Dimension in Puritanism*. Chapel Hill: University of North Carolina Press, 1988.

———. *The Precisionist Strain: Disciplinary Religion and Antinomian Backlash in Puritanism to 1638*. Chapel Hill: University of North Carolina Press, 2004.

Breen, Louis A. *Transgressing the Bounds: Subversive Enterprises among the Puritan Elite in Massachusetts, 1630–1692*. New York : Oxford University Press, 2001

Bremer, Francis J. *The Puritan Experiment*. New York: St. Martin's, 1976.

Bremer, Francis J., and Lynn A. Botelho, eds. *The World of John Winthrop: Essays on England and New England, 1588–1649*. Charlottesville: University of Virginia Press, 2005.

Bush, Sargent, Jr., ed. *The Correspondence of John Cotton*. Chapel Hill: University of North Carolina Press, 2001.

Byrd, James P. *The Challenge of Roger Williams*. Macon, Ga.: Mercer University Press, 2002.

Cooper, James F., Jr. *Tenacious of Their Liberties: The Congregationalists in Colonial Massachusetts*. New York: Oxford University Press, 1999.

Cowing, Cedric B. *The Saving Remnant: Religion and the Settling of New England*. Urbana: University of Illinois Press, 1995.

Delbanco, Andrew. *The Puritan Ordeal*. Cambridge, Mass.: Harvard University Press, 1989.

Donnelly, Marian Card. *The New England Meeting Houses of the Seventeenth Century*. Middletown, Conn.: Wesleyan University Press, 1968.

Dunn, Richard S., and Laetitia Yeandle, eds. *The Journal of John Winthrop, 1630–1649*. Cambridge, Mass.: Harvard University Press, 1996.

Fairbanks, Jonathan L. *New England Begins*. 3 vols. Boston: Museum of Fine Arts, 1982.

Foster, Stephen. *The Long Argument: English Puritanism and the Shaping of New England Culture*. Chapel Hill: University of North Carolina Press, 1991.

Gaustad, Edwin Scott. *Liberty of Conscience: Roger Williams in America*. Grand Rapids, Mich.: Eerdmans, 1991.

Godbeer, Richard. *Escaping Salem: The Other Witch Hunt of 1692*. New York: Oxford University Press, 2005.

Gordis, Lisa M. *Opening Scripture: Bible Reading and Interpretive Authority in Puritan New England*. Chicago: University of Chicago Press, 2003.

Grasso, Christopher. *A Speaking Aristocracy: Transforming Public Discourse in Eighteenth-Century Connecticut*. Chapel Hill: University of North Carolina Press, 1999.

Hall, David D., ed. *The Antinomian Controversy, 1636–1638: A Documentary History*. Durham, N.C.: Duke University Press, 1990.

———. *The Faithful Shepherd: A History of the New England Ministry in the Seventeenth Century*. Chapel Hill: University of North Carolina Press, 1972.

———. *Witch-Hunting in Seventeenth-Century New England: A Documentary History*. Boston: Northeastern University Press, 1991.

———. *Worlds of Wonder, Days of Judgment: Popular Religious Belief in Early New England*. New York: Knopf, 1989.

Hall, Michael G. *The Last American Puritan: The Life of Increase Mather, 1639–1723*. Middletown, Conn.: Wesleyan University Press, 1988.

Hambrick-Stowe, Charles E. *The Practice of Piety: Puritan Devotional Disciplines in Seventeenth-Century New England*. Chapel Hill: University of North Carolina Press, 1982.

Heimert, Alan, and Andrew Delbanco, eds. *The Puritans in America: A Narrative Anthology*. Cambridge, Mass.: Harvard University Press, 1985.

Henigman, Laura. *Coming into Communion: Pastoral Dialogues in Colonial New England*. Albany: State University of New York Press, 1999.

Holifield, E. Brooks. *The Covenant Sealed: The Development of Puritan Sacramental Theology in Old and New England, 1570–1720*. New Haven, Conn.: Yale University Press, 1974.

Hoopes, James. *Consciousness in New England*. Baltimore: Johns Hopkins University Press, 1989.

Innes, Stephen. *Creating the Commonwealth: The Economic Culture of Puritan New England*. New York: Norton, 1995.

Karlsen, Carol F. *The Devil in the Shape of a Woman: Witchcraft in Colonial New England*. New York: Norton, 1987.

Knight, Janice. *Orthodoxies in Massachusetts: Rereading American Puritanism*. Cambridge, Mass.: Harvard University Press, 1994.

Knoppers, Laura Lunger, ed. *Puritanism and Its Discontents*. Newark: University of Delaware Press, 2003.

McGiffert, Michael, ed. *Puritanism and the American Experience*. Reading, Mass.: Addison-Wesley, 1969.

McKenna, George. *The Puritan Origins of American Patriotism*. New Haven: Yale University Press, 2007.

Middlekauff, Robert. *The Mathers*. Berkeley: University of California Press, 1999.

Miller, Perry. *Errand into the Wilderness*. Cambridge, Mass.: Harvard University Press, 1956.

———. *The New England Mind: From Colony to Province*. Cambridge, Mass.: Harvard University Press, 1962.

———. *The New England Mind: The Seventeenth Century*. Cambridge, Mass.: Harvard University Press, 1963.

———. *Orthodoxy in Massachusetts, 1630–1650*. 1933. Reprint, New York: Harper and Row, 1970.

Miller, Perry, and Thomas H. Johnson, eds. *The Puritans: A Sourcebook of Their Writings*. 2 vols. New York: Harper and Row, 1963.

Moore, Susan Hardman. *Pilgrims: New World Settlers and the Call of Home*. New Haven: Yale University Press, 2007.

Morgan, Edmund S. *The Puritan Dilemma: The Story of John Winthrop*. Boston: Little, Brown, 1958.

———. *The Puritan Family*. New York: Harper and Row, 1966.

———. *Visible Saints*. New York: New York University Press, 1963.

Norton, Mary Beth. *In the Devil's Snare: The Salem Witchcraft Crisis of 1692*. New York: Knopf, 2002.

Peterson, Mark A. *The Price of Redemption: The Spiritual Economy of Puritan New England*. Stanford, Calif.: Stanford University Press, 1997.

Pettit, Norman. *The Heart Prepared: Grace and Conversion in Puritan Spiritual Life*. 2d ed. Middletown, Conn.: Wesleyan University Press, 1989.

Porterfield, Amanda. *Female Piety in Puritan New England*. New York: Oxford University Press, 1992.

Stannard, David E. *The Puritan Way of Death*. New York: Oxford University Press, 1977.

Stoever, William K. B. *'A Faire and Easie Way to Heaven': Covenant Theology and Antinomianism in Early Massachusetts*. Middletown, Conn.: Wesleyan University Press, 1978.

Stout, Harry S. *The New England Soul: Preaching and Religious Culture in Colonial New England*. New York: Oxford University Press, 1986.

Tipson, Baird. "New England Puritanism." *EARE* 1:467–80.

Walker, Williston. *The Creeds and Platforms of Congregationalism*. 1893. Boston: Pilgrim, 1960.

Weir, David A. *Early New England: A Covenanted Society*. Grand Rapids, Mich.: Eerdmans, 2005.

Westerkamp, Marilyn J. *Women and Religion in Early America: The Puritan and Evangelical Traditions*. New York: Routledge, 1999.

Winship, Michael P. *Making Heretics: Militant Protestantism and Free Grace in Massachusetts, 1636–1641*. Princeton: Princeton University Press, 2002.

Wood, Timothy L. *Agents of Wrath, Sowers of Discord: Authority and Dissent in Puritan Massachusetts, 1630–1655.* New York: Routledge, 2006.

Youngs, J. William T. *The Congregationalists.* New York: Greenwood, 1990.

5. PRESBYTERIANISM

(*SEE ALSO* S.1–10 AND T.)

Balmer, Randall, and John R. Fitzmier. *The Presbyterians.* Westport, Conn.: Greenwood, 1993.

Bruggink, Donald J., and Carl H. Droppers. *Christ and Architecture: Building Presbyterian/ Reformed Churches.* Grand Rapids, Mich.: Eerdmans, 1965.

Coalter, Milton J., John M. Mulder, and Louis B. Weeks, eds. *The Mainstream Protestant "Decline": The Presbyterian Pattern.* Louisville, Ky.: Westminster/John Knox, 1990.

———. *The Organizational Revolution: Presbyterians and American Denominationalism.* Louisville, Ky.: Westminster/John Knox, 1992.

———. *The Pluralistic Vision: Presbyterians and Mainstream Protestant Education and Leadership.* Louisville, Ky.: Westminster/John Knox, 1992.

———. *The Re-Forming Tradition: Presbyterians and Mainstream Protestantism.* Louisville, Ky.: Westminster/John Knox, 1992.

Fisk, William Lyons. *The Scottish High Church Tradition in America.* Lanham, Md.: University Press of America, 1995.

Le Beau, Bryan F. *Jonathan Dickinson and the Formative Years of American Presbyterianism.* Lexington: University Press of Kentucky, 1997.

Leyburn, James G. *The Scotch-Irish: A Social History.* Chapel Hill: University of North Carolina Press, 1962.

Longfield, Bradley J. *The Presbyterian Controversy.* New York: Oxford University Press, 1991.

McKim, Donald K. *Presbyterian Beliefs.* Louisville, Ky.: Geneva Press, 2003.

Melton, Julius. *Presbyterian Worship in America.* Richmond, Va.: John Knox, 1967.

Morrison, Jeffrey H. *John Witherspoon and the Founding of the American Republic.* Notre Dame, Ind.: University of Notre Dame Press, 2005.

Noll, Mark A. *Princeton and the Republic, 1768–1822.* Princeton, N.J.: Princeton University Press, 1989.

———, ed. *The Princeton Theology, 1812–1921.* Grand Rapids, Mich.: Baker, 2001.

Pryor, Mark. *Faith, Grace, and Heresy: The Biography of Rev. Charles M. Jones.* Writer's Showcase Press, 2002.

Schmidt, Leigh Eric. *Holy Fairs: Scottish Communions and American Revivals in the Early Modern Period.* Princeton, N.J.: Princeton University Press, 1989.

Slosser, Gaius Jackson, ed. *They Seek a Country.* New York: Macmillan, 1955.

Smylie, James H. *American Presbyterians: A Pictorial History.* Philadelphia: Presbyterian Historical Society, 1985. (*Journal of Presbyterian History* 63 [Spring/Summer 1985].)

Tait, L. Gordon. *The Piety of John Witherspoon.* Louisville, Ky.: Geneva Press, 2001.

Trinerud, Lionel. *The Forming of an American Tradition.* Philadelphia, 1959.

Weeks, Louis. "Presbyterianism." *EARE* 1:499–510.

Weston, William J. *Presbyterian Pluralism.* Knoxville: University of Tennessee Press, 1997.

6. CONGREGATIONALISM AND THE PURITAN TRADITION
(*SEE ALSO* R.3., S.1–10, AND T.)

Cayton, Mary Kupiec. "Congregationalism from Independence to the Present." *EARE* 1:481–98.

Goddard, Carolyn E., ed. *On the Trail of the UCC: A Historical Atlas of the United Church of Christ.* New York: United Church Press, 1981.

Howe, Daniel Walker. "The Impact of Puritanism on American Culture." *EARE* 2:1057–74.

Phillips, Joseph W. *Jedidiah Morse and American Congregationalism.* New Brunswick, N.J.: Rutgers University Press, 1983.

Rohr, John von. *The Shaping of American Congregationalism, 1620–1957.* Cleveland: Pilgrim, 1992.

Scott, Donald W. *From Office to Profession: The New England Ministry, 1750–1850.* Philadelphia: University of Pennsylvania Press, 1978.

Stoever, William K. B. "The Calvinist Theological Tradition." *EARE* 1:1039–56.

7. OTHER REFORMED CHURCHES

Balmer, Randall H. *A Perfect Babel of Confusion: Dutch Religion and English Culture in the Middle Colonies.* New York: Oxford University Press, 1989.

Bratt, James D. *Dutch Calvinism in Modern America.* Grand Rapids, Mich.: Eerdmans, 1984.

Brinks, Herbert J., ed. *Dutch American Voices: Letters from the United States, 1850–1930.* Ithaca, N.Y.: Cornell University Press, 1995.

Bruins, Elton J. *The Americanization of a Congregation: A History of the Third Reformed Church of Holland, Michigan.* Grand Rapids, Mich.: Eerdmans, 1970.

Butler, Jon. *The Huguenots in America.* Cambridge, Mass.: Harvard University Press, 1983.

Coalter, Milton J., and John M. Mulder. "Dutch and German Reformed Churches." *EARE* 1:511–24.

De Klerk, Peter, and Richard R. De Ridder, eds. *Perspectives on the Christian Reformed Church.* Grand Rapids, Mich.: Baker Book House, 1983.

DeJong, Gerald F. *The Dutch Reformed Church in the American Colonies.* Grand Rapids, Mich.: Eerdmans, 1978.

DiPuccio, William. *The Interior Sense of Scripture: The Sacred Hermeneutics of John W. Nevin.* Macon, Ga.: Mercer University Press, 1998.

Fabend, Firth Haring. *Zion on the Hudson: Dutch New York and New Jersey in the Age of Revivals.* New Brunswick, N.J.: Rutgers University Press, 2000.

Graham, Stephen R. *Cosmos in the Chaos: Philip Schaff's Interpretation of Nineteenth-Century American Religion.* Grand Rapids, Mich.: Eerdmans, 1995.

Hamstra, Sam, Jr., and Arie J. Griffioen, eds. *Reformed Confessionalism in Nineteenth Century America: Essays on the Thought of John Williamson Nevin.* Lanham, Md.: ATLA/Scarecrow, 1995.

Harinck, George, and Hans Krabbendam, eds. *Sharing the Reformed Tradition: The Dutch–North American Exchange, 1846–1996.* Amsterdam: VU Uitgeverij, 1996.

Hoeksema, Gertrude. *A Watered Garden: A Brief History of the Protestant Reformed Churches in America.* Grand Rapids, Mich.: Reformed Free Publishers Assn., 1992.

House, Renee S., and John W. Coakley. *Patterns and Portraits: Women in the History of the Reformed Church in America.* Grand Rapids: Eerdmans, 1999.

Kidd, Thomas. *The Protestant Interest: New England After Puritanism.* New Haven: Yale University Press, 2004.

Knowles, Anne Kelly. *Calvinists Incorporated: Welsh Immigrants on Ohio's Industrial Frontier.* Chicago: University of Chicago Press, 1997.

Kroes, Rob. *The Persistence of Ethnicity: Dutch Calvinist Pioneers in Amsterdam, Montana.* Urbana: University of Illinois Press, 1992.

Nichols, James Hastings, ed. *The Mercersburg Theology.* New York: Oxford University Press, 1966.

Penzel, Klaus. *Philip Schaff.* Macon, Ga.: Mercer University Press, 1991.

Schneider, Carl Howard. *The German Church on the American Frontier.* St. Louis: Eden Publishing house, 1939.

Swieringa, Robert P. *They Came to Stay: Essays on Dutch Immigration and Settlement in America.* New Brunswick, N.J.: Rutgers University Press, 1984.

VandenBrege, Peter N. *Historical Directory of the Reformed Church in America, 1628–1978.* Grand Rapids, Mich.: Eerdmans, 1978.

Wentz, Richard E. *John Williamson Nevin.* New York: Oxford University Press, 1997.

O. Baptist Tradition
(*SEE ALSO* S.1–10, especially S.6)

Brackney, William Henry. *The Baptists.* Westport, Conn.: Greenwood, 1988.

———. *Baptists in North America.* Malden, Mass.: Blackwood, 2006.

———. *Historical Dictionary of the Baptists.* Lanham, Md.: Scarecrow, 1999.

Ernst, Eldon G. "The Baptists." *EARE* 1:555–77.

Freeman, Curtis W., et al., eds. *Baptist Roots.* Valley Forge, Pa.: Judson, 1999.

James, Sydney V. *John Clarke and His Legacies: Religion and Law in Colonial Rhode Island 1638–1750.* University Park: Pennsylvania State University Press, 1999.

Leonard, Bill. *Baptists in America.* New York: Columbia University Press, 2007.

———. *Baptist Ways: A History.* Valley Forge, Pa.: Judson Press, 2003.

———. "Independent Baptists: From Sectarian Minority to 'Moral Majority.'" *Church History* 56, no. 4 (Dec. 1987): 504–17.

McLoughlin, William G. *Isaac Backus and the American Pietist Tradition.* Boston: Little, Brown, 1967.

———. *New England Dissent, 1630–1833.* 2 vols. Cambridge, Mass.: Harvard University Press, 1971.

———. *Soul Liberty: The Baptists' Struggle in New England, 1630–1833.* Hanover, N.H.: University Press of New England, 1991.

Wardin, Albert W., Jr. *Baptist Atlas.* Nashville: Boardman, 1980.

P. The Peace Churches

1. THE SOCIETY OF FRIENDS (QUAKERS)

Baltzell, E. Digby. *Puritan Boston and Quaker Philadelphia.* Boston: Free Press, 1979.

Barbour, Hugh, and J. William Frost, eds. *The Quakers.* New York: Greenwood, 1988.

Barbour, Hugh, et al., eds. *Quaker Crosscurrents: Three Hundred Years of Friends in the New York Yearly Meetings.* Syracuse, N.Y.: Syracuse University Press, 1995.

Endy, Melvin B., Jr. "The Society of Friends." *EARE* 1:595–614.

———. *William Penn and Early Quakerism.* Princeton, N.J.: Princeton University Press, 1973.

Frost, J. William, and John M. Moore, eds. *Seeking the Light: Essays in Quaker History.* Philadelphia: Pendle Hill, 1986.

Hamm, Thomas D. *Earlham College: A History, 1847–1997.* Bloomington: Indiana University Press, 1997.

———. *The Quakers in America.* New York: Columbia University Press, 2003.

———. *The Transformation of American Quakerism.* Bloomington: Indiana University Press, 1988.

Hickey, Damon D. *Sojourners No More: The Quakers in the New South, 1865–1920.* Greensboro: North Carolina Yearly Meeting, 1997.

Ingle, H. Larry. *Quakers in Conflict: The Hicksite Reformation.* Knoxville: University of Tennessee Press, 1986.

Lapsansky, Emma Jones. *Quaker Aesthetics: Reflections on a Quaker Ethic in American Design and Consumption.* Philadelphia: University of Pennsylvania Press, 2003.

Larson, Rebecca. *Daughters of Light: Quaker Women Preaching and Prophesying in the Colonies and Abroad, 1770–1775.* New York: Knopf, 1999.

Oliver, John W., ed. *J. Walter Malone: The Autobiography of an Evangelical Quaker.* Lanham, Md.: University Press of America, 1993.

Russell, Elbert. *The History of Quakerism.* New York: Macmillan, 1942.

Selleck, Linda B. *Gentle Invaders: Quaker Women Educators and Racial Issues during the Civil War and Reconstruction.* Richmond, Ind.: Friends United Press, 1995.

Steere, Douglas V. *Quaker Spirituality: Selected Writings.* New York: Paulist, 1984.

Tolles, Frederick B. *Meeting House and Counting House.* Chapel Hill: University of North Carolina Press, 1948.

Weddle, Meredith Baldwin. *Walking in the Way of Peace: Quaker Pacifism in the Seventeenth Century.* New York: Oxford University Press, 2001.

2. ANABAPTISTS AND PIETISTS

Atwood, Craig D. *Community of the Cross: Moravian Piety in Colonial Bethlehem.* University Park: Penn State University Press, 2004.

Atwood, Craig D., and Peter Vogt, eds. *The Distinctiveness of Moravian Culture.* Bethlehem, Pa.: Moravian Historical Society, 2006.

Bender, Harold S., and Henry C. Smith, eds. *The Mennonite Encyclopedia.* 4 vols. Hillsboro, Kans.: Herald Press, 1955–59.

Bowman, Carl E. *Brethren Society: The Cultural Transformation of a "Peculiar People."* Baltimore: Johns Hopkins University Press, 1995.

Bush, Perry. *Dancing with the Kobzar: Bluffton College and Mennonite Higher Education, 1899–1999.* Newton, Kans.: Faith & Life Press, 2000.

———. *Two Kingdoms, Two Loyalties: Mennonite Pacifism in Modern America.* Baltimore: Johns Hopkins University Press, 1998.

Faull, Katherine M., trans. *Moravian Women's Memoirs*. Syracuse, N.Y.: Syracuse University Press, 1997.

Gollin, Gillian Lindt. *Moravians in Two Worlds*. New York: Columbia University Press, 1967.

Gundy, Jeff. *A Community of Memory*. Urbana: University of Illinois Press, 1996.

Homan, Gerlof D. *American Mennonites and the Great War, 1914–1918*. Scottsdale, Pa.: Herald Press, 1994.

Hostetler, Beulah Stauffer. *American Mennonites and Protestant Movements*. Scottsdale, Pa.: Herald Press, 1987.

Hostetler, John A. *Amish Society*. Baltimore: Johns Hopkins University Press, 1963, 1968.

Juhnke, James C. *Vision, Doctrine, War: Mennonite Identity and Organization in America, 1890–1930*. Scottsdale, Pa.: Herald Press, 1989.

Kasdorf, Julia. *Fixing Tradition: Joseph W. Yoder, Amish American*. Telford, Pa.: Pandora, 2002.

Keim, Albert N. *Harold S. Bender, 1897–1962*. Scottsdale, Pa.: Herald Press, 1998.

Kraybill, Donald B. *The Riddle of Amish Culture*. Baltimore: Johns Hopkins University Press, 1989.

Kraybill, Donald B., and Carl F. Bowman. *On the Backroad to Heaven: Old Order Hutterites, Amish, and Brethren*. Baltimore: Johns Hopkins University Press, 2001.

Kraybill, Donald B., and James P. Hurd. *Horse-and-Buggy Mennonites*. University Park: Pennsylvania State University Press, 2006.

Loewen, Roydon. *Hidden Worlds: Revisiting the Mennonite Migrants of the 1870s*. North Newton, Kans.: Bethel College, 2001.

Longenecker, Stephen L. *Pietism and Tolerance: Pennsylvania German Religion, 1700–1850*. Metuchen, N.J.: Scarecrow Press, 1994.

Miller, Keith Graber. *Wise as Serpents, Innocent as Doves: American Mennonites Engage Washington*. Knoxville: University of Tennessee Press, 1996.

Nolt, Stephen M. *Foreigners in Their Own Land: Pennsylvania Germans in the Early Republic*. University Park: Penn State University Press, 2002.

O'Malley, J. Steven. *"On the Journey Home": The History of Mission of the Evangelical United Brethren Church, 1946–1968*. New York: General Board of Global Ministries, United Methodist Church, 2003.

Redekop, Calvin, Stephen C. Ainlay, and Robert Siemens. *Mennonite Entrepreneurs*. Baltimore: Johns Hopkins University Press, 1995.

Redekop, Benjamin, and Calvin Redekop, eds. *Power, Authority, and the Anabaptist Tradition*. Baltimore: Johns Hopkins University Press, 2001.

Reschly, Steven D. *The Amish on the Iowa Prairie, 1840 to 1910*. Baltimore: Johns Hopkins University Press, 2000.

Reynolds, Margaret C. *Plain Women: Gender and Ritual in the Old Order River Brethren*. University Park: Penn State University Press, 2001.

Roth, John D., ed. *Mennonite Quarterly Review* 73, no. 2 (Apr. 1999). Special issue on Anabaptist-Mennonite spaces and places of worship.

Schlabach, Theron F. *Peace, Faith, Nation: Mennonites and Amish in Nineteenth-Century America*. Scottsdale, Pa.: Herald Press, 1988.

Schmidt, Kimberly D., et al. *Strangers at Home: Amish and Mennonite Women in History.* Baltimore: Johns Hopkins University Press, 2002.

Smaby, Beverly Priot. *The Transformation of Moravian Bethlehem.* Philadelphia: University of Pennsylvania Press, 1988.

Sommer, Elisabeth W. *Serving Two Masters: Moravian Brethren in Germany and North Carolina, 1727–1801.* Lexington: University Press of Kentucky, 2000.

Stoeffler, F. Ernest, ed. *Continental Pietism and Early American Christianity.* Grand Rapids, Mich.: Eerdmans, 1976.

Thorp, Daniel B. *The Moravian Community in Colonial North Carolina.* Knoxville: University of Tennessee Press, 1989.

Toews, Paul. *Mennonites in American Society, 1930–1970.* Scottsdale, Pa.: Herald Press, 1996.

Umble, Diane Zimmerman. *Holding the Line: The Telephone in Old Order Mennonite and Amish Life.* Baltimore: Johns Hopkins University Press, 1996.

Wagner, Walter H. *The Zinzendorf-Mühlenberg Encounter.* Bethlehem, Pa.: Moravian Church of America, 2002.

Weaver, J. Denny. *Keeping Salvation Ethical: Mennonite and Amish Atonement Theology in the Late Nineteenth Century.* Scottsdale, Pa.: Herald Press, 1997.

Weaver-Zercher, David. *The Amish in the American Imagination.* Baltimore: Johns Hopkins University Press, 2001.

Wentz, Richard E. *Pennsylvania Dutch: Folk Spirituality.* New York: Paulist, 1993.

Williams, George H. *The Radical Reformation.* Philadelphia: Westminster, 1962.

Wilson, Laura. *Hutterites of Montana.* New Haven, Conn.: Yale University Press, 2000.

Yoder, Don. "Sects and Religious Movements of German Origin." *EARE* 1:615–34.

Q. Methodism
(*SEE ALSO* S.1–10)

Allen, Charles L. *Meet the Methodists.* Nashville: Abingdon, 1986.

Andrews, Dee E. *The Methodists and Revolutionary America, 1760–1800.* Princeton: Princeton University Press, 2000.

Bucke, Emory Stevens, ed. *The History of American Methodism.* 3 vols. New York: Abingdon, 1964.

Campbell, Dennis M., William B. Lawrence, and Russell E. Richey, eds. *Doctrines and Discipline.* Nashville: Abingdon, 1999. (Vol. 3 of *United Methodism and American Culture*)

Collins, Donald E. *When the Church Bell Rang Racist: The Methodist Church and the Civil Rights Movement in Alabama.* Macon, Ga.: Mercer University Press, 1998.

Davies, Horton. *Worship and Theology in England.* Vol. 3. Princeton, N.J.: Princeton University Press, 1961.

Halevy, Elie. *The Birth of Methodism in England.* Chicago: University of Chicago Press, 1971.

Hardt, Philip F. *The Soul of Methodism: The Class Meeting in Early New York City.* Lanham, Md.: University Press of America, 2000.

Hatch, Nathan O., and John H. Wigger, eds. *Methodism and the Shaping of American Culture.* Nashville, Tenn.: Kingswood Books, 2001.

Heitzenrater, Richard P. *The Poor and the People Called Methodists, 1729–1999.* Nashville, Tenn.: Kingswood Books, 2002.

Hempton, David. *Methodism: Empire of the Spirit.* New Haven: Yale University Press, 2005.

Kaufman, Paul Leslie. *"Logical" Luther Lee and the Methodist War against Slavery.* Lanham, Md.: Scarecrow, 2000.

Kimbrough, David L. *Reverend Joseph Tarkington, Methodist Circuit Rider: From Frontier Evangelism to Refined Religion.* Knoxville: University of Tennessee Press, 1997.

Kinghom, Kenneth C. *The Heritage of American Methodism.* Nashville: Abingdon Press, 1999.

Kirby, James E., Russell E. Richey, and Kenneth E. Rowe. *The Methodists.* Westport, Conn.: Greenwood, 1996.

Knotts, Alice G. *Fellowship of Love: Methodist Women Changing American Racial Attitudes, 1920–1968.* Nashville: Abingdon, 1996.

Lawrence, William B., Dennis M. Campbell, and Russell E. Richey, eds. *The People(s) Called Methodist: Forms and Reforms of their Life.* Nashville: Abingdon, 1998. (Vol. 2 of *United Methodism and American Culture*)

Murray, Peter C. *Methodists and the Crucible of Race, 1930–1975.* Columbia: University of Missouri Press, 2004.

Norwood, Frederick A. *The Story of American Methodism.* Nashville: Abingdon, 1974.

Outler, Albert C., ed. *John Wesley.* New York: Oxford University Press, 1965.

Owen, Christopher H. *The Sacred Flame of Love: Methodism and Society in Nineteenth-Century Georgia.* Athens: University of Georgia Press, 1998.

Richey, Russell E. *The Methodist Conference in America.* Nashville: Kingswood, 1996.

Richey, Russell E., Dennis M. Campbell, and William B. Lawrence, eds. *Connectionalism: Ecclesiology, Mission, and Identity.* Nashville: Abingdon, 1997. (Vol. 1 of *United Methodism and American Culture*)

———. et al., eds. *Questions for the Twenty-First Century Church.* Nashville: Abingdon, 1999. (Vol. 4 of *United Methodism and American Culture*)

Schmidt, Jean Miller. *Grace Sufficient: A History of Women in American Methodism, 1760–1939.* Nashville: Abingdon, 1999.

Schneider, A. Gregory. *The Way of the Cross Leads Home: The Domestication of American Methodism.* Bloomington: Indiana University Press, 1993.

Semmel, Bernard. *The Methodist Revolution.* New York: Basic Books, 1973.

Sutton, William R. *Journeymen for Jesus: Evangelical Artisans Confront Capitalism in Jacksonian Baltimore.* University Park: Pennsylvania State University Press, 1998.

Tucker, Karen B. Westerfield. *American Methodist Worship.* New York: Oxford University Press, 2001.

Tuell, Jack M. *The Organization of the United Methodist Church.* Nashville: Abingdon, 1982.

Turley, Briane K. *A Wheel within a Wheel: Southern Methodism and the Georgia Holiness Association.* Macon, Ga.: Mercer University Press, 1999.

Wallace, Charles I., Jr. "Wesleyan Heritage." *EARE* 1:525–38.

Wigger, John H. *Taking Heaven by Storm: Methodism and the Popularization of American Christianity.* Urbana: University of Illinois Press, 2001.

Yrigoyen, Charles, Jr. *The Global Impact of the Wesleyan Traditions and Their Related Movements.* Lanham, Md.: Scarecrow, 2002.

———. "United Methodism." *EARE* 1:539–54.

R. Religious Liberalism

1. ENLIGHTENMENT AND EUROPEAN BACKGROUND

Aldridge, Alfred Owen. *Benjamin Franklin and Nature's God*. Durham, N.C.: Duke University Press, 1967.

Bailyn, Bernard. *The Ideological Origins of the American Revolution*. Cambridge, Mass.: Harvard University Press, 1967.

Bainton, Roland H. *Hunted Heretic: The Life and Death of Michael Servetus*. Boston: Beacon, 1953.

———. *The Reformation of the Sixteenth Century*. Boston: Beacon, 1952. See especially chapter 7, "The Free Spirits".

Becker, Carl L. *The Heavenly City of the Eighteenth-Century Philosophers*. New Haven, Conn.: Yale University Press, 1952.

Boorstin, Daniel J. *The Lost World of Thomas Jefferson*. Chicago: University of Chicago Press, 1993 (c. 1948).

Corrigan, John A. "The Enlightenment." *EARE* 2:1089–1102.

———. *The Hidden Balance*. Cambridge: Cambridge University Press, 1987.

———. *The Prism of Piety: Catholick Congregational Clergy at the Beginning of the Enlightenment*. New York: Oxford University Press, 1991.

Cragg, G. R. *The Church and the Age of Reason*. New York: Atheneum, 1961.

Gay, Peter. *The Enlightenment*. 2 vols. New York: Knopf, 1966, 1969.

Kloos, John M., Jr. *A Sense of Deity: The Republican Spirituality of Dr. Benjamin Rush*. Brooklyn, N.Y.: Carlson, 1991.

Koch, Adrienne, ed. *The American Enlightenment*. New York: Braziller, 1965.

May, Henry F. *The Divided Heart: Essays on Protestantism and the Enlightenment in America*. New York: Oxford University Press, 1991.

———. The *Enlightenment in America*. New York: Oxford University Press, 1976.

Schmidt, Leigh Eric. *Hearing Things: Religion, Illusion, and the American Enlightenment*. Cambridge, Mass.: Harvard University Press, 2000.

Walters, Kerry S. *Benjamin Franklin and His Gods*. Urbana: University of Illinois Press, 1999.

Ziff, Larzer, ed. *The Portable Benjamin Franklin*. New York: Penguin Books, 2005.

2. UNITARIANISM, TRANSCENDENTALISM, AND UNIVERSALISM

Ahlstrom, Sydney E., and Jonathan S. Carey, eds. *An American Reformation: A Documentary History of Unitarian Christianity*. Middletown, Conn.: Wesleyan University Press, 1985.

Albanese, Catherine L. *The Spirituality of the American Transcendentalists*. Macon, Ga.: Mercer University Press, 1988.

———. "Transcendentalism." *EARE* 2:1117–28.

Allen, John. *Unitarianism in the Antebellum South*. Tuscaloosa: University of Alabama Press, 2001.

Bressler, Ann Lee. *The Universalist Movement in America 1770–1880*. New York: Oxford University Press, 2000.

Capper, Charles, and Conrad Edick Wright, eds. *Transient and Permanent: The Transcendentalist Movement and its Contexts*. Boston: Northeastern University Press, 1999

Cassara, Ernest, ed. *Universalism in America: A Documentary History.* Boston: Beacon, 1971.

Cayton, Mary Kupiec. *Emerson's Emergence.* Chapel Hill: University of North Carolina Press, 1989.

Delano, Sterling F. *Brook Farm.* Cambridge, Mass.: Harvard University Press, 2004.

Field, Peter S. *Ralph Waldo Emerson: The Making of a Democratic Intellectual.* Lanham, Md.: Rowman and Littlefield, 2002.

Frothingham, Octavius Brooks. *Transcendentalism in New England.* 1876. Reprint, New York: Harper, 1959.

Grodzins, Dean. *American Heretic: Theodore Parker and Transcendentalism.* Chapel Hill: University of North Carolina Press, 2002.

Harris, Mark W., ed. *Unitarian Universalist Association Directory.* Boston: The Association. Annual.

Howe, Daniel Walker. *The Unitarian Conscience.* Cambridge, Mass.: Harvard University Press, 1970.

Hutchison, William R. *The Transcendentalist Ministers.* New Haven, Conn.: Yale University Press, 1959.

Marini, Stephen M. *Radical Sects of Revolutionary New England.* Cambridge, Mass.: Harvard University Press, 1982.

Miller, Perry, ed. *The Transcendentalists.* Cambridge, Mass.: Harvard University Press, 1950.

Miller, Russell E. *The Larger Hope.* 2 vols. Boston: Unitarian Universalist Association, 1979, 1985. (History of Universalism.)

Robinson, David. *The Unitarians and the Universalists.* Westport, Conn.: Greenwood, 1985.

Rose, Anne C. *Transcendentalism as a Social Movement, 1830–1850.* New Haven, Conn.: Yale University Press, 1981.

Siry, Joseph M. *Unity Temple.* Cambridge: Cambridge University Press, 1996.

Versluis, Arthur. *The Esoteric Origins of the American Renaissance.* New York: Oxford University Press, 2001.

Wider, Sarah Ann. *Anna Tilden: Unitarian Culture and the Problem of Self-Representation.* Athens: University of Georgia Press, 1997.

Wilbur, Earl Morse. *A History of Unitarianism: Socinianism and Its Antecedents.* c. 1942. Reprint, Boston: Harvard University Press, 1977.

———. *A History of Unitarianism in Transylvania, England and America.* c. 1945. Reprint, Boston: Beacon, 1978.

Williams, George Hunston. *American Universalism.* Rev. ed. Boston: Skinner House, 1976.

Williams, Peter W. "Unitarianism and Universalism." *EARE* 1:579–94.

Wright, Conrad. *The Beginnings of Unitarianism in America.* Boston: Beacon, 1966.

———. *The Liberal Christians.* Boston: Beacon, 1970.

———, ed. *A Stream of Light: A Sesquicentennial History of American Unitarianism.* Boston: Unitarian Universalist Association, 1975.

———. *Three Prophets of Religious Liberalism.* Boston: Beacon, 1961.

Wright, Conrad Edick, ed. *American Unitarianism, 1805–1865.* Boston: Northeastern University Press, 1989.

3. PROTESTANT LIBERALISM, URBANIZATION, AND THE SOCIAL GOSPEL

Abell, Aaron I. *The Urban Impact on American Protestantism, 1865–1900.* 1943. Reprint, Hamden, Conn.: Archon, 1962.

Averill, Lloyd J. *American Theology in the Liberal Tradition.* Philadelphia: Westminster, 1967.

Cauthen, Kenneth. *The Impact of American Religious Liberalism.* New York: Harper and Row, 1962.

Christiano, Kevin J. *Religious Diversity and Social Change: American Cities, 1890–1906.* New York: Cambridge University Press, 1987.

Croce, Paul Jerome. *Science and Religion in the Era of William James.* Chapel Hill: University of North Carolina Press, 1995.

Curtis, Susan. *A Consuming Faith: The Social Gospel and Modern American Culture.* Baltimore: Johns Hopkins University Press, 1991.

Dorn, Jacob H. *Socialism and Christianity in Early 20th Century America.* Westport, Conn.: Greenwood, 1998.

———. *Washington Gladden, Prophet of the Social Gospel.* Columbus: Ohio State University Press, 1967.

Dorrien, Gary J. *The Making of American Liberal Theology: Idealism, Realism, and Modernity, 1900–1950.* Louisville, Ky.: Westminster John Knox Press, 2003.

———. *The Making of American Liberal Theology: Imagining Progressive Religion, 1805–1900.* Louisville, Ky.: Westminster John Knox Press, 2001.

Duke, David Nelson. *In the Trenches with Jesus and Marx: Harry F. Ward and the Struggle for Social Justice.* Tuscaloosa: University of Alabama Press, 2003.

Edwards, Wendy J. Deichmann, and Carolyn De Swarte Gifford, eds. *Gender and the Social Gospel.* Urbana: University of Illinois Press, 2003.

Evans, Christopher Hodge. *The Kingdom Is Always But Coming: A Life of Walter Rauschenbusch.* Grand Rapids, Mich.: Eerdmans, 2004.

———, ed. *Perspectives on the Social Gospel.* Lewiston, N.Y.: Edward Mellen, 1999.

———. *Social Gospel Liberalism and the Ministry of Ernest Fremont Tittle.* Lewiston, N.Y.: Edward Mellen, 1996.

Handy, Robert T., ed. *The Social Gospel in America.* New York: Oxford University Press, 1966.

Hopkins, C. Howard. *The Rise of the Social Gospel in American Protestantism, 1865–1915.* New Haven, Conn.: Yale University Press, 1940, 1967.

Hutchison, William R. *The Modernist Impulse in American Protestantism.* Cambridge, Mass.: Harvard University Press, 1976.

King, William McGuire. "Liberalism." *EARE* 2:1129–46.

Lippy, Charles H. "Social Christianity." *EARE* 2:917–32.

Massa, Mark A., S.J. *Charles Augustus Briggs and the Crisis of Historical Criticism.* Minneapolis: Fortress, 1990.

May, Henry F. *Protestant Churches and Industrial America.* New York: Harper, 1949.

Minus, Paul M. *Walter Rauschenbusch.* New York: Macmillan, 1988.

Seager, Richard Hughes. *The World's Parliament of Religions.* Bloomington: Indiana University Press, 1995.

White, Ronald C., Jr. *Liberty and Justice for All: Racial Reform and the Social Gospel (1877–1925)*. San Francisco: Harper and Row, 1990.

White, Ronald C., Jr., and C. Howard Hopkins. *The Social Gospel*. Philadelphia: Temple University Press, 1976.

Zahniser, Keith A. *Steel City Gospel: Protestant Laity and Reform in Progressive-Era Pittsburgh*. New York: Routledge, 2005.

4. SECULARISM AND FREE THOUGHT

Kirkley, Evelyn A. *Rational Mothers and Infidel Gentlemen: Gender and American Atheism, 1865–1915*. Syracuse, N.Y.: Syracuse University Press, 2000.

Kraut, Benny. *From Reform Judaism to Ethical Culture*. Cincinnati: Hebrew Union College Press, 1979.

Krauthammer, Charles. "The Humanist Phantom." *New Republic*, July 25, 1981, 20–25.

Marty, Martin E. "Free Thought and Ethical Movements." *EARE* 2:731–40.

———. *The Infidel: Freethought and American Religion*. Cleveland: World, 1961.

Persons, Stow. *Free Religion: An American Faith*. New Haven, Conn.: Yale University Press, 1947.

Turner, James. *Without God, without Creed*. Baltimore: Johns Hopkins University Press, 1985.

Walters, Kerry S. *The American Deists*. Lawrence: University Press of Kansas, 1992.

S. Conservative Protestantism

1. JONATHAN EDWARDS, THE GREAT AWAKENING, AND ITS AFTERMATH

Brown, Robert E. *Jonathan Edwards and the Bible*. Bloomington: Indiana University Press, 2002.

Bushman, Richard L., ed. *The Great Awakening: Documents on the Revival of Religion, 1740–1745*. Chapel Hill: University of North Carolina Press, 1989.

Butler, Jon. *Awash in a Sea of Faith: Christianizing the American People*. Cambridge, Mass.: Harvard University Press, 1990.

Chai, Leon. *Jonathan Edwards and the Limits of Enlightenment Philosophy*. Oxford: Oxford University Press, 1998.

Cherry, Conrad. *The Theology of Jonathan Edwards*. Bloomington: Indiana University Press, 1990.

Coalter, Milton J., Jr. *Gilbert Tennent, Son of Thunder*. New York: Greenwood, 1986.

Conforti, Joseph A. *Jonathan Edwards, Religious Tradition, and American Culture*. Chapel Hill: University of North Carolina Press, 1995.

Crawford, Michael J. *Seasons of Grace: Colonial New England's Revival Tradition in Its British Context*. New York: Oxford University Press, 1991.

Danaher, William J., Jr. *The Trinitarian Ethics of Jonathan Edwards*. New York: Columbia University Press, 2004.

Daniel, Stephen H. *The Philosophy of Jonathan Edwards*. Bloomington: Indiana University Press, 1994.

Edwards, Jonathan. *The Works of Jonathan Edwards*. Various titles and editors. New Haven, Conn.: Yale University Press, 1957–. Continuing series.

Faust, Clarence H., and Thomas H. Johnson, eds. *Jonathan Edwards.* New York: Hill and Wang, 1935.

Fitzmier, John R. *New England's Moral Legislator: Timothy Dwight, 1752–1817.* Bloomington: Indiana University Press, 1998.

Gaustad, Edwin Scott. *The Great Awakening in New England.* New York: Harper, 1957.

Goen, Clarence C. *Revivalism and Separatism in New England, 1740–1800.* New Haven, Conn.: Yale University Press, 1962.

Grasso, Christopher. *A Speaking Aristocracy: Transforming Public Discourse in Eighteenth-Century Connecticut.* Chapel Hill: University of North Carolina Press, 1999.

Hall, Timothy D. *Contested Boundaries: Itinerancy and the Reshaping of the Colonial American Religious World.* Durham, N.C.: Duke University Press, 1994.

Hart, D. G., Sean Michael Lueus, and Stephen J. Nichols, eds. *The Legacy of Jonathan Edwards: American Religion and the Evangelical Tradition.* Grand Rapids, Mich.: Baker Academic, 2003.

Heimert, Alan, and Perry Miller, eds. *The Great Awakening.* Indianapolis: Bobbs-Merrill, 1967.

Helm, Paul, and Oliver D. Crisp, eds. *Jonathan Edwards: Philosophical Theologian.* Burlington, Vt.: Ashgate, 2003.

Juster, Susan. *Disorderly Women: Sexual Politics and Evangelicalism in Revolutionary New England.* Ithaca, N.Y.: Cornell University Press, 1994.

Kidd, Thomas S. *The Great Awakening.* New Haven: Yale University Press, 2007.

———. *The Protestant Interest: New England after Puritanism.* New Haven: Yale University Press, 2004.

Kimnach, Wilson H., Kenneth P. Minkema, and Douglas A. Sweeny, eds. *The Sermons of Jonathan Edwards.* New Haven, Conn.: Yale University Press, 1999.

Lacey, Barbara E. *The World of Hannah Heaton: The Diary of an Eighteenth-Century New England Farm Woman.* DeKalb, Ill.: Northern Illinois University Press, 2003.

Lambert, Frank. *Inventing the "Great Awakening."* Princeton, N.J.: Princeton University Press, 1999.

———. *"Pedlar in Divinity": George Whitefield and the Transatlantic Revivals, 1737–1770.* Princeton, N.J.: Princeton University Press, 1994.

Lee, Sang Hyun, and Allen Guelzo, eds. *Edwards in Our Time: Jonathan Edwards and the Shaping of American Religion.* Grand Rapids, Mich.: Eerdmans, 1999.

Lovejoy, David O. *Religious Enthusiasm and the Great Awakening.* Englewood Cliffs, N.J.: Prentice-Hall, 1969.

Marini, Stephen A. "The Great Awakening." *EARE* 2:775–98.

Marsden, George. *Jonathan Edwards: A Life.* New Haven: Yale University Press, 2003.

McClymond, Michael J. *An Approach to the Theology of Jonathan Edwards.* New York: Oxford University Press, 1998.

McDermott, Gerald R. *Jonathan Edwards Confronts the Gods: Christian Theology, Enlightenment Religion, and Non-Christian Faiths.* Oxford: Oxford University Press, 2000.

Miller, Perry. *Jonathan Edwards.* 1949. Reprint, Westport, Conn.: Greenwood, 1959.

Pauw, Amy Plantinga. *"The Supreme Harmony of All": The Trinitarian Theology of Jonathan Edwards.* Grand Rapids, Mich.: Eerdmans, 2002.

Pointer, Richard W. *Protestant Pluralism and the New York Experience.* Bloomington: Indiana University Press, 1988.

Seeman, Erik R. *Pious Persuasions: Laity and Clergy and Eighteenth-Century New England.* Baltimore: Johns Hopkins University Press, 1999.

Smith, John E., Harry S. Stout, and Kenneth P. Minkema, eds. *A Jonathan Edwards Reader.* New Haven, Conn.: Yale University Press, 1995.

Stout, Harry S. *The Divine Dramatist: George Whitefield and the Rise of Modern Evangelicalism.* Grand Rapids, Mich.: Eerdmans, 1991.

Valeri, Mark. *Law and Providence in Joseph Bellamy's New England.* New York: Oxford University Press, 1994.

Ward, W. R. *The Protestant Evangelical Awakening.* Cambridge: Cambridge University Press, 1992.

Winiarski, Douglas L., "Jonathan Edwards, Enthusiast? Radical Revivalism and the Great Awakening in the Connecticut Valley," *Church History* 74, no. 4 (Dec. 2005): 683–739.

2. NINETEENTH CENTURY EVANGELICALISM

Bebbington, David W. *The Dominance of Evangelicalism: The Age of Spurgeon and Moody.* Downers Grove, Ill.: InterVarsity Press, 2005.

Brekus, Catherine A. *Strangers and Pilgrims: Female Preaching in America 1740–1845.* Chapel Hill: University of North Carolina Press, 1998.

Conkin, Paul. *The Uneasy Center: Reformed Christianity in Antebellum America.* Chapel Hill: University of North Carolina Press, 1995.

Grammer, Elizabeth Elkin. *Some Wild Visions: Autobiographies by Female Itinerant Evangelists in Nineteenth-Century America.* New York: Oxford University Press, 2003.

Hackett, David G. *The Rude Hand of Innovation: Religion and Social Order in Albany, New York, 1652–1836.* New York: Oxford University Press, 1991.

Handy, Robert T. *A Christian America.* 2d ed. New York: Oxford University Press, 1984.

Hanley, Mark Y. *Beyond a Christian Commonwealth: The Protestant Quarrel with the American Republic, 1830–1860.* Chapel Hill: University of North Carolina Press, 1994.

Hart, D.G., Sean Michael Lucas, and Stephen J. Nichols. *The Legacy of Jonathan Edwards: American Religion and the Evangelical Tradition.* Grand Rapids, Mich.: Baker Academic, 2003.

Hatch, Nathan. *The Democratization of American Christianity.* New Haven, Conn.: Yale University Press, 1989.

Johnson, Curtis D. *Islands of Holiness: Rural Religion in Upstate New York, 1790–1860.* Ithaca, N.Y.: Cornell University Press, 1989.

Marty, Martin E. *Protestantism in the United States: Righteous Empire.* 2d ed. New York: Scribners, 1986.

McLoughlin, William G., ed. *The American Evangelicals, 1800–1900.* New York: Harper and Row, 1968.

Rabinowitz, Richard. *The Spiritual Self in Everyday Life.* Boston: Northeastern University Press, 1989.

Sassi, Jonathan D. *A Republic of Righteousness: The Public Christianity of the Post-Revolutionary New England Clergy.* New York: Oxford University Press, 2001.

Smith, John E., Harry S. Stout, and Kenneth P. Minkema, eds. *A Jonathan Edwards Reader.* New Haven, Conn.: Yale University Press, 1995.

Sweeney, Douglas A. *Nathaniel Taylor, New Haven Theology, and the Legacy of Jonathan Edwards.* New York: Oxford University Press, 2003.

Sweet, Leonard I., ed. *The Evangelical Tradition in America.* Macon, Ga.: Mercer University Press, 1984. Contains extensive bibliographical essay.

———. "Nineteenth-Century Evangelicalism." *EARE* 2:875–900.

Taves, Ann, ed. *Religion and Domestic Violence in New England.* Bloomington: Indiana University Press, 1989.

Wallace, Dewey D., Jr. *Sherlock Bristol. The Pioneer Preacher: Incidents of Interest, and Experiences of the Author's Life.* Urbana: University of Illinois Press, 1989.

Wells, Colin. *The Devil and Doctor Dwight: Satire and Theology in the Early American Republic.* Chapel Hill: University of North Carolina Press, 2002.

3. REVIVALISM

(*SEE ALSO* SUBSECTIONS 1, ABOVE, AND 4, BELOW)

Blumhofer, Edith L., and Randall Balmer, eds. *Modern Christian Revivals.* Urbana: University of Illinois Press, 1993.

Brown, Kenneth O. *Holy Ground: A Study of the American Camp Meeting.* New York: Garland, 1992.

Carwardine, Richard. *Transatlantic Revivalism.* Westport, Conn.: Greenwood, 1978.

Corrigan, John. *Business of the Heart: Religion and Emotion in the Nineteenth Century.* Berkeley: University of California Press, 2002.

Dorsett, Lyle W. *Billy Sunday and the Redemption of Urban America.* Grand Rapids, Mich.: Eerdmans, 1991.

Eslinger, Ellen. *Citizens of Zion: The Social Origins of Camp Meeting Revivalism.* Knoxville: University of Tennessee Press, 1999.

Evensen, Bruce J. *God's Man for the Gilded Age: D. L. Moody and the Rise of Modern Mass Evangelism.* New York: Oxford University Press, 2003.

Hambrick-Stowe, Charles E. *Charles G. Finney and the Spirit of American Evangelicalism.* Grand Rapids, Mich.: Eerdmans, 1996.

Hardman, Keith. *Charles Grandison Finney, 1792–1875.* Syracuse, N.Y.: Syracuse University Press, 1987.

Henry, Stuart C. "Revivalism." *EARE* 2:799–812.

Kling, David W. *A Field of Divine Wonders: The New Divinity and Village Revivals in Northwestern Connecticut, 1792–1822.* University Park, Pa.: Penn State University Press, 1993.

Knickerbocker, Wendy. *Sunday at the Ballpark: Billy Sunday's Professional Baseball Career, 1883–1890.* Lanham, Md.: Scarecrow Press, 2000.

Long, Kathryn Teresa. *The Revival of 1857–58.* New York: Oxford University Press, 1998.

Martin, Robert F. *Hero of the Heartland: Billy Sunday and the Transformation of American Society, 1862–1935.* Bloomington: Indiana University Press, 2002.

McClymond, Michael J., ed. *Embodying the Spirit: New Perspectives on North American Revivalism.* Baltimore: Johns Hopkins University Press, 2004.

McLoughlin, William G. *Modern Revivalism.* New York: Ronald, 1959.

———. *Revivals, Awakenings, and Reform.* Chicago: University of Chicago Press, 1978.

Perciaccante, Marianne. *Calling Down Fire: Charles Grandison Finney and Revivalism in Jefferson County, New York, 1800–1840.* Albany: State University of New York Press, 2003.

Robertson, Darrel M. *The Chicago Revival, 1876.* Metuchen, N.J.: Scarecrow, 1989.

Sims, Patsy. *Can Somebody Shout Amen!: Inside the Tents and Tabernacles of American Revivalists.* Lexington: University Press of Kentucky, 1996.

Weisberger, Bernard A. *They Gathered at the River.* Boston: Little, Brown, 1958.

4. THE SECOND GREAT AWAKENING(S)

Birdsall, Richard D. "The Second Great Awakening and the New England Social Order." *Church History* 39, no. 3 (Sept. 1970): 345–64.

Boles, John B. *The Great Revival, 1787–1805.* Lexington: University Press of Kentucky, 1972.

Cross, Barbara M., ed. *The Autobiography of Lyman Beecher.* 2 vols. Cambridge, Mass.: Harvard University Press, 1961.

Cross, Whitney R. *The Burned-over District.* Ithaca, N.Y.: Cornell University Press, 1950.

Fitzmier, John R. *New England's Moral Legislator: Timothy Dwight, 1752–1817.* Bloomington: Indiana University Press, 1998.

Johnson, Paul E., and Sean Wilentz. *The Kingdom of Matthias.* New York: Oxford University Press, 1994.

Keller, Charles Roy. *The Second Great Awakening in Connecticut.* New Haven, Conn.: Yale University Press, 1942.

McLoughlin, William G., ed. *Lectures on Revivals in Religion by Charles G. Finney.* Cambridge, Mass.: Harvard University Press, 1960.

Mead, Sidney E. Nathaniel *William Taylor, 1786–1858: A Connecticut Liberal.* Chicago: University of Chicago Press, 1942.

Payne, Rodger M. *The Self and the Sacred: Conversion and Autobiography in Early American Protestantism.* Knoxville: University of Tennessee Press, 1998.

5. REFORM, ANTISLAVERY, THE CIVIL WAR, AND RECONSTRUCTION

Note: The literature on antebellum reform in general and antislavery in particular is vast. The following is only a sampling of some important scholarly studies of these topics.

Abzug, Robert. *Cosmos Crumbling.* New York: Oxford University Press, 1994.

Blum, Edward J. *Reforging the White Republic: Race, Religion, and American Nationalism, 1865–1898.* Baton Rouge: Louisiana State University Press, 2005.

Blum, Edward J., and W. Scott Poole, eds. *Vale of Tears: New Essays on Religion and Reconstruction.* Macon, Ga.: Mercer University Press, 2005.

Bodo, John R. *The Protestant Clergy and Public Issues, 1812–1848.* Princeton, N.J.: Princeton University Press, 1954.

Boylan, Anne. M. *The Origins of Women's Activism: New York and Boston, 1797–1840.* Chapel Hill : University of North Carolina Press, 2002.

Carwardine, Richard J. *Evangelicals and Politics in Antebellum America.* New Haven, Conn.: Yale University Press, 1993.

Cayton, Mary K. "Social Reform from the Colonial Period through the Civil War." *EARE* 3:1429–40.

Cherry, Conrad, ed. *God's New Israel.* Chapel Hill: University of North Carolina Press, 1998.

David, Hugh B. *Leonard Bacon.* Baton Rouge: Louisiana State University Press, 1998.

Davis, David Brion. "Some Themes of Countersubversion." In *The Fear of Conspiracy,* edited by Davis, pp. 9–22. Ithaca, N.Y.: Cornell University Press, 1971.

Dollar, Kent T. *Soldiers of the Cross: Confederate Soldier-Christians and the Impact of War on Their Faith.* Macon, Ga.: Mercer University Press, 2005.

Dorsey, Bruce. *Reforming Men and Women: Gender in the Antebellum City.* Ithaca, N.Y.: Cornell University Press, 2002.

Fahey, David M. *Temperance and Racism: John Bull, Johnny Reb, and the Good Templars.* Lexington: University Press of Kentucky, 1996.

Filler, Louis. *The Crusade against Slavery, 1830–1860.* New York: Harper, 1960.

Fornieri, Joseph R. *Abraham Lincoln's Political Faith.* DeKalb: Northern Illinois University Press, 2003.

Foster, Charles I. *An Errand of Mercy: The Evangelical United Front, 1790–1837.* Chapel Hill: University of North Carolina Press, 1960.

Fuller, Wayne W. *Morality and the Mail in Nineteenth Century America.* Champaign: University of Illinois Press, 2003.

Griffin, Clifford S. *Their Brothers' Keepers.* New Brunswick, N.J.: Rutgers University Press, 1960.

Guelzo, Allen C. *Abraham Lincoln, Redeemer President.* Grand Rapids, Mich.: Eerdmans, 1999.

Howard, Victor B. *The Evangelical War against Slavery and Caste: The Life and Times of John G. Fee.* Selinsgrove, Pa.: Susquehanna University Press, 1996.

Johnson, Curtis D. *Redeeming America: Evangelicals and the Road to Civil War.* Chicago: Ivan R. Dee, 1993.

Johnson, Paul E. *A Shopkeeper's Millennium: Society and Revivals in Rochester, New York, 1815–1837.* New York: Hill and Wang, c. 1978.

Kaufman, Paul Leslie. *"Logical" Luther Lee and the Methodist War against Slavery.* Lanham, Md.: Scarecrow, 2000.

Kelley, Robert. *The Cultural Pattern in American Politics.* New York: Knopf, 1979.

McKanan, Dan. *Identifying the Image of God: Radical Christians and Nonviolent Power in the Antebellum United States.* New York: Oxford University Press, 2002.

Merrill, Walter M. *Against Wind and Tide: A Biography of William Lloyd Garrison.* Cambridge, Mass.: Harvard University Press, 1963.

Miller, Randall M., Harry S. Stout, and Charles Reagan Wilson, eds. *Religion and the American Civil War.* New York: Oxford University Press, 1998.

Mintz, Steven. *Moralists and Modernizers.* Baltimore: Johns Hopkins University Press, 1995.

Noll, Mark A. *The Civil War as a Theological Crisis.* Chapel Hill: University of North Carolina Press, 2006.

Perry, Lewis. *Radical Abolitionism.* Ithaca, N.Y.: Cornell University Press, 1973.

Quist, John W. *The Roots of Antebellum Reform in Alabama and Michigan.* Baton Rouge: Louisiana State University Press, 1998.

Rothman, David J. The *Discovery of the Asylum.* Boston: Little, Brown, 1971.

Salerno, Beth A. *Sister Societies: Women's Antislavery Organizations in Antebellum America.* Dekalb: Northern Illinois University Press, 2005.

Smith, Timothy L. *Revivalism and Social Reform.* 1957. Reprint, Baltimore: Johns Hopkins University Press, 1980.

Speicher, Anna M. *The Religious World of Antislavery Women: Spirituality in the Lives of Five Abolitionist Lecturers.* Syracuse, New York: Syracuse University Press, 2000.

Stout, Harry S. *Upon the Altar of the Nation: A Moral History of the Civil War.* New York: Viking, 2006.

Strong, Douglas M. *Perfectionist Politics: Abolitionism and the Religious Tensions of American Democracy.* Syracuse, N.Y.: Syracuse University Press, 1999.

Tyler, Alice Felt. *Freedom's Ferment.* Minneapolis: University of Minnesota Press, 1944.

Walters, Ronald G. *American Reformers, 1815–1860.* New York: Hill and Wang, 1978.

Winger, Stewart. *Lincoln, Religion, and Romantic Cultural Politics.* Dekalb: Northern Illinois University Press, 2003.

Wolf, William J. *The Religion of Abraham Lincoln.* New York: Seabury, 1963. Originally published as *The Almost Chosen People.*

Woodworth, Steven E. *While God Is Marching On: The Religious World of Civil War Soldiers.* Lawrence: University Press of Kansas, 2001.

Wyatt-Brown, Bertram. *Lewis Tappan and the Evangelical War against Slavery.* 1969. Reprint, Baton Rouge: Louisiana State University Press, 1997.

Ziegler, Valarie H. *The Advocates of Peace in Antebellum America.* Bloomington: Indiana University Press, 1992.

6. THE SOUTH AND APPALACHIA

Alabama Sacred Harp Convention. *White Spirituals from the Sacred Harp.* Notes by Alan Lomax. New World Records. New York, 1977.

Aldridge, Marion D., and Kevin Lewis, eds. *The Changing Shape of Protestantism in the South.* Macon, Ga.: Mercer University Press, 1996.

Bailey, Kenneth K. *Southern White Protestantism in the Twentieth Century.* New York: Harper and Row, 1964.

Barnes, William Wright. *The Southern Baptist Convention, 1845–1953.* Nashville: Boardman, 1954.

Bealle, John. *Public Worship, Private Faith: Sacred Harp and American Folksong.* Athens: University of Georgia Press, 1997.

Bryan, G. McLeod. *These Few Also Paid a Price: Southern Whites Who Fought for Civil Rights.* Macon, Ga.: Mercer University Press, 2001.

Burton, Thomas. *The Serpent and the Spirit: Glenn Summerford's Story.* Knoxville: University of Tennessee Press, 2004.

———. *Serpent Handling Believers.* Knoxville: University of Tennessee Press, 1993.

Calhoon, Robert M. *Evangelicals and Conservatives in the Early South, 1740–1861.* Columbia: University of South Carolina Press, 1988.

Campbell, Will D. *Providence.* Waco, Tex.: Baylor University Press, 2002.

Clarke, Erskine. *Dwelling Place: A Plantation Epic.* New Haven: Yale University Press, 2005.

———. *Our Southern Zion: A History of Calvinism in the South Carolina Low Country, 1690–1990.* Tuscaloosa: University of Alabama Press, 1996.

Crowley, John G. *Primitive Baptists of the Wiregrass South : 1815 to the Present.* Gainesville: University Press of Florida, 1998.

Daly, John P. *When Slavery Was Called Freedom: Evangelicalism, Proslavery, and the Causes of the Civil War.* Lexington: University Press of Kentucky, 2002.

Dorgan, Howard. *Giving Glory to God in Appalachia: Worship Practices of Six Baptist Subdenominations.* Knoxville: University of Tennessee Press, 1987.

———. *In the Hands of a Happy God: The "No Hellers" of Central Appalachia.* Knoxville: University of Tennessee Press, 1997.

———. *The Old Regular Baptists of Central Appalachia.* Knoxville: University of Tennessee Press, 1989.

Eighmy, John Lee. *Churches in Cultural Captivity: A History of the Social Attitudes of Southern Baptists.* Knoxville: University of Tennessee Press, 1972.

Farmer, James Oscar, Jr. *The Metaphysical Confederacy: James Henley Thornwell and the Synthesis of Southern Values.* Macon, Ga.: Mercer University Press, 1986.

Flynt, Wayne. *Alabama Baptists.* Tuscaloosa: University of Alabama Press, 1998.

Fuller, A James. *Chaplain to the Confederacy: Basil Manly and Baptist Life in the Old South.* Baton Rouge: Louisiana State University Press, 2000.

Gardner, Robert G. *A Decade of Debate and Division: Georgia Baptists and the Formation of the Southern Baptist Convention.* Macon, Ga.: Mercer University Press, 1995.

Glass, William R. *Strangers in Zion: Fundamentalists in the South, 1900–1950.* Macon, Ga.: Mercer University Press, 2001.

Goen, C. C. *Broken Churches, Broken Nation: Denominational Schisms and the Coming of the American Civil War.* Macon, Ga.: Mercer University Press, 1985.

Goff, James R., Jr. *Close Harmony: A History of Southern Gospel.* Chapel Hill: University of North Carolina Press, 2002.

Grammich, Clifford A., Jr. *Local Baptists, Local Politics: Churches and Communities in the Middle and Uplands South.* Knoxville: University of Tennessee Press, 1999.

Hankins, Barry. *Uneasy in Babylon: Southern Baptist Conservatives and American Culture.* Tuscaloosa: University of Alabama Press, 2002.

Harrell, David Edwin, Jr., ed. *Varieties of Southern Evangelicalism.* Macon, Ga.: Mercer University Press, 1981.

Harvey, Paul. *Freedom's Coming: Religious Culture and the Shaping of the South from the Civil War through the Civil Rights Era.* Chapel Hill: University of North Carolina Press, 2005.

———. *Redeeming the South: Religious Cultures and Racial Identities among Southern Baptists, 1865–1925.* Chapel Hill: University of North Carolina Press, 1997.

Hawkins, Merrill M., Jr. *Will Campbell: Radical Prophet of the South.* Macon, Ga.: Mercer University Press, 1997.

Heriot, M. Jean. *Blessed Assurance: Belief, Actions and the Experience of Salvation in a Carolina Baptist Church.* Knoxville: University of Tennessee Press, 1994.

Heyrman, Christine Leigh. *Southern Cross: The Beginnings of the Bible Belt.* New York: Knopf, 1997.

Hill, Samuel S., ed. *The New Encyclopedia of Southern Culture.* Vol. 1, *Religion.* Chapel Hill: University of North Carolina Press, 2006.

———. *On Jordan's Stormy Banks.* Macon, Ga.: Mercer University Press, 1983.

———. *Religion and the Solid South.* Nashville: Abingdon, 1972.

———. "The South." *EARE* 3:1493–1508.

———. *Southern Churches in Crisis.* New York: Holt, Rinehart and Winston, 1967.

———. *Southern Churches in Crisis Revisited.* Tuscaloosa: University of Alabama Press, 1999.

———. *Varieties of Southern Religious Experience.* Baton Rouge: Louisiana State University Press, 1988.

Hill, Samuel S., and Charles H. Lippy, eds. *Encyclopedia of Religion in the South.* 2nd ed. Mercer University Press, 2005.

Hood, Fred J. *Reformed America: The Middle and Southern States, 1783–1837.* University: University of Alabama Press, 1980.

Irons, Charles F. *The Origins of Proslavery Christianity.* Chapel Hill: University of North Carolina Press, 2008.

Israel, Charles A. *Before Scopes: Evangelicalism, Education, and Evolution in Tennessee, 1870–1925.* Athens: University of Georgia Press, 2004.

Jones, Loyal. *Faith and Meaning in the Southern Uplands.* Urbana: University of Illinois Press, 1999.

Kell, Carl L., and L. Raymond Camp. *In the Name of the Father: The Rhetoric of the New Southern Baptist Convention.* Carbondale: Southern Illinois University Press, 1999.

Kimbrough, David L. *Taking Up Serpents: Snake Handlers of Eastern Kentucky.* Chapel Hill: University of North Carolina Press, 1995.

Leonard, Bill J., ed. *Christianity in Appalachia.* Knoxville: University of Tennessee Press, 1999.

———. *God's Last and Only Hope: The Fragmentation of the Southern Baptist Convention.* Grand Rapids, Mich.: Eerdmans, 1990.

Lippy, Charles H. *Bibliography of Religion in the South.* Macon, Ga.: Mercer University Press, 1983.

Mathews, Donald G. *Religion in the Old South.* Chicago: University of Chicago Press, 1977.

Matthews, Donald G., and Beth Barton Schweiger, eds. *Religion in the American South.* Chapel Hill: University of North Carolina Press, 2004.

McCauley, Deborah Vansau. *Appalachian Mountain Religion: A History.* Urbana: University of Illinois Press, 1995.

McCauley, Deborah Vansau, and Laura E. Porter. *Mountain Holiness: A Photographic Narrative.* Knoxville: University of Tennessee Press, 2003.

McMillen, Salley G. *To Raise Up the South: Sunday Schools in Black and White Churches, 1865–1915.* Baton Rouge: Louisiana State University Press, 2001.

Miller, Randall M. *Catholics in the Old South.* Macon, Ga.: Mercer University Press, 1983.

Morgan, David T. *The New Crusades, the New Holy Land: Conflict in the Southern Baptist Convention, 1969–1991.* Tuscaloosa: University of Alabama Press, 1996.

Mulder, Philip N. *A Controversial Spirit: Evangelical Awakenings in the South.* New York: Oxford University Press, 2002.

Neville, Gwen Kennedy. *Kinship and Pilgrimage: Rituals of Reunion in American Protestant Culture.* New York: Oxford University Press, 1987.

Newman, Mark. *Getting Right with God: Southern Baptists and Desegregation, 1945–1995.* Tuscaloosa: University of Alabama Press, 2001.

Norman, Corrie E., and Don S. Armentrout, eds. *Religion in the Contemporary South.* Knoxville: University of Tennessee Press, 2005.

Ownby, Ted. *Subduing Satan: Religion, Recreation, and Manhood in the Rural South, 1865–1920.* Chapel Hill: University of North Carolina Press, 1990.

Patterson, Beverly Bush. *The Sound of the Dove: Singing in Appalachian Primitive Baptist Churches.* Urbana: University of Illinois Press, 1995.

Peacock, James L., and Ruel W. Tyson, Jr. *Pilgrims of Paradox: Calvinism and Experience among the Primitive Baptists of the Blue Ridge.* Washington, D.C.: Smithsonian Institution Press, 1989.

Proctor, Samuel, and Louis Schmeir. *Jews of the South.* Macon, Ga.: Mercer University Press, 1982.

Rohrer, S. Scott. *Hope's Promise: Religion and Acculturation in the Southern Backcountry.* Tuscaloosa: University of Alabama Press, 2005.

Scales, T. Laine. *All that Fits a Woman: Training Southern Baptist Women for Charity and Mission, 1907–1926.* Macon, Ga.: Mercer University Press, 2000

Schweiger, Beth Barton. *The Gospel Working Up: Progress and the Pulpit in Nineteenth-Century Virginia.* New York: Oxford University Press, 2000.

Shepherd, Samuel C., Jr. *Avenues of Faith: Shaping the Urban Religious Culture of Richmond, Virginia, 1900–1929.* Tuscaloosa: University of Alabama Press, 2001.

Snay, Mitchell. *Gospel of Disunion: Religion and Separatism in the Antebellum South.* Cambridge: Cambridge University Press, 1993.

Spain, Rufus B. *At Ease in Zion: A Social History of Southern Baptists, 1865–1900.* Nashville: Vanderbilt University Press, c. 1961, 1967.

Sparks, Elder John. *The Roots of Appalachian Christianity: The Life and Legacy of Elder Shubal Stearns.* Lexington: University Press of Kentucky, 2001.

Sparks, Randy J. *Religion in Mississippi.* Jackson: University Press of Mississippi, 2001.

Startup, Kenneth Moore. *The Root of All Evil: The Protestant Clergy and the Economic Mind of the Old South.* Athens: University of Georgia Press, 1997.

Stephens, Lester D. *Science, Race, and Religion in the American South: John Bachman and the Charleston Circle of Naturalists, 1815–1895.* Chapel Hill: University of North Carolina Press, 2000.

Stricklin, David. *A Genealogy of Dissent: The Culture of Progressive Protest in Southern Baptist Life, 1920–1995.* Lexington: University Press of Kentucky, 1999.

Thompson, James J., Jr. *Tried as by Fire: Southern Baptists and the Religious Controversies of the 1920s.* Macon, Ga.: Mercer University Press, 1982.

Titon, Jeff Todd. *Powerhouse for God: Speech, Chant and Song in an Appalachian Baptist Church.* Austin: University of Texas Press, 1988. Also recordings published under same title by University of North Carolina Press, Chapel Hill, 1982.

Tyson, Ruel W., Jr., James L. Peacock, and Daniel W. Patterson, eds. *Diversities of Gifts: Field Studies in Southern Religion.* Urbana: University of Illinois Press, 1988.

Wardin, Albert W., Jr. *Tennessee Baptists: A Comprehensive History, 1779–1999.* Brentwood, Tenn.: Tennessee Baptist Convention, 1999.

Williams, Michael E. *Isaac Taylor Tichenor: The Creation of the Baptist New South.* Tuscaloosa: University of Alabama Press, 2005.

Wills, Gregory A. *Democratic Religion: Freedom, Authority, and Church Discipline in the Baptist South, 1785–1900.* New York: Oxford University Press, 1997.

Wilson, Charles Reagan. *Baptized in Blood: The Religion of the Lost Cause, 1865–1920.* Athens: University of Georgia Press, 1980.

——, ed. *Cultural Perspectives on the American South. Vol. 5: Religion.* New York: Gordon and Breach, 1991.

——. *Judgment and Grace in Dixie: Southern Faiths from Faulkner to Elvis.* Athens: University of Georgia Press, 1995.

——. *Religion in the South.* Jackson: University Press of Mississippi, 1985.

Young, Jeffrey Roberts. *Domesticating Slavery: The Master Class in Georgia and South Carolina, 1670–1837.* Chapel Hill: University of North Carolina Press, 1999.

7. NINETEENTH-CENTURY PROTESTANTISM: EDUCATION, THOUGHT, GENDER, AND CULTURE

Boylan, Anne M. *Sunday School.* New Haven, Conn.: Yale University Press, 1988.

Brown, Candy Gunther. *The Word in the World: Evangelical Writing, Publishing, and Reading in America, 1789–1880.* Chapel Hill: University of North Carolina Press, 2004.

Caskey, Marie. *Chariot of Fire: Religion and the Beecher Family.* New Haven, Conn.: Yale University Press, 1978.

Elson, Ruth Miller. *Guardians of Tradition: American Schoolbooks of the Nineteenth Century.* Lincoln: University of Nebraska Press, 1964.

Gorn, Elliott J., ed. *McGuffey Readers: Selections from the 1879 Edition.* Boston: Bedford/St. Martin's, 1998.

Haynes, Carolyn A. *Divine Destiny: Gender and Race in Nineteenth-Century Protestantism.* Jackson, Miss.: University Press of Mississippi, 1998.

Hedrick, Joan D. *Harriet Beecher Stowe: A Life.* New York: Oxford University Press, 1994.

Hewitt, Glenn A. *Regeneration and Morality: A Study of Charles Finney, Charles Hodge, John W. Nevin, and Horace Bushnell.* Brooklyn, N.Y.: Carlson, 1991.

Hill, Patricia R. "The Missionary Enterprise." *EARE* 3:1683–96.

Kemeny, P.C. *Princeton in the Nation's Service.* New York: Oxford University Press, 1998.

Kilde, Jeanne Halgren. *When Church Became Theatre: The Transformation of Evangelical Architecture and Worship in Nineteenth-Century America.* New York: Oxford University Press, 2002.

Laderman, Gary. *The Sacred Remains: American Attitudes toward Death, 1779–1883.* New Haven, Conn.: Yale University Press, 1996.

Livingstone, David N., D. G. Hart, and Mark Noll, eds. *Evangelicals and Science in Historical Perspective.* New York: Oxford University Press, 1999.

Marsden, George M. *The Evangelical Mind and the New School Presbyterian Experience.* New Haven, Conn.: Yale University Press, 1970.

McDannell, Colleen. *The Christian Home in Victorian America, 1840–1900.* Bloomington: Indiana University Press, 1986.

Miyakawa, T. Scott. *Protestants and Pioneers.* Chicago: University of Chicago Press, 1964.

Moorhead, James. *American Apocalypse: Yankee Protestants and the Civil War, 1860–1869.* New Haven, Conn.: Yale University Press, 1978.

Mulder, John M. *Woodrow Wilson: The Years of Preparation.* Princeton, N.J.: Princeton University Press, 1978.

Mullin, R. Bruce. *Miracles and the Modern Religious Imagination*. New Haven, Conn.: Yale University Press, 1996.

———. *The Puritan as Yankee: A Life of Horace Bushnell*. Grand Rapids, Mich.: Eerdmans, 2002.

Rudolph, Frederick. *The American College and University*. New York: Vintage, 1962.

Smith, H. Shelton. *Changing Conceptions of Original Sin*. New York: Scribners, 1955.

Stephens, Bruce M. *The Prism of Time and Eternity: Images of Christ in American Protestant Thought from Jonathan Edwards to Horace Bushnell*. Lanham, Md.: American Theological Library Association, 1996.

Stewart, John W., and James H. Moorhead. *Charles Hodge Revisited*. Grand Rapids, Mich.: Eerdmans, 2002.

Sweeney, Douglas A. *Nathaniel Taylor, New Haven Theology, and the Legacy of Jonathan Edwards*. New York: Oxford University Press, 2003.

White, Barbara Anne. *The Beecher Sisters*. New Haven: Yale University Press, 2003.

Wosh, Peter J. *Spreading the Word: The Bible Business in Nineteenth-Century America*. Ithaca, N.Y.: Cornell University Press, 1994.

Wright, Louis B. *Culture on the Moving Frontier*. Bloomington: Indiana University Press, 1955.

Zink-Sawyer, Beverly Ann. *From Preachers to Suffragists: Woman's Rights and Religious Conviction in the Lives of Three Nineteenth-Century American Clergywomen*. Louisville, Ky.: Westminster John Knox, 2003.

8. MISSIONS

(*SEE ALSO* F. ON NATIVE AMERICAN MISSIONS)

Ayer, H. D. *The Christian and Missionary Alliance: An Annotated Bibliography of Textual Sources*. Lanham, Md.: Scarecrow Press, 2001.

Bays, Daniel H., and Grant Wacker, eds. *The Foreign Missionary Enterprise at Home*. Tuscaloosa: University of Alabama Press, 2003.

Boyd, Nancy. *Emissaries: The Overseas Work of the American YWCA, 1895–1970*. New York: Woman's Press, 1986.

Carpenter, Joel A., and Wilbert R. Shenk, eds. *Earthen Vessels: American Evangelicals and Foreign Missions, 1880–1980*. Grand Rapids, Mich.: Eerdmans, 1990.

Clymer, Kenton J. *Protestant Missionaries in the Philippines, 1898–1916*. Urbana: University of Illinois Press, 1986.

Cunnigham, Floyd T. *Holiness Abroad: Nazarene Missions in Asia*. Lanham, Md.: Scarecrow, 2003.

Graham, Gael. *Gender, Culture, and Christianity: American Protestant Mission Schools in China, 1880–1930*. New York: Peter Lang, 1995.

Harris, Paul William. *Nothing but Christ: Rufus Anderson and the Ideology of Protestant Foreign Missions*. New York: Oxford University Press, 1999.

Holtrop, Pieter N., and Hugh McLeod, eds. *Missions and Missionaries*. Rochester, N.Y.: Boydell, 2000.

Hutchison, William R. *Errand to the World: American Protestant Thought and Foreign Missions*. Chicago: University of Chicago Press, 1987.

Porterfield, Amanda. *Mary Lyon and the Mount Holyoke Missionaries*. New York: Oxford University Press, 1997.

Robert, Dana L. *American Women in Mission.* Macon, Ga.: Mercer University Press, 1996.

———. *Occupy until I Come: A. T. Pierson and the Evangelization of the World.* Grand Rapids, Mich.: Eerdmans, 2003.

Ruoff, E. G., ed. *Death Throes of a Dynasty: Letters and Diaries of Charles and Bessie Ewing, Missionaries to China.* Kent, Ohio: Kent State University Press, 1990.

Shenk, Wilbert R., ed. *North American Foreign Missions, 1810–1918.* Grand Rapids, Mich.: Eerdmans, 2004.

Stanley, Brian. *Missions, Nationalism, and the End of Empire.* Grand Rapids, Mich.: Eerdmans, 2003.

Swanson, Jeffrey. *Echoes of the Call: Identity and Ideology among American Missionaries in Ecuador.* New York: Oxford University Press, 1995.

Taylor, Wilma Rugh, and Norman Thomas Taylor. *This Train Bound for Glory: The Story of America's Chapel Cars.* Valley Forge, Pa.: Judson, 1999.

Underwood, Elizabeth. *Challenged Identities: North American Missionaries in Korea, 1884–1934.* Seoul: Royal Asiatic Society Korea Branch, 2003.

Wacker, Grant, ed. "Special Issue: the Missionary Impulse in American History" *Church History* 72, no. 4 (Dec. 2003).

Walker, Randi. *Protestantism in the Sangre de Cristos, 1850–1920.* Albuquerque: University of New Mexico Press, 1991.

Willis, Alan Scot. *All According to God's Plan: Southern Baptist Missions and Race 1945–1970.* Lexington: University Press of Kentucky, 2004.

Xi, Lian. *The Conversion of Missionaries: Liberalism in American Protestant Missions in China, 1907–1932.* University Park: Pennsylvania State University Press, 1997.

Zwiep, Mary. *Pilgrim Path: The First Company of Women Missionaries in Hawaii.* Madison: University of Wisconsin Press, 1991.

9. THE VICTORIAN ERA THROUGH THE 1920S

Braude, Ann. *Radical Spirits: Spiritualism and Women's Rights in Nineteenth-Century America.* Boston: Beacon, 1989.

Brighten the Corner Where You Are: Black and White Urban Hymnody. New World Records. New York, 1978.

Carroll, Bret E. *Spiritualism in Antebellum America.* Bloomington: Indiana University Press, 1997.

Carter, Paul A. *The Spiritual Crisis of the Gilded Age.* DeKalb: Northern Illinois University Press, 1971.

Cashdollar, Charles D. *A Spiritual Home: Life in British and American Reformed Congregations, 1830–1915.* University Park: Pennsylvania State University Press, 2000.

Douglas, Ann. *The Feminization of American Culture.* New York: Knopf, 1977.

Findlay, James F., Jr. *Dwight L. Moody.* Chicago: University of Chicago Press, 1969.

Foster, Gaines M. *Moral Reconstruction: Christian Lobbyists and the Federal Legislation of Morality, 1865–1920.* Chapel Hill: University of North Carolina Press, 2002.

Gusfield, Joseph R. *Symbolic Crusade: Status Politics and the American Temperance Movement.* 2d ed. Urbana: University of Illinois Press, 1986.

Hobbs, June Hadden. *"I Sing for I Cannot Be Silent": The Feminization of American Hymnody, 1870–1920.* Pittsburgh: University of Pittsburgh Press, 1997.

Hohner, Robert A. *Prohibition and Politics: The Life of Bishop James Cannon, Jr.* Columbia: University of South Carolina Press, 1999.

Kerr, K. Austin. *Organized for Prohibition: A New History of the Anti-Saloon League.* New Haven, Conn.: Yale University Press, 1985.

Kicich, John J. *Ghostly Communion: Cross-Cultural Spiritualism in Nineteenth-Century American Literature.* Hanover, N.H.: Dartmouth College Press, 2004.

Mayer, John A. "Social Reform after the Civil War to the Great Depression." *EARE* 3:1441–61.

Rieser, Andrew C. *The Chautauqua Movement: Protestants, Progressives, and the Culture of Modern Liberalism.* New York: Columbia University Press, 2003.

Rorabaugh, W. J. *The Alcoholic Republic.* New York: Oxford University Press, 1979.

Rose, Anne C. *Victorian America and the Civil War.* New York: Cambridge University Press, 1992.

Sinclair, Andrew. *Era of Excess: A Social History of the Prohibition Movement.* New York: Harper and Row, 1964.

Sizer, Sandra S. *Gospel Hymns and Social Religion.* Philadelphia: Temple University Press, 1978.

Timberlake, James H. *Prohibition and the Progressive Movement, 1900–1920.* Cambridge, Mass.: Harvard University Press, 1963.

10. FUNDAMENTALISM

(*SEE ALSO* SECTIONS S.13 AND Y.4)

Ammerman, Nancy Tatom. *Bible Believers: Fundamentalists in the Modern World.* New Brunswick, N.J.: Rutgers University Press, 1987.

Abrams, Douglas C. *Selling the Old-Time Religion: American Fundamentalists and Mass Culture, 1920–1940.* Athens: University of Georgia Press, 2001.

Bendroth, Margaret Lamberts. *Fundamentalism and Gender, 1875 to the Present.* New Haven, Conn.: Yale University Press, 1993.

———. *Fundamentalists in the City: Conflict and Division in Boston's Churches, 1885–1950.* New York: Oxford University Press, 2005.

Brasher, Brenda. *Godly Women: Fundamentalism and Female Power.* New Brunswick, N.J.: Rutgers University Press, 1998.

Brereton, Virginia Lieson. *Training God's Army: The American Bible School, 1880–1940.* Bloomington: Indiana University Press, 1990.

Carpenter, Joel. *Revive Us Again: The Reawakening of American Fundamentalism.* New York: Oxford University Press, 1997.

DeBerg, Betty A. *Ungodly Women: Gender and the First Wave of American Fundamentalism.* Minneapolis: Fortress, 1990.

Hankins, Barry. *God's Rascal: J. Frank Norris and the Beginnings of Southern Fundamentalism.* Lexington: University Press of Kentucky, 1996.

Hart, D. G. *Defending the Faith: J. Gresham Machen and the Crisis of Conservative Protestantism in Modern America.* Baltimore: Johns Hopkins University Press, 1994.

Kraus, C. Norman. *Dispensationalism in America.* Richmond, Va.: John Knox Press, 1958.

Larson, Edward J. *Summer for the Gods: The Scopes Trial and America's Continuing Debate over Science and Religion.* Cambridge, Mass.: Harvard University Press, 1998.

Lienesch, Michael. *In the Beginning: Fundamentalism, the Scopes Trial, and the Making of the Antievolution Movement.* Chapel Hill: University of North Carolina Press, 2007.

Marsden, George M. "Fundamentalism." *EARE* 2:947–62.

———. *Fundamentalism and American Culture.* New York: Oxford University Press, 1980, 2006.

———. *Reforming Fundamentalism: Fuller Seminary and the New Evangelicalism.* Grand Rapids, Mich.: Eerdmans, 1987.

Marty, Martin E., and R. Scott Appleby, eds. *Accounting for Fundamentalisms.* Chicago: University of Chicago Press, 1994.

Moran, Jeffrey P. The *Scopes Trial: A Brief History with Documents.* Boston, Mass.: Bedford/ St. Martin's, 2002.

Russell, C. Allyn. *Voices of American Fundamentalism.* Philadelphia: Westminster, 1976.

Sandeen, Ernest. *The Roots of Fundamentalism.* Chicago: University of Chicago Press, 1970.

Trollinger, William Vance, Jr. *God's Empire: William Bell Riley and Midwestern Fundamentalism.* Madison: University of Wisconsin Press, 1990.

Weber, Timothy P. *Living in the Shadow of the Second Coming: American Premillennialism, 1875–1925.* Enlarged ed. Chicago: University of Chicago Press, 1987.

11. HOLINESS

Brasher, J. Lawrence. *The Sanctified South: John Lakin Brasher and the Holiness Movement.* Urbana: University of Illinois Press, 1994.

Eason, Andrew Mark. *Women in God's Army: Gender and Equality in the Salvation Army.* Waterloo, Ont.: Wilfred Laurier University Press, 2003.

Hamilton, Barry W. *William Baxter Godbey: Itinerant Apostle of the Holiness Movement.* Lewiston, Me.: Edwin Mellen Press, 2000.

Jones, Charles Edwin. *Perfectionist Persuasion: The Holiness Movement and American Methodism, 1867–1936.* Methuen, N.J.: Scarecrow, 1974.

Leclerc, Diane. *Singleness of Heart: Gender, Sin, and Holiness in Historical Perspective.* Lanham, Md.: Scarecrow, 2001.

Messenger, Troy. *Holy Leisure: Recreation and Religion in God's Square Mile.* Philadelphia: Temple University Press, 2000.

Murdoch, Norman H. *Origins of the Salvation Army.* Knoxville: University of Tennessee Press, 1994.

Oden, Thomas C., ed. *Phoebe Palmer: Selected Writings.* New York: Paulist, 1988.

Raser, Harold E. *Phoebe Palmer.* Lewiston, N.Y.: Mellen, 1987.

Schmidt, Jean Miller. "Holiness and Perfection." *EARE* 2:813–30.

Smith, Timothy L. *Called unto Holiness.* Kansas City, Mo.: Nazarene Publishing House, 1962.

Stanley, Susan Cunningham. *Feminist Pillar of Fire: The Life of Alma White.* Cleveland: Pilgrim, 1993.

Stanley, Susie C. *Women Preachers' Autobiographies and the Sanctified Self.* Knoxville: University of Tennessee Press, 2002.

Taiz, Lillian. *Hallelujah Lads & Lasses: Remaking the Salvation Army in America, 1880–1930.* Chapel Hill: University of North Carolina Press, 2001.

Weiss, Ellen. *City in the Woods: The Life and Design of an American Camp Meeting on Martha's Vineyard.* New York: Oxford University Press, 1987.

Winston, Diane. *Red Hot and Righteous: The Urban Religion of the Salvation Army.* Cambridge, Mass.: Harvard University Press, 1999.

12. PENTECOSTALISM
(*SEE ALSO* G. AND V.)

Adair, Peter, and Blair Boyd. *The Holy Ghost People.* Contemporary Films/McGraw Hill film (1968) subsequently released in several videocassette versions, e.g., CRM/McGraw Hill Films, 1984. Documentary on a snake-handling congregation in West Virginia.

Anderson, Allan. *An Introduction to Pentecostalism.* Cambridge: Cambridge University Press, 2004.

Anderson, Robert Mapes. *Vision of the Disinherited: The Making of American Pentecostalism.* New York: Oxford University Press, 1979.

Baer, Jonathan R. "Redeemed Bodies: The Functions of Divine Healing in Incipient Pentecostalism." *Church History* 70, no. 4 (Dec. 2001): 735–71.

Blumhofer, Edith L. *Aimee Semple McPherson.* Grand Rapids, Mich.: Eerdmans, 1993.

———. *Restoring the Faith: The Assemblies of God, Pentecostalism, and American Culture.* Urbana: University of Illinois Press, 1993.

Blumhofer, Edith L., Russell P. Spittler, and Grant A. Wacker, eds. *Pentecostal Currents in American Protestantism.* Urbana: University of Illinois Press, 1999.

Burgess, Stanley M., and Gary B. McGee, eds. *Dictionary of Pentecostal and Charismatic Movements.* Grand Rapids, Mich.: Regency Reference Library, 1988.

Crews, Mickey. *The Church of God: A Social History.* Knoxville: University of Tennessee Press, 1990.

Dayton, Donald W. *Theological Roots of Pentecostalism.* Metuchen, N.J.: Scarecrow, 1987.

Goff, James R., Jr. *Fields White unto Harvest: Charles F. Parham and the Missionary Origins of Pentecostalism.* Fayetteville: University of Arkansas Press, 1988.

Goff, James R., Jr., and Grant Wacker, eds. *Portraits of a Generation: Early Pentecostal Leaders.* Fayetteville: University of Arkansas Press, 2002.

Griffith, R. Marie. *God's Daughters: Evangelical Women and the Power of Submission.* Berkeley: University of California Press, 1997.

Hardesty, Nancy A. *Faith Cure: Divine Healing in the Holiness and Pentecostal Movements.* Peabody, Mass.: Hendrickson, 2003.

Harrell, David Edwin, Jr. *All Things Are Possible: The Healing and Charismatic Revivals in Modern America.* Bloomington: Indiana University Press, 1975.

Jacobsen, Douglas. *Thinking in the Spirit: Theologies of the Early Pentecostal Movement.* Bloomington: Indiana University Press, 2003.

Jones, Charles Edwin. *A Guide to the Study of the Pentecostal Movement.* 2 vols. Metuchen, N.J.: Scarecrow, 1983.

Miller, Donald E., and Tetsunao Yamamori. *Global Pentecostalism.* Berkeley: University of California Press, 2007.

Poloma, Margaret M. *The Assemblies of God at the Crossroads.* Knoxville: University of Tennessee Press, 1989.

———. *Main Street Mystics: The Toronto Blessing and Reviving Pentecostalism.* Walnut Creek, Calif.: AltaMira, 2003.

Pullum, Stephen J. *"Foul Demons, Come Out!": The Rhetoric of Twentieth-Century American Faith Healing.* Westport, Conn.: Praeger, 1999.

Robins, R. G., and A. J. Tomlinson. *Plainfolk Modernist.* New York: Oxford University Press, 2004.

Stephens, Randall J. *The Fire Spreads: Holiness and Pentecostalism in the American South.* Cambridge, Mass.: Harvard University Press, 2008.

Sutton, Matthew Avery. *Aimee Semple McPherson and the Resurrection of Christian America.* Cambridge, Mass.: Harvard University Press, 2007.

Synan, Vincent. *The Holiness-Pentecostal Movement in America.* Grand Rapids, Mich.: Eerdmans, 1971.

Wacker, Grant. "The Functions of Faith in Primitive Pentecostalism." *Harvard Theological Review* 77, nos. 3–4 (1984): 353–75.

———. *Heaven Below: Early Pentecostals and American Culture.* Cambridge, Mass.: Harvard University Press, 2001.

———. "Pentecostalism." *EARE* 2:933–46.

13. THE LATER TWENTIETH- AND EARLY TWENTY-FIRST CENTURIES

Allen, L. Dean. *Rise Up, O Men of God: The "Men and Religion Forward Movement" and the "Promise Keepers."* Macon, Ga.: Mercer University Press, 2002.

Balmer, Randall. *Blessed Assurance: A History of Evangelicalism in America.* Boston: Beacon Press, 1999.

———. *Mine Eyes Have Seen the Glory: A Journey into the Evangelical Subculture in America.* 4th ed. New York: Oxford University Press, 2006.

———. *Thy Kingdom Come: How the Religious Right Distorts the Faith and Threatens America.* New York: Basic Books, 2006.

Brickner, Bryan W. *The Promise Keepers.* Lanham, Md.: Lexington, 1999.

Bruce, Steve. *Pray TV: Televangelism in America.* New York: Routledge, 1990.

Buss, Doris. *Globalizing Family Values: The Christian Right in International Politics.* Minneapolis: University of Minnesota Press, 2003.

Capps, Walter H. *The New Religious Right.* Columbia: University of South Carolina Press, 1990.

Claussen, Dane S., ed. *The Promise Keepers: Essays on Masculinity and Christianity.* Jefferson, N.C.: McFarland, 2000.

Cochran, Pamela D. H. *Evangelical Feminism.* New York: New York University Press, 2005.

Critchlow, Donald T. *Phyllis Schlafly and Grassroots Conservatism.* Princeton, N.J.: Princeton University Press, 2005.

Di Sabatino, David. *The Jesus People Movement: An Annotated Bibliography and General Resource.* Westport, Conn.: Greenwood, 1999.

Elzey, Wayne. "Popular Culture." *EARE* 3:1727–42.

Eskridge, Larry, and Mark A. Noll, eds. *More Money, More Ministry: Money and Evangelicals in Recent American Culture.* Grand Rapids, Mich.: Eerdmans, 2000.

Fitzgerald, Frances. "Liberty Baptist." In *Cities on a Hill,* by Frances Fitzgerald, 121–202. New York: Simon and Schuster, 1986.

Fogel, Robert W. *The Fourth Great Awakening and the Future of Egalitarianism*. Chicago: University of Chicago Press, 2000.

Forbes, Bruce David, and Jeanne Halgren Kilde, eds. *Rapture, Revelation, and the End Times*. New York: Palgrave Macmillan, 2004.

Frady, Marshall. *Billy Graham*. Boston: Little, Brown, 1979.

Frankl, Razelle. *Televangelism: The Marketing of Popular Religion*. Carbondale: Southern Illinois University Press, 1987.

Giuliano, Michael J. *Thrice Born: The Rhetorical Comeback of Jimmy Swaggart*. Macon, Ga.: Mercer University Press, 1999.

Griffith, R. Marie. *Born Again Bodies: Flesh and Spirit in American Christianity*. Berkeley: University of California Press, 2004.

———. *God's Daughters: Evangelical Women and the Power of Submission*. Berkeley: University of California Press, 1997.

Harding, Susan Friend. *The Book of Jerry Falwell: Fundamentalist language and Politics*. Princeton, N.J.: Princeton University Press, 2000.

Harrell, David Edwin, Jr. *Oral Roberts*. San Francisco: Harper and Row, 1985.

———. *Pat Robertson*. San Francisco: Harper and Row, 1987.

Hart, D. G. *Deconstructing Evangelicalism: Conservative Protestantism in the Age of Billy Graham*. Grand Rapids, Mich.: Baker Academic, 2004.

———. *That Old-Time Religion in Modern America: Evangelical Protestantism in the Twentieth Century*. Chicago: I. R. Dee, 2002.

Hendershot, Heather. *Shaking the World for Jesus: Media and Conservative Evangelical Culture*. Chicago: Univ. of Chicago Press, 2004.

Hunter, James Davison. *American Evangelicalism*. New Brunswick, N.J.: Rutgers University Press, 1983.

———. *Culture Wars*. New York: Basic Books, 1991.

Ingersoll, Julie. *Evangelical Christian Women*. New York: New York University Press, 2003.

Kaplan, Esther. *With God on Their Side: George W. Bush and the Christian Right*. New York: New Press, 2005.

Kazin, Michael. *The Populist Persuasion*. Ithaca, N.Y.: Cornell University Press, 1995.

Kintz, Linda, and Julia Lesage, eds. *Media, Culture, and the Religious Right*. Minneapolis: University of Minnesota Press, 1998.

Ladd, Tony, and James A. Mathisen. *Muscular Christianity: Evangelical Protestants and the Development of American Sport*. Grand Rapids, Mich.: Baker Books, 1999.

Liebman, Robert C., and Robert Wuthnow, eds. *The New Christian Right*. Hawthorne, N.Y.: Aldine, 1983.

Lienisch, Michael. *Redeeming America: Piety and Politics in the New Christian Right*. Chapel Hill: University of North Carolina Press, 1993.

Loveland, Anne C. *American Evangelicals and the U.S. Military: 1942–1993*. Baton Rouge: Louisiana State University Press, 1996.

Martin, William. "Mass Communications." *EARE* 3:1711–26.

———. *A Prophet with Honor: The Billy Graham Story*. New York: W. Morrow, 1991.

———. *With God on Our Side: The Rise of the Religious Right in America*. New York: Broadway, 1996.

McGirr, Lisa. *Suburban Warriors: The Origins of the New American Right*. Princeton, N.J.: Princeton University Press, 2001.

Miller, Donald E. *Reinventing American Protestantism: Christianity in the New Millennium*. Berkeley: University of California Press, 1997.

Neal, Lynn. *Romancing God: Evangelical Women and Inspirational Fiction*. Chapel Hill: University of North Carolina Press, 2006.

Numbers, Ronald L., ed. *Creationism in Twentieth-Century America: A Ten-Volume Anthology of Documents, 1903–1961*. New York: Garland, 1995.

———. *The Creationists*. Cambridge, Mass.: Harvard University Press, 2006.

Quebedeaux, Richard. "Conservative and Charismatic Developments of the Later Twentieth Century." *EARE* 2:963–76.

Shea, William M. *The Lion and the Lamb: Evangelicals and Catholics in America*. New York: Oxford University Press, 2004.

Smith, Christian. *Christian America? What Evangelicals Really Want*. Berkeley: University of California Press, 2000.

———. *Divided by Faith: Evangelical Religion and the Problem of Race in America*. New York: Oxford University Press, 2000.

———. *Evangelicalism, Embattled and Thriving*. Chicago: University of Chicago Press, 1998.

Stone, John R. *On the Boundaries of American Evangelicalism: The Postwar Evangelical Coalition*. New York: St. Martin's, 1997.

Tamney, Joseph B. *The Resilience of Conservative Religion: The Case of Popular, Conservative Protestant Congregations*. Cambridge; New York: Cambridge University Press, 2002.

Turner, John G. *Bill Bright and the Campus Crusade for Christ*. Chapel Hill: University of North Carolina Press, 2008.

Wacker, Grant. "Searching for Norman Rockwell: Popular Evangelicalism in Contemporary America." In *The Evangelical Tradition in America,* edited by Leonard I. Sweet. Macon, Ga.: Mercer University Press, 1984.

Wagner, Melinda Bollar. *God's Schools*. New Brunswick, N.J.: Rutgers University Press, 1990.

Watt, David Harrington. *Bible-Carrying Christians: Conservative Protestants and Social Power*. New York: Oxford University Press, 2002.

———. *A Transforming Faith: Explorations of Twentieth-Century American Evangelicalism*. New Brunswick, N.J.: Rutgers University Press, 1991.

Wilcox, Clyde. *God's Warriors: The Christian Right in Twentieth Century America*. Baltimore: Johns Hopkins University Press, 1992.

Williams, Rhys H., ed. *Promise Keepers and the New Masculinity*. Lanham, Md.: Lexington Books, 2001.

Wills, Garry. *Under God: Religion and American Politics*. New York: Simon & Schuster, 1990.

14. OVERVIEWS AND BIBLIOGRAPHY

Blumhofer, Edith L., and Joel A. Carpenter, eds. *Twentieth-Century Evangelicalism: A Guide to the Sources*. New York: Garland, 1990.

Boyer, Paul. *When Time Shall Be No More: Prophecy Belief in Modern American Culture*. Cambridge, Mass.: Harvard University Press, 1992.

Brereton, Virginia Lieson. *From Sin to Salvation: Stories of Women's Conversions, 1800 to the Present.* Bloomington: Indiana University Press, 1991.

Collins, Kenneth J. *The Evangelical Moment.* Grand Rapids, Mich.: Baker Academic, 2005.

Dayton, Donald W., and Robert K. Johnston, eds. *The Variety of American Evangelicalism.* Downers Grove, Ill.: InterVarsity, 1991.

Emerson, Michael O., and Christian Smith. *Divided by Faith: Evangelical Religion and The Problem of Race in America.* New York: Oxford University Press, 2000.

Gallagher, Sally K. *Evangelical Identity and Gendered Family Life.* New Brunswick, N.J.: Rutgers University Press, 2003.

Hunt, Stephen. *Christian Millennialism.* Bloomington: Indiana University Press, 2001.

Krapohl, Robert H., and Charles H. Lippy. *The Evangelicals: A Historical, Thematic, and Bibliographical Guide.* Westport, Conn.: Greenwood, 1999.

Lovegrove, Deryck W. *The Rise of the Laity in Evangelical Protestantism.* New York: Routledge, 2002.

Magnuson, Norris A., and William G. Travis. *American Evangelicalism: An Annotated Bibliography.* West Cornwall, Conn.: Locust Hill, 1990.

Marsden, George M. *Understanding Fundamentalism and Evangelicalism.* Grand Rapids, Mich.: Eerdmans, 1991.

Peshkin, Alan. *God's Choice: The Total World of a Fundamentalist Christian School.* Chicago: University of Chicago Press, 1986.

Pope-Levinson, Priscilla. *Turn the Pulpit Loose: Two Centuries of American Women Evangelists.* New York: Palgrave Macmillan, 2004.

Reimer, Samuel Harold. *Evangelicals and the Continental Divide: The Conservative Protestant Subculture in Canada and the United States.* Montreal: McGill-Queen's University Press, 2003.

Schuster, Robert D., James Stambaugh, and Ferne Weimer, comps. *Researching Modern Evangelicalism: A Guide to the Holdings of the Billy Graham Center.* Westport, Conn.: Greenwood, 1990.

Sweeney, Douglas A. *The American Evangelical Story.* Grand Rapids, Mich.: Baker Academic, 2005.

Thuesen, Peter J. *In Discordance with the Scriptures: American Protestant Battles over Translating the Bible.* New York: Oxford University Press, 1999.

Weber, Timothy P. *On the Road to Armageddon: How Evangelicals Became Israel's Best Friend.* Grand Rapids, Mich.: Baker, 2004.

T. "Mainline" Protestantism

Balmer, Randall. *Grant Us Courage: Travels along the Mainline of American Protestantism.* New York: Oxford University Press, 1996.

Balmer, Randall, and Lauren F. Winner. *Protestantism in America.* New York: Columbia University Press, 2005.

Baltzell, E. Digby. *The Protestant Establishment.* New York: Vintage, 1964.

Bendroth, Margaret Lamberts. *Growing Up Protestant: Parents, Children, and Mainline Churches.* New Brunswick, N.J.: Rutgers University Press, 2002.

Bendroth, Margaret Lamberts, and Virginia Lieson Brereton, eds. *Women and Twentieth-Century Protestantism.* Urbana: University of Illinois Press, 2002.

Brown, Charles C. *Niebuhr and His Age.* Philadelphia: Trinity Press International, 1992.

Brown, Robert McAfee, ed. *The Essential Reinhold Niebuhr.* New Haven, Conn.: Yale University Press, 1987.

———. *Reflections over the Long Haul: A Memoir.* Louisville, Ky.: Westminster John Knox Press, 2005.

Bucher, Glenn R., and L. Gordon Tait. "Social Reform since the Great Depression." *EARE* 3:1441–62.

Carroll, Jackson, and Wade Clark Roof, eds. *Beyond Establishment: Protestant Identity in a Post-Protestant Age.* Louisville, Ky.: Westminster/John Knox, 1993.

Chaves, Mark. *Ordaining Women: Culture and Conflict in Religious Organizations.* Cambridge, Mass.: Harvard University Press, 1997.

Crow, Paul A., Jr. "The Ecumenical Movement." *EARE* 2:977–96.

Davie, Jody Shapiro. *Women in the Presence: Constructing Community and Seeking Spirituality in Mainline Protestantism.* Philadelphia: University of Pennsylvania Press, 1995.

Duke, David Nelson. *In the Trenches with Jesus and Marx: Henry F. Ward and the Struggle for Social Justice.* Tuscaloosa: University of Alabama Press, 2003.

Ellingson, Stephen. *The Megachurch and the Mainline.* Chicago: University of Chicago Press, 2007.

Ellwood, Robert S. *The Fifties Spiritual Marketplace.* New Brunswick, N.J.: Rutgers University Press, 1997.

Evans, Christopher H., ed. *The Social Gospel Today.* Louisville, Ky.: Westminster John Knox, 2001.

Evans, Sara M., ed. *Journeys that Opened Up the World: Women, Student Christian Movements, and Social Justice, 1955–1975.* New Brunswick, N.J.: Rutgers University Press, 2003.

Ferm, Deane William. "Religious Thought since World War II." *EARE* 2:1159–72.

Fox, Richard. *Reinhold Niebuhr.* New York: Pantheon, 1985.

Fox, William L. *Willard Sperry.* New York: Peter Lang, 1991.

Friedland, Michael B. *Lift Up Your Voice like a Trumpet: White Clergy and the Civil Rights and Antiwar Movements, 1954–1973.* Chapel Hill: University of North Carolina Press, 1998.

Gallup, George, Jr., and Jim Castelli. *The People's Religion: American Faith in the 90s.* New York: Macmillan, 1989.

Goldstein, Warren. *William Sloane Coffin, Jr.* New Haven: Yale University Press, 2004.

Handy, Robert T. *A History of Union Theological Seminary in New York.* New York: Columbia University Press, 1987.

Hudnut-Beumler, James. *Looking for God in the Suburbs: The Religion of the American Dream and Its Critics, 1945–1965.* New Brunswick, N.J.: Rutgers University Press, 1994.

Hulsether, Mark. *Building a Protestant Left:* Christianity and Crisis *Magazine, 1941–1993.* Knoxville: University of Tennessee Press, 1999.

Hutchison, William R., ed. *Between the Times: The Travail of the Protestant Establishment in America, 1900–1960.* New York: Cambridge University Press, 1989.

Johnson, Dale A., ed. *Vanderbilt Divinity School.* Nashville: Vanderbilt University Press, 2001.

Lawrence, William T. *Sundays in New York: Pulpit Theology at the Crest of the Protestant Mainstream, 1930–1955.* Lanham, Md.: Scarecrow, 1996.

Lotz, David W. *Altered Landscapes: Christianity in America, 1935–1985.* Grand Rapids, Mich.: Eerdmans, 1989.

Marty, Martin E. *Modern American Religion.* Vol. 1: *The Irony of It All*: 1893–1919. Chicago: University of Chicago Press, 1986. Vol. 2: *The Noise of Conflict*: 1919–1941. Chicago: University of Chicago Press, 1991. Vol. 3: *Under God, Indivisible*: 1941–1960. Chicago: University of Chicago Press, 1996.

———, ed. *Where the Spirit Leads: American Denominations Today.* Atlanta: John Knox, 1980.

Michaelsen, Robert S., and Wade Clark Roof. *Liberal Protestantism: Realities and Possibilities.* New York: Pilgrim, 1986.

Moorhead, James H. *World without End: Mainline American Visions of the Last Things, 1880–1925.* Bloomington: Indiana University Press, 1999.

Nesbitt, Paula D. *Feminization of the Clergy in America.* New York: Oxford University Press, 1997.

Paris, Peter J., et al. *The History of the Riverside Church in the City of New York.* New York: New York University Press, 2004.

Piper, John F., Jr. *Robert E. Speer: Prophet of the American Church.* Louisville, Ky.: Geneva Press, 2000.

Purvis, Sally B. *The Stained Glass Ceiling: Churches and Their Women Pastors.* Louisville, Ky.: Westminster/John Knox, 1995.

Pyle, Ralph E. *Persistence and Change in the Protestant Establishment.* Westport, Conn.: Praeger, 1996.

Roof, Wade Clark. *Spiritual Marketplace: Baby Boomers and the Remaking of American Religion.* Princeton, N.J.: Princeton University Press, 1999.

Roof, Wade Clark, and William McKinney. *American Mainline Religion.* New Brunswick, N.J.: Rutgers University Press, 1987.

Rossinow, Doug. *The Politics of Authenticity: Liberalism, Christianity, and the New Left in America.* New York: Columbia University Press, 1998.

Schenkel, Alfred F. *The Rich Man and the Kingdom: John D. Rockefeller, Jr., and the Protestant Establishment.* Minneapolis: Fortress, 1995.

Trost, Theodore Louis. D*ouglas Horton and the Ecumenical Impulse in American Religion.* Cambridge, Mass.: Harvard University Press, 2002.

Voskuil, Dennis N. "Neo-Orthodoxy." *EARE* 2:1147–58.

Warren, Heather A. *Theologians of a New World Order: Reinhold Niebuhr and the Christian Realists, 1920–1948.* New York: Oxford University Press, 1997.

Wellman, James K. *The Gold Coast Church and the Ghetto: Christ and Culture in Mainline Protestantism.* Urbana: University of Illinois Press, 1999.

Wuthnow, Robert. *The Restructuring of American Religion.* Princeton, N.J.: Princeton University Press, 1988.

Wuthnow, Robert, and John H. Evans. *The Quiet Hand of God: Faith-Based Activism and the Public Role of Mainline Protestantism.* Berkeley: University of California Press, 2002.

U. The West and the Pacific Rim

Banker, Mark T. *Presbyterian Missions and Cultural Interaction in the Far Southwest, 1850–1950.* Urbana: University of Illinois Press, 1993.

Buerge, David M., and Junius Rochester. *Roots and Branches: The Religious Heritage of Washington State.* Seattle: Church Council of Greater Seattle, 1988.

Carnett, Daniel R. *Contending for the Faith: Southern Baptists in New Mexico, 1935–1995.* Albuquerque: University of New Mexico Press, 2000.

Denton, James A. *Rocky Mountain Radical: Myron W. Reed, Christian Socialist.* Albuquerque: University of New Mexico Press, 1997.

DeRogatis, Amy. *Moral Geography: Maps, Missionaries, and the American Frontier.* New York: Columbia University Press, 2003.

Engh, Michael E. *Frontier Faiths: Church, Temple, and Synagogue in Los Angeles, 1846–1888.* Albuquerque: University of New Mexico Press, 1992.

Frankiel, Sandra Sizer. *California's Spiritual Frontiers.* Berkeley: University of California Press, 1988.

Guarneri, Carl, and David Alvarez, eds. *Religion and Society in the American West.* Lanham, Md.: University Press of America, 1987.

Kerstetter, Todd M. *God's Country, Uncle Sam's Land: Faith and Conflict in the American West.* Urbana: University of Illinois Press, 2006.

Luchetti, Cathy. *Under God's Spell: Frontier Evangelists, 1722–1915.* New York: Harcourt Brace Jovanovich, 1989.

Maffly-Kipp, Laurie F. *Religion and Society in Frontier California.* New Haven, Conn.: Yale University Press, 1994.

Pascoe, Peggy. *Relations of Rescue: The Search for Female Moral Authority in the American West, 1874–1939.* New York: Oxford University Press, 1990.

Phillips, Michael. *White Metropolis: Race, Ethnicity and Religion in Dallas, 1841–2001.* Austin: University of Texas Press, 2006.

Shipps, Jan, and Mark Silk, eds. *Religion and Public Life in the Mountain West.* Walnut Creek, Calif.: AltaMira, 2004.

Soden, Dale E. *The Reverend Mark Matthews: An Activist in the Progressive Era.* Seattle: University of Washington Press, 2001.

Szasz, Ferenc M. *The Protestant Clergy in the Great Plains and the Mountain West, 1865–1915.* 1988. Reprint, Lincoln: University of Nebraska Press, 2004.

———. *Religion in the Modern American West.* Tucson: University of Arizona Pres, 2000.

Szasz, Ferenc M., and Richard W. Etulain, eds. *Religion in Modern New Mexico.* Albuquerque: University of New Mexico Press, 1997.

Tucker, Cynthia Grant. *Prophetic Sisterhood: Liberal Women Ministers of the Frontier, 1880–1930.* Boston: Beacon, 1990.

Walker, Randi Jones. *Emma Newman: A Frontier Woman Minister.* Syracuse, N.Y.: Syracuse University Press, 2000.

Yohn, Susan M. *A Contest of Faiths: Missionary Women and Pluralism in the American Southwest.* Ithaca, N.Y.: Cornell University Press, 1995.

V. Latino Religion

Arreola, Daniel D., ed. *Hispanic Spaces, Latino Places.* Austin: University of Texas Press, 2004.

Avalos, Hector. *Introduction to the U.S. Latina and Latino Religious Experience.* Leiden: Brill, 2004.

Badillo, David A. *Latinos and the New Immigrant Church.* Baltimore: Johns Hopkins University Press, 2006.

Barton, Paul. *Hispanic Presbyterians, Methodists and Baptists in Texas.* Austin: University of Texas Press, 2006.

Bremer, Thomas S. *Blessed with Tourists: The Borderlands of Religion and Tourism in San Antonio.* Chapel Hill: University of North Carolina Press, 2004.

Canedo, Lino Gomez, O.F.M., "Religion in the Spanish Empire." *EARE* 1:187–200.

Carroll, Michael P. *The Penitente Brotherhood: Patriarchy and Hispano-Catholicism in New Mexico.* Baltimore: Johns Hopkins University Press, 2002.

Castro, Rafaela. *Chicano Folklore.* New York: Oxford University Press, 2001.

Chávez, Ernesto. *"Mi Raza Primero!" (My People First!): Nationalism, Identity, and Insurgency in the Chicano Movement in Los Angeles, 1966–1978.* Berkeley: University of California Press, 2002.

Cunningham, Hilary. *God and Caesar at the Rio Grande: Sanctuary and the Politics of Religion.* Minneapolis: University of Minnesota Press, 1995.

Dahm, Charles W. *Parish Ministry in a Hispanic Community.* New York: Paulist, 2004.

Dalton, Frederick John. *The Moral Vision of César Chávez.* Maryknoll, N.Y.: Orbis Books, 2003.

Díaz-Stevens, Ana María. *Oxcart Catholicism on Fifth Avenue: The Impact of the Puerto Rican Migration upon the Archdiocese of New York.* Notre Dame, Ind.: University of Notre Dame Press, 1993.

Díaz-Stevens, Ana María, and Anthony M. Stevens-Arroyo. *Recognizing the Latino Resurgence in U.S. Religion.* Boulder, Colo.: Westview, 1998.

Dolan, Jay P., and Allan Figueroa Deck, S.J., eds. *Hispanic Catholic Culture in the U.S.* Notre Dame, Ind.: University of Notre Dame Press, 1994.

Dolan, Jay P., and Jaime R. Vidal, eds. *Puerto Rican and Cuban Catholics in the U.S., 1900–1965.* Notre Dame, Ind.: University of Notre Dame Press, 1994.

Durand, Jorge, and Douglas S. Massey. *Miracles on the Border: Retablos of Mexican Migrants to the United States.* Tucson: University of Arizona Press, 1995.

Elizondo, Virgilio, et al., eds. *The Treasure of Guadalupe.* Lanham, Md.: Rowman & Littlefield, 2006.

Griffith, James S. *Beliefs and Holy Places: A Spiritual Geography of the Pimería Alta.* Tucson: University of Arizona Press, 1992.

Journal of the American Academy of Religion 67, no. 3 (Sept. 1999). Special issue on Latino religion.

Lara, Jaime. *City, Temple, Stage: Eschatological Architecture and Liturgical Theatrics in New Spain.* Notre Dame, Ind.: University of Notre Dame Press, 2004.

León, Luis D. *La Llorona's Children: Religious, Life, and Death in the U.S.–Mexican Border-lands.* Berkeley: University of California Press, 2004.

Machado, Daisy L. *Of Borders and Margins: Hispanic Disciples in Texas, 1888–1945.* New York: Oxford University Press, 2003.

Madsen, William. *The Mexican-Americans of South Texas.* 2d ed. New York: Holt, Rinehart and Winston, 1973.

Martinez, Juan Francisco. *Sea La Luz: The Making of Mexican Protestantism in the American Southwest, 1829–1900.* Denton: University of North Texas Press, 2006.

Martinez, Richard E. *PADRES: The National Chicano Priest Movement.* Austin: University of Texas Press, 2005.

Matovina, Timothy M. *Horizons of the Sacred: Mexican Traditions in U.S. Catholicism.* Ithaca, N.Y.: Cornell University Press, 2002.

———. *Tejano Religion and Ethnicity: San Antonio, 1821–1860.* Austin: University of Texas Press, 1995.

Matovina, Timothy M., and Gerald E. Poyo, eds. *Presente! U.S. Latino Catholics from Colonial Origins to the Present.* Maryknoll, N.Y.: Orbis, 2000.

Morales, Ed. *Living in Spanglish: The Search for Latino Identity in America.* New York: LA Weekly Books/St. Martin's Press, 2002.

Nabhan-Warren, Kristy. *The Virgin of El Barrio: Marian Apparitions, Catholic Evangelizing, and Mexican-American Activism.* New York: New York University Press, 2005.

Poyo, Gerald E. *Cuban Catholics in the United States, 1960–1980.* Notre Dame, Ind.: University of Notre Dame Press, 2007.

Román, Reinaldo L. *Governing Spirits: Religion, Miracles, and Spectacles in Cuba and Puerto Rico, 1898–1956.* Chapel Hill: University of North Carolina Press, 2007.

Romero, C. Gilbert. *Hispanic Devotional Piety.* Maryknoll, N.Y.: Orbis, 1991.

Sánchez Walsh, Arlene M. *Latino Pentecostal Identity.* New York: Columbia University Press, 2003.

Schulte, Francisco. *Mexican Spirituality: Its Sources and Mission in the Earliest Guadalupan Sermons.* Lanham, Md.: Rowman & Littlefield, 2002.

Sklar, Deidre. *Dancing with the Virgin: Body and Faith in the Fiesta of Tortugas, New Mexico.* Berkeley: University of California Press, 2001.

Steele, Thomas J. *Santos and Saints: The Religious Folk Art of Hispanic New Mexico.* Santa Fe, N.M.: Ancient City Press, 1994.

Torres, Eliso "Cheo", and Timothy L. Sawyer, Jr. *Curandero: A Life in Mexican Folk Healing.* Albuquerque: University of New Mexico Press, 2005.

Treib, Marc. *Sanctuaries of Spanish New Mexico.* Berkeley: University of California Press, 1993.

Treviño, Roberto R. *The Church in the Barrio: Mexican-American Ethno-Catholicism in Houston.* Chapel Hill: University of North Carolina Press, 2006.

Tweed, Thomas A. *Our Lady of the Exile: Diasporic Religion at a Cuban Catholic Shrine in Miami.* New York: Oxford University Press, 1997.

Vanderwood, Paul J. *Juan Soldado: Rapist, Murderer, Martyr, Saint.* Durham, N.C.: Duke University Press, 2004.

Vásquez, Manuel A. *Globalizing the Sacred: Religion across the Americas.* New Brunswick, N.J.: Rutgers University Press, 2003.

Vecsey, Christopher. *On the Padres' Trail.* Notre Dame, Ind.: University of Notre Dame Press, 1996.

Weigle, Marta. *Brothers of Light, Brothers of Blood: The Penitentes of the Southwest.* Santa Fe, N.M.: Ancient City Press, 1989.

W. Islam in North America

Abdo, Geneive. *Mecca and Main Street: Muslim Life in America After 9/11.* New York: Oxford University Press, 2007.

Alvi, Sajida Sultana, Homa Hoodfar, and Sheila McDonough, eds. *The Muslim Veil in North America: Issues and Debates.* Toronto: Women's Press, 2003.

Austin, Allan D. *African Muslims in Antebellum America.* New York: Routledge, 1997.

Curtis, Edward E., IV. *Black Muslim Religion in the Nation of Islam, 1960–1975.* Chapel Hill: University of North Carolina Press, 2006.

———. *The Columbia Sourcebook of Muslims in the United States.* New York: Columbia University Press, 2008.

Dannin, Robert. *Black Pilgrimage to Islam.* New York: Oxford University Press, 2002.

Diouf, Sylviane A. *Servants of Allah: African Muslims Enslaved in the Americas.* New York: New York University Press, 1998.

Dodds, Jerrilyn D. *New York Masjid: The Mosques of New York City.* New York: PowerHouse Books, 2002.

Gottschalk, Peter, and Gabriel Greenberg. *Islamophobia.* Lanham, Md.: Rowman and Littlefield, 2008.

Haddad, Yvonne Yazbeck. *Muslim Communities in North America.* Albany: State University of New York Press, 1994.

———, ed. *The Muslims of America.* New York: Oxford University Press, 1991.

Haddad, Yvonne Yazbeck, and Jane Idleman Smith, eds. *Mission America: Five Islamic Sectarian Communities in North America.* Gainesville: University Press of Florida, 1993.

Haddad, Yvonne Yazbeck, and John L. Esposito, eds. *Muslims on the Americanization Path?* New York: Oxford University Press, 2000.

Martin, Richard C. *Encyclopedia of Islam and the Muslim World.* New York: Macmillan Reference, 2003.

McCloud, Aminah Beverly. *African American Islam.* New York: Routledge, 1995.

McGinty, Anna Mansson. *Becoming Muslim: Western Women's Conversions to Islam.* New York: Palgrave Macmillan, 2006.

Metcalf, Barbara Daly, ed. *Making Muslim Sacred Space in North American and Europe.* Berkeley: University of California Press, 1996.

Mohammad-Arif, Aminah Unif. *Salaam America: South Asian Muslims in New York.* London: Anthem Press, 2002.

Moore, Kathleen M. *Al-Mughtaribun: American Law and the Transformation of Muslim Life in the United States.* Albany: State University of New York Press, 1995.

Turner, Richard Brent. *Islam in the African-American Experience.* Bloomington: Indiana University Press, 1997.

Walbridge, Linda S. *Without Forgetting the Imam: Lebanese Shi'ism in an American Community.* Detroit: Wayne State University Press, 1997.

Waugh, Earle H., Baha Abu-Laban, and Regula B. Quereshi, eds. *The Muslim Community in North America.* Edmonton: University of Alberta Press, 1983.

X. Asian and Asian-American Religions

Bromley, David G., and Larry D. Shinn, eds. *Krishna Consciousness in the West.* Lewisburg, Pa.: Bucknell University Press, 1989.

Bryant, Edwin F., and Maria L. Eckstrand, eds. *The Hare Krishna Movement.* New York: Columbia University Press, 2004.

Carnes, Tony, and Fenggang Yang, eds. *Asian American Religions.* New York: New York University Press, 2004.

Chen, Carolyn. *Getting Saved in America: Taiwanese Immigration and Religious Experience.* Princeton, N.J.: Princeton University Press, 2008.

Daner, Francine Jeanne. *The American Children of Krsna.* New York: Holt, Rinehart and Winston, 1976.

Dempsey, Corrine G. *The Goddess Lives in Upstate New York: Breaking Convention and Making Home at a North American Hindu Temple.* New York: Oxford University Press, 2006.

Downton, James V., Jr. *Sacred Journeys: The Conversion of Young Americans to Divine Light Mission.* New York: Columbia University Press, 1979.

Eck, Diana L. *On Common Ground: World Religions in America.* New York: Columbia University Press, 1997. CD-ROM and hardcopy "Guide for Teachers and Students."

Fenton, John Y. *Transplanting Religious Traditions: Asian Indians in America.* New York: Praeger, 1988.

Fenton, John Y., et al. *Religions of Asia.* 2d ed. New York: St. Martin's, 1988.

Fields, Rick. *How the Swans Came to the Lake: A Narrative History of Buddhism in America.* Boulder, Colo.: Shambala, 1981.

Fitzgerald, Frances. "Rajneeshpuram." In *Cities on a Hill,* edited by Frances Fitzgerald, pp. 247–82. New York: Simon and Schuster, c. 1981, 1983, 1986.

Frykenberg, Robert Eric. *Pandita Ramabai's America: Conditions of Life in the United States.* Grand Rapids, Mich.: Eerdmans, 2003.

Guest, Kenneth J. *God in Chinatown: Religion and Survival in New York's Evolving Immigrant Community.* New York: New York University Press, 2003.

Haaland, C. Carlyle. "Shinto and Indigenous Chinese Religion." *EARE*: 669–709.

Hammond, Phillip E, and David W. Machacek. *Soka Gakkai in America.* New York: Oxford University Press, 1999

Hayashi, Brian Masaru. *"For the Sake of Our Japanese Brethren": Assimilation, Nationalism, and Protestantism among the Japanese of Los Angeles, 1895–1942.* Stanford, Calif.: Stanford University Press, 1995.

Jackson, Carl T. *Vedanta for the West.* Bloomington: Indiana University Press, 1994.

Jeung, Russell. *Faithful Generations: Race and New Asian American Churches.* New Brunswick, N.J.: Rutgers University Press, 2005.

Judah, J. Stillson. *Hare Krishna and the Counterculture.* New York: Wiley, 1974.

Khandelwal, Madhulika S. *Becoming American, Being Indian: An Immigrant Community in New York City.* Ithaca : Cornell University Press, 2002.

Kurien, A. Prema. *A Place at the Table: The Development of American Hinduism.* New Brunswick, N.J.: Rutgers University Press, 2007.

Kwon, Ho-Youn, Kwang Chung Kim, and R. Stephen Warner, eds. *Korean Americans and Their Religions.* University Park, Pa.: Pennsylvania State University Press, 2001.

Layman, Emma McCoy. *Buddhism in America.* Chicago: Nelson Hall, 1976.

Matsuoka, Fumitaka, and Fernandez, Eleazar S., eds. *Realizing the America of Our Hearts: Theological Voices of Asian Americans.* St. Louis, Mo.: Chalice Press, 2003.

Min, Pyong Gap and Kim, Jung Ha, eds. *Religions in Asian America: Building Faith Communities.* Walnut Creek, Calif.: AltaMira Press, 2002.

Moore, Dinty W. *The Accidental Buddhist.* Doubleday: New York, 1997.

Morreale, Don, ed. *The Complete Guide to Buddhist America.* Boston: Shambala, 1998.

Palmer, Susan Jean. *Moon Sisters, Krishna Mothers, Rajneesh Lovers: Women's Roles in New Religions.* Syracuse, N.Y.: Syracuse University Press, 1994.

Phan, Peter C. *Christianity with an Asian Face: Asian American Theology in the Making.* Maryknoll, N.Y.: Orbis, 2003.

Prebish, Charles S. *American Buddhism.* North Scituate, Mass.: Duxbury Press, 1979.

———. *Luminous Passage: The Practice and Study of Buddhism in America.* Berkeley: University of California Press, 1999.

Prebish, Charles S., and Kenneth K. Tanaka, eds. *The Faces of Buddhism in America.* Berkeley: University of California Press, 1998.

Prothero, Stephen. *The White Buddhist: The Asian Odyssey of Henry Steel Olcott.* Bloomington: Indiana University Press, 1996.

"Racial Spirits: Religion and Race in Asian American Communities." Religious theme issue, *Amerasia Journal* 22, no. 1 (Spring 1996).

Seager, Richard Hughes. *Buddhism in America.* New York: Columbia University Press, 1999.

———. *The World's Parliament of Religions.* Bloomington: Indiana University Press, 1995.

Tweed, Thomas. *The American Encounter with Buddhism, 1844–1912.* Bloomington: Indiana University Press, 1992.

Tweed, Thomas, and Stephen Prothero, eds. *Asian Religions in America: A Documentary History.* New York: Oxford University Press, 1998.

Williams, Raymond Brady. *Religions of Immigrants from India and Pakistan.* Cambridge: Cambridge University Press, 1988.

Yoo, David K. *New Spiritual Homes: Religion and Asian Americans.* Honolulu: University of Hawai'i Press, 1999.

Y. Mormonism and Other Indigenous Religious Groups

1. GENERAL

Conkin, Paul K. *American Originals: Homemade Varieties of Christianity.* Chapel Hill: University of North Carolina Press, 1997.

2. MORMONISM (LATTER-DAY SAINTS)

Arrington, Leonard J. *Brigham Young.* New York: Knopf, 1985.

Arrington, Leonard J., and Davis Bitton. *The Mormon Experience*. New York: Knopf, 1979.

Arrington, Leonard J., Feramorz Y. Fox, and Dean L. May. *Building the City of God: Community and Cooperation among the Mormons*. 2d ed. Urbana: University of Illinois Press, 1992.

Avery, Valeen Tippetts. *From Mission to Madness: Last Son of the Mormon Prophet*. Urbana: University of Illinois Press, 1998.

Barlow, Philip L. "Jan Shipps and the Mainlining of Mormon Studies." *Church History* 73, no. 2 (June 2006): 412–26.

———. *Mormons and the Bible*. New York: Oxford University Press, 1991.

Bates, Irene M., and Gary Smith. *Lost Legacy: The Mormon Office of Presiding Patriarch*. Urbana: University of Illinois Press, 1996.

Bennion, Janet. *Women of Principle: Female Networking in Contemporary Mormon Polygyny*. New York: Oxford University Press, 1998.

Bergera, Gary J. *Conflict in the Quorum: Orson Pratt, Brigham Young, Joseph Smith*. Salt Lake City, Utah: Signature Books, 2002.

Bringhurst, Newell G., and Lavinia Fielding Anderson, eds. *Excavating Mormon Pasts: The New Historiography of the Last Half Century*. Salt Lake City: Greg Kofford Books, 2004.

Brodie, Fawn M. *No Man Knows My History: The Life of Joseph Smith*. New York: Knopf, 1971.

Brooke, John L. *The Refiner's Fire: The Making of Mormon Cosmology, 1644–1844*. New York: Cambridge University Press, 1994.

Bushman, Richard L. *Joseph Smith: Rough Stone Rolling*. New York: Knopf, 2005.

———. *Joseph Smith and the Beginnings of Mormonism*. Urbana: University of Illinois Press, 1984.

Bushman, Richard L., and Claudia L. Bushman. *Mormons in America*. New York: Cambridge University Press, 1999.

Bushman, Richard L. Edited by Jed Woodworth. *Believing History: Latter-day Saint Essays*. New York: Columbia University Press, 2004.

Compton, Todd. *In Sacred Loneliness: The Plural Wives of Joseph Smith*. Salt Lake City: Signature, 1997.

Cornwall, Marie, Tim B. Heaton, and Lawrence A. Young, eds. *Contemporary Mormonism: Social Science Perspectives*. Urbana: University of Illinois Press, 1994.

Davies, Douglas J. *An Introduction to Mormonism*. Cambridge, England: Cambridge University Press, 2003.

Daynes, Kathryn M. *More Wives than One: Transformation of the Mormon Marriage System, 1840–1910*. Urbana: University of Illinois Press, 2001.

Embry, Jessie L. *Black Saints in a White Church: Contemporary African American Mormons*. Salt Lake City: Signature, 1994.

Erickson, Dan. *"As a Thief in the Night": The Mormon Quest for Millennial Deliverance*. Salt Lake City: Signature, 1998.

Flake, Kathleen. *The Politics of American Religious Identity: The Seating of Senator Reed Smoot*. Chapel Hill: University of North Carolina Press, 2004.

Forsberg, Clyde R., Jr. *Equal Rites: The Book of Mormon, Masonry, Gender, and American Culture*. New York: Columbia University Press, 2004.

Francaviglia, Richard V. *The Mormon Landscape*. New York: AMS Press, 1978.

Givens, Terryl L. *By the Hand of Mormon: The American Scripture that Launched a New World Religion.* New York: Oxford University Press, 2002.

———. *The Viper on the Hearth: Mormons, Myths, and the Construction of Heresy.* New York: Oxford University Press, 1997.

Gordon, Sarah Barringer. *The Mormon Question: Polygamy and Constitutional Conflict in Nineteenth-century America.* Chapel Hill: University of North Carolina Press, 2002.

Hamilton, C. Mark. *Nineteenth Century Mormon Architecture and City Planning.* New York: Oxford University Press, 1995.

Hanks, Maxine. *Women and Authority: Re-Emerging Mormon Feminism.* Salt Lake City: Signature, 1992.

Hardy, B. Carmon. *Solemn Covenant: The Mormon Polygamous Passage.* Urbana: University of Illinois Press, 1992.

Hill, Marvin S., ed. *The Essential Joseph Smith.* Salt Lake City: Signature, 1995.

Larson, Stan, ed. *Prisoner for Polygamy.* Urbana: University of Illinois Press, 1993.

Launius, Roger D., and Linda Thatcher, eds. *Differing Visions: Dissenters in Mormon History.* Urbana: University of Illinois Press, 1994.

Leone, Mark P. *Roots of Modern Mormonism.* Cambridge, Mass.: Harvard University Press, 1979.

Lieberson, Goddard, producer. The *Mormon Pioneers.* Columbia Records Legacy Collection. New York, 1965.

Madsen, Carol Cornwall. *In Their Own Words: Women and the Story of Nauvoo.* Salt Lake City: Deseret, 1994.

O'Dea, Thomas F. *The Mormons.* Chicago: University of Chicago Press, 1957.

Patzwald, Gari-Anne. *Waiting for Elijah: A History of the Megiddo Mission.* Knoxville: University of Tennessee Press, 2002.

Paul, Erich Robert. *Science, Religion, and Mormon Cosmology.* Urbana: University of Illinois Press, 1992.

Prince, Gregory A. *Power from on High: The Development of Mormon Priesthood.* Salt Lake City: Signature, 1995.

Quinn, Michael D. *Early Mormonism and the Magic World View.* Salt Lake City: Signature, 1987.

———. *The Mormon Hierarchy: Origins of Power.* Salt Lake City: Signature, 1994.

———. *Same-Sex Dynamics among Nineteenth-Century Americans: A Mormon Example.* Urbana: University of Illinois Press, 1996.

Shipps, Jan. "The Latter-day Saints." *EARE* 1:649–68.

———. *Mormonism.* Urbana: University of Illinois Press, 1985.

———. *Sojourner in the Promised Land: Forty Years among the Mormons.* Urbana: University of Illinois Press, 2000.

Smith Research Associates. *New Mormon Studies CD-ROM: A Comprehensive Resource Library.* Salt Lake City: Signature, 1998.

Solomon, Dorothy Allred. *The Sisterhood: Inside the Lives of Mormon Women.* New York: Palgrave Macmillan, 2007.

Stark, Rodney. *The Rise of Mormonism.* New York: Columbia University Press, 2005.

Taber, Susan Buhler. *Mormon Lives: A Year in the Elkton Ward.* Urbana: University of Illinois Press, 1993.

Underwood, Grant. *The Millenarian World of Early Mormonism.* Urbana: University of Illinois Press, 1993.

Van Wagoner, Richard S. *Mormon Polygamy.* Salt Lake City: Signature, 1989.

———. *Sidney Rigdon.* Salt Lake City: Signature, 1994.

Vogel, Dan, ed. *Early Mormon Documents.* Vols. 1 and 2. Salt Lake City: Signature, 1996, 1998.

Walker, Ronald W. *Wayward Saints: The Godbeites and Brigham Young.* Urbana: University of Illinois Press, 1998.

Walker, Ronald W., David J. Whittaker, and James B. Allen, eds. *Mormon History.* Urbana: University of Illinois Press, 2001.

Westergren, Bruce N., ed. *From Historian to Dissident: The Book of John Whitmer.* Salt Lake City: Signature, 1995.

Whitsel, Bradley C. *The Church Universal and Triumphant: Elizabeth Clare Prophet's Apocalyptic Movement.* New York: Syracuse University Press, 2003.

Whittaker, David J. *Mormon Americana: A Guide to Sources and Collections in the United States.* Provo, Utah: BYU Studies, 1995.

Wicks, Robert S., and Fred R. Foister. *Junius and Joseph: Presidential Politics and the Assassination of the First Mormon Prophet.* Logan: Utah State University Press, 2005

3. CHRISTIAN SCIENCE, METAPHYSICAL RELIGION, AND "HARMONIALISM"

Ahlstrom, Sydney E. "Mary Baker Eddy." In *Notable American Women,* edited by Edward T. James, Janet W. James, Paul Boyer, 1:551–61. Cambridge, Mass.: Harvard University Press, 1971.

Albanese, Catherine L. *A Republic of Mind and Spirit: A Cultural History of American Metaphysical Religion.* New Haven: Yale University Press, 2007.

Braden, Charles. *Spirits in Rebellion.* Dallas: Southern Methodist University Press, 1963.

Ellwood, Robert S. "Occult Movements in America." *EARE* 2:711–22.

Fuller, Robert C. *Mesmerism and the American Cure of Souls.* Philadelphia: University of Pennsylvania Press, 1982.

George, Carol V. R. *God's Salesman: Norman Vincent Peale and the Power of Positive Thinking.* New York: Oxford University Press, 1993.

Gill, Gillian. *Mary Baker Eddy.* Reading, Mass.: Perseus, 1998.

Gomes, Michael. *Theosophy in the Nineteenth Century: An Annotated Bibliography.* New York: Garland, 1994.

Gottschalk, Stephen. "Christian Science and Harmonialism." *EARE* 2:901–16.

———. *The Emergence of Christian Science in American Religious Life.* Berkeley: University of California Press, 1973.

———. *Rolling Away the Stone: Mary Baker Eddy's Challenge to Materialism.* Bloomington: Indiana University Press, 2006.

Harley, Gail M. *Emma Curtis Hopkins: Forgotten Founder of New Thought.* Syracuse, N.Y.: Syracuse University Press, 2002.

Ivey, Paul Eli. *Prayers in Stone: Christian Science Architecture in the United States 1894–1930.* Urbana: University of Illinois Press, 1999.

Judah, J. Stillson. *The History and Philosophy of the Metaphysical Movements in America.* Philadelphia: Westminster, 1967.

Knee, Stuart E. *Christian Science in the Age of Mary Baker Eddy.* Westport, Conn.: Green-wood, 1994.

Meyer, Donald. *The Positive Thinkers.* Middletown, Conn.: Wesleyan University Press, 1988.

Moore, R. Laurence. *In Search of White Crows: Spiritualism, Parapsychology, and American Culture.* New York: Oxford University Press, 1977.

Parker, Gail Thain. *Mind Cure in New England.* Hanover, N.H.: University Press of New England, 1973.

Peel, Robert. *Christian Science.* New York: Holt, 1958.

———. *Mary Baker Eddy.* 3 vols. New York: Holt, Rinehart and Winston, 1966, 1971, 1977.

Satter, Beryl. *Each Mind a Kingdom : American Women, Sexual Purity, and the New Thought Movement, 1875–1920.* Berkeley: University of California Press, 1999.

Schoepflin, Rennie B. *Christian Science on Trial: Religious Healing in America.* Baltimore: Johns Hopkins University Press, 2003.

Wessinger, Catherine, ed. *Women's Leadership in Marginal Religions.* Urbana: University of Illinois Press, 1993.

4. MILLENNIALISM AND ADVENTISM

Bull, Malcolm, and Keith Lockhart. *Seeking a Sanctuary: Seventh-day Adventism and the American Dream.* New York: Harper and Row, 1989.

Collins, John J., Bernard McGinn, and Stephen J. Stein, eds. *The Encyclopedia of Apocalypticism.* 3 vols. New York: Continuum, 2000.

Doan, Ruth Alden. *The Miller Heresy, Millennialism, and American Culture.* Philadelphia: Temple University Press, 1987.

Edwards, Calvin W., and Gary Land. *Seeker after Light: A. F. Ballenger, Adventism, and American Christianity.* Berrien Springs, Mich.: Andrews University Press, 2000.

Forbes, Bruce David, and Jeanne Halgren Kilde, eds. *Rapture, Revelation, and the End Times.* New York: Palgrave Macmillan, 2004.

Frykholm, Amy Johnson. *Rapture Culture: Left Behind in Evangelical America.* New York: Oxford University Press, 2004.

Gaustad, Edwin S., ed. *The Rise of Adventism.* New York: Harper and Row, 1974.

Gibson, Scott M. *A. J. Gordon: An American Premillennialist.* Lanham, Md.: University Press of America, 2001.

Harrison, Barbara Grizzuti. *Visions of Glory: A History and Memory of the Jehovah's Witnesses.* New York: Simon and Schuster, 1978.

Hunt, Stephen, ed. *Christian Millenarianism: From the Early Church to Waco.* Bloomington: Indiana University Press, 2001.

Knight, George R. *Millennial Fever and the End of the World.* Boise, Idaho: Pacific Press, 1993.

———. *A Search for Identity: The Development of Seventh-Day Adventist Belief.* Hagerstown, Md.: Review and Herald, 2000.

Land, Gary. *Adventism in America.* Grand Rapids, Mich.: Eerdmans, 1986.

Lippy, Charles H. "Millennialism and Adventism." *EARE* 2:831–44.

Moorhead, James H. "Searching for the Millennium in America." *Princeton Seminary Bulletin,* n.s., 8, no. 2 (1987): 17–33.

Morgan, Douglas. *Adventism and the American Republic.* Knoxville: University of Tennessee Press, 2001.

Numbers, Ronald L. *Prophetess of Health: A Study of Ellen G. White.* New York: Harper and Row, 1976.

Numbers, Ronald L., and Jonathan M. Butler, eds. *The Disappointed: Miller and Millenarianism in the Nineteenth Century.* Bloomington: Indiana University Press, 1987.

Penton, M. James. *Apocalypse Delayed: The Story of the Jehovah's Witnesses.* Toronto: University of Toronto Press, 1985.

Rogerson, Alan. *Millions Now Living Will Never Die: A Study of Jehovah's Witnesses.* London: Constable, 1969.

Rowe, David L. *Thunder and Trumpets: Millerites and Dissenting Religion in Upstate New York, 1800–1850.* Chico, Calif.: Scholars Press, 1985.

Sanders, Carl E. II. *The Premillennial Faith of James Brookes.* Lanham, Md. University Press of America, 2001.

Vance, Laura L. *Seventh-day Adventism in Crisis.* Urbana: University of Illinois Press, 1999.

Wessinger, Catherine. *How the Millennium Comes Violently.* New York: Seven Bridges Press, 2000.

5. RESTORATIONISM

Casey, Michael W. *The Battle over Hermeneutics in the Stone-Campbell Tradition, 1800–1870.* Lewiston, N.Y.: Mellen, 1998.

Harrell, David Edwin, Jr. *The Churches of Christ in the 20th Century: Homer Bailey's Personal Journal of Faith.* Tuscaloosa: University of Alabama Press, 2000.

———. *Quest for a Christian America: The Disciples of Christ and American Society to 1866.* Nashville: Disciples of Christ Historical Society, 1966.

———. "Restorationism and the Stone-Campbell Tradition." *EARE* 2:845–58.

———. *The Social Sources of Division in the Disciples of Christ, 1856–1900.* Nashville: Disciples of Christ Historical Society, 1973.

Hughes, Richard T., ed. *The American Quest for the Primitive Church.* Urbana: University of Illinois Press, 1988.

———, ed. *The Primitive Church in the Modern World.* Urbana: University of Illinois Press, 1995.

———. *Reviving the Ancient Faith: The Story of Churches of Christ in America.* Grand Rapids, Mich.: Eerdmans, 1996.

Hughes, Richard T., and C. Leonard Allen, eds. *Illusions of Innocence: Protestant Primitivism in America, 1630–1875.* Chicago: University of Chicago Press, 1988.

Hughes, Richard T., C. Leonard Allen, and R. L. Roberts, eds. *The Churches of Christ.* Westport, Conn.: Greenwood Press, 2001.

McAllister, Lester G., and William E. Tucker. *Journey in Faith: A History of the Christian Church (Disciples of Christ).* St. Louis: Bethany, 1975.

Machado, Daisy L. *Of Borders and Margins: Hispanic Disciples in Texas, 1888–1945.* New York: Oxford University Press, 2003.

Tristano, Richard M. *The Origins of the Restoration Movement.* Atlanta, Ga.: Glenmary, 1988.

Verkryuse, Peter A. *Prophet, Pastor, and Patriarch: The Rhetorical Leadership of Alexander Campbell.* Tuscaloosa: University of Alabama Press, 2005.

Williams, D. Newell. *Barton Stone.* St. Louis: Chalice, 2000.

———. *A Case Study of Mainstream Protestantism: The Disciples' Relation to American Culture, 1880–1989.* Grand Rapids, Mich.: Eerdmans, 1991.

6. COMMUNITARIAN SOCIETIES

Andrews, Edward Deming. *The People Called Shakers.* New York: Dover, 1963. (See also numerous other titles by Andrews)

Ashcraft, W. Michael. The *Dawn of the New Cycle: Point Loma Theosophists and American Culture.* Knoxville: University of Tennessee Press, 2002.

Bach, Jeff. *Voices of the Turtledoves: The Sacred World of Ephrata.* University Park: The Pennsylvania State University Press, 2003.

Carden, Maren Lockwood. *Oneida.* Baltimore: Johns Hopkins University Press, 1969.

Cook, Philip L. *Zion City, Illinois: Twentieth-Century Utopia.* Syracuse, N.Y.: Syracuse University Press, 1996.

Fogarty, Robert S. *All Things New: American Communes and Utopian Movements, 1860–1914.* Chicago: University of Chicago Press, 1990.

———, ed. *Desire and Duty at Oneida: Tirzah Miller's Intimate Memoir.* Bloomington: Indiana University Press, 2000.

Foster, Lawrence. *Religion and Sexuality: Three American Communal Experiments of the Nineteenth Century.* New York: Oxford University Press, 1981.

———. *Women, Family, and Utopia: Communal Experiments of the Shakers, the Oneida Community, and the Mormons.* Syracuse, N.Y.: Syracuse University Press, 1991.

Garrett, Clarke. *Origins of the Shakers.* Baltimore: Johns Hopkins University Press, 1997.

Gutek, Gerald and Patricia. *Visiting Utopian Communities: A Guide to the Shakers, Moravians, and Others.* Columbia: University of South Carolina Press, 1998.

Guthrie, John J., Jr., Phillip C. Lucas, and Gary Monroe, eds. *Cassadaga: The South's Oldest Spiritualist Community.* Gainesville: University Press of Florida, 2000.

Hayden, Dolores. *Seven American Utopias.* Cambridge, Mass.: Harvard University Press, 1976.

Humez, Jean M., ed. *Mother's First-Born Daughters: Early Shaker Writings on Women and Religion.* Bloomington: Indiana University Press, 1993.

Kanter, Rosabeth Moss. *Commitment and Community.* Cambridge, Mass.: Harvard University Press, 1972.

Lippy, Charles H. "Communitarianism." *EARE* 2:858–74.

Noyes, George Wallingford, comp. *Free Love in Utopia: John Humphrey Noyes and the Origin of the Oneida Community.* Urbana: University of Illinois Press, 2001.

Patterson, Daniel. *The Shaker Spiritual.* Princeton, N.J.: Princeton University Press, 1979.

Promey, Sally M. *Spiritual Spectacles: Vision and Image in Mid-Nineteenth-Century Shakerism.* Bloomington: Indiana University Press, 1993.

Stein, Stephen J. *The Shaker Experience in America.* New Haven, Conn.: Yale University Press, 1992.

Terri, Salli, arranger. *Music of the Shakers.* Pleiades Records. Carbondale, Ill., n.d.

Thomas, Robert David. *The Man Who Would Be Perfect: John Humphrey Noyes and the Utopian Impulse.* Philadelphia: University of Pennsylvania Press, 1977.

Thurman, Suzanne R. *O Sisters, Ain't You Happy? Gender, Family, and Community among the Harvard and Shirley Shakers, 1782–1918.* Syracuse, N.Y.: Syracuse University Press, 2002.

Whitson, Robley Edward, ed. *The Shakers: Two Centuries of Spiritual Reflection.* Mahwah, N.J.: Paulist, 1983.

Z. "Cults," New Religions, the New Age, and Turn-of-the-Century Religious Pluralism

Adler, Margot. *Drawing Down the Moon: Witches, Druids, Goddess-Worshipers, and Other Pagans in America Today.* Boston: Beacon, 1986.

Berger, Helen A. *A Community of Witches: Contemporary Neo-Paganism and Witchcraft in the United States.* Columbia: University of South Carolina Press, 1999.

Bloch, Jon P. *New Spirituality, Self, and Belonging: How New Agers and Neo-Pagans Talk about Themselves.* Westport, Conn.: Praeger, 1998.

Body Mind Spirit. *The New Age Catalogue.* New York, 1988.

Brown, Michael F. *The Channeling Zone.* Cambridge, Mass.: Harvard University Press, 1997.

Chidester, David. *Salvation and Suicide: An Interpretation of Jim Jones, the Peoples Temple, and Jonestown.* Bloomington: Indiana University Press, 1988.

Chryssides, George D. *The Advent of Sun Myung Moon.* New York: St. Martin's, 1991.

Comstock, Gary David. *Unrepentant, Self-Affirming, Practicing: Lesbian/Bisexual/Gay People within Organized Religion.* New York: Continuum, 1996.

Drury, Nevill. *Exploring the Labyrinth: Making Sense of the New Spirituality.* New York: Cassell and Continuum, 1999.

Eck, Diana L. *A New Religious America: How a "Christian Country" Has Become the World's Most Religiously Diverse Nation.* San Francisco: HarperSanFrancisco, 2001.

Ellis, Bill. *Raising the Devil: Satanism, New Religions, and the Media.* Louisville: University of Kentucky Press, 2000.

Ellwood, Robert S. *Alternative Altars.* Chicago: University of Chicago Press, 1979.

———. *The Eagle and the Rising Sun: Americans and the New Religions of Japan.* Philadelphia: Westminster, 1974.

———. *Eastern Spirituality in America.* New York: Paulist, 1987.

———. *The 60s Spiritual Awakening.* New Brunswick, N.J.: Rutgers University Press, 1994.

Elwood, Robert S., and Harry B. Partin. *Religious and Spiritual Groups in Modern America.* 2d ed. Englewood Cliffs, N.J.: Prentice-Hall, 1988.

Emerson, Michael O. *People of the Dream: Multiracial Congregations in the United States.* Princeton, N.J.: Princeton University Press, 2006.

Farrell, James J. *The Spirit of the Sixties: The Making of Postwar Radicalism.* New York: Routledge, 1997.

Fuller, Robert C. *Spiritual, but not Religious: Understanding Unchurched America.* New York: Oxford University Press, 2001.

Gallagher, Eugene V., and W. Michael Ashcraft. *Introduction to New and Alternative Religions in America*. Westport, Conn.: Greenwood, 2006.

Gardell, Mattias. *Gods of the Blood: The Pagan Revival and White Separatism*. Durham, N.C.: Duke University Press, 2003.

Hall, John R. *Gone from the Promised Land: Jonestown in American Cultural History*. New Brunswick, N.J.: Rutgers University Press, 1987.

Hanegraaff, Wouter J. *New Age Religion and Western Culture*. Leiden: E. J. Brill, 1996.

Hartman, Keith. *Congregations in Conflict: The Battle over Homosexuality*. New Brunswick, N.J.: Rutgers University Press, 1996.

Harvey, Graham. *Contemporary Paganism*. New York: New York University Press, 1997.

Heelas, Paul. *The New Age Movement*. Cambridge, Mass.: Harvard University Press, 1996.

Janzen, Rod. *The Rise and Fall of Synanon: A California Utopia*. Baltimore: Johns Hopkins University Press, 2001.

Jenkins, Philip. *Mystics and Messiahs: Cults and New Religions in American History*. New York: Oxford University Press, 2000.

Kripal, Jeffrey J. *Esalen: America and the Religion of No Religion*. Chicago: University of Chicago Press, 2007.

Kyle, Richard. *The New Age Movement in American Culture*. Lanham, Md.: University Press of America, 1995.

Laderman, Gary, ed. *Religions of Atlanta: Religious Diversity in the Centennial Olympic City*. Atlanta: Scholars Press, 1996.

Lau, Kimberly J. *New Age Capitalism: Making Money East of Eden*. Philadelphia: University of Pennsylvania Press, 2000.

Lewis, James R. *Odd Gods: New Religions and the Cult Controversy*. Amherst, N.Y.: Prometheus, 2001.

Lewis, James R., and J. Gordon Melton, eds. *Perspectives on the New Age*. Albany: State University of New York Press, 1992.

McCloud, Sean. *Making the American Religious Fringe: Exotics, Subversives, and Journalists, 1955–1993*. Chapel Hill: University of North Carolina Press, 2004.

Mickler, Michael. *The Unification Church in America: A Bibliography and Research Guide*. New York: Garland, 1987.

Miller, Timothy. *The 60s Communes*. Syracuse, N.Y.: Syracuse University Press, 1999.

Miller, Timothy, ed. *America's Alternative Religions*. Albany: State University of New York Press, 1995.

Oppenheimer, Mark. *Knocking on Heaven's Door: American Religion in the Age of Counterculture*. New Haven: Yale University Press, 2003.

Orsi, Robert A., ed. *Gods of the City*. Bloomington: Indiana University Press, 1999.

Pike, Sarah M. *Earthly Bodies, Magical Selves: Contemporary Pagans and the Search for Community*. Berkeley: University of California Press, 2001.

———. *New Age and Neopagan Religions in America*. New York: Columbia University Press, 2004.

Porterfield, Amanda. *The Transformation of American Religion: The Story of a Late-Twentieth-Century Awakening*. New York: Oxford University Press, 2001.

Reavis, Dick J. *The Ashes of Waco*. Syracuse, N.Y.: Syracuse University Press, 1998.

Richardson, James T., Joel Best, and David G. Bromley, eds. *The Satanism Scare.* New York: A. de Gruyter, 1991.

Robbins, Thomas, and Dick Anthony. "'Cults' in the Late Twentieth Century." *EARE* 2:741–54.

Robbins, Thomas, and Susan J. Palmer, eds. *Millennium, Messiahs, and Mayhem: Contemporary Apocalyptic Movements.* New York: Routledge, 1997.

Roszak, Theodore. *The Making of a Counter Culture.* Garden City, N.Y.: Doubleday, 1969.

Salomonsen, Jone. *Enchanted Feminism: Ritual, Gender and Divinity among the Reclaiming Witches of San Francisco.* New York: Routledge, 2002.

Shupe, Anson D., and David G. Bromley. *The New Vigilantes.* Beverly Hills, Calif.: Sage, 1980.

Stein, Stephen J. *Alternative American Religions.* New York: Oxford University Press, 2000.

Sutcliffe, Steven. *Children of the New Age.* New York: Routledge, 2003.

Sutcliffe, Steven J., and Marion Bowman. *Beyond New Age: Exploring Alternative Spirituality.* New York: Columbia University Press, 2000.

Tabor, James D., and Eugene V. Gallagher. *Why Waco?* Berkeley: University of California Press, 1995.

Teasdale, Wayne, and George F. Cairns. *The Community of Religions: Voices and Images of the Parliament of Religions.* New York: Continuum, 1996. On the 1993 event.

Tipton, Steven M. *Getting Saved from the Sixties.* Berkeley: University of California Press, 1982.

York, Michael. *The Emerging Network.* Lanham, Md.: Rowman and Littlefield, 1995.

Warner, R. Stephen, and Judith G. Wittner, eds. *Gatherings in Diaspora: Religious Communities and the New Immigration.* Philadelphia: Temple University Press, 1998.

Wright, Stuart A., ed. *Armageddon in Waco: Critical Perspectives on the Branch Davidian Conflict.* Chicago: University of Chicago Press, 1995.

Wuthnow, Robert. *After Heaven: Spirituality in America Since the 1950s.* Berkeley: University of California Press, 1998.

Zaretsky, Irving, and Mark Leone, eds. *Religious Movements in Contemporary America.* Princeton, N.J.: Princeton University Press, 1974.

Index

PETER W. WILLIAMS is Distinguished Professor of Comparative Religion and American Studies at Miami University in Oxford, Ohio. He is the author of *Houses of God* and *Popular Religion in America* and coeditor of *The Encyclopedia of the American Religious Experience*, *The Encyclopedia of American Social History*, *The Encyclopedia of American Cultural and Intellectual History*, and *The Encyclopedia of Religion in America*.

The University of Illinois Press
is a founding member of the
Association of American University Presses.

―――――――――――――――――――――――

Composed in 11/14 Adobe Minion Pro
by Jim Proefrock
at the University of Illinois Press
Designed by Dennis Roberts
Manufactured by Sheridan Books, Inc.

University of Illinois Press
1325 South Oak Street
Champaign, IL 61820-6903
www.press.uillinois.edu